A treatise of Episcopacy; confuting by scripture, reason, and the churches testimony, that fort of Diocesan churches, prelacy, and government .. Volume 1-2

Baxter, Richard, 1615-1691

A

TREATISE

OF

EPISCOPACY;

CONFUTING BY

SCRIPTURE, REASON, and the CHURCHES
TESTIMONY, that fort of

Diocefan Churches,

PRELACY, and GOVERNMENT,

Which cafteth out

The *Primitive Church-Species, Epifcopacy, Miniftry* and *Difcipline,*
and confoundeth the Chriftian World by Corruption, Ufurpation, Schifm, and Perfecution.

Meditated in the Year 1640. when the *Et cætera* Oath was impofed. Written 1671. and caft by. Publifhed 1680, by the importunity of our Superiours, who demand the Reafons of our Nonconformity.

By *RICHARD BAXTER.*

LONDON,

Printed for *Nevil Simmons* at the Three Cocks at the Weft end of S. *Paul's,*
and *Thomas Simmons* at the Princes Arms in *Ludgate-ftreet.* 1681.

The History of the Production of this Treatise, with its Design and Sum ; to prevent mis-understanding.

Because many of late, as well as Justice *Roger L'Estrange*, do seem to believe themselves in their accusation of me, as *changing with the Times*; though I greatly affect the change of a Proficient, and know not at what age it is that such men would fix us that we may grow no wiser, nor ever repent of former Ignorance or Errour ; yet I will here confess to them that if what I here write against be good and right, I have been forty years unchanged in my Errour.

My mutability hath been little to my advantage for this world, For further than I was for the King, I never was one year on that which was called the *upper* or *stronger* prevailing side, as far as I understand it. Nor to the very day that I was turned out of all, did my Preferments, or Riches ever serve me, so much as to have a House, or keep a Servant man, (save in Travail) or Woman (save one aged Woman that provided me necessaries, in a few top rooms of another mans House ;) which I mention for the sake of the mistaken *French* stranger, Mr. *Durel*, that tells the World another story.

And as to this Subject, this is the Breviate of its History, *ab origine*. I was in my Child hood, first bred up under the School, and Church-teaching, of eight several men, of whom only two preached once a month, and the rest were but Readers of the Liturgie, and most of very scandalous lives. After that I fell into the hands of a Teacher, that studied for preferment, and reviled Puritanes ; and after that I fell into the happier acquaintance of three ancient Divines, that were called then Conformable Puritanes ; and all of them bred in me an Opinion, that *Nonconformists* were *unlearned men, addicted to* humorous, causeless Singularity: For I knew but one * who was an honest plain Preacher but of little learning: And to settle me, the Divines that I followed, made me read Bishop *Downame's* Defence, Bishop *Andrews*, and others for Episcopacy, and Mr. *Sprint*, Dr. *Burges*, and others for the Ceremonies: And I verily judged them to be in the right: But as soon as I was ordained, I removed into a Countrey where were some Nonconformists, some few of them Learned Ministers, and many Laymen ; of whom, one in the house with me, was oft disputing the Case with me, and I thought I had still the better: And the *Nonconformable Ministers* there, were men of so much Holiness, and

Where Dr. Ackfree was bred : His next Neighbor.

A 2   Peace,

Peace, that they would scarce ever talk of the matters in difference, but of *Holiness* and *Heaven*, and repressing the over-much heat of the Lay-men: And the famous *William Fenner* being lately of the next Parish, a Conformist of learning, yet plain and affectionate in preaching, God had blest his Ministry with so great success in the Conversion of many ungodly Persons; as that the reverence of him, kept up the honour of Conformity among the Religious people thereabouts.

But in 1640. I was removed to *Brignorth*, and the Canons newly made, imposed on us an *Oath*, which had these words, [I A. B. *do swear that I do approve of the Doctrine, and Discipline, or Government of the Church of* England, *as concerning all things necessary to Salvation*——*Nor will I ever give my* CONSENT *to alter the Government of this Church, by Arch-Bishops, Bishops, Deans, and Arch-Deacons,* &c. *As it stands now established, and as by right it ought to stand*——*And all these things I do plainly and sincerely acknowledge and swear, according to the plain and common sence and understanding of the same words, without any equivocation, or mental evasion, or secret reservation whatsoever; And this I do heartily, willingly, and truly, upon the Faith of a Christian: So help me God in Jesus Christ.*]

Though every Minister in the Countrey, as well I, was for Episcopacy; yet this Oath so startled them that they appointed a meeting at *Brignorth* to consult about it. It fell out on my Lecture day, and at the meeting, it fell to my lot to be the Objecter, or Opponent, against Mr. *Christopher Cartwright* (a good Man, incomparably beyond me in Learning, the Defender of K. Ch. 1. against the Marquess of *Worcester*, and the Author of the Rabbinnical Commentary on *Gen.* whose Papers of Justification, I since answered) He defended the Oath; and though my Objections were such as were none of the strongest, the Ministers thought he failed in answering them, and we broke up more dubious than before.

I had a little before set my self to a more serious study of the Case of the Ceremonies than before; and upon the reading of Dr. *Ames Fresh suit*, and some others (having before read little on that side) I came to see that there was a great difference between the determination of such Circumstances of *Order* as the Law of Nature, or Scripture allow and oblige men to determine one way or other, the *Genus* being necessary, and the making of new mystical significant teaching Ordinances, and Symbols of Christianity (of which see Bishop *Jer. Taylor* cited in my 2d. Plea.) And hereupon I had setled my Judgment only against the imposed use of the Cross in Bap-

Baptifm, and the abufe of undertaking Godfathers.

But now I refolved before I took fuch an Oath as this, to ftudy over again the Controverfie of Epifcopacy, (which elfe I think I fhould fcarce have done) For I faw 1. That fuch an *Oath and Covenant*, fo Univerfally impofed, was made the teft and terms of Church concord, and fo would be an Engine of divifion by fhutting out all that could not take it. The Scotch Oath, and Covenant was not the firft impofed on us: The Bifhops Oath and Covenant to the contrary went here before it. 2. I faw that the whole frame of the prefent Church-Government, was about to be fixed, as by an Oath of Allegiance, on the Land, as if it were as neceffary as Monarchy, and to be woven into the fundamental unchangeable conftitution, and it were true, *No Bifhop, no King.* 3. I askt, *What was the meaning of the Et cætera,* and could have no folution, but from the following words [*As it ftands now eftablifhed*] And underftood not well how far Lay-chancellous, Officials, Surrogates, Regifters, Proctors, Advocates, were part of the eftablifhed Government; but I faw it certainly included, Arch-bifhops, Deans, and Archdeacons. 4. I askt whether the King and Parliament had not power to fet up a Bifhop in every Corporation? and to take down Deans, Arch-Deacons, Chancellours, Officials, &c. and few denied it. 5. I askt my felf, if the King and Parliament make fuch a change, and command my Confent, whether I muft difobey them, and foreftall my obedience by a Covenant and Oath? 6. I thought that what is impofed on all the Clergie to day, may be impofed on the Laity next; And then all Parliament men will be Sworn and Covenanted never in Parliament fo much as to Confent to change any of the Church-Government now eftablifhed. 7. I found that I muft alfo fwear [*That it ought fo to ftand.*] which could mean no lefs, than by a Divine Law, when Mans Law may not alter it. 8. I found fuch Heartinefs, Willingnefs required in the Swearer, as required very full fatisfaction in all this. And that with the terrible re-nunciation of the *Help of God in Chrift,* if I do not all that I fwear to. 9. And I muft be deprived of my Office (for Benefice I had none) and caft out of the miniftry, if I refufed to take this Epifcopal Covenant and Oath. 10. And I knew that he that made no Confcience of deliberate Perjury, had little reafon to hope that he had any good Confcience, true Grace, or Honefty; and fpecially if he concurred to involve all the Clergie, or Nation in the guilt.

Upon thefe Confiderations, I fet my felf to a more fearching ftudy of the matter: I read *Gerfom Bucer, Didoclave, Jacob,* (and after *Parker, Bains,*) and others on one fide, and all that I could get

on

on the other, (*Downam* again, *Bilson, Hooker, Saravia, Andrews,* and many more) And the result of my search was this, I wondered to find so many write *for* and *against* Episcopacy, without distinguishing the sorts of Episcopacy: For I found reason to think one sort at least Tolerable, yea, desirable; but that which the Oath of 1640, would have bound me to, I found great reason to judge to be but what I have described it in this Book: And I here give notice to the Reader, that whereever he findeth me speak, as against the *English Diocesane Prelacy*; I mean it as described by *Coustns*, and Dr. *Zouch*; and as relating to that Oath and Canon, and not in opposition to the Laws of the Land.

This Judgment then setled, I never could see cause to change, but the more I read of the Ancients, Church History, Counsels,&c. And many other Writers for Episcopacie, (*Petavius, Sancta Clara Spalatensis,* Dr. *Hamond* and many more) the more was I confirmed in it to this day. When Usurpation was at the highest, I wrote accordingly in my book, called *Disputations of Church Government.* When the King came home I accordingly used my Endeavours as a Reconciler with the Ministers here called Presbyterians, who seemed mostly of the same mind, And how little an alteration of the Church Goverment in the Kings Declaration of Ecclesiastical Affairs, did we receive with thankfulness, and it would have been with a conforming joy, but that we knew the leading Men, that treated with us, too well to hope that they had any intention to continue it, but to use it——they knew to what, till they had done their work and got *this* Act of *Vniformity.*

In 1668. After I had been in the Goal, and yet men called for the reasons of my Nonconformity, I drew up some of my thoughts rudely: And in 1671. The call being renewed I wrote this Book, as now it is (saving a few additional Notes): But cast it by my Friends and my experience perswading me, that the Bishops, and their Parliament adherence could not patiently bear it.

Many years after some Letters past between Mr. *Henry Dodwell* (then of *Ireland*) and me: And his last being tedious, and he seeming not to intend or desire a publication of them, I gave him but a short general return, instead of a voluminous particular Answer, especially because I had this Book written by me, in which I had more than answered him, and was not willing or at leasure to write over the same things again: But when I had lately wrote in my *Book of Concord* a *summary* confutation of Mr. *Dodwels* schismatical Volumne, in which he degradeth, unchurcheth, if not unchristeneth, so many of the Protestants, as having no

Sacrament

Sacraments, no Covenant-right to Salvation, but sinning against the Holy-Ghost; and all for want of a Ministery derived by an uninterrupted succession of Episcopal Ordination from the Apostles, (and could not by importunity prevaile with him to answer *Voetius de desperata causa Papatus*, or my *Dispute of Ordination*, at last I received a Letter from him, signifying his purpose, upon his Friends desire to Publish his long Letter written to me out of *Ireland*: So that I saw a necessity of Publishing my Treatise which contained more than an Answer to him: And the rather because some R. Reverend Bishops and others had urged me, to give an Account of the Reasons of my Nonconformity: So that I had not leave to suppress this book, nor be longer silent. And yet I fear that they that so called for it, will not easily bear it.

The *summe* of Mr. *Dodwels* Letter to me, now in the press, is to prove the possibility of right Discipline, by our Diocesane Government as it is, 1. Because Magistrates can exercise theirs by as few : 2. Because the Ancients *de facto* did it by such : Therefore it may be done.

To answer these two is to answer his Letter, which one would think should be so easy, that no Scholar should have need of help to do it.

1. If any man can by an harrangue of words be brought to renounce his reason and experience, so far as to believe that the Office of a Pastor may be performed to as many Parishes, as the Office of a Major or Justice of Peace may, and that Pastors have no more to do in watching over particular Souls, instructing, exhorting, convincing, comforting, visiting, worpshing, Governing, &c, than the works of a Justice of Peace amount to, and that Dr. Stillingfleet (*e. g.*) shall be excused if he do no more for his Parish, than Justice *Rog. L'Estrange* doth, I undertake not to convince that man of any thing. Read over the work of a Bishop as I have here discribed it from the Scripture and Dr. *Hamond* and compare it with a Justices work, and if you can yet be deceived by Mr. *Dodwel* be deceived.

And yet I think there are in divers Parishes about us many Justices for one Pastor : I am confident *London* Diocess hath a great number for one Bishop.

And either our *Justices* are bound (besides what now they doe) to labour as much to bring some to Repentance, and such other work, as the Pastors are bound to do, or not : If not, it will not follow that as large a Circuit may be Governed by one Pastor as by one Justice : If yea, then he doth but condemne the Justices for unfaithfulness ; which will not prove, that a Pastor must be as bad.

And

2. And as to his appeal to the discipline *of the* Ancients; I leave the Reader to the deceit of this mans arguings, 1. If he cannot find it fully proved in this Book, that the Churches of the ancient Bishops were not so big as our greatest Parishes, as to the number of Souls, much less as our Dioceffes. 2. And if in my abstruct of *Church-History* of *Bishops* and *Counsels*, I have not fully proved, that Discipline was neglected, corrupted or overthrown dy degrees as Bishops-Churches overswelled. When we read such doleful complaints in History, Fathers, Counsels and their Canons of the corruption of the Churches, is this the true use to be made of all, *that we must be like them, and not blame them, lest we open the nakedness of our Fathers?* 3. And if men can make themselves willingly so blind, as by a story that the Fathers did such things among People and circumstances which we know not, to renounce *common* experience that it is not now any where done, nor can possibly be done; If men can be so ignorant what our Parishes and Dioceffes are, and what a Bishop and Chancellor do and can do, Let such err, for I am unable to cure them, any more than if they were confident, that my Lord Major can Govern all the Families of *London* as their Masters, by stewards, without Family-Masters, or that one Physitian, or one Tutor, could serve instead of many for the City.

Indeed they that have as low an esteem of true Discipline, as Mr. *D.* in his Letter seems to have, may easily believe that a few men may do it. And those Papists that can let the Church be the sink of common uncleanness, and a Nursery of Ignorance, Vice, and Prophaneness; so they may but keep up their Wealth, and Ease, and Honour, by crying up *Order, Government,* and *Unity*, may accordingly believe, that no more knowledge, Piety or Discipline is a duty, than serveth the ends of their worldly Dominion.

I must again give notice to the Reader that whereas the Common Objections of the greatness of Bishops Churches in the second Centurie, are fetcht from the instances of *Rome,* and *Alexandria,* I have answered even those two in the beginning of my Breviate of *Church-History,* to which I must refer you, and not again repeat it here.

I know that poor ingnorant Persons must expect such a shameful Cant of old reproach as this, to cheat them into the hatred of Christs Church-order, and Government, into a love of Clergie bondage, a scornful smile shall tell them [Mr. *Baxter would have as many Bishops as Parishes, and a Pope in every Parish; when men think one in a Diocess too much: When every ignorant or rash Priest shall be the Master of all the Parish, and you have no remedy against his Tyranny; what a brave reformation will this be?*] And such a deceitful scorn will serve to delude the ignorant and ungodly,

But if they truly understood the case, they would see the shame of this deriding objection. 1. A Pope is a Monarch or Governour of the world, and a Diocesan of a multitude of Parishes. And sure he usurpeth not so much, who will be but the Church-guide of one? A man is abler to guide one School, Colledge, Hospital, or Family, than a hundred or thousand, without any true Master of a Family, School, Colledge, &c. under him.

2. Why is not this foolish scorne used against these foresaid relations also? Why say they, not every Master maketh himself a Pope or Bishop to his own house, and every School-Master to his School, whereas one Master over a thousand would do better with bare Teaching Ushers, that had no Government.

3. Let it be remembred that we would have no Parish Pastor to have any forceing power, by Fines, Mulcts, Imprisonments, &c. But only to prevaile so farr as his management of Divine authority on mens Consciences can prevail: And we would not have Magistrates punish men meerly because they stand excommunicate, or because they tell not the Clergy that they repent. True excommunication is a heavy punishment fitted to its proper use, and not to be corrupted by the force of the Sword, but to operate by it self; And *valeat quantum valere potest.* He that despiseth it will not say he is enslaved by it. But is this all that the Bishops desire?

4. We would have no man become the Pastor of a Church without the peoples *consent* (if not choice) no more than a Physician should be forced on the sick. And as the Servant that consenteth to be a Servant, consenteth to his Masters Authority, and he that consenteth to a Physician, consenteth to be ruled by him for his health, and neither take this for a slavery: So he that consenteth to a Pastor, consenteth to his Pastoral conduct: And if he think it to his injury, he may choose.

5. And yet we believe that the Magistrate may constrein Atheists, Infidels, and such as refuse all proper Church Communion, to hear Gods word Preached, and make all the Parish allow the Teacher his tythes and maintenance due by Law: But he may force no man to Receive the great gift of the Body and Blood of Christ, or a pardon delivered and sealed by

B

baptism

Baptism or the Eucharist, and to be a member of the Church as such, against his will. For none but desirous consenters are capable of the gifts, so that the same Minister may be the common Teacher of all the Parish, and yet the Church-Pastor only of fit consenters. And when Sacraments are free and no Minister constrained to deliver them against his Conscience, nor any unwilling man to receive them, who is by this enslaved?

6. And if a Church-Pastor do displease the Church, and the main body of them withdraw their consent, we would not have any man continue their Pastor while they consent not, but disclaim him. Though in case of need the Rulers may continue him in his Benefice as the publick Preacher, if the people be grosly and obstinately culpable in refusing him.

7. And we would have that Parish-Pastor to have no power to hinder any other Minister from giving any one the Sacrament whom he denyeth it to, or that refuseth it from him. Though he that for a common cause is cast out of our Church, should not be received by others, till he repenteth, yet that holds not in all private causes, between the particular Pastor and him; nor in case of unjust excommunication: And other Ministers must judge of their own actions, whom to receive; and an injuring Minister may not hinder any other, nor the injured person from communicating elsewhere.

8. And we would have Parish Churches be as large as personal communion doth require or allow, and every Church to have divers Ministers; and if one be chief or Bishop, and the rest assistants; and if three or four small Parishes make one such communicating Church, we resist not.

9. And we desire frequent meeting or Synods of neighbour Pastors; and that there every single Pastor be ready to give an account of his Ministry, and to answer any thing that shall be alledged against him. And that the vote of the Synod obligeth all against unnecessary singularity.

10. We refuse not that one in every such Synod be the moderator; and if as of old every City (πόλις) or Corporation had a Bishop, so if but every Corporation or market Town, or every circuit that hath as many Communicants as

cans

can know one another by neighbourhood and some conversation and sometimes assembling (like a great Parish with
many Chappels) had but so much power, as is essential to a
true particular Pastor and Church; yea or but the power that
a free Tutor, Philosopher or Physician hath, to manage his
office by his skill, and not as an Apothecary or meer executor
of a strangers dictates, we should quietly submit.

11. And as we refuse not such Bishops (even *durante vita &*
capacitate) in every Church or City that is Corporation; so if
it please either the King, or the Churches by his permission
to give one grave and able man a general care of many
Churches, (as even the Scots superintendents had at their reformation, as *Spotswood* of *Lothian*, &c.) not by violence
to silence, and oppress, but by meer Pastoral power, and only
such as the Apostles themselves used to instruct junior Pastors,
to reprove, admonish, &c. we resist not: And so if Godly
Diocesans will become Arch-bishops only of this sort, and
promote our work instead of hindering it, we shall submit,
though we cannot Swear approbation, it being a thing that
Christian Ministers may doubt of, and no Article of our
Creed.

12. And if the King do cumulate wealth and honour on
them, and give them their place in Parliaments, to keep the
Clergy from contempt, yea, or trust any of them under him
as Magistrates with the Sword, whether we like it or not,
we shall peaceably submit, and obey them as Magistrates.

13. And if for order sake these Diocesans should have a
negative voice (unless in cases of forfeiture or necessity) in
the ordination of Ministers to the Church universal, not taking away the power of particular Churches to choose, or at
least freely consent or dissent, as to the fixing of Pastors o-
ver themselves, we would submit to all this for common peace.
Specially if the Magistrate only choose men to Benefices and
Magistracies, and none had the Pastoral power of the Keyes,
but by the Election of the Clergy and the peoples consent,
which was the judgment and practice of the universal Church,
from the beginning of Episcopacy till of late.

14. And lastly, we hold the Magistrate the only Governour by the Sword, as well of Pastors as of Physicians and all

others

others; And though he may not take the work of our proper calling out of our hands no more than the Physician, yet he may (by justice and discretion) punish us for male-administration, and drive us to our duty, though not hinder us from it; And we consent to do all under his Government. Judge now, whether we set up Popes or Tyrants.

By all this it is apparent that it is none of the designe of this Treatise to overthrow or weaken the Church of *England*; but to strengthen and secure it against all its notorious dangers. 1. By reforming those things, which else undoubtedly will cause a succession of dissenters in all generations, though all we the present Nonconformists are quickly like to be past troubling them, or being troubled by them, even of themselves many will turne upon the same reasons which have convinced us. 2. By uniting all Protestants, and turning their odious wrath and contentions, into a reverence of their Pastors, and into mutual Love and help.

This Treatise being hastened in three presses since Mr. *Dodwel* sent me his Letter that required it, I have not time to gather the Printers Errata, but must leav ethem to the discretion of the Reader. Only for [*English Prelacy*] before the first Chapter and in many other places should be [*The described Prelacy*].

I will end with the two following Testimonies, *One ad rem, the other ad hominem.*

The Lord pity his Ship that is endangered by the Pilots.

October 14. 1680.

Richard Baxter.

Justin Martyr's Apolog. We had rather die for the confession of one Faith, then either lie or deceive them that examine us: Otherwise we might readily use that Common saying, my Tongue is sworn, my mind is unsworn (*vid. Rob. Abbot: old way* p. 51.)

Thorndike of forbearance of Penalties. It is to no purpose to talk of reformation in the Church unto regular Government, without restoring the Liberty of choosing Bishops, and the Priviledge of Injoying them, to the Synods, Clergy and people of each Diocess. So evident is the right of Synods, Clergy and people in the making of this of whom they consist, and by whom they are to be governed, that I need make no other reason of the neglect of Episcopacy, than the neglect of it.

THE

THE
CONTENTS.

PART. I.

PART. II.

A
TREATISE
OF
EPISCOPACY.

Confuting, by

SCRIPTURE, REASON,

And the

CHURCHES TESTIMONY,

That fort of Dioceſan Churches, Prelacy and Government, which caſteth out the Primitive Church-ſpecies, Epiſco-pacy, Miniſtry and Diſcipline, and confoundeth the Chriſtian world by Corruption, Uſurpation, Schiſmes, and Perſecution.

Meditated 1640 when the &c. Oath was impoſed: Written. 1671 and caſt by: Publiſhed 1680 by the Call of Mr. *H. Dodwel*, and the Importunity of our Superiors, who de-mand the Reaſons of our Nonconformity.

The deſigne of this book is not to weaken the Church of *England*, its Government, Riches, Honour or Unity: But to ſtrengthen and ſe-cure it, 1. By the concord of all true Proteſtants who can never u-nite in the preſent Impoſitions: 2. And by the neceſſary reformati-on of Pariſh-Churches, and thoſe abuſes, which elſe will in all ages keep up a ſucceſſion of Nonconformiſts.

As an Account why we dare not *Covenant* by Oath or Subſcription *never to endeavour* any (amending) *alteration of the Church Government* (by lawful meanes, as Subjects) nor make our ſelves the juſtifying vouch-ers for all the unknown perſons in the Kingdom, who vowed and ſwore it, that none of them are obliged to ſuch (lawful) endeavours by their vow.

By *RICHARD BAXTER*, a Catholick Chriſtian, for love, con-cord and peace of all true Chriſtians, and obedience to all lawful com-mands of Rulers; but made, called and uſed as, a Nonconformiſt.

London, Printed for *Nevil Simmons* at the three Cocks at the Weſt end of *Saint Pauls*, and *Thomas Simmons* at the *Prince's* Armes in *Ludgate-*ſtreet, MDCLXXXI.

There are lately published of this Authors these two Books following, and sold by Thomas Simmons *at the Princes Armes in Ludgate-street.*

CHurch-History *of the Government of Bishops and their Councils, Abbreviated.* Including the chief part of the Government of Christian Princes and Popes, and a true account of the most troubling *Controversies* and *Heresies* till the *Reformation.* Written for the use especially of them, I. Who are ignorant or misinformed of the state of the *Antient Churches.* II. Who cannot read many and great *Volumes.* III. Who think that the *Universal Church* must have one *Visible Soveraign,* Personal or Collective, Pope or General Councils. IV. Who would know whether *Patriarchs, Diocesans, and their Councils,* have been, or must be the cure of *Heresies* and *Schismes.* V. Who would know the truth about the great *Heresies* which have divided the *Christian World,* especially the *Donatists, Novatians, Arrians, Macedonians, Nestorians, Eutychians, Monothelites,* &c. By *Richard Baxter,* a Hater of False History.

A Moral Prognostication, I. What shall befal the Churches on Earth till their Concord, by the Restitution of their *Primitive* Purity, Simplicity and Charity. II. How that Restitution is like to be made, (if ever) and what shall befal them thenceforth unto the End in that *Golden Age* of *LOVE.* Written by *Richard Baxter,* when by the Kings Commission, we (in vain) treated for Concord, 1661. And now published not to instruct the Proud, that scorn to learn; nor to make them Wise, who will not be made Wise: But to Instruct the Sons of *Love* and *Peace,* in their *Duties* and *Expectations.* And to tell *Posterity,* That the Things which befall them, were Fore-told: And that the Evil might have been prevented, and Blessed *Peace* on Earth attained, if Men had been but willing; and had not shut their Eyes, and hardened their Hearts, against the Beams of *Light* and *Love.*

THE
English Diocesan
AND
PRIESTHOOD
TRYED, &c.

CHAP. I.

The Reasons of this Writing.

I Am not ignorant how displeasing it will be to the Prelates, that I publish these Reasons of my Nonconformity to the Subscriptions and Oaths by which they would have me become an obliged Approver of their Function. Nor am I ignorant what Power, Wit and Will they have to express and exercise their displeasure: And consequently, how probable it is that I shall suffer by them for this work. And I well know that peaceable subjects should not unnecessarily say any thing against that which is required by their Rulers Laws, nor cherish the Peoples discontents, but do all that is lawful for the common Peace: And I am not of so pugnacious or self-hating a disposition, as to be willing of mens displeasure, especially my Superiours, or to be ruined in this World, and all that I may but vent my Opinion, in a case wherein I have published already so much that is still unanswered, as in my Disputations of Church-Government is to be seen.

And

And upon such Reasons (but above all, that I might not cast away my opportunity for some more useful writings, nor put an end to my own labours before God put an end to them) I have been silent in this Cause since our publick debates in 1661, above ten years. I have lived peaceably; I have endeavoured to preserve the due reputation of the publick Ministry, and to perswade all others to due subjection, love and quietness: I have by Word and Writing opposed the Principles of such as are exasperated by their sufferings into the Dividing and Separating extream; Though I knew, that by so doing, I was like to incur the displeasure and bitter censure of the Separatists, as much as I had before of the Prelates, (though not to suffer so much by them.) And I thought that the Prelates themselves who would not understand the true state of the People, nor the tendency of their way, by our informations, and evident Reasons, might yet come in time to know all by experience, and so to amend what they have done amiss.

But now I dare be no longer silent for the Reasons given *Apol. ch. 1.* which I will stay the Reader briefly to sum up. 1. I find that experience it self doth not Teach some men, but Harden them.

2. I perceive that those that are now convinced by experience, and wish they had taken another course, and rather have united the Ministry, than silenced them, are not able to undo what they have done, nor to amend what is done amiss, much less to retrieve all the doleful consequents; but the matter is gone out of their hands and beyond their power.

3. I see that while we wait, the Devil's work goeth on, by the silence and by the Divisions of the Ministers: Popery greatly increaseth; Quakers multiply; Atheism and Infidelity go bare-faced among those that are accounted men of reputation: Malice, and bitter hatred of each other, with common backbitings, censurings and slanders, instead of sweet Love and Concord, do notoriously encrease. Thousands are every day committing these sins, to the increase of their guilt, and the hastening of Gods judgments on the Land: The sufferers call the Prelates persecuters, and wolves in sheeps cloathings, who are known by their fruits, their teeth and claws. The Prelatists still say that the Nonconformists are unreasonable, discontented, peevish, factious, unpeaceable, unruly schismaticks; that will rather see all confounded than they will yield to things indifferent. And shall we still stand by, and silently see this work go on?

4. And to love and defend Truth, Honesty and Innocency is to be like to God. It is pity that those that Christ hath done so much to justifie, and will so gloriously justifie at the last, should have nothing said on their behalf by men. But we are much more obliged to justifie a righteous cause, than righteous men; For all men have somewhat that is unjustifiable, but so hath not the truth of God.

5. And he that in his Baptismal Covenant is engaged against the Flesh, the World, and the Devil, should be loath to see all their work go on

and

and not oppose it; and to fee, that which he taketh to be no better than deliberate Lying, or Juftifying fin, and Perjury it felf, and covenanting never to obey God in lawful and neceffary Church-reformation, to be all called; Things indifferent.

6. Nature and Scripture teach us to have a due and moderate regard of our own reputation as men; but much more as Minifters of Chrift; feeing the doctrine of Chrift which we preach or write, is ufually difhonoured in the Minifters difhonour, and the edification of the fouls of them that hear us or read our writings, is greatly hindered by it.

7. While Noblemen, Knights, Gentlemen, conformable Clergy-men, and many others of all Ranks, are poffeffed with thefe thoughts of us, that we are perfons who hypocritically pretend to Godlinefs, while indeed we are fo humourfome, that we will forbear our Miniftry, and our Maintenance, and fuffer any thing, and divide the Church, rather than yield to indifferent things; this is a fcandal, a grievous fcandal, either given or taken, and tendeth to wrong their fouls that are fcandalized: And if we give them this fcandal, it is our heinous fin: But if they take it by mifinformation, we are obliged to do our part to heal it: Souls are precious; and fcandal doth endanger them, even to diftaft Religion it felf, for the fakes of fuch as they take us to be: And we muft not ftand by and fee men perifh, if we can do any thing to fave them.

8. The fufferings of many of the Minifters are very great, that have not bread for their children, nor cloaths to cover them, and are afhamed to make known their wants: And if with all this, we fuffer the burden of unreproved calumny to lie on them, and keep them not to the neceffary comfort which confcience fhould find in fufferings with innocency, we fhall be guilty of uncharitablenefs our felves.

9. It is part of our Honouring the King and Parliament and other Magiftrates, not to defpife or flight their cenfures: And the judgment which they have publickly paffed on us, in an Act of Confinement, which impofeth the Oath for Prelacy, is fo hard and grievous, that if we are guilty, it is fit we fhould be made the common reproach of men; And if we are not, (as Non-conformifts) it is our duty to rectifie the judgment of our fuperiours where they are mifinformed. And as *Auguftine* faith, that no good Chriftian fhould be patient under an imputation of Herefie; fo I may fay that no good Subject fhould be fenflefly patient under an imputation of difloyalty and fedition: That better befeemeth the anarchical and truly difloyal and feditious, who take it for no crime.

10. And we know how pleafantly the Papifts infult to hear us ftigmatized for Villains and feditious Perfons by our brethren, and what ufe they will make of it at prefent and in furure Hiftory to the Service of their malice, and injury to the truth: which we ought not filently ftill to fuffer; while we fee how hereby they do already multiply.

B 2   11. And

11. And how unlikely foever it be, it is not impoffible, that our Superiours, that at once depofed and filenced about 1800 Minifters of
Chrift, when they fee what Reafons we have for our Non-conformity,
may be moved to reftore thofe that yet furvive: And then how many
thoufand fouls would have the joy and benefit?

12. Laftly, Truth and the juft information of Pofterity, is a thing
exceedingly defirable to ingenuous minds: It is a great trouble to
think that the Ages to come, fhould be injured by falfe Hiftory.
Therefore we muft do our beft, that they may but truly know our
Cafe; and then let them judge of the Perfons and Actions of this
our Age, as they fhall find Caufe, when Truth is opened to them.

Upon all thefe Reafons, though to my own great labour, and to the
greater contradiction of my natural love of filent quietnefs, and to
the probable incurring of mens difpleafure, I take it to be my duty
to give my *Superiours, Neighbours* and *Pofterity,* a true Account of the
Reafons which have moved my felf and others of my mind, to refufe to Subfcribe and Swear to the prefent *Englifh* Diocefan Prelacy:
Committing my Life and Liberty to the pleafure of God, in obedience
to whom I have both refufed to Conform, and written thefe Reafons
of my Non-conformity.

CHAP.

CHAP. II.

The English *Diocesan Prelacy, and Church-Government, truly described; that it may be known what it is which we disown.*

IT being not Episcopacy in General, but (the Popish and) the *English* Species of Prelacy, which our Judgments cannot approve, and which we cannot swear to as approvers, it is necessary that we tell strangers, what this Prelacy is, that the subject of our Controversie be not unknown, or misunderstood. But the subject is so large, that the very naming of the parts of our Ecclesiastical Government, in Tables by Dr. *Ri. Cosins*, maketh up a Volume in 16 Tables, and many hundred branches. Which being written in *Latin* I must refer the Foreign Reader to it; Not at all for the understanding of our Practice, but only of our Rule, or Laws with our Church-Constitution: seeing it would take up a considerable Volume to open but one half of his Scheme. All that I shall now do is to give you this brief Intimation.

That in *England* there are 26 or 27 Bishopricks: of which two are Archbishops: In all these set together there was when *Speed* numbred them, nine thousand seven hundred twenty five Parish Churches, but now many more. In the Diocess that I live in (*Lincoln*) there is above a 1000 or 1100. In very many of these Parishes, besides the Parish-Churches, there are Chapels, that have Curates, in some Parishes one Chapel, in some two, in some three, if not more. In these Parishes the number of Inhabitants is various, as they are greater or lesser: The greatest about *London*, such as *Stepny, Giles-Cripplegate, Sepulchres, Martins, &c.* have some about 50000 persons, (some say much more) some about 30000, some about 20000, &c. But ordinarily in Cities and Market-Towns through the Country, the number is about 2000, or 3000, or 4000, or 5000 at the most, except *Plimouth*, and some few great Parishes that have far more. And in Villages, in some 2000, in some 1000, in some small ones 500, or 300, or in some very small ones fewer. There are in *England* 641 Market-Towns (saith *Speed*) which are of the greater sort of Parishes, and such as in old times were called Cities, though now a few have got that title; at least a great number of them are equal, and some much greater and richer than some that now are named Cities. The Diocess that I live in is about six-score Miles in length. By all this you may conjecture how many hundred thousand souls are in some Diocesses, and at what a distance from each other: and what personal Communion.

munion it is that they are capable of: I my felf who have travelled o-
ver moſt of *England* never ſaw the face or heard the name of one Perſon
(I think) of many thouſands in the Dioceſs that I live in : Nor have we any
other Communion with the reſt of the Dioceſs (even with above a thouſand
Pariſhes in it) than we have with the People of any other Church or Dioceſs in the land about us, ſave that *One* Biſhop and his Chancellor and o-
ther Officers, are over us all.

The Magiſtrates Civil Governmeut of the Church I ſhall not meddle
with, as having no exceptions againſt it. The Sacerdotal or Spiritual
Power, called the Power of the *Keys*, determineth who ſhall be Members
of the Church, and partake of its Communion, and exerciſeth other acts
of Spiritual Diſcipline, of which more anon. This power is ſaid to be
in Archbiſhops and Biſhops *in foro ecclefia publico vel exteriore*, though
alſo in the Governed Presbyters, *in foro privato interiore*, as they may
privately comfort a penitent perſon, and declare God's promiſe of the
pardon of his ſin. [*a*] The Archbiſhops have it in eminency: As alſo the
power of confirming the Election of the Biſhops of their Provinces ; and
the power of Confecrating Biſhops with two others : and the power of
Convocating Provincial Synods upon the Kings Prefcript; and of mode-
rating in them. The power of receiving Appeals, and of Viſiting the
whole Provinces : yea to receive Appeals from the lower Judges, omit-
ing the middle ones ; and to exercife Ecclefiaſtical Jurifdiction in any
vacant Dioceſs under them. They have [*b*] power of Diſpenfation in
all Caufes (not judged contrary to Gods word) wherever the Pope had
power ; and where the Pope had not power, if the King or Council permit it them. They may difpenfe with the Eating of fleſh on Faſting-days,
with Marrying without previous publication ; with divers irregularities,
and ſometime may aboliſh *fimoniacum ambitum*. They may grant Commen-
dams, and Difpence with Non-reſidence, and with the keeping of divers
Churches called Benefices, in feveral Cafes, and with a Sons ſucceeding
his Father, and with Lay-mens poffeffing the Church-maintenance, called
Prebends.

The Biſhops (who take place in Parliament of other Barons, as the
Archbiſhops do of Dukes) [*c*] are all chofen really by the King, who
nominateth in a Writ to the Dean and Chapter the man whom they muſt
chufe ; who *pro formâ* do chufe him, never contradicting the Kings
Nomination.

Their proper Office conſiſteth in the powers of *Order* and of *Jurifdiction*, (as they diſtinguiſh them:) Their power of Order is threefold, 1. To
Ordain Prieſts and Deacons. 2. To Confecrate Churches and Burying places ; 3. To Confirm Children after Baptiſm , when they can fpeak and
ſay the Creed, Lords Prayer and Decalogue, and others that were not
Confirmed in their Childhood. Befides, that they may be Privy-Coun-
fellors, Lord-Keepers of the Great Seal, Lord Treaſurers, Embaſſadours,
&c. Their ordinary Ecclefiaſtical Jurifdiction extendeth, 1. to the Inter-
diction

(margin notes:)
a *Cofins* Tab. 3.

b *Cofins* Tab. 4.

c *Cofins* Tab. 5.

diction of Divine Offices, 2. to publick Admonitions and Penances, 3. to suspension from the Sacrament, and from ingress into the Church, and 4. to Excommunication and Absolution, and 5. to Anathematisms. And as to Ministers, 1. They may Sequester Benefices. 2. They may Suspend *ab officio & beneficio*, and forbid them to Preach or Pray; Or grant License to such as shall be tolerated to Preach. 3. They may deprive; 4. And depose Ministers by *sentence* verbal, and *degradation* actually.

This Church Jurisdiction of Bishops is distinguished into *Voluntary* and *Contentious*; [d] The Voluntary extendeth to abundance of things granted them by Statute, and by Common Law, which I pass by: That which d *Cof.* Tab. they claim both by Municipal Law and Ecclesiastical, is, 1. The probate *6.* of the Testaments of the dead; 2. The granting Administration of Goods to the next of Kin, 3. Keeping the *bona caduca* where none claimeth the Inheritance, 4. To receive Reasons of Administring, and to be Judges of them. 5. To confer Benefices, or Institute such as others present. 6. To grant Induction to the Instituted. 7. To receive the Fruits of vacant Benefices. 8. To allow the Vicar a fit proportion. 9. To grant Letters Dimissory, or Testimonial. 10. To Visit their Diocess once in three years. In which Triennial Visitation, they usually go to one Town in a County, (and never see the face of the people in the many score or hundred Churches about them;) and thither they summon the Ministers, and the Church-Wardens and Sides-men; Where one Minister preacheth, and then the Ministers must dine with the Bishop; and in Court he (or his Officer) giveth a Book of Printed Articles, containing a multitude of particulars, which the Church-warden must swear to present by, where because of the *quality* of them some Church-Wardens refuse, and others because of the number; some saying it is *unlawful* to undo their Ministers and Neighbours by such Presentments (as for omitting a Ceremony, for preaching or keeping a Fast in private, &c.) and some saying it is impossible to keep the Oath, and some saying that if they do it, they shall be hated of their Neighbours: Whereupon those that refuse are prosecuted to punishment; And the rest take the Oath and Articles; but not one of many doth present accordingly; though the Canon enquires after the perjured. And many that fear perjury or persecution themselves, do hire some poor man to be Church-Warden in their stead, that will venture upon all. I must intreat the Reader to peruse some of their Books of Articles (especially such as Bishop *Mountagues* and Bishop *Wrens*) to see what was then enquired after. Dr. *Zouch de Jud. Eccles.* p. 37. §. 1. *Part.* 3. saith, *Ad judices quod attinet statuto ordinatum, quod personæ conjugatæ dummodo Doctores Juris Civilis fuerint, qui ad officium Cancellarii, Vicarii Generalis, Officialis, vel Commissarii à Majestate Regia, Archiapiscopo, Episcopo, Archidiacono aut alio quocunque potestatem habente deputati sunt, omnem Jurisdictionem Ecclesiasticam exercere, & quam libet censuram sive coercitionem errogare possint.*

This Jurisdiction of Bishops is exercised either Universally by a Vicar General, usually a Lay-man; or particularly by a Commissary. [e] And e *Cof.* Tab. when he please the Bishop may do it himself.   The *2.*

The other part of their Jurisdiction is called Contentious; And here the
Bishop may himself judge in some Cases [f] but in the ordinary course
of Jurisdiction, a Civil Lawyer called his Chancellor is the Judge : This
Chancellor is and must be a Lay-man, which even Bishop *Goodman* of
Gloucester, [*Myst. Rel. Epist.* ' I have it and can produce it at this time,
' under the Kings own Hand and Seal, wherein he forbids that any Church-
' man or Priest in Holy Orders be a Chancellor : and this was the occasion
' of all the corruption of the Spiritual Courts : For Chancellors live only
' on the Fees of the Court : and for them to dismiss a Cause, it was to lose
' so much blood. See further in him.] a Papist Bishop of a Protestant
Diocess, complaineth in Print, that he could not get Reformed. This
Chancellor keepeth an Ordinary Court, in the form of a Civil Court,
where are Advocates for Council, and Proctors for pleading : [g] Certain men called Apparitors (whose name is commonly a scorn among
the people,) do from abroad the Country bring them in Accusations,
and Summon the persons accused ; besides those that by Plaintiffs are accused. Here are judged Causes about Church Materials, and Causes
Criminal ; which he that readeth the whole Book of Canons and the Vi-
sitation-Articles may see, they being too many for me to recite. [h] Besides a multitude of Cases about Marriages (to be contracted, dissolved,
separation) and Testaments, and the Goods of Intestate persons. [i]
Priests, Deacons and Lay-men are judged in these Courts ; The final
constraining penalty is Excommunication, or before that Suspension, and
other degrees of Church punishment before mentioned as belonging to
the Bishop : The supposed offenders are no otherwise dealt with to bring
them to true Repentance, than as in Civil Courts by other Lay-Judges.
They that appear not, and they that pay not the Fees of the Court and
Officers, are Excommunicate, and they that obey not the Orders of the
Court. In Excommunications and Absolutions the Lay-Chancellor is Judg,
but he writeth the Decree in the Bishops name : And (at least sometimes)
pro forma, some Priest or other is procured to be present (no Bishop,)
to utter the Sentence which the Lay Judge Decreeth : This Sentence is
sent by the Chancellor to the Minister of the Parish where the offender
liveth, who must publish it in the Church openly (as the Cryer doth the
Kings Proclamation;) But if it be the Minister himself that is Excommunicated, another Minister readeth it. The whole process of their
Judicial Tryals, Sentences and Executions you may see in *Cosin's, Tab.*
9. 10.

Besides the Chancellor's Courts (called the Bishops) the Archdeacons
have certain inferiour Courts, where they enquire after faults, and return the great ones to the Bishops Courts. [k] And they Induct or give
possession of Benefices.

As for the Parish Priests or Ministers, ordinary Parishes have but one
to each ; but Great Parishes cannot be served (as they call it) without a
Curate ; and each Chapel hath a Curate ; but all under *One*, that hath the
sole

f *Cos. Tab.* 8.

g *Cos. Tab.* 2. & *Tab.* 8.

h *Cos. ibid.*

i *Cos. ibid.*

k *Cos. Tab.* 2.

sole poſſeſſion of the Benefice, whether he be Parſon or Vicar. Theſe Prieſts are Ordained by the Biſhop (ſome one, two, or three Presbyters if preſent alſo impoſing hands:) They are choſen to the Church and Benefice by the Patron who preſents them to the Biſhop; who giveth them Inſtitution for Title, and Induction for poſſeſſion. When he is Ordained, Inſtituted and Inducted, he muſt not Preach to his People, till he hath got a [*l*] Licenſe from the Biſhop of that Dioceſs; no though he were before Licenſed in another Dioceſs : Nor muſt he Preach or Officiate, or have any Benefice or Church, till he have ſub-ſcribed, and done as is expreſſed in the Act of Uniformity: And he muſt declare his Aſſent and Conſent to all things contained in and pre-ſcribed by three Books (the Liturgy, the Book of Ordination, and the Articles.) And he muſt ſwear obedience to his Biſhop.

His Office is (when after Licenſed) to Preach, to Read the Scriptures, and the Apocrypha, and many Acts of Parliament, and Homilies; to read the Liturgy, or Prayers; To give notice of Holy-days and Faſting-days : To Baptize all Children, without exception, that are offered him, by Godfathers and Godmothers (the Parents not Covenanting for them, but others;) To Marry perſons ; To Church Women after Child-bear-ing; To hear Children in Church ſay the Catechiſm that is in the Liturgy (but many have been forbidden by the Biſhops to expound it, or tell the Children the meaning of the words which they ſay by rote:) To celebrate and give the Sacrament to the Pariſhioners : To viſit the Sick, and abſolve them, if they ſay they repent : To bury the Dead, af-firming of them all that God in mercy hath taken their ſouls, as our dear brethren, to himſelf; excepting only, 1. Thoſe that die unbaptized, (though Children of Princes or godly Parents) 2. Thoſe that are Excom-municate (uſually ſuch as durſt not Conform to them:) 3. And thoſe that kill themſelves (though in a Frenſie:) To uſe the Croſs, Surplice, and other Ceremonies of the Church: And to joyn with the Church-War-dens (if they pleaſe) in preſenting ſuch to the Biſhops Courts, as break their Laws; And if he deny any notorious offender the Sacrament, he muſt become his Accuſer before the Chancellour, or Biſhops Court. [*m*] This is the Office of a Pariſh Prieſt.

Where you muſt note 1. in *general*, that he hath no *Judicial Admini-ſtration in the Church:* [*n*] They ordinarily ſay, that he hath no *Juriſ-diction*, but meer *Prieſtly Orders*; As if they knew not that *Prieſtly Order* is nothing but the Sacred Office; and that that Office is the Power of the Keys, or eſſentially containeth the *Power* of *Guiding* the *Flock* in *Teach-ing, Worſhip* and *Diſcipline; under* Chriſt the Chief Prophet, Prieſt and King. Civil Juriſdiction over the Church is the Kings, and Spiritual is part of the Prieſtly Office or Order (as to the ſubject people to be go-verned.)

2. Particularly note, 1. that the Miniſter hath in *England* no power to Judge whom to Baptize, and whom not, but muſt Baptize all that are

offered,

C

l Act of Uniform.

That Pa-riſh Prieſts have no Govern-ing power, ſee Dr. Zouch ; as alſo that the King is the Ec-cleſiaſtical Supream.

m Coſ. Tab. 13.

n Coſ. Tab. 11.

offered, though the Children of Jews, Infidels, Turks, Apoftates.

2. That he hath no power to hinder the admiffion of any fo baptized, into the ftate of adult Members by the Bifhops Confirmation. For though it be faid Children fhall bring his Certificate, that they can fay the Catechifm, yet 1. thofe Children may go without it, and do ordinarily: When I was confirmed my felf, none was required, nor did I ever fee any given. 2. And if it were, the poor Children feldom underftand any thing that they fay, or much. 3. There is not one of multitudes in our Churches that ever fought or minded fuch Confirmation, becaufe of its abufe.

3. That he hath no power to hinder any confirmed, or adult perfons from the Sacraments, on the account of the groffeft ignorance or infidelity: when multitudes among us know not what the Sacrament is, nor know the effentials of the Chriftian Faith.

4. He hath no power to convent any open offender before him, to call him to repentance: They may chufe to come to him, or to open their doors to him, or fpeak to him, if he come to them.

5. He hath no power to call them to Repentance openly before the Church, or pray by name for their Repentance, or admonifh them.

6. He hath no power to judge any perfon to be Excommunicate.

7. Nor to abfolve any that is penitent after Excommunication; But only to read the Lay-Chancellours fentences, fent him in the Bifhops name.

8. He hath no power to forbear giving the Lords Supper to any one how notorious an offender foever, unlefs he will profecute him at the Bifhops Court, nor then, but for once: So that if he pay his Fees and be Abfolved there, though the Minifter know him to be never fo bad, he muft give the Sacrament the next time. And the profecution is fo odious and fruitlefs that I never knew any do it, except againft the Nonconformifts.

9. He that feeth never fo great figns of Impenitency in any man that is fick, or will but fay that he is fick, hath no power to deny him private Abfolution and the Sacrament, if he do but fay, I Repent.

10. He hath no power to forbear pronouncing of all Traytors, Murderers, Adulterers, Perjured, Atheifts, &c. that never profeft Repentance, at their Burial, that *God hath of his mercy taken to himfelf the foul of this our dear brother*; except the unbaptized, &c. aforefaid.

And note, 1. that the Parifh Prieft hath no power to do thefe things either by himfelf, or in conjunction with the Bifhop, or any other.

2. And that there is not one Suffragan Bifhop or Chorepifcopus in *England* under the 26 Bifhops, to do any part of their work in thefe 97025 Parifhes.

CHAP.

CHAP. III.

Our Judgment of the History of the Antient Church-Go-
vernment, and of the rife of the Diocefan Prelacy.

I Shall anon fhew more fully, that there are two things efpecially in
which we think the very *Species* of our Diocefan Prelacy to be altered from the antient Epifcopacy. One is in the Extent of their
Office, as to their fubject Charge, a Bifhop *infimæ fpeciei*, of the
loweft *fpecies*, having then but *One Church*, and now a Bifhop *infimæ fpe-*
ciei having many hundred Churches made into one, or nullified to make
One. 2. In the *Work* of their Office, which was then purely Spiritual or
Paftoral, and is now mixt of Magiftratical and Minifterial, exercifed by
mixed Officers in Courts much like to Civil Judicatures. The Hiftory of
their rife I fuppofe is this.

1. Chrift made a difference among his Minifters himfelf, while he
chofe twelve to be Apoftles, and fpecial Witneffes of his Doctrine, Life,
and Refurrection, and Afcenfion, and to be the Founders of his Church,
and the Publifhers of his Gofpel abroad the World.

2. As thefe Apoftles preached the Gofpel themfelves, and planted
Churches, fo did many others as their helpers, partly the feventy fent
by Chrift, and partly called by the Apoftles themfelves; And all thefe
exercifed indefinitely a preparing Miniftry, before particular Churches
were gathered abroad the World, and afterwards went on in gathering
and calling more.

3. Befides this preparing unfixed Miniftration, the fame Apoftles alfo
placed, by the peoples confent, particular fixed Minifters over all the feveral Churches which they gathered.

4. Thefe *fixed Minifters* as *fuch*, they named indifferently, Bifhops,
Elders, Paftors and Teachers. Whereas thofe of the fame Office in general yet unfixed, are called either by the General name of *Chrift's Mini-*
fters, or *Stewards of his Myfteries*; And in regard of their fpecial works,
fome were called Apoftles, fome Prophets, and fome Evangelifts.

5. Thefe Apoftles though unfixed and having an Indefinite charge, yet
went not all one way, but as God's Spirit and prudence guided them, they
difperfed themfelves into feveral parts of the World.

6. But as they did many of them firft ftay long at *Jerufalem*, fo afterward in planting and fetling Churches, they fometimes ftayed feveral
months or years in one place, and then went to another. And fo did the
Evangelifts or Indefinite Affiftants whom they fent forth on the fame
work.

Acts 14.
23. Tit.
1.

C 2 7. While

7. While they ſtayed in theſe newly planted Churches they were themſelves the chief Guides of the People: And alſo of their fixed Biſhops.

8. This abode in ſettling the particular Churches and their particular Biſhops or Elders, occaſioned Hiſtorians, afterward to call both Apoſtles and Evangeliſts (ſuch as *Timothy*, *Titus*, *Silas*, *Silvanus*, *Luke*, *Apollo*, &c.) the Biſhops of thoſe Churches; though they were not ſuch as the fixed Biſhops were, who undertook a ſpecial Charge and care of one particular Church alone, or above all other Churches.

9. On this account the ſame Apoſtle is ſaid to be the firſt Biſhop of many Churches; (as *Peter* of *Antioch*, and *Rome*; *Paul* of *Corinth*, *Epheſus*, *Philippi*, &c.) When indeed the Apoſtles were the particular fixed Biſhops of no Churches, but the Biſhops equally of many, as a ſort of unfixed Epiſcopacy is included in Apoſtleſhip.

10. On this account alſo it is that *Timothy* is ſaid to be Biſhop of *Epheſus*, becauſe he was left there for a time to ſettle that and other Churches of *Aſia* near it, as an Aſſiſtant of the Apoſtles: And ſo *Titus* is called the Biſhop of *Crete*, becauſe he ſtaid in that Iſland (which was ſaid to have an hundred Cities) on this work, which belonged not to a particular Biſhop, but to the more indefinite Miniſtry.

11. How many ſuch fixed Biſhops, Elders, Paſtors, or Teachers, each particular Church muſt have, the Apoſtles never determined by a Law: But did *de facto* ſettle them according to the number of ſouls, and ſtore of qualified perſons: In ſome Churches it is poſſible there might be but one (with Deacons:) In others it is evident that there were many; as at *Jeruſalem*, *Corinth*, &c.

12. The particular Churches which were the charge of theſe fixed Biſhops or Elders were Societies of Chriſtians conjoyned for *Perſonal Communion in God's Worſhip, and mutual aſſiſtance in holy living*: And though for want of convenient room, or liberty, they did not always meet all in the ſame place, yet were they ordinarily no more than *could* meet in one place when they had liberty: and never more than could hold *perſonal Communion*, if not at once, yet at ſeveral times in publick worſhip: (As it is now in thoſe places where one part of the Family goeth to Church one part of the day, and another on the other part.) And thoſe by-Meetings which any had that came not conſtantly to the publick Aſſemblies, were but as our Houſe-Meetings, or Chapel-Meetings, but never as another Church: Nor were their Churches more numerous than our Pariſhes, nor near ſo great.

13. At the firſt they had no Conſecrated nor Separated places for their Church-Meetings, but Houſes or Fields, as neceſſity and opportunity directed them. But as ſoon as they could, even nature taught them to obſerve the ſame appointed and ſtated places for ſuch Aſſemblies: Which as ſoon as the Churches had peace and ſettlement, they appropriated to thoſe ſacred uſes only, though they had not yet the ſhape or name of Temples.   14. Though

14. Though the Pastors of the Church were all of one *Office*, now called *Order*, being all subordinate Ministers of Christ, in the Prophetical, Priestly and Regal parts of his Office, in the Power and Duty of Teaching, Worshiping and Government; yet was the disparity of Age, Grace and Guifts to be observed among them, and the younger Pastors (as well as people) owed a meet reverence and submission to the Elder, and the weaker to the stronger who had notoriously more of God's Grace and Guifts. So that in a Church where there were many Pastors it was not unlawful nor unnecessary, to acknowledge this disparity, and for the younger and weaker to submit much to the judgment of the elder and more able.

15. While they kept only to the exercise of the meer Pastoral work of Teaching, and Worshiping, and that Government which belongeth hereunto, they had little temptation (comparatively) to strive for a preeminence in Rule, or for a Negative Voice; But aliene or accidental work, did further that as followeth.

16. The Apostles did reprove those Worldly contentious and uncharitable Christians, who went to Law before Heathen Judges: And the thing shewed so little of the Christian Spirit of Love, and was also of so ill consequence, by scandals and dissentions, that it was worthy to be reproved, especially in Christians that were persecuted by those Magistrates. Therefore almost all the differences of Christians were necessarily decided by Arbitration: And none were thought so fit to be the Arbitrators, as the Elders or Pastors of the Churches. By which it came to pass, that where Churches were great, and the ceasing of persecution (which came but as storms that passed away) did restore that peace which cherished dissentions, the work of the Elders in these Arbitrations, was not small; especially as added to their greater proper Office-work.

17. At the same time many Heresies arose, which occasioned Divisions in the Churches, and sometimes among the Officers themselves.

18. And the Ministers being, though holy, yet imperfect, as well as other Christians, the remnants of self conceitedness and pride, occasioned also the trouble of the Churches: For when the Apostles themselves while Christ was with them strove who should be the Greatest, and have the highest place, it is no wonder if they did so afterward, who had not so great a measure of Grace as they.

19. Besides all this, when the Apostolical Virtues ceased, there were few Philosophers or Learned men that turned Christians, and few that had excellent Gifts of Oratory, fit to be Teachers of the Churches; And the most of the Elders were good men but of inferiour parts; Like the better, sort of our unlearned godly Christians. By which means it came to pass, that some one of the Clergy in every Church, (when there were many) having so much Knowledge, and Oratory as to overtop the rest, he was ordinarily more esteemed than the rest.

20. By these four means conjunct it quickly came to pass, that in every
Church

Church that had many Elders, some one was chosen by the rest and by the people, to be the chief, and to have some special power of Church affairs: And 1. In cases of frequent Arbitration, there seemed a kind of necessity, that some One be Umpire: For if half go one way and half the other, there can be no end: 2. And in case of Heresies and different Opinions in Religion, if One had not in each Church some deciding, over-ruling power, or Negative Voice, it is no wonder if Divisions were the hardlier prevented, and the Churches Unity hardly kept. 3. And especially when some *One* was really *wiser* and *abler* than the rest, it was thought but suitable to Nature, that he rather ruled the juniors and weaker sort, than that their Votes should rule him, or rule without him. 4. And when all men have too much self-love and Pride, which enclineth them to desire pre-eminence, and maketh them judge too high of themselves, it was thought safer for all the Clergy and People, to judge who among them was really the best and wisest man, than to leave every man to be judge of himself and of the rest: For so it was too likely that every man would think himself the wisest. Therefore one was chosen as supposed by others (even by the whole Church) as the fittest man to have a deciding and overseeing power among the rest, to avoid contention, which their own strife about pre-eminence would cause.

21. And there was a fifth cause, which was not much less than any of the rest: which was, that often through the scarcity of fit persons, One man was first settled over a new-gathered Church, before any others could be had to joyn with him. And therefore he being there first alone, and that in sole power, it was thought unfit that any that came after him, should come in without his consent or Ordination, because he was the sole Governour; so that, 1. because they came *after* him, 2. and that, by his *Will*, if not Ordination, it must needs follow that he would usually have the pre-eminence. As it is now among us, where the Rector of the Parish where there are divers Chapels, chusing his Curates, who are usually his Juniors, he is constantly of greater power than they, and ruleth them accidentally, though his Office be the same as theirs.

22. As by these means one Pastor got a pre-eminence of esteem and power above the rest, so in a short time he got the title of *Episcopus*, Bishop, to be appropriated to himself alone, leaving the name of Elders, and Pastors, and Priests unto the rest in common with himself: For he was now become the prime Overseer of the whole Church, both people and Elders.

23. Our own experience sheweth us how it came to pass, that the people themselves not only consented to all this, but also desired and promoted it: (especially then when the effects of Clergy-ambition had not fully appeared to the World:) For even now when a great Parish can get one Learned able Pastor, they say, we will allow you so much, but your Curates must take less: And they will not endure that the young and weak Curates, have either equal maintenance, or equal honour or power

over

over them, as the chief Paſtor of the Pariſh hath; ſo that the people themſelves are againſt an equality of power, where there is not an equality of worth.

24. Though we cannot prove that this fixed Epiſcopacy was either ſet up by the Apoſtles, or countenanced by them, nor yet that it was begun and in being in their days; yet it could not be long after their days that it begun; And if *Hierome* miſtake not, it began at *Alexandria* ſome years before the death of St. *John* the Apoſtle.

25. All this while the Biſhop was not ſuppoſed to be of a diſtinct Office, or *ſpecies* of Miniſtry, (now called *An Order*) but only an Overſeer and chief of perſons in the ſame Office with him; being in common with the reſt, *Epiſcopus plebis*, and extraordinarily, *Epiſcopus Cleri vel Epiſcoporum ſeu Presbyterorum*. As one of the Monks is made Abbot in a Monaſtery, or as one Juſtice among many is of the *Querum*, or one Judge on the Bench is the chief Juſtice: Or as the Preſident in an Academick College.

26. The chief thing in which a ſpecial power was given to the Biſhops above their fellow Presbyters was in *Ordination*, that none ſhould be Ordained without them; It being a matter of exceeding great conſequence to the Churches, what Miniſters were ſet over them, and therefore put chiefly in the power of theſe choſen men. And the next part of their power was in having the chief diſpoſal of all Church affairs, as our Pariſh Paſtors have now among their Curates: ſo that nothing was to be done in the Church without and againſt their conſent and pleaſure.

27. This Epiſcopacy did ſo univerſally obtain, that I remember not to have read of any ſort of Chriſtians, Orthodox or Heretical, Catholick or Schiſmatical, who ever refuſed it, or ſpake againſt it, till *Ærius*'s time. And even he ſpake not againſt it as flatly unlawful, but as unneceſſary, as far as I can gather from *Epiphanius*. And after him all ſorts and Sects of Chriſtians ſtill owned it: Even the *Donatiſts* and *Novatians*, who had their Biſhops as well as others.

28. In Scripture times we read not of any meer fixed Biſhops of particular Churches, who Ordained either Biſhops or Presbyters; but only Apoſtles and their unfixed Aſſiſtants, who had an equal charge of many Churches. Not that the *Office* of the *Indefinite unfixed* Miniſtry was not the ſame with the *Office* of the *fixed* Biſhops *in ſpecie*: (For both had power to do all the Miniſterial work, as they had a call and opportunity to exerciſe it.) But becauſe it being the employment, of the Indefinite or unfixed Miniſters to Gather and plant Churches, before they could be Governed, the Ordination of Elders over them, was part of the planting of them; and ſo fell to their lot, as part of their conſtituting work.

29. How it came to paſs that the Itinerant or Indefinite exerciſe of the Miniſtry for planting Churches, ſo quickly almoſt ceaſed after the Apoſtles days, is a matter worthy to be enquired after: For whereas ſome

think,

think, that *de jure & obligatione*, it ceased with the Apostles, as being their proper work, that cannot be true, 1. Because many others were employ- ed in the same work in the Apostles days: 2. Because it is Christ's own description of that Ministry to whom he promiseth his presence, to the end of the Age or World, *Mat.* 28. 19, 20. 3. Because to this day, there is still lamentable necessity of such: Five parts in six of the World being yet Infidels.

30. It is most probable that this service abated and withered gradually by the sloth and selfishness of Pastors. And that it was the purpose of the Apostles, that the fixed Bishops should do their part of both these works; that is, Both to preach. for the Converting of all the Infidel Countries near them, and also Govern their particular Churches (yet not but that some others might be deputed to the Gathering of Churches alone.) And then these Bishops finding so much work at home, and finding that the Itinerant work among Infidels, was very difficult, by reason of La- bour, Danger, and their want of Apostolical gifts, hereupon they spared themselves, and too much neglected the Itinerant work. Yet I must confess that such Evangelists did not yet wholly cease. *Eusebius Hist. lib.* 5. *cap.* 9. saith, *Pantænus* is said to have shewed such a willing mind to- wards the publishing of the Doctrine of Christ, that he became a Preach- er of the Gospel to the *Eastern Gentiles*, and was sent as far as *India*: For there were, I say there were then, many Evangelists prepared for this purpose, to promote and plant the Heavenly Word with Godly Zeal, after the manner of the Apostles.

31. It was the ordinary custome of the Apostles to preach and plant Churches first, in Cities, and not in Country Villages. Because in Ci- ties there were, 1. the greatest number of Auditors, and 2. the greatest number of Converts; And so there only, were found a sufficient num- ber to constitute a Church. Not that this was done through any pre- eminence of the City, or ignobility of Villages; but for the competent numbers sake. And had there been persons enow for a Church in Vil- lages, they would have placed Churches and Pastors there also (as at *Cenchrea* it seems they did.)

32. When there was a Church of Christians in the City, and a few Converts in the Country Villages that joyned with them, they all made up but one full Assembly, or Church, fit for personal Communion, for a long time after the Apostles days; the main body of the people being still Infidels: so that the Christian Churches stood among the Infidels as thin, as the Churches of the Anabaptists, Separatists and Independants did among us here in *England*, in the days when they had greatest Li- berty and countenance.

33. Though at first the Bishops being men of the same Office with the other Presbyters, were not to do a work distinct and of any other kind than the Presbyters might do, but only Lead them and Preside among them in the same work as their Conductors (as I said before of a chief Justice, &c.)

Yet

Yet afterward the Bishop for the honour of his calling appropriating certain actions to himself alone, the Presbyters not exercising those acts in time, the not exercising them seemed to signifie a want of Office or power to exercise them; and so subject Presbyters (who were never made by the Apostles that can be proved, nor by their command) were like a distinct Order or Species of Church-Officers, and grew from syn-Presbyters or assessours of the same Office *in specie* to be as much subjects to the Bishops, as the Deacons were to the Presbyters.

34. All this while the Bishop with his fellow Elders and Deacons dwelt together in the same City, and often in the same House, and met in the same Church, the Bishop sitting in the midst on a higher seat, and the Presbyters on each hand him in a semi-circle, and the Deacons standing; And the Presbyters Preaching and otherwise officiating as the Bishop appointed, who ruled the action. And the Converts of the Villages came to this City Church as Members of it, and joyned with the rest. In the days of the Author of the Epistles ascribed to *Ignatius*, every Church had but One Altar, and One Bishop with his Fellow Elders and Deacons as the note of its Unity; or Individuation. For so many people as had personal Communion at *One Altar*, with the *Bishop or Elders* were the constitutive parts of the Churches.

35. Thus it continued also in the days of *Justin, Tertullian* and *Cyprian,* no Bishop having more than *one Church* or *Altar,* without any other formed *self-communicating Church* under him, but only Oratories in City or Country.

36. The first that brake this Order were *Alexandria* and *Rome,* where Converts soon multiplyed to a greater number than could meet in one place, or Communicate at one Altar: wherefore sub-assemblies with their particular Presbyters, were there first formed, who Communicated distinctly by themselves. (Though there is no proof that they Communicated there in the Sacrament of a long time after that they met for Preaching and Prayer.) Yet even in *Rome* and *Alexandria* the only places that had more than one stated Assembly for 200 years or more, there were not so many Christians then as in the Parish that I now live in; See more of my Proof in the beginning of my *Church History abridged*: whose first and second Chapters belong specially to this Treatise, and therefore I must refer the Reader to them.

37. Even in *Epiphanius* time about 370 years after Christ, it is noted by him as a singularity in *Alexandria*, that they had distinct Assemblies besides the Bishops; whereupon *Petavius* himself largely giveth us notice, that in those days, except in a few very great Cities, there was but one Church-assembly in a Bishops charge.

38. After that in Cities, or Country Villages, the Converts multiplyed into more than could meet in one Assembly, and had allowance to Communicate in their sub-assemblies; yet were they appointed on certain great and solemn Festivals, to Communicate all with the Bishops at the chief City Church, which sheweth that the sub-assemblies then were few and small.

D

39. Thus

39. Thus was the Apostles Order by degrees subverted; and whereas they settled distinct Churches with their distinct Bishops, no Bishop having two Churches under him, (that had not also their proper Bishop) now One Church was made of many without many Bishops; sub-Presbyters first in the same Church being introduced, at last sub-Churches also were set up. And when they should have done as we do with Bees, let every new Swarm have a new Hive, and should have multiplyed Bishops and Churches, homogeneal, as sufficient numbers of Converts came in, instead of this, the City Bishops kept all *under them* as if they had been still *one Church* (yet not as Archbishops that have Bishops under them) and kept their sub-Presbyters as their Curates to officiate in the several Churches that had all no Bishops but One.

40. The causes of this were apparently most of the same which are mentioned before for the making of sub-Presbyters: Especially, 1. The selfishness of the Bishops, who were loth to let go any of the people from under their superiority: Because it was more honour to rule many than one single Congregation; and he was a greater man that had many sub-Presbyters and whole Assemblies at his command, than he that had not: And also *many* afforded greater maintenance than a *few*. And 2. the same Reasons that made men at first set up one Presbyter as Bishop over the rest, to avoid Divisions, and to determine Arbitrations, did now seem strong to them, for the keeping up the Authority of the City Bishop over the sub-Assemblies round about them. 3. And Cities only having been possessed of Bishops for many Years if not Ages, before there were Christians enow to make up Country Churches, both the Bishops and the City Inhabitants, (easily overlooking the Reason of it) took this for their Prerogative, and did plead Prescription; As if *Schools* being planted only in Cities first, the Cities and Schoolmasters should thence plead, that none must be setled in Country Villages, but what are ruled by the City School-Masters. And thus the Cities being far the strongest, and the Interest of the Citizens and Bishops in point of honour being conjunct, and none being capable of a Country charge, but such as the City Bishops at first Ordained to it (because then there were no other Bishops,) without resistance it came to pass that both Churches and Presbyters were subjected to the City Bishops. 4. And it greatly advanced this design that the Churches which were planted in the *Roman* Empire, did seek to participate of all secular honour that belonged to the place of their Residence: And (as Dr. *Hammond* hath largely opened, though not well justified) did form themselves according to the Model of the Civil Government: so that those Cities that had the Presidents or chief Civil Rulers and Judicatures in them, did plead a right of having also the chief Bishops and Ecclesiastical Judicatures: And thus not only Cities ruled the Country Villages, but in time the distinct powers and pre-eminences of Archbishops, Metropolitans, Primates, Patriarchs, and the *Roman* chief Patriarch or Pope came up: And the Pagan Common-
wealth

Vid. Epist. 2. Edict. Anacleti de forma provincia-li, Metro-pol. &c. Turrian, pro Epist. desr. c. 24. De novita-te hujus formæ leg. Blondel. cont. Decr. p. 1. 27. who giv-eth full testimony of it, cont. Anaclet. Ep. 2. 41.

wealth and Chriſtian Church, within the *Roman* Empire, (and the neighbouring parts that were influenced by them) had a great reſemblance.

41. But that which moſt notably ſet up this exort ſwelling and degenerate Prelacy, was the miſtaken zeal of *Conſtantine*, together with his Policy, and the ambition of Chriſtians and Biſhops that were gratified by it. For, 1. As *Conſtantine* perceived that it was the Chriſtians that were his ſureſt ſtrength, and when the Heathen Soldiers turned from one Emperour to another, as they were tempted, he knew that if he only did own the Chriſtians they would unanimouſly own him, and be conſtant to him; ſo alſo his Judgment and Zeal for Chriſtianity did concur with his Intereſt and Policy: And as all the Secular and Military Rulers depended on him for honour and power, throughout the *Roman* world, he thought it not ſeemly to give the chief Chriſtians who were the Biſhops, leſs honour than he did to the Heathens, and to common men: Nor did he think meet to deny to the Chriſtian Churches ſuch priviledges, as might ſomewhat ſet them higher than his other ſubjects. 2. And the Biſhops and Chriſtians coming from under long ſcorn and contempt, and coming newly from under the cruel Perſecution of *Dioclſian*, and affrighted anew by *Maxentius*, and *Licinius*, they were not only glad to be now honoured and advanced, but greatly lifted up with ſuch a ſudden wonderous change, as to be brought from ſcorn and cruel torments, to be ſet up above all others: As we ſhould have been, had we been in their caſe, and it's like ſhould no more have feared the ill conſequents of too much exaltation than they did. 3. And the Chriſtian people thought that the exaltation of their Biſhops was the honour and exaltation of their Religion it ſelf, as well as of their perſons.

42. Whereas (as is aforeſaid) the Chriſtians had commonly ſtated the power of Arbitrating all their Civil differences in the Biſhop alone (when the Apoſtle intimated that any *Wiſe man* among them, as ſuch, was fit for that buſineſs) it grew preſently to be accounted a heynous crime or ſcandal, for any Chriſtians to go to Law, before the Civil Magiſtrate. And *Conſtantine* finding them in poſſeſſion of this cuſtom, did by his Edict confirm it and enlarge it: decreeing that all Biſhops ſhould be Judges of all the Chriſtians cauſes by conſent, and that no Civil Judge or Magiſtrate ſhould compel any Chriſtian to his bar: Inſomuch that in *Theodoſius* his days, when one of *Ambroſe* his Presbyters had a cauſe to be tryed, he denyed himſelf to be a Chriſtian, that he might have it decided by the Civil Magiſtrate, that was Chriſtian alſo. So that even Chriſtian Magiſtrates might not judge unwilling Chriſtians but the Biſhops only. Yet had not the Biſhops then the power of the Sword, but decided all as Arbitrators, and enforced their Sentences with rigorous penances and Church-cenſures: By which means, 1. many the more turned Chriſtians (without the Faith and Holineſs of Chriſtians) that they might both partake of the Chriſtians honour and immunities, and ſpecially that they might be free from corporal penal-

ties

ties for their crimes. (And who would not do fo, if it were now our cafe.) 2. And by this means the rigorous penalties of the Church by penances were the more eafily fubmitted to, as being more eafie than corporal pains and mulcts. And when thus by the Laws and countenance of fo great an Emperour, the Bifhops were made the Judges of all that were Chriftians at prefent, and all that would turn Chriftians that defired it, it is eafie to underftand, 1. what a Lordfhip they muft needs have as to the kind of power; 2. How their Office muft degenerate from purely fpiritual, into fecular or mixt : 3. And how numerous their Flocks, and large their Provinces would foon be.

And here you muft note thefe things, 1. That the Bifhop of every Church was made Judge of thefe caufes; not alone by himfelf, but with his Presbyters or Clergy, who judged with him. 2. That yet this power was not then taken to be any effential or integral part at all of the Paftoral Office; but an Accidental work, which Lay-men might do as well as Paftors; and that it was committed to the Bifhop only as the beft able for Arbitration; becaufe of his abilities and intereft, and that as a matter of meer convenience; and alfo for the honour of his place. 3. That therefore this Judging power for ending ftrife and differences, might be alienated from the Clergy and done by Lay-men, where there was caufe. 4. And that the Bifhop had fo much more power than the Presbyters that he could commit it from them to Lay-men. All this that one inftance of *Silvanus* in *Socrates, lib. 7. cap. 37.* (and in *Hanmer, cap. 36.*) whofe words were thus [Silvanus *alfo no lefs expreffed in his other acts and dealings, the good motion of his Godly mind. For when he perceived that the Clergy refpected nothing but gain in deciding the Controverfies of their Clients, (O woful Clergy!) he thenceforth fuffered none of the Clergy to be judge, but took the fupplications, and requefts of fuiters, and appointed. One of the* Laity, *whom for certain he knew to be a juft and godly man, and gave him the hearing of their caufes, and fo ended quietly all contentions and quarrels.*] (And the likelieft way it was.) You fee here, 1. that when Princes will needs make the Clergy Magiftrates to honour them, the wife and good men of the Clergy will return fuch power to the Laity, as ufually fitter for it. 2. And that it is no wonder that when Law-bufinefs is caft upon the Clergy, if they grow worfe than Lawyers in covetoufnefs and injuftice. 3. And yet this was not a making Lay-men to be Chancellors that had the power of the Keys! For *Silvanus* did only appoint Lay-men to do Lay-mens work; to arbitrate differences : but not to excommunicate, nor to judge men to excommunication, as they do now. 4. And this was not a making of Ecclefiaftical Elders that were not Paftors : and therefore it is no countenance for fuch : but it was a prudent cafting back that work on the Laity, which good Emperours had in imprudent piety caft upon the Clergy, that each might do his proper work. 5. But this was but one good Bifhop that was fo wife and honeft ; and therefore it proved no general reformation.

This

This Judicial power went so far and took up so much of the Clergies time, that the Synod *Taraconens.* was after this put to Decree, *Can.* 4. that the Clergy should not judge Causes on the Lords day; and *Can.* 10. that no Bishop or Clergy-man should take rewards or bribes for Judgments.

And the *Canons* so deterred Christians from seeking Justice from the Civil Judicatures, that they had few but Heathens to be Judges of. Yea the Christians thought so hardly of the Judges themselves (for punishing men by the Sword, when the Bishops even for murder it self did punish them but with Penance,) that they doubted sometime whether those Christians that exercised Magistracy or Civil Judgment after Baptisme, were not therefore to be taken for sinners; as is visible in *Innocent* 1. his *Epist.* to *Epist.* 3. to *Exuper. Tholesan. cap.* 3. in *Crab. Tom.* 1. *p.* 459.

And before in *Silvester's Concil. Rom. apud Crab Vol.* 1. *p.* 280. *Can.* 16. it is Decreed [*Nemo Clericus vel Diaconus aut Presbyter propter causam suam quamlibet intret in curia, quum omnis curia à cruore, dicitur, & immolatio simulachrorum est: Quod siquis Clericus in curiam introierit, anathema suscipiat, nunquam rediens ad matrem Ecclesiam: A Communione autem non privatur propter tempus turbidum.* And *Constantine* is said to be a Subscriber, with 284 Bishops, 45 Presbyters, and 5 Deacons. And in former *Conc. sub Silvest.* [*Nullum Clericum ante judicem stare licet.*]

I know that *Duarenus* and *Grotius* describe not the Bishops power as so large as the Canonists do. But *Duarenus* confesseth that *Theodosius* made a Law, that *lites omnes & controversiæ forenses ad judicium Ecclesiæ remitterentur, si alter uter litigatorum id postularet.* That all strifes and controversies forensick should be remitted to the judgment of the Church, if either of the contenders required it: And that *Charles* the Great renewed and confirmed the same Law: *Duar. lib.* 1. *p.* 8. And *Grotius de Imper. sum pol. p.* 236. saith, *This Jurisdiction by consent the Bishops received from* Constantine, *with so great power, that it was not lawful further to hazzle any business which the Bishops sentence had decided;* that is, saith he, *remotâ appellatione.* And he there sheweth that three sorts of Jurisdiction were by the Emperours given to the Bishops: 1. *Jure ordinario,* and so they judged of all matters of Religion (and which the Canons reached, which went very far in heinous crimes.) 2. *Ex consensu partium,* when the parties chose the Bishop for their Judge (*Vid. Concil. Chalced. c.* 9.) 3. *Ex delegatione;* which yet went further: And even to the *Jews* such kind of power had been granted.

But of this whole matter of the Rise of such Prelacy, their Courts and power, *Pardre Paulus* hath spoken so well and truly in his *Histor. Concil. Trident. pag.* 330, 331, &c. that I would intreat the Reader to turn to it and peruse it, as that which plainly speaketh our judgment of the History now in question: Read also his History of Benefices.

43. The countenance of the Emperour with these honours and immunities, having brought the *World* into the Church, or filled the Churches with Carnal-temporizers, the numbers were now so great, that quickly the great-

great Cities had many Parifh Churches, and the Country Villages about had fome ; fo that now about 400 or 500 Years after Chrift, moft Bifhops of great Cities had more Churches than one, even feveral fub-Affemblies, and Altars, as dependant on their Mother Church.

44. Yet were their Dioceffes (whch at firft were called Parifhes) fomewhat bounded, by the Canon and Edicts, which decreed that every City where there were Chriftians enow to make a Church, fhould have a Bifhop of their own, and that no Bifhop (except two, who bordered one on Scithia a rude unconverted Countrey, and the other on the like cafe, of which more in due place.)

45. And then every *oppidum* or populous Town, like our Market-Towns and Corporations, was called πόλις, a City, and not only a few among many that have that name by priviledge, as it is in *England* now. So that even at this height of Prelacy, about 500, 600 or 700 Years after Chrift, they were but as if every Corporation or Market-Town in *England* had a Bifhop, who ruled alfo the adjacent Villages. For though when they began to fwell, it was once decreed by one Council, that Villages and every fmall City fhould not have a Bifhop, left the Name of a Bifhop fhould grow vile or cheap ; yet this was but with this addition, [thofe Villages or fmall Cities where there was not a fufficient number of Chriftians:] (whereas *Gregory* at *Neocefarea* thought feventeen a fufficient number to have a Bifhop.) And the Canons, that every City fhould have a Bifhop, remained ftill in force.

45. Yet was it for about 440 Years fo far from thefe great Bifhops to ufurp the Sword, or any coercive or coactive power, on mens Bodies or Eftates, that they unanimoufly held that the Magiftrate himfelf was not to punifh mens Bodies for Herefie or a falfe Religion. Till at laft the bloody violence of the *Circumcellian Donatifts*, did caufe *Auguftine* in this to change his mind, and think them meet for the Magiftrates coercion.

46. When Bifhops grew carnal and ungodly, and more regarded the keeping up their Power, Parties and Opinions, than Charity, they began to diftruft the Spiritual Weapons of their warfare; and inftead of true vigilancy againft errours, and confutation of them, by clear reafon and a holy life, they fled to the Rulers to do it by the Sword. But though *Ithacius* and *Idacius* with their Synod of Bifhops, excited *Maximus* to take this courfe againft the *Prifcilianifts*; yet not only St. *Martyn* did therefore to the death avoid their Synods and Communion, and petitioned the Emperour, for the Hereticks peace ; but even St. *Ambrofe* alfo at *Milan* would have no Communion with thofe Bifhops, that had done this thing.

47. About the Year 430, or after, *Cyril* at *Alexandria* did lead the way, and actually ufed the Sword againft the Lives, Eftates and Liberties of Offenders : An example which others quickly followed : And eafily did he ftep from the great Judicial Power before defcribed, to a forcing power, the preparations being fo great, and the Emperour fo ready to exalt them, and the people of *Alexandria* fo turbulent and inclined by pride and paffion to fuch ways.
48. As

Vit. Ambrof. per Baron.

48. As the Prelacy thus swelled, so the Churches grew suddenly more corrupted with all manner of Vice. The Bishops began with sorrow to confess unto the Hereticks, that the greater number in the Churches were naught. When they should chuse their Bishops they could seldom agree; but frequently instead of holy peaceable Votes, did turn to Devilish rage and blood-shed, and covered the Streets and Church-floors with the Carkasses of the slain; (especially in the Case of *Damasus* and others at *Rome*, and oft at *Alexandria* and *Constantinople.*) Frequently they fell into fewds, and fought it out, and murdered people by multitudes: Even the strict holy Monks of the *Egyptian* Desarts, were as forward as others to fighting, blood-shed and sedition: Even in their ignorance, for such a paultry and sottish an Opinion, as that of the *Anthropomorphites*, as that God hath the shape and parts of a man: so that they forced that deceitful treacherous Bishop *Theophilus Alex.andr.* to flatter them, and curse the Books of *Origen* (not for his errours, but for the opposite truth) and to take on him to hold as they did. When God tryed them with a *Julian* (who did persecute them very little,) they reproached him to his face, and tryed his patience as well as he did theirs. The *Antiochians* scornfully bid him shave his Beard and make Halters of it. In a word, when *Constantine* had brought the World into the Church, the Church grew quickly too like the World. *Socrat.l.3. c. 15.*

49. But it was not the people only, but the Pastors, both Prelates and Presbyters, that grew licentious, wicked, proud, contentious, turbulent, and the shame of their Order and Profession, and the great disturbers and dividers of the Churches: except here and there an *Ambrose*, an *Augustine*, a *Chrysostome*, a *Basil*, a *Gregory*, an *Atticus*, a *Proclus*, and a few such that so shined among a darkened degenerate Clergy, as to be singled out for Saints. Abundance got these great and tempting Prelacies by Simony, and more by making friends to Courtiers: And not a few by Carnal compliances with the people: what abundance of most sharp Epistles did *Isidore Pelusiota* write to *Eusebius* the Bishop, and to *Sosinus*, *Martianus*, *Eustathius*, &c. of all their horrible wicked lives, and yet could never procure their Reformation? What abundance of Epistles did he write against them to other Bishops, and yet could not procure their correction or removal? What a sad character doth *Sulpitius Severus* give of the Bishops that prosecuted the *Priscilianists*, and in particular of their Leader *Ithacius*, of his own knowledge? What abundance of Prelates are shamefully stigmatized, by *Socrates*, *Sozomen*, *Theodoret*, *Euagrius*, &c? When a Rebel rose up against his Prince, and got but the stronger party, and possession, how quickly did they flatter him and own him. I find but one Bishop besides St. *Martin* in all *France* and that part of *Germany*, that disowned *Maximus* that murdered *Gratian*: The rest applauded him for their own ends: Nor in that part of *Italy* I find not any besides *Ambrose* and one *Hyginus* that disowned him: (Not that I think it my part to condemn all the holy Bishops who professed subjection to Usurpers in possession:

fion : Even holy *Ambrofe* could write to the odious Tyrant *Eugenius*, [*Clementiffimo Imperatori Eugenio*] concluding [*Nam cum privato detulerim corde intimo, quomodo non deferrem Imperatori.*] *When I honoured thee a private man from the bottom of my heart, how can I but honour thee being Emperour ?*] And how far have the *Roman* Bifhops gone in this, even to *Phocas*, and fuch as he ?)

When good *Gregory Nazianz.* was chofen and fettled Bifhop of *Conftantinople*, and loved and honoured by a good Emperour, yet was he rejected (though he eafily yielded) even by the Synod of Bifhops, in the arrogancy of their minds, becaufe that he came not in by them. With what pride, what falfhood, what turbulency did *Theophilus Alexand.* carry on all his bufinefs with the Monks, and for the depofing of *Chryfoftome ?* And how arrogantly and turbulently did *Epiphanius* joyn with him ? and even *Hierome* make himfelf partaker ? And how eafily did he get a Synod even where *Chryfoftome* lived to fecond them ? fuch lamentable inftances are more eafie than pleafant to be cited.

And that Epifcopacy which was fet up to prevent Herefie and Divifions, did afford the Heads of moft of the Herefies and Divifions that befell the Churches. How few of all the Herefies mentioned by *Epiphanius*, after that Prelacy was in force, were not Headed and carried on by Prelates ? And when the *Arian* Herefie fprung up by a Presbyter, the Prelates fo numeroufly received it, that they feemed to be the far greater part, if not the main body of the Imperial Church : Witnefs the perverting of many Emperours ; the many Councils at *Sirmium*, *Ariminum*, &c. And the many new Creeds which *Socrates* and *Hilary* fo fhamefully enumerate and declaim againft. So that it was faid that the World groaned to find it felf turned *Arian*.

And their fewds and inhumane contentions were fo many and odious, that it is a fhame to read them. Multitudes of Cities had Bifhops fet up againft Bifhops, and fome Cities had more than two, or three : The people reviling and hating each other, and fometime fighting tumultuoufly unto blood, for their feveral Prelates. The Chriftian World was made as a Cockpit, and Chriftian Religion made a fcorn, by the Contentions of the Bifhops. *Conftantines* wifdom, confcience and intereft, engaged him to ufe all his fkil, his *kindnefs* and his *power*, to reconcile them : And if he had not done what he did, how unfpeakably wretched would their odious contentions have rendered them ? And yet he profeffeth his heart almoft broken by their diffenfions ; and while he chid them bitterly and exhorted them kindly, he could not prevail. His Sons that fucceeded him laboured to unite the Bifhops, (though in different ways) and could not do it. *Jovianus* the little time he reigned, declared his hatred of their contentions, and how much he loved a peaceable man : but that did not cure them, even when they came new from under a *Julian*. I will look no lower, to the more degenerate Prelacy ; but recite the doleful words of *Eufebius* ; even of thofe that were not at the worft, and came but newly

from

Theodoret Ecclef. Hift. l. 1. cap. 10. Leg. Valentiniani & Valentus ; Legem feu Literas in Theodoreti Eccl. Hift. l. 4. c. 7. & Heftor. Andeanorum, c. 9. & Meffalianorum c. 10. cum interpretatione D. Hookeri, li. 7. p. 65. de Andio.

From under the persecutions of former Emperours, when they had but a little prosperity, immediately before *Dioclesans* persecution, they are thus described. [*How great and what manner of glory and liberty the doctrine of piety due to Almighty God, preached in the World by Christ, hath obtained before the persecution of our time, among all mortal men both Grecians and Barbarians, it requireth more labour to declare, &c. The clemency of the Emperours (when Heathen) towards the Christians was so increased, to whom also they committed the Government of the Gentiles; And for the great favour they bare to our Doctrine, they granted liberty and security to the Professors of Christianity. What shall I say of them, that in the very Palace of the Emperours, and in the presence of Princes lived most familiarly: which esteemed of their Ministers so highly, that they granted them in their presence freely to deal in matters of Religion, both by word and deed; together with their wives and children and servants? And thus one might then have seen the Bishops of all Churches in great reverence and favour among all sorts of men, and with all Magistrates. Who can worthily describe those innumerable heaps, and flocking multitudes, throughout all Cities and famous Assemblies, frequenting the places dedicated to prayer: Because of which circumstances, they not contented with the old and ancient buildings (which could not receive them) have throughout all Cities, builded them from the Foundation wide and ample Churches: These things thus prevailed in process of time, and daily increased far and nigh: So that no malice could intercept, no spiteful fiend bewitch, no wight with cunning at all hinder it, as long as the Divine and heavenly hand of God upheld and visited his People, whom as yet he worthily accepted. But after that our affairs through too much liberty, ease and security, degenerated from the Natural rule of piety; and after that one pursued another with open contumely and hatred; and when that we impugned our selves by no other than our selves, with the armour of spite, and sharp spears of approbrious words, so that Bishops against Bishops, and People against People, raised sedition; last of all, when that cursed hypocrisie and dissimulation had swam even to the brim of malice; The heavy hand of Gods high judgment after his wonted manner (whilest as yet the Ecclesiastical Societies assembled themselves nevertheless) began softly by little and little to visit us; so that the persecution that was raised against us took first his Original, from the Brethren that were under Banner in the Camp. When as we were touched with no sense thereof, nor went about to pacifie God, we heaped sin upon sin, thinking like careless Epicures, that God neither cared, nor would visit our sins; And they which seemed our Shepherds, laying aside the rule of piety, practised contention and schism among themselves, and whilst they aggravated these things, that is, contentions, threatnings, mutual hatred and enmity, and every one proceeded in Ambition, much like Tyranny it self, then I say, then did the Lord make the daughter of Zion obscure, and overthrew from above the glory of Israel, &c.* — c. 2. *We saw with our eyes the Oratories thrown down to the ground, the foundations digged up, the holy Scriptures burned to ashes in the open Market-place, and the Pastors of the Churches some shamefully hid themselves.* — *Yet is it not our drift to describe the bitter calamities of these men, which at length they suffered,*

Euseb. l. 8. c. 1. Dr. Hammer's Translat. p. 144, 145.

E

nor

nor to record their diffension and infolency practifed among themselves, before the perfecution, &c.]

Note that all this was before *Arius* his Herefie, even before *Dioclefians* cruelties; but not before the beginning of Church-Tyranny and ambition, as is faid.

But after this, alas, how much greater were their enormities and diffentions, when their Tyranny was much encreafed; It would grieve any fober Chriftian to read how the Chriftian World hath been toffed up and down, and the people diftracted, and Princes difturbed and dethroned, and Herefies fomented, and horrid Perfecutions, and bloodfhed caufed, by the pride and contentioufnefs of Prelates : And moft of all this, in profecution of that Controverfie, which Chrift decided fo long ago, *viz. Who fhould be greateft. It was not Religion,* faith *Socrates, l. 5. c. 22. that the two* Arian *Sects of* Marinus *and* Agapius *was about, but Primacy : They ftrove which of them fhould be the chief : wherefore many Clergy-men under the jurifdiction of thefe Bifhops, perceiving the ambition, the rancour and malice of thefe proud Prelates, forfook them, &c.*

Macedonius at *Conftantinople* was fo Tyrannical, that as he came in by cruelty, fo he caufed more, by prefumptuous removal of the bones of *Conftantine,* to another Church, that he might pull down that, and this without *Conftantius* the Emperours knowledge : where the people in Factions fought it out, till the Church and Streets were full of Carkalfes and ftreams of blood, faith *Socrates.* The fame man, fet four Companies of Souldiers on the *Novatians* in *Paphlagonia,* till he enraged the people with Clubs and Bills to kill them all. And he was fo Tyrannical in forcing Conformity, that he not only forced men to the Sacrament, but gagged their mouths and popt it in.

Nor was this only the vice of the Heterodox but the Orthodox, as is aforefaid. And as the *French* and *German* Bifhops aforefaid did againft the *Prifcillinaifts,* fo for their own intereft againft one another, they flattered and reftlefly inftigated the Civil power, even Ufurpers to execute their Wills : and favoured that power that moft favoured them. When the forefaid *Maximus* had killed *Gratian* and reigned in *France,* and entered *Italy;* (after that *Ambrofe* had ftopt him a while) *Theophilus Alexandr.* fendeth an Agent Presbyter with two Letters, and a rich prefent, one to *Maximus* and one to *Theodofius;* ordering him to ftay the iffue of the Fight; and give the Prefent with his Letter to him that proved the Conqueror : But a Servant ftole the Letters from the Prieft, and opened the whole bufinefs, and caufed the Prieft to fly and hide himfelf.

50. Thefe contentions of the Bifhops and corruption of manners, fo diftafted the more Religious fort of the people, that it occafioned the multiplying of feparating Herefies : and greatly encreafed and confirmed others, efpecially the *Donatifts,* and *Novatians;* becaufe men thought them to be of better lives than the Orthodox.

51. Yea, by their very abufe of good and holy men, they drove even

the

[margin note:] Socrat. l. 2.
c. 3.
Id. ib.

the Orthodox often to separated Societies, as thinking so bad Prelates unfit to be communicated with. As in *Constantinople* their abuse, ejection and banishment of *Chrysostome* caused great numbers of his faithful people to forsake the Church; and meet only in separated Conventicles; And though they differed in no point of Doctrine, Worship or Discipline from the rest, all that they could do by tyranny and threats would never bring them again to the Church; but they were called *Joannites*, and assembled by themselves; till *Atticus* by wise and honest means first began the reconciliation, by the publick inserting of *Chrysostome*'s name among their honoured Bishops in the daily Liturgy of the Church, and *Proclus* after wisely perfected it, by fetching the bones of *Chrysostome* with honour, from the place of his banishment into the Church. But *Theodoret*, *Hist. Eccl. l. 5. c. 36.* ascribeth it to that good Emperour *Theodosius* Junior: It's like a good Bishop and he consented. For saith *Socrates, c. 40. Proclus behaved himself fairly* *Socrat. l. 7.* *towards all men, perswading himself that it was far easier for him by fair means* *c. 44.* *to allure men to the Church, than by force to compel them to the Faith.*

52. The multitudes of Schismes and horrid enormities in the Church of *Rome*; the grand corruption of Religion by them; the shameful divisions between the *Greek* and *Western* Churches, began so long ago and continued to this day, with much more such evidence, do tell the World that is willing to see, what all this tended to as it's perfection.

53. And having thus shewed how the Bishops of the Flock came to be Bishops of Bishops, and how they grew from the Pastoral Office to a pompous denomination mostly secular, and how the Bishops of single Churches, did grow to be the Bishops of multitudes of Churches turned into one Diocesan Church of another species, we shall leave it to those that are wise and impartial, to judge whether a true Reformation must retrieve them, and what Age and state of the Church must be our pattern, to which we should endeavour to return; and in what point it is that it is meet or possible, for Christians unanimously to fix between the Apostolical institution and the height of Popery? And what satisfying proof any man can give that in a line of 1500 Years, that it is the right point that he hath chosen.

CHAP.

CHAP. IV.

*The Judgement of those Nonconformists (now silenced)
who 1660. addressed themselves to King Charles the
Second for Concord in the matter of Church-Government : what they then offered, and what those of the
Authors mind now hold, as to the Right of what is before Historically related.*

AS I have delivered our Judgment about the History of Prelacy,
so shall I next freely and truly express my own Judgment and
those that have concurred with me about the right of Church-
Government it self, (supposing those 100 *Propos. ad Lud. Moli-
næum* which I have published about the Nature of Church-power, and the
extent of the Magistrates power in Church-matters.) For Truth hath great
advantage when it appeareth, 1. compact, and entire, 2. and in the o-
pen light. Since the writing of this our judgment is more fully published
in the Nonconformists first and second Plea for Peace.

Joh. 5.11.
Gen. 3.15.
Joh. 17.2.
Mat. 28.
18, 19.
Eph. 1.
21, 22.
 Prop. 1. Since the Fall of Man, as God hath given a Saviour to the
World, by whom he hath made a new Covenant with or for Mankind ;
so hath he delivered all things into the Redeemer's hands, and given him
all power in Heaven and Earth, making him the Administrator General,
and Head over all things to the Church.

 2. Some things are under Christ as *Utensils*, viz, *Inanimates and Bruites* ;
some are under him as *meer enemies* subdued, as *Devils* ; some are under
him as *generally Redeemed*, and *subjects de jure*, or *quoad obligationem*, to be
Ruled and used upon terms of Mercy ; And so are all Mankind in general, till the day of life and grace is past : some are under him as Visible
Consenters, and Professed subjects ; so are the Baptized and visible professors of Christianity : And some are under him as sincere Heart-Cove-
nanters, Justified and Sanctified, and to be Glorified by him.

 3. As *Nature* it self is now delivered up to Christ, and the *Law of Nature* is now part of *his Law*, and the *Instrument of his Government*, both
for the *common good* and *order* of the *Redeemed World*, and also as *sanctified*
to the *special good* and *order* of *his Church* ; Even so is the Office of *Magistracy* now under him, and derived from him, and dependant on him,
in both these forementioned respects. (Notwithstanding all the vain
arguments which Mr. *Brown* a *Scotch* Divine, *Cont. Velthusium* hath written to the contrary ; which need no confutation to an intelligent Reader.))

                        4. But

4. But the Office of the Sacred Ministry is much of *Grace* and *Institution*, and less of *Natural original* than Magistracy. For though it be of *Natural* obligation, that one man teach another, and that there be some fitter persons than the multitude to instruct the people and guide them in Gods Worship; Yet that in *specie* there should be *Preachers of the Gospel*, and Administrators of this instituted worship and Church-discipline, this is it self of *Chrifts Inftitution*, as the *Doctrine*, *worship* and *discipline* which are their Office-work are of his Institution.

5. And though a great part of a Christian Magistrates work be also Instituted, *viz.* to promote Chrifts Inftituted Doctrine, Worship and Discipline, yet so much also of his work is natural, as that he may be called a *Magiftrate*, though he be not a Christian Magistrate, while he executeth Gods Laws of Nature, for the common good: But he is (at least) less fitly called a Minister or Priest of God, who shall only teach the Law of Nature, and guide an Assembly in meer Natural Worship, (omitting all that is by Institution:) Or if any think otherwise, it being but *de nomine*, at least this is certain, that the Christian or Evangelical Ministry is by Institution.

6. Therefore, though so far as the Mosaical Magistracy was founded in Nature, or in any Revelation expounding the Law of Nature, we may under the Gospel fetch proofs thence for the Christian Magistrates Authority and Obligation; Yet can we fetch no Model of a Gospel Ministry, nor proof of our Authority or obligation as instituted, from the Instituted Ministry of the Mosaical Church: Because the Law of *Mofes* is abrogate, and indeed did never bind the *Gentiles*, (as I have fuller proved in my Treat. of the Lords day.) Nor is it safe to argue from parity of reason that we muft now be or do as they did, in point of pure institution, while we so little know the total reason of God's institutions, and when he himself hath taken them down and set up new ones we muft not then plead our Reason against the alterations which God himself hath made.

7. Therefore though Christ be now the Head and Fountain of Power, both to Magistrates and Ministers, yet he did not institute a new Office of Magistracy, but add new Laws for them to rule by as part of their Rule of Government; Because their Office was so much founded in Nature, and so much of their work lay in ruling mankind according to their common Natural Law: But a Ministry he did institute a-new, as to the species and great essentials of the Office.

8. Christ changing both the Inftituted Mosaical Law, and Priesthood, did begin himself in his own person as the Great Prophet, High Priest and King of his Church, to exercise his Office in the *Jewish* Nation.

9. Being not to continue corporally on earth, nor his bodily presence being ubiquitary, he designed that the Holy Ghost should be his *Agent internally* to carry on his work in the World; And he appointed the Sacred Office of the Ministry, that meet men might be his Agents externally,

ly, in the Teaching and Governing of his Redeemed ones in a holy order, and in conducting them in holy worship, in a Ministerial subordination to his Prophetical, Regal and Priestly Office.

10. As he himself did Officiate among the *Jews*, so he first placed this Ministerial Power in twelve chosen men, and seventy Assistants with some relation to the twelve Tribes and seventy Elders of *Israel*, to whom he sent them.

11. During the time of Christ's abode among them in the flesh, they were but as Pupils and Learners while they were Teachers; and their *Abilities, Commissions, Office* and *Work*, and so their *success* were all yet imperfect: They were not yet authorized openly and commonly so much as to declare Christ to be the Messiah and Saviour, but only to prepare men for that belief: Because those works were not yet done, which must be the *Evidences* of their Doctrine and the Instruments of mens Conviction, *viz.* Christ's Death, Resurrection, Ascension, and his sending the miraculous gift of the Holy Ghost.

12. When Christ was risen before his Ascension, he perfected their Commission, both as to their Work and Province; but appointed them to stay till the descent of the Holy Ghost upon them, (as the sealing and full delivery of it, giving them full ability for their work) before they set themselves about the solemn performance of it.

13. Their Commission and Office was, 1. to Teach men and make them Christians (or Christ's Disciples,) 2. and then to Baptize them into the name of the Father, the Son, and the Holy Ghost, and so to take them into his Covenant and Church; and, 3. to Teach them as Covenanted and en-Churched persons, to observe all his commands; The first part of their work was to be exercised unlimitedly on all the World, as far as they were able; The second part on the new Converted Believers (and their infant seed;) And the third part on the Baptized (that were adult:) And he added the promise of his presence with them to the end.

14. As he now enlarged their Commission to *All the World* as the object of the first part of their Office; so, he added one (*Paul*) by a voice from Heaven, unto the number of the Apostles, who was especially made an Apostle to the Gentiles, to shew the rest that they were no more confined to the twelve Tribes of *Israel*.

15. Because these Apostles were entrusted not only with a common Preaching of the Gospel, but as Founders of the Churches, to be the eye and ear-witnesses, of the life, miracles, resurrection and doctrine of Christ, and to acquaint men certainly with the Laws of Christ; therefore he promised them the extraordinary gift of the Holy Ghost, to lead them infallibly into all truth, and to bring all things to their remembrance, which he had taught and given them in Charge; and so to enable them to perform all their Commission, which he gave them accordingly, and so made them the Foundations of his Church, and the infallible deliver-

ers

ers of his Will to the World, by their preaching and practice first, and afterwards by their Writings.

16. Therefore since their miraculous reception of the Spirit, all their Doctrines Writings and Establishments which were done in the Execution of their Commission, are ascribed to the Holy Ghost : It was the Holy Ghost that Indited the Sacred Scriptures ; and it was the Holy Ghost that settled the Churches, and that wrought the Miracles, and that bare witness of Christ, and the Christian verity. For the Apostles spake not of themselves, but as the Holy Ghost inspired them.

17. As others in that time were employed as their assistants in propagating the Christian Faith, so had they also the same spirit, though in several measures, and gifts. And so far as they had that spirit, he was the seal of their doctrine : But because it was the Apostles that had the promise of Infallibility, we have greater assurance of the Infallibility of their writings, than of others ; It being *their approbation*, which is much of our assurance that the writings of their Assistants were infallible, and the testimony which they give of the persons that wrote them (*viz. Mark* and *Luke*.)

18. These Apostles with their many Assistants, (Prophets and Evangelists) did by *preaching*, *holiness* and *miracles*, (the effects of Divine *Wisdome*, *Goodness* and *Power*) convert multitudes, and baptize them, and did not only thus gather them into the Catholick Church to Christ, but also settled them in a holy Order in particular Churches, for personal communion among themselves in holy worship and holy living: And they made such regular Church-communion a duty to all that could obtain it.

19. By the authority of Christ and the Holy Ghost they ordained others to the sacred Office of the Ministry ; The same office with their own as to the common works of *Preaching* and *Teaching* the Gospel, *Worshiping* and *Guiding* the Churches by holy *Discipline* ; which are the common essentials of the sacred Ministry: But not the same in respect of their extraordinary endowments and works before described (as eye and ear witnesses, infallibly delivering the will of Christ.)

20. Though in the Nature of the Office all Christs Ministers have the Power before mentioned, (1. to convert men to the Faith by preaching, 2. to take them into the holy Covenant and Church by Baptism) 3. to teach, worship and rule, in particular Churches ; or, 1. to gather Churches by preaching and baptizing, 2. and then to teach and guide them ;) Yet all are not called equally to the exercise of all these parts ; But some were by the Apostles and the Holy Ghost indefinitely employed in an unfixed course, in converting men and gathering Churches, yet officiating also in gathered Churches where they came ; And others were fixed in the stated relation of Pastors to particular gathered Churches, to teach and rule them, and worship among them ; yet so as also to Preach for the conversion of unbelievers, as far as they had ability and opportunity.

21. The

21. The unfixed Officers were called Minifters in General, and Stewards of God's Myfteries, and Evangelifts: But the fixed Officers, were alfo efpecially called Bifhops, Paftors, and Elders: Though fometime rarely the other alfo had fuch Titles, becaufe of their doing the fame work tranfiently in the Churches where they came.

22. They that were unfixed Preachers or Evangelifts, had not that fpecial and particular Charge of all the fouls in particular Churches, and in fome one Church above all the reft, as fixed Bifhops or Paftors have: But they had a greater Obligation than thefe Bifhops to preach to Infidels, becaufe it was their ordinary chief work.

23. The Paftors of particular Churches had fuch a Charge of thofe particular Flocks, above all other Flocks (materially,) as that they were not obliged equally to do the fame for others as they did for them: Though yet when they had a particular call, they might tranfiently or occafionally perform the work of the Paftoral Office, to other Churches.

24. This relation to their particular Flock, was not fuch as difobliged them from their higher regard of the Univerfal Church: For our relation to that is ftricter and more indiffoluble than to any particular Church: And we muft always *finally* prefer the Church Univerfal, though *materially* we are to labour in our particular Churches principally (and fometimes only) becaufe by fuch Order the Church Univerfal is beft edified.

25. The Apoftles ufually (but not only) planted Churches in great Cities; rather than in Country Villages.

26. This was not that hereby they might oblige others to confine Churches to Cities only, nor becaufe they had any fpecial honour for a City, but becaufe they were the places of greateft Concourfe, and had beft opportunity for Affemblies, and moft materials to work upon.

27. Neither the Apoftles nor others for fome Ages after Chrift, did divide the Countries about fuch Cities, and affign part of them to be the Diocefs of one Bifhop, and the other part to the Bifhop of the next adjoyning City: Nor was there any bounding of Parifhes or Diocefs, nor any determination, to which Bifhop fuch and fuch ground, or Villages of unconverted Infidels did belong. Only as natural prudence guided them (and the fpirit of God,) they fo difperfed themfelves that none might hinder another in his work; but as moft tended to the propagation and orderly governing of the Churches.

28. Therefore no City Bifhop had fuch a Particular Charge of the fouls of all the individual Infidels, either in his City or the Country round about him (which fome feign to have been his Diocefs) as he had of the fouls of the Church which he was Paftor of. Though he was bound to do all that he could to convert all as he had opportunity, he ftood not in any Paftoral relation to this or that individual Infidel, as he did to all the individual Chriftians of his charge. *Ignatius* requireth the Bifhop to

know

know all his Flock by name, and enquire after them, even the servants; but not so of all Infidels in his City or Circuit.

29. No man was therefore the Pastor of any Christians in a particular Church-relation meerly because he converted them: Nor was there ever any Law made by Christ or his Apostles, that all should be members of that particular Church whose Overseer did convert them; much less that at a distance they should be the members of his Episcopal charge, though in another Church.

30. The Apostles setled in every particular Church, one or more with the Pastoral power of the Keys, to teach and govern that Church, and to lead them in publick worship. And every such Body should still have one or more Pastors with such power . And no Pastor or Bishop should have more particular Churches under his special immediate Charge, than one, unless as an Archbishop who hath Bishops in those particular Churches under him.

31. A particular Church of Christ's Institution by his Apostles, is [*A sacred Society consisting of one or more Pastors, and a capable number of Christian Neighbours, consociate by Christs appointment and their own consent, for personal communion in God's publick worship and in holy living.*] In this definition, 1. The Genus is [*a sacred Society*] so called, 1. to distinguish it from a meer community, or unbodied company of Christians; 2. and to distinguish it from Civil and prophane Societies, (For the *Genus* is subalternate, and the species of a superiour *Genus*.) 2. The constitutive parts are Pastor and People. 3. I say [*Pastors*] as distinguishing it from all other societies as headed by other Officers or Rulers; As Kingdoms by Kings, Colleges by their Governours, Schools by School-masters, Families by Parents, &c. For Societies are specified by their Governours. 4. I say [*one or more*] because it is the *Office in some person* that is the constitutive part, the number being indifferent as to the *Being*, though not as to the *well being* of the Society. 5. The *People* being the other material part of the Society, I call them [*Christians*] that is *Baptized Professing Christians*, to distinguish them from all. Infidels, who are uncapable to be members. 6. I call them [*Neighbours*] because the Proximity must be such as rendereth them capable of the Ends of the *Society*, For at an uncapable distance they cannot have Church-communion. 7. I put in [*a capable number*]-because *too few or too many* may be utterly uncapable of the Ends: One or two are uncapable defectively: such multitudes as can have no Church communion, are uncapable through excess (of which more after.) 8. The *form* is the *Relative Union* of Pastor and People, in reference to the Ends; Which I mean in the word [*Consociate.*] 9. The foundation or prime efficient, is [*Christ's Institution.*] 10. The Condition, *sine qua non*, is [*their mutual consent.*] 11. The end or *terminus* is their [*Communion.*] 12. The *matter* of this Communion, is both [*God's publick worship*] and a *holy life*; which distinguisheth them from such as associate for civil ends, or any other besides these. 13. The proper species of this holy Communion is that it be [*Personal.*] By

F   which

which I mean such as Pastor and People may ordinarily exercise in *presence*; to distinguish it from that sort of Communion, 1. which we have only in *spirit*, in *faith*, *judgment* and *affection*, with Christians in all parts of the World: And, 2. from that external Communion which several Churches hold together by Messengers, Delegates, or Letters. For if that kind of distant Communion would serve to the being of a particular Church, we might be of the same particular Church with men in the several parts of the World.

32. Deacons are subordinate Officers, or Ministers to Christs Ministers, not essential to the Church, but only Integral, as needful to its well being, in such Churches, where the *number* and *benefit* of the People do require them.

33. The necessity of these Individual or particular Churches, is founded, in the necessity of the foresaid publick worshiping of God, and in the use of the mutual assistance of Christian Neighbours in the matters of salvation, and in the need of the personal inspection and conduct of the Pastors over all the Flock.

34. The difference between this *personal Communion*, and the distant Communion by Letters or Delegates, or meerly internal in Faith and Love, is so great and notorious, as must make those Societies *specifically* distinct, which are associated for such distinct Ends.

35. Yet do we not hold that all true Churches do Assemble together in one place; or that they consist of no more than can meet at once: For whole Families seldom go all at once to the Assembly: Therefore if one part go to day, and another the next day, they worship God publickly in personal Communion, though not all at the same time. 2. And many may be sick, and many infants, and many aged, and the great distance of some may make a Chapel or subordinate Meeting often needful. And yet, 1. they may all come together in one place at several times for Church-communion. 2. And they may live so near, that one may be capable of neighbourly converse with others, and of admonishing, exhorting and encouraging each other, in their Christian Course.

36. Where a Church is so small as to need but one Pastor, Christ doth not require that they have more; And One can neither be superiour or inferiour to himself.

37. But it is most desirable that a Church be as numerous or great, as will consist with that sort of Communion which is the end of the Society; and consequently that they have many Pastors; Because this tendeth to their *strength* and *beauty*, and it is a joyful thing to worship God in full Assemblies.

38. The work of a Bishop or Pastor of a single Church is, (to mention it more particularly) to Teach the Church the meaning of the Scriptures, especially of all the Articles of Faith, and the things to be Desired in Prayer, and the matters and order of Obedience to all the commands of Christ. To instruct the Children in the Catechistical or Fundamental verities.

verities. To Baptize, to Pray in the Affembly, to praife God, to cele-brate the Lords Supper, to vifit the Sick, and pray for them: To vifit the feveral Families, or perfonally inftruct thofe ignorant ones, that un-derftand not publick Preaching, as far as he hath opportunity: To watch over the Converfations of the feveral Members, and to receive informa-tions concerning them: To refolve the doubts of thofe that feek refolu-tions, and to offer help to them that are fo fenflefs as not to feek it, when their need appeareth: To comfort the fad and afflicted: To reprove the fcandalous: To admonifh the obftinate before all: To cenfure and caft out the impenitent that continue to reject fuch admonition: To abfolve the penitent: To take care of the Poor: And to be exemplary in holinefs, fobriety, juftice and charity. I pafs by Marriage, Burials, and fuch o-ther particular Offices. And I meddle not here with Ordination, or any thing that concerneth other Churches; but only with the work of a Bifhop or Paftor to the People of his proper Flock.

39. The ableft Man among us, for mind and body, may find full and needful employment of this fort, among an hundred perfons, efpecially fuch as our common Chriftians are: But if he have five hundred or a thou-fand, he hath fo much to do, as will conftrain him to leave fomething un-done which belongeth to his Office. Therefore our Market-Towns, and large Country Parifhes, where there are ordinarily two, three, or four thoufand in a Parifh, have need of many paftors, to do that for which the Paftoral Office was ordained: Much more our greateft City and Town Parifhes that have ten thoufand, twenty thoufand, and fome above thir-ty, if not forty or fifty thoufand in a Parifh.

40. The office of a Paftor, containing the *Power of the Keys*, as fub-ordinate Minifterially to Chrift in his Teaching, Ruling and prieftly work, is not by man to be divided and part of it to be given to one fort, and part to another (though they that have the *whole power* may varioufly *exercife it*, as there is caufe.) But every Church muft have fuch as have the *whole power*, as far as concerneth the People of that Church.

41. To divide the effential parts of the Sacred Office, (as to give one the power of *Teaching* only, another of *Worfhiping* only; and another of Ruling only; or any two of thefe without the third, is to deftroy it, and change the *fpecies*, as much as in them lieth that do it.) And as no one is a *man* without his Animal, Vital and Natural parts; fo no one is a true Pa-ftor without the threefold power forementioned, of Teaching, Rule-ing that Church by Paftoral means, and Conducting them in publick Worfhip. He may be a Paftor that is hindered from the exercife of fome one of thefe or more; but not he that hath not the *Power* in his Office. Dividers therefore make new Church-Offices, and deftroy the old.

42. Churches headed by fuch a new fort of Officers, fpecifically di-ftinct from the old of Chrift's Inftitution, are Churches fpecifically differ-ing from the Churches which Chrift Inftituted.: Becaufe the Society is fpe-cified by the *fpecies* of its Head or Governour.

F 2

43. To

43. To make a new fort of Church-Heads or Rulers, as their Conftitutive parts, is to make a new fort of Churches.

44. The three forfaid Effential parts of the Paftoral Office are not to be exercifed by any Lay-man, nor by any man that hath not that Office: Nor may the Paftors do that work *per alios*, or delegate Lay-men, or men of another Office to do it as in their ftead. For the Office is nothing but juft *Authority* and *Obligation* to do that work: And if they convey fuch *Authority* and *Obligation* to another, they convey the *Office* to another; And fo he is no longer a Lay-man, or of another Office only.

45. Therefore though many Paftors of the fame Office may in a great Church diftribute the work among them, yet none of them muft do it only as the delegate of another, not having himfelf from God the Office which containeth the power of doing it.

46. But the *Accidentals* of the Paftoral Office may be committed to a Lay-man, or one that is no Paftor (As to fummon Affemblies, to keep Regifters, or the Church Books, Goods, Buildings, with many the like:) And fo fome think that the Apoftles inftituting Deacons was but a communicating the Accidentals of their Office to other men. Therefore if Chancellors did only thefe accidental works (or Lay Elder either) and meddled not with the facred power of the Keys, we fhould not be fo quarrelfome, as to condemn their undertaking, unlefs it were for the abufe.

47. We doubt not but in a Church that hath many Paftors, thofe that are young and weak fhould much fubmit to the elder and more able, and be as far ruled by them, as the difference of age, experience and abilities, without a difference of Office, doth require.

48. And we doubt not, but where Temples and Church-maintenance are at the difpofe of Patrons, People or Magiftrates, they may give them to fome one Paftor as the prefent poffeffor, fo that no other fhall have part but by his conceffion. And this difference there is between the Parfon and his Curates in our Parifhes, and an accidental fuperiority and inferiority thereby, without a difference of Office.

49. If Magiftrates, or Councils, or Cuftome, fhould in each particular Church that hath many Paftors, give one a Governing, that is a negative voice among the reft, in the management of the affairs of that Church, fo that the reft fhould not go againft him or without him, as Archbifhops now are over Bifhops, and Archpresbyters were formerly over Presbyters, and Archdeacons over Deacons, and Prefidents over Colleges, and Courts of Juftice, without claiming a diftinct Office; though the fad experience of Mens inclination to Church-tyranny, make us doubtful whether we fhould wifh for fuch an inequality, yet would we not unpeaceably difturb or quarrel with fuch an Order, when it is fettled: Our Parifh Order aforefaid being indeed but fuch.

50. Whether God himfelf hath appointed another fort of Bifhops who may be better called Archbifhops, as Succeffors of the Apoftles in the

Ruling

Ruling part of their Office; and whether these have not a Power above particular Church Pastors in Ordinations, and in the oversight of the Pastors themselves, and in the Care of many Churches, I have long ago confessed, is a Case of too much difficulty for me to determine. On the one side, though the Apostles have no Successors in the extraordinary and temporary part of their Office, yet Church-government being an ordinary and permanent part, as doctrine is, I can hardly think that when we find one Form of Church-government instituted by Christ himself, and continuing till the end of that Age, that we should presume to say that this Form then ceased and another must succeed it without good proof. What we find enacted and setled must stand, till we can prove it abrogate. And unless it were a thing which in the nature of it were temporary, it seemeth a harsh imputation of mutability, to feign Christ to set up a Church-government which should be in force but for an hundred years. And on the other side it puzleth me: 1. to find it so hard to prove, that the Apostles themselves did indeed exercise any Office power over other Pastors, which one may not do towards another, over and above that which accrewed to them from the meer extraordinary advantage of their gifts and Apostolical proper work: 2, And to find it so obscure, whether they setled any as their Successors in that superiority of power which they had.

51. But being in such doubt, and being uncertain whether such Arch-Bishops or Apostolical Successors in the points of Ordination and oversight of many Churches, be of Divine right or not, I resolve not to contend against any such Order, nor to disobey any just commands of such, nor to reproach the *custome* of the Churches.

52. And though I know that Pastors should not unnecessarily be diverted by any aliene works, yet if it please the Magistrate to commit some of his power of Church-government by the Sword, (about things extrinsick, to the Pastoral Office) into the hands of some Ministers as his Officers, and if he call them Bishops, and command us to obey them, and if he make them Barons, and endow them with Lordships and great revenues, though I see the great peril to the Church from hence, by reason of mens pride and worldliness; yet will I not reproach this Order, nor deny any just obedience to any such Officers of the King.

53. If any acknowledging the Pastors of each Church to have the whole Pastoral Office, and *power of the Keys* of that Church which he overseeth, shall yet affirm that the aforesaid superiour General Bishops (or Arch-Bishops) have a *superiour power of the Keys*, and therefore shall have the decision of controversies that arise in particular Churches between the Pastors and the People, and that appeals may be made by the people to them, and that they may visit the particular Churches at their pleasure, and have power to censure the particular Bishops (or Pastors) when they deserve it, or to Ordain Ministers, remove them, and depose them as there is just cause, (by bare sentence, and the peoples consent,) and all this *jure divino*, as Successors to the Apostles in their Government, or

to

to such Archbishops (or General Bishops) as *Timothy* and *Titus*. I shall not contend against any of this, for the reasons aforesaid, being uncertain of the thing in question. But if I must be put to subscribe, that I believe all this to be true, (as if it were an Article of my Faith) the same uncertainty would forbid me.

54. And here I must take occasion to say, that I take unnecessary Subscriptions, Declarations, Promises and Oaths, to be one of the chiefest of the Devil's Engines, to divide Christ's Churches, and to fish out those Ministers that make conscience of perjury and lying, and to turn them out of the work of Christ, and to leave in those that do not, (when Conscience can find but any shifting pretence,) And how fit such are for the Sacred Ministry, and whose servants really they are, and how they are like to do Christ's work, and what a Case the Churches will be in that have such, and what the effects will be with the common people, and how the lovers of Godliness will resent all this, and what else will follow hereupon, I leave to the Reader that hath the brains of a man, or ever opened his eyes to mark what is done abroad in the World, or that ever read with observation the things that in other Ages have befallen the Churches, or that knoweth what relation light hath to darkness, good to evil, and Christ to *Belial*. I think that the *Articles* of our *Faith* and the matters of our *practice* are so to be distinguished, as that there is a *necessity* of *Believing* the *former*, and therefore we may be called to profess that we do *Believe them*; And for the other, (the *Agenda*) we must be called to *Do* them; (and if they be plain and necessary duties of our Religion, being to be *Believed* to be *Duties* before we do them, we may sometime be put to profess that Belief.) But *duties* of humane imposition, or of doubtful nature, may *be done* as *things lawful* by thousands of peaceable men, that cannot say or swear that they are duties; or may be done as of humane obligation by those that cannot say they are of Divine obligation.

55. We hold that the first Churches that did divolve all arbitrations of differences among Christians upon the Pastors, did that which brought no great present inconvenience, when the People were but few and the Pastors had sufficient leisure; but that which prepared for the degenerating of the Ministry and the Churches lamentable corruption; And therefore that they should have foreseen this, and done as St. *Paul* directed them, and referred matters to any fit [*wise man among them.*] And when they saw the mischief, they should have quickly reformed it, as *Silvanus* Bishop of *Troas* aforementioned did: And that if there were Lay Elders in any of the ancient Churches, (as one passage in *Origen*, and one in *Ambrose*, and this of *Silvanus* in *Socrates* have made some think) they were truly Lay, and appointed only to such Arbitrations as these, and such other Animadversions over the rest, as Lay-men may do; (A help that I once tryed and found to be very great.)

56. We hold that when *Constantine* gave the Clergy the sole Power of Judging the Causes (Civil and Criminal) of all the Christians, he shewed

ed more ignorant zeal, than true discretion, and did let in a pestilence into the Church; and that instead of that he should have only left Arbitrations to mans free choice, and have set up a Christian or Righteous Magistracy, to whom both Bishops and all other Christians should submit.

57. We hold that when Christians so multiplyed, as that they grew uncapable of *Personal Communion*, at one *Altar*, it was the duty of them and the Bishops, to have ordered them into new Churches, which should every one have had its proper Bishop, or plenary Pastoral Office among them; and not to have kept them all still in the name of one particular Church (*infimi ordinis*) when they were uncapable of the nature and end.

58. We hold that it was sinfully done, to make a new Office or Order of *subject Presbyters*, that had not the Governing power of their particular Churches, neither alone, nor conjunct; but had only the power to Teach and Worship, the Government being reserved only to the Bishop of another (called a Mother) Church.

59. But we believe that this came not in till many hundred Years after Christ, and that but by slow degrees, and that after subordinate Churches and Altars were invented, and set up, yet the Pastors under the name of Presbyters, had much of the Governing power (of the Keys) though with and under the Bishop of the Mother Church.

60. The deposing of all the first rank or Order of Bishops, which were before over each particular Church, the making of a new Office of half Presbyters, the making of Churches of a new *species*, as being under a new sort of Officers, the making Archbishops, who should have many Churches and Bishops under them, to become the Bishops of the lowest rank, having none under them; but above all these, the making of the Pastoral work, especially discipline become utterly impossible, by putting that into one mans hand, that cannot be done but by many (or many hundred,) these and such like are the things that we can neither swear to nor approve.

61. We hold that though the Magistrate may shape his part of the Church-Government variously, according to the interest of the common good, yet that the Spiritual or Pastoral part should not have been molded into the shape of the Civil Imperial Government; And that so doing did give the Papacy that countenance which is the ground of its usurpation.

62. For we hold that the *essential constitution* of the *Pastoral Office*, and *its work*, and the essential constitution of the *Church Universal*, and of *Individual* (or particular) *Churches*, are all of Divine unalterable Institution; And that all Laws of Christ for such Constitution, and for Administration, are unalterable by man: Though we hold that Circumstancials and Accidentals are alterable, as being not fixed by any Divine determination. (As *e.g.* how many Ministers shall be in each Church, which of them

them shall be more regarded than the rest, as being of greater wisdom, how oft and when and where they shall assemble, with many the like.)

63. We hold that as all Christians (ordinarily) should have *personal Communion* in particular Churches, so those Churches and their Bishops should hold such Communion as is needful to their strength and concord, and the common good.

64. This Communion of Churches is to be held internally by Concord in the same *Faith* and *Love* and *Religion*, and externally by the same *profession*, and *instrumentally*, 1. by Messengers and Letters, and, 2. by Delegates and Synods when there is need; (which as is said, for Time, Place, Numbers, Provinces, Orders, are left to humane Prudence.)

65. If any that divide the Country into Provinces, will settle Synods accordingly, and settle over them Presidents for the ordering of their proceedings, and will give power to one above others, to call such Synods, and will call these Provinces, or Nations, or Empires, by the name of Provincial, National, or Imperial Churches, and the Bishops so exalted by the name of Metropolitans, Primates, Patriarchs, &c. We contend not against this as unlawful in it self (though we easily see the accidental danger, being taught it by long and sad experience;) so be it, 1. that none of these be pretended to be of Divine Institution, but of humane determination; 2. and that they meddle with nothing but such accidentals as are left to humane prudence; 3. and that they equal not their humane Association with the Christian Worshiping Churches, which are of Christ's Institution, 4. and that much less they do not oppress their brethren, and tyrannize, nor deprive the particular Pastors and Churches of their proper priviledges and work. But alas when were these Rules observed by humane Churches?

66. The Canons of such Synods or Councils of Bishops, may be made Laws indeed by the Civil power, and they are (if just) obligatory to the people, by virtue of the Pastoral Authority of the Bishops: But as to the particular Bishops, they are only *Agreements*, and no proper Laws (the Major Vote of Bishops being not proper Governours of the rest) and bind only by virtue of Christ's General Laws for Love and Concord.

67. The Pastoral power is not at all Coactive by secular force, on body or estate, but only Nunciative and persuasive, commanding in Christ's name as authorized by him, and executed no otherwise than by a *Ministerial word*, and by with-holding our own acts of Administration, and denying our Communion to offenders: Nor did the Apostles themselves pretend to any other than this power of the *Word* (for the Keys are exercised but thus) excepting what they did by Miracle. And if Bishops would go no further, they would work on none but Voluntiers, and their usurpations might be the more easily born.

67. And indeed we are fully perswaded, that none but Voluntiers are fit for the great priviledge of Church-Communion, and that giving it to the

the unwilling that had but rather endure it than a Prison, is a great pro-fanation of it, and a cheat to poor souls, and a horrid corrupting of Christ's Churches and Ordinances.

68. If wilful Church-corruptions have made any places uncapable of a present conformity to Christ's Institutions, their incapacity must not be-come the measure and rule of our Reformation; But a true Conformity to the Institution must be intended and endeavoured, though all cannot come up to it at the first.

69. We do not hold that every Corruption in Number, or Officers, or Order, nullifieth a Church, or maketh all Communion with it unlawful, as long as the essential constitution doth remain. Yea, though my own judgment is, that every Church in Town or Country should have a Bishop, yet if they would but set up one Bishop with his assistant Presbyters in every Corporation and Great Town, with the neighbour Villages, ac-cording to the antient practise, from the middle of the third Century for many following; so that true discipline might but be made possible to them that had a heart to practice it, I should greatly rejoyce in such a Reformation; much more, if every Parish Pastor were restored to all the parts of his Office, though he exercised all under the Government of Bi-shops.

70. We hold the Parish Churches of *England*, that have true Ministers (that are, not utterly uncapable through Ignorance, Heresie, Insufficiency, or Wickedness,) to be true Churches of Christ; But that is, because we hold the particular Ministers to be true Bishops (*Episcopos Gregis etsi non Episcoporum,*)and to have the power of the Keys over all their Flocks: And that is, because we hold that it is not in our Bishops power to deprive them of it though they would; And because we hold that when Christ hath instituted and described the Office of a Pastor or Presbyter, and the Or-dainers ordain a man to that Office, their power shall be judged of by Christs' institution, and not by the Ordainers will, though he mistake or would maim and change it by his wrong description. And that the Or-dainer is but a Ministerial Invester, delivering possession according to his Masters will and not his own: And as long as Christ giveth to Pastors the power of the Keys, and they themselves consent to receive and use them, (especially if the People also consent to the exercise of them) it is not the Bishops *will* or *words* that can nullifie this power. And if this Answer were not good, I confess, I were not able to Answer a *Brownist*, who saith, that we have no true Publick Churches of God's Institution, Diocesan Churches being but Humane, if they had Bishops in each Church under them, and being sinful when they have none, and Parochial Chur-ches being Humane or null, as having no Bishops of their own, nor Pa-stors of Christ's Institution, but half Pastors; and therefore being but part of a Diocesan Church. But all this is sufficiently answered by our foresaid Reasons; which no high Prelatist can soundly answer.

71. I do hold that those Parish Assemblies, that have no Ministers, [but

G

such as are incapable, either through notorious Ignorance, or Heresie, or utter Insufficiency as to the Essentials of their Office, or by disclaiming themselves any Essential part of the Pastoral Office, or by notorious Preaching against Godliness, and opposing the Churches necessary good,] are indeed no true Churches of Christ, but only are Analogically or Equivocally so called; As you may call a Community of Christians that have no Pastor or Church, which is no Organized or Political Society.

72. But yet I think it not simply unlawful to joyn at any time with such an Assembly: For I may joyn with a Christian Family, or occasional Assembly, though not as with a Church.

73. We hold that all the Christians in the World (in particular Churches or our) do make up one Catholick or Universal Church: which is Mystical and Invisible, in that, 1. the Faith of Mens minds is Invisible, 2. and Christ is Invisible to us Mortals now he is in Heaven. But it is also Visible, 1. In respect of the Members and their outward Baptism and Profession, 2. and because that Christ the Head was once Visible on Earth, and is still Visible in Heaven to the Glorified part (as the King is to his Courtiers, when the rest of the Kingdom seeth him not.) and will Visibly appear again to all.

74. We hold that this Universal Church is One in Christ alone, and that it hath no other King or Head; That he hath Instituted no Vicarious Head, either Pope or General Council; Nor is any mortal man or men capable of such an Office.

75. We hold therefore that the *Roman* Pope (and General Councils, if they claim such an Headship) is an Usurper of part of Christ's Prerogative; which having usurped he hath used against Christ, and his interest; against the Soveraignty of Princes, and against the true Unity, Concord, Peace and Holiness of the Churches.

76. And we hold that it was the modelling of the Church to the Policy of the *Roman* Empire, which gave the Pope the advantage for this usurpation: And that the *Roman* Catholick Papal Church is a meer Humane Form, and an Imperial Church, as much as the Archbishop of *Canterbury* as Superiour to the rest of *England* is of Man, and that Body so united is a National Church: And that the General Councils were never truly General, as to all the Churches in the World, but only as to the *Roman* Imperial Church; None considerable ever coming to such Councils, but those that were or had been in the *Roman* Empire, or some very few that closely bordered on them: Nor had the *Roman* Emperour (who usually called, or gave his Warrant for such Councils, or Governed them) any power over the Clergy of all the rest of the Christian World, (in *Ethiopia*, the outer *Armenia*, *Persia*, *India*, &c.) Nor did the Imperial Pope then exercise any power over them. And we are perswaded that the power of the Patriarchs of *Alexandria*, *Antioch*, *Jerusalem*, *Constantinople*, and of the Metropolitans, Primates, &c. stood on the same foundation with the Primacy of the Pope, and that one is no more of Divine right than the other; But

But that the Papacy is the far more wicked Usurpation, as pretending to more of Christ's Prerogative.

77. We hold therefore that the *Roman* Church, as such, that is, as pretending to be the Church-Catholick, Headed by an (Usurping) Universal Bishop, is no true Church of Christ, but a Humane and traiterous Usurpation and conspiracy, therefore by Protestants called Antichristian: Though those that are true Christians among them are Parts of Christ's Catholick Church, and those that are true Pastors among them, may be the Guides of true particular Churches.

78. We hold therefore that no Power on Earth, Popes, Council or Prince, hath power to make Universal Laws to bind the whole Church of Christ on Earth, because there is no Universal Head or Soveraign but Christ.

79. By all this it is evident that we grant all these following disparities in the Church: 1. The disparity of Age, standing, and Gifts among Ministers of the same Order: 2. A kind of paternal priority where one was the Teacher, Educater, or Ordainer of the other. 3. An accidental disparity, when one only by the Patron or Magistrate hath the sole possession of the Maintenance and power of the Temple. 4. We will not unpeaceably contend against the guiding power or negative Vote of One Bishop in a particular Church over the rest of the Pastors of the same Office; Nor do we take such a power to make a distinct Office. 5. We do not strive against the Presidency of one, in Synods, as Moderator; No though it were *durante vitâ* (which Bishop *Hall* thought would serve to heal us.) 6. We do not deny Obedience to any Bishop, who is Commissioned by the King, to exercise as a Church-Magistrate, his part of the Church-Government. 7. Much less do we strive against the Power of Kings and Lawful Magistrates *Circa Sacra*, (of which *Grotius* hath excellently written *de Imper.*) But we take the Magistrate to be the necessary and only Ruler by the Sword, to keep Peace and Order among Church-men, as well as among men of all other Professions. 8. Yea, I do not contend against the Divine Right of General Bishops, (or Archbishops) such as *Timothy* and *Titus*, nor will deny Obedience to them, who take care as Visitors of Many Churches, which have every one their proper Bishop, one or more, with true plenary Pastoral power of the Keys, to guide the people of their charge. 9. We refuse not to receive Ordination from such General Bishops. 10. Nor do we refuse to be responsible to them, when we are accused of any male Administration, or to admit of Appeals from us to them.

80. By all which it appeareth, 1. How falsly we are charged to be against all Episcopacy. 2. And how falsly and deceitfully all those Writers state the Case and plead against us, that only plead for a Congregational or Parochial Episcopacy, or any of this which we grant; and how they cheat their Readers, who make them believe, that our Controversie is, whether there should be *any Episcopacy*, and not what *kind* of E-

piscopacy

piscopacy it should be. 3. What friends they will prove to the Church, that will rather do all that is done against it, than endure those that grant all this which we do grant them.

The London Ministers Thanksgiving to the King is to be seen in Priors As also their desire of B. Usher's Primitive Model of Government.

81. That I am not singular in all this, I prove in that it was only Archbishop *Usher's* Reduction of Episcopacy to the Primitive state, which the Nonconformists, (malitiously called Presbyterians) did offer to his Majesty and the Bishops, 1660. as the means of our Concord, and which was rejected: Yea, that they * thankfully accepted (though not totally approved) that higher Model expressed in his Majesties Declaration about Ecclesiastical Affairs.

And now, I suppose, I have given *Strangers* and *Posterity* a truer Description of the Judgment of the present Nonconformists, than malicious turbulent ambitious Persons use to give of them, or than the extreams and freaks of a few Sectaries would allow men to receive.

CHAP. V.

Concerning the Writers of this Controversie; With a Summary Answer to the Chief that write against the Cause which I defend.

Now 18 years, this being written 9 years ago.

I Have not been altogether negligent to read the Controversies on this Subject, nor I hope partial in Reading them; If I have, it hath been because I had rather have found Conformity to the Prelacy to be lawful; for then I had not above * nine years been silenced, and denied not only all Church maintenance, but leave to preach Christ's Gospel, nor had I been exposed as I have been to so much wrath and malice, expressed in so many scurrilous lying invectives and libells, besides other ways. Even when I doubted of the use of the transient Image of the Cross, I was of opinion that Prelacy was lawful, and so was likely to continue, if the Prelates would have given me leave: But in 1640, they put a New Oath upon us, *Never to Consent to the Alteration* of the present frame of Prelacy, as under Archbishops, Bishops, Deans, Archdeacons, &c. and that it *ought so to stand.* And I thought it was then time, when I was put to such a solemn Oath, to search more throughly into all the matter before I sware. And in searching, I found in general that almost all Writers for Episcopacy, either confound Diocesan Prelacy, such as ours, with the Episcopacy of a single Church, or at least all their proof extendeth to no more than I have here granted. When they

offer.

offer us the definition of a Bishop (which few of them do) it is such as neither supposeth any more Churches than one to be his Charge, nor any Presbyters under him at all; but only a Power of Ordaining Presbyters, and ruling them when he hath them, whether in one Church or more.

And I find that they are so far from proving that ever the Apostles appointed a distinct Office of Presbyters which had not the power of the Keys over the People, *in foro interiore & exteriore* (as they call them) but had only power to Teach and Worship, under Bishops as a superior Office or Order, as that they prove not any such to have ever been under the Apostles themselves; and some of themselves do plainly deny it: Nor do they prove that long after the Presbyters were any more subject to the Bishops, than the Deacons are now to the Archdeacon, or the Bishops to the Archbishop, who are of the same Order. So that whoever else they speak to, they say nothing to me, and seem not to know where the Controversie lyeth, *viz.* 1. *Whether a Bishop of the lowest rank* (being *no Archbishop*, or having no Bishops under him) over many Churches, (or Societies of Christians stated under their proper Pastors, or Presbyters, for ordinary personal Communion in all God's publick Worship,) be of *Divine*, or Lawful Humane, Institution? 2. Whether an Order or Office of Presbyters that have not the power of the Keys even *in foro exteriore*, be of Divine, or Lawful Humane Institution? (whom for brevity I shall hereafter call *half-Presbyters.*) So that the Question is not, whether one Man was after sometime called peculiarly the Bishop, and in the same Church sate over Presbyters of the same Office, as Archpresbyters, or as Archdeacons over Deacons, or Archbishops over Bishops; Nor yet whether there were or should be a General sort of Bishops (or Archbishops) over the Bishops of particular Churches? But whether any stated Body of Worshiping Christians, as afore described (like our Parish-Churches that have *unum altare*) should be without a Bishop of their own, or without a Pastor that hath the threefold power before described, of Leading the People in Doctrine Worship and Discipline, called the power of the Keys? And whether he be a true Presbyter or Minister of Christ that wants this power? And whether they that depose the Parish Ministers of this power, do not degrade the Presbyters, nullifie the Churches under them, and depose the ancient sort of Episcopacy *quantum in se?* and set up another Humane sort of Churches called Diocesan, and of Archbishops turned into Bishops, *infimi gradus*, in their stead, together with a new *Species* of *half-Presbyters?*

1. How far *Whitgift's* Disputations against *Cartwright* are guilty of this overlooking the true Question, I leave to the Reader: Only I must say for him, that when his Adversarie standeth most upon the denial of all superior Episcopacy, it was his part to prove what was denied. And I need say no more than that *Whitgift* oft professeth (as Dr. *Stillingfleet* hath collected out of him,) that God hath in Scripture prescribed no one sort of

of Church-Government: And therefore not the Prelatical.

Saravia. 2. I do not expect that ever this Controversie should be handled by two more judicious Adversaries than *Saravia* and *Beza* were. And as *Beza* protesteth against a Parity, and pleadeth for a *Prostasie*, *desireth* that which he calleth Divine Episcopacy, tolerating and submitting to that which he calleth *Humane Episcopacy*, and flatly opposing only that, which he calleth Satanical Episcopacy; So *Saravia* professeth, *p.* 1, 2. & *p. Defens.* 4, 5. that the General nature of the *Evangelical Ministry*, common both to Bishops and Presbyters, containeth these three things, 1. The Preaching of the Gospel. 2. The Communication of the Sacraments, 3. The Authority of Church-Government: And only pleadeth that in this last, the Power of Bishops and Presbyters is not equal, but the Bishops power is principal in Government. Which granteth the main Question which we Nonconformist now contend for. And I confes that *Saravia*'s Writings were the first and chief that brought me to suspect that the Apostles have Successors in the point of Government, as being but an ordinary and durable part of their Office: which Argument he hath better managed than any man else that I have seen. And *p.* 12. *ib.* He granteth that the 70 Disciples were not under the Government of the 12 Apostles. He granteth that chosen *Seniors* of the Laity may be great

Vid. & p. *104. &* *110, 111,* *120, 121.* Assistants in the Government: Yea, *Def.* 1. 8. *p.* 83. He saith, that in the absence of *Paul* and his Assistants, the Churches of *Crete* were wholly ruled, till *Titus* Ordained them Pastors, by such Elders. [*A senioribus quos ratio & natura in quavis Societate dat, non Ordinatio: quales sunt natu majores, & quotquot aliqua virtute in populo excellunt: quibus deferre natura omnes gentes docuit: quibus addo eos quos tunc temporis passim, dona Sp. sancti venia excitabant, sed nulli loco alligabant.*] And no wonder, for he affirmeth, that in times of publick corruption of Doctrine, any man that is learned and able and fit, must propugne and defend the truth, as he hath ability and opportunity; or else be judged for hiding his talents as the unprofitable servant, *pag.* 23. *cap.* 2. Yet doth he most improbably imagine that *Rome* and *Corinth* had no proper Pastors, when *Paul* wrote his Epistles to them. When as *Paul* had dwelt a year and half at *Corinth*, when it was the practice of the Apostles to Ordain Elders in every Church, and when among the *Corinthians* there were so many Prophets, Instructers, Speakers of Languages, Interpreters, &c. that *Paul* is fain to regulate and restrain them in their Church-meetings, that they might not over-do, and hinder one another. And yet were these People without any proper Pastor? Without a Prelate? it's like they were. Yea, when *Paul* directeth them to deliver the incestuous man to Satan, and to exercise Church-discipline upon others that were scandalous, doth not this intimate that they had among them such as were impowred to do it? If only transiently and occasionally, they could Worship God publickly and deliver Sacraments, and Govern the Church but transiently and rarely: How did they spend the Lords days, when those transient guides were absent?

abſent? Did the major part of the people, who *Saravia* thinketh were to exerciſe the foreſaid Diſcipline, alſo Conſecrate and Adminiſter the Sacrament, or publickly pray and worſhip God without a Paſtor? Were they every Lords day to depoſit their Collections, and have no Paſtors, and ſo no Church-Aſſemblies? Had they ſo many Sects and falſe Teachers to trouble them, and yet no Paſtors? When *Clem. Rom.* ſo ſhortly after writeth ſo much to reconcile the Paſtors and People that diſagreed. And when *Paul* tells the *Romans* and *Corinthians* what Officers God ſetteth in the Church, is it like there was none fixed among them? *1 Cor.16. 1, &c.*

And I muſt note how great a charge he layeth on the Biſhops, when, *Reſp. ad N. p. 10. Art. 12.* He ſaith that [the Biſhop is *æque imo magis proprius ſingularum Eccleſiarum ſua Dioceſeos Paſtor, illis qui ibi præſunt & reſident, utpote ad quem cura præcipua illorum locorum pertineat:* The Biſhop hath more Charge or Care of all the Pariſhes in his Dioceſs than the preſent Paſtors have: (O dreadful undertaking.) *Ad quem prima & præcipua Cura omnium incumbet: ita ut, ipſe ſuum agnoſcit gregem, & ſingulis quibus manus imponit, &c.* How many hundred thouſand individuals then hath the Biſhop of *London* this particular Charge of, whoſe names he never heard, and whoſe faces he never ſaw? *Oportet enim Epiſcopum omnes quantum fieri poteſt, qui ipſius cura commiſſi ſunt, noſſe.* The Biſhop muſt know all his Flock, if poſſible; And muſt he have a Flock then which he cannot poſſibly know, nor never ſaw one of a hundred or thouſand of them, with any particular knowledge at leaſt?

And *Cont. quæſt. & Reſp. Bezæ, p.* 103. He approveth of *Zanchy's* judgment [that Ceremonies and things indifferent be left free] [and the Churches free in them.]

And *Defenſ. p.* 286. He ſaith, [*Primum Epiſcoporum omnium & Presbyterorum unum eſſe Ordinem Conſtituo.*] I maintain that there is one Order of all *Biſhops* and *Presbyters*] Therefore they cannot differ but *Gradu*, as a *Deacon* and *Archdeacon*. And again, *ib. p.* 286. *Miniſterii autem Evangelici unitas, probatur ab horum unitate; & ut ita loquar, identitate: Eandem enim veritatis doctrinam, omnes Orthodoxi docent, eadem Sacramenta Miniſtrant, eandem cenſuram exercent; tantum Provinciarum eſt inæqualitas & graduum diverſitas,*] [The Unity of the Goſpel Miniſtry is proved from the Unity, or as I may ſay, Identity of theſe: All (that are Orthodox) teach the ſame true Doctrine, Adminiſter the ſame Sacraments, exerciſe the ſame Cenſures; Only there is an inequality of Provinces, and a diverſity of degrees.] Thus the moſt Learned and rational Defender of Prelacy giveth away their Cauſe.

3. Biſhop *Bilſon*, a moſt Learned and judicious man alſo, ſaith more for Epiſcopacy than any of our late Writers; and in my judgment ſaith more againſt the Office of Eccleſiaſtical Elders diſtinct from Paſtors, than can be anſwered. But to our two main Queſtions before-mentioned,

ed, (of a Bishop over many Churches without Bishops under him, and of half-Presbyters) how little he saith the Reader will soon see (yea how much on our side.)

4. As for *Hooker*, till his *7th* Book came lately out, we had nothing in him considerable of this subject: And in that Book it self, so little to the purpose, as to our foresaid two Controversies, as is next to nothing, nor worthy a Reply. In his §. 2. *p.* 4. He attempts (that which few do) to give us the definition of a Bishop, which is [*A Bishop is a Minister of God, unto whom with permanent continuance, there is given not only power of Administring the Word and Sacraments, which power other Presbyters have, but also a further power to Ordain Ecclesiastical persons, and a power of Chiefty in Government over Presbyters as well as Lay men, a power to be by way of Jurisdiction a Pastor even to Pastors themselves.*] And then he distinguisheth of *Bishops at large* or indefinite, and *Bishops* with *restraint*, and faith he meaneth the later. And so you have what must be expected from Mr. *Hooker* for the information of you, what Episcopacy he pleads for: Where it is obvious how fraudulently (through oversight or partiality I know not) he dealeth: For whereas he durst put no more into the definition of Episcopacy about Jurisdiction but [*a power of Chiefty in Government over Presbyters as well as Lay-men.*] yet would not tell us, whether *Government* of *Lay-men*, (under the Bishop) belong to the Presbyters or not : His words seem plainly to imply it.; what use else is there for his [*Chiefty*] and [*as well as Lay-men.*] And yet twice over he would name nothing but, *Teaching* and *Sacraments* which belong to the Pastor as a Pastor in general; leaving it as a thing which he would neither affirm nor deny, whether Pastors Governed their Flocks. Yet all that Decantate Book turneth on the Hinges of this lame Definition (which hath other defects which I pass by;) And without this we cannot know what Subject he disputeth of. Whereas *Saravia* well noted and acknowledged three Essential parts of the Ministry in General, Mr. *Hooker* who leaveth out one of them, and yet durst not deny it, should have told us, whether he include it or not; seeing it is the matter of most of our difference; and we take him for no Pastor or Presbyter that is without the *power* of Government, nor that to be a true Church (*in sensu politico*) that hath no other Pastor.

2. And when as one part of his Adversaries deny not (at least) the Lawfulness of one Bishops superiority in a single Church, as far as his description speaketh, but only in many Churches; no, nor one Archbishops power over many Churches that have their own Bishops, but only his power to depose all the Bishops of particular Churches and turn them all into one Diocesan Church; his Definition visibly reacheth to no other sort of Bishops, but such as we oppose not; and so he saith nothing at all against us, to any purpose through all his Book: For where after he confidently tells us that the extent of his Jurisdiction alters not
the

Hooker answered as far as our cause requireth.

Remember also that Hooker's third Book is written to prove that no one Form is commanded in Scripture: Therefore not the Prelatical.

the *Species*, it is but barely said, and by his leave I shall fully prove the contrary anon. And *pag. 4. l. 7.* He confesseth that *de facto* [*Many things are in the state of Bishops, which the times have changed; Many a Parsonage at this day is larger than some ancient Bishopricks were.*] It's well confest: And I shall try among other things, whether the Name of a Bishoprick will make a Parsonage and a Diocess to be *ejusdem speciei*, and whether magnitude do not make a specifick difference, between the Sea and a Rivulet or a glass of water, or between a Ship and a Nut-shel.

And whereas *page 6.* He undertaketh to prove a *Coercive Power* in Bishops, either he speaketh according to the common use of men, or not: If not, he would not be understood: *& Qui non vult intelligi, debet negligi:* If he do, then by *Coercive* he must mean, by *Outward force upon the body;* which is false, and is proper to the Magistrate, Parents or Masters; and is disclaimed by all sober Protestant Divines, yea by Papists, as not at all belonging to the Pastoral Office. Though we easily grant that Pastors may *Coercere* by *word* (and so may Presbyters sure,) yet no otherwise but by *word.* For *Excommunication* and *Degradation* as far as belongs to them, are but *words* (and an after forbearing of their own acts of Communion.) But this is not the common use of the word *Coercive* as applyed to Government by way of distinction. How much wiselier doth the (more Learned and judicious) Bishop *Bilson* still distinguish by the *Power of the Word,* as differing from the Magistrates Coercive *or by the Sword?*

Yet note that *page 8. §. 5. l. 7.* He is brought to acknowledge [*that All Churches by the Apostles erected received from them the same Faith, the same Sacraments, the same Form of publick Regiment: The Form of Regiment by them established at first was, that the Laity be subject to a College of Ecclesiastical persons, which were in every such City appointed for that purpose: These in their writings they term sometime Presbyters and sometime Bishops. To take one Church out of a number for a pattern, what the rest were, the Presbyters of* Ephesus, *as it is in the History of their departure from the Apostle* Paul *at* Miletum, *are said to have wept abundantly all; which speech doth shew them to have been many: And by the Apostles exhortation it may appear, that they had not each his several Flock to feed, but were in common appointed to feed that one Flock the Church of* Ephesus, *for which cause the phrase of his speech is this* Attendite gregi, *Look to all that one Flock over which the Holy Ghost hath made you Bishops: These persons Ecclesiastical being termed then Presbyters and Bishops both, &c.*] How little doth this agree with Dr. Hammond.

And page 9. he saith, [*The outward being of a Church consisteth in the having of a Bishop.*] Then the *Brownists* must carry it, that our Parishes are no true Churches (but parts of a Church) because they have no Bishop: Only a Diocesan Church hath a Bishop : Therefore only a Diocesan is a true Church; (which anon shall be proved to be but Humane.)

And

And *page* 12. He thus expoundeth *Hierome*, as holding Episcopacy alterable [*The Church hath power by Universal consent upon urgent cause to take it away; if thereunto she be constrained through the proud tyrannical and unreformable dealing of her Bishop———Wherefore lest Bishops forget themselves, as if none on earth had authority to touch their states, let them continually bear in mind, that it is rather the force of custome than any such true heavenly law can be shewed, by the evidence whereof it may of a truth appear, that the Lord himself hath appointed Presbyters for ever to be under the Regiment of Bishops in what sort soever they behave themselves. Let this consideration be a bridle to them; Let it teach them not to disdain the advice of their Presbyters, but to use their Authority with so much the greater humility and moderation, as a Sword which the Church hath power to take from them.*] This is Mr. *Hooker.*

And yet must I swear never to consent to any alteration.

And *page* 14. He confesseth that according to the Custom of *England,* and a Council at *Carthage,* Presbyters may impose hands in Ordination with the Bishop, though not without him : So that by this they have the the power of Ordination to, though he have a Negative Voice in it. And indeed if all Ordination must be done by one of a Superiour Order, who shall Ordain Bishops, or Archbishops, or *Patriarchs,* or the *Pope ?*

And *page* 18. He saith, [*Most certain truth it is that Churches Cathedral and the Bishops of them are as glasses, wherein the face and countenance of Apostolical antiquity remaineth even as yet to be seen———*] Which is it that we also affirm, every City or Church having a Bishop and Presbytery of their own.

And whereas *page* 19. He saith, [*If we prove that Bishops have lawfully of old ruled over other Ministers, it is enough; how few soever those Ministers have been, how small soever the circuit of place which hath contained them.*] If this be so, we grant you *enough,* when we grant *Parochial Bishops.*

But no where doth he more palpably yield our Cause, than *page* 21, 22. where to *Cartwright's* Objection, that [*the Bishop that* Cyprian *speaketh of is nothing else but such as we call Pastor, or as the common name is Parsons, and his Church whereof he is Bishop is neither Diocess nor Province, but a Congregation which met together in one place to be taught by one man.*] He hath no better answer to this, than to tell us, that *If it were true, it is impertinent;* and that it is not true, because *Cyprian* had many *Presbyters under him, so as they might have every day change for performance of their duty :* And he never once attempteth to prove that *Cyprian* had more Churches, yea, or Assemblies than One ; but only that he was over the Presbyters in one Church or Assembly, and as an Archbishop was over Bishops. The same thing which I submit to ; but nothing against the things that I assert against him. A Parson may have divers Curates under him, and not divers Churches, much less a thousand that have no other Bishop ?

And

And whereas *page* 33. It is objected that many things are innovated in our Discipline, as imposing Ministers on the People without their consent, Bishops Excommunicating alone, Imprisoning, &c. His answer is, that the Church may change her customes; And on that ground alloweth the Ordination of Presbyters alone, because the Church can give them power: For he goeth in Church-matters as he doth in point of Civil Government, on his false supposition, that all Power is Originally in the whole Body, saying, *page* 37. [*The whole Church visible being the true Original subject of all power, it hath not ordinarily allowed any other, than Bishops alone to Ordain. Howbeit as the ordinary course is ordinarily in all things to be observed, so it may be in some cases not unnecessary that we decline from the ordinary ways.*] (What is more contrary than *Saravia* (*Tract. de Obedient.*) and *Hooker* in their Principles of Government ?) From hence also, *page* 38. He inferreth the no *necessity of continued Succession of Bishops in every effectual Ordination.* And it is very observable which he granteth (for it cannot be denied.) [*The Power of Orders I may lawfully receive without the asking consent of any multitude: but the power I cannot exercise upon any certain People against their wills.*]

And *page* 38. He cannot deny but the ancient use was for the Bishops to excommunicate with the College of his Assistant Presbyters ; but he taunteth *Beza* for thinking that this may not be changed. These are the men that build upon Antiquity, and the Custom of the Universal Church.

And *page* 69. when the Canons for Bishops spare course of living are objected, he saith, that those *Canons were made* when *Bishops lived of the same Purse which served as well for a number of others as for them, and yet all at their disposing;* Intimating the old Course, when every Church had its Bishop and inferiour Clergy. But Innovation is lawful for our Prelacy.

And now he that can find any thing in *Hooker* against the points which I defend, or for that Prelacy which I oppose, any more worth the answering than this that I have recited, let him rejoyce in the perfection of his eye-sight. And if thus much be worthy to be confuted, or such as this, let them do it that have nothing else to do. So ridiculous is the Challenge of one that glorieth to write a Book with the same Title [of *Ecclef: Policy,*] who insultingly provoketh us to write a full Confutation of *Hooker,* who saith so little to the main point in Controversie, our Diocesan Form of Prelacy, and writeth his whole Book in a tedious Preaching stile, where you may read many leaves for so much Argumentation, as one Syllogism may contain ; that I think I might as wisely have challenged himself to construe Mr. *Fox's* Book of Martyrs, or *Baronius* his Annals, almost, or at least may say as Dr. *John Burges* doth of Mr. *Parker* (another sort of *Parker*) his Book of the Cross, which Dr. *Ames* saith was never answered, that *if any will reduce that gawdy Treatise into Argument* (it being indeed almost all made up of the

fruits

fruits of Reading, History, Sentences, &c. of purpose to confute them that said the Nonconformists were no Schollars) *he should quickly have an Answer to it.* So if any will reduce all that is in Mr. *Hooker's* 8 Books (in tedious Discourses into Syllogism, (which is against what I maintain,) I believe it will not all fill up one half or quarter of a page; and it shall, God-willing, be soon answered. In the mean time the popular Principles of his First and Eighth Book, subverting all true Government, I have already confuted elsewhere (in my *Christian Directory*.)

Bishop *Downame* Answered.

5. Bishop *Downame* hath said much more to the main Points, in the defence of his Consecration Sermon, and as much as I can expect to find in any. But, 1. as to the mode he is so contrary to *Hooker*, that (being a very expert Logician) he wasteth so much of his Book about the *Forms* of Arguments and Answers, that he obscureth the matter by it, and ensnareth those Readers, who do not carefully distinguish between Matter and Words, and between the *force* of the *reason*, and the *form* of a Syllogism. And he so adorneth (or defileth) his Style with taunts, insulting scorns, and contemptuous reproaches, that it is more sutable to the Scold at *Billings-gate* than so learned and godly a Divine, and occasioneth his Adversaries to say, You have here a taste of the Prelatical Spirit.

He fell after under the frowns of Bishop *Laud* himself, his Book of perseverance being prohibited.

2. As to the *matter* of his first Book, I am of his mind (against meer ruling Elders) He and *Bilson* have evinced what they hold in that. But as to the points in which we differ he indeed saith much to little purpose, and finally giveth away his Cause, or as he merrily telleth his Adversary, *pag. 62. l. 3. c. 47.* he useth it as Sir *Christopher Blunt's head was used, after his apprehension, first healed, and then cut off.* For, 1. in his *lib. 3.* Where he speaketh of the power of Ordination, he not only confesseth that it is in Presbyters with the Bishops, and that the Bishops have but a superiority of power therein, but is angry with his Adversary for supposing the contrary, saying *ch. 3. p. 68.* [*But where good Sir, do I say, they must have the sole power in Ordination, which you have so oft objected, and now again repeat? make you no conscience of publishing untruths? Cannot Bishops be superiour to other Ministers in the power of Ordination and Jurisdiction, which is the thing which I maintain, unless they have the sole power?* so p. 64, &c.

* *Ambrose in Eph. 4. Aug. qu. in vet. & N. Test. q.101. Cypr. l. 3. ep. 17. Concil. Carth. Græc. c. 43. Carth. 2. c. 4. Conc. Arausic. c. 2.*

Therefore he granteth, that *extraordinarily in case of necessity Presbyters may Ordain* (that is without a Bishop.) *page 69.* and *page 108.* he giveth this reason for the validity of their Ordination; Because Imposition of hands in Confirmation of the Baptized and Reconciliation of Penitents, were reserved to Bishops as well as Ordination, and yet in the absence of Bishops may be done by Presbyters. * And that the Papists themselves grant that the Pope may license a Presbyter to Ordain Presbyters: [*If therefore (saith he) by the Popes license a Presbyter may Ordain Presbyters, much better may a Company of Presbyters, to whom in the want of a Bishop the Charge of the Church is devolved, be authorized thereto by necessity.*] And if all

all this be so, no doubt but the Power of Ordination is in Presbyters, as such, though they are not to exercise it alone, nor without or against the Bishop (And so formerly they were not to Preach, or Baptize, nor Congregate the Church without him.) For why cannot a Lay-man Ordain with the Bishop but because he hath no such authority?

And *Cap.* 5. as to the power of *Jurisdiction* he saith the same, p. 110. 111. [*I deny not Presbyters (which have charge of souls) to have Jurisdiction; both severally in their Parishes, and jointly in Provincial Synods. And I have confessed before, that Presbyters have with and under the Bishops exercised some Jurisdiction. I grant that Godly Bishops, before they had the countenance and assistance of Christian Magistracy* * *and direction of Christian Laws; used in all matters of moment, to consult with their Clergy. This was practised by* Cyprian, Ambrose *also (in 1 Tim. 5. 1.) teacheth, that there was a time when nothing was done without the advice of the Presbyters; which therefore by* Ignatius *are called the Counsellors and Co-assessors of the Bishops: Which course if it were used still, as it would ease the Bishops burden very much, so would it nothing detract from their superiority in Governing.*————

And page 115. [*The thing which I was to prove, if it had been needful, was, that whereas Presbyters did Govern each one the People of a Parish, and that privately,* † *the Bishop Governeth the People of the whole Diocess and that publickly.*

So that both Ordination and Jurisdiction belong to the Presbyters Office; though in the exercise of it they must be governed themselves. Is not this the very sum of Archbishop *Usher's* Model of Primitive Episcopacy, which we offered his Majesty and the Bishops at first, for Concord, and the Bishops would not once take it into their Consideration, nor so much as vouchsafe to talk of it, or bring it under any deliberation? When, alas, we poor undertrodden Persons, not only desired to be low our selves, but yielded to submit to all their heights, their Lordships, Parliament dignities, grandure, and to let them alone with their (real) sole Ordination and Jurisdiction over us poor Presbyters, and to have taken as much care of the People as they would, so we could but have obtained any tolerable degree of Government to be setled in each particular Church, either in all the Presbyters or in one Bishop, and not have had all the particular Churches deprived of Bishops and all the Pastoral Jurisdiction.

But our great Controversie is handled by Bishop *Downame* in his second Book, wherein he laboureth to prove that the Bishops Church, or rather Charge, was not a *Parish,* but a *Diocess.* And first, page 4. he giveth us a scheme of the Scripture acception of the word [*Church*] as preparatory to his design: In which there are many Texts cited, not only without any shew of proof, that they speak of what he affirmeth them to speak, but contrary to the plain scope of the places. And he tells us that the word [*Church*] *is used in Scripture for the Church Militant Congregated in an Universal or Oecumenical Synod.* And offereth us not one Text for instance, which

*The Prelates pretence for innovation: All the cause Is laid on Magistrates.

† Doth a publick Church Pastor govern but privately? what meaneth he by that which can be good hence? A private man may rule privately, that is, by Counsell: *Judicium publicum* is the Officers judgement.

which he doth though injurioufly, for all the reft: Nor is there any that
fo fpeaketh.

He tells us that the word is ufed *particularly to fignifie the Church of a Na-*
tion in the fingular number; but could name no fuch place as to any Church
fince Chrift, but only the Jewifh Church, *Acts* 7. 38.

And he faith, it is ufed to fignifie, *particularly and definitely the Church*
of a Nation in the plural number. And is not this a ftrange kind of Allegati-
on? The Scripture fpeaketh of [*the Churches in a Nation.*] Therefore it
ufeth the word for the *Church of a Nation, in the plural number.* Is *one*
Church and *many* all one with him: Would he have applauded that man
that would have faid, that fuch an Author ufeth the word [*College*] (for
the College of an Univerfity in the plural number,) becaufe he named the
College in an Univerfity? and this to prove that an Univerfity is one College? Had it not been better faid, The New Teftament never ufeth the
word *Church* for all the Churches in one Nation (fince Chrift) definitely,
but ever calleth them plurally Churches: Therefore to call them all *One*
(*National*) *Church* is not to imitate the Scripture.

His firft Inftance is, *Rom.* 6.4. *All the Churches of the Gentiles.* A fad
proof of a *National Church!* What Nation is it that the word [*Gentiles*]
fignifieth? No doubt the Gentile Churches were in Gentile Nations: But
that doth not prove that the Chriftians in any Nation are ever called in
Scripture (fince the Jews Nation) *One Church* but *Churches.*

His next inftance is, 1 *Cor.* 16. 1. *The Churches of Galatia*: And the
reft are all fuch, *v.* 19. 2 *Cor.* 8. 1. *Gal.* 1. 2. 22. The Churches of *Afia,*
Macedonia, Judæa: But I hope he intended no more than to tell you that
the Chriftians of feveral Nations, are never called a *Church,* but *Chur-*
ches, as having any fort of Union than National.

He giveth many inftances when the word [*Church*] is ufed definitely to
fignifie the *Church of a City and Country adjoyning*: But to prove it
ufed to fignifie *feveral Churches* in City and Country adjoyning, but *one*
only.

Two Texts he alledgeth to prove that the word [*Church*] is ufed definitely
to fignifie thefe Churches Congregate into a Synod or Confiftory: But I believe his word of neither place. One is *Mat.* 18. 17. *Tell the Church, &c.*
If I fay that [*tell the Church*] fignifieth [*tell the Society containing Paftors and*
Chriftians] though it is the Paftors that you muft immediately fpeak to
and the offender muft hear, I give as good proof of my expofition as he
doth of his. If I fpeak to a *man,* and hear a *man,* though it be only his
ears that *hear* me, and his *tongue* that fpeaketh to me, yet by the word
[*man*] I mean not only *ears* and *tongue.* If the King fend a Command to
a *Corporation* to expel a feditious member, though the Mayor or Aldermen
only do it Authoritatively, and the People but executively, yet the
word [*Corporation*] doth not therefore fignifie the Officers only. The other
Text is, *Act.* 15. 22. But I will not believe him that [*the whole Church*]
fignifieth the Synod only: For though they only *decreed* it, I think the reft
con-

confented and approved it, and are meant in the word [*the whole Church.*]

I grant him that (*Rom.* 16. 1.) the word fignifieth the Church of a Village or Town ; But he will never prove that it is not meant of a Church of the fame *Species* as City Churches were.   And as to the Houfe or Family Churches which he mentioneth. *Rom.* 16. 5. 1 *Cor.* 16. 19. *Col.* 4. 15. *Phil.* 2. Dr. *Hammond* expoundeth, *Col.* 4 15. of the Church that did *meet in his houfe,* and fo fome do all the reft : But that we ftand not for, nor doth it concern us.

But when he addeth a multitude of Texts, as ufing the word Church *indefinitely,* not defining the place, Society of a Nation or City, quantity, &c. moft of the inftances brought are of Churches definite, as to *place,* and of the fame Species as the Apoftles Inftituted ; though when the Church of fuch a place is faid to do a thing, it's no determination what number of the members did it.   His firft inftance is *Acts* 4. 31. and next *Acts* 15. 3, 9, &c. *The Churches had reft through all Judæa, and Gallile, and Samaria: Acts* 15. 3. Speaks of the Church of *Antioch,* which *v.* 27. it's faid they gathered together: *v.* 4. mentioneth the Church at *Jerufalem, v.* 11. mentioneth the Churches of *Syria* and *Cilicia. Acts* 18. 22. Speaketh of the Church at *Cæfarea. Rom.* 16. 16. Speaks of the Churches where *Paul* lately travelled. *v.* 23. *Gaius* was the *Hoft* of a definite whole Church, at *Corinth.*   And when 1 *Cor.* 4. 17. he fpeaketh of his teaching in *every* Church, it is an Univerfal enunciation, but of Churches of a certain or definite *fpecies,* and fo of the reft.

Then *p.* 5. he telleth us what *is truly and properly a Church on Earth ;* and faith, *Every company of men profeffing the true faith of Chrift is both truly a Church and a true Church.*   Anf. Yes, As *Canis cæleftis* is *truly a Dog,* and a *true Dog :* but not properly, but equivocally : A Church in its moft famous fignification is a *Society* conftituted of the *Paftor* and Flock , as a School of the Schoolmafter and Schollars: And an accidental meeting of Chriftians in a Market or Ship, is no more properly called a Church, than School-boys meeting in fuch places are a School : No nor occafionally praying together neither.

So *p.* 5. He concludeth that the Chriftian People of one City, and Country adjoyning, whether Province or Diocefs are one Church ; yea of any Nation or part of the World, not becaufe under one Spiritual Government or Prieft-hood, but becaufe one People or Commonwealth ruled by the fame Laws, profeffing the fame Religion.   All this is *de nomine* only. But are we not likely to difpute well, when we never agree of the Subject, or terms of the Queftion ?   We have no mind to contend about Names : Let him call the World, or a Corporation, or Kingdom, or *Eclefiam Malignantium* by the name of a Church if he will, fo that we firft agree what *Church* we difpute of.   We talk not of any accidental meeting or Community, but a Society before defined, *conftituted of the pars gubernans* and *pars fubdita.*   And of this fort we know of Divine Inftitution,

an

an *Univerſal Church Headed by Chriſt*, and *particular Churches* headed under him by their Biſhops or Paſtors: A Church without a *Head*, (in Fair, Ship, or Temple) we talk not of: Nor yet of a Church that hath but an Accidental, Extrinſick, and not an Eſſential Conſtitutive Head, to them, as they are Churches of Chriſt's Inſtitution: Whether it be the Emperour of *Germany*, or of *Conſtantinople, Mahometan*, Chriſtian, Papiſt, or Proteſtant, we believe that every Soveraign is ſo the Head, that is the Ruler of the Church, that is, of the Chriſtians in his Dominions. We denominate *à formâ*: Biſhop *Downame* may denominate whence he pleaſe, *à materiâ* or *ab accidente*, *&c.* and ſay, They are one Church that are under one Prince, Law, of one Religion. Do with your Equivocals what you will; But forget not that it is a *Paſtoral particular* Church of the Holy Ghoſt's Inſtitution that we Diſpute about. Otherwiſe I deny not Dioceſan, or Patriarchal Churches, nor deny that the Papal Kingdom is a Church of a certain *ſpecies* right or wrong.

And forget not his Conceſſion p. 6. and we need no more, [*Indeed at the very firſt converſion of Cities, the whole number of the People converted (being ſometimes not much greater than the number of the Presbyters placed among them) were able to make but a ſmall Congregation. But thoſe Churches were in Conſtituting, they were not fully Conſtituted, till their number being increaſed they had their Biſhop or Paſtor, their Presbyters and Deacons, without which*, Ignatius *ſaith, there was no Church, &c.*] Of which after.

He next, *Cap.* 1. laboureth much to prove, that the words *Eccleſia, Parœcia*, and *Diocæſis*, of old were of the ſame ſignification; About words we have no mind to ſtrive: But all the proofs that he brings of the extent of a Church to more than one Congregation or Altar, are fetcht from later times, when indeed Churches were transformed into Societies much different from thoſe before them.

He citeth *Concil. Carth.* 2. *c.* 5. *&* 3. 42, 43, *&c.* that places that had no Biſhops before ſhould not receive Biſhops without the conſent of the Biſhop whom they were before under. Indeed by theſe Canons we ſee much of the ſtate of the Church in thoſe times, and partly how the Caſe was altered. Every Church had a Biſhop of its own: Thoſe Churches were almoſt all firſt planted in Cities: The multitudes were Heathens: but the City Chriſtians with thoſe in the Country near them, were enow to make a Church or Congregation. In time ſo many were Converted in the Country Villages, that they were allowed Aſſemblies like our Chappels at home: And ſome of them had Country Biſhops ſet over them: And in many places greater Towns (which they then called Cities) were anew converted. The Presbyters that were abroad among theſe new Converts or ſcatered Chriſtians, made them know that every Church ſhould have a Biſhop, and that they might chooſe one of their own: And few Presbyters being then Learned able men in Compariſon of the Biſhops, by this advantage of preſence among them, many raw and ſchiſmatical Presbyters crept into the Peoples affections, and perſwaded them to chooſe
them

them for their Bishops: when they were chosen and ordained, they encroached on the rest of the old Bishops Diocess, and also refused to come to the Synods, lest their failings should be known, pretending that they must stay with their own People. Now the Bishops that complained of this, did not alledge, 1. That no Bishop should be made but in a City, 2. Nor that when Christians multiplyed, they must not multiply Bishops accordingly, but all be under their first Bishop only, 3. Nor that a new Congregation had not as good right to have and chuse a Bishop of their own, as the first City Congregation had. But only to keep ignorant Schismatical Presbyters from deceiving the People for their own exaltation, and from hindering Synodical Concord, they Decreed that none in their Diocesses should have Bishops, without the first Bishops consent; And that being so Consecrated they should frequent Synods, and should be Bishops only of that People that first chose them, and not encroach on the rest of the Diocess. And whereas he hence gathereth that tha Country Churches [ever from the beginning belonged to the City Bishops.] There were no such things as Appendant Country Churches from the beginning of the City Churches: But it's true, that from the beginning of the Country Peoples Conversion, when they were not enow to make Churches themselves, they belonged to the City Churches as Members (Even as now the Anabaptists and Independent Churches consist of the People of Market-Towns, and the adjoyning Country Associated into one Assembly.) After that the Country Meetings were but as Oratories or Chappels: And when they came to be enow to make distinct Churches of, some good Bishops had the Wit and Grace to help them to *Chorepiscopi*, Bishops of their own; but most did choose rather to enlarge their own Possessions or Powers, and set Subject Presbyters only over the People.

And that these new Bishopricks must be by the old Bishops consent, is apparently a point of Order to avoid inconveniences (if not of Usurpation:) For what power had the old Bishop to keep any Church of Christ without a Bishop of their own, when it was for there good?

That he hath some countenance from *Leo*, for the New Church Form (without Bishops) I wonder not, when *Leo* was one of the hottest that betimes maintained the *Roman* Primacy, if not Universal Soveraignty.

And as the Care against placing Bishops in small places, *ne vilescat nomen Episcopi*, came in late, so 1. It intimateth that it was otherwise done, at least by some before, 2. And it is but the Prelatical grandure which *Constantine* had pufft up, which is then alledged as the Reason of this Restraint.

His Argument is, [*That which was judged unlawful by the Canons of approved Councils, and Decrees of Godly Bishops, was never Lawfully, regularly and ordinarily practised: But, &c.*] I deny the Major. Kneeling at Prayer or Sacrament on the Lords day, the Marriage of Priests, the Reading of the Heathens Writings, and abundance such-like, were forbidden by such approved Councils; especially a multitude of things depending on the new

I   Impe-

Imperial shape of the Churches, which are now lawful, and were lawful, and ordinarily practised before : *Paul* Kneeled and Prayed on the Lord's day, *Acts* 20. *&c.* Therefore the placing of Bishops in Country Parishes was not unlawful before, because the Councils of Bishops afterward forbad it, nor was it ever unlawful by Gods Law. Methinks a Bishop that subscribeth to the 39 Articles of the Church of *England*, which mentioneth General Councils erring, even in matters of Faith, should never have asserted that they cannot erre in matter of Government, nor retract and alter that which was well practised before them.

His next Argument is this, If there were any Parish Bishops then, they were the *Chorepiscopi*, But the *Chorepiscopi* were not such.

Anf. 1. I deny the Major : There were then many City Bishops that were but Parish Bishops, or had but one Church, as shall be further proved. 2. Yet as to a great number it is granted that their Diocesses had many Churches, at the time of *Concil. Eliber. Sardis. &c.* which he mentioneth. But it followeth not that therefore it was so with any in the time of *Ignatius*, or with many in *Cyprian's* time. 3. If it were all granted *de facto*, it will not follow, that *de jure*, it was well done, and that the old Form was not sinfully changed. 4. The *Chorepiscopi* themselves might have many Congregations under them, like our Chapels, and yet be Parish Bishops ; And it's most probable that at first they had no more than one of our Country Parishes, though afterwards they had many Churches under them, as City Bishops had.

His next Argument is, [*Churches endued with Power Ecclesiastical, sufficient for the Government of themselves, having also a Bishop and Presbytery, had the power of Ordination : But Country Parishes had not the Power of Ordination : Ergo, &c.*

Anf. 1. Government is Inferiour or Superiour : They might have sufficient Inferiour power of Government, though they had none of the Superiour power, such as belongeth to Archbishops, to whom Appeals were made : As a Corporation that hath a Mayor and Assistants hath sufficient Inferiour power, but not Regal, nor such as Judges, Lord Lieutenants, &c. have. And if it were proved, (as some hold) that only General, or unfixed Ministers, like the Apostles, and Evangelists, or Archbishops that were over many Churches, had the power of Ordination, and not the Inferiour Bishops of single Churches, it would not follow that these Inferiour Bishops had not the power of Governing their own Churches with assisting Presbyters : And if he will prove for us, that every fixed Bishop hath the power of Ordination, who hath but the Inferiour power of Governing his single Church, by Admonitions, Excommunications, and Absolutions, he will but do our work for us.

2. I deny his Minor Propof. If by [Country Parishes] he mean [the Bishops of Country Parishes] they had the *Power* of Ordination : And all that he saith against it, is only to prove, that *de facto*, they had not the *Exercise* of it in the times he mentioneth, and that *de jure humano*, it was

not

not allowed them by Canons. But, 3. We grant so much of the Conclusion, as that *de facto*, few Country Parishes had a Bishop and Presbytery: Because there were but few Country Parishes in the World, till the third Century, that were really Christian Churches, or fixed Societies of Christians that had ordinary Church-communion together in the Sacrament, or had an Altar. But our Case is, *About single Churches*, now called Parish Churches, and not about [*Country Churches.*] For they might be but *single* Parish Churches, though they were in Cities only, and the Country Members joyned with them in the Cities.

And his own Confession is, *page 35.* that besides *Rome* and *Alexandria,* [that had many Churches in the City, *there is not the like evidence for multitude of Parishes in other Cities, imediately after the Apostles times.*] I suppose by his Citations, he meaneth till the third Century. And if this be granted us of all the great Cities of the World, that they cannot be proved to have many Churches, we have no great reason to look for many in the Country Villages.

His next Argument is, [*Churches containing within their Circuit, not only Cities with their Suburbs, but also whole Countries subject to them, were Diocesses. But the Churches, subject to the ancient Bishops in the Primitive Church, contained, &c. Therefore they were Diocesses:*

Ans. Either this is his Description of a Diocess, or we have none from him that I can find: And let who will Dispute about the Names of Diocess and Parish, for I will not. And if by a *Diocess* he meaneth a Church consisting of all the *Christians* in City and Country associated for Personal holy Communion, having One Altar and One Bishop, this is that which we call a *single Church*, or some a Parish-Church, and if he call it a Diocess he may please himself.

But if he mean that in these Cities and whole Countries were several such Churches, that had each an Altar, and were fixed Societies for personal holy Communion, not having any proper Bishop of their own, but one Bishop in Common, with whose Cathedral Church, they did not, and could not Communicate, (through Number or distance) I deny his Minor proposed in this sense, as to the two first Centuries; though not as to the following Ages. But if by [*Cities, Suburbs, and whole Countries subject*] he mean all the unconverted Infidels of that space (for doubtless he calls not the soil or place, the Church) I deny the very subject; There were no such Churches: Infidels and Heathens make not Churches, (Though Hereticks made somewhat like them, *sicut vespæ faciunt favos,* as *Tertullian* speaketh.) If the Diocesan Churches Disputed for, be Churches of Pagans and Infidels, we know no such things.

But if he mean that all the Heathens in that Circuit are the Bishops Charge in order to Conversion, I answer, 1. That maketh them no parts of the Church: Therefore the Church is of never the larger extent for the foil or Infidel Inhabitants. 2. The Apostles, and other General Preachers (like the Jesuits in the *Indies*) may divide their Labourers by Provinces

I 2   for

for the Peoples Converſion, before there be any Churches at all. 3. This diſtribution is a meer prudential Ordering of an accident or circumſtance; and therefore not the Divine Inſtitution of a Church Form or Species. 4. Neither Scripture nor prudence ſo diſtributeth Circuits or Provinces to Preachers, in order to converſion of Infidels, as that other Preachers may not come and Preach there, as freely as one that claimeth it as his Province. For, 1. Chriſt ſent out his Apoſtles by two and two at firſt. 2. *Paul* had *Barnabas* or ſome other Evangeliſt or General Preacher uſually with him. And *Peter* and *Paul* are both ſaid to be at *Rome*, at *Antioch*, and o-ther places: And many Apoſtles were long together at *Jeruſalem*, even many years after Chriſt's Reſurrection. Chriſt that bid them go into all the World, never commanded that one ſhould not come where another was, nor have power to Preach to Infidels in that Dioceſs.

And what is the Epiſcopal power over Infidels, which is claimed? It is not a power to *Ordain*, or to *Excommunicate* them. It can be no other than a power to Preach to them, and Baptize them when converted. And this is confeſſed to belong to Presbyters. If the Biſhops would divide the World into Dioceſſes, and be the only Preachers in thoſe Dioceſſes, it would be no wonder if the World be unconverted. It is not Biſhops that are ſent by the Papiſts themſelves to convert the *Indians*.

But perhaps you may ſay that the Biſhops rule thoſe Presbyters that do it. I anſwer, 1. It's an imperfect kind of Government, which a Biſhop in *England* can exerciſe over Presbyters that daily Preach, as Mr. *Eliat* his hel-pers to the Natives in a Wilderneſs many thouſand Miles from them. 2. But if they do rule the Preachers, that maketh not the Soil nor the Heathens to be any parts of their Church, but the Preachers only. Therefore a Dio-ceſs with them, and a Church, muſt be different things.

His firſt Reaſon therefore, *page* 36. from the Circuit is vain. His ſe-cond, *page* 37. that the City Biſhops had a right from the beginning over many Churches, (that had no other Biſhops) and did not after uſurp it, he proveth not at all: For the words of Men three or four hundred years after Chriſt, alledging *ancient cuſtome* are no proof: When the 25 *Can. Trull.* cited by himſelf, maketh thirty years poſſeſſion enough againſt all that would queſtion their Title. And abundance of things had Cuſtome and Antiquity alledged for them ſo long after, that were known Innova-tions.

His third Reaſon is from the *Chorepiſcopi*, as the Biſhops ſuffragan, which ſheweth no more, but that the City Biſhops (whether juſtly or by uſurpa-tion) were at laſt really Archbiſhops, or Rulers of Biſhops: But of this before.

His fourth Reaſon, from Succeſſion will be good, when he that affirm-eth that no Church was governed by the Pariſh Diſcipline, hath proved that all, many, yea, or any Biſhops from the Apoſtles days, had many Churches under them that had no Biſhops of their own. Till then he ſaith nothing.

As

As to his inftance of the *Scythians* having but one Bifhop, the Reafon was, becaufe it was but little of their Country at firft that were made Chriftians, or that were at all in the *Roman* Empire : So that the Bifhop was fetled at *Tomis*, in the borders of the Empire (in the Maritine part of the *Euxine* Sea,) that thence he might have an influence on the reft of the *Scythians* over whom the *Romans* had no power, and where there were many Cities indeed, but few Chriftians : as may be feen in *Theodoret, Tripart. Nicephor.* and many others. Of his other three or four inftances, I fhall after fpeak.

Chap. 3. *lib.* 2. He pretends to prove that the feven *Afian* Churches were Diocefan, and not Parochial, and never defineth a Diocefs and Parifh ; which is loft labour.

His firft Argument is, [*Churches, whofe Circuit contained Cities and Countries adjoining, were Dioceffes. But, &c.*

This is before anfwered: Our Queftion is, Whether they were as our Diocefan Churches, fuch as had in thefe Cities and Countries many Altars and Churches without Bifhops under them : Trees, and Houfes, and Fields, and Heathen People, make not Churches, nor yet fcattered Chriftians, that were Members only of the City Church.

His proof of the Minor is, 1. Thefe Churches comprized all the Churches of *Afia.*

Anf. If he mean that all the reft of the Churches of *Afia* had no Bifhops, but Parifh Presbyters under thefe feven Bifhops he fhould prove it, (and confute Dr. *Hammond* that is fo contrary to him, (had he then lived:) Till then we take it as a contemptible incredible affertion, that *Afia* had but feven Bifhops, and yet a multitude of Churches : If he mean only that thefe feven were Archbifhops, his impertinency is too palbable.

Particularly, he faith, *The Church of* Ephefus, Smyrna, &c. *Contained a great City, and the Country belonging to it, &c.*

Anf. We talk of Churches under Churches, and he talketh only of *Cities* and *Countries*; Again, I fay, Let him take his Diocefs of Infidels, Houfes and Ground, we know no fuch Churches.

Page 46. He faith [*Cenchrea was fubject to the Church of* Corinth, *and never had a Bifhop of their own.*] But not a fyllable of proof: It is not a *Family Church*, which we fpeak of, therefore he need not here have mentioned that : But a Church affociated for ordinary Communion in God's publick worfhip, which cannot be celebrated without a Paftor. Let him prove that *Cenchrea* was fuch a Church and yet had no Bifhop.

In §. 6. p. 49. He would prove that the *Circuit of a Church was in the Intention of the Apoftles, or firft Founders, the fame from the beginning, before the divifion of Churches as after :* Which I fhall in due place difprove. His reafons are, 1. *Becaufe the whole Church fince the Apoftles days hath fo underftood the intention of the Apoftles.*

Anf. 1. This is not proved. 2. I fhall anone prove the contrary ; that the Apoftles had no intention that Churches fhould be defined by the limits

of

of the place and Country : nor did they themselves ever appoint any such bounds to any one Church, and say *so far it shall extend*: Nor did they ever take any but Christians in any Circuits for Members of the Church. And I shall prove that all Churches were but such as I described, single Churches with their Bishops at the first, and that some Villages had Bishops four or five hundred years after : And his own Reason that *Churches followed the Civil Form*, proveth the mutability of their bounds, seeing the Civil Forms were mutable.

His next Reason is because [*that division of Churches which was* 300 *or* 400 *Years after Christ, with their Limits and Circuits, were ordinarily the same which had been from the beginning, as divers Councils testifie.*

Ans. Those Councils mean no more, than that it had been an old or setled Custome, (as many Learned men have proved.) And if they could be proved to mean that from the Apostolical plantations the bounds of all the Diocess were set, I marvel that any man could believe them. But they say no such thing, as were it not tedious to the Reader, an examination of each particular would shew. Else no new Churches and Bishops must be setled in the World, but those that the Apostles converted in any Cities between or near them; For the unconverted Cities in the inter-spaces, were as much those Bishops Diocesses as the Villages of equal distance : And then the making of new Cities would have made one a Bishop of many Cities, contrary to the Canons.

His third Reason is, that *the Distribution of the Churches usually followed the division of the Common wealth.*

Ans. 1. If so (as is said) they must be various and mutable. All the World was not divided just as the *Roman* Empire was : And the Imperial divisions had great changes. 2. I think it lost labour to dispute with him that holdeth this assimilating the Church to the Civil Form, was of Divine Apostolical Institution. If any can think so, let him give us his proof that the Church Constitution must vary as Monarchical, Aristocratical and Democratical States do; As Empires and free Cities do : And that from the King to the Constable, we must have a correspondent Officer : And that the Papacy as Capital in the *Roman* Empire, was of Gods Institution. And that an Emperour, King, or popular State may change the Form of the Churches, as oft as they may the Form of their subordinate Governments. Are not these small Reasons to prove, that when the Apostles planted Bishops in all single Churches, they intended that those Bishops should be the sole Bishops of many hundred Churches, when they should be raised in the Circuit of ground, which now is called their Diocesses. But more of this in due place.

But next he appealeth to *mens consciences, Whether it be not unlikely that there was but one Congregation belonging to these famous Cities towards the end of the Apostles days.* Of which more afterward.

In *Chap.* 4. *p.* 69. He argueth, [*The Presbyteries ordained by the Apostles, were appointed for Diocesses, and not to Parishes : Therefore the Churches endued*
with

with the power of Ecclesiastical Government were not Parishes but Dioceses.

Anf. Our Queftion is, Whether they were fingle Churches as before defined, or only One Diocefan Church made up of many fuch fingle Churches: 1. If by *Presbyteries* be meant many Presbyters, a College, or *Confessus*, I deny the Confequence; becaufe every Church that had Government had not fuch a Presbytery; But one Bifhop or Paftor did ferve for fome of the lefser Churches, and yet that one had Governing power. 2. I deny the Major: It was fingle Churches that had then many Elders fet over them. 3. Reader, it feemeth to me no fmall difparagement to the Diocefan Caufe, that the grand Patrons of it fo extreamly differ among themfelves. Dr. *Hammond* holdeth that in all the Scripture times, no one Church had any Presbyters at all, fave only one fingle Bifhop. This Bifhop *Downame* feemeth to hold, that *every Governed Church* had a Presbytery. And [*no one*] and [*every one*] extreamly differ: Yet either of them would have cenfured him that had gain-fayed them.

His proof of the Antecedent is this. [*They who were appointed to whole Cities and Countries to labour fo far as they were able the converfion of all that belonged to God, were appointed to Dioceffes, not to Parifhes : But, &c.*]

Anf. Is not here fruftration inftead of edification to the Reader, for want of defining a Diocefs and a Parifh. I thought we had talkt of a Diocefan Church; and here is a Diocefs defcribed which may be a *fingle Church*, or no Church at all as the Bifhop pleafeth. Here is not fo much as any Chriftians, much lefs Congregations of them mentioned as the Bifhops Flock: But many an Apoftle, Evangelift, and Converting Preacher, hath been fet over Cities and Countries to labour mens Converfion, as far as they were able, before they had converted any, or at leaft enow to make a Church; and after that, before they had converted more than one Affembly. The Jefuits in the *Indies* thus laboured in feveral Provinces, before they were Bifhops of thofe Provinces, or called them Provincial Churches. But now we perceive what he meaneth by a Diocefs, even a /pace of Ground containing Inhabitants to be converted if we can.

I will fhorten my Anfwer to the reft of his Reafonings for fuch Diocefan Churches.

I will put a few Queftions, more pertinent than his Queries *p.* 67. about the ftate of fuch Diocefan Churches.

Q. 1. Whether the Apoftles were not, by this defcription, Bifhops of all the World as their Dioceffes? And whether therefore it follow that there were no Bifhops under them in particular Churches?

Q. 2. Whether Apoftles and Evangelifts did not go from City to City, fometime ftaying fome Months or Years at one, and then pafling to another? And whether this made all the interjacent Countries their Dioceffes, changing their Bifhops as oft as they thus changed their Habitations?

Q. 3. Whether more than one fuch Apoftle or Evangelift were not both at once, and fuccefsively in the fame place, to labour the converfion of all they could? And whether therefore there were many Bifhops to a Diocefs?

Q. 4

Q. 4. Where we shall find the proof that the Apostles or Evangelists set the bounds of Diocesses? And whether this description of his own do make Diocesses bounded by circuit or space of Ground, or by the Abilities of the Bishop to endeavour conversion?

Q. 5. When the Apostles forbad any other to labour mens conversion in their Cities or Countries where they or others had been before them? And did not one plant and another water, (and usually more than one at once?)

Q. 6. Whether (*Mat.* 28. 19, 20.) Discipling or Preaching to convert men, and then baptizing them, be not the way of gathering Churches; and therefore proveth that before conversion they are no Churches? and are not Christians only members of the Church? And are those Diocesan Churches that are no Churches?

Q. 7. If one be setled in a single Congregation in the City, with a purpose to endeavour the conversion of the Country; is not a Diocesan Church there the same as a single Congregation, though the Diocess be larger?

Q. 8. If when Congregations multiplyed, Bishops were not multiplyed, but one would keep many Churches under himself alone, doth it prove that this was well done because it was done? and that God consented to this change?

His next Reason is, *because Churches were not then divided into Parishes?* Which in due place I shall prove to be a sufficient Reason against him. Churches were Societies constituted of Pastors and their Christian Congregations, as afore defined: And his inference is vain, that [*Presbyteries were not settled in Parishes, because the Churches were not yet divided into Parishes.* For they were Parishes, that is, *single Churches,* without *dividing.* The space of Ground called Parishes was not then marked out; Nor was a Diocesan Church (like ours) that hath no subordinate Bishops divided into Parishes; for there were no such Diocesan Churches to be so divided. But the Universal Church and the Apostolical Provinces were made up (or constituted) of Parishes, I mean of particular *Churches,* as greater numbers are of unites, and as Villages are of Houses. But to say that *Churches were not divided into Parishes,* in the sence in question, is all one as to say, *Churches were not divided into Churches.*

Our Controversie is like this, Whether all the Families in the Town should have but One common Master? And he that affirmeth it, should argue thus; Masters were not at first appointed to Families but to Villages; For Villages were not at first divided into Families, (when there were none but single Houses erected.) True; but Families were Families before there were Villages to be divided. As Villages were not made before Houses, and then divided into Houses, nor Cities before Streets, and afterwards divided into Streets; nor Kingdoms before Cities and Corporations, and then divided into Corporations, (or inferiour Societies) Nor Academies before Colleges, and then divided into Colleges; so neither were Provincial, or Diocesan Churches made before *single Churches,* and after divided into

into them ; but were made by the coalition of many single Churches ; which should not have been changed for that use *in specie*, by altering the *species* of their Pastors, and depriving them of their Proper Bishops.

In his *5th Chap.* He pretendeth to confute the Assertion that for the first 200 years, the City Churches were but single Congregations. Here we use to except only *Alexandria* and *Rome* in all the World : And we confidently extend the time to 150 years, and very probably to 200 ; and moreover say, that till the fourth Century, most or very many Churches were no other, if not long after in many Kingdoms.

All his talk, p. 80. against *shallow giddy Heads, that see no further than their Nose end*, because it was denied that Pastors were set in single Congregations to convert also the Infidels about, I have nothing to do with : For I assert that as all Ministers are bound to endeavour the conversion of such, if they have opportunity (not wanting power,) so those are most bound to it that have best opportunity, which is the Neighbour Bishops. But till men are converted they are no parts of the Church ; no, nor of that particular Church, *eo nomine*, because converted by that Bishop (as shall be proved,) without some further consent and ground. The rest about the largeness of the Church of *Jerusalem*, &c. shall be considered in due place.

In his *Chap.* 6. p. 104. I desire it may be noted that he saith, [*I do not deny but that at the first, and namely in the time of the Apostle* Paul, *the most of the Churches so soon after their conversion, did not each of them exceed the proportion of a populous Congregation.* And p. 114. that *Metropolitans he thinks were intended by the Apostles, or at least, suadente naturâ & necessitate flagitante,* as *Beza* saith : And I suppose a Diocesan Church will find no better ground than a Metropolitan, *viz.* Humane Prudence, or (I think intended.)

In *chap.* 7. He pretendeth to prove, that in the Apostles times Parishes began to be distinguished under one only Bishop, &c. But what's the proof ? *Rome* and *Alexandria* are all the Instances. † But, 1. his proof that *Evaristus* divided Parishes about *An.* 100 is worth nothing, as having no sufficient evidence, but fabulous reports. 2. He allegeth *Eusebius, l.* 2. *c.* 15. saying of St. *Mark,* that *he is said first to have constituted the Churches* of Alexandria. But this is no proof. 1. Because *Eusebius*'s following words out of *Philo* do make it most probable, that by [*the Churches of* Alexandria] he meant [*the Churches in and about* Alexandria,] which proveth not many in the City it self. 2. If he had planted many Churches in the City, it is no proof that he varied from the practice of the other Apostles, who (as *Act.* 14. 23.) placed Elders (that is, faith Dr. *Hammond*, Bishops) in every Church : Or that the Elders of each Church had not the true Pastoral or Episcopal power of Governing the Flock, (which is all that we plead for.) And if it had been proved that *Mark* had been over them : it followeth not that he was not over them as an Archbishop, but as a meer Bishop only. 3. *Grotius* and Dr. *Hammond* think they prove that

† In my Treat. of the true way of Concord, I have also disproved the Instances of *Rome* and *Alexandria.*

K   *Rome*

Rome and other great Cities then had more Bishops than one, by reason of the peoples diversity in Languages, &c. As *Peter* of the Circumcision, and *Paul* of the Uncircumcision. 4. *Eusebius* mentioneth not this as a certainty, but with an [*it's said*] which is the usual note of his uncertain reports (of which he hath not a few, as is commonly confessed.) 5. Dr. *Hammond* is so far from believing this (that many Parishes were committed so early to Presbyters under one Bishop) that he thinketh there is no proof that any such Presbyters were in being in the Scripture times. And though we confess that *Alexandria* and *Rome* had divers Churches in them long before other places, there is no proof or probability that it was so in the Apostles days. And *l. 3. c. 4. Eusebius* expresly saith, [*But how many and what sincere followers have governed the Churches planted by the Apostles, it cannot be affirmed, but so far as may be gathered from the words of* Paul. And *c.* 19. he mentioneth in the singular number the *Church* (not the Churches) of *Rome, Antioch,* and *Jerusalem.* And *l. 4. c.* 11. he saith *Celadion* succeeded *Mark* in the *Church* of *Alexandria.*

But he saith *l. 5. c. 9.* that *Julianus* was chosen Bishop over the Churches of *Alexandria*: And *c.* 22. *Demetrius* came in his place. And *l. 6. c.* 1. *Demetrius* took upon him the oversight of the Congregations there. And *c.* 35. *Dionysius* received the Bishoprick of ruling the Churches in or about *Alexandria, &c.*

Ans. 1. So long after it is not denied, but that *Alexandria* had more Assemblies than one. 2. Yet it is most likely that by the Churches in and about *Alexandria, Eusebius* meant the Churches under the Archbishop of *Alexandria*, which had Bishops of their own. 3. Before they had a Temple there might be several lesser Meetings in the City, which were but as our Chapels, or the Independants Meeting in several Houses at once, when yet the Church was but one, because they were associated for *Personal Communion.* 4. When the Parishes were divided to several Presbyters, yet then each Presbyter had the true Episcopal Office as to the People, though not the Name; and though they were under a superiour Bishop; that is, they had the whole Office of a Presbyter or Pastor, to *Govern* the People as well as *Teach* them and *Worship* with them. And so there was then no Parish like ours, which is but part of a Diocesan Church, and no Church of it self (as the Bishops Form it) because it hath but a half Pastor. 5. And is not the case of all other Churches in the World, that to this time were but single Churches, more considerable than the case of *Rome* and *Alexandria*, which differed from all the rest.

Obj. But all the rest did the same, as soon as they had People enow to make many Churches?

Ans. 1. I have told you *Grotius* and Dr. *Hammond* think that there were more Bishops than one in a City for some time. 2. This multiplication was not till long after in the third Century, and with most in the fourth, when it was no wonder that the Church fell into the Imperial Form: And when they did so, the *Roman* Primacy arose with the rest. 3. Yet even
then

then the Presbyters were *Epifcopi gregis*, and had the true, full, Paftoral power as to their Flocks, as aforefaid. So that there were no Bifhops that yet depofed the Presbyters as now.

Page 125. He faith, [*Neither was this a thing peculiar to the Bifhops of A-lexandria, but common to others.*———Ignatius *was Bifhop not only of Anti-och, but of* Syria: Irenæus, *the Bifhop of* Lyons, *was Bifhop of* [the Churches in France, &c.

Anf. 1. This openeth the former cafe: Thefe were not Diocefanes, depofing all the *Epifcopos gregis*, and become fole Bifhops, but Archbi-fhops that had under them Bifhops in each particular Church. Yet note, that it is the *French* Synod of Bifhops which *Eufeb. ib. l. 5.c. 2 3. Iren.*is faid to overfee, as it's faid, *ibid.* that *Palmas* did fo among the Bifhops of *Pon-tus* in their Synod, and that *Victor* was Prefident in the Bifhops Synod at *Rome*, and *Theophilus* of *Cefarea*, and *Narciffus* of *Jerufalem* in the *Pale-ftine* Synod: Which is nothing to our cafe.

It is further faid, that *Optatus* faith, that in *Rome* were 40 Churches, and that *Theodoret* had 800.

Anf. 1. It is granted, that in *Optatus*'s days *Rome* had 40, which is nothing to our cafe in hand. 2. In thofe 40 fo late, there were no half Presbyters, but as this Doctor confeffeth, they had not only a joynt pow-er in Governing the Flocks, but in Ordination too. 3. I confefs *Theodo-ret*'s cafe feemeth ftrange, and though of late date is fo incredible as con-trary to the cafe of other Churches, that I do the rather for that claufe believe that Epiftle to *Leo* to be a forgery, or corrupted at leaft. And befides this Reafon, I have thefe alfo for it. 1. Becaufe he himfelf faith, that *Cyrus*, where he was Bifhop, was but two days journey from *Antioch, Hift. Sanct. Patr. de Juliano.* And he that knoweth how great the Diocefs of *Antioch* was, will not eafily believe that a Town within two days jour-ney (to Monks that went on foot) was like to have eight hundred Chur-ches in it at that time. 2. And we know out of whofe fhop *Theodoret*'s Epiftles come. *Nicephorus* faith, he read above 500 of his Epiftles. *Ba-ronius* faith there is a Book in the *Vaticane* containing 150 of them: *Metin-us* tranflated thefe into *Latine.* But faith *Rivet. Crit. Sacr. l. 4. c. 21. p.* 455. the Reader muft remember that they have been kept all this while in the Adverfaries Cabinets, and by them are brought into light and in-to Latine, fo that they have no authority, further than other Hiftory con-firmeth them. 3. Efpecially feeing *Leontius de Sectis* faith, as *Baronius* confeffeth, that Hereticks fained Epiftles in *Theodoret*'s name; And *Bel-larmine de fcript. Eccl.* mentioneth one that hath his name in *Concil. Ephef.* that neither *Theodoret* nor any Chriftian is to be charged with. 4. And that this one Epiftle to *Leo* fhould be cull'd out of all the reft to be alone Print-ed after *Theodoret*'s Works, fheweth the defign, and what credit is to be given to it. 5. And I fhall anon cite much out of *Theodoret* himfelf, to fhew the improbability that Diocefses had then fo many Churches.

And

And fo much as a juft confutation of Bifhop *Downame*, not as referring to other men with whom he dealt, but to the caufe which we have in hand. And that I anfwer not the whole Book, is becaufe I know of no more in it than what I have culled out, which needeth an anfwer as to the caufe which I defend : Of which I make the judicious Reader Judge.

Bifh. Hall.   6. Bifhop *Hall*'s Defence of Epifcopacy meddleth fo little with the point now in Queftion, that I have no need to fay any thing to it, more than is already faid. And he granteth all that I defire.

Petavius.   7. As for *Petavius*, I need not confute him ; for he granteth me moft, as to matter of Fact, that I defire, as I fhall after further fhew. His Fundamental Affertion is, That the two Offices of Bifhops and Presbyters, were both placed in the fame perfon, in the Apoftle's days ; at which *Salmafius* juftly laugheth : For what is that but to fay, that then there was no fuch perfon as a Subject Presbyter (much lefs as our half-Presbyters:) And *Salmafius* juftly congratulateth his conceffion, [that *folo confenfu hominum & vitandi fchifmatis gratia, unus enumero Epifcoporum, eorundemq; Presbyterorum, electus eft qui præeffet cæteris: Quod nemo dici prohibet——Nam etfi Epifcopalis ordo jure divino introductus eft, non eodem tamen illo jure decretum eft, ut unus in fingulis civitatibus & Ecclefiis, effet Epifcopus, fed Ecclefiæ authoritate conciliorumque fanctionibus.* viz. [*It was only by Mans confent and for the avoiding of Schifm, that one was chofen out of the number of Bifhops, who alfo were Presbyters, to be above the reft : This faying none forbiddeth. For though the Epifcopal Order was introduced by Divine Right, yet was it not by the fame right decreed, that One fhould be a Bifhop in each City and Church, but by the authority of the Church and the fanctions of Councils.* Of this fober Jefuit more anon.

Bifh. Andrews.   8. The Learned Bifhop *Andrews* in his Epiftles to *Pet. Molinæus*, hath faid fomewhat ; but in his Scheme (Printed at *Oxford*, 1641. before the Treatifes for Epifcopacy) much more. But as to his Defcription of the *Jewifh* Form, we dare not thence gather that Chriftians may imitate them, while we know that the ceffation of the *Jewifh* Policy and Law is fo largely pleaded for by *Paul*, and that Chrift is the perfect Lawgiver to his Church, and that we muft not add or alter on pretence of fuppofed parity of reafon. And as to his Reafons for Diocefanes from the New Teftament, though the well ordering of them make them very taking, yet when examined, they are no other but what we have found and anfwered in others.

B. Ufher.   9. The truly Learned, Reverend, and Godly Primate *Ufher*, in the fame forementioned Collection of Treatifes hath one of the Original of Bifhops and Metropolitans, and another of the Proconfular *Afia*. But, 1. The utmoft which he pleadeth for is no more than we acquiefce in, as
that

that it was his Model or Reduction (publiſhed ſince by Dr. *Bernard*) which we humbly offered to his Majeſty as the means of our common concord. And he hath himſelf told me his Judgment, that Biſhops and Presbyters differ not as two *Orders*, but in *Degree*; And that *Ordinis eſt Ordinare*, or that he that hath the *Order* hath intrinſical power to Ordain; though he is regularly to do it under the Biſhops overſight; And therefore it is not invalid, and null, but only irregular or ſchiſmatical, when it is done diſobediently againſt the Biſhop (and ſo may be diſabled *in foro exteriore*,) which Dr. *Bernard* alſo hath publiſhed of him; and Dr. *Maſon* in the ſame Treatiſe fuller proveth. And he took Presbyters to be Governours of the Flocks; and the Synods of Biſhops to be but for Concord, and not to have a proper Governing power over the particular Biſhops, as he hath himſelf expreſſed to me. Him therefore that is for us, we need not confute. And yet I muſt confeſs, that the great Argument which he and Biſhop *Andrews*, and *Saravia*, and all others uſe, from the title of *Angel* given to the Biſhops, *Rev.* 2. and 3. did never ſeem of any weight to me; nor moved my underſtanding that way at all: Believing that *Tyconius* his old Expoſition mentioned by *Auſtin* † is liker to be true, and that indeed, it is neither one Prelate nor all the Clergy, but the *whole Churches* that is meant by the *Angel of the Churches.*

For the Prophecy coming by Viſion, the word [*Angel*] is mentioned in the Viſion phraſe, and oft in that book is by all confeſſed to ſignifie collective Bodies, and more than ſingle Individuals: As *Uſher* (*de Babilone*) himſelf holdeth, that by [*the falſe Prophet*] in the ſingular number, is meant the *Roman* Clergy. It would be more tedious than neceſſary to recite the inſtances in that Book. I therefore who, becauſe of its obſcurity, am apt to be diſtruſtful of almoſt all Arguments that are fetcht from the dark Prophecies of *Daniel*, or the *Revelations*, am little ſatisfied with this from the name *Angel*. And who can believe them that ſay *Timothy* was then the Biſhop of *Epheſus*, and ſo excellent a perſon, as that none *was like minded*, as *deſcribed* by *Paul*; and yet that Chriſt had this againſt him, that he *had loſt his firſt love*, and muſt remember from whence he is fallen and *repent*, and do his firſt works or be rejected, *Rev.* 2. 4, 5. And in a word, that the Apoſtles, who placed holy perſons in the Miniſtry, had ſet ſuch over thoſe eminent Churches, as were neither hot nor cold, and had the reſt of the faults that are mentioned by Chriſt. And the whole ſtyle of the Text doth eaſily prove this Expoſition againſt theirs, *Rev.* 2. 2, 4, 7. As the praiſes and diſpraiſes there ſeem to refert to the whole Church, ſo *v.* 7. what can be more expreſs than [*Hear what the Spirit ſaith unto the Churches.*] And *v.* 10. *Behold the Devil ſhall caſt ſome of you into priſon, that ye may be tryed, and ye ſhall have tribulation ten days: be thou faithful, &c.* And again, *v.* 11. *He that hath an ear, let him hear what the Spirit ſaith unto the Churches*] which is repeated and ſpoken to every one of the ſeven. *v.* 14, 15. It is liker to be the whole Society than the Biſhop that is reproved for having falſe Teachers and Hereticks among them, and are called quick-

ly

† *Lib.* 3. *c.* 30. *de Doctrin. Chriſtian.* which *Auguſtine* ſeemeth to approve.

ly to repent: And *v. 20.* that suffered the Woman *Jezebel* to teach: For the Bishops could not hinder false Teachers, but by Excommunicating them, and disswading the People from hearing them: But the People could have done more, even refused to hear them.

V. 23. And all the Churches shall know] seemeth to intimate that this was written to the Church.

V. 24. Unto you I say, and to the rest in Thyatira, *as many as have not this Doctrine, and have not known the depth of Satan, &c.* Was this spoken to the Bishop only?

Chap. 3. v. 1. Was it the Bishop of *Sardis* only that *had a name to live and was dead,* and that was warned to be *watchful and strengthen the things which remain that are ready to die, whose works were not perfect before God? that must remember how he had received and heard — that had a few Names in* Sardis, *&c.* And so of the rest.

Obj. But it is said, Chap. 1. v. 20. *The seven Stars are the Angels of the seven Churches; and the seven Candlesticks are the seven Churches.*

Ans. And what can a man gather hence to satisfie himself in this point? whether the sense be [*As the heavenly Angels, are the Guardians of the Churches, so these Stars are those Angels, in whose Person I speak to the Churches themselves that are signified by the Candlesticks:*] Or [*As the Angels are the Guardians of the Churches, so by that title, I signifie the whole Ministry that guide them, and by the Candlesticks the Churches, and I write to the whole.* For as every Message begins with [*To the Angel,*] so it endeth with [*To the Churches.*

Obj. The Bishop was to deliver it to the Churches.

Ans. This is precarious. 1. The Apostle wrote it, that both Pastors and People might immediately read it, and did not intrust it as an unwritten tradition to one, to be delivered to the rest. 2. All the Pastors were to deliver or teach it to the People, and not one Bishop only. This therefore is no cogent Argument.

The Dispute at the Isle of Wight. 10. As for the Disputers for Episcopacy at the Isle of *Wight,* with King *Charles,* they manage *Saravia's* Argument (fetcht from the Continuance of the Ordinary part of the Apostles Office) as he did before them (and many others) so well, that for my part I cannot confute them, but remain in doubt; and therefore have nothing to say against them. But that's nothing to our Case, whether every particular Organized Church should have a Bishop or the full Pastoral Office in it.

John Forbes 11. As to *Joh. Forbes* his *Irenic.* he maintaineth but such an Episcopacy as we offered to his Majesty in Bishop *Usher's* Reduction: He pleadeth for such a Bishop as is the Moderator of a Presbytery, *p.* 242, 243. and as must be subject to censure himself, *p.* 145. and that shall do nothing of weight without the Presbyteries consent, *p.* 145. and as is still bound to the Work of a Presbyters Office, *p.* 146. And that an Orthodox Church
that

that hath no Bishop or Moderator hath but a certain Oeconomical defect, but is still a true Church, and hath the power that other Churches have that have Bishops, *p.* 158. And that *jure divino* Presbyters have the Power of Ordaining as well as of Preaching and Baptizing, though they must use it under the Bishops inspection in those places that have Bishops, *page* 164. And he is more full for the Power of Presbyters Ordaining, and the validity of it, than any man that I now remember.

12. The two Books of the *Bohemian* Government of the *Waldensian* Churches, Written by *Lascitius* and *Commenius*, contain that very Form of Government, which I think the soundest of any that I have yet seen.

13. The Learned and Judicious *Grotius*, (before he turned to *Cassander's* *Grotius*, and *Erasmus's* temperament in Religion) in his book *de Imper. sum. pot. circa sacra*, in almost all things speaketh the same which I approve and plead for ; though he be for some Episcopacy.

1. As to the Pastoral power, it self in whomsoever, he affirmeth it to be but Nuntiative, Declarative, Suasory, and *per consensum*, and not any *Imperium*; Like the power of a Physitian, a Counsellor, and an Embassadour.

Chap. 4. But then by *Imperium* he meaneth that which is *coactive* by the Sword: And he acknowledgeth the power of the Ministry by the Word upon Consenters, to be of Divine Institution, so that they sin against God, who do reject it. And if the Pastors of the Church did meddle with no other power, we should the sooner be agreed. For my part I take the very power of the Keys, to be no other, than a power of applying God's Word to the Consciences of the Penitent and Impenitent, and the Church ; and a power of judging who is fit or unfit for Church-communion according to God's Word, which judgment we can no otherwise execute but by the same Word, and by forbearing or exercising our own Ministerial actions to the person: (As a Physitian may refuse to Medicate the unruly.)

In *chap.* 6. He speaketh justly of the Princes power (as in the former.) And so he doth *chap.* 7. of the use and power of Synods or Councils.

Chap. 8. He well vindicateth the Magistrate, and denyeth to the Church or Bishops, the Legislative power, *circa sacra* : and sheweth that Canons are not proper Laws.

Chap. 9. He sheweth the Jurisdiction, properly so called, belongeth to the Magistrate, and not to the Pastors as such, (Though of old they might be also Magistrates.)

He sheweth that the use of the Keys is called Jurisdiction, but by the same figure by which Preaching is called Legislation (which is true as to the Declaration who is bound or loose, *in foro cæli*; but Pastors more properly judge who is to be taken into Church-communion or excluded.)

The

The prescript of Penance he saith is no Jurisdiction, but as the Councel of a Physitian, or Lawyer, or Philosopher. That the denying of the Sacraments is not properly Jurisdiction, he thus (excellently) explaineth [p.229. *As he that Baptizeth, or as the old custome was, puts the Eucharist into ones mouth or hand, doth exercise an act of Ministry and not of Jurisdiction; so also he that abstaineth from the same acts. For the reason of the visible signs, and of the audible is the same: By what right therefore a Pastor denounceth by words to one that is manifestly flagitious, that he is an utter alien to the Grace of God; by the same right also he doth not Baptize him, because it is the sign of remission of sin; or if he be Baptized, giveth him not the Eucharist, as being the sign of Communion with Christ. For the sign is not to be given to him that the thing signified doth not agree to; nor are pearls to be given to swine: But, as the Deacon was wont to cry in the Church [Holy things are for the Holy] Yea it were not only against Truth, but against charity, to make him partaker of the Lords Supper, who discerneth not the Lords Body, but eateth and drinketh judgment to himself: In these things while the Pastor doth only suspend his own act, and doth not exercise any Dominion over the acts of others, it is apparent that this belongeth to the use of Liberty, and not to the exercise of Jurisdiction. Such like is the case of a Physician refusing to give an Hydropick water when he desireth it, or in a grave person who refuseth to salute a profligate fellow, and in those that avoid the company of the Leprous.* (Only it must be remembred that this avoidance is by a Society governed therein by an Officer of Divine Institution.)

Next he proceeds to the Churches duty, and sheweth, 1. That as *Cyprian* saith, *The Laity that is obedient to God's commands, ought to separate themselves from a sinful Pastor or Prelate* (that is, that is grosly bad.) 2. That they ought to *avoid familiarity with scandalous Christians: As a Schollar may forsake a bad Teacher, and as an honest Man may leave the friendship of the flagitious.* As for the names of *Deposition* and *Excommunication*, he saith, That we must interpret the *name* by the *thing*, and not the *thing* by the *name*; And that the Church deposeth a Pastor when they forsake him or refuse to use him, *and Excommunicateth a man, when they avoid his communion,* (and declare him unmeet for communion.) *In all which the Church useth her own right, but taketh not away another mans.*

Then for the Canonical Enquiries after faults, and impositions of Penence, or delays of absolution, he sheweth that both the Canons and Judgments by them being but prudential Determinations of Modes and Circumstances, bound none but Consenters, without the Magistrates Law, except as the Law of Nature bound them to avoid offences. (He should add, [and as obedience in general is due to Church-guides of Christ's appointment.]) And how the Magistrate may constrain the Pastors to their duty.

Chap. 10. He sheweth that there are *two perpetual Functions in the Church, Presbyters and Deacons: I call them Presbyters* (saith he) *with all the Ancient Church, who feed the Church with the Preaching of the Word, the Sacraments*

and

Be it known to posterity that if the Prelates would have granted us but so much liberty, our distracted Churches might have had Concord.

and the Keys, which by Divine Right are individual (or inſeparable.) (Note that.)

And §. 27. He ſaith, *It is doubtful whether Paſtors where no Biſhops are, and ſo are under none, though over none, are to be numbered with Biſhops or meer Presbyters.*

§. 31. His counſel for the choice of Paſtors is, that (as in *Juſtinian's* time) *none be forced on the People againſt their wills, and yet a power reſerv'd in the chief Rulers to reſcind ſuch elections as are made to the deſtruction of Church or Commonwealth.*

Chap. 11. §. 10. He ſheweth that *Biſhops are not by Divine precept.*

And §. 1. That therefore the different Government of the Churches that have Biſhops, or that have none, ſhould be no hindrance to Unity.

And §. 10, 11. That ſome Cities had no Biſhops, and ſome more than one: And that not only in the Apoſtles days, but after, one City had ſeveral Biſhops, in imitation of the *Jews*, who to every Synagogue had an Archiſynagogus. *Page* 357. He ſheweth that there have been at *Rome* and elſewhere long *vacancies* of the Biſhops See, in which *the Presbyters Governed the Church without a Biſhop*; And ſaith, that all the Ancients do confeſs, that *there is no act ſo proper to a Biſhop, but a Presbyter may do it, except the right of Ordination.* Yet ſheweth, p. 358. that Presbyters ordained with Biſhops, and expoundeth the Canon thus, that *Presbyters ſhould Ordain none, contemning the Biſhop.*

And p. 359. He ſheweth that where there is no Biſhop, Presbyters may Ordain, as *Altiſiodorenſis* ſaith among the Schoolmen. And queſtioneth again whether the Presbyters that have no Biſhops over them be not rather Biſhops than meer Presbyters; citing *Ambroſe's* words [*He that had no one above him, was a Biſhop*] (what would he have ſaid of our City and Corporation Paſtors that have divers Chapels and Curates under them: Or of our Preſidents of Synods: or ſuch as the Paſtor of the firſt Town that ever I was Preacher in (*Bridgnorth* in *Shropſhire*) who had ſix Pariſhes in an exempt Juriſdiction, four or five of them great ones, and kept Court as ordinary like the Biſhops, being under none but the Archbiſhop.)

And §. 12. He ſheweth that there was great cauſe for many Churches to lay by Epiſcopacy for a time.

And p. 366. he ſaith [*Certainly Chriſt gave the Keys to be exerciſed by the ſame men, to whom he gave the power of Preaching and Baptizing. That which God hath joyned let no man ſeparate.*] (But then how ſhould Satan have uſed the Churches as he hath done?) And he ſheweth of meer ruling Elders (as he had done of Biſhops) that they are not neceſſary, but are lawful; and that it may be proved from Scripture that they are not diſpleaſing to God; and that formerly the Laity joyned in Councils. Only he puts theſe Cautions (which I conſent to) 1. That they be not ſet up as by God's command. 2. That they meddle no otherwiſe with the Paſtoral Office, or Excommunication, than by way of Counſel. 3. That none be choſen that are unfit. 4. That they uſe no coactive power, but what

L   is

is given them by the Soveraign. 5. That they know their power to be mutable, as being not by Gods command, but from man.

And *Chap.* 11. §. 8. He delivereth his opinion of the Original of Episcopacy, that it was not fetcht from the Temple pattern so much as from the Synagogues,) where as he said before, every Synagogue had a chief Ruler.)

14. As for *J. D.* and many other lesser Writers, (Sir *Thomas Aston*, &c.) who say but half the same with those forementioned, it is not worth your time and labour to read any more Animadversions on them.

J. D. &c.

15. But the great Learned *M. Ant. de Dominis Spalatensis* deserveth a more distinct consideration: who in his very learned Books *De Repub. Ecclesf.* doth copiously handle all the matter of Church-Government. But let us consider what it is that he maintaineth. In his *lib.* 5. *c.* 1. he maintaineth that [*the whole proper Ecclesiastical Power is meerly Spiritual.* In *cap.* 2. that *no Power with true Prefecture, Jurisdiction, Coaction and Domination belongeth to the Church.* In *c.* 3. he sheweth that an improper Jurisdiction belongs to it. Where he overthroweth the old Schoolmens Description of *Power of Jurisdiction*, and sheweth also the vanity of the common distinction of Power of Order and of Jurisdiction; and maintaineth, 1. that Power of Jurisdiction followeth, *ab Ordine*, as Light from the Sun: 2. That all the Power of the Keys which is exercised for Internal effects, although about External Matters, (of Worship or Government) belongeth directly to the *Potestas Ordinis*: 3. That the *Power* of *Jurisdiction* as distinct from *Order*, and reserved to the Bishops, is but the power about the Ordering of External things, which is used *Principally* and *Directly* for an *External* Effect (that is *Church* order.) §. 5. *p.* 35. 4. That it is foolish to separate power of Order from any power of Jurisdiction whatsoever, that is properly Ecclesiastical, it being wholly Spiritual. 5. The Episcopal Jurisdiction (not properly Ecclesiastical) he maketh to consist in ordering Rites and Ceremonies and Circumstances, and Temporals about the Church, and about such Modal Determinations about particular persons and actions as are matters of humane prudence, (which have only a General Rule in Nature or Scripture. 6. By which (though he hold Episcopacy *Jure Divino*) that it is but such things that he supposeth proper to the Bishop (which the Magistrate may determine and make Laws for, as *Grotius* and others prove at last, and himself after; and as Sir *Roger Twisden* hath Historically proved to have been used by the Kings of *England, Histor. Def. Cap.* 5. 7. That *all Ecclesiastical power whatsoever is fully and perfectly conjunct with Order.* page 36. 8. *That this plenitude of power is totally and equally in all Bishops and Presbyters lawfully Ordained: and that it is a meer vanity to distinguish in such power of Order, Plenitudinem potestatis à parte solicitudinis.* 9. That this equal power of the Bishop and Presbyter floweth from Ordination; and is the *Essential Ordinary Ministerial power*. 10. That this vain separating power of Order and Jurisdiction

M. Ant. de Dom. Spalatensis.

is

is the whole Foundation of Popery. §. 7. p. 36. & *passim* 37, &c. 11. He frequently calleth that [*the Essential power*] in which Bishops and Presbyters are equal, and so taketh the rest but for Accidental. 12. He thus describeth the Bishops power of Jurisdiction, *c.* 3. p. 39. §. 13. [*About those things which are constituted in the Church, only by Humane Ecclesiastical Right, there is in the Church true Jurisdiction not necessarily depending on the Sacred Order it self, if there be any at all separate from Order.* Such as Licensing a Bishop to Ordain in anothers Diocess, &c. For these *acts are not Actus Sacri neque spirituales, neque attingunt directè quicquam supernaturale, sed sunt merè temporales, & circa rem externam & temporalem quæ est mera applicatio,* &c. *These are not Sacred nor Spiritual, nor touch any thing directly that is Supernatural, but are meerly Temporal, and about an External and Temporal matter, Et his solis verum est, &c.* So that it is most evident, that as God hath left to Humane Prudence the Ordering of some Modes and Circumstances of Worship and Discipline and Church-Order, and by his General Laws, so *Spalatensis* thought that all the Bishops proper Jurisdiction lay in these things, which were of Humane Right, and that all things of divine appointment were equally belonging to the Presbyters. Where again I desire it may be observed. 1. That Magistrates may determine of such things, and so make void or needless such an Episcopacy. 2. That it is most certain that many things of External Order belong to a Presbyter to determine, as to one that is the Conducter of the Sacred Assemblies: As what Text to preach on, what Method to use, what Chapter to read: where and at what hour the People shall meet, how long they shall stay, what Tune to sing a Psalm in, and abundance of the like. So that even that Jurisdiction which he excepteth to the Bishop is common to him with the Presbyter that officiateth: And all that can be pretended is that it belongeth to him, to determine such Circumstances as equally belong to many Churches (which yet Synods of Presbyters may do as effectually for Concord.) 3. That indeed there is no true Ecclesiastical act which tendeth not to Internal Spiritual effects: Publick Admonitions and Confessions as well as private are for the humbling of the Sinner, and the exercise of Repentance; and Excommunications and Absolutions in publick are not only nor chiefly for the external Order of the Church, but for the preserving of the peoples souls from sin, and for the warning of others, and for the preserving in their minds a due esteem of the holiness of our Religion, and the necessity of holiness in us, and to convince those without, that God's Laws and Ways and People are more holy than those of the World. This is a clear and certain truth: and therefore according to *Spalatensis*, Presbyters must in publick as well as private Admonitions, and Absolutions, and Excommunications, have equal power with Bishops, except as to the ordering of the Circumstantials of it. Which though he sometime seem to reserve for the Bishop, yet (to do him right) when he doth so, he saith that it is a mixt power: As it is the exercise of the Keys, it is Essential to the Sacred Office, common to both; but as it is a prudential determination

mination

mination of Circumſtances according to Humane Right, directly and principally for *outward* and not for *inward effects*, it is the Biſhops Juriſdiction.
So that really he maketh the Biſhop, as ſuch, to be but the Maſter of Order
and Ceremonies, where the Magiſtrate doth not do it himſelf, and where it
belongeth not to the Officiating Paſtor as ſuch.

His *cap.* 4. is to prove that the power for Internal Effects of Grace in
the Church by External acts, is exerciſed only Miniſterially, by Miniſters
as ſuch, Inſtanced *cap.* 5. in Baptiſme *cap.* 6. in the Lords Supper, *cap.* 7.
in Confeſſions and Penance ; and *cap.* 9. in that Excommunication which
is the exerciſe of the Keys (for he miſtaketh in excluding Baptiſm from
the Keys, which indeed is the firſt uſe for intromiſſion.) *Cap.* 12. He a-
gain purpoſely ſheweth who are the Miniſters of each Ordinance. And
firſt again Vindicateth his Uniting of Order and proper Juriſdiction Eccleſiaſtical as before.

§. 4. p. 465. He confidently ſaith, that *to him it is a moſt certain thing*
that the power of Order, is of the Word, Sacrament and Keys, and that it
is, plena, tota, integra, fully, totally, intirely in every Biſhop and lawful Preſ-
byter.

§. 22. p. 472. He ſaith, that *Confirmation is neither a true Sacrament, but*
a part of the Ceremonies of Baptiſm ; nor is it at all of Divine, but of humane Ec-
cleſiaſtical Inſtitution ; nor doth it ſuppoſe any ſpecial power given by God to him
that adminiſtreth it, for any ſpecial ſupernatural effect. But the Church for
honour reſerveth this Ceremony to the Biſhop.

And §. 24. He ſaith, [*And why are Biſhops ſo rigid that they will not per-*
mit to their Pariſh Miniſters the Faculty of Confirming, ſpecially when they them-
† Yea, ne- *ſelves come very ſeldome* † *into thoſe Pariſhes to viſit. And verily thoſe Biſhops*
ver into *which have large Dioceſſes of Chriſtians in the* Turkiſh *Dominions, as my Arch-*
one *Biſhoprick of* Spalato, *ought (if this Ceremony were of any great account) to give*
Pariſh of *their Pariſh Miniſters there living free power of Confirming : Yea, if the Bi-*
ten or *ſhops deny it them, the Pariſh Miniſters may and ought to exerciſe this Ceremo-*
twenty. *ny by their own Authority.*

☞ And here I will tell Poſterity, that if we could have but got our Prelates,
&c. to have Confirmed to us but one *Word*, which the King granted us,
pro tempore, only in his *Declar. of Eccleſ. Affairs*, viz. that *Confirmation* as
a ſolemn Tranſition from Infant Church-State, into the Adult, ſhould be
but by the Miniſters [CONSENT] (as knowing his People better than
the Biſhop that never before ſaw them, or heard of them, or examined
them) it had healed one of the greateſt of our Breaches : But our Concord
was not thought worth this little price ; Though there is not in all the
places that ever I lived in, one Perſon of an hundred (if five hundred)
that I can hear of, that ever was Confirmed, or ever ſought it or regarded it. And yet their Rubrick ſaith, that we muſt not give the Lords Supper to any that are *not Confirmed*, or *ready for it* : Yet have we no power to
require of any Man a Proof or Certificate of his Confirmation, nor can
we know whether he be Confirmed or not ; Nor can we refuſe any at the
Lords.

Lords Table that refuseth to be examined by us, whether he be *ready to be Confirmed,* (save Infants.)

And in that 12. chap. §. 25, 26, 27. p. 473. *Spalatensis* again sheweth, that the *Power of the Keys for binding and loosing, belongeth to* Bishops and Presbyters as Ministers. And though he reserve the *Publick use* of them to the Bishop, he saith, *that he may commit it to a Presbyter.* For it is *Mixt, and hath partly the External Jurisdiction which the Bishop received by his proper Episcopal Ordination ; and partly, yea much rather* (or more*) the Internal, by the Keys, which they have by virtue of their Presbyterial Ordination, in equality with the Presbyters. The External, because it is External, may therefore be delegated to another, even a Lay-man :* (which is it, which the Parliament of *Scotland* have lately declared to be in the King.) And doth not all this shew what Episcopacy is? Even a Magistrates Office, *Circa Sacra, vindicated* by *Grotius* and others. But (saith he) *they cannot delegate the inward power which is properly of the Keys, because this dependeth of the Sacred Presbyterial Order,* both *in fieri, in esse, in conservari & operari.* For the *Presbyterial Order hath always the Keys annexed.——For when any is Ordained Presbyter, the Keys are given him, and Jurisdiction, with Orders, by Divine Right.*

And §. 28. p. 474. *Seeing the Apostles gave the Keys equally to all Bishops and Presbyters,—— No man can by Divine Right, reserve part of the Keys to himself alone, and leave another part to others.*

Moreover in *lib. 2. c. 3. §. 61. p. 210.* He sheweth that *Clement, Linus,* and *Anacletus,* were all Bishops in *Rome* at once.

Lib. 2. c. 9. §. 1. p. 282. He sheweth, that *Bishops and Presbyters are wholly equal in all Essentials, which belong to the Ecclesiastical Ministries to be exercised towards the People.* And that even in Government, *the rest of the Presbyters* (without excepting any) *in every Church make one College, of which the Bishop is the Head ; all Ordained to the same Cure and Government of Souls.* (So this Diocess hath between a thousand and two thousand Ministers, living some of them an hundred or sixscore Miles distance, to make a College to the Bishop that is usually at *London.*) How the Bishop is bound to Govern with them, see him, §. 4.

And §. 5. To be plainly understood, he saith, *We Bishops therefore must all remember, that All the Presbyters are our Brethren, and Collegues in the Ministry ; not our Servants or Slaves, and that by Divine Right they have no less power in feeding the people of God than we have : And if we exercise any External ampler Jurisdiction over them, not properly Ecclesiastical, it is not of our own power , but delegated from the Magistrates power,* as I shall prove *lib. 6.* and 10.

Yet plainer, §. 8, 9. p 285. *These Parish Presbyters have by Divine Right, full Power in the Ministry of Christ, and in these Parishes are the Ordinary Ministers, but under the Bishop.* For the Bishop alone hath a General Ecclesiastical Government to settle Ministers in their Diocess —— But being applyed to the Government of their Church, they have the ordinary power, but Presbyterial in that Church.———*By positive Right only Bishops are deputed to certain Seats.*——

Yet

Yet Presbyters have so this Ordinary power, that they cannot by Humane Ecclesia-stical Right reduce it into Act, till applyed by the Bishop in his Diocess.———

And *c*. 9. §. 11. *p.* 286. §. 1 3. *p.* 287. He sheweth, that in Vacancies, or the Bishops Absence, the Clergy of Presbyters have the whole Episcopal power of Government.

And *p.* 288, 289. He laboureth to prove, that one Church had many Bishops, and that it is but Ecclesiastical Law or Custome that one Church should have but one Bishop.

And §. 15. That if the Canons prohibited not, a Bishop might make all his Parish Presbyters full Bishops, as (§. 16.) in the *Ministerial Essenti-als towards the Faithful, they are by Divine Right equals. Vid.* & §. 20. *page* 291.

This is enough to say of *Spalatensis*, save that all that he saith for Bishops against us, is so little a part of what is said by the rest, that it can require no new Answer. And if this great Moderator, (who returned to *Rome*, though for a miserable imprisonment and end) because we are not yet near enough to Antiquity, (or rather being flattered into covetous and ambitious hopes) be able to prove no greater a difference between Bishops and Presbyters, we need not think that any other is like to do it.

Dr. *Ham-mond* an-swered. 16. The last great, Learned, Sober Defender of Episcopacy, and the last that I need to mention here, is Doctor *Hammond*, who in his Annotations, and his Treat. of the Keys, and especially his Dissertations against *Blondel*, and his Defence of them against the *London* Ministers, hath said much in this Cause. But his way is new (save that he followeth *Petavius* in the main supposition:) He forsaketh almost all the Fathers, and almost all the Patrons of Episcopacy of later times (who have written for it) in the Exposition of all the Texts of Scripture which mention the Elders and Bishops of Churches in those times, supposing that they all speak of Bishops only.

In his Treat. of the Keys, he maintaineth that the power of them was given to the Apostles onely by Christ, and to Bishops as their Successors by the Apostles. But I take it for undeniable truth, that the Bishops and Elders settled in every Church by the Apostles in *their own time*, had this power, and I need not expect a contradiction in it. And how fitly those are called the *Apostles Successors*, whom they set over the Churches in their own time, even from the beginning that they settled Churches, and with whom they continued in the same Churches many Months or Years (as *Paul* in *Asia*, I leave to others to judge.

But the Question is not whether Bishops have the power of the Keys, but whether *all Presbyters* have it not also? And 1. He sheweth that (according to the Canons,) the Presbyters might do nothing in this or in other Acts of Ministration, without the Bishop. 2. That our *English* Ordainers, though they say, *Receive the Holy Ghost, whose sins you do remit,* it

shall

shall be remitted, &c. Do not give the Presbyters *all the Power of binding and loosing but so much as the Bishops or the Governours are presumed to have thought fit to impart to them* (which he saith is. 1. The declaring in the Church the absolution of penitents after the Confession. 2. The absolving them by way of prayer before the Sacrament. 3. And by Baptismal washing, and 4. Upon Confession to the sick, and in private Conference, and Confession, &c. Which yet he saith, [*Is by Christs Authority committed to the Presbyters.*] 3. He saith,[*All this will not extend to the absolving from the bond of excommunication, or proportionably to such power of binding, any further (at most,) than to confer the first power of it ; which if it be then given, doth yet remain (as the other Power of Preaching, and administring the Sacraments)bound and restrained from being exercised, till they be further loosed by the donation of a Second Power.*]

Ans. But 1. Either he was not *able*, or not *willing*, to tell us whether this Power be given the Presbyters or not. For he avoideth it, by saying [*at most*] and *if it be given.*] If not able, his ability must be plainly deficient as to the decision of our main controversie of the difference between Bishops and Presbyters, which dependeth on it : If unwilling, he was unwilling to give us any solid satisfactory decision of this Case.

2. Being his Neighbour, I wrote in his Life time, a Confutation of that Assertion, that the ordained received their Office and Power properly from theOrdainer as the neerest Efficient of it,(in my Disput.ofOrdination, in my Disput.of Church-Government)and I proved that thePower or Office is immediately from Christ, and that the Ordainers do but design the Person that shall receive it, and Ministerially deliver him possession by an investing Sign.

3. Either the Office of a Presbyter is of Divine *Institution*, or of *Humane* : Either fixed by the Holy Ghost in the Apostles, immutably ; or made, and alterable by the Bishops ? If the Office be of Divine institution, and fixed for the Churches constant use, whether by Christ immediately or by the Holy Ghost in the Apostles,) than it is not in the Bishops Power to Altar it : And so whatever the Ordainers *please to give them*, is none of the measure of their Power : As the Arch-Bishop may Crown or anoint the King, and yet not give him what Power he please : Or rather as it is of Divine appointment, that the Husband shou'd be the Governour of the Wife : And she that chooseth him, and he that Marrieth them, cannot alter it, nor do they give him his measure of Power as they please, but suppose him endowed with that by God, and do only choose the Person that shall receive it ; and Ministerially invest him in the Possession of it. And if the Priest that marrieth them should by any words Contradict, or limit this institution of God, it were a Nullity, and invalid. If he do but say, *I pronounce you Husband and Wife.* He therefore pronounceth the man to have that Power of a Husband which God hath given him, though he vainly say after, you shall have but so much, or so much of it. And so it is in present Case : If God have made the Ministerial Office, he hath made it *something*

con-

conftituted of its effential parts ; And if fo what man hath Power to alter it. But if it be *humane*, yea, and made by the Bifhops then I confefs they may alter it, or deftroy it. . And if a Presbyter have what power the Ordainers pleafe to give him, every Ordainer may alter the Office and make a new *Species* of Church Minifters at his pleafure : Prove that and our difpute is at an end. But Papifts, Greeks, and Proteftants are agreed againft it.

4. If Presbyters receive that which he calleth [*the firft Power*] (which he would not deny, though he would not grant) it is all that at prefent I am pleading for it : And it isall that in their ordination they receive (as he faith) as to the *Word* and *Sacraments*. If then the Office of a Presbyter continue the fame Power of the Keys as to Excommunication, and Abfolution, as it doth of adminiftring the Word and Sacraments, at prefent I reft fatisfied with this (In which Learned *Spalatenfis*, and thofe that go with him, cannot be confuted)For this proveth that theirDivinely-inftitutedOffice Effentially containeth this Power of the Keys, though to be exercifed under the infpection of a Superiour.

5. And if this Infpection would prove that they have not the Power or that their Office, or Order is therefore diftinct, it will alfo prove that Bifhops have not the Power of the Keys, becaufe they exercife it under the Infpection of Metropolitans, Arch-Bifhops, Primates, or Patriarchs : And alfo that they are of a diftinct Order from all thefe : And that a Phyfition hath no Power to Guide or Govern his voluntary Patients in order to Cure, and that he is off a diftinct Office from the Colledge and Prefident, becaufe he is under their infpection. And are not all Bifhops under the Government of the King, as well as Phyfitions and other Subjects : And have they no Power of the Keys, becaufe he ruleth them.

And as a Presbyter might do nothing without the Bifhop, fo no one Bifhop could do any thing without other Bifhops : For he had no Epifcopal Power till they ordained him.

And as to after Government or that which he calleth the grant of a Second Power.

6. Is it any thing but *Humane Licenfe* to Exercife the Power of Office of Divine inftitution before received ? And is not the Magiftrates *Licenfe* as neceffary to the Bifhop and the Presbyter too, as the Bifhops is to the Presbyter.

7. And I take it for undenied among Chriftians, that humane Power of Government, extendeth but to the *Ordering* and not the *Nulling* of a Function inftituted by God. It is not referred to King or Bifhop, whether there fhall be a Preaching or none, Sacraments, or none, Church difcipline and exercife of the Keys, or none ; no more than whether there fhall be a Scripture, and Divine Law, a Chrift, a Heaven, and whether men fhall be good or bad, faved or damned : But only by whom, and when, and how, this Divine Function fhall be fo exercifed, as may beft attain the end, as to thofe circumftances not determined of by God ; and not contradicting Gods Inftitutions. Therefore if the Bifhops fay that the Preachers of the Gofpel

fhall

shall be silenced (perhaps by hundreds or thousands) while the necessity of the Peoples Souls is undeniable, their Authority in this should hinder no man from going to Preach (further than their violence hindreth.) And so by his own Rule it must be as to Discipline, if Discipline be a Work belonging to a Presbyter. And as *Spalatensis* saith of *Confirmation*, the Presbyter should do it, though the Bishop forbid him.

8. The *Second Power* which the Presbyter must receive from the Prelate for Teaching, Worshipping, and Governing the Flock, is either, 1. For the *exercise* of it in *General to any fit persons*, or else for the limitation of him to such a particular Flock. 2. And it is either a General License or power at once given to do all his Work, or to do this of Government whenever there is cause, or else it is a particular License for each particular act.

1. We deny not, but that as a Physician Licensed to practice, is not thereby made the Physician of this or that Person, Hospital or City, but have a particular Call for such an Exercise or Application of his skill. So an Ordained Minister of Christ hath no prepared Object on which to Exercise a Pastoral Office, but by a particular Call to such a Flock. But however you Censure our simplicity for it, we are resolved to believe, till you say more against it, 1. That the same may be said of a Bishop too ; and therefore by your Argument, when this Bishop is fixed in a particular Flock, he receiveth a *second power* as you call it, and so without it hath not the power of the Keys any more than the Presbyter ; and so must be of a distinct Order from the Bishops that give him his second power : And who giveth them theirs? And if you rise to a Patriarch or Pope, what Superiour of another Order giveth them their *second* Power ? 2. That Institution or fixing a man (before Ordained) to a particular Flock, doth not make him of another Order or Office, nor is a new Ordination ; nor is he as oft Ordained and made of another Office, as he changeth his Flock, or receiveth a new License from the Bishop or the King, (from whom I had rather have it.) 3. That the People as well as the Bishop (if not much more) do give the Minister this opportunity for the exercise of his Office, (as the Patient chooseth his Physician.) And yet it is my Opinion that this will not prove that the People are his Governours, much less that they give him a new Order or Office. And of old the People chose their Bishops themselves : It will be as much honour for you Learnedly to prove that there were no Kings in the World till Bishops made them, as to confute D. *Blondel's* Historical proof of the Peoples ancient choice of their Bishops.

2. And as to a General License, I will thank the King for it, yea, or any man that hath power to hinder me, that he will give me leave to Preach and Exercise my Office : But I do not think that every man that doth not hinder me when he can, doth give me power. And if a Bishop be so extraordinary good as not to silence nor hinder a Minister from Preaching Christ, I do not think that this man is an Usurper in Preaching the Gospel,

M   for

for want of a Licenfe or fecond Power : Nor yet in exercifing the reft of his Office, where he and the People do confent. Thefe things feem plain to us, and they that (whether by Learning, or the Love of Riches and Honour and Domination) are made wifer than we, may fuffer fuch Fools gladly, while themfelves are (*in re vel fpe*) Rich, Honourable and wife. 3. And what is Ordination but a General Inveftiture in the power of performing the Minifterial Office? And why may not the *General Power* or Licenfe be given at once as at twice? I think [*Take thou Authority to Preach the Word of God, and Adminifter the Holy Sacraments, and the Difcipline of the Church, when thou art thereto lawfully called,* (that is, haft opportunity and fit Objects) *is a General Licenfe* : And a Man may prefently Exercife this Office on Confenters : Unlefs the fence be [*Take thee power when it fhall be given thee.*]

3. But if it be a *Particular Licenfe* that is here meant by the grant of *fecond power,* I confefs that there is fomewhat confiderable in it, and that in old time the Bifhop and his Clergy living together, and meeting in the fame Church, the Presbyters (like our Parifh Curates now) were in all the Worfhip of the day, and in their privater Miniftry to the People to be ruled by the Bifhop, and to Modifie and Circumftantiate all as he directed them : And fo may it be again. But fure a Minifter is not to travel an hundred miles to the Bifhop, to know whether he fhall vifit this fick man, or give the Sacrament to the other, and to know what Chapter he fhall read, and fuch like? If it be not a *General Licenfe* that is meant, it muft needs fuppofe the Bifhops prefence.

9. And feeing the Bifhops may *Licenfe* a Presbyter to ufe the Keys, the opening of this will help our underftandings about the nature of the Bifhops Office. There is no act of Jurifdiction which they do not Ordinarily commit to others. The fentence of Excommunication and Abfolution is ordinarily decreed by a Lay-Chancellor. (And *Spalatenfis* faith, that Epifcopal-Jurifdiction may be done by a Lay Delegate.) The fame fentence is *Pronounced* in Court by a Lay-Man, or a meer-Presbyter. The fame fentence is publifhed in the Church by a Presbyter or Deacon. And a Prince may give a Licenfe to exercife the Miniftry to which we were Ordained.

I enquire then, 1. Whether the granting of this Epifcopal Power, be a making that Man a Bifhop that it's granted to? If fo, a Bifhop, a Prefbyter, and a Chancellor are all of one Office, when thus impowred. If not fo, then a Lay-man, or one of another Office, may have power to do the Work of the Bifhops Office. And what is the Office (tell me if you can) befide *Authority* and *Obligation* to do the Work? A Lay-man and Prefbyter may by the Bifhop be Authorized and Obliged to do the Work of a Bifhop, and this *ordinarily* as an Office: (For fo they do,) *Ergo,* a Chancellor and a Presbyter may be made really a Bifhop, and yet in their efteem remain a Lay-man and a Presbyter ftill. And is not that a Lay Office which a Lay-man may be Commiffioned to do? If a Lay-man were but Commiffioned to do the Work of a Presbyter (to Teach a Church ordinarily,

narily, to Administer the Sacraments, and to Excommunicate and Absolve *in foro internæ pœnitentialis*, either it would make the Man a Presbyter, or it would be a Nullity. And if it be not so with the Bishops Office, what is the Reason? Is it not because it is not of Divine Specification and Institution, but Humane, and therefore mutable, or such as Men may parcel out, and commit to Lay-men by pieces as they please? So much to Dr. *Hammond*'s Appropriation of the Power of the Keys in that Treatise.

As to his Annotations, I shall have occasion to recite them hereafter, *The Anno- tations.* among those that give up the Diocesan Cause (as opposed by us) and therefore shall here pass them by.

His Dissertations against *Blondel*, have a Premonition about Ordination, which though most confident, I shall manifest, when I come to the point of Ordination, to be most weak; and indeed have done it before his death in my Disput. of Ordin.

His first Preliminary Dissertation of Antichrist, of the Mystery of Iniquity and of *Diotrephes*, I will not be so needlesly tedious as to meddle with any further then to say that I will believe Dr. *Hammond* here, and in his Annot. on 2 *Thes.* 2. when I am fallen into so deep a sleep, as to dream, 1. That the famous Coming of Christ, and our gathering together to him, (which is a great Article of the Christian Faith) is but *Titus* his Destruction of *Jerusalem*; and that the reward promised to all that love his appearing, is meant to all that love the said Destruction of *Jerusalem*; 2. And that this Destruction was not to be called *nigh*, or at *hand*, which fell out so few Years after. 3. And that the *Gentiles* of remote Countries were so shaken in mind and moved about a Question of a few Years distance of the Destruction of the *Jews*, more than about Christ's coming to the Common Judgment. 4. And that the *Gnosticks* were indeed such terrible Persecutors of the Church, (who were dispersed Subjects) when their Doctrine was but that they might dissemble to escape Persecution themselves; and greater Persecutions were near? and not the *Gnosticks*, nor *Jews*, but *Nero* beheaded *Paul*; and the *Jews* themselves were banished *Rome*? 5. And that *Simon Magus* was indeed so famous a Fellow, as to be taken for the supream God, when Church Writers speak so uncertainly of his conflicts with *Peter* as of a doubtful story, and the evidence is so obscure, and the *Roman* Histories say so little of him? He might as well have thought the Apostle would have made all that ado about *James Naylor*, if he had been then alive. 6. And that there were not many other Hereticks as well as the *Gnosticks* that troubled the Churches, if *Epiphanius* knew how to name them and describe them rightly, or *Irenæus* before him, or *John* in *Rev.* 2. and 3. before them. 7. And that *Simon Magus* and his Heresie was a Mystery of Iniquity *not revealed* when *Paul* wrote the second Epistle to the *Thessalonians*. 8. And that many had not then followed him and fallen away to Heresie. 9. Or that by the *Apostasie* that must first come, is meant the Apostles separation from the *Jews*, and *Moses*'s Law; As if

he

he had said, we will firſt ſeparate, and that ſhall bring perſecution on you, but till we do that, it is withheld. 10. Or that the ſaid ſeparation was not done by degrees, ſome before this, and ſome after. 11. Or that the difference between the *Jews* perſecution of the Chriſtians, before the Apoſtles Apoſtaſie, and after it, was indeed ſo great as to be the Criſis of the Antichriſts Revelation. 12. And that poor *Simon* ſhould be the Man that *ſitteth in the Temple of God, and oppoſed and exalted himſelf above all that is called God,* when as the Scripture never once nameth him after his deprecation of the Apoſtles curſe or threatning; though *Nicolaitanes* are named, and *Alexander, Hymeneus* and *Philetus* named, and other Adverſaries, and all the terrible things foretold, which are here ſuppoſed to be done by *Simon,* and his Doctrine? What, were all the Sacred Writers afraid to name him when they recited all the Evils that he muſt do, and are ſuppoſed to make it a great part of all the Epiſtles, and the Hiſtory in *Acts* 15. and when he had been ſo ſharply rebuked and humbled before, *Act.* 8. 13. That the ό και χων, he *that with-holdeth, till he be taken out of the way,* is not meant of any perſon, *power* or *ſtate,* but the aforeſaid ſeparation of the Apoſtles. 14. That *verſe* 8. that *the breath of Chriſt's own mouth,* ſignifieth St. *Peter's* words that caſt down *Simon* when he fell and hurt him; and that the *brightneſs of his coming, or the appearing of his own preſence,* is nothing but the foreſaid Deſtruction of *Jeruſalem.* 15. And ſo many of the *Gnoſticks* and Hereticks, that troubled all the Churches of *Aſia* and other Countries, were got together into *Jeruſalem,* as that they might be ſaid to be conſumed and deſtroyed there, who ſo long after troubled the Churches. 16. And when I can believe that the Revelation is made up of ſuch a ſence, and that moſt or much of it, was fulfilled before it was revealed and written, and all the reſt fulfilled long ago (about *Conſtantine's* days) except one Parentheſis, or a few Verſes in the 20*th* Chapter. And that the Reſurrection and Thouſand Years reign of the Martyrs, is that 1000 Years from *Conſtantine's* beginning, in which the Biſhops had Wealth and Honour, and ſate on Thrones, and judged the People in Courts, as our Lay-Chancellors now do; and that this Glory, Wealth, and Grandure of Prelates, is the Churches Reſurrection, Glory and Felicity: And that theſe happy thouſand Years continued 700 Years after the riſing of *Mahomet*; and included thoſe 8*th,* 9*th,* 10*th,* and 11*th* Ages, which *Eraſmus* and all learned men (even *Bellarmine* himſelf) ſo dolefully bewail. And that when Boys, and Whores, and Sorcerers, and Murderers, and Hereticks, and Schiſmaticks ruled the Church, they were *happy that had a part in this firſt Reſurrection* to all this Glory, yea, that theſe are *Holy* too, *Rev.* 20. 6. And that the ſecond death ſhall have no power on them; that is while they are drowning the true Churches of Chriſt in the Floods of all abomination, and bringing in all corruption, and laying the grounds of all diviſion, ſubduing Kings, and murdering Chriſtians by thouſands, till the Year 1300. Bleſſed and holy and happy are they, becauſe though they perſecute the Godly, they are free from being perſecuted

cuted themselves, which is the second death : Yea, that the Church was freed from persecution in the Ages when the poor *Waldenses*, and *Albigenses* were murdered in greater numbers than ever the Heathens murdered the Christians heretofore. When I can believe abundance of such things as these, I will believe Dr. *Hammond*'s first Dissertation.

His second Dissertation which is to vindicate the Epistles of *Ignatius*, I little regard, as not concerning me. I leave it to Dr. *Pierson* (who they say is about it) to answer *Dallaeus* his numerous Arguments against him (with *Dronysius*.) For my part, I wish Dr. *Pierson* may prevail ; For there is no Witness among all the Ancients whom I more trust to (at least *ad hominem*) as a plain undoubted destroyer of our Prelacy, than *Ignatius*, who is the confidence of the Prelatical Champions. I am possest with admiration as much at their glorying in *Ignatius*, as the Patron of Diocesans, who is so much against them, as I am at their glorying in *Rich. Hooker* as a Defender of Monarchy and the Prelates Loyalty : Of *Ignatius* I shall say more anon.

His third Dissert. about Scripture passages more concerneth us.

Cap. 1. which tells us of Chrifts Episcopacy, concerneth not our Cause.

Cap. 2. Whether the παλιγγενεσία, the Regeneration, be the New Church State, and the Apostles Episcopal Thrones be there meant, as setled in several Provinces (which cannot be proved ever to have been) is little to our business. Nor yet whether he will prove that it is not Prelacy but Secular Coactive power and grandure that is denyed to the Apostles, and that it was those that grudged at the Precedency desired for *James* and *John*, which Chrift intended to reprehend, because it was not an injurious Secular power, but a labour that was to be in the Prelates of the Church. It sufficeth me that so much is here confessed. And it cannot be denied : For that Precedency and Power which Chrift alloweth in the Rulers of the Nations, is it which he denyeth to his Disciples : But it is not Tyranny, proud Domination and Oppression, but just Secular Government, which he alloweth in the Rulers of the Nations : *Ergo*, it is this and not the former which he denyeth to his Disciples.

And let all the Prelates here remember, that the Question, Whether they be Above their Brethren by Dr. *H*'s Confession, is, Whether they may take more care and pains for Mens Salvation ? When one of us poor Ministers were not able night and day to Catechise, instruct and oversee a Congregation of two or three thousand Souls, without much help or many sad unavoidable Omissions, the Question shall be, whether the Bishop may not undertake to Teach and oversee many hundreds or a thousand Parishes, and Catechise, Pray with, and Exhort a thousand times more than any Parish Minister doth or is able to do ; And to do all this without ever coming into those Parishes , or ever seeing the Faces, or hearing the names of one of a multitude of the People ; or ever speaking one word to them, but summoning them by Apparitors to a Lay-Chancel

lors

lors Court, to be Excommunicated firſt, and after impriſoned while they live, if they do not what the Chancellor bids them. O what is mans underſtanding! when a Carnal intereſt hath there clothed it ſelf with a Sacred name.

Cap. 3. He telleth us of the Power of the Keys commited to the Apoſtles, and by them to the Biſhops, as their Succeſſors: But whether all the Biſhops Ordained by them, and living with them, (and ſome dying before them it's like) were their *Succeſſors*, and whether all true Paſtors were not ſuch Biſhops as had the Power of the Keys; and whether by thoſe Keys be meant the Government of the Flocks, or alſo of the Governors themſelves, and of what extent the Churches under each Biſhop was, and to what end and uſe, are the things in Queſtion, which he here ſaith nothing to.

Cap. 4. He proveth by ſtrong affirmation, that the Apoſtles were by Chriſt's laſt Commiſſion, *Mat.* 28. 19, 20. to be the Biſhops of their ſeveral aſſigned certain Provinces. But confidence goeth not for proof with us. He tells us of the name of Epiſcopacy, *Acts* 1. 29. We never queſtioned, whether the Apoſtles had the Overſight of the Church; but we hold, 1. That the World was the firſt Object of their Office, from whence they were to gather Churches. 2. That the Place, Courſe, or Circuit of their Travels and Miniſtry, was not of any Divine Inſtitution, but left to their prudent choice, by the Common Rules of Nature (doing all things in Order, and to Edifying) and ſometime directed in their motions by the preſent inſpiration of the Holy-Ghoſt. 3. That more than one Apoſtle was oft in the ſame Cities and Countries, none claiming it as his peculiar Province, nor denying the right of others to be there. And where one was this Year, another was the next. 4. That when an Apoſtle planted a Church in any City, and ſettled Biſhops over the People, they themſelves were called by many of the Ancients, the firſt Biſhops of thoſe Cities; in which ſence, one Man had many Biſhopricks. 5. That the Apoſtles were Itinerant unfixed Biſhops, and not fixed Biſhops, ſuch as they themſelves confined to any one limited Church or Province. Nor can it be proved out of all Antiquity, that any one of all the Apoſtles, was confined to any one limited Province, much leſs what that Province was; but only that their Ability, Opportunity, Time and Prudence limited every Man, and directed him as the End required. 6. And that if the Apoſtles had fixed themſelves in particular limited Provinces, they had diſobeyed their Commiſſion, which was, to go Preach the Goſpel to all the World. And no Man did ever yet ſo dote, as to pretend that they divided the whole World into twelve Provinces, and there fixed themſelves: And ſuch twelve Provinces as they had been capable of overſeeing, would have been but a little of the World: And it was but a little part, comparatively, that they Preacht the Goſpel to: Moſt Kingdoms of the World they never ſaw: And thoſe which they came into, were ſo great and many, that they Preached but to a few of the People. Yet this was not their culpable Omiſſion, becauſe caufe they were limited by Natural Impotency, and fo by Impoffibilities of doing more : But had it been by a Voluntary fetling themfelves in twelve Provinces to the neglect of all the reft, the Cafe had been otherwife. But whilft they did their beft for the whole World themfelves, and Ordained others to do the reft, they performed their Office.

There needeth no more to be faid as to thofe Ancients that name the Apoftles *Bifhops* : Nor is their Epifcopacy, if proved, any thing to our Cafe, as fhall be manifefted.

Cap. 5. He thought he had proved that *Power in the Church is given by the Apoftles to the Bifhops only.* Whereas (with *Spalatenfis*, and moft Chriftians) we hold it given to Chrift's Minifters, as fuch, and therefore to them all, though in an Eminency the Apoftles only had it. And, 1. Whereas he denyeth the Power of the 70, becaufe they were not Apoftles, but Difciples: We Anfwer, 1. That Evangelifts and other Minifters that were not Apoftles, had the Power of the Keys. 2. That to deny that the 70 were at leaft Temporary Apoftles limited to the *Jews*, and had the power of Preaching and working Miracles, would be to deny the letter of the Text. And the Apoftles themfelves could not Govern Churches, till they were gathered.

2. And yet if neither they, nor *John* Baptift, in Baptizing, did exercife any power of the Keys (which he can never prove) it is nothing to our Cafe.

3. When will he prove that the Evangelifts and the Itinerant Affiftants of the Apoftles, had not the power of the Keys ? When themfelves commonly fay, that the higher Orders contain the powers of the lower ? And are the Bifhops higher than the Evangelifts ?

4. Nay, when will he prove, that ever any Prefbyter was Ordained by the Apoftles, or by any others as they appointed, without the power of the Keys? It would weary one that loveth not confufion and loft labour, to read long Difcourfes of the Power of the Keys or Government, which diftinguifh not the Government of the Laity or Flocks, from the Government of the Minifters themfelves? and that abufe the Church by feigning an Office of Prefbyters that are not Prefbyters, and proving that Church-Governors are not Church-Governors? For what is the Office of the Prefbyter or Paftor effentially, but a Stated Power and obligation to Teach and Govern the People, and Worfhip as their mouth and guide ?

Cap. 6. He feemeth, by denying the *Evangelifts* the power of the Keys, and of Church-teaching, and making them meer Preachers to the Infidels, to favour the Independants Opinion, who think the Laymen fent forth are to do that work. But, 1. *Mat.* 28, 19, 20. Chrift maketh fuch Officers as muft Preach and Baprize and gather Churches among the Infidels before they govern them, to be them that he will be with to the end of the World. And the fame men had the Power of teaching the Churches when they were gathered, as is there expreffed. 2. Call them by what name you will, fuch *Itenirants* were ufual in the Apoftles daies, as *Silas*, *Apollo*, and ma-

ny.

ny more. 3. It was not the twelve Apoſtles only that Converted the World, but ſuch other Miniſters, that were called thus to labour by them, or by the Spirit immediately. *Joſeph* of *Arimathea* is ſaid by many to have preached here, and in other Countries. 4. What man will dream that when theſe went abroad the World to convert men, they were the fixed Biſhops of particular Churches firſt, which they thus forſook? 5. Who will believe that *Joſeph, Silas, Apollo, Luke, Mark, Nathaniel, Philip,* or any other, when they had converted any City, or Countrey, had no power after to teach them as a Church, or give them the Lords Supper, no nor to Baptize them firſt, nor to ordain them Biſhops, and ſettle them in order, but muſt either have an Apoſtle or a City Biſhop to come thither after them to do it? Such Fancies are obtruded on the Church, becauſe the one Miniſterial or Prieſtly Office is firſt diſmembred, and then new Officers feigned to be made up of the ſeveral Limbs.

Cap. 7. As he rob'd the *Evangeliſts* of the Power of the Keys, he would now rob all the meer Presbyters of it; and all (without ſhew of Scripture proof) from ſuch words of Canons or Ancients as ſay the Presbyters ſhall do nothing without the Biſhops. 1. As if the Presbyters were no Rulers of the Flocks, becauſe the Biſhops are Rulers of the Presbyters? As if a Judge or a Juſtice were no Governour, becauſe he is under the King? 2. O Cruel Biſhops that will undertake to do that for the Souls of many hundred Pariſhes, which many hundred Miniſters are too little for, that the Souls of men and their own together may be damn'd by the Omiſſion of it! If the power of the Keys be appointed for mens Salvation, they perfidiouſly betray them that thruſt out the many hundreds that ſhould do it, pretending that it belongeth to one man among the many hundred that cannot do it. But of the Biſhops great undertaking, I muſt ſay more anon.

Cap. 8. Of the *Chorepiſcopi* there is little that concerneth us, ſaving that he cometh near to grant us all that we deſire, while that §. 15 he ſaith that *Learned men believe that in the Church of one Region, of old there was but one Altar, ſo that* Ignatius *rightly conjoyneth* ἐν θυσιαστήριον *and* ἕνα ἐπίσκοπον: *And all Schiſmaticks were ſaid to ſet up Altar againſt Altar.* As Cypr. de Unit. Eccle. Ep. 40. 72, 73] This is the ſum of all that we plead for. And §. 29. he mentioneth the *Chorepiſcopis* as immitating the 70, when yet he had denied the 70, to have the power of the Keys, which he ſuppoſeth the *Chorepiſcopi* to have under the Biſhops. Of *Clemens* words in due place.

Cap. 9. About the ſence of a Canon variouſly read.

And *Cap.* 10. Whether *Eutychius Alexandrinus* erred in one thing; and therefore were not to be believed in another, are little pertinent to our buſineſs.

In his 4th. Diſſert. the *Cap.* 1. is but *Proem,* but *Cap.* 2. he tells us that the Apoſtles as Biſhops Governed the Churches which they had planted, *without* the *mediation* of a *Colledge* of *Presbyters* (all ways) and he bringeth not a word to prove it, but 1 Cor. 3. 6. *You have not many Fathers in Chriſt,*

Chrift, I have begotten you by the Gofpel, c. 4. 1 5, 16. *I have planted* ,and c. 9. 19, 21. *I will come to you, will ye that I come with the Rod ?* and c. 5. 3, 4. *I as abfent in Body but prefent in Spirit have judged*———This is all. And will not the impartial Reader wonder at humane frailty, how eafily men believe what they would have to be true, and what, an evident *Nothing* will go for undenyable proof. Let the Reader Note, 1. That the queftion is not whether an Apoftle after that he had planted a Church remain ftill an Apoftle to them as well as others, and have the Apoftolical eminency of Power, which is greater than any meer Bifhop had. 2. But firft, Whether the Apoftles had any fixed Provinces, or Cities undertaken as their fpecial charge, in which no other Apoftle had Apoftolical Power? And 2. Whether there were not fixed Bifhops fetled by them in all the Churches which they planted? 3. And whether it was not fo in the Church of *Corinth* in particular? Yea, whether they had not more Bifhops or Presbyters than one? For by [*Unius*] which here he applyeth to *Paul*, he meaneth *Unicus, Paul only*, or elfe he abufeth his Reader and himfelf. And 1. He that will follow *Paul* in his Travels, will find that he went the fame way that fome other Apoftles went, *viz. John* and *Peter*, and therefore that they muft have the fame Diocefes, or have their Diocefes notably intermixt: *John* was in *Afia* as well as *Paul*, and no man can prove that he was the Second Bifhop of *Ephefus*, or *Afia*, as *Paul's* fucceffor only when he was dead. Nor will the *Romans* be willing to grant that *Peter* was Bifhop of no more at *Rome* but the Jews only (as this Dr. elfewhere intimateth) left that prove not that the Gentile Church of *Rome* was founded by *Peter*, but by *Paul* alone. 2. What proof hath he that befides *Peter* and *John*, there were not many other Apoftles *per vices* in the fame Cities where *Paul* had been? And that when they did come thither, they had not Apoftolical Power there? 3. Doth not the Text exprefly fay that *Paul* and *Barnabas* long travelled together? And doth it any where intimate that *Paul* was the Governour of *Barnabas*, or the fole Bifhop of the Churches planted by them both together? Sure the people that would have worfhipped *Barnabas*, as *Jupiter*, and *Paul* but as *Mercury*, did fee no Sign of fuch a Prelacy in *Paul*. And the Apoftles feem fo to have ordered the matter, by going by Couples (as Chrift fometimes fent two and two before him,) as if they had done it purpofely to prevent thefe Monarchical conceits. *Peter* and *John* were together at the healing of the Criple, and the fuccefsful preaching that followed thereupon. Sometime *Paul* and *Barnabas* are together; fometime *Paul* and *Silas*, and *Barnabas* and *Mark*: *Paul* and *Softhenes* are the infcribed Names who fend the firft Epiftle to the *Corinthians*, and *Paul* and *Timothy* the fecond. And in the Text alledged, it is faid, *One faith I am of* Paul, *and another I am of* Apollo; and c. 1. 12. *Every one of you faith, I am of* Paul, *and I of* Apollos, *and I of* Cephas.—And *Paul* baptized none of them fave *Crifpus* and *Gaius*, and the houfhold of *Stephanus*. By which it appeareth that *Peter* was among them as well as *Paul*; and if *Peter* had been only the Bifhop of

N   the

the *Jews* here also, *Apollos* would not have been brought in as a third in a way of equality : And the Controversie would have been otherwise decided by *Paul*, by telling the *Jews* that *Peter* was their sole Bishop, and the *Gentiles* that *Paul* was theirs, and all of them, that *Apollos* was but their Subject. But he goeth quite another way to work, preferring none, nor dividing Dioceses, but levelling Ministers, as being but the helpers of their Faith. And though they had Apostolical preeminence above *Apollos*, yet *Peter* and *Paul* are not said to have a proper Episcopacy over him.

And now to his Arguments. 1. *Paul planted*; *Paul onely was their Father*. What then ? *Ergo*, *Paul* onely was their Bishop. I deny the Consequence, and may long wait for a syllable of proof. Contrarily, *Paul* onely was not their Apostle : *Ergo*, *Paul* onely was not their Bishop. For every Apostle you say hath Episcopal Power included in the Apostolical : and none of them ceased to have Apostolical Power where-ever they came, (though they were many together, as at *Jerusalem*) *Ergo*, None of them ceased to have Episcopal Power. The conceit of Conversion and Paternity entituling to sole Episcopacy, I shall confute by it self anon.

2. But *Paul judged the incestuous person*, and *speaketh of coming with the rod*. And what followeth ? *Ergo*, None but *Paul* might do the same in that Diocess. I deny the Consequence. Any other Apostle might do the same. Where is your Proof ? And if all this were granted, it is nothing against the Cause that we maintain.

And next let us inquire, whether this Church had no Bishops or Presbyters but *Paul*? As here is not a word of proof on their side, so I prove the contrary :

1. Because the Apostles ordained Elders or Bishops in every Church and City, *Acts* 14. 23. *Tit.* 1. 5. Therefore the Church of *Corinth* had such.

2. If they had not Presbyters or Bishops, they could hold no ordinary Christian Church-Assemblies, for all Gods publick Worship; *e. g.* They could not communicate in the Lords Supper; for Lay-men may not be the Ministers of it, nor the ordinary Guides and Teachers of a Worshipping Church. But they did hold such ordinary Assemblies, communicating in the Lords Supper. And to say, that they had onely Pastors that were itinerant *in transitu* as they came one after another that way, is to speak without book, and against it; and to make them differ from all other Churches, without proof.

3. 1 *Cor.* 14. doth plainly end that Controversie, with 1 *Cor.* 11. when they had so many Prophets, and Teachers, and gifted Persons in their Assemblies, that *Paul* is put to restrain and regulate their Publick Exercises, directing them to speak but one or two, and the rest to judge : and this rather by the way of edifying plainness, than by Tongues, &c. And *c.* 11. they had enow to be the ordinary Ministers of the Sacraments. And *ch.* 5. they had Instructions for Church-Discipline, both as to the incestuous man, and for all the scandalous for the time to come, and are chidden for not
using

using it before. And who but the Separatists do hold, that the power of the Keys for the exercise of this Discipline is in the Peoples hands ? Therefore most certainly they had a Clergy. And if all this go not for proof against a bare Affirmation of the contrary, we can prove nothing.

4. And 1 *Cor.* 4. 15. I scarce think that *Paul* would have had occasion to say [*Though you have ten thousand instructers*] if they had not had qualified Persons enow to afford them one or two for Presbyters.

Cap. 2. proving no more of any one Apostles fixed Episcopacy, he cometh to their secondary Bishops or Apostles : And whereas we judge, that Apostles, and Evangelists, and the Apostles Assistants were unfixed Ministers, appropriating no Churches or Dioceses to themselves in point of Power, but planting, setling, and confirming Churches in an itinerant way, and distributing their Provinces onely arbitrarily and changeably, and as the Spirit guided them at the present time of their work ; and that Bishops and Elders were such Pastors as these Church-gatherers fixed in a stated relation to particular Churches ; so that an Apostle was a Bishop *eminenter*, but not *formaliter* ; and that a Bishop, as such, was no Apostle in the eminent sense, but was also an *itinerant Preacher* limitedly, because while he oversaw his Flock he was also to endeavour the conversion of others, as far as his opportunity allowed him : I say, this being our judgment, this learned Doctor supposeth Apostles, as such, to be Bishops, and the fixed Bishops, as such, to be second Apostles. And I so avoid contending about *Names*, even where it is of some importance to the Matter, that I will not waste my time upon it till it be necessary. In § 1. he telleth us, that these *second Apostles were made partakers of the same Jurisdiction and Name with the first, and either planted and ruled Churches, or ruled such as others had planted.* *Answ.* 1. We doubt not but the Apostles had indefinite itinerant Assistants, and definite fixed Bishops placed by them as aforesaid : But the indefinite and the definite must not be confounded. 2. And were not *Luke, Mark, Timothy*, and other itinerant Evangelists, as such, of the Clergy, and such Assistants or secondary Apostles ? Exclude them, and you can prove none but the fixed Bishops : But if they were, why did you before deny Evangelists, *Dissert.* 3. *cap.* 6. the power of the Keys, and make them meer converting Preachers, below Doctors and Pastors, and the same with Deacons ? whereas *Paul, Ephes.* 4. 11. doth place them before Pastors and Teachers. But avoiding the Controversie *de nomine*, call them what you will, we believe that these itinerant Assistants of the Apostles were of that One sacred Office commonly called the Priesthood or Ministry, though not yet fixed ; and that the assigning them to particular Churches did not make them of a new Order, but onely give them a new object and opportunity to exercise the Power which they had before ; and that *Philip* and other Deacons were not Evangelists meerly as Deacons (which term denoteth a fixed Office in one Church), but by a further Call : And that you never did prove, that ever the Scripture knew one Presbyter that had not the power of the Keys, as Bishops have ; yea, you confess your self the contrary. All therefore

N 2   that

that followeth in that Chapter, and your Book, of *James the Just*, and *Mark*, and others having Episcopal power, is nothing against us: The thing that we put you to prove is, that ever the Apostles ordained such an Officer as a Presbyter that hath not Episcopal Power and Obligation too, as to his Flock; that is, the Power of governing that Church according to God's Word.

And I would learn, if I could, whether all the Apostles which staid long at *Jerusalem*, while *James* is supposed to be their Bishop, were not Bishops also with him? Whether they ceased to be Apostles to the People there? Or whether they were Apostles, and not Bishops? And whether they lost any of their Power by making *James* Bishop? And whether one Church then had not many Bishops at once? And if they made *James* greater than themselves, Whether according to your Premonition they did not give a Power or Honour which they had not (which you think unanswerable in our Case)?

Cap. 4. come in the *Angels of the Churches, Rev.* 1, 2, & 3. of which (though the matter be little to our Cause) I have said enough before, why I prefer the Exposition of *Ticonius*, which *Augustine* seemeth to favour. And I find nothing here to the contrary that needeth a Reply.

Cap. 5. he would prove the Angels to be Archbishops; which if done, would not touch our Cause, who meddle not with Archbishops, but onely prove, that the full Pastoral or Episcopal Office or power of the Keys as over the Flock, should be found in every particular Church that hath *unum Altare*.

To prove Metropolitans (again) he tells us, how that in *Provinces* we find [*Churches*] mentioned in the Plural number, and in *Cities* onely [*a Church*] singularly: not perceiving how hereby he overthrows his Cause, when he can never prove that in Scripture *many particular Churches* are called [*A Church.*] Diocesane or Metropolitan, as united in one Bishop, as our Diocesane and Metropolitan Churches now are. Nay, indeed, though the Society be specified by the Government, yet the Name sticketh in their teeth here in *England*, and they seldom use the Title of *the Church of Canterbury and York*] for the whole Province; and they use to say the *Diocese* of. *Lincoln, London, Winchester, Worcester, Coventry and Litchfield, &c.* rather than [*the Church of Lincoln, London, Coventry and Litchfield, &c.*] lest the Hearers would so hardly be seduced from the proper sense of the word [*Church*] as not to understand them.

His Proofs of the Civil or Jewish distinction of Metropolitans, §. 4, 5, &c. let them mind that think it pertinent: But § 9. we have a great word, that [*It may be proved by many examples, that after this Image the Apostles took care every where to dispose of the Churches, and constituted a subordination and dependence of the lesser on the more eminent Cities, in all their Plantations.*] *Answ.* This is to some purpose, if it be made good. The first Instance is *Acts* 14. 26. 16. 4. and 15. 2, 3, 22, 23, 30. Not a word else out of Scripture. And what's here? Why, "*Paul* and *Barnabas* are sent to *Je-*
"*rusalem*

" *rusalem* from *Antioch*, to the Apostles and Elders, about the Question,
" and were brought on their way by the Church, and passed thorow *Phe-*
" *nice* and *Samaria*: Chosen men are sent to *Antioch* with *Paul* and *Barna-*
" *bas*, *Judas* and *Silas*, with Letters from the Apostles, Elders, and Bre-
" thren, even to the Brethren of the *Gentiles*, in *Antioch*, *Syria*, and *Cili-*
" *cia*: And when they came to *Antioch* they delivered the Letters; and
" *Paul* and *Timothy* as they went thorow the Cities delivered them the *De-*
" *crees* to keep, that were ordained by the Apostles and Elders that were at
" *Jerusalem*.] Doth not the Reader wonder where is the Proof? And wonder he may for me, unless this be it: The Apostles and Elders were at *Je-*
rusalem when they wrote this Letter, and thence sent it to *Antioch*, *Syria*,
and *Cilicia*.: *Ergo*, They established the Bishop of *Jerusalem* to be the Governour and Metropolitan of *Antioch*, *Syria*, and *Cilicia*. The Apostle *Paul*
went from *Antioch* to other Cities, and delivered them these Decrees:
Ergo, *Antioch* is the governing Metropolis of those Cities. I think the
major Propositions are, [Every City from which Apostles send their Letters to other Cities, and every City from which an Apostle carrieth such
Letters or Decrees to other Cities, is by those Apostles made the Governing Metropolis of those other Cities.] What dull Heads are the Puritans,
to question such a Proposition as this? But it is not given to all Men to be
wise: And we ignorant Persons are left in doubt, *Q.* 1. Whether the
Universal Headship or Papacy of the Bishop of *Jerusalem* be not of Apostolical Institution? and that more than by one Apostle, even by all of
them that were then at *Jerusalem*? *Q.* 2. Whether the Apostles did not
this as they did other parts of Church-settlement, by the Spirit of God?
and so, whether it be not *jure Divino*? yea, by a more eminent Authority
than the Scriptures, which were written by parts, by several single Men,
some Apostles, and some Evangelists? when this is said to be done by all
together. *Q.* 3. Whether Christ's Life, Death, Resurrection, Ascension,
and sending the Apostles thence into all the World, (and not into the *Ro-*
man Empire onely) do not incomparably more evidently make *Jerusalem*
the Universal Metropolis of the Earth, and so set it above *Rome*, which is
but the Metropolis of one Empire? *Q.* 4. Whether then an Universal
Head of the Church or Vicar of Christ be not *jure Divino*? and so, a
Jerusalem Papacy be not essential to the true Church and Religion?
Q. 5. Whether then all the Emperours, Bishops, and Churches, that did
set up *Rome*, *Alexandria*, *Antioch*, and *Constantinople* above *Jerusalem*,
were not Traytors against the Universal Sovereign of the Church, and guilty of Usurpation and gross Schism? *Q.* 6. To what purpose this Sove-
reignty was given to *Jerusalem*, which was never possess'd and exercised?
Q. 7. Whether *Peter*'s being at *Rome* could alter this Church-Constitution?
and one Apostle could undo what all together had done? *Q.* 8. Whether
the Apostles carried this Metropolitical Prerogative with them from place
to place, where-ever they came? And whether it did belong to the *Men* or
the *Place*? And whether to the Place whence they first set out, or to every
Place

place where they came? or to the place where they dyed? Judge what is the proof of any of these. *Q.* 9. When they were scattered, which of their Seats was the Metropolitan to the rest? or were they all equal? *Q.* 10. If the Power followed the Civil Power of the Metropolitane Rulers, whether *Cæsar* did not more in constituting the Church-Order, and giving power comparatively to the Metropolitanes, than Christ and his Apostles? *Q.* 11. Whether it was not in *Cæsar's* power to unmake all the Church Metropolitans and Bishops at his pleasure, by dissolving the Priviledges and Charters of Cities? *Q.* 12. If it please any King, or be the Custom of any Kingdom (as it is in many parts of *America*) that the Kingdom have no Cities or Metropolis, whether it must have any Churches, Bishops, or Metropolitane? *Q.* 13. Whether when *Paul* wrote his Letters from *Corinth* to *Rome* he thereby made the Bishop of *Corinth* the Governour of the Bishop and Diocess of *Rome*? And whether little *Cenchrea* was over them also, because *Phœbe* carried the Letter? And did his writing from *Philippi* to *Corinth* subject *Corinth* to the Bishop of *Philippi*? And did his writing from *Rome* to *Galatia, Ephesus, Philippi*, the *Colossians*; and from *Athens* to the *Thessalonians*, and from *Laodicea* and *Rome* to *Timothy*, and from *Nicopolis* to *Titus*, and *John's* writing from *Patmos* to the *Asian* Metropolitanes produce the same effect? *Q.* 14. If *Paul's* carrying the Letters from *Antioch* to other Cities, proved *Antioch* the Governour of the rest? whether when he returned from the other to *Antioch* again, he made not the other the Governours of *Antioch*? I am ashamed to prosecute this Fiction any further. His following Citations from the Fathers I think unworthy of an Answer, till it be proved, 1. That these Fathers took the Metropolitane Order, as such, to be of Apostolical Institution, and not in complyance with the *Roman* Government, by meer humane, alterable policy. And, 2. That this Opinion rose as early as he pretendeth. 3. And that these *Ancients* were not deceived, but our *English* Bishops rather (*Bilson, Jewel, &c.*) who took Patriarchs and Metropolitanes, as such, for Creatures of Humane Original.

While *Ignatius* his being Bishop of [*a Church in Syria*] shall prove him the Bishop of all *Syria*; and [*the Church of God dwelling in* Syria *in* Antiochia] shall be equivalent with [*the Church in* Antiochia *governing all* Syria] I shall not undertake to hinder such men from proving any thing that they would have believed.

His *Cap.* 6. of the promiscuous use of the Names of Bishop and Presbyter, and *Cap.* 7. that prepareth the stating of the Controversie, need no answer, but to say, that we deny not but where a single Presbyter was, he had himself the power of Governing that Church; but where there were many, though all had the full Office severally, they were bound to use it in Concord. And whether one amongst them shall have a precedency or guidance of the rest, we think (as *Dr. Stillingfleet* hath proved) to be a matter alterable by humane prudence, according to the various condition of the Churches: And if any take both such Bishops and Arch-

bishops

bishops to be *Jure Divino*, with Dr. *Hammond*, it will be somewhat to his Cause, but nothing to ours.

Cap. 8. he openeth his conceit (which in time I shall shew doth yield us the whole Cause) that every place of Scripture which mentioneth *Bishops* or *Presbyters*, meaneth *Diocesan superéminent Bishops only*. And first he proveth it of the Elders Bishops of *Ephesus*, *Acts* 20. because the *whole flock* is meant of all *Asia*: Fully proved, because *Irenæus* said (as he thought) that the Bishops were convocate from *Ephesus* and the nearest Cities. But, 1. *Irenæus* saith not [*Bishops*] only, but *Bishops* and *Presbyters*, conjoining them as two sorts, and not [*Bishops or Presbyters*] as the Doctor doth. 2. The *nearest Cities*, and *all Asia*, we take not for words of the same importance. 3. We take not your bare word for the validity of the Consequence, that because the Bishops of several Cities were there, therefore it is all *Asia* that is singularly called πᾶν τὸ ποιμνιον, the whole Flock, and not each Bishops Flock respectively; *q. d.* Each of you *look to your several Flock.* 4. We think if you calculate the time, *Acts* 20 and 21. and consider *Paul's* haste *Acts* 20. 16. that few impartial men will believe that *Paul's* Messengers (that were wont to go on foot) did so quickly go all over *Asia*, and so quickly get together all the Bishops of *Asia* to *Miletum*; unless they all resided at *Ephesus*, as our *English* Bishops do at *London*, and Governed their unknown people by a Lay-Chancellour. 5. And *Irenæus*, *ibid.* p. 312. saith [*Et omnia hujusmodi per solum Lucam cognovimus*, we know all such things by Luke *alone*, pretending no other Tradition. And if it be in *Luke* it is yet to be thence proved. 6. But he pleadeth our Cause too strongly, by supposing that each City then had a Bishop without any subject half Presbyter, and so that no such Office was yet made.

Cap. 9. Of *Timothy's* Episcopacy concerneth not our Cause. Though I hope that neither he nor his Church were so bad as the Angel or Church in *Rev.* 2. is described: And it's easier to answer the strength of Dr. *Hammond*, than for him to answer the Evidence brought by *Prin* in his *Unbishoping Timothy and Titus*, to shew the itinerant life and Ministry of *Timothy*, contrary to the life of a fixed Bishop. And if non-residency have such Patrons, and *Timothy* have taught men to leave their Churches year after year, and play the Pastor many hundred Miles distant, it will make us dream that non-residence is a duty. And if all these years *Timothy's* Metropolitan Church at *Ephesus* had no *ordained Presbyter* (but Passengers that fell in) I blame them not, or wonder not at least, that they lost their first love; for it's like they seldom had any Church Assemblies to Communicate and Worship God together.

Cap. 10. Cometh to the case of *Philippi*, *Phil.* 1. 1, 2. And, 1. §. 3. he saith, *It is manifest that* Epaphroditus *Bishop of* Philippi *was at* Rome *with* Paul *when he wrote this Epistle* (and he supposeth that there were yet no Presbyters, but Bishops.) And so when *Paul* wrote *to all the Saints which are at* Philippi, *with the Bishops and Deacons,*] he meant [*to those that are not at*

Philippi,

Philippi *where there was no Bishop*, but in other Cities of *Macedonia* that had every one a Prelate without ever a Presbyter under him.] With some this expounding may go for modest, if not true.

Two probable Arguments I object against his improbable Expositions of this Text and that *Acts* 20. before mentioned: 1. Where did he ever read that all the Province of *Macedonia* was called *Philippi* ; and the Saints said to dwell at *Philippi* that dwelt all over *Macedonia* ? 2. Where did he ever read in Scripture many Episcopal Churches under one Metropolitan, called *One Church* in the singular Number, as in *Acts* 20. 28. or One Flock either ? 3. Will any knowing man deny that he contradicteth not only *Hierom* and *Theodoret*, but the common Exposition of the Fathers, by this his odd Opinion ? And is it not gross partiality for the same man that can so easily cast off the judgment of almost all the Ancients at once, to lay so much of the whole stress of his Diocesan and Metropolitan Cause upon the Fathers assertions, yea doubtful reports ; and to take it for so immodest a thing in others, to deny belief to them in such uncertain matters ?

But he setteth *Epiphanius* his words against *Ærius* against them all : Even that *Epiphanius* who ordained in the Bishop of *Jerusalem*'s Diocess to his displeasure, and that combined with that *Theophilus Alexand.* (of whom *Socrates* writeth such horrid and unchristian practices) to root out *Chrysostom*, and raise a flame in the Church of *Constantinople* ; who liker a mad man than a sober Bishop, came from *Cyprus* not only into the City, but the Church where *Chrysostom* used to officiate, to inflame his people, and declame against, and censure their Bishop, to whom he was an inferiour ; and that parted with him in a wrathful Prognostick, and dyed by the way home : And yet even this one man saith nothing to his advantage, but that the Apostles placed Bishops only with Deacons in some Churches that had not fit men to make Presbyters of : which we not only grant, but doubt whether ever they made any but Bishops, (though in great Cities there were many of them.)

And §. 8, 9, 10. when it seemed to serve his turn, he yet further gratifieth us, by granting, yea maintaining that *one* Congregation had not two Bishops, yet [*nothing hindreth but that in the same City there might sometimes be two distinct Assemblies, converted by two Apostles, perhaps of distinct dialects and rites, and these governed by distinct Bishops, with a divided or distinct Clergie,*] which is almost as much as we desire. If any more be necessary he granteth it us, §. 11. where having feigned and not proved that the people of all the Province of *Macedonia* were said by *Paul* to be at *Philippi* ; he confesseth that then every City had a Bishop, and *none of those that we now call Presbyters.* And it is more this Bastard sort of Presbyters Office that we deny than the Bishops : And granting this he grants us all ; even that then there was no such half Officers, nor Bishops that had the rule of any Presbyters : which he further proveth, §. 19, 20, 21. And by the way, §. 16, 17. he giveth us two more Observations, 1. That the πρεσβυτερια

gave

gave precedency to some Churches. Where I would learn whether the Holy Ghost still observed the order in converting men, to begin at the highest Metropolis, and descend by order to the lowest, and so to the Villages? Or whether our Doctor do not here contradict what he said before, of the Apostles every where disposing of the Churches according to the Civil Metropolitical Order? I doubt his memory here failed him.

2. *Philippi* and *Thessalonica* being both in *Macedonia*, and these Epistles being each written to all the Province, we hence learn that the Epistle to the *Thessalonians*, and that to the *Philippians*, were written to the same men. Whether each Epistle, *Rev.* 2. & 3. to the seven Churches of *Asia* was written to all *Asia*, and so all the faults charged on all that are charged on any one, I leave to your arbitrary belief. For none of these are proved, whatever proof is boasted of.

Cap. 11. he further gratifieth us in expounding 1 *Tim.* 3. in the same manner, One Bishop with Deacons then serving for a whole Diocess, that is for one Assembly, not having such a thing as a half Presbyter subject to any Bishop.

Cap. 12. he is as liberal in expounding *Tit.* 1. By *Elders in every City*, is meant a single Bishop that had no half Presbyter under him, and whose Diocess had but one Assembly. We are not so unreasonable as to quarrel with this liberality.

Cap. 13. And about *Heb.* 13. we are as much gratified in the Exposition of the word [ἡγέμονοι] of which more afterwards. And *Cap.* 14. and 15. he saith the same of Ποιμὴν and Διδάσκαλος, Pastors and Teachers, that they both are meant of none but Bishops. And *that Presbyters now adays are permitted and tyed to teach the people, and instruct them from the Scriptures, this apparently arose hence, that Bishops in ordaining Presbyters gave them that power, but not to be exercised till licensed by the Bishops Letters.*] Of this detestable Opinion (worse than the *Italians* in the Council of *Trent*, that would have derived the Episcopal Power from the Pope) I have said somewhat before, and intend more in due place. The Bishops do only ministerially give them possession: Christ is the only Instituter of the Office by himself (and his Spirit in his Apostles.) Can the Bishops any more chuse to deliver this possession by Ordination, than to preach the Gospel? Could they have made Presbyters that had no power to teach the people? Is the Bishops liberality the original of the Office? How much then is Christ beholden to Bishops, that when a thousand Parishes are in some one of their Diocesses, they will give leave to any Presbyter to teach any of the people? and that when eighteen hundred of us were silenced in one day (*Aug.* 24. 1662.) that all the rest were not served so too?

Cap. 16. he exerciseth the same naked affirming Authority of the words [*Ministers of the word*] *Luke* 1. 2. and *Stewards*] all are but Bishops. And he asketh *whether ever man heard of more Stewards than one in one house? or of several bearers of one Key?* And he foresaw that we would tell him that Gods Catholick Church is one House of God, and that at least all the

O   Apostles

Apoſtles were Stewards and Key-Bearers in that one Church; and that by his Doctrine none but one of them ſhould be Steward of Gods Myſteries, or have the Keys : And therefore he ſaith, that [*Though the Apoſtles are called Stewards of the Myſteries of God,* 1 *Cor.* 4. 1. *that is to be reckoned as pertaining to the many divided Families, that is the many particular Churches, diſtinct parts of the Univerſal Church, which the Apoſtles divided among themſelves. Anſw.* Unleſs his *etiam* here be a ſelf-contradicting cheat, it will hence follow, 1. That the Apoſtles are not Stewards of Gods Myſteries in gathering Churches, but only to the Churches gathered. 2. That in Baptizing and giving the Holy Ghoſt, to ſuch as yet entered not into a Particular Church, they excerciſed not any of their ſaid Stewardſhip or Power. 3. That thay have no Power of the Keyes at all, over any that are not Members of a Particular Church, (ſuch as the *Eunuch, Act.* 8. And many Merchants, Embaſſadors, Travellers, and many thouſands that want Paſtors or opportunity, or hearts, yea and all Chriſtians in the firſt Inſtant as meerly Baptized Perſons ſeeing Baptiſme entereth them only into the Univerſal Church, and not into any particular (as ſuch) 4. And that till the Apoſtles gathered particular Churches, and diſtributed them, they had no Stewardſhip, nor uſe (at leaſt) of the Keyes. And what if it can never be proved that ever the Apoſtles diſtributed the univerſal Church into Apoſtolical Provinces, but only *pro re nata* diſtributed themſelves in the World, were they never Stewards then nor Key-bearers? Verily if I believed ſuch a diſtribution of the World into twelve or more Provinces by them, I ſhould queſtion the power that altered that Conſtitution, and ſet us up but four or five Patriarches. And were the ſame Apoſtles no Stewards or Key-bearers out of their (feigned) ſeveral Provinces? If we muſt be ſilenced unleſs we ſubſcribe to the Dictates of ſuch ſelf conceited Confident men, who ſhall ever *Preach* that is not born under the ſame Planet with them? *Cap.* 17. he proceedeth ſtill to maintain our Cauſe, that even in *Juſtin Martyrs* writings, and others of that Age, by the προεςωτις are meant the Biſhops of the ſeveral Churches who had not one Presbyter under them, but Deacons only, and therefore had but ſingle Congregations; but did themſelves alone with the Deacon perform all the publick Offices in the Church. And that no equal Presbyter was placed with them, offendeth us no more than that our Pariſh Miniſters now are preſented and inſtituted alone, yea and have power to take Curates under them as their helpers.

Cap. 18. He proveth truly that the Names *Sacerdos* and *Sacerdotium* are uſually by old Writers ſpoken of ſole Biſhops and Epiſcopacy. By which we are the more confirmed in our Opinion, that he that is not *Epiſcopus gregis* a Biſhop over the Flock, is not *Sacerdos,* true Paſtor, but hath only a limb of the Miniſterial Office, being a thing of preſumptuous Prelates inſtitution.

Cap. 19. He further ſtrengtheneth us by maintaining that the word *Presbyter,* in the places of the New Teſtament cited by him, doth mean only

a Bi-

a Bishop, that is a Pastor of one only Congregation, that had no Presbyter under him, but Deacons: and that *no mention is made* by the Apostles of *other Presbyters*, § 6. And he gratifieth us with *Epiphanius* his
Reasons, § 4. [*because as yet there was not a multitude of Believers:*] And
that the Elders that *Paul* speaketh to *Timothy* of ordaining and rebuking,
and those that were worthy of double honour, were only Bishops that had
no subject Presbyters. Whether they were set over the Churches as *Moses*
was over *Israel*, with a design that they should make subordinate Officers
under them, I shall enquire in due place.

Cap. 20. He goeth over most of the other Texts in the New Testament that mention Elders, shewing that they mean such Bishops; and that
even at *Hierusalem*, the Elders *Acts* 15. were not our new half Priests,
but the Bishops of all the Churches of *Judaa*; and so of others here
again repeated by him. But it sticketh with me, that these Bishops having no subject Presbyters, are found so oft in the Metropolitane City,
and so oft in travel, and so oft many hundred Miles from home, that I
doubt it was but a few Churches in the world that kept the Lords day,
and assembled for publick Worship, or had any Sacraments frequently,
but lived as the Atheists and impious contemners of Church-Communion
now do; or else that with the Fanaticks we must hold that Lay-men or
Deacons did play the Priests in all Church Offices.

Cap. 21. He vindicateth that one remaining Text, *Jam.* 5. 14. which
mentioneth Presbyters visiting the sick, as meant only of Bishops, and not
of mungrel Priests: And so being secured that these were never found in
the Scripture times, and consequently no Bishop (except Archbishops)
that had more worshipping Churches than one, we must look who presumed to institute another Office. And here, § 3. he perswadeth us to
be so civil to *Ignatius*, as thankfully to acknowledge him the first Patron
of our Office-dignity; intimating that there is no earlier proof of the invention of this mungrel Office, than the Epistles of *Ignatius*.

Cap. 22. He tells us that the word *Presbyter* is also taken for Bishops by
Polycarp, Papias, Irenaus, Tertullian, and *Clemens Alexand.* so that our cause
will be carried beyond Scripture times. But again finding so many Bishops with *Polycarp*, I doubt he maketh Bishops too unwearied Travellers,
and too great non-Residents, and Gods Publick Worship too often interrupted by their absence.

Cap. 23, 24, 25, 26. He speaketh of Deacons, the word and Office,
which we have now no business with, but to note that *cap.* 26. § 8. he is
again at *Epiphanius* allowing a single Bishop without Presbyters, but not
without Deacons, because he cannot be a Bishop without Deacons, (which
I believe not, nor do our Prelates) but without subject Presbyters he
may (better than with them.) And § 10. he excellently argueth from
the Epistle to *Timothy*, that seeing *Paul instructeth him in all things belonging
to the Church of God*, 1 Tim. 3. 15. and yet *never mentioneth these Medio-
xumos* Presbyteros, *mungrel or middle Priests, it is plain that the reason is*

O 2　　　　　　　　　　　　　　　*because*

because none fuch were inftituted when the *Apoftle wrote :* To which I add; nor afterward by the Apoftles, as far as can be proved, and therefore never fhould have been.

Cap. 27. He fpeaketh of the Πρεσβυτας and πρεσβύτιδας *Tit.*1. and 2.and 1 *Tim.*5. fhewing that thefe Women were *in Orders* : Of which I have no mind to contend, fo that by the Name it be not inferred that they are fhe-Bifhops ; and that they argue not as a Preacher did fince we were filenced (I can name the Man and place) from St. *John*'s Epiftle [*to the Elect Lady*] to prove that there were Lord-Bifhops in the Apoftles daies, *viz.* an Elect Lady fuppofeth an Elect Lord : But there are no Elect Lords, but Elect Lord-Bifhops: *Ergo——*

We have not yet feen all Dr.*Hammond*'s confutation of our Diocefan Prelacie. In his fifth Differtation we have more.*Cap.* 1. He fpeaketh of *Clemens Rom.* and whereas we think that the confufion among Hiftorians, came partly from the little notice that came down from thofe times of fuch particulars, and partly from the identity of the Office of *Linus, Cletus,* and *Clemens* ; being all Bifhops at once of a great Church (the Half-Presbyters being not yet ordained) he gratifyeth us by proving that not only at *Rome,* but alfo in *Antioch, Ephefus, Corinth,* and *Jerufalem,* there were more Churches than one, with their feveral Bifhops : Even one of the *Jews* and one of the *Gentiles* (how the local Diocefe were then divided is hard to tell, and where it was that one Apoftle had Power of the Keys, and where not) I fhall improve this Conceffion in due place.

Cap. 2. Of *Clements* Epiftle he firft takes notice of the Infcription [*to the Church of God, dwelling* (or fojourning) *at Corinth*] The fame Phrafe as *Philip.* 1.1,2. And by this *Church* he proveth (by confident affirming) that all the Churches of *Achaia* are meant. And that the fame is to be faid of *Paul*'s Epiftle to the *Corinthians,* he unrefiftibly proveth, by faying that *Quifquis eas vel leviter deguftaverit (tuo fcilicet guftu)hoc omnino pronunciandum effe nobifcum ftatuet. Nec igitur de hac Clementis ambigi poterit.*] And fo all that Controverfie is ended. But though (without Scripture proof) imagination might handfomely feign, that the many Churches of *Achaia* are called fingularly [*the Church of Corinth,*] as one, becaufe of the Unity of the *Metropolitane* ; yet, 1. I would have heard fomewhat llike reafon for, and fome inftances of the ufe of fuch a fpeech, as this [ἐκκλησία τῦ Θεῦ ἡ παροικῦσα Ρώμην, τῇ ἐκκλησία τῦ Θεῦ παρκῦσα κόρινθον] The Church of God dwelling (or fojourning) at *Rome,* to the Church of God dwelling (or fojourning) at *Corinth.* And why and where, and by what good writers, all *Achaia* is called *Corinth,* or all *Macedonia, Philippi* (or all the Cities about it) indeed as the County of *Worcefter,* the County of *York,* of *Warwick,* &c. are ufual Titles, fo may the *Church of York, Worcefter, Warwick,* be in the Diocefans fenfe. But whoever faid of all the County or Diocefs [*To the County, Diocefs, dwelling at York, Worcefter, Warwick?*] As if all the Countrey and Towns belonging to that Circuit were called *Warwick,* &c.

2. Doth

2. Doth not his own proof evidently confute him. 2 Cor. 1. 1. *To the Church of God which is at* Corinth, *with all the Saints which are in all* Achaia. Are the last words Tautological ? doth [*with*] signifie no addition at all. If by [*the Church which is at* Corinth] be meant all the Church s and Christians in *Achaia*, what sense is there in the addition of [*with all the Saints which are in* Achaia?]O what kind of proof will satisfie some Learned Men!

3. Was it all the Churches of *Achaia* that the incestuous person. 1 Cor. 5. dwelt with ? and that are chidden for suffering him in their Communion ? and that are directed when they meet together to cast him out, and not to eat with him ?

4. Would it not be Calumny according to all rational Laws, to accuse all the Churches of *Achaia*, of all those Crimes which the Church at *Corinth* is accused of, without a better proof than this ?

5. Was it all the Churches of *Achaia*, which 1 Cor. 14. are said to meet all in one place, and to have so many Prophets and Interpreters in that one. Assembly ? I am not at leisure to say more of this.

But who denieth that the same Epistle which was directed first to the *Corinthians*, was secondarily directed to the rest of *Achia*, and to be Communicated to them ? And yet not the Churches of *Achaia* be all said to be or dwell at *Corinth*.

When 2 Cor. 1. 10. *Paul* speaketh of [*the Regions of* Achaia(εν τοις κλ ιμασι) he saith that sheweth that the matter belonged [*to the whole Church of* Achaia.] But how long have they all been challenged to name one Text of *Scripture*, that speaketh singularly of the *Church of a Province* or *Countrey*, consisting of many particular Churches : Yet addeth he [*In re manifesta non pluribus opus est.*]

Cap. 3. He only mentioneth the occasion of *Clements* Epistle, where without any Proof he extendeth the Sedition then raised by them, to the disturbance of the Civil Government and Peace : And if he had proved as he endeavoureth that by τοις ηγεμένοις is meant the Civil Rulers (which is utterly uncertain) yet the commendation of their Obedience, formerly to the Civil Power, as part of the Character of their orderliness and peaceableness, doth not prove that Rebellion against them was part of their following disorder.

Cap. 4. Is to tell us, 1. That *Clemens* puts Obedience to Rulers, and due honouring of Presbyters as a Law of God (which is not to be doubted of.) 2. That Bishops were sent by the Apostles, as the Apostles by Christ, but were joyned only with Deacons to attend them. Mark here Reader, that he doth not only acknowledge that *de facto* the Order of Mungrel or Half-Priests was not yet Existent, but also that none such were sent by the Apostles, and so not Instituted, and that *Clemens* himself taketh notice of no such even in his times. But how the Dr. will prove that no great Churches (and particularly this of *Corinth*) had but one Bishop, you shall see with little satisfaction.) 3. He noteth that these Bishops thus *sent* were *constituted every where, Ecclesias nondum natas, sed ad partum (bonis Dei auspiciis) festinantes,*

tes, brachiis atq; ulnis suis susceptum & administratum; to receive in their Arms and Arms the Churches not yet born, but (by Gods Blessing) *hastning to the Birth*] whereas of his own Head he had before said that the *Bishops were sent* by the Apostles (when *Clement* saith no such thing) but only that they were *Constituted* (*sending* being the word used of Itinerant Preachers gathering and visiting Churches, and *Constituting* with Ordaining the usual word of Bishops and Presbyters, who as such are *fixed* to particular Churches;) so now he more boldly feigneth that Bishops were (yea every where) to receive Churches that were yet no Churches: Where he contradicteth both Scripture and common use of the word Bishop, and abuseth *Clement*. 1. Let any Man that can shew us that in the New Testament the word Bishop is ever used of any Pastor that was not related to a Church, and as signifying that Relation, and that *Bishop and Flock* are not as much Relatives as King and Kingdom. 2 Let him shew that can, that the word was used otherwise by Christians, for many a hundred years after Christ. Though I grant that Ministers in general were (and may be) ordained *sine titulo*, to Preach and gather Churches, and help others, yet never *Bishops*, the word signifying an Over-seer of the Flock or Church to which he is related. 3. If it were certain that the *futurity* of *believing* mentioned by *Clemens* had relation to the Constitution of Bishops, and not to the Apostles Preaching only, yet *Clemens* saith not that *there were yet no Believers* or *no Churches* where they were constituted Bishops: Where there were but a few Believers, the Apostles placed Bishops and Deacons over those few, who should receive others into the same Society (till it was full and no further) who should after believe. It is an abuse of *Clemens* to say, it was [*to Churches yet not born*] when he hath no such word! As if it could not be for *future Believers*, unless at present there were no Believers. And it is an abuse of him to feign him to assert that the Apostles did *every where* as soon as they had once Converted one Man, presently make that new Baptized Novice a Bishop before they Converted any more, saving perhaps one or two to be his Deacons: Or that they used to make Deacons (or Bishops either) to Churches future, that were yet no Churches: When as the Scripture telleth the contrary most expresly, that the Church at *Jerusalem*, was before the Deacons, *Act.* 7. That they ordained Elders in *every Church*, Act. 14. 23. and not in *no Church*, as he implyeth: And *Tit.* 1. 5. every City is equivalent to every Church, for it was not in every Infidel City that had no Christians: Which beyond all modest contradiction is proved by the Rules given to *Timothy* and *Titus* for the Ordination of Bishops and Deacons: Who were to be approved chosen persons, that had ruled their own Houses well, *not Novices, apt to teach, well reported of those without* (which supposeth *some* to be *within*) Tim. 3. 14, 15. *These things I write unto thee, that thou mayest know how to behave thy self in the House of God, which is the Church of the Living God, a Pillar and Basis of the truth.*] The first that were converted did not always prove the fittest to be Bishops; perhaps they might be Women or weakly guifted: To feign that the Apostles did that *every where*, which none

can

can prove that *ever* they did once (to make a Bishop and Deacons of the two
or three first Novice-converts before there were any more Converted, and
to make Bishops and Deacons before there were any Christians to constitute Churches, meerly for future Churches,) this is not *Clemens* act, whoever else will own it.

4. Lastly he noteth here that this was done by the *Revelation* of the *Spirit*,
whereby they *examined and tryed who was worthy of that Dignity*. And,
1. What use for *examination* who was worthy, where there was no other to
stand in Competition, and where the first Convert still was taken? Election is *è multis*. And if he be compelled to grant that there were more Christians over whom the Bishop was set, it is a Contradiction to say that a *Bishop and his Flock*, though small, is *no Church*. 2. It is hard to believe that
the multitude of ignorant Lads, and wicked Men that are now set over
Churches, are Constituted by this Apostolical choice and Tryal, by the
Holy Ghost.

Cap. 5. §. 5. He now acknowledgeth that where many were at first
Converted, not always the first but the fittest was chosen Bishop. And
how prove you that he and his Flock were no Church? The same he maintaineth, §. 11. And after from the *choice* usually made by *suffrages* and other
reasons, well confuteth the former conceit, when he took it to be *Blondels*;
but sure he could not believe that they were *Ecclesiæ nondum natæ*, or *future
Believers* that chose Bishops by Suffrages? But having so fully in this Chapter confuted his former, as *Blondel's* opinion, I doubt not but *Blondel* is in
this as easily reconciled to him as he to himself, and meant no more, but,
1. That the Apostles used (not to make Bishops of the first Converts simply, but) to choose them out of the ancient, grown, and proved Christians. 2. And that being so chosen (not he that was first Baptized, but)
he that was first *ordained*, had the presidence in the *Consessus* of their Presbyters: Which the Dr. might easily have seen, and spared his insulting
upon the contrary supposition.

But let it here again be noted, that §. 9. he expresly and confidently asserteth all that I now *desire*, viz. That Clemens *doth speak of that time of the
Churches beginning, in which there were not yet many Believers, and therefore without doubt, neither Presbyters instituted.* If he means [no *Subject Presbyters*]
or if he means [not *many in a Church but one Bishop*] I desire no more: For
then no Bishop had more Church Assemblies than one, not any half-Presbyters were ordained by the Apostles. For *Clemens* doth not tell us what the
Apostles did in the *beginning* of their Preaching only, but giveth us this as
an account of all their course, in setling Offices in the Churches where
they came.

Cap. 6. He confesseth that *Clemens* mentioneth but two Orders, Bishops
and Deacons, (and we would have no more) and §. 4. is over angry with
Blundel for gathering hence, that he did not do as those that from the *Jewish* Elders, or Priests, or the 70 gather another order, what is there in this
Collection that deserveth the sharp words of that §.

Cap. 7. Whether *Clemens* well cited *Isai.* 60.17. we need not debate. But if yet any think that the Dr. hath not fully granted us our Cause, let him take these additions : §. 7. He well gathereth from *Clemens* that this *form of Government, founded in Bishops and Deacons* (in each Church) *being setled by Men entrusted by Christ, is no less to be ascribed to Gods Command than if Christ himself had constituted* Bishops and *Deacons in every City.* (Let who dare then approve of the alteration by the Introduction of another Order of Priests.) And §. 8. He noteth also out of *Clemens* that the *foresight* of the *contention* that would be about Episcopacy caused this establishment of Bishops and Deacons : No doubt God foreknew both that the popular fort would oppose Government, and that the Monarchical Prelates would depose all the Bishops of the same Church save themselves, and the Arch-Prelates would depose all the Bishops of particular Churches, and set up half Priests in their stead. And he doth well not to pass the following words in *Clemens* (though hard, yet plainly subverting the Doctors opinion) that from this same foresight the Apostles constituted the foresaid Bishops and Deacons (in every Church) ϰ μεταξὺ ἐπινομὴν δεδώκασιν, &c. *ac descriptas deinceps ministrorum officiorumq; vices reliquerunt, ut in defunctorum locum alii viri probati succedere, & illorum munia exequi possent,* (as *Pat. Junius* translateth it.) The word [ἐπινομὴν] can allow no such doubt as shall make this much of the sense to be questionable, 1. That upon the foresight of the Contentions about Episcopacy the Apostles made (by the Spirit) an established Description of the Orders and Offices which should be in the Church, not only in their times, but afterwards. 2. And that the approved men that should hereafter be ordained, should succeed in those same Orders which the Apostles had established and described, even to the same Work or Office, (τὴν λειτουργίαν αὐτῶ.) 3. That the Apostles thus setled or described no mungrel or half Priests, but only Bishops and Deacons, nor any Churches that had not each a Bishop and Deacon. 4. Therefore no such half Priests should be brought in, but only such as the Apostles instituted or described.

I can scarce speak my thoughts plainlier, than by the Doctors next words, § 9. [*It is evident that by the immediate impulse of the Spirit of God Bishops were constituted (Deacons only joyned to them) in every Church, and so at* Corinth, *and the rest of the Cities of* Achaia : *And that by the command of the same Divine Prophesie or Revelation, successors were assigned to them after their departure* :(not a new order invented)*Christ thus consulting and providing for the Churches peace,* &c.] And §. 14. he well granteth, 1. *That the form of Church Government was no where changed by the Apostles* (and so no middle order instituted by them.) 2. *That through all their Age, and when they were consummate in the middle, under their Disciples,* the Government of every Church was in the power of the *Bishops and Deacons in common.*

But whereas §. 13, &c. he layeth this as the ground of his Cause, 1. That it was not the Church at *Corinth* alone, but of all *Achaia* that *Clemens* writeth to under this name. 2. And that there were not many Bishops in one Church, but

but one to each of these particular Churches : I desire the Reader, 1. To try impartially whether in all the Drs. Book there be one word of cogent Evidence to prove what he saith, yea or to make it credible or likely. 2. To consider these Reasons following for the contrary.

1. As is said, whether Scripture custom of speech will allow us to call all the Churches of a Region [*A Church*] in the singular Number : Shew one Text for it if you can.

2. Whether any ancient Ecclesiastical use of speech will allow us to say that the Churches of *Achaia* dwell at *Corinth* (as *Clemens* speaketh, p. 1.)

3. Whether I have not proved from 1 *Cor.* 14. *&c.* that the Church of *Corinth* had more Ministers, or Clergy men, or Pastors in it than one in *Paul's* time ? And therefore was not without so soon after.

4. Whether it be credible that when it was but *one* or *two* Persons (p. 62.) by whom or for whose cause the Presbyters were ejected ; that it is like either this *one* or *two* were members of more particular Churches in *Achaia* than *one* or *two* ? Or that all the Churches of *Achaia* would so far own *one* or *two* mutineers in a particular Church, as to cast out many of their Ministers for their sakes ?

5. Yea when *Clemens* whole scope intimateth that this one or two did this because they aspired after Power or Preeminence themselves : Could they expect themselves to be made the Rulers of more than one or two Churches ?

6. And what was the cause of this one or two like to touch the Bishops of the other Churches ? And what Cognisance was all *Achaia* like to have of the cause of one or two distant persons, so as for them to rise up against their own Bishops.

7. If it was not all nor many Pastors that were thus turned out (as *Clemens* words import) why should all *Achaia* be called seditious, and blamed for it ?

8. Doth not the common Law of Charity and Justice forbid us to extend those words of reproof to a whole Province, which cannot be proved to extend farther than to a single Church, and principally toucht but one or two.

9. I have before proved that *Paul* by [the Saints at *Corinth*] meaneth but one Church : Therefore it's like that *Clemens* doth so too.

10. The Bishops and Deacons that *Clemens* speaketh of, were set up συνδοκησάσης τῆς ἐκκλησίας πάσης, *Cum consensu totius Ecclesiæ*, or as the Dr. will needs have it [*applaudente aut congratulante tota Ecclesia*] indeed [*with the good liking, Pleasure*, or *Approbation of the whole Church.*] And shall we be perswaded that all the Cities and Countrey of *Achaia* were that *whole Church*, which *approved*, or *consented* to these particular Pastors that were put out ? Or that had Cognisance of them or acquaintance with them ?

11. He expresly saith, pag. 62. κορινθίων ἐκκλησίαν, *That the Church of Corinth for the sake of one or two, moved Sedition against the Presbyters.*] And why doth he never say [*it was the Church of* Achaia.]

12. p. 63. He supposeth the Person Emulating to be [*a Believer of power in explaining Doctrine, wise in judging of Speeches,* &c. And would have the concern'd Person say (p. 69.) *If the Sedition be for me,* and the *Contention and Schisms, I will remove, I will be gone whither you will, and will do what the People pre-determine of* (or *command,*) *only let the Flock of Christ with the Presbyters set over them live in peace.*] And is it like that the Flock that this Person must say so to, was all *Achaia*?

13. And p. 73. He requireth [*those that begun the Sedition, to be obediently Subject*

P   to *to the Presbyters* (and not to their Bishop onely.) And is it like to be the Bishops of other Churches through all *Achaia*, that this *one or two* is required to *Obey* and be in *Subjection to*.

I have given my Reasons, to prove that these Presbyters were in the One Church of *Corinth*: Compare his (if you can find them) to the contrary, and Judge Impartially as you see cause.

Cap. 8. Hath nothing that concerneth us, but the recitall of his grand Confession, lest we should think that in *Clemens* days, the great Bishop of *Corinth*, or any in *Achaia*, had any more Church-assemblies than one to whom he could do all the Pastoral Offices himself, he thus concludeth, §. 9. [*Indeed mention is found only of Bishops (with Deacons) constituted in each City, sometimes under the Title of Bishops, sometimes of Presbyters; there being no token or foot-step at all appearing of such as we now call Presbyters,* &c.] To which I wholly agree; though not that there was but one Presbyter in *Corinth*.

Cap. 9. He is offended much with *Blondel*, for reproaching *Hermas*, and yet using his Testimony: As if a Hereticks, or an Infidels Testimony might not be used in point of History: And, §. 14. he again cometh to his supposition of Bishops without Subject Presbyters, as if it served his turn more than ours.

Cap. 10. About *Pius* words, hath nothing that I find the cause concerned in.

Cap. 11. Is of little moment to us, both parties have little that is cogent, but velitations about dubious words.

Cap. 12. Is but about the sense of the word applyed to *Irenæus*, which Dr. *H.* taketh here and by many after to mean a Bishop, and wonders that *Blondel* pleadeth for a parity of order from a common Name. But it is not so much without reason as he maketh it: For if Bishops and Presbyters were in the first times called by one Name; and the highest Person in the Church then was ordinarily known by the name Presbyter, and the appropriating of [*Bishop*] to one sort, and *Presbyter* to another, came afterwards in by such insensible degrees, that no man can tell when it was; it founds very probable, that it was the true Episcopal Power, or the same Office and Order, that was first commonly possessed by them to whom the name was Common.

And so much of Dr. *Hammond*'s Dissertations, wherein I must desire the Reader to note, 1. That I meddle not with other mens Causes, nor particularly with the question: Whether one man in each Church, had of old, a guiding superiority over the rest of the Presbyters? Nor yet, whether the Apostles had such successors in the General care of many Churches, (such as Visiters, or Arch-Bishops) but only, 1. Whether every Presbyter were not Essentially a Bishop, or Governour of the Flock, having the power of Keys, as they call it, *in foro interiore & exteriore*, both for resolving Consciences and for Church-order. 2. Whether every particular Church, which ordinarily communicated together in the Lords Supper, and had *unum Altare*, had not one or more such Bishops. 3. Whether it was not a sinful corrupting change, to bring in another Species of Presbyters; and so to depose all the particular Churches and Bishops, and set up a *Diocesane* Bishop, *infimi ordinis*, with half-Churches and half-Priests, under him in their stead. 2. And note, That as it concerned me not to speak to all that the Doctor hath said, so I have carefully chosen out all that I thought pertinent and of a seeming weight, as to the cause which I mannage, and have past by nothing in the whole

Book,

Book, which I thought an understanding Reader needeth an answer to.

There is yet the same Authors Vindication of his Dissertations to be considered : But I find nothing new in them to be answered by me, nor that I am concerned for the Cause in hand any further than to give you these few Observations.

1. That again, *p.* 5. he saith, [*That by observing the paucity of Believers in many Cities in the first Plantations, which made it unnecessary that there should by the Apostles be ordained any more than a Bishop and Deacon (one, or more) in each City, and that this was accordingly done by them at the first, is approved by the most undenyable ancient Records.*]

2. That *p.* 7. he again well averreth that the Jewish and Gentile Congregations occasioned several Churches and Bishops in the same Cities. And *p.* 14. 15. That *Timothy* was placed by *Paul*, Bishop of the Gentiles at *Ephesus*, and *S. John*, and another after him, Bishop of the *Jews.* Pag. 16. He thinketh that *Timothy* was Bishop of *Ephesus* (or Angel) when *Rev.* 2. was wrote. Pag. 17. From *Epiphanius* he reckoneth above 50 years from the *Revelation of John, Rev.* 2. to the writing of *Ignatius's* Epistles. By which we may Calculate the time when the Office of half-Presbyters began to be invented, according to his own Computation. That *pag.* 21. *& passim,* his supposition of the 24 Bishops of *Judæa,* sitting about the Throne of *James* Bishop of *Jerusalem,* and his other supposition of their being so ordinarily there. And of the Bishops of Provinces in other Nations, being so frequently many score, if not hundred Miles off their people in the *Metropolitane* Cities, when the people had no other Priest to Officiate, doth tend to an *Atheistical* conceit, that the Ordinary use of Sacred Assemblies and Communion is no very needful thing, when in the best times by the best men, in whole Countreys at once, they were so much forborn.

Pag. 26. Again you have his full and plain Assertion, [*That there were not in the space within compass of which all the Books of the new Testament were written, any Presbyters, in our modern Notion of them, created in the Church, though soon after certainly in Ignatius time, (which was above 50 years after the Rev.) they were*].

Pag. 60. He supposeth that *whoever should settle Churches under a Heathen King among Heathens, must accordingly make the Churches gathered subordinate to one another, as the Cities in which they are gathered were* (though Heathen) *subordinate to one another,* of which more in due place.

Pag. 76, 77. He saith that [*As Congregations, and Parishes are Synonimous in their Style, so I yield that Believers in great Cities were not at first divided into Parishes, while the number of Christians in a City was so small that they might well assemble in the same place, and so needed no Partitions, or Divisions. But what disadvantage is this to us, who affirm that one Bishop, not a Colledge of Presbyters, presided in that one Congregation, and that the Believers in the Regions and Villages about did belong to the care of that single Bishop, or City Church*] *A Bishop and his Deacon were sufficient at the first (to sow their Plantations—[For what is a Diocess but a Church in a City with the Suburbs and Territories, or Region belonging to it ? And this certainly might be and remain under the Government of a single Bishop. Of any Church so bounded there may be a Bishop, and that whole Church shall be his Diocess, and so he a Diocesan Bishop, though as yet this Church be not subdivided into more several Assemblies.*] So that you see now what a Diocess is. And that you may know that we contend not about Names, while they call the Bishop of one

Con

Congreation, a *Diocesane*, we say nothing against him: A *Diocesan* in our sense is such as we live under, that have made one Church of many hundred or a thousand.

But Reader be not abused by words, when it is visible Countreys that we talk of. As every Market-Town, or Corporation is πολις a City in the old sense, so the Diocess of *Lincoln* (which I live in) at this reckoning hath three or fourscore Diocesses in it, and the Diocess of *Norwich* about 50 Diocesses in it, &c. That is such Cities with the interjacent Villages.

Pag. 73. He saith [*When they add these Angels were Congregational, not* Diocesan, *they were every of them Angels of a Church in a City, having authority over the Regions adjacent and pertaining to that City, and so as* CHURCH *and* CONGREGATION, ARE ALL ONE, AS IN ORDINARY USE IN ALL LANGUAGES THEY ARE: *Thus were Congregational and Diocesan also. What follows of the paucity of Believers, in the greatest Cities, and their meeting in one place, is willingly granted by us.*

I must desire the Reader to remember all this, when we come to use it in due place. And you may modestly smile to observe how by this and the foregoing words, the Dr. forgetfully hath cast out all the *English Diocesans*: While he maketh it needful that the Cities be Ecclesiastically subordinate as they are Civilly, and maketh it the very definition of a *Diocesan* Bishop, to be a Bishop of a City with the Country or Suburbs belonging to it: But in *England* no lesser Cities (ordinarily at least) nor Corporation-Towns are at all Subject to the great Cities: Nor are any Considerable part of the Countrey Subject to them; nor do the Liberties of Cities, or Corporations, reach far from the Walls, or Towns. So that by this Rule the Bishop of *London, York, Norwich,* and *Bristow* would have indeed large Cities with narrow liberties: But the rest would have Diocesses little bigger than we could allow to conscionable Faithful Pastors.

But he yet addeth more, *p.* 79. he will do more for our cause than the Presbyterians themselves, who in their disputes against the Independents say that *Jerusalem* had more Christians belonging to the Church than could conveniently meet in one place; But, saith the Dr. [*This is contrary to the Evidence of the Text, which saith expresly, v. 44. that all the Believers were* ἐπὶ τὸ αὐτὸ, *meeting in one and the same place. The like may be said of the other places,* Act. 4. 4. and 5. 14. *For certainly as yet though the number of believers increased, yet they were not distributed into several Congregations.*

Will you yet have more? p. 80, 81. When the *London* Ministers say that [*the Believers of one City made but one Church in the Apostles days*] he answereth [*This observation I acknowledge to have perfect truth in it, and not to be confutable in any part: And therefore instead of rejecting, I shall imbrace it, and from thence conclude that there is no manner of incongruity in assigning of one Bishop to one Church, and so one Bishop in the Church of* J. rusalem, *because it is a Church, not Churches,* BEING FORCED TO ACKNOWLEDGE THAT WHERE THERE WERE MORE CHURCHES, THERE WERE MORE BISHOPS.] I am almost in doubt by this whether the Dr. were not against the *English* Prelacy, and he and I were not of a mind, especially remembring that he said nothing against my disputations of Church Goverument written against himself, when I lived near him. Observe Reader,

der, 1. That even now he confessed that a *Church* and *Congregation* is all one. 2. And here he confesseth, that *where there were more Churches, there were more Bishops*; and his words [*Because it is a Church, not Churches*] seem to import that *de jure* he supposeth it is no Church without a Bishop, and that there should be no fewer Bishops than Churches. And then I ask, 1. Where and when do all the Christians in this Diocess, of above an hundred miles long, *Congregate*; who meet but in above a thousand several Temples, and never know one of a thousand of the Diocess? 2. Doth not this grant to the *Brownists*, that the Parish Churches are no Churches, but onely parts of the *Diocesane* Church? 3. And then if it be proved that the *Diocesane* Church-form, is but of humane invention, what Church in *England* will they leave us, that is of divine institution? This is the unhappiness of *overdoing* to *undo all*; and of aspiring too high, to fall down into nothing.

And doth he not speak much to the same purpose, p. 87. [*One City with the Territories adjoyning to it, being ruled by one single Bishop, was to be called a singular Church: And therefore that which is said to be done in every Church, Act. 14. 23. is said to be done in every City, Tit. 1. 5. The sum of which observation is only this, that one City with the Territories adjoyning to it, never makes above one Church in the Scripture Style.* (And yet he largely proveth the contrary, that there was one Church and Bishop of *Jewish* Christians, and one of Gentiles) *whereas a Province, or Countrey, or Nations consists, of many Cities, and so of many Episcopal Sees or Churches.*] The like he hath again p. 90. §. 53.

But whereas p. 88. he would Prove that a Province, or Nation, of *many Churches, may be called one Church; because the Churches in all the World are so called in our Creed, and in the Scripture:* I answer, That he can never prove that many Churches are ever in Scripture called one, save only the *Universal Church*, which is but one, being Headed by *one Head*, even Christ. The Universal Church (as he said before of a *Church* compared to *Persons*) is One Collective body, as a Political Society related to Christ or constituted of Christ and all Christians: And a particular *Church is one as constituted of the Ministerial Pastors and People*: But find any Text of Scripture that calleth the Churches of a Nation, or Province, one Church, in all the new Testament if you can.

In *pag.* 103. he giveth Reasons for his singularity in interpreting so many Texts of Scripture; and sheweth that as the Fathers differ from each other, (as *Tirinus* sheweth) so we may also differ from them, (and I know not of any Expositor that ever wrote that hath more need of this Apology than *Grotius* and he.) And I mislike not his Reasons. But then how unsavoury is it for the same person to expect that we should in reverence to one expository word in *Irenæus*, and another in *Epiphanius*, forsake the common sense of the Fathers where they do agree? or that we must bow to every ancient Canon?

But I would not have him thought more singular than he is, lest when I have answered him the Prelatists forsake him, and say that they are still unanswered, therefore I crave the Readers special observation of his words, p. 104, 105. [*I might truly say that for those minute considerations and conjectures wherein this Doctor differs from some others who have written before him, as to the manner of interpreting some few Texts, he hath the Suffrages of many of the learnedst men of this Church at this day, and as far as he knows. OF ALL that embrace the same cause with him.*] Of

which

which I only say, that if he do but minutely differ from others, and not at all from the moſt, I hope my confutation of him will not be impertinent as to the reſt. But if he lay the very ſtreſs of his cauſe upon novel Expoſitions of almoſt every Text which mentioneth Biſhops, Presbyters, Paſtors, and quite croſs the way of almoſt all (ſave *Petavius*) that ever went before him; then think whether that cauſe ſtand on ſo firm ground, as ſome perſwade, which needeth ſuch new foundations or ways of ſupport at this Age, in the judgement of ſuch learned men as theſe.

Pag. 119, 120, 121. He proveth that *Dioceſane* Biſhops are the only Elders of the Church which *James* adviſeth the ſick to ſend for : ſuppoſing the City Churches (even of *Jeruſalem*,) to be yet no bigger than that one Biſhop and a Deacon (who yet was not this Viſiter of the ſick) might do all the Miniſterial work. Where I confeſs he quite outgoeth me in extenuating the Churches in S. *James*'s time. If the Church of *Jeruſalem* had ſeven Deacons, I will not belive him (pardon the incivility) that they had but one Presbyter. And (pardon me a greater boldneſs in ſaying) if he had tryed but as much as I have done what it is to do all the Paſtoral work for one Pariſh of 2 or 3000 Perſons in publick and private, he could not poſſibly have been of this Opinion. Nor do I think it likely, that when it is a *ſingular Perſon* that *James* bids ſend for the *Elders* of the *Church*, but that it implyeth that the Church where he was had more Elders than one. I confeſs that if it had been ſpoken either to Perſons, plurally, or of Churches plurally, the phraſe might well have ſignified the ſingle Elders of the ſeveral Churches : But to ſay to each ſick man ſingularly, *Let him ſend for the Elders of the Church* (ſingularly) in common uſe of ſpeech ſignifieth that there were many Elders for that man to ſend for in the Church. And whereas he asketh whether a ſick man muſt ſend for the Colledge of Presbyters? I anſwer, that a ſick man may well ſend for the Presbyters or Miniſters, either one after another, as there is occaſion, or more than one at once if need require for his Reſolution. If we ſay to a ſick man in *London*, (ſend for the *Phyſicians of the City, and let them adviſe you*, &c.) it ſignifieth that the City hath more Phyſicians than one, and that he may adviſe with one, or more at once, or *per vices* as he findeth Cauſe : and no man would ſpeak ſo to him, if *London* had but one Phyſician, and *Norwich* another, and *York* another, &c. And when, p. 121. he ſuppoſeth the Objection, that *they have a mean opinion of viſiting the ſick*, becauſe they ſay, it is not the Biſhops work (which he well maketh it to be) methinks this ſhould ſuit with no *Engliſh* Ears, who will quickly underſtand, that they ſpeak *de facto* of our Biſhops, to whom a ſick man may ſend an hundred, or fifty, or twenty Miles, to deſire him to come preſently, and pray with him, if his diſeaſe be a Phrenſie which depriveth him of his Wits, and all about him be as mad : And the Biſhop with us may be ſaid to viſit the ſick of his Dioceſs, as a man may be ſaid to weed a Field that pluckth up a weed or two where he goeth ; or to build a City, becauſe he knockt up a Nail or two in his own Houſe.

Pag. 120. It is obſervable which he ſaith [*Indeed, if it were not (the Biſhops work to viſit the ſick) how could it be by the Biſhop, when other parts of his Office became his full Employment, committed to the Presbyter. For, 1. he could not commit that to others, if he firſt had it not in himſelf : And, 2. This was the only Reaſon of ordaining inferior Officers in the Church, that part of the Biſhops task might be performed by them.*

Anſ. Either he believed that the Office of a Subject Presbyter (or Order as they

call

call it) was inftituted by God, and fetled in the Church as neceffary by his Spirit, and Law, or not: If he do, then *Qu.* 1. Whether the work of thefe Presbyters, after the inftitution, be not the work of their *own* Office, and not (in the individual acts) the Bifhops? As *Eve* was a Rib of *Adam* materially, but when fhe was a woman, fhe was no part of *Adam*, nor her acts like his acts; and fo of all woman-kind thereafter. *Qu.* 2. Whether the Bifhop any other way commit the work or Office to him, than by calling him to an Office which God himfelf had made or inftituted, and Minifterially invefting him in it as a Servant (that hath no land of his own) may be fent by his Mafter to inveft another in fome Land which he hath given him, by a Legal Solemn delivery of poffeffion; or as a Steward may fend fuch Reapers into his Mafters field as his Mafter did before exactly defcribe to him? Chrift being the only maker of the Office, and punctual defcriber of it, and the Bifhop, people, and Magiftrates altogether, doing no more but choofe the Perfon defcribed as fit, and deliver him poffeffion of the place.

But if he thought that the Bifhop himfelf doth make the Presbyters Office, by parting his own, and fo giving him as much as he thinketh fit, I fhall fhame this Opinion in due place.

Pag. 132. (and in his *Differt.*) he would make us believe that (*Polycarp*'s Epiftle, and fo) *Clement*'s [*to the Church* παρικῆσαν Κόριντον] were to be interpreted extenfively as relating to παροικία, to the Church in that Parifh, that is the Diocefs, of *Corinth*, or Province of *Achaia*. And fo he diftorteth *Phil.* 1. 1. and other places; but in all his Citations giveth us not a word of proof, that παροικέω fignifieth to dwell in the Circuit or extent of a Diocefs, and not fimply to *fojourn* or *dwell*. As if παροικέω were derived from παροικία, and as if the firft notion of παροικία were a Diocefs, or a City with its Territories: As *Put: Young* faith on *Clement*'s Epift. *p.* 1. [*cum idem fit* παρικεῖν *quod* παροικεῖν *ut videre eft ftatim in initio libri Ruth & alibi apud* 70: which he further proveth) yea and by an old Infcription of an Altar brought from *Delos*, &c. fee the place. And we took it to be agreed on that παροικέω in its ftrict fenfe is but *habito tanquam peregrinus, advena fum*; and in its ufual larger fenfe, *juxta habito, accolo, fum proximus, vicinus, accola*. And παροικία & παροικηfις but *incolatus & vicinia & habitatio propinqua*; a place of cohabitation, or a neighbourhood: As we ftill take *cohabitation* to be a neceffary qualification or *difpofitio materiæ* of a Church-member (of the fame particular Church, contrary to the Diocefan ftate, where the Members never fee each other, nor hear of their Names.) And though παροικία in procefs of time (as Bifhops enlarged their Diocefs or Church) came to fignifie a whole Country, or Circuit as large as a Diocefs did, yet no man can prove that it was fo from the beginning of the Churches; or fignified any determined fpace of ground, beyond the habitation of the members of one Worfhipping Church or Congregation: Even as παροικὸ δομέω is not to build in the fame Diocefe, but near or in the fame Neighbourhood; and παροικίζω is not to fet ones dwelling in the fame Diocefs, but vicinity: That πάροικ⊙ alfo in its ftricteft fignification is but *inquilinus* a *fojourner*, and in its largeft οἶκος⊙ a *cohabitant*, but in both fignifieth a *Neighbour* (and not ftrangers dwelling out of the notice of each other through a Diocefs) is fo fully fhewed out of many Authors by the *Bafil.* Lexicon (publifhed by *Henr. Petr.* 1568.) that I need not add to it. And the Authors of that Lexicon fuppofe, that the third (the Church) fignification is primarily but from *πάροικος, ut accola*, that [*Paraci huic dicuntur qui fanum aliquod accolunt* (not that dwell near a thousand or many hundred several Churches) *unde & παροικία curia & vicinia conventus* (not many hundred Conventions) *accolarum coitio & congregatio, hoc parochiam dicunt absurde.* Much more would they call the newer Notion of a Diocess-Parish like ours, absurd. In *Heb.* 11. 9. and *Luk.* 24. 18. *Act* 7. 6. 1 *Pet.* 2. 11. 1 *Pet.* 1. 17. *Act.* 13. 17. *Act.* 7. 29. *Eph.* 2. 19. (which are all the places in the new Testament where these words are used that I know of) the Dr. himself in his *Annotations* doth not once pretend that the word is used in his Province sense: And is not *Clemens* and *Polycarp* liker to use the word in the Scripture sense, than in this aliene sense, that since came into the Church? We must therefore take leave, till better proof of the contrary, to expound *Clemens, Polycarp*, and *Ignatius*, meerly by [*sojourning and cohabiting in such a vicinity* as Personal and Congregational Communion required.

But his only seeming proof is (again) because *Paul*'s Epistle to the *Corinthians*, was to the Province of *Achaia*. To which again I answer, that *Paul*'s Epistle to the *Corinthians* was to be communicated to all *Achaia* (and after to all the World;) but that maketh not *Corinth*, and *Achaia*, nor [the Church at *Corinth*,] and [the Churches of all Achaia] to be the same: Nay, *Paul* expresly distinguisheth them by the Conjunction, as aforesaid; else his words were Tautological, if by [*To the Church of God, which is at* Corinth, *with all the Saints which are in all* Achaia] he had meant [*To the Church of God, which is in all* Achaia, *with the Saints that are in all* Achaia] And I had thought all *Achaia* had been more than a Parish, even as the word *παροικία* was used Ecclesiastically in those times, in the opinion of the *Diocesane* Divines themselves. And so much of Dr. *Hammond*, and all that have written for our Prelacy.

The Opposers of Prelacy.

To name the Authors that write on the other side (or some of them) is enough, viz. 1. *Beza*, 2. *Cartwright*, 3. *Jacob* against *Downame*, 4. *Didoclave* alias *Calderwood*'s *Altare Damascenum*, 5. Learned *Parker de Polit. Ecclesiast.* (not so florid as his Treat. of the Cross, but more nervous) 6. Holy and Learned *Paul Baine* (*Perkin*'s Successor) his *Diocesan*'s Tryal, short and nervous, in *Syllogisms.* 7. *Salmasius* in 2 Books (*Apparat. ad primat. P. & Walo. Messalinus*,) 8. Before him *Gersom Bucer differt. de Gubern. Ecclesiæ*, against *Downame*, large and learned. 9. *Jer. Burroughs*, in 2 or 3 sheets, Argumentatively. 10. *Prins* unbishoping of *Timothy* and *Titus*, 11. Dr. *Bastwick*'s *Flagellum Pontificis & Episcoporum Latialium* (oratorical) 12. And such are *Miltons.* 13. *Smectymnuus*, that is, *Steph. Marshal, Edw. Calamy, Tho. Toung, Mat. Newcomen*, and *Will. Spurstow*: And a defence of it. 14. The *Lond.* Ministers *Jus Divinum, Presb. & Minist.* 15. The Isle of *Wight* Papers. 16. *Dav. Blondel* (that wonder of the world, for Chronology and History.) A few leaves of whose over-large Collections, Dr. *Hammond* hath Answered, as you have heard, and given his reason for going no further, because *Blond.* extendeth the Ministerial Parity but to 140. But to us it is not so inconsiderable to see by what degrees the Prelacy rose, and to see it proved so copiously, that even in after Ages the species extent of Churches, and the *Order* or *Species* of *Presbyters* were not altered, notwithstanding accidental alterations. And therefore I shall undertake to bring proof enough of what I now plead for, from times much lower than 140, such as I think the impartal will rest satisfied in, though interest and preconceived Idea's are seldom satisfied, or conquered by a Confutation.

Cap.

CHAP. VI.

That it is not of Gods institution, nor is pleasing to him that there be no Churches and Bishops but in Cities; or that a City with its territories, or Country adjacent, be the bounds of each Church.

SOme late most esteemed defenders of *Diocesanes*, especially Dr. *Ham-mond*, lay so great a stress upon the supposition, that the Apostles set-led the Churches in the Metropolitane and Diocesane order, and that they did partly in imitation of the Jewish policy, and partly as a thing necessary by the nature of the thing, that even in Heathen Kingdomes, when Churches are gathered in any Cities, they must have a difference of Church power over each other as they find the Cities to have a civil pow-er (as you heard before from Dr. *H.*) that I think it meet here briefly to prove, 1. That it was not of the Apostles purpose to have Churches and Bishops placed only in Cities, and not in Villages. 2. Nor that Church power should thus follow the civil; 3 Nor that a City with its territories should be the measure of the habitation of each Churches members. The *licet* in some cases I deny not, but the *oportet* is the question, yea and the *licet* in other cases. The two first are proved together by these reasons, following.

1. Christ himself our grand examplar did not only preach and con-vert Christians in Cities, but in Country villages, where he held assem-blies, and preacht and prayed, yea in mountains and in Ships: And though he planted no particular Churches with fixed Bishops there, yet that was because he did so no where. He performed all offices in the Country which he did in the Cities, except that which was appropriated to *Jerusalem* by the Law and the institution of his last supper, which could be done but in one place.

2. There is no Law of God (direct or indirect) which maketh it a duty to settle Churches and Bishops in Cities only, and forbiddeth the settling them in Country villages: This is most evident to him that will search the Scripture, and but try the pretended proofs of the late Prelatists; for the vanity of their pretensions will easily appear; They have not so fair a pretense in the New Testament for asserting such a Law, as the Pope hath for his supremacy in [*Peter feed my sheep*]. And where there is no Law, there is no obligation on us unto duty, and no sin in omission.

If they say that [*the Apostles did plant Churches only in Cities compre-hending their territories*] I answer, 1. They prove that they planted them in Cities; but the silence of the Scriptures proveth not the Negative, that

Q   they

they planted none in Villages. 2. Nor have they a word of proof that each Church contained all Christians in the Cities, with all the interjacent Villages. 3. Much less that they must contain all such, when all the Countries were converted, and the Christians were enow for many Churches. 4. Nor can they ever prove that the Apostles planting Churches only in Cities, was intended as a Law, to restrain men from planting them any where else; Any more than their not converting the Villages or the generality of the Cities, will prove that they must not be converted by any other: Or than that their setting up no Christian Magistrates, or converting no Princes, will prove that there must be no such thing. Whoever extended the obligation of Apostolical example to such Negatives, as to do nothing which they did not? 5. The reason is most apparent why they preached first in Cities, because there is no such fishing as in the Sea; They had there the frequentest fullest auditories: And so they planted their first Churches there, because they had most converts there. And it is known that *Judea* (a barren mountainous Coutrey of it self) had been so harressed with Wars, that there was little safety and quiet expected in Countrey Villages; and the Roman Empire had been free from the same plague by such short intervals, that as many people as could got into the Cities: (for all that know by experience what War is, do know the misery of poor Country people who are at every wicked Soldiers mercy.) It was therefore among poor scattered labourers, a hard thing to get a considerable auditory: which maketh Mr. *Eliot* and his helpers work go on so heavily among the scattered Americans, who have no Cities or great Towns, because they can rarely speak to any considerable numbers. Now to gather from hence either that Villages must have no Churches or no Bishops, is an impiety next to a concluding that they must not be assembled, taught, or worship God.

3. The reasons are vain and null, which are pretended for such a modelling of Churches to the form of the civil Government, and thus confining them to Cities. For, 1. There is no need that one Bishop be the Governour of another at all; 2. And therefore no need that the Bishop of a Metropolis govern the Bishop of a lesser City, or he, the Bishop of a Village. 1. God hath not given one Bishop power over another, as meer Bishops. As *Cyprian* saith, in his *Carth. Council, none of us are Bishops of Bishops,* but Colleagues. Dr. *Hammond* himself saith, that the Bishops are the Apostles Successors, and the Apostles were equal in power and Independent, *Annot. in 1 Tim.3.c. p.732. Jesus Christ dispensing them (all the particular Churches of the whole world by himself and administring them severally, not by any one Oeconomus, but by the several Bishops as inferiour heads of unity to the several bodies so constituted by the several Apostles in their plantations, each of them having* αυτοκεφια *a several distinct commission from Christ immediately, and subordinate to none but the supreme donor or plenipotentiary.]* Indeed if it be not Bishops, but Archbishops or Bishops of Bishops which are the Apostles Successors, in order over the Bishops as they are supposed to be over the

Priests

Priests, then, such an order of Arch-Bishops is of divine right; But not as Metropolitanes, or for the Cities sake, but as general Officers to take care of many Churches, succeeding the Apostles.

2. And that Apostolical succession is not the foundation of the Metropolitan or City power is plain; 1. Because if the Bishop or Arch-Bishop be the immediate successors of the Apostles, there must be but just 13 or 14 in the whole world, if they succeed them fully in the accidentals of their office: But if not, than their residence in Cities, will not prove that they must succeed them in that accident, any more than in the number. 2. Because (as is shewed) the Apostles tyed not themselves to Cities only; and what they did in preferring Cities was occasional (as is said before): 3. Nor is there the least proof (beyond an ostentation of vain words and confidence) that ever the Apostles setled Churches according to the civil form, and put the Bishops of lesser Cities under the Metropolitans: No more than that among themselves that Apostle was Ruler of the rest, who had the Metropolis for his Seat: The Papists themselves not pretending that Peter was Ruler of the rest, because Rome was his Seat, but that Rome must have the ruling Universal Bishop, because it was the Seat of Peter. And if the Metropolis made not one Apostle Ruler of the rest, why should it do so by their successors? And I never heard any attempt to prove, that Mathew, Bartholomew, Lebbeus, James the Apostle, Thomas, Philip and every one of the Apostles had a distinct independent Metropolis for his Episcopal Seat. 4. Indeed its but vain words of them that pretend that the Apostles fixed themselves in any Seat at all; but it is certain by their Office and by History that they oft removed from place to place, in order to call as much of the world as they were capable, and were sometimes in Metropoles and sometimes in other places: and though the ancients make them the first Bishops of Churches, they do not say that they were Bishops of any particular Churches only, exclusively to all others: But the same Apostle that Planted ten or twenty Churches was the first Bishop of them all pro tempore, setling fixed Bishops to succeed them. 5. And whoever dreamed that Mark who was no Apostle, was the Ruler of other Apostles, (at least that came into his Province) because Alexandria was the second Metropolis.

4. This pretended forming of the Churches as aforesaid is contrary to the Ends of Church Institution and Communion: which are the publick worshipping of God, and personal Communion of Parochians or Cohabitants in that worship, Sacraments and holy living, in mutual assistance. Whereas in a great part of the world, Country Villages are so far from any Cities, that if they must travel to them for this publick Communion, they must spend all the Lords day in travalle, and yet miss their Ends, and come too late. Nor can Women, Children and aged ones possibly do t at all. But if they are to have no such personal Communion with the City Churches, but have it ordinarily among themselves, then (whatever men may say that strive about the Name) they are not of that particular

City

City Church as such, but are of another Church at home, which must have a Bishop because it is a Church.

5. Their Civil and City or Diocesan frame contradicteth the plain institution or Law of Christ and of his Spirit. For 1. *Math.* 28. 19. 20. it is the very Commission of the Apostles and their successors (with whom Christ will be to the end of the world) to Teach or Disciple all Nations, and then to Baptize them, and so gather them into the Church Universal, and then Teach them as Disciples all his Laws, which includeth Congregating them in perticular Churches where they must be so taught. Now as it is all Nations, even the whole Countryes and not the Cities only that must be Discipled or convicted and Baptized, so it is the whole Nations, Villages and all of Baptized persons that must thus be *Congregated into perticular Churches* and taught. 2. To which add. *Act.* 14. 23. the positive exemplary and so obliging ordinary practice of the Apostles. *They ordained them Elders in every Church* : so that 1. It is Gods will that *Villages* have Churches. 2. And it is Gods will that every Church have a Bishop (at least) therefore it is Gods will that every Village have a Bishop which have a Church; or that some Villages have Bishops.

And though [*every* City be mentioned *Tit.* 1. 5. that only sheweth that *de facto* then and there, Village Churches were rare or none, but not *de jure* they must not be gathered : nor doth he say [*ordain Elders in Cities only*] : much less [give them Rule according to the City power.]

And as *Cenchrea* had a Church, which was no City, so *Act.* 14. 23. will prove that they should have a Bishop. For every Church is to have a Bishop. And *Cenchrea* was not a family-Church; and so the name not used equivocally : And Bishop *Downams* assertion that it was a Church with a mean Presbyter under the Bishop of *Corinth*, is a naked unproved saying that deserveth no credit ; and is contradicted by Doctor *Hammond*, who saith there was there no meer Presbyter in being.

6. Had this form been setled as they Pretend (in Cities only and Diocesses) there would have been uncertainty and contentions what places should have Bishops and Churches, and what places should have none. For it is uncertain and litigious, what place is to be taken for a City and what not. For πολις sometimes signifieth any great Town, and sometimes strictly Towns incorprate, and sometimes more strictly eminent Corporations now called *Cities* with us here in *England*. And how great would the difficulty have been to determine when a Town was big enough to pass for a City, or when it had privileges enow for that title. If it be said, that the account and name then and thus used was the directory, they will then make Gods Church to depend for being upon a *Name* with heathen people. If they will call *Cenchrea* a City, it shall have a Church; otherwise it shall have none. But there was no such controversie in those times.

7. According to their model Churches shall be mutable and dissolvible at the will of the Magistrate, yea of every Heathen Magistrate : For

if he will but change the priviledges and title of a Town and make it no City, it must have no Church or Bishop: And if he will remove the privileges and title, the Church and Bishop must remove: And if he will endow a big Village or Town with City privileges and name, a Church and Bishop must be then made anew. But who can believe that Christ thus modled his Churches in his institution?

8. Yea after their model, an infidel or Christian King *a iud agens*, that never thinketh on it or intendeth it, shall change the Churches, and destroy them. If by war a City be turned into no City, or if the King for other reasons un-city it, or if change of Government put it into another Princes power, that shall for his convenience un-city it, the Church in City and Country is at an end, though there remain people enow to constitute a Church.

9. Yea a fire or an Earthquake by this Rule may end a Church, by Wood and stone, though the Country still have never so many Christians: and when the City is gone, the Church is gone. 10. Yea it will be in the power of every king, even of Heathens, whether Christ shall have any Church or Bishop in his kingdoms, or not. Because he can un-city or dis-priviledge all the Cities in his kingdom at his pleasure, and consequently unchurch all the Churches.

11. And by their way Christ hath setled as various Church forms as there be forms of Government in the world: For all Dominions are not divided into Provinces, under Prisidents &c as the Roman Empire was: In many Countries, the Metropolis hath no superiority over the other City or the Country, and so that will be of divine institution in one Country, which will be a sin in others.

12. Yea by this Rule many vast Countries must have no Bishops or Churches at all, because they have no Cities (as is known among the Americans); and others must have but one Church and Bishop in a whole Country of many hundred Miles.

13. And by their Rule all the Bishops of *England* are unbishoped, and their Diocesan *Churches* are unchurched. For 1. Some of them (in *Wales* and *Man*) have no Cities now called such. 2. Others of them have many Cities (not only *Coventry and Lichfield, Bath and Wells* now called Cities, but) abundance of Corporations really Cities. 3. And the Cities in *England, Scotland* and *Ireland* have no Civil Government over all the Countries, Corporations, Villages of the Diocese at all: nor are they Seats of Presidents or Lieutenants that have such Rule, so that our Dioceses are not modelled to the form of the Civil Government. What subjection doth *Hartfordshire, Bedfordshire, Buckinghamshire,* &c owe to the Town of Lincolne?

14. By their model it is not Bishops and Metropolitans alone that are of divine right: For if the Church Government must be modelled to the Civill, the Imperial Churches must have had Officers to answer all the Proconsuls and Prefects, the Lieutenants, the Vicars, the Consular

Prefi-

Presidents, the Correctors &c. For who can prove that one fort or two only muft be imitated and not others.

15. They muft by their rule, fet up in *England* an inconfiftent or felf deftroying form. For in many if not moft Counties our Lord Lieutenants, Deputy-Lieutenants, and Sherifs, and moft Juftices dwell in Countrey mannors and Villages, and not in Cities. And fo either Cities muft not be the Seats of Bifhops and Churches, or elfe the Seat of Civil Government muft not be the Seat of the Ecclefiaftical. If they fay that *Affizes* and Seffions are kept in the County Towns, I anfwer. 1. So Church affemblies called Synods or Councils may be held in them, and yet not be the Bifhops Seat. For they are not the Judges or Juftices Seat, becaufe of Affizes, and quarterly Seffions. 2. The obfervation is not univerfally true: Yea no Affizes or Seffions at all are therefore held in any Town becaufe it is the County Town, but becaufe it is the convenienteft place for meeting. The choice of which is left to the Judges and Juftices; who fometimes choofe the County Town, and fometimes another, as they pleafe (As *Bridgnorth* in *Shropfhire*, *Alesbury* (not *Buckingham*) ordinarily in *Buckinghamfhire*, and fo of others. 3. And thefe County Towns are few of them either Cities or Bifhops Seats: As *Buckingham*, *Hartford*, *Bedford*, *Cambridge*, *Huntington*, *Warwick*, *Darby*, *Nottingham*, *Sherwsbury*, *Ipfwich*, *Colchefter*, *Lancafter*, *Flint*, *Denbigh*, *Montgomery*, *Merioneth*, *Radnor*, *Cardigan*, *Carnarvon*, *Pembrook*, *Carmarthen*, *Brecknock*, and divers others.

16. This model of theirs is in moft parts of the world or many, quite contrary to the Intereft of the Church: and therefore forbidden by God in Nature and Scripture, by that rule, *Let the end be preferred, and the means which beft ferve it: Let all things be done to edification:* For in moft of the world the Rulers are enemies to Chriftianity, and difpofed to perfecute the Paftors of the Church; therefore they will leaft endure Ecclefiaftical Courts and Bifhops in their Imperial Cities, and under their nofes (as we fay) *Obj.* The *Romans* did endure it. *Anf.* For all the ten perfecutions, the *Romans* gave ordinarily more liberty of Religion than moft of the world doth at this day. Bifhops and Paftors, are glad to keep out of the way of Infidel and Heathen Rulers. (And I think verily our moft Zealous Englifh Prelates would be loath, (if they had their language) to go fet up a Church and Bifhops feat at *Madrid*, *Vienna*, *Ingolfted*, yea at *Florence*, *Milan*, *Ravenna*, *Venice*, *Lisbone*, *Warfaw*, &c. And if they muft needs be in thofe Countries, they would rather chofe a more private and lefs offenfive feat.

17. I think that few Churches or Bifhops in the world, except the *Italian* (if they) are of the opinion now oppofed by me. * The *Greek* Church is not: For though for honor fake they retain the name of the ancient Seats, yet they ordinarily dwell in Countrey Villages. And fo doth the *Patriarck* of *Antioch* himfelf often, or at leaft *Antioch* is now no City, of which he hath the name. And *Socrates*, and after him other

Hiftorians

* *Quemadmodum hodie ab aliquot feculis Antioch ina fedes*

Historians tell us, that of old this practise varied as a thing indifferent, *Patr. non* in several Countries according to their several customes, which had no *est in ea* Law of God for them, and therefore were not accounted necessary. *urbe unde*

18. Our English Bishops have been for the most part of another mind *ter, sed in* till Dr. *Hammond* and others turned this way of late: Not only *Jewel,* *Meredin ad* *Bilson* , and many others have asserted that *Patriarks* , *Metropoli-* *tipam Cha-* *tans* and *Primates*, and such like are of human right, and mutable, but *bar, in fi-* few if any were found heretofore to contradict them. And at this day *niliusMelo-* many Bishops ordinarily dwell in their Country houses, (As the Bishop *Jos.* of *Lincolne* did at *Bugden,* the Bishop of *Coventree* and *Lichfield* , (former- *Scaliger* ly) at *Eccleshall* Castle ; the Bishop of *Chester* (now) at *Wigan,* and so *in Eusebs.* of others). And I think that is the Bishops Seat where usually his *pag. 232.* dwelling is, and not where a Lay-Chancellor keepes a Court, or where a Dean and Chapter dwell who are no Bishops.

19. There have (as Dr. *Hammond* hath well proved) been of old several Churches in one City ; one of *Jews* and one of *Gentiles,* with their several Bishops and Clergy. Therefore one City with its terri- tories is not *jure Divino* the measure or boundaries of one only Church.

20. If the Church Government must be modelled to the Civil, then in every Monarchie or Empire there must be one Universal Pastor to rule all the rest as there is one King: And in every Aristocracy, there must be a Synod of Prelates in Church Supremacy ; and in every *De-* *mocracy* —— who or what —— But then the Papacy will be proved not only lawful, but of Divine institution , as the Head or Church Soveraign of the *Roman* Empire (though not of all the world) (at *Rome* first and at *Constantinople* after) And indeed I know no word of rea- son that can be given to draw an impartial man of Judgment to doubt, but that *Metropolitans, Primates, Patriarcks,* and the Pope as Head of the Churches in the Empire, stood all on the same ground, and had the same Original ; as all Fathers Councells and History shew, which true- ly proveth that (as an Universal Papacy is a Treasonable Usurpation, so) an Imperial Papacy (that is, through the *Roman* Empire) is but a human Creature, and *Metropolitans, Patriarcks, &c.* are the like ; and they that will feigne the one to be of Gods institution or necessary, must say that the other is so to.

But after all this, one consequence puts the world in hope that *Dioce-* *sans* may come in time to be reformed : For seeing Kings may make and unmake Cities, and consequently Bishop-pricks at their pleasure, when- ever it shall please his Majesty, or any other wise and Holy Prince, to declare every Corporation and Market Town to be a *City,* we must needs have a Bishop in every one of them (according to the principles of the Prelates themselves. And then the Diocese will not be so great, but a di- ligent Pastor may possibly sometimes, see the greater number of his flock.

Obj. But they that do say that the *Apostles* took this course do not say that it is so obligatory but that in cases of necessity we may do otherwise.

Ans. 1.

Anf. 1. They alledge the very Law of nature for it, that it must be so even in Heathen Empires *ex natura rei*, as Dr. *Hammond* before cited. 2. All meer positves give places to natural duties, *ceteris paribus :* in cases of true necessity we may break the rest of the Lords day, we may omit the Lords Supper, we may stay from the Church assemblies, we may forbear to preach or pray or meditate or read. So that the exception only of necessity will but equal this *Diocesan* model, to other positive ordinances, which are indeed Divine.

Obj. What if we prove but the Lawfulness of it, though not the Duty?

Anf. If you prove it not of Divine institution, I have proved it to be sinful, and shall do much more, by all the evils which attend it. And so much for these City Diocese and Metropolitans and modelling the Church Government to the state.

CHAP. VII.

The Definition and reasons of a Diocesan Church considered, and overthrown.

I Have already shewed, that we dispute not about aery notions, nor Non-existence, but about such Dioceses as we see and have ; and that by a Diocese we Non-conformists mean only a large circuit of ground with its inhabitants conteining many perticular Parishes: And by a *Diocesan* Church, we mean all the Christians within that circuit, who have but one Bishop over them, though they be of many Parish Churches, yea few *Presbyterians* take the word so narrow as this. For (I think too) many of them do with *Rutherford* distinguish between a worshipping Church and a Governed Church (and sadling the horse for Prelacy to mount on) do affirm that many (about twelve usualy) of these worshiping Churches (like our Parishes) may make but one Governed or Presbyterial Church: But a Diocese in England conteineth many hundred, and some above a thousand Parishes (as is said.)

But the *Diocesans* (*Hammond* and *Downam*) define not a Diocese (as we see it) as conteining many Churches or holy assemblies ; but only as being the Church of one City with its territories. Now the question is, what it is that is the specifying difference by which a *Diocesan* Church is distinguished from others, and constituted. 1. Not that it is in a City: For an Independent Church, or a Presbyterian Church may be in a City: When there is but *one Church* there, or many Independent ones, these are no other than those allow, whom you take for your chief adversaries.

2. Is it then the circuit of *ground* that is the boundary of these

Churches, either this ground is inhabited, or not; if not, then earth and trees make their Churches. If inhabited, it is by Infidels, or by Christians, or both. If by Infidels they are no *members* of any Christian Church, and therefore not of a *Diocesan* Church. Unless they will professe to have Churhes of Infidels:

If they be *Christians*, either they are no more, nor more distant than as that they may (at least the main body of them) come on the Lords daies to the City Church into one assembly, or else they are enow to make more or many Church assemblies. If the former, than what differ they from a *Parish Church*, or an *Independent Church*, which is planted in a City? When each of them are but one congregation, where is the difference but in the arbitrary Name?

But if the City and territories have Christians enow for *many Churches*, then either they are formed into many or not. If they are, they should (by their own confession) have many Bishops: If not, either Church Societies are Gods ordinance or not. If not, the City should have none: If they are, where hath God exempted the Country from the priviledge or duty any more than the City?

But if they should say that a *Diocesan* Church is one Church in a City and its territories consisting of Christians enow to make many, of whom the most part take up with oratories for Churches, this would suite our Notion of a *Diocesan* Church, but not theirs. For they say that it is not necessary that a *Diocesan* Church have more than one Congregation.

Therefore it must needs follow that their *Diocesan* Church must differ from our Parish or Congregational Churches only *in potentiâ* and not *in actu*, or else earth or Infidels must be the differencing matter. Unless they will say that the *Order of Prelacy* in it maketh the difference, which is the office of a Pastor who is actually Governour but of one congregation, but is *in potentia* to be the Governour of more when he can convert them, and then is the Governour of them all in that territory when they are converted. But if *one* congregation or *many* make not the difference, a meer possibility in the Infidels of becoming Christians cannot make the difference, because the Subjects of that possibility are no members of the Church at all. Therefore the difference must be only in the office of the Bishop. And if so, then an *Independent* Church that hath a Bishop is a *Diocesan* Church; And so an *Independant* and a *Diocesan* Church may be all one. And then if a Bishop were but setled in a Parish Church in the City or Country, it would make it a *Diocesan* Church. And then when we have proved that the Country should have Churches, and not meer Oratories, and that every Church should have a Bishop, and so that a Bishop is not to be appropriated to a City and its territories, we have done all. And that society which should have all Gods Church ordinances, should have a Pastor necessary for the exercising of them all. Let every true Parish Church, should have

R   al

all Gods ordinances (belonging to a fingle Church) therefore they fhould have a Paftor (at leaft) to exercife them. And, a Paftor authorized to exercife all particular Church ordinances of Chrifts is a true Bifhop. But every true particular Church fhould have fuch a Paftor. Therefore they fhould have a Bifhop. By the *Church ordinances* I mean 1. Teaching. 2. Minifterial Worfhip, in Prayer, Praife and Sacraments. 3. Difcipline fecret and publick in that Church. And let them remember that they that inftead of proof, do but crudely affirme, that Cities only may be Bifhops Seats, do but beg the queftion.

But becaufe he that pu's us hardeft to it (*Downame*) doth lay fo much on thefe two differences of a *Diocefan* Church from a Parochial. 1. That a Diocefe conteineth the City and territories, though at firft it have but one Congregation. 2. That converting the reft of the City and territories, giveth the Bifhop a right to Govern them all : I will further diftinctly confider of both thefe.

CHAP. VIII.

Whether the Infidel Territories or Citizens do make part of a Diocefane Church.

1. WE diftinguifh between a Diocefe and a Diocefane Church. 1. The word Diocefe firft was of civil fignification, and fo we have nothing to do with it. 2. It may fignifie a Country of Infidels whom a Minifter of Chrift endeavoureth to convert : And fo it is no Church of it felf, nor no part of a Church, if a Church be in it : (as is paft all queftion.) And fo we deny not but that, 1. Every Minifter fhould convert as many Infidels as he can. 2. That he that is refident on the place as Paftor of a Cohabiting Church hath better opportunity than a ftranger ufually to convert the neighbour infidels ; And therefore hath more obligation to endeavour it ; becaufe men muft divide and order their work as their opportunities do invite and guide them. 3. But yet that God fet no man his Minifterial Charge by the meafure of ground : And therefore that if fuch a City-Bifhop have a fmaller number of Infidels in his territories, than will take up his time and labour (befides the care of his Church) he ought not to confine his labour to them, nor neglect other territories that need his help, but may, muft and fhould go further in his endeavours, as *Auguftine* and other later Bifhops among the Saxons, notwithftanding the neighbourhood of the Brittains ; and as *Wilfred* alias *Boniface* among the Germans, &c. And if any other Minifter come among the Infidels in the Territories of a City that hath a Church, while they have need of fuch help, the Bifhop were a beaft if he

fhould

should forbid him on pretense that it is his Diocess where another hath nothing to do. But as unoccupied Countries belong to any occupant, so an Infidel Country belongeth to any preacher that hath opportunity to convert them. And if a Diocesane prohibit such preaching, he is to be neglected or reprehended, but not obeyed. Yet I deny not, but prudence may direct preachers (as it would do occupants in the aforesaid case) to distribute their labours so as one may not hinder but help another: But that is not a Law of propriety otherwise than as mutual consent obligeth. And it is, but the determination of circumstances, and that not about any part of a Church, and therefore nothing to the constitution of a Church.

And as is shewed, as Christ sent his Disciples out by two and two, so the Apostles oft went two together, or an Apostle and an Evangelist, which shewed that no one claimed the Diocess. But still, were it otherwise, Infidels are not of the Church.

CHAP. IX.

Whether converting a Diocese give right to the Converter to be their Bishop or Governour.

1: WE deny not, but that Converts owe a peculiar love and respect to those as their fathers in Christ which did convert them; which *Paul* claimeth of the *Corinthians.* 2. And we deny not but *cæteris paribus,* that man being as fit a man as others, and his abode being nearer, and his Church being not full, but capable of them, this advantage should encline his converts, to choose him rather than another for their Pastor,

But yet converting them as such giveth him not a right to govern them as their Pastor, nor necessitateth them to choose him: As I prove.

1. Because a Layman (as *Frumentius* and *Edesius* and *Origen,* &c.) may convert men, who are not Pastors to them or any.

2. Because Conversion and Baptism as such is but mens admission into the *Universal* Church (as in the Eunuchs case, *Act.* 8. is manifest) and not into any particular Church: It uniteth them to Christ, but not to any particular Pastor: For they Baptize not into their own name.

3. Because when two or three go together, as *Paul* and *Barnabas, Silas, Timothy, Luke,* &c. it is to be supposed that one converteth not all, but one some and another some; and therefore it converting gave right there must be many Bishops and Churches in a place.

4. Because when a Church is settled, a strange preacher that converts

R 2

after, yea one that hath a charge elsewhere, may convert many neighbours, that were not Converted, and yet it will not follow that he must come, and set up another Church there for that, nor that they must remove their dwelling to follow him.

Yet I confess that he that converteth men cæteris paribus is 5. Because a man may (and abundance of excellent preachers have done it) convert many souls in many Countries where they go at great distances from each other : But he cannot be the Bishop of so many people or Churches so far dispersed.

fittest to be chosen for their Pastor : on which account Greg. Nazianz. was chosen at Constantinople , for the Success of his Ministry against Arianism : And in my Church-History , I have told you of a Council that decreed, that if a Bishop neglected to turn any of his City from heresie, he that converted them should have them for his flock : which sheweth that there might on just cause be then more Bishops and Churches than one in a City ; and that they were not necessarily measured by the compass of ground, but Churches might be mixt among each other as to habitation, on such occasions.

6. Because it would make it uncertain who it is that hath any where the Episcopal power. For Conversion is, 1. a secret work known only to the person converted. 2. And it is an obscure and usually a gradual work, not done at once, but by such degrees, that the convert seldome knoweth himself who it was that converted him : Though he may know that one mans ministry so far convinced him, and another so far, and so on ; It will be hard to say just when it came to a conversion. And if you say it is he that perswaded him to be baptized, that may be a lay man, or long after his Conversion. Princes in some Countries force or perswade thousands to be baptized. If you say, that it is he that *baptized* him, than *Paul* should be Pastor but to few of the *Corinthians,* who thanked God that he baptized none of them but *Stephanus* houshold, *Gaius* and *Crispus* ; as being not sent to baptize, but to preach the Gospel.

7. Because else many persons should be necessitated to choose a bad or very weak man, if not a heretick for their Bishop, when they may have far better and abler men. For it hath been known that a bad Minister, and a heretical Minister, much more a very weak Minister hath converted men. But God doth not allow such converts therefore to cast their Souls under the danger and disadvantage of such a ones Ministry, or oversights when much fitter may be had.

8. Because both nature and Scripture example direct men to another course ; that is, 1. To be members of the Church where they are cohabitants, if there be a worthy Pastor ; 2. And to get the best they can. For cohabitation or proximity or vicinity is necessary to Church ends, both to publick and private communion and mutual help. But the Minister that converth them may dwell far off, that.

Therefore indeed the Reasons why all in a City and vicinity were wont to be of the same Church (if there were room) was not because that Minister converted them, but because they were fit for such Communion by cohabitation.

2. And.

9. And were it otherwise the Bishop and his Presbyters preaching to the same people, the Presbyter might convert more and become joint Bishop.

10. And certainly it would unbishop all the English Bishops almost that I am acquainted with, who nether converted their Dioceses from Infidelity, nor baptized them, nor convert many that ever we hearof from a wicked life, to serious holiness: which the Presbyters have done by very many, and so must there be made the Bishops (if they would.)

CHAP. X.

That a particular Church of the first or lowest order, must consist of Neighbour Christians associated for Personal Communion in local presence, in holy worship and conversation; and not of strangers so remote, as have only an Internal Heart-Communion, or an External Communion by the mediation of others.

LEt it be here noted (that none dally with the Name [Church] as an equivocal, that, 1. I speak of no meer Community of Christians, nor of any accidentall assembly, which have no Pastors, or no intent of sacred ends; Call them what you will: But of a proper Christian society constituted of the *Pars gubernans* and the *Pars gubernata*; the Pastor and Flock. 2. That I speak not of a Family Church, which consisteth of the Master and the Family. 3. Nor yet of the Universal Political Church, as visible or as mystical: which consisteth of Christ the head, and all visible or sincere believers. 4. Nor of any *Christian Churches* confined by Agreement for *Concord of Churches*, being many. 5. Nor of any such Churches accidentaly united in one kingdom, under one king or Civil Governor, whether Christian or Infidel. 6. Nor of many Churches headed by humane appointment with one Metropolitane, Primate or Patriack, being a Pastor thus exalted by men above the rest. 7. Nor yet of many Churches under one Arch-Bishop or general Apostolical Visitor or Pastor, claiming this general oversight by Divine right (whether rightly or wrongfully I now take no notice) 8. But the Church which I treat of is, only the political society of Christians of the first ranck (and so of a Bishop of the lowest ranck, or a meer Bishop that is no Arch-Bishop). Not of an Oratory, or Chappel of ease, where part of a true Church often meet; but of a true entire Church of the first magnitude or rank.

And I take it for granted 1. That such Churches there should be, 2.

R 3

and

and that every true Church should have its Bishop, as Doctor *Hammond* and many others grant, taking the Church in this political notion; or if that be not granted I will proove it further anon.

And that these lowest true political or Organized Churches, must be Neighbours united for Personal Communion, as aforesaid, I prove.

1. First from all the Scripture instances: The Churches at *Jerusalem*, *Antioch*, *Ephesus*, *Corinth* &c. were all such as is fuller to be opened in the 2d. Part.

2. From the instances of all the Churches of the first and second age, of which also more is after to be said.

3. From the dutyes of Church members, which are as followeth.

1. To assemble together for Gods publick service; *Act.* 4. *Heb.* 10. 25. 1. *Cor.* 14. &c. And how can they do this that are utterly out of reach, and never know or see each other ?

2. To have the same Pastors that are among them, and over them, and preach to them the word of God, and go before them by the example of an holy life. 1 *Thef.* 5. 12, 13. *Heb.* 13. 7, 17, 24. 1 *Tim.* 3. 6, 7, &c. And how can they hear the Pastors that never Preach to them, or be Guided by those that never see them, or follow their example whom they never knew, or come for counsel to them that are out of their reach and knowledg ?

3. To send to their Pastors when they are sick, to pray with them, and advise them: which they cannot do to them that are out of their reach. *Jam.* 5. 4. To provoke one another to Love and to good works, and to *consider* one another (*κατανοωμεν*) to that end: A word that signifieth *knowledge* and more, even *Observation* of that which we see or know. In which and *v.* 25. saith Dr. *Hammond* [*Let us weigh and consider all advantages we can have upon one another to provoke and excite one another to Charity and all actions of piety, such as are joyning in the publick service. And not suffer our selves to proceed so far towards defections as to give over the publick assemblies, (the forsaking of which is not is not only deserting the publick profession of Christ, but also of the meanes of growth in grace) but stir up one another to the performance of this*] All which suppose propinquity, and and consist not with the distance of uncapable strangers. *Heb.* 3. 13. *To exhort one another daily while it is called to day, left any be hardened by the deceitfulness of sin.* Which we cannot do by men of another Countrey, with whom we have no converse.

All is plainly expressed, 1 *Thef* 5. 11. 12, 13. *Wherefore comfort your selves together, and edifie one another even as also ye do. And we beseech you brethren to know them which labour among you, and are over you in the Lord, and admonish you, and to esteem them very highly in love, for their work sake,* and to be at *peace among your selves.* But how can they comfort themselves together that never came together, or see each other ? There can no peace but Negative be among them, that are not among each other, and have no converse. They cannot edifie utter strangers. How can I know the

Bishop

Bilhop of the Diocefe who never faw him, nor ever had opportunity to see him, tho I live about an hundred miles neerer him (being at *London*) than fome parts of his Diocefe are? I know thofe that *Labour among us* in this Parilh, but the Bilhop never laboured among us, nor was here that ever I heard of; nor do I know one in the Parilh, that ufeth not to *Travaile*, that ever faw him, and few that by hearfay know his name.

Rom. 15.7. 14. *Receive ye one another as Chrift alfo received us, to the Glory of God.* 6. *That ye may with one mind and one mouth glorifie God* —— of which faith Dr. *Hammond*, [*That ye may joyn unanimoufly* Jews *and* Gentiles *into one, and affembling together, worlhip and ferve the Lord, wherefore in all humility of condefcenfion and kindnefs, embrace and fuccour one another, help them up when they are fallen, inftead of defpifing and driving them from your communion v.* 14. [*Able alfo to admonilh one another fo* Col. 3. 16. *Teaching and admonilhing one another in Pfalms, and Hymns* —— But more of this in the 2d. part.

5. Laftly it is their part to admonilh a brother that offendeth, and if he hear not, to take two or three witneffes, and if he hear not to tell the Church *Matth.* 18. 15. (of which fee Dr. *Hammonds Annot.* and of the Keys). But all this requireth perfonal knowledge and propinquity.

Obj. *It is not neceffary to the being of Church members, that every one that is a Church member know them: many in* London *know not their next Neighbours.*

Anf. I fpeak not. 1. Of the Act, but of the *Power* or *Capacity* and the *Relation* with its end. 2. I fpeak not of every member, but of fo great a part as denominateth the Church.

1. As a Paftor who by ficknefs or other impediment preacheth not of a long time, may yet be a Paftor, becaufe he hath. 1. The Power. 2. And a Relation whofe end is the Inftructing of the Flock. 3. And he intendeth the exercife as foon as the impediment is removed (or if lazynefs or any culpable neglect be the caufe, that altereth not the nature of the office, but proveth him faulty): So a member that is. 1. Capable. 2. Related to the end, may be a member, though neglect or impediments keep them from the exercife of much of that which they otherwife may do. He that dwelleth in the Neighborhood may do all thefe Offices to another, if he will, when opportunity calleth for it; and therefore may be fo obliged to it: But fo cannot he that dwelleth out of reach. Citizens or members of Corporations are in a capacity for offices belonging to the fociety, though fome may neglect them, and others want opportunity to do them; but one out of reach is uncapable of the duty and therefore *uncapable* of the Relation, which is made up of *obligation* to that duty when there is caufe. The *Relation* is effentially a *Power* and *obligation* to the Duty: And the *Difpofitio materie* is neceffary to the *reception* of the *forme.* He therefore that is not in a capable means by *cohabitation*, is not *materia*

materia disposita, and can neither have *Power* nor *obligation* to the dutyes of a Church member towards the rest, and so cannot have the Relative form, or be indeed a member. And therefore all that write judiciously of the definition of a particular Church, do make Propinquity or Cohabitation, to be the *Dispositio materiæ sine qua non*; From which they are called *Parishioners*. They are not a Church because a *Parish*; but they are therefore the *materia disposita* as to this part of the capacity extrinsick (Christianity being it that maketh them intrinsecally fit materials).

2. And I deny not but some few members may be several waies uncapable naturally of the ordinary offices of members: Some by infancy, some by distraction, some by sickness, some by the restraint of Parents Masters or Husbands, and some by a retired disposition, &c. And some Churches may be so sinfully over-great, as that the number hindereth many of the members from a capacity of the ordinary duty of the relation; which is the case of some great Parishes in *London*: But either this is the case of the greater part and main body of the Society, or but of a few. If but of a few, it may prove it a *disordered* Church, but it cannot prove it *no Church*; no more than a few Hereticks can denominate the Church *Heretical*, or a few mad, or leprous persons, can denominate it mad or leprous, or than the family of *Noah*, *David*, *Christ*, was denominated from a *Cham*, an *Absolom*, a *Judas*. But if it be the main body (though in intrinsick qualifications, the Church may be denominated from the *better* part sometimes and not from the greater, yet) in extrinsick qualifications, it is now to be denominated a Church only from the Pastor and that number who are capable of the relation (as being the two constitutive parts) and all the rest are none of the Church: And if there be no such *body* united to the Pastor for true Church ends, and capable of them, it is no Church.

Obj. But it is enough to make one *Church*, if they be all united in one *Bishop* or *Governour*, though their distance make them uncapable of knowing one another, and doing what you have described.

Ans. It is enough indeed to make a Church of another *species*, such as I before named, either the Catholick Church throughout the world, or a Church composed of many particular Churches (if it may be called a Church): Because their Communion is not to be Local or *present*, nor to the ends of a particular Church; but only intrinsical in Faith and Love, and extrinsical by Delegates or Mediators. But this is not enough to the *being* of a Church of the first order which now we speak of, which should have a Bishop of their own, and is not composed of many united Churches. For else the Church of a Patriark or a Primate, or an Arch-Bishop or Metropolitane, should be a Church of the first order, and have no Church or Bishop under it. For such a Church is united in one Governour. (To say nothing of the Papal Church, which yet pretendeth not to depose all Bishops.) Therefore the unity of the Governour

will

will not suffice of it self to make one Primary Church ; though it may make one Compounded or General Church conteining many Churches and Bishops. 2. And the nature of the thing telleth us, that as the *People*, have their *Duties* and *Priviledges* as well as the Pastors, so the people must be united among themselves, by some common Relation, conteining *Power* of and *Obligation* to that duty, and capacity of that priviledge : Which is past all *doubt* among knowing men. Therefore an uncapable body cannot be made one Primary Church, by the unity of a Prelate. 3. But as we distinguish of a *Church single* and *compounded of many, particular and General, Primary and Secondary*, (all which termes I use to be clearly understood), so do we also of Bishops or Pastors : which are *particular* Bishops of one Church , or *General* Bishops of many Churches. Of the first sort we confess all that is said positively, that is, that *one such Bishop* maketh one *Church*. Because the very nature of his office, as shall be after shewed, doth suppose a capable society. It being his office in presence personally to conduct them ; which a General distant Bishop cannot do, so that indeed, *one Present Pastor* (or more) of a *flock by Christianity and Vicinity capable, and by consent united with him and one another for presential Communion in publick worship and holy conversation*, are the constitutive parts by which a Primary Church is essentiated and must be defined.

Obj. *But even the Presbyterians say that many worshiping congregations may make up one Governed Church, though each congregation have ordinary Communion in the Sacrament, &c. among themselves distinct from the rest ; because they may be all united in the Government of one Presbytery. And our ordinary Parishes have Chappels in them, and yet are one Church.*

Ans. 1. We must be excused from submitting now to the opinions of *Presbyterians* or any other party, while we are giving an account of our own judgment in the case.

2. The *Presbyterians* are not all of a mind in that point, whether each of those Parishes be not a true political Church, and have not its own plenary Pastor or Bishop, and such a Government as belongeth to a particular Church, though (as they all think) subordinate to a *Presbytery* of many Churches conjunct (or as some call it) of one Church denominated so from the higher Government.

3. And as to our Chappels ordinarily they are but places for the Assembling of such as by age or foul weather or weakness cannot travaile to the Parish Churches, and they are for distance and number in those Parishes that have them, no more or other, than may consist not only with the personal acquaintance of the members of the Parish Church, but also with the frequent Communion of them all , *by turnes* in the same Parish Church, if they please to travaile to it, as they may. So that these *Chappels of ease*, as they are commonly called, are not inconsistent with all the fore-described ends and dutyes of Church-members : And even the Independants do confess, that age, distance , persecution, &c.

S

may

may allow one of their Churches to meet at once in several houses or places, where several Pastors may *pro tempore* officiate : and yet, this consisteth with all the forementioned ends of the relation.

4. And indeed disorders and confusions in Churches, must not be our measure, to judge of their Nature and constitution by, though one in a Swoone may be hardly discerned from a dead man, yet life is nevertheless essential to a man. The Principalities in *Germany* may be so curtailed, and intangled, that it shall be hard, for Lawyers to judge whether the Princes be proper Soverains and Monarchs or not. And yet what doth constitute Monarchy and Soveraignity is known. A Ship may be made so little, and a Barge so big, as that it may be hard to distinguish them by name : and yet a Ship and Barge are divers. If in one great house, there be several men with their Wives Children and Servants, in several rooms or parts, and one have some superiority over the rest, they being free journy-men or labourers under him, the degree of the Power of the chief Master here may be in several cases so various, as that it shall be hard for any man to say, whether this be *one Family* only or *many*. But must we therefore remove all distinction of Families, or forsake the old and usual definition. The same I say of *Primary perticular Churches*. *Stepney* Parish, or *Giles Criplegate*, or *Martins* in the fields may be so great, as to make a doubt of it, whether they are single Churches ; and so may some *Lancashire* Parishes, that have very distant and large Chapelries. But shall the disease or extaordinary case, or dicffiulty of such a Parish, make us change the old and true definition of a Church?

And thus some Presbyterians have argued from the Multitude of Converts at *Jerusalem* and *Ephesus*, that they could not be one particular Church, so as to meet all in one place (which is the common and strongest objection against us). But 1. undoubtedly there were many strangers there, that were ready to pass away to other places. 2. And the Spirit knew that the Church was quickly by persecution to be scattered. 3. And on a suddain there was not time to settle them in exact order, as afterward they did in all the Churches. *Acts.* 14. 23. But many Apostles being there they might transiently have divers meetings at once. 4. And the number and distance of them all was no greater then might consist with the forementioned Church Ends and *definition*. They that meet one day with one Apostle, might meet the next day with another, and might have *Personal Communion* and *Conversation*. And 5. The text saith that they did meet all in one place : and as Doctor *Hammond* aforecited saith, they deny the plain text that do deny it : they were not distributed into divers assembles ; and the [*All*] *that meet together*, must mean the *greater part* of the Church members at once. And I my self have Preached to a Congregation, supposed by understanding persons in it, to be six thousand, and all to have heard : and as many more might have heard the next day : and so twenty thousand might make a Church, when vicinity maketh them otherwise capable ; and in *Judea* we find that men speaking to Armies, yea the Enemies Armies, shew that far more could hear at once, then can do with us (whether voices or aire did make the difference I Know not) and if the fore-named Parishes that have but one ordinary meeting place, have 30000 or 40000 or 50000 souls in them, we may conjecture at the case of *Jerusalem* hereby; For though among those new Converts, there were not so many neglecters of the Assemblies, yet the passing strangers might be many.

To make the case plain, I would but desire the dissenters to consider. 1. Whether that Gods publick worship be not a duty? Even the Communion of Christians in Doctrine, Prayer and Sacrament?

2. Whether there must not be some present Pastors to officiate before the Church in all these?

3. Whether this Congregation must not be Christians, and persons qualified for Communion? and whether the Churches have not alwaies (by the holy Spirits appointment) differenced between *Christians* and Infidels, and between Heretical or flagitious persons, and the orderly and obedient? and admitted the first sort only to Communion?

4. Whether he that is present and delivereth the Sacrament, should not know what he doth, and to whom he giveth it, and should not in the administring make a difference, and keep away the Infidels, Hereticks and openly flagitious, and should not know the people whom he overseeth?

5. And whether he can do all or any of this, to a transient multitude, that as the waters of a river are passing away, when he still seeth strange faces only, and those are his Auditors, and Commuicants, whom he never saw before, or knoweth: how can he know whether they are Baptized Christians, or unbaptized, Jews or other Infidels?

6. Therefore is not an ordinary Cohabitation, or vicinity, of necessity to a fixed Church and Pastor, that he may know them, and they may know each other? These things I suppose are past dispute.

7. And then I ask whether such a society as this be not a true Church? and such as is described in scripture? and such as should ordinarily be continued in the world? whether it be part of a more compounded general Church, and under the general oversight of Apostolical Bishops, is none of my question now; but whether this be not an ordinary political Church, of the first order?

8. And if so, whether every such Church by *Acts.* 14. 23. should not have such Elders as are there mentioned, which Doctor *Hammond* maintaineth to be Bishops? or should not have such *Episcopos gregis* overseers of this flock, as are impowered to do all the foresaid works of their proper Office? of which next.

CHAP.

CHAP. XI.

That a Bishop or Pastor of a particular Church of the first rank afore-described, must Govern it statedly, as present by himself, and not as in absence by another.

[Holy Chry-]
[sostom de]
[sacerdotio]
[cap.17.p.57]
[Even about]
[so small a]
[part of a]
[Bishops or]
[Pastors]
[charge as]
[the care of]
[Virgins.]
[faith. But if]
[any one say]
[that there is]
[no need of a]
[Bishop to]
[meddle]

NOthing hath more deceived men (next to Infidelity and Carnality) in this controversie, than want of *experience*: Judging by a noise of words of such matters as they never faithfuly tryed. Had men well tryed a few years what it is to do the Office of a Pastor, they would easily know to whom it belongeth. But when either University students, or Nominal Pastors do stand by and look on, or read and hear only of the *name* of Church-Power and Government, and never did more themselves, than to preach and say the service of the Church, or now and then visit a sick man, or dine or talk on the by with a neighbour, or at most hear Children say their Catechism, it is no wonder if they talk at randome, and think that a man may be the only Bishop of many hundred Churches, and Govern them *per alios*, or at twenty, or fourty, or an hundred miles distance, by meer visiting or meeting the Clergy, and dining with them once in three Years.

with such things as these; Let him know that upon him will fall all the cares of Virgins duty, and so all the accusations which shall be cast on Virgins: And therefore it is much better if he administring the business himself he shall be void of those causes, which he must susteine by others offences; thus leaving that administration to live in fear of giving account or being judged for the sins which others do commit. Adde also, that he that performeth this office by himself, transacteth all with great facility. But he that is necessitated to do it by the vicarious labour of others, besides that it is a great business to him to perswade all mens minds well to performe the work; certainly he himself hath not so much remission of his labour by abstaining from that office, as he must sustaine business and troubles from them that resist, and strive against his judgment and opinion.] And if so great a Bishop as the Patriarks of Constantinople *must not do so small a part of his work* per alios, alas, *what a life do our Diocesans live!*

I shall here therefore prove that the nature of the *Primary Episcopacy (* or *Particular,* if the word *Primary* be cavilled at *)* is such, as cannot be done in *absence*, nor *per alios* by substitutes, in any of its *Proper parts*, but only by a *present Bishop* or *Pastor* himself.

And here first remember that I say [*in any of its proper parts*, as distinguishing the proper works of the sacred Ministry, from those that are *common* to other men, and those that are but Accidents or Circumstantial. As a Bishop may plow his land, or build his house, or saddle his horse, by another, so I doubt not but he may appoint another to toll the Bell to Church, to cover the holy Table, to receive Collections, to read Proclamations, to keep the Church doors, to repair the building, to bring relief to the Poor, to do that about sacred things, which is common to Lay men

with

with Minifters; even to read the Pfalm, to chufe it, to fet the tune, to publifh Marriages, to name to the people the times of meeting, to read the Scriptures, to be meffengers to fummon accufed offenders, to tell the Church, to fummon witneffes, to hear witneffes and confeffions; All thefe he may appoint a fervant or another to do, becaufe they are but accidental to his Office, and no part of his proper work; but that his *proper work* muft be done by *himfelf*, and that as prefent ordinarily with the people whom he Governeth, the enumerations of the particular will evince.

1. The work of fuch a Bifhop is Publick in the facred Affemblies.

2. Or out of the Affemblies by way of application to particular Perfons and cafes.

1. In the Affemblies, 1. It is the Bifhops office to be the *chief Teacher* of the Church; to preach, inftruct, exhort and comfort them ufually himfelf; And when he doth it not himfelf to appoint another, and judge of his performance. (I fhall referve the proof to the 2d. part, where all this is to be reviewed to a further ufe.) And this is the work of one that is prefent.

2. He is to be the mouth or Interceffor of the people, as a Prieft under Chrift the Great high Prieft and Interceffor: To pray in the Affembly, to be their mouth in the common confeffion of fins: To praife God and give thanks with and for them; to whom they are to joyn in confent with their Amen, (at leaft.) And this is the work of a *prefent* Perfon.

3. He is to Baptize and admit perfons into the vifible Church; Or to try and judg who is fit to be Baptized, and to admit them by fome other Minifter of Chrift; but he can neither Baptize, nor try and judge particularly who is to be baptized (at leaft of the Adult) unlefs he be prefent and know the perfons, and hear his confeffion and receive his claime.

4. He is to Celebrate the Supper of the Lord, to confecrate the Bread and Wine, to be the Meffenger of Chrift in his name to deliver them as his body and blood, and the Seals of his Love, and of Remiffion of fins unto the people, and fo to commemorate his death till he come, and as his Steward to give his houfehold meat in feafon; but this is all the work of a *Prefent* and not an *abfent Perfon*.

5. He is to be the judge of the claime and title of the perfons that come to the Churches Communion; to fee that Infidels and incapable perfons be not there, which is not well done by one that is not ordinarily prefent, even in the Adminiftration to fee to whom it is adminiftred.

6. He is to be the chief publick reprover, and admonifher of Scandalous perfons by name, who are fo to be openly reproved and admonifhed in the Church, which he cannot well do if he be not in the Church himfelf.

S 3   7. He

7. He is to be the chief publick Excommunicator of the obstinately wicked, to declare before all that such a person is uncapable of communion with the Church: which is not well done by one that is not there to do it; as shall anon be further opened.

8. The same is to be said of publick Absolution, when the Penitent is publikely taken into the Church, or judged and declared to be Absolved.

That Christ Mat. 18. in his tell the Church, meaneth tell the con- gregation, assembly or multitude, and not only go tell an ab- sent Dioce- san Bishop (when per- haps one must go 20, 40,50 miles to tell him), see Grotius himself in his Annot. on the Text and his proof out of Tertullian and others. See also Erasmus on the place. And many others say the same, though some would have

9. And the blessing of the people in the name of the Lord, at the dismission of the Assembly hath of old been reserved to the Bishop as his part which is to be done by one that is there present.

11. And as for those acts of *Application* to persons and cases which are to be done out of the Assembly, 1. To be at hand for the people to repair to in their greater doubts for resolution, and greatest difficulties for direction (as a Physician among the sick) is not the least part of the true Bishops work. And this requireth his usual presence and some acquaintance usually with the persons life: No man will expect that all such doubting people travaile to a strange Bishop many score miles distant, or out of their reach.

2. To hear the confessions and cases of burdened penitent souls and to direct them in the true way to peace and comfort, is a special part of the Bishops work besides his resolution of Doctrinal doubts which requireth presence, and acquaintance (usually) with the person.

3. It is part of the Bishops work to watch over the peoples conversa- tion, and to see that they live not in mortal sins or scandalous courses; and to reprove them that do, and draw them to repentance. And all this is a present persons work.

4. It is the Bishops work to see that the families of the flock be or- dered in the fear of God, and that Parents and Masters do their duties, and indulge not wickedness in their houses, which is also a present per- sons work.

5. It is the Bishops work to visit the sick and to pray with and for them, which requireth presence.

the Church to be only the Bishop, or as others the Presbytery. Rutherfords contrary reason is but a fallacy, viz. [The same Church that must be heard must be told, but it is not the Congregation but the Elders that must be heard. Ergo &c. Ans. The Church consisting of the Pastor and people must be told, and they have all ears that without confusion can hear at once, but they cannot without confusion all speak at once, there- fore one must speak for all. For this argument would equally prove that it is not any Presbytery or Court, or many Ministers that should be told, if it be but one that is to speak to the sinner: And it is not necessary that they all speak to him. As the chief Judge speaketh for all the Bench, and the Prolocutor for all the Synod, and yet the Court or Synod may be complained to; so is it here: The same man may see with two eyes and hear with two ears, and yet speak but with one tongue (yet this reason once deceived me.) Seeing then that Christ, instituted thus much of discipline in each particular Church; it is clear that by his institution every particular Church (associated for presential Communion) should have one or more pastors authorized for so much discipline which is that which we plead for.

6. It

6. It is the Bishops work to stir up the people that are dull and backward to their several duties, in publick and in private, and to provoke them to love and to good works which is the work especially of *present* and not of absent men.

7. And it is his duty to have a special care of the poor, and to see that they be relieved; which he will never do well in absence and to the unknown.

8. And it is confessed to be the Bishops work to admonish the unruly, to reprove and exhort ungodly persons, to convince gainsayers, to hear the accused speak for themselves, to hear what accusers and witnesses say against them; which requireth presence, as shall be further shewn anon.

Obj. Other men may examine witnesses and reprove offenders; therefore this may be committed to another.

Ans. Other men may do it on another obligation, in another manner, to another end: But to do it from the Pastoral obligation, in a Pastoral manner; to Pastoral ends, is proper to the Pastors of the Church.

Obj. A Bishop may receive accusations by presentments, or by information, and may summon offenders, examine witnesses, and judge at a distance of persons that are to him unknown.

Ans. He may do what he can that way, when necessity hindereth him from doing better, but not with any true satisfaction to God, the Church or Conscience to discharge the office of a particular Church Bishop. In case of *title* to lands or goods a civil Judicature may judge of persons that are unknown: Because the title dependeth not on the moral qualities of the persons: And in criminal cases where the question to be judged or resolved is, whether the person shall live or die, or shall be fined, imprisoned, banished or not, the case may be judged of unknown persons *secundum allegata & probata*: For outward punishments must go upon outward proved crimes, and the Judges can possibly do no more, because about twelve must judge a whole Kingdome. And yet even there they greatly regard *qua mente*, with what mind and intent the deed was done, and they greatly regard the moral qualifications of a Witness as to his credibility, as far as they can find it out. But in Church cases, it is mens consciences that are to be wrought upon. The first intention of the Pastor is to bring the sinner to repentance; yea though he continued impenitent never so long before, he is not to be excommunicated till at the present also he shew impenitency. Therefore it is more necessary to be acquainted with the person, and many an admonition or exhortation (ordinarily) should go before. And when it cometh to excommunication, the principal part of that Act is to acquaint the Congregation that the impenitent person is unfit for Church communion, and to charge and exhort them to avoid him. And to do this it is necessary that the Church be taught to abhor the sin, and to do it in abhorrence

horrence of the sin, and therefore that they be convinced that the person is such a one indeed. For seeing God commandeth them to Love all the faithful and to live with them in the exercises of that Love in peace, if Godly men be unjustly excommunicated, by a Diotrephes, who receiveth them not and excommunicateth such as do receive them, the Church must not disobey God in obeying such a wicked excommunicater. And though its true, that for order sake, they must oft rest satisfied in the Pastors judgment, when they have no reason to question it; Yet it is as true, that it is a thing to be done before the Congregation, that they may not only exercise a bare obedience to the Pastor in it, but also an abhorrence of the sin, which they cannot do that have no satisfactory notice of the case; And also that all suspitions of injustice and Church tyranny in their Pastors may be avoided: And that the offender may be convinced before all, that he may be ashamed: And seeing no man is to be excommunicated for any ordinary great sin, without impenitency in it; so that the question is not then so much whether the man have sinned, as whether he be Penitent, what man of any experience in these matters can believe that a Bishops, or a Chancellors Court among strangers, and also when he is in fear of being imprisoned and utterly undone if he be excommunicated, is so fit to try a mans repentance, as the face of the Congregation where he is known, and hath no such motives to constrain him to lie, and use hypocrisie. Nay in very truth such judicatures may as easily know beforehand, that all the impenitent persons that almost ever come before them, (who are not conscientious persons that take the sin for a duty) will say they *repent*, and play the dissemblers, as that a Child will cry for forgiveness to escape a whipping.

Obj. But is it not so much the better? The Church must have hypocrites: we cannot change the heart; that belongs to God: If we bring men to profess repentance it is all thats our part to do.

Ans. Hypocrites that cannot be lawfully detected must be in the Church: But we must not therefore make men hypocrites, that they may be in it; and constrain them to apparent lying, and then make lying to be the Church Title, and the very constituting qualification of a visible Christian; else you may set men on the rack till they say they repent, and then absolve them and pronounce them the pardoned Sons of God; which will be a surer way than an imprisonment. And in this practice this doctrine which I leave all Christians to judge of, is included, [*Every Blasphemer, Heretick Adulterer, Drunkard,* &c. who had rather say that he repenteth, than lie in a Gaol and be undone, ought to be a communicating member of the Church, and to be declared pardoned by absolution.

Yea if there were no Penalty, the face of strangers is no fit trial of repentance. If the sinner be obstinate, he will easilier stand it out before strangers that know him not, than before the Congregation which is acquainted with his guilt. But usually he will think, that it is no great shame to say, I *repent* before a few strangers, who are never like to see him more.

more, and therefore this he will easily yield to, that would not yield to confession and repentance before the Church that is acquainted with them: Experience proveth all this to be true: And I regard not their reasonings which are against common experience.

Obj. But we see that many now will rather stand it out, and go to prison, than they will profess repentance before a Bishop, or at a chancellours Court.

Ans. But who be those? Not drunkards or fornicators or any wicked livers: But men that more fear to sin against God, who can cast both soul and body into Hell, than to lie in prison: perhaps it is such Ministers as now are silenced for not saying, subscribing or swearing as they are bid: or it is some Church-Wardens who fear that they should be guilty of *Persecution* or *Perjury* (which in their opinion are neither of them *things indifferent*) if they should take the Oaths with the Articles that sometimes are offered them. Or perhaps it is some one for not receiving the Sacrament, either when a troubled Conscience maketh them fear lest they should eat and drink damnation to themselves, or from a Minister, or with a Church, which they think the Scripture commandeth them to avoid: whether such be in the right or in the wrong, no wonder if they refuse to repent, though they suffer, when they fear a greater suffering from God.

Obj. But the Minister of the place, though he excommunicates none, may seek to bring the sinner to repentance, and may satisfie the Church of the justness of the excommunication.

Ans. 1. In the nature of the thing, they go together, and are the work of the same persons: And therefore *Tertullian* assureth us, that in his time, Discipline was exercised in the Church-meeting, when they had been worshipping God. 2. Who is either so fit, or so obliged to satisfie the Church of the Act, as he that doth it, and hath examined all the Cause? A parish Minister cannot bring any unwilling person to come over to speak with him, (not that we would have him have a forcing power: but he cannot do his own Ministerial part, which is to refuse to be the Pastor of such a man as refuseth to speak with him at all, or to take him for his Pastor, nor to forbear himself to give him the Sacrament): so that he that neither heard the examination of the Cause by the Chancellor, nor perhaps can have any speech with the person, or at least with the Accuser, or any of the Witnesses, is very unfit to justifie another mans act, and to satisfie the Church that it is well done; much less to exhort the offender to repent, who to him perhaps (if he vouchsafe to speak to him) will justifie his own cause, when he cannot call witnesses to convince him. And (to speak to that which is our common case) we have few persons excommunicated (that ever I saw or knew of in forty years time) save only the Conscientious persons beforementioned: And when the parish Minister oft taketh them for the godliest persons in his Parish, and the Bishop or Chancellor excommunicates them as Impe-

nitent fchifmaticks, how fhall fuch a parifh Minifter juftifie that, and fatisfie the perfon or people of the juftice of it, which he himfelf lamenteth as a hainous fin, which tendeth to the diffipation of his
flock.

But I come nearer to enquire into this *officiating per alium* by which
an *abfent Bifhop* is fuppofed to do his office in the feveral Parifhes of his
Diocefe.

1. That *alius* or Official is either a *Layman*, or a *Clergyman*. 2. If a
Clergyman, he is either one of the *fame Order with the Bifhop* or *another*.
3. Either it is the meer accidentals of his facred function, which he
committeth to another, or the *proper Acts* of it. 4. Either it is *pro hac
vice* in fome cafe of neceffity, or it is as by an ordinary ftated Official.

1. If it be a Layman and the work be but Accidental or Extrinfick
to the facred function, I grant that he may do it: But for fuch works
we need no Bifhop: For what a Layman may do when he bids him, he
may do when the *King* or his Magiftrates bids him. This is not the
thing in queftion. But if it be a *proper Paftoral Act*, this Layman that
doth it, either receiveth from *the Bifhop power and obligation to do it*, or
not. If *not*, he cannot do it as his Official: If he do, then he is a *Paftor* or *Bifhop* himfelf, and is *Ordained*, and fo no *Layman*: For I provoke
any diffenter living to tell me wherein the facred office (or any other)
lieth, but in a *Power* (or *Authority*) and an *Obligation to do the proper works*
of that office, fo that undeniably here is a contradiction.

And if any were of opinion that *pro tempore* in a cafe of neceffity a
Layman might do any Minifterial facred act, as Preach, Baptize, Confecrate the Sacrament of Chrifts body and blood, excommunicate, abfolve, *&c.* 1. I anfwer, if that were true, it would but prove that thofe
Acts are not *proper* to the facred function in fuch a cafe of neceffity as
fingle Acts, but only as ordinarily and ftatedly done by one feparated
to them. 2. And therefore this would not at all concern our cafe,
which is not about extraordinary Acts in cafes of neceffity, but
about an ordinary ftated courfe, by Courts, Chancellors, and Officials.

2. But if the Agent or Official were not a Lay Chancellor but a
Clergyman, if he be of the fame *Order* with the Bifhop, than I grant all,
for it granteth me all; even that every Church fhould have an (ordinarily) prefent Bifhop. But if he be fuppofed to be but of an inferi-
or Order, then I proceed as before; either the Bifhop giveth him *power*
and *obligation* to do the *proper work* of the Bifhop or not: If nor, he is
not hereby enabled to do it. If yea, then he hath thereby made him
a Bifhop: For to be a Bifhop is nothing elfe than to *have Authority* and
Obligation to do the proper *work* of a Bifhop. But if it be but an *Accidental* or a *common* work, which another may do, it is not that in queftion, nor do we need the Office of a Bifhop for it.

More-

Moreover either the Bishop *pro hic & nunc* was himself obliged to do that *Act* which he committeth to another, or not he but the *other* was by office obliged to do it. If he himself was obliged to do it, he sinned in not doing it. If he were not, it was not truly his act or part of his office work: nor did he do it by another, but that other did only his own work; for which not the Bishop, but he shall have the reward.

Obj. *But doth not he that sendeth his servant to pay a debt, himself in Law-sense pay it per alium? what another doth as his Instrument, reputatively he doth himself.*

Ans. I grant it; because it is none of the debtors proper work, nor is he at all obliged to it, to bring the money and deliver it himself, but to cause it to be delivered : Therefore in *sending* it, he doth all that he is obliged to do, and when another is his instrument, it is supposed that he is not obliged himself to do that which his instrument doth, but only to *cause* the doing of it, by himself or an Instrument, as he please: so that still this is nothing to the case of a work that is proper to the Bishops Office.

Obj. *But we therefore grant that it is not proper to the Bishops Office to Judge, Excommunicate, or Absolve, but only to Rule the Action, by giving another power to do it.*

Ans. 1. If so, then nothing but Commissioning others, is the proper work of the Episcopal order: and then any Presbyter may *in foro interno vel externo* ordinarily exercise the whole power of the Keys upon the flocks, he may Excommunicate and absolve publikly, as an act common to his Office with the Bishops, if it please the Bishop to give him *Power*, which he may do without making him a Bishop. And if so, I enquire whether God be not the maker of the Presbyters office, and not the Bishop? and whether God only (describing it) give not all the power by way of Law, Charter or Institution, and the Bishop give it not only by way of ministerial solemnization and investiture ? and if so, whether he that is duely called to the Pastoral office, which God only made and described, must not (in season) do the works of that office? whether men commission him or not ? or whether at least he any more need the Bishops commission for Church Government, Excommunication and Absolution, than for Preaching and Celebrating the Lords supper, seeing both are now thus confessed acts common to the order of the Presbyter and the Bishop? I think all this is past contradiction

And I ask then whether that *all giving of power to another* be proper to the Bishops order? If yea, than a Minister cannot give his Clerk power to chuse the Psalm, or tune, &c. If not, then may not a Bishop if he please also give power to the Presbyters to *ordaine*, and to give other men power ? For if it be his proper work only to *give power* to others to do all the sacred acts of office, he may give others power to ordain; and if so, then *Ordination will be like Preaching*, Sacraments, and Discipline, which are none of them proper to the Bishops order.

T 2

And

And is not Church difcipline the exercife of the power of the keys ? If then the power of the keys may be exercifed by the Presbyters, when e-ver the Bifhops pleafe, it feems it is common to them, with him, as well as Sacraments, and therefore belongeth not to a Bifhop as a Bifhop, but as a Presbyter.

* Difput. of Church Go-ver. 2. And if in my difpute of ordination * I have fully proved that the power of the Miniftry is given by Chrift fo far immediatly, as that it paffeth not through the hands of Electors or Ordainers to the receiver, but is given by the meer Inftrumentality of the Law or inftitution, and that the Electors and Ordainers do no more than determine of the qualified perfon that receives it, and publickly inveft him, or minifterially folemnize his Poffeffion, (as the Burgeffes chufe, and the Steward or Recorder invefteth the Major of a Corparation, whofe power floweth immediatly from the Charter granted by the King)then all this controverfie is at an end : and I doubt not but that's fully proved.

And if commanding another to do an office work be all that is proper to the Bifhop, I ask *whether any thing there be proper to him ?* and fo whether we muft have fuch an office ? For may not the King command the Mi-nifter to do all the work which belongeth to his function ? may he not appoint Magiftrates, and make Law to command it ? may he not punifh thofe that do it not ? Is he not *cuftos utriufq, tabule ?* and muft he not corect mal-adminiftration in minifters, and drive them to do their duty ? No doubt he may.

Obj. *But he doth not ordaine Minifters, though he command them to do their duty when ordained.*

Anf. 1. Our prefent queftion is not about Ordination, but command-ing men to Govern the Church by Difcipline or fully to Rule by the Keys the people of a particular Church. If this fo far belong to the Presbyters office that he may do it by the Bifhops Licence, let him that can, tell me why he may not do it by the *Kings* Licence ? and then (as they were wont to fay of old) *excepta ordinatione,* nothing but ordination only is pro-per to the Bifhops office.

And that this is not proper neither, 1. This objection it felf doth in-timate, feeing the Bifhop may give another *Power to ordaine :* (and then why may not the King ?) 2. Many of the Schoolmen, and the Papifts themfelves confefs, that the Pope (fay fome), or Prelates (fay others) may impower an Abbot or Presbyter to ordaine; of which fee that un-anfwerable book of *Voetius de defperata caufa Papatus* againft *Janfenius* for Presbyters ordination. 3. And our Church of *England* caufeth Pref-byters to impofe hands with the Bifhops, and Bifhop *Downam* aforecited is angry with his anfwerer, for fuppofing that he pleaded for fole power of ordination in the Bifhop, when he fpaks but for a cheif power.

And if nothing but a *cheif power* in ordaining be proper to a Bifhop; why then are the Churches fo confounded, and beggered, and altered, by a contrary practice ? And why is a new office of Bifhops fet up in the world? whofe work is to hinder the Minifters of Chrift from their office-work, under pretence of a power of Licenfing them to it? when God licenceth them to the work, when he calleth them to that office, which effentially, confifteth in a *power* and *Obligation* to do it, when they have opportunity

Moreover my Lord *Bacon* iu his confiderations hath well manifefted (if impartiall wife men could have bin heard) that the office of a Bifhop is a *function* confifting in the exercife of *perfonall skill*, or abilities: and therefore muft be done by him that hath them, and not committed to another, as the office of a Judg, or Lawyer, of a Phifitian, of a Tutor, &c. no man choofeth a Tutor or Phifitian meerly to fend another to him for his Tutor or Phifitian, but to do the work himfelf. It is not like the place of a King, whofe right dependeth not on his parts or skill, becaufe he may Govern by others that are able.

And *Grotius* (who one would think by their refpect *to him*, fhould have been regarded by them) truly faith *de Imperio fum. poteft.* Pag. 290 [*Nam illud [Quod quis per alium facit, per fe facere videtur] ad eas tantum pertinet actiones quarum caufa efficiens proxima a jure indefinita eft*] that is [*For this faying, That whofe a man doth by another he feemeth to do by himfelf, belongeth only to thofe actions, whofe necreft efficient caufe is not defined by the Law*] But fure when God made the Paftoral office, he meant that the perfons called to it, fhould do the work and not only appoint other men to do it.

And I would know whether the work of a Presbyter (as to confecrat and celebrate the Sacrament &c) may be done *per alium*, by one that is no Presbyter. If not (as all fay not) then I ask, whether the Bifhops work or the Presbyters be the more facred? If the Presbyters, then his Office is more facred: If the Bifhops (or both alike) then that Bifhops work, may no more be done *per alium then* the Presbyters.

Moreover I know no Bifhops but would willingly be more Refpected and Honoured than the Presbyters, and if they defire, it fhould be only by way of *fear*, they neither think or wifh like Minifters of Chrift, nor like fober men. But if by way of love, who *knoweth not what advantage the prefent* Paftor hath above the abfent, *cæteris paribus*, to get the people's love? and *Paul* would have it to be fo, 1 Thef. 5. 12, 13. *It is thofe that Labour among them and admonifh them, whom they muft efteem highly in Love*, not for their titles and dignities, but for *their work fake*. And who knoweth not that he that Loveth a man for Preaching the word of falvation to him, is likelier to come to him, whofe doctrine daily edifieth him, and comforteth him, than to him whom one of a hundred of his Dioceffe never heard a Sermon or a good word from, in all their lives? If it be for the work fake that they muft or will be Loved, is not he liker to be moft Loved who is ftill with them, and prayeth and praifeth God with them, and comforteth, and confirmeth them, and refolveth their doubts, and quieteth their troubled Confciences, and vifiteth them in ficknefs, and taketh care of the poor, and vifiteth them from houfe to houfe, than he that once or never came among them, and is unknnown? And if the

people

people be Rebellious and wicked, it is the *present Pastor* who shall be most hated and opposed (which if it be for Christ is a good and comfortable thing, and hath a special promise *Mat.* 5, 10. 11, 12.) And that Pastor who is most beloved of the good people, and most hated by the bad, is he that will *do most* good for mens salvation, and will have most comfort in his Soul, and at last the greatest reward from God; and that is *cæteris paribus* the present Pastor.

And it were worth the noting (if blind men would see) that this is our great reason of the common calamities of the Churches: that when the best of the people love their *present* faithfull *Pastors* and the worst *hate* them most, and *love best* the *Absent Bishops* that trouble them (as they do the dead Saints for whom they keep holy daies) these wicked people fly to the Bishop and seek to make the *present* Pastors suspected, or odious to him, as Schismaticks, or such as are against the Bishops mind and honour: and because these Villains Love the absent Bishop better then the present Pastors, therefore the Bishop (that knoweth them not but by hearsay) taketh such for the honestest men in the Parish, and so taketh their words against the Ministers: and (to the utmost of my experience I speak it) ordinarily, that Minister shall pass with the Bishop for a Schismatick, a Puritan, a seditious Fellow, or a stark knave, let him be more Learned than *Hierom*, more industrious than *Augustin*, more holy than *Macarius*, or at least as suspected of these crimes, whom the flattering malignant, will so represent to him: especially if he be a sensual Gentleman, that cannot endure to have his lusts and licentiousnes reproved, or controlled by a Minister of Christ. And when these lies and slanders have encouraged the ungodly accusers by their successe, while they engage the Bishop against the present Pastors, and cause him to turn their troubler, hinderer or persecutor, then is the Prelate and the Pastor become as enemies, whose interests are grown inconsistent, and then they come to have their several Parties, and the debauched take one side, and the sober and religious the other, and what followeth upon this, he is mad in this age who is ignorant after so great experience.

But I shall add more of this subject in the Chapter following.

CHAP. XII.

The just opening and understanding of the true nature of the Pastoral office and Church Government, would end these controversies about Episcopacy.

THe name of *Church Government* so far deceiveth undistinguishing gross or inconsiderate wits, as that they take the controversie to be

but

but whether we shall have order or anarchie, Church Government or none. As if neither the Magistrates Government of the Sword were any thing, nor yet the Pastors Government by the word. But I would fain know of these men what more it is that they would have, and what is the Church Government which they so much contend for?

1. Is it an *Universal Legislation*? It is high and damnable Treason against Christ for any mortal men to claime it. Universal Legislation is the prerogative of the Universal King. There is no Universal King but Christ, who else is Governour of all the world or all the Churches in the world? And Christ hath in nature and Scripture given the world already an Universal Law. If he hath done it well, take not on you to amend it. If you say he hath done it ill, either take not on you to be Christians, or else call your self the Christ, that is Anti-Christ, if you will take Christs place and take upon you to amend his work. If you dream of an Universal Pope or General Council as having this power, you will but make true Anti-Christs of them, and foolishly confound a humane constitution with a Divine, and the *Roman* Empire with *all the world*. For you are ignorant in Church History if you see not plainly that Popes, Patriarks, and Primates stand all on the same foundation; And that both they and Councils (falsly called, General,) were but Imperial, or confined to one Princes Dominion, called or ruled usually by the Emperours, who had no power in other Princes Territories: No Councils conteining any considerable members, but such as were in that one Empire, or formerly had been of it, and so kept the custome which then they had received, except that the *Romans* placed one Bishop on the borders of *Scythia* or *Tartary*, and one on the borders of *Persia*, in hope that he might have influence further into the Countries, and rarely one or two such might be at a Council called General, so that certainly there is no Universal Law-giver or Judge but Christ. This therefore is not the Church Government of Bishops which men contend for.

2. What is it then, is it an Universal Exposition of the Scripture or of Christs Laws? why an exposition truly Universal is for Regulation as the Law it self: And none ever had such power (even in civil Government) but the Law-givers themselves: Else the Expositor of the Lawes should be King, and not the maker, seeing it is his sence that the subject must be ruled by. But if it be a particular *decisive* exposition which you meane, such as a Judge in deciding particular controversies, I shall say more to that anon.

3. If it be any Coactive or Coercive power of Church Government that you meant, by mulcts or Corporal penalties, no Bishops as such have any thing to do with it; not only *Bilson*, but the generality of the Prelatists disclaime it, and confess that it belongeth only to the King and Magistrates and that they receive it from the King, if ever they excercise any such.

4. What

4. What is it then, is it to be the Kings Ecclesiastical Council, to prepare such Canons as he shall enact? Of Canons I shall say more anon. But though Pastors may be the fittest to Council Kings, yet that giveth them no power, nor doth aptitude make an office, nor is the King tyed to them, but may advise whith whom he please. And experienced present Pastors, are usually fitter to give advice in the matters of Religion, than they. And even Civil impartial Noblemen have usually proved wiser, soberer and more peaceable and happy Church Councellours, then the interessed partial Clergy.

I am not of *Erastus* mind, that all Church Government belongeth to the Magistrates. I have lately published my judgment of that matter in certain Propositions to *Ludov. Molinæus.* But I grant to him, and all sober impartial Divines do grant, that all forceing Government by the Sword, belongeth to Magistrates (and Parents) only, and not to any Bishops as such.

It followeth therefore that no Bishops power extendeth to any other effect, but only to work on the Consciences of Volunteers, unless as the Magistrates or Parents may constraine them by penalties to submit to it. Suppose therefore a while that the Magistrates force were withdrawn from your discipline, and left it to it self, you would then know better by experience wherein its strength consisted. That man would then Rule the people most, who did most effectually convince their reason, and prevaile with Conscience : and further nothing would be done, Are not our Bishops well aware of this —— Do they not themselves confess how little their Government would signifie above the Government of present Presbyters, unless they could give clear convincing Reasons to the people, which absent strangers are unlike to do? What do you think your peculiar power would signifie in one year above a Presbyters, if the Magistrate left all at liberty in their Church obedience to their Pastors, would not the present Pastors carry almost all, with the best and soberest of the flocks? Especially where Bishops make it their office to forbid the Pastors to do theirs, and to keep them from Preaching the word of life? Their holding fast the secular conjunct power, and using it so much doth shew what they trust to ! they say themselves, what would the Keys signifie without the Sword? and the Bishops Government prevail, where none are punished for despising it if the Bishop excommunicate a faithfull Preacher, neither he nor his flock will much regard it, but goe on in the service of the Lord. And perhaps some will excommunicate the Bishop and be even with him. O! that the Magistrates would a few Years try what the Keys can do in *England* of themselves, and *valeant quantum valere possunt.* Not that I would wish him to leave off his own duty, to punish sin ; but let it not be mixed with Church Offices, so, as that all that shall be imputed to the Bishops Keys, which is effected only by the Magistrates Sword. I deny not but the Magistrate may moderately drive men to hear Gods word, and to do

the

the immediate duties of their places? But not to profess that they are Christians when they are not, or that they consent to Church Communion, when they do not: Nor to take those Privileges which belong not to them: *No man hath right to Church Communion, who had rather be excommunicated then repent of sin*: Therefore if Gods word and an excommunication will not bring him to profess Repentance, he should not be either Rackt or Imprisoned, to force him to say he doth repent, when it is certain that he doth not indeed repent, who will not profess it by easier means: Nor hath that man right to absolutiaon and Church Communion, who only prefereth it before a Goale. The effects of the Church Keyes are talked of but are indeed unknown, where secular force doth deterr men into lyeing professions of repentance and drive unwilling persons in to the Communion of the Church: No unwilling person should have the Seal of pardon put into his hands.

Obj. But we cannot say they are unwilling who consent, though moved by the penalty of the Law and Sword.

Ans. Yes; he is to be called *unwilling*, who hath not the willingness which Christ maketh necessary: He that is not *willing* to have *Church Communion for it self*, and *for Christ* and *his salvation*, is not willing of it at all indeed, nor in Gods account: For it is *only freedome from a Prison* that he is willing of, and of Church Communion as a *means* to that, and not as a means to the end that God appointed it: As he that consenteth to be Baptized only to heal the Kings evil, or to save his life, is not to be Baptized nor taken for a Christian, nor is it Baptism indeed, but *touching only* which he consenteth to; so is it in this case.

Obj. But how know you but them that hath righter ends together with these, punishment brings many a man to reason and true repentance.

Ans. You suppose your selves that *the word and Keys will not prevail* with him of themselves; and therefore it is that you desire force; your own Consciences tell you that it is but to avoid punishment that you suppose him to profess repentance: Otherwise when your threats have brought him to repentance, try what is the cause by remitting the penalty on his body, and after freely leaving him to himself.

Obj. But some are like Children that will hear reason when their stubbornness is taken down: Therefore it may also have better motives for ought you know.

Ans. 1. Men that are dealt with in the matters of Salvation, are not to be thus used as Fools and Children about common things; but as men that must live and die as they choose. 2. And God hath left us no such means to bring men into a right Choice in things of this nature: Otherwise you might set Infidels on the Rack till they consent to be Baptized, or send them to Prison, and then say, how know you but this, as the Rod doth Children, hath brought them to their witts. But the Church of Christ never took this course, nor never thus understood his will. 3. The case is plain to men that will understand: When God hath made mens *free consent* the *Condition* of their *Salvation* and the *pro-*

V

fession

feffion *of a free consent* to be the Condition of Church Communion (and what wife man would have lower that will not make the Church a fwine ftie)? It followeth that the Paftors muft have the *evidence* of fuch a *Profeffion of free* and *voluntary consent*, or elfe they muft not receive fuch perfons: Now fuch a one *that hath* been long tried by the word, and by the penalty of Excommunication it felf, and refufeth to profefs Repentance, but only protefteth it when no other means will efcape a Prifon, doth not give the Paftor an evidence in the Court of Reafon acceptable, to fignifie a voluntary Repentance or confent; and therefore what ever poffibly may be known to God, he is not to be taken into the Church: For we muft judge by evidence, and that is by fuch free profeffion of Repentance, as Chrift hath taught us to expect: and therefore we can only Judge that perfon to be one, that had rather fay he repenteth than be imprifoned, but not as one that indeed repenteth or defireth Church Communion as fuch, and for true ends.

Obj. But if he be in the Church though without Repentance, he may there be brought to Repentance afterward.

Anf. Poffibilities are no Rule for us to go by in fuch cafes, fo you may fay if *one be Baptized*, before he profefs to believe or repent, he may be brought to it after by hearing in the Church: But this is but to make Lawes for the Church inftead of Chrifts, when we have caft out his Lawes, and to confound the world and the Church by our foolifh adverfe reafon. He that is in the Church notorioufly againft or without his will, ftands there but as a teftimony of the Bifhops perfidioufnefs: And he that will not come in by any reafoning or intreating, without the violence of the Sword, is in all procefs of humane Judgments to be efteemed unwilling: The ancient Churches would indeed importune men to Baptifm; but they never baptized any (at age) that did not intreat to be baptized, and voluntarily make profeffion of faith and repentance. And Papifts and Proteftants commonly affirm, that none fhould be conftrained to be baptized, or to make profeffion of Chriftianity. But the Papifts come after and tell us that yet when *one is baptized*, he may be compelled by force to all his duty, and fo may be conftrained to ftay in the Church, or to return if he forfake it: Their Reafons are, 1. Becaufe now he is obliged by his own confent. 2. Becaufe he hath put himfelf under the Government of the Church, and therefore muft be Governed by it. *Anf.* But 1. to confent to be a Chriftian Ruled by Chrift, and to confent to be conftrained by force to continue this confent, are two things. Prove the latter if you can to be included in our Baptifm? Contrarily as we *freely* and not forcedly confent, it is fuppofed that we are accordingly to continue it as we began it. 2. And to put our felves under the Government of the Church, is not to put our felves under the fword: the Church punifhment reacheth no further then excommunication: and where a man is fully excommunicated, he is caft out of the Church again: and when he is out of it, he is not under its Government: Indeed he is under the
Magiftrates,

Magistrates Government: But if that will prove that he may be punished for not repenting and returning to the Church when Excomunicate, it will prove too that he might be punished before Baptifm, for not repent. ing and being baptized. For though there be fome aggravations of his fin that Apostatizeth to it, yet that differeth the cafe but as to the *degree*. It is for the quality of the crime it felf, that the Magistrate is to punish (as Murder, Theft, Adultery, Blafphemy &c.) Whether it be in the unbaptized, or baptized, or excomunicate: But it *is for Impenitency* only in fome crime that the Church doth excommunicate. And if the Magistrate muft imprifon or kill men properly for Impenitencie, it muft be as it aggravateth the *crime* it felf, and it may be as well the unbaptized as the baptized, for he is the Governour of both: It is therefore a meer fiction of Papifts Church Tyrants, that there is fuch a difference between the unbaptized and the excommunicate, as that the first muft not have Church priviledges till they difire them, and the later may have them if they be but commpelled to keep them, or return to them by the fword.

And fo fchifmaticaly different are they from the Catholick Church for many hundered years after Chrift, as directly to contradict them. For all the Canons as well as the Hiftory tell us, that all the antient Churches when they had excommunicated a finner, would not receive him till he had penitently begged readmiffion : Yea they ufed to caft down themfelves on the earth(as even great *Theodafius* did before *Ambrofe* when but fufpended), and to beg pardon and readmiffion with tears : nay for great faults, this was not received till many months or years continued penitence, fhewed their defires to be fincere ; and now Prelates muft have a Blafphemer, or a common Drunkard, compelled by the fword to fay that he repenteth, that he may the next day have the honour and priviledge of a Chriftian Communicant, whether he will or not. O kind-natured-cruell-Church!

And when *Cyril* of *Alexandria* began to ufe the fword, and when the Circumcellian *Donatifts* tempted *Auguftine* to change his opinion about ufing force in matters of Religion ; yea and when *Ithacius* and his par-takers offended *Martin* and *Ambrofe* by ftirring up *Maximus* against the *Prifcillianifts*, none of all this was to force thefe Hereticks by the fword, to Communicate in the Church before they had fhewed a voluntary re-pentance, nor to make them Church members against their wills, even that *Ithacius* whom *Hooker* himfelf acknowledgeth fo bad, was not fo foolifh : But only they would have forced them to their own wales, and punifhed them as feducers of the people, and as difturbers of the Churches purity and peace. Though yet it is too evident, that the pride and paffion of the Prelates that were orthodox, did quickly and fiercely flame out to the conflagration of the Churces, when they found that the Chriftian Emperours were ready to ferve their paffions with the fword.

It is then paft denial, that all the power of Bifhops or any Paftors is but the *management of the word of God, upon the Confciences of men*
V 2   that

that believe them and voluntarily receive that word: only with this advantage, that they do not this as *private men,* but as *Officers appointed* so to mannage this *word.* And therefore he that disobeyeth the word of God truly delivered and applied by them, committeth a double sin; one as he disobeyeth Gods word as such, in the matter in hand, and the other as he disobeyeth that particular word of God, which commandeth him to hear and obey his Pastors. But if men will so sin, we have nothing but that *word of God,* which they despise to cure them by.

For instance, 1. In our admonitions and reproofs, of the greatest sinners, we can do no more but shew them Gods Law, which they have broken, and which threatneth damnation to them, and to perswade them by Scripture arguments to repent that they may escape.

2. In *excommunication* it self, we have nothing to do but to shew them the same word, and shew them how God hath threatned to punish them, and to shew them and the Church that word which commandeth us to have no Communion with them but to avoid them, and according to that word to declare them (Impenitency openly Characterizing them) to be persons unmeet for Christian Communion, and such as (till they repent) are under the wrath of God, and must expect his dreadful judgment; and to command the Church in Christs name to withdraw from the Impenitent person, and to have no Communion with him. And all this is but the application of Gods word to his Conscience and the Churches. If his seared Conscience deride it all, we can do no more. If he will forcibly intrude into the Communion of the Church against their wills, it is like ones breaking into my house; the Magistrate must restrain him as a violater of the peace as well as of the Churches liberties: If the Magistrate will not, the Church must remove from him. If they cannot, they must pronounce him morally absent, as a forcible intruder and none of their Communion. If the Church will not obey the Pastors sentence, he hath no instrument but the same word to bring them to it. Now all this being past denial, let us come more particularly to enquire in all this, what part there is essential to a Bishops office as such.

1. Is it the making of Church Lawes or Canons? About what? 1. Either these Canons are but the Commanding of that which Gods Law made a duty before, or of somewhat newly made a duty by themselves: 2. Either they are Lawes or Commands to the Laity only, or to the Presbyters, or to the particular Bishops, or all.

1. If they do but urge the performing of some duty already made such by God, in Scripture or Nature, who ever doubted, but Presbyters may do that even to teach and charge the people from God to obey his Laws.

And note that God daily maketh new duties by the Law of nature, even providentially altering the Nature of things; And so he maketh

this

this or that to become *Decent* and *Orderly* and fo a duty. And maketh it my duty to fpeak this or that word, to this or that perfon, or to do this or that particular good work. Even by varying occafions, accidents and circumftances of things.

2. But if thefe Canons make new duties which God hath not made, 1. If it be to the *Laity*, the *Presbyters* may do the like; for they are Guides alfo of the Laity, unlefs they are forbidden by a fuperior power: If it be only to the Presbyters, that will not reach our prefent cafe, as fhall be further fhewed afterward. 3. If it be to the Bifhops themfelves, they cannot be Laws, but meer agreements, becaufe one Bifhop is not the proper Governour of another; nor *many of one*; nor the prefent in Council of the abfent as fuch.

And here by the way it is worthy to be noted how much the Dicoefines contradict themfelves, in this claim of Government: They fay that they are of a diftinct order and office from meer Presbyters, becaufe they have power to Govern them. And yet they make, 1. A Council of Bifhops to have as high a governing power over particular Bifhops of the fame order: 2. And an Arch-Bifhop to be the Governour of Bifhops; 3. And a Primate or Patriarch to be the Governour of Arch-Bifhops; and yet not to be of a diftinct *Order*, or office, but only of a diftinct *degree* in the accidentals of the fame order. If Government prove a diftinct *Order*, or *Office* in one, it will do fo in the other. And why may not the Magiftrate make all the fame Canons who ruleth them all?

But let us confider what thefe Canons may be. 1. The Bifhops make Canons, how often Synods or Councils fhall be held, and when and where, and when they fhall be diffolved. But, 1. May not the *King* do the fame? And can that be proper to Bifhops which the King may do? Yea which all Emperours have formerly ufed? 2. And is not this Cannon made to rule *Bifhops themfelves*? who is it but Bifhops (or fo much as them) that you think fhould be called unto Councils? And are the Bifhops in Council of another *order* than themfelves out of Council? Need we an office of Bifhops to rule Bifhops of the fame office?

2. Canons are made about Temples, Buildings, Tithes, Glebes, Bells, Pulpits, Seats Tables, Cups, Fonts, and other utenfils. And 1. who doubteth but the Magiftrate may do all this? yea that it belongeth to him to regulate fuch things as thefe? 2. And who knoweth not that even Bifhops are under thefe Canons alfo, who are of the fame order? 3. And that Presbyters (even in *England*) are members of thefe Synods, and fo make Canons to rule the Bifhops? Ergo, they are of a fuperior order to Bifhops by your reafoning.

3. Canons are made for the regulating of Minifters attire, in the Church and out, and for officiating garments, as furplices &c. And of thefe I fay the fame as of the former. The King may do the fame as Bifhops may do, and Bifhops themfelves are bound by them, and

V 3   Presbyters

Presbyters make them, which three things prove that it is not the proper work of Bishops as a distinct order from meer Presbyters.

4. Canons are made for worship Gestures; in what gesture to pray, to receive the Sacrament, to use the Creed, &c. And the same three answers serve to this also, as to the case in hand.

5. Canons are made for Holidaies, publick Fasts, and Thanksgivings, and Lecture daies. And the same three considerations fall in here.

6. Canons are made for the ordering officers, fees, and such like in Bishops Courts. And here all the same three things fall in, 1. The King may do it, 2. It is Bishops that are ruled, 3. Presbyters also make the Canons, therefore it is not *jure divino* the proper work of a distinct Order.

7. Canons are made for the choice of what *Translation* of the *Bible* shall be used in all the Churches, and what version or meetre of the singing Psalmes. And of this also the three former things hold true.

8. Canons are made to impose a Liturgie, in what words Ministers shall speak to God and to the people. And, 1. This also the King may do and doth, 2. And it obligeth Bishops. 3. And Presbyters make it.

9. Canons are made against Schismaticks, new Discipline and constitutions, non-subscribers, unlicensed Preachers, for the book of Articles, of ordination, for Catechizing, Preaching, Marrying, Burying, Christing, and such like: In all which each of the said three answers hold.

10. Canons are made to keep Parents from open covenanting to God for their Children in Baptism, that they shall not be urged to be present, that God-fathers do that office and not they; As also that none be baptized without the transient *Image* of a *Cross*, and such like: whether this be well or ill done, the three former answers all hold in this.

11. All the Canons that are for the restraint of sin, as neglect of Church worship, prophaning of it, and other abuses, have the same censure.

12. The circumstantiating Canons, how oft Bishops shall confirm, and whom they shall ordaine, and how oft, and how oft the Common prayer be read, the Surplice worne, the Sacraments administred, in what place, what Registers to be kept, what order to be observed in reading the Scriptures and the *Apocrypha*, with abundance the like, have all the foresaid answers to prove that they are no proper work of a distinct order.

There remaineth therefore but the determination of present circumstances, which are part of the Ministers proper work, or the Lecturer or Clerkes at least. As, 1. What text to Preach on to day. How to expound it, and apply it: In what method to Preach: What words to use: How long to Preach: 2. In what method, words and length to Pray (where free Prayer is allowed.) 3. What particular Psalm to

Sing,

Sing, and in what tune ; 4. On what particular daies to adminiſtꝛ the Lords Supper, beſides the great daies (Eaſter , Whitſontide) &c. At what hour to go to Church, and when to end, 5. What particular ſick-perſon to viſit, and when: And what ſinner to reprove or admoniſh perſonally. And who is to be taken for a true penitent and abſolved *in foro pænitentiali* or privately (as they diſtinguiſh, all theſe are either the perſonal work of him that officiateth) (as chewing his meat of a man before he ſwallow it and degeſt it ; or as chooſing his medicaments is to the Phyſician) and belongeth to his calling, which none ſhould hinder him in (of which I make no queſtion) And if ſo, it is not the proper work of a Biſhop. Or elſe it is fit that this liberty be taken from him, and that other men chooſe for him every day his Text, his Method, his words, his tune, his hour and the reſt. And if ſo, when this alſo ſhall be made a Canon, no doubt but the King and Parliament and Preſby-ters in convocation, will all have a hand in it ; and perhaps the Biſhops be under the Canon as well as others. Yet then we have not found out a Biſhops proper work unleſs it were when he is preſent in the ſame aſ-ſemblies to governe the work in all theſe circumſtances, in which I do not contend againſt him.

11. If then it lie not in Legiſlation or Canon making, let us conſider whether it lie in *judging* or *executing*. And this muſt be chiefly about *Excommunication* and *Abſolution*, as it concerneth the Laity. And here, 1. The buſineſs is not to judge of the Law, but of the *Perſon by the* Law. It is not to judge in plaine caſes, whether we muſt avoid an impenitent Fornicator , a Drunkard, a Blaſphemer, an Heretick, &c. For if the Biſhops ſay nay, we muſt not believe him or obey him. And for diffi-cult inſtances, of the *ſpecies* of ſins deſerving, it is partly the work of an expoſitor of Scripture, to determine of them, and partly of the Canons and Laws of the land, where Magiſtrates and Preſbyters are efficient, an l Biſhops themſelves obliged as well as Preſbyters.

The buſineſs therefore is to judge whether *this* perſon be guilty of ſuch a *Crime*, and. 2. Whether he be impenitent therein. And that this is the work of a *Parochus*, that is, a Cohabiting Paſtor, who is upon the place, and knoweth the parties, and not of a ſtrange Biſhop over a thouſand or many hundred Churches, I have partly ſhewed before, and partly ſhall ſhew now, and partly hereafter. At the preſent let the unexperienced conſider of this which any Novice that is upon the place may know.

l. 1. pag. 112. Col. 2. & Gregor. Sayrus To. 2. l. 1c. 17. num. 2. &. 8. &c. And indeed they con-clude that out of the caſe of ſcandal, Magiſtrates Laws, nnull materially, that is, to the Common hurt, or that are againſt common good, bind not in Conſcience ; ut Id. Fragoſo ib. p. 112. n. 224. ... W·t cteth the conſent of Silveſt. Tabien. Cald. Bartol. Hoſtienſ. & Doctorum Communiter. So that Mr. John Humfrey is not ſingular in his reſtrictive of this Caſe, though I leave him many cautions and li-mitations in the Letter, part of which he hath printed in the end of his book.

1. A Bishop (especially armed with penal terrour) or a Chancellour's Court, is not like to know of one scandalous Impenitent person of a hundred, which the present Pastor is like to know of. For experience telleth us that few, honest men will accuse their neighbours, where they shall but get hatred, and foresee no more probality of procuring the persons repentance by it : And that Church-Wardens do not and will not do it. Many men that fear perjury, refuse the oath, lest they should break it, or sin in keeping it, as it bindeth them to prosecute many men for Conscientious Nonconformity : And those that take the Oath, before they fear an oath, will make no Conscience at all of breaking it. So that a matter of notorious fact is past dispute. The land knoweth that not one Swearer, Curser, Fornicator, Adulterer, Railer, Thief, Derider of Scripture and Religion, &c. of a multitude, is ever accused at the Bishops Court. Whereas the Present Pastor can scarce choose but know the greatest part of these in his Parish, by dwelling among them, where he shall have frequent notice of it. Say as long as you will that this is long of the Minister, or Long of the Church-Wardens, or of the Apparitor, we know that the thing is so.

2. And in Church judgments, where a mans repentance is the cause in question, he hath the advantage an hundred fold that is present. For the tenor of his life before, and after, will be of great signification in judging of this : A man that never fell into such a sin before, and that quickly lamenteth it by free confession (known to the Pastor) may easily be believed to be penitent. But a man that hath many years continued in a wicked life, and that after all admonition and persuasions to repent, confessing one day and sinning the next, and perhaps deriding the Pastor, and making a jest of his own confessions, is not so quickly to be believed. And yet the strange *Diocesans* or Chancellour shall not know the difference, nor hear any more at the best, than [I repent] And whereas they say, if he sin again he is to be accused again] 1. They know *de facto*, that this is seldome done, except against some Conscientious Nonconformists. 2. And when neighbours see that the man whom they enraged against them by an accusation, cometh home again, by saying *I Repent*, and paying his fees, and doth but watch to execute his malice against the accusers, they will meddle in such unprofitable work no more.

3. And whereas the Chancelor or Diocesane must go upon the witnesses report. 1. The credit of the witnesses will be unknown to them; because it lyeth upon the honesty of the persons, whom they know not but by other persons; nor those other but by others; and they are forced to take all our slight reports, usualy from some flatterers of themselves, almost the worst men in the Parish, accounted by them the best and most credible, because they know not them aright, nor the rest at all. 2. And how unsatisfactory a thing it is to a mans Conscience, to Judge at random, or upon the uncertain credit of they scarce know who, in a case

of

of Excommunication or Absolution; whereas the present Pastor may goe on far more cleare and satisfactory grounds.

4. Moreover the Conviction of a sinner before Excommunication or Absolution, requireth a great deal of time, and a great many words, and those chosen with the greatest skill, and set home with the greatest Life, and Light, and Love, that can be manifested by the speaker; Many a time I have tried it, and could never satisfie my Conscience without more frequent, long and earnest exhortation, and prayer with it, than ever I knew Chancelor or Bishop use to fourty delinquents set together. The present Pastor hath opportunity to do this: But the Chancelor or Diocesane hath not. I never heard of any such means used in their Courts that was of such a nature as true Pastoral exhortations are, to melt a sinners heart into repentance. But of this before.

2. Another case of perticular *judgment* is, what sinner in his sicknnnes before death, is fit for Absolution. Here they cannot make the Bishop Judge, who is many a mile off; nor can they tell how to deny it to be without the office of the Parish Pastor, and therefore they allow him to be the Absolver; and yet, left he be the Judge, they bind him to Absolve all that require it, and do but say they repent: which must needs be a pernicious deceiving course to impenitent souls, when it is known that nothing is more ordinary with many in sicknes and in health, than to say I repent of some one gross disgraceful sin, and live in others worse without any profession of repentance, and die so at last. And must I absolve him from that sin which he repenteth of without the rest? or from all because he repenteth *of one*? yea, commonly men have a Confession which is like a Profession of their sin, and a Repentance which declareth it self to be Impenitence it self: some stoutly some stupidly saying [I confess I am a swearer and a drunkard, a whoremonger, but you Precisians are as bad and worse, for you are but hypocrites: I repent of my sins daily, and aske God mercy, though I commit them daily, and I doubt not of forgiveness, for all are sinners] and if one of these say also on his sick bed, he repenteth, without any signs of serious contrition or change of heart, we must Absolve him: But yet though we are not free in this, it is no Diocesanes proper work, and therefore requireth not their office.

3. Another Judgment of individuals necessary is *who is to be baptized, at least of persons at age; in Infidell Countries, or such as ours, where many thousand Anabaptists Children are unbaptized till they come to age?* The question is not what shall be the Law and Rule (whether Scripture or Canon) but who shall judge whether the person be capable according to the rule. Dotb elses every one hath not faith: The profession that entitleth to baptisme must be, 1. Of the whole essence of our part of the Covenant, faith, consent and future obedience. 2. With tolerable understanding of what they say. 3. With seeming seriousness. 4. With seeming Voluntarines and fixed resolution. Now how can a *Diocesan* judge of this, that is not within many miles of the place, nor never saw

X   the

the perfon in his life? It hath ever been confeffed to be part of the Baptizers work, though under the Government of Magiftrates, and in the Church the prefent Bifhop is not denyed a negative vote or a guiding judgment in the affair.

4. The very fame throughout is to be faid of judging what individual perfons in a Parifh are grown up to a capacity of the Lords Supper; (whither it be done in confirmation or at any other time) certainly they muft renew their baptifmal Covenant, and moreover underftand the fenfe of the Sacrament, &c. But fhall the Diocefan that never feeth one of an hundred of his Diocefe judge of every one of thefe? I will ftay no longer on fuch inftances; I think we need no more.

III. If the cafes of Teftaments, Adminiftrations, Licenfes to marry, judgement of cafes of divorce, difpenfations and fuch like be pretended as the proper works of Bifhops, I think I need not ftay to confute them, while it is known that fo much as is not every Paftors work in it, belongeth to the Magiftrate, and is done among us by his Commiffion, and that ufually by Laymen.

IV. We have therefore the Government of the Minifters themfelves to fpeak of next, which confifteth, 1. In ordination, 2. Inftituting and inducting, 3. Licenfing, 4. Sufpending, ejecting, filencing and degrading.

1. And *ordination* being that great and notable work, which anciently was taken to be all that was *proper* to the Bifhop, by many of the Fathers, as well as *Hierome*, this above all muft be well confidered. And 1. Let us confider of the Reafons for it; and 2. Of the different cafes.

1. The reafons given for appropriating ordination to *Diocefans*, or Bifhops are thefe, 1. Becaufe no man can give that which he hath not: 2. Becaufe it is an act of fuperiority: 3. Becaufe none but Bifhops ever did it in Scripture times, or fince without the Churches condemnation.

1. The firft of thefe reafons Dr. *Hammond Præmon. Differt.* is earneft in urging. To which I fay, 1. It is granted, that *no man giveth that which he hath not.* But *Presbyters have the office of Presbyters, therefore* by your fuppofition) they may give it.

Obj. But (faith he) *Presbyters had never a power given by the ordainers to ordain.*

Anf. I deny it, and prove the contrary (whatever the ordainers mean) 1. Thofe who in their ordination had an Office, Power or Keys of Chrifts making, conteining the power of ordination, delivered to them Minifterially, had the power of ordination delivered to them Minifterially: But all true Paftors or Presbyters ordained in *England* had an Office, Power or Keys of Chrifts making, conteining the power of ordination delivered to them Minifterially. *Ergo* they had the power of ordination fo delivered. Nothing needs proof but the Minor. And, 1. That

That Chrift and not the Bifhops made the true Paftoral Office, or Keyes, is paft doubt among fober Chriftians, 2. And that it was the ordainers meaning to deliver them no new humane office, but that which Chrift (by his Spirit and Apoftles at leaft) made, inftituted and defcribed, I will ftand to the ordainers own profeffion, 3. And if fo, I think they will confefs, that if they did miftake, and think that the office conteined nor, what it conteined indeed, their miftake will not difable the ordained Minifter; no more than the Errour of a Recorder or Steward, who thinketh when he giveth the Mayor his Oath, that his office hath leffer power than it hath: But Gods making and not mans meaning muft determine of the power, 4. Therefore all the queftion is whether God put the power of ordination into the Paftoral office. Of which now I will fay but this, that Dr. *Hammond* confeffeth that there was no Paftor ordained in Scripture times that had not the power of ordination: And I fhall after prove, that no other fhould be introduced fince by men.

2. And farther the Church of *England* appointeth Minifters to impofe hands with the *Diocefan* in ordination: Therefore they take not *ordination*, but only a *Superiority* in *ordination*, to be proper to their office; As Bifhop *Downame* and other of them alfo openly hold and profefs.

2. The, 2d. Reafon, that ordination is an Act of *Superiority*. 1. Is granted; becaufe the perfon to be ordained is yet no Minifter of Chrift, and therefore is Inferior to the Presbyters that ordain him, till he have received his office. 2. But that *afterward* the ordainer muft be of an higher order (as well as greater antiquity in office) than him that is ordained by him, I deny: For than Bifhops could not ordain Bifhops; nor Arch-Bifhops ordain Arch-Bifhops: and who fhall ordain the Patriarcks, or (if you be for him) the Pope? Have they all fuperiours to do it?

3. The third Reafon from Hiftory I fhall confute in due place: only here retorting it thus: In Scripture times no fixed *Diocefan* ever did ordain, therefore none fuch fhould now ordain.

2. But next let us diftinguifh, 1. Between ordaining to the Miniftry in the Univerfal Church without affixing to a particular Charge, and the fixing of a Paftor in that particular Church. And, 2. Between ordaining a Bifhop or Plenary Paftor, and a half Paftor called now a Presbyter.

1. As Baptifm as fuch doth joyn a man to no particular Church, but only to the Univerfal, but yet they that have opportunity fhould fecondarily by a farther act of confent alfo joyn themfelves to the particular Church where they live; but if they live where they have no fuch opportunity, they muft do it after as foon as fuch opportunity cometh: Even fo ordination to the facred Miniftry as fuch doth fix a man to no particular Church, but make him a Minifter of Chrift to the world for mens con-

X 2   verfion,

version, and to the Universal Church for Christians edification, as he shall have any particular opportunity for exercise (which the Church of *England* expresseth by the words [*when thou shalt be thereunto Lawfully called*] meaning a call *ad exercitium*, to the exercise of the office received : But yet where there are not many unchurched Infidels to be converted, but all profess Christianity, it is not fit such shall be ordained *sine titulo*, as they speak, lest it occasion irregularity and poverty in the Clergy, but be at once affixed to a particular Church, which fixed Ministers are in Scripture usually called Bishops, Presbyters and Pastors, with relation to their particular *flock or Church*, besides their primary relation to the *World* and to the *universal Church*, from which the extraordinary Officers were called Apostles and Evangelists, and the ordinary ones *Ministers* of Christ in general. Though I deny not but even the unfixed may be called Bishops, Elders and Pastors, as being *virtually* such, and in an Office which wanteth nothing but a particular Call to that fixation and exercise.

Now 1. To call a Minister already made such to a particular Church, and so to make a Bishop or Pastor or Presbyter of him, doth not necessarily require a *Diocesan* : For, 1. The people that are at liberty may do it, and ordinarily have done (as *Blondel* hath fully proved) And in our times if a free people only choose a man already ordained, and take him for their Pastor, no man taketh this for a nullity, no not the Prelatists themselves. 2. And a Pastor Magistrate or Prince may do it without a Bishop, as none deny. 3. And a Minister may frequently on just occasion be removed from place to place, and needeth not a Bishop for every change, at least as to the being of his office.

2. And as to the first ordination of a *Minister* as such, if there must be a *Diocesan* to do it, this is gathered either from the *nature of the thing*, or from *divine institution*.

1. As to the *nature of the thing*, it sheweth no such necessity, but rather contradicteth it ; for 1. As to *Efficiency*, if a Bishop or Arch-Bishop or Primate or Patriark may be made without the agency of any one of a higher order, then so may a Presbyter. For the reason is the same.

2. And as to the object ; 1. The first object of the sacred *Ministry* as such, is the Infidel world; to whom they are to Preach the Gospel, and offer Christ and Salvation, and beseech them in Christs stead to be reconciled to God, to call them from darkness to light, and the power of Satan unto God. And to think that none but Apostles should do this, and that all the world must be left to the Devil when the Apostles were dead, is an unchristian thought: To those that must do this, Christ promised his presence to the end of the world. Now, 1. The Infidel world is no more under the power of a *Diocesan* than of a Presbyter : If it be, it is either. 1. As he is a Prelate. 2. Or as a *Diocesan*. 1. Not as a Prelate in general. For if the *world* be the object of the Ministers office, it can be no more of the Prelates as such. 2. Not as a *Diocesan* : For the

2 Cor. 5. 19.
Act. 26. 18.
Mat. 28. 20.

the Infidel world, [Egypt, Tartary, Japan, China, Persia, &c.] is no part of any Bishops Diocese. 2. And as to the *work* of a Preacher to the Infidels, it is the very same whether it be done by a Bishop or a Presbyter: There is nothing to do for them but preach and baptize, and neither of those is a work proper to a Bishop.

If it be said that it is not because of the object or the work are proper to a Bishop, but because the *sending forth* a man for that work is proper to him; I answer, that when I have proved past contradiction that he sendeth a man to do as high a work as he could there do himself, and to the very same, it sheweth that *ex natura rei* there needeth no *higher order* than the Ministers to send him: No more than there needeth a higher progenitor than a man to beget a man,

2. And as his office is related to the *Church-Universal*, all the same argumentation will hold good. For the Church-Universal is the object of the Ministers office as well as of the Prelates; and no more than his own Diocese is the special charge of a *Diocesan* as such; and the work to which the Minister is ordained in general to the whole Church can no otherwise be proved less than the Prelates, unless by proving a Divine institution (which they will grant.)|

2. And as for a Divine institution as to the ordaining power, I will say but this much, (which may take with cordate men) till I come to speak more largely of the point. 1. That Doctor *Hammond* (and as far as he knew, all that owned the same cause with him) doth grant that the Apostles (nor any other) in Scripture times did not so much as institute the office of a Presbyter as distinct from a Bishop, much less ever ordain any one to such an office: And that in all their Instructions to *Timothy* and *Titus* about ordination of Bishops or elders and Deacons, they have not a syllable about any ordination or qualification of such subject Presbyters, but only about ordaining Bishops. Therefore if Bishops be the successors of the Apostles in ordination, they cannot do more than they did; nor ordain any other Presbyters than Bishops.

2. That if Bishops were the Institutors of Presbyters, as distinct from them by a Power of parcelling out their office to others than Bishops, yet have power to make more sorts of sacred Ministers, by subdivision of their power. They may make one office only to Preach, and another only to baptize, and another only to pray, and another only to administer the Lords Supper, and another to Excommunicate, and why not another to ordaine; and so ordination shall not be proper to a Bishop. And so a Chancellor that hath the parcel of excommunicating and absolving, is as true a Clergy man, and of as high original as a Presbyter.

3. But that which Dr. *Hammond* betaketh himself to at last (in his Answer to the *London* Ministers) is as miserable a shift as ever a poor cause was reduced to (that had never stood if it had not been more beholden

X. 3.
holden

'holden to the Sword than to such foundations) he durst not say that the Presbyters office is not of Divine institution : And yet it was not instituted in Scripture times: But it was instituted in Saint *Johns* time by him alone after the writing of his Gospel (which according to *Jerome* was about a year or two before he dyed) and the Revelation (which according to *Ireneus* li. 5.) was about four or five years before he dyed. And so all the Bishops power of ordaining subject Presbyters dependeth, 1. On one Apostles Institution, 2. Not proved at all by Scripture, 3. But only by Church-History, which hath not a syllable of such a thing, as that Saint *John* did institute the Presbyters office ; 4. And this is feigned to be done by Saint *John* many years after *Peter* and *Paul*, are said to be Bishops of *Rome* and *James* of *Jerusalem*, and *Peter* of *Antioch*, and *Mark* of *Alexandria*. Yea about thirty two years after *Mark* was put to death according to *Eusebius* ＊ see then what proof the Doctor giveth us that even at *Rome* and *Alexandria* all that time, there was no Bishop over Presbyters, nor any that ever ordained a Presbyter that was not a Bishop.

＊ Hierome saith he dyed in the eighth year of Nero. *vid.* Jos. Scaliger. *Anim. in* Euseb. *Dorothæ in refutanuem,* pag. 195.

3. But suppose the Divine institution be proved of Bishops ordination of subject Presbyters, let these three things more be noted.

1. That at least we have brought it to the Ancients measure, that *excepta sola ordinatione*, except only *ordination*, here is no work for to make a Bishops office of, but what a Presbyter may do.

2. That in this ordination they themselves acknowledg that the Presbyters may joyn, even in imposing hands, which is the note of Superiority (the lesser being blessed by the greater); and so Presbyters also (by *Epiphanius*'s leave) do *generare patres* : And Bishops have not the *sole power* of ordination, but the *chief*.

3. And whether a *chief power* in investing men in the Ministerial office, do make a distinct order or office *de nomine*, let them contend that please *de re*; if this were all, we were agreed: For my part, I had rather that Bishops had not only a *chief power* as moderators, but even a Negative voice in *ordination*, yea and in Removals and fixing of Ministers, than not: For in so weighty a business two Locks and Keyes to keep out bad men, are surer than one. And the poor silenced Nonconformists have yielded to much more than this.

But yet there remaineth one part of the *Diocesans* work to be considered, *viz.* The judging of Heresie and Schism, and the *silencing*, *suspending* and *degrading* of Ministers that deserve it. The Question is, whether this be not *proper* to the Prelates office.

And here no man can wish us to swallow the terms of the question whole, without distinguishing, as if they signifyed but one thing.

1. As judging is, 1. Either *private* by discerning ones own duty, which belongeth to every private man. 2. Or publick for the deciding of a controversie; and this is. 1. Civil, 2. Or properly Ecclesiastical;

fo in several manners and to several ends, Private men, Magiſtrates and Paſtors may judge of Hereſie &c.

2. And as for *ſuſpending, ſilencing* and *degrading,* either. 1. It ſignifieth ſome *Correction by* the *Sword or force* ; and that undoubtedly belongeth only to the Magiſtrate, and to no private man, nor Clergy man at all, as ſuch.

2. A Private man and much more a Congregation, may and muſt refuſe a notorious Intolerable Miniſter ; whether *Inſufficient, Heretical* or *wicked* and *Malignant,* they muſt withdraw from him, and not take him for their guide, and Paſtor, nor truſt their Souls upon his care and conduct. If *Cyprian* had never ſaid [*Plebs maximam habet poteſtatem, vel ſacerdotes dignos eligendi, vel indignos reenſandi,* the Law of nature ſaith enough ; as it doth warrant a man to refuſe an unskilful or malicious murdering Phyſician. And Scripture requireth every man to take heed of falſe Teachers , and deceivers, and from ſuch to turne away.

3. To *ſilence* a falſe Teacher by Argument, (by word or writing) belongeth to every man that is called to contend earneſtly for the faith, and to anſwer a fool according to his folly.

4. To perſwade him by Argument to give over Preaching, or to reform his errours. 1. A private man may do it privately ; 2. Any Miniſter of Chriſt may do it both *ex charitate & ex officio & authoritate,* as a Miniſter of Chriſt in his name. For as a Phyſician doth medicate another Phyſician, not as another man, but as a Phyſician, and a judge doth judge the cauſe of another Judge, not as a private man, but as a Judge ; ſo a Miniſter of Chriſt doth Preach to a Miniſter. and perſwade him, not as a private man but as a Miniſter, not as his ſuperiour, but as a Meſſenger of Chriſt who is his Soveraigne.

5. Yea, to *Command* ſuch a man *ex authoritate Nuntii vel Miniſtri,* by *Miniſterial authority in the name of Chriſt* to forſake his Hereſie and wickedneſs, or to forbear the Sacred Miniſtry, belongeth to Miniſters of the ſame office. For if a Miniſter Preach or ſpeak to another Miniſter as a Miniſter himſelf, and in Chriſts name, then no doubt but he may *command* in Chriſts *name* ; which is but by Miniſterial office to publiſh the Commands of Chriſt : No doubt but he may ſay to another Miniſter [I Counſel, yea Command you in the name of Chriſt, by vertue of my office and his word, to forbear Adultery, Theft, Blaſphemy, Hereſie, or elſe to forbear the Sacred Miniſtry] Yea he may ſay thus (with due reverence) to a Biſhop, ſo that for a ſilencing by Reaſon or force, or by Miniſterial authority and command as from Chriſt, there is no need of the office of a *Dioceſan.*

6. The queſtion therefore is whether we muſt have a Biſhop to ſilence men by *bare Authority without convincing effectual argument* ſatisfying his Conſcience ? or elſe by a diſtinct *Superior Authority,* more powerful than the Miniſters ?

And

And. 1. Seing the *Diocefan* as fuch hath not the Sword, it is certain that he filenceth no further than he prevaileth with the Confcience, either of the Minifter to be filent, or of the people not to *bear him*, or of the *Magiftrates* to filence him by force.

Now to do this, either he muft prove to them from the word of God, by argument, that each of thefe are thus far obliged by God ; or elfe that God hath made him as *Diocefan* the *Judge* , and they are bound to do it, becaufe he bids them do it.

For the firft, as is faid, it belongeth to every Minifter, even with office-authority to tell both Magiftrates, Minifter and people their duty, in the name of Chrift: Thus [God hath commanded Adulterers, Hereticks, &c. To forfake their fins or forbear the Miniftery , and commanded me to publifh this in his name, even to particular perfons : But thou art an Adulterer, Heretick &c. go &c. Or [God commandeth me to tell the people that it is their duty to avoid a Heretick, and the Magiftrate that it is his duty to filence him by force: Therefore I require this of you in his name].

2. But if the *Diocefan* claim a Superiour Nuntiative power , as one more to be *believed* than the Minifter, this is. 1. But to the doing of the fame work which a Minifter may do. 2. And he muft prove that Superiour credibility. 3. But Minifterial conviction is efficacious according to the evidence that is brought to do the work. If the hearer believe not that the Major is Gods word (that an Heretick e.g. muft give over Preaching). Or if he deny the Minor [but thou art an Heretick] it is not a Bifhops word that will convince him, but a Minifter that is better at proving it may do more.

Obj. *but we will command him to be filent.* Anf. And he will deride you and command you to be filent again.

Obj. *Then we will convince the Magiftrate of his duty to filence him by force.* Anf. 1. That was not the way for 300 years after Chrift : And what was *Epifcopacy* for till then ? 2. What if the Magiftrates believe you not, will you convince him *by Scripture* or by your *Authority* over the Magiftrate? It by Scripture a wifer Presbyter can do that better, or as well. It by authority, of that anon.

Obj. *But at leaft we will convince the people that it is their duty to forfake that Preacher.* Anf. Again I fay, if you will do it by Scripture , a Minifter can do it as well. And thus many Minifters now do filence the *Diocefans* and Conformifts, that is, they perfwade the people not to hear them, or own them. But if by *authority*, it muft come to this at laft, that you are made by God the Judges , and this muft be believed.

And remember ftill you *filence no further than you perfwade the Confcience to believe that God hath given you this authority.* And. 1. I ask whether it be ever likely that you will filence any Hereticks , falfe Teacher, or Schifmatick this way by making him take you for one authorized by by God to forbid him to Preach. For it muſt be in one of theſe three caſes or all that you have this power. 1. Either to ſilence him as a Heretick that is no Heretick, or not proved ſuch. 2. Or to ſilence him as a Heretick that notoriouſly and provedly is a Heretick. 3. Or to ſilence him as a Heretick in a doubtful caſe to others, but judged Heretic &c. by you.

1. In the firſt caſe neither the injured perſon, nor any that know that you injure him will or muſt obey you. Elſe a malignant Prelate might ſilence all the holieſt and worthieſt Miniſters of Chriſt, and it would be at ſuch mens mercy, whether Chriſt ſhould have Churches, or the people ſhould be Chriſtians or be ſaved. I am one of the 1800 that have been ſilenced by better authority than the Prelates alone, and yet I think I am bound in Conſcience to exerciſe the Miniſtry which I received, whatever I ſuffer, to the utmoſt of my opportunity. And if the Sword ſtreightened my opportunity no more than my Conſcience of the *Dioceſans* Prohibition, I ſhould be but very little hindered.

2. In the 2d. caſe (of notorious Hereſie) all good Chriſtians are bound by God to avoid ſuch a man, though you never ſilenced him, yea though you licenſed him; yea though you commanded them to hear him: And ſo Magiſtrates are bound to do their duty in reſtraining him, Can you deny this? Muſt the peoples Souls be poyſoned and damned, till the Biſhop pleaſe to take away the poyſon and to ſave them? muſt the Magiſtrate let Hereticks alone till it pleaſe the *Dioceſan* to judge them?

2. And in this caſe, no ſober Chriſtian will deny, that a Presbyter ought to call upon people and Magiſtrates to do their duty, as well as the *Dioceſans*. Yea, and to command men in Chriſts name, to avoid a notorious or proved heretick.

Obj. But a *Presbyter cannot examine the caſe and ſo get proof.* *Anſ.* He may examine it as far as Reaſon with Miniſterial authority will perſwade the *guilty* or the *witneſſes* to be examined. And his care of the Church and the peoples Souls obligeth him ſo to do. And a Prelate cannot bring men by force to examination or witneſſing.

3. But let his guilt be never ſo notorious to others, is it like that the perſon himſelf will be *ſilent* through Conſcience of obedience to a Prelate.

Conſider. 1. that if he will not obey a Miniſter that ſheweth him the word of God, it is unlikely that he will obey a Prelate that ſaith I have authority to ſilence you.

2. A Heretick doth not know that he is a Heretick, nor any erroneous perſon know that it is an errour which he believeth: For it is a contradiction to err in judgment, and to know it to be any errour. And then 1. He knoweth that his office is *durante vita*, and that he is bound not to ceaſe it without cauſe. 2. He knoweth that you have no power to ſilence Orthodox Preachers as Hereticks, but thoſe that are Hereticks indeed.

Y   deed.

deed. 3. He taketh himself for Orthodox and you for the Heretick.
4. And all his followers are of his mind. How then will you silence
a Heretick without the Sword? If you convince him of his errour, you
shall not need to silence him; for he will leave his errour rather than
his Ministry: But if you convince him not of his errour, you will hardly
convince him, that because of that errour, he must be silent; (nor convince his followers that they must not hear him).

3. All the question therefore that remaineth, is, *whether in unknown
doubtful cases, you are the Judges of Heresie, Errour, Schism, and of mens
unworthiness to Preach.* And here. 1. I need not tell you that by this
way you can never silence either the *Arrians*, or any that deny your authority. Of which sort you know are most that you silence in this age
and Nation. No, nor a Donatist, a Novatian, or any one that is for
the office of Bishops, but taketh you for no Bishop as being unduely called: Of which sort were abundance of Christians towards each others
Bishops in former ages; and such are the Papists now towards you.
So that neither Papist nor Protestant that I ever knew silenced by you,
doth forbear upon Conscience of this your pretended authority at all.
And what a silencing power is that which scarce any man would be ever
silenced by? You cannot choose but know this to be true.

2. And really, should Magistrates themselves be so servile to you
as to silence all Ministers by the Sword, whom a Prelate judgeth to be
silent, while he knoweth not whether it be deservedly or not; God
forbid that Protestants, like the Popes, should make Kings to be their
Executioners, or hangmen. A meer Executioner indeed is not bound
to know or examine, whether the sentence was just or not
(though in most cases to forbear if it be notoriously unjust), but what a
King or Magistrate doth, he must do as a publick Judge, and therefore
must hear the cause himself, and try whether he be really guilty or not,
and not only whether a Bishop judged him so. Else Magistrates will either be involved in the bloody sin of persecution, as oft as a Prelate will
but command them; and so must be damned and help to damn others,
when Prelates please: Or else it is no sin for a Magistrate to silence all
the holyest Ministers of Christ, to the damnation of thousands of ignorant untaught Souls, so be it the Prelates do but bid him, and he
keep himself unacquainted with the cause. And next they must obey
the Counsel at *Laterane sub. Inoc.* 3. And exterminate all subjects
out of their Dominions (though it be all that are there) and must
burn Holy-Christians to ashes, because the Pope or Prelates bid
them.

3. I need not make also a particular application of this case to the
people: When they know nothing but wise and sound and holy in the
Doctrine or life of their Pastors, and God bids them *know such as labour
among them and are over them in the Lord, and highly esteem them in Love
for their work sake;* they will hardly be so debauched as to violate this
command;

command of God, as oft as a *Diocesan* will but say [*I know some Heresie or Crime by your Teacher which you do not, and therefore he must Preach no more, and you must no more use his ministry.*] Were I one of these people, I would be bold to ask the *Diocesan* [Sir what is the *Heresie or Crime* that he is guilty of ? If he refuse to tell me I would slight him as a Tyrant : General Counsels told the people of the Heresies for which they did depose their Pastors. If he told me what it was, I would try it by Gods word: If I were unable, I would seek help. If the *Diocesan* silenced my Teacher, and ten neighbour Bishops wiser than he, did tell me that it was for Truth and Duty, and that the Heresie was the Bishops, I would hear my Teacher, and believe the other Bishops before him, (without taking them to be of a higher order.)

The objections against this, and what is before said shall be answered in the next Chapter. You see when it is but opened, how the *Diocesans* power vanisheth into the air.

CHAP. XIII.

That there is no need of such as our Diocesans for the Unity or the Government of the particular Ministers, nor for the silencing of the unworthy.

IT stuck much in the minds of the Ancient Doctors and Christians that *Episcopacy* was necessary to avoid Schism and discord among the Ministers and the people ; and that it was introduced for that reason. And I am so averse to singularity in Religion, that I will not be he that shall gainsay it. A double, yea a treble *Episcopacy*, though I cannot *prove* instituted of Christ, yet will I not contradict, because one sort I cannot *disprove*, and the other two I take to be but a prudential humane determination of the Circumstances of one and the same sacred Ministerial office-work. 1. That which I cannot disprove as to a *Divine Institution*, is a General Ministry over many Churches (like the Scots Visiters at their Reformation) who as Successors to the Apostles and Evangelists in the durable parts of their office, were by a conjunction of Scripture evidence and Divine authority of office, to perswade Pastors and people to their several duties, and to have a chief hand in ordaining and removing Ministers. 2. That which I will not contradict antiquity in, is a Bishop in every particular Church, to be as the chief Presbyter, like the chief Justice on the bench or one of the *Quorum*, as our Parish Ministers now are in respect to all their Curates of the Chappels under them. 3. And I would not deny but at all Ministerial Synods, one man may be Moderator, either *pro tempore*, or for continuance, as there is cause.

Thele

Thefe two laft are but Prudential circumftances, as Doctor *Stilingfleet* hath proved. And in all thefe I like the Difcipline of the *Waldenfes*, *Bohemian* and *Polonian* Churches.

But no Government of the Presbyters, no concord, no keeping out of Herefie, requireth fuch as our *Diocefans*; 1. Who put down all the Bifhops of the particular Churches, under them, 2. And pretending Spiritual Power, Govern by the force of the Magiftrates Sword: 3. And obtrude themfelves on the people and Paftors, without their con- fent, and againft their wills, being by multitudes taken for the ene- mies of the Church. 4. And vifibly before the world introducing fo many bad Minifters, and filencing fo many faithful ones, as in thisage they have done.

Without them we have all thefe means of concord following. 1. We have a clear defcription of the duty of Minifters and people in Gods word. 2. We have Minifters to Preach up all thefe duties by Office. 3. The people are taught by Scripture what Minifters to choofe. 4. We find it natural to the people to be for Learned and godly Minifters, though many of them be bad themfelves. And though it be not fo with them all, yet the fober part do ufually perfwade the reft: So that in *Lon- don* and elfe where, thofe Parifhes where the people choofe, had ufually far worthier Paftors than the reft, efpecially than thofe in the Bifhops prefentation. 5. The people are obliged by God to marke thofe Mini- fters that caufe divifion and contention and avoid them. 6. The Mini- fters are bound to give notice to the people of falfe teachers and Schif- maticks, and to command them to avoid them; And themfelves to re- nounce Communion with them after the firft and fecond admonition. 7. Thefe Minifters may have correfpondence by Synods, to keep up con- cord by agreement among themfelves. So we have over all a Chrifti- an King and Magiftracy, who are the rightful Governours of the Cler- gy as well as of all other fubjects; and may conftrain the negligent to their duty, and reftrain the Heretical, Schifmatical and wicked from their fin. And may not all this do much to keep up Concord?

2. What our *Diocefans* really effect in order to concord or order, they do it by the Magiftrates power, and not by the Keys; without the Magiftrate they would be fo contemned a fort of men, that inftead of fi- lencing us by their keyes, one of us now filenced could do more to fi- lence them, were that according to our Judgment; I mean, it were eafier to perfwade ten people from Hearing one of them (fpecially of late) than for them to perfwade one from hearing us, in many places. And what the Magiftrate doth, he can do by others if he pleafe, as well as now he doth by them.

3. The Churches that have no Bifhops have incomparably leffe He- refie, Schifm, Wickednefs, and more concord than we have here. The Church of *Scotland* is an eminent inftance, which hath known but little by experience what Schifm or Herefies are. And fo are the Proteftant

Proteſtant Churches of *France*, of *Geneva*, of *Helvetia*, and other places:

4. Were but the true *Epiſcopacy* forementioned reſtored, we ſhould yet leſs know any ſhew of need for our *Dioceſane*, Magiſtrate Miniſters, and they would ſuffice, to do what on earth may be expected.

Obj. Were not Biſhops the meanes of the Churches concord in all ages?

Anſ. True Biſhops ſuch as afore deſcribed, did their parts, but when ſuch as our *Dioceſans* ſprang up, the Church was preſently broken into pieces, and by odious contentions and diviſions became a ſcandal and ſcorne to unbelievers. To read but the Acts of Counſels and the Hiſtory of the Church, and there find the horrid contentions of Prelates againſt each others, the parties which they made, their running up and down the world, to Princes and Rulers, and Synods to bear down one another, it will do as much to grieve and amaze the Soul of a Sober Chriſtian, almoſt as an Hiſtory in the world that he can peruſe.

Obj. But they ſilenced Hereticks and depoſed them, and ſo kept Doctrine ſound and ſafe. *Anſ.* Before they had the Sword of the Magiſtrate to ſecond them, they ſilenced none: For how could they do it? They only judged them to be caſt out of their Communion, and depoſed, which they could no way execute but by avoiding them, and perſwading the people to diſown them and avoid them: For they neither did nor could hinder them from gathering Churches and Preaching to their followers: And there the rejected ones did reject their Rejecters, and excommunicate their excommunicaters, and in the eyes of their followers were the better men, and only Orthodox: So that their ſilencing was but changeing their Congregations. And ſo numerous were the ſects that followed ſuch Teachers, that they ſometimes ſeemed more than the Orthodox: *Epiphanius* found enow in his time to fill a large Volume. And the Donatiſts alone were ſo numerous in *Africa* as to pretend to be the Catholick Church, and by their numbers and inſolency deterred *Auguſtine* into a change of his opinion, and to call for that help from the Princes Sword, which before he had denyed. Never had the Church in any place, ſo many Sects and Hereſies, as ſince the times that Prelacy grew up, and in thoſe Countries, and where it was moſt exerciſed. And indeed the ignorance and pride of Prelates was not the leaſt cauſe. For ſome of them (and no ſmall number) became the Authors of Hereſies themſelves, ſuch as *Paulus, Samſſatenus*, the *Apolinarii*, the great Patriarcks, *Dioſcorus, Neſtorius, Macedonius*, and alas how great a number more and others of them did by their domineering inſolency riſe up with ſo much pride and wrath againſt thoſe that humoured them not, eſpecially if indeed they erred, as that they forced ſome into Schiſms, and by ſilenceing the diſſenters, did but drive them to ſet up for themſelves in ſeparated aſſemblies; And they ſo diſ-

affected

affected the zealous people, as drove them away from the Orthodox Churches, to the Sects and Hereticks, as the English Prelates do at this day; so that multitudes of the most strict and temperate Christians followed the *Novations*, the *Donatists*, and much worser sects.

And when the Prelates grew up to a secular terrour, and twisted with the Civil power, and were backed by the Sword, 1. They made the more sober and mortified Christians the more dislike them; as may appear by what *Eusebius*, *Socrates*, and others write of them, and the Characters that are given of *Cyril* and *Theophilus*, *Alexander*, and such others: And by *Martins* separation from *Ithacius* and *Idacius*, and their Synods, and by the increase of the Priscilianists by their pride and violence, mentioned by *Sulp. Severus*, and others. 2. And it was not by the Keys indeed, but by the Sword which backt them, that they did all that they did, be it good or evil, in silencings, and in keeping up their order. 3. And they did but teach the Hereticks to strengthen themselves, by the same means : So that the Priscilianists once got countenance from *Gratians* Courtiers against the Bishops; And *Ambrose* was persecuted or endangered by *Valentinian*, as *Athanasius* at last was by *Constantine* himself, and *Chrysostome* deposed, and many others by such means : Yea till at last the Bishops found that evil is more commonly befriended by corrupted nature than good; and that Goodness is usually lowest where wealth and honours make men highest, and that few Princes were the best of men, and therefore that if one befriended the truth, many were like to be against it, and till the *Arrians* by the help of Emperours, and *Vandal* and *Gothish* Kings, had almost turned all the Church into *Arrians*, and had got the General Councels on their sides, and had cruelly persecuted the Orthodox Bishops, and taught them what it was to trust to the Sword, for the clensing and concord of the Churches. And when the controversie of Images came up, one Emperour was for them and another against them : By which means and by the contending of the Eastern and Western Patriarcks and Prelates, who should be the greatest, the Churches have been torne to pieces, and so continue lamentably to this day (as in the History was before declared.)

And it was the Prelatical Tyranny of the Romanists, that since raised so many parties against them, and then had no way to Curb them, but by prosecuting them by the Sword and flames, as in the case of the *Waldenses*, *Albigenses*, and *Protestants* appeareth: And as the Murders of many hundred thousands in *Piedmont*, *France*, *Germany*, *Ireland*, *England*, &c, Besides their Inquisitions shew. Thus *Solitudinem fecerunt*, *& unitatem & pacem vocarunt*. When they have hanged, burnt and slain the people and Priests, they have quieted and silenced them, and when they have made a solitude and depopulation by killing those that differ'd from them, they have brought all to concord, and been all of a mind.

And

And let none be offended that I mention the Papists in describing Prelacy. For I do it not to raise an Odium on them; but I refer it to the consideration of sober men, 1. Whether as *Herbarists* give us the picture and description of herbes, not in their spring, but in their full grown stalk, blossom and fruits, and as he that will know the nature and difference of fruits, or animals, must stay till they are come to their full growth and ripeness, and not take them green and young; so he that will judge either of *Schism* or of *Church-tyranny* must do. 2. And whether the *Quakers, Ranters, Familists* and *Minister-monsters* be not *Schismaticks* ripe and at full growth, and therefore a young Schismatick is not to tell us what Schism is, but should himself see what he will be when he is ripe. And so whether Popery be not the *Diocesane* Prelacy full grown and ripe; and whether they should not therefore see what they would come to, if that which withholdeth in the several Kingdoms were taken out of the way, as the Pope hath removed it in the Empire. If the *Diocesans,* Metropolitanes, Patriarks, and Pope (as to his Primacy in the Empire) did not all stand on the same humane foundation, then are they not the things that I am speaking of.

Obj. But the late and present Schismes in England shew that it is the Adversaries of Prelacy that are the causes.

Ans. Very true, for Prelacy maketh it self adversaries, and so maketh some of the Schismaticks. There are two sort of *Schismaticks*; some *Prelatists* (as the Papists, the *Novatians,* the *Donatists,* and most of the old Schismaticks were); and some Anti-prelatists. And there are two sorts of Anti-prelatists: Some Catholick being for the Primitive *Episcopacy,* and some Schismaticks. And these last the Prelates make, and then complain of them. It is their state, and practice, hereafter described, that driveth men to distast them, and so precipitateth the injudicious into the Contrary extreme. It is Prelacy that maketh almost all the Sects that be in *England* at this day: When they see how the Spiritual Keys are secularly used by Laymen in their Courts, when they see what Ministers and how many hundred of them are silenced, and what Fellows in many places are set up in their stead, they think they can never fly far enough from such Prelates: To tell the world, It is Schismaticks that we silence, and they are obedient and Orthodox persons that we set up, may signifie something in another land or age, but it doth but increase the disaffection of those that are upon the place, and know what kind of men the Prelates commend, and who they discommend and silence. A very Child when he is eating his apple, will not cast it away, because a Prelate saith it is a Crab, nor when he catcheth a Crab, will he eate it, if a Prelate Swear it is a sweat apple. Though he that doth but look on them may possibly believe him.

I believe they that thought that Prelacy was the only cure of our Schismes, do know by this time by experience, that by that time the Prelates had again ruled but seven years, there were seven and seven
against

against them for one that was so before: And we that dwell among them, do take those that dislike their course and waies, to be the Generality of the most Religious and sober people of the land (alwaies excepting the King and Parliament and those that must be still excepted).

CHAP. XIV.

The true Original of the warrantable Episcopacy in particular Churches, was the notorious disparity of abilities in the Pastors: And the original of that tyrannical Prelacy into which it did degenerate, was the worldly Spirit in the Pastors and people, which with the world came by prosperity into the Church. Quære, Whether the thing cease not, where the reason of it ceaseth?

GOd doth not carry on his work upon mens Souls, by names and empty titles; but by such real demonstrating evidences of his *Power*, *Wisdome* and *Goodness*, as are apt to work on the Reason of man. And therefore he that would make his Apostles the Foundations or chief Pillars and Instruments in and of his Churches, would accordingly endow them with proportionable abilities, that in the *Miraculous* demonstrations of *Power*, and the convincing demonstrations of *Wisdome*, and he amiable holy demonstrations of *goodness*, they might as far excel others as they did in authority.

And nature it self reacheth us to difference men in our *esteem* and *affection*, as they really differ in worth and lovelines. And this Law of Nature is the Primary Law of God: And the holy Scriptures plainly second it, telling us oft of the diversity of Gods gifts in his Servants, which all make for concord, but not for equality of esteem; and that there are greater and lesser in the Kingdom of God, and that Gods gifts in all men must be honoured, *Math.* 12. 1 *Cor.* 12. *Eph.* 4. *Hb.* 5. 10. 11. 12. & 6. 1. 2. 3. 4.

And God that would have his various gifts variously esteemed, did in all ages himself diversifie his Servants gifts. All were not Apostles, nor all Prophets, nor all Evangelists: And after their daies all the Ministers or Elders of the Churches were not men of Learning, nor of so full acquaintance with the sacred Doctrine, nor so grave, prudent, staied, holy, charitable, or peaceable as some were usually when miraculous gifts did cease, and very few Philosophers or men of learning turned Christians. Any man may know that had not been told it by Church-History, that their Elders or Pastors were such as the better sort of our unlearned Christians are; who can pray well, and worship

C

God sincerely, and read the Scripture, and in a plain familiar manner, can teach the Catechistical points, and perswade to duty and reprove vice: But as for Sermons in a methodical accurate way, as now used, and defending the truth, and opposing Heresies, and stopping the mouths of gainsayers, they must needs be far below the Learned. But yet here and there a Philosopher was converted; and of those that had no such Learning (then called secular, and the Learning of the Gentiles) some few were far better Learned than others in the sacred Scriptures, and the customes and Learning of the Jews: And it was long before the Christians had Schools and Academies of their own.

That this was so, appeareth. 1. In the reason of the thing. For no effect can exceed the total cause. Therefore they that had not the inspirations prophetical, or miraculous guifts, nor Academies and Schools of secular Learning, nor so much as Riches and leisure, but Poverty and persecution and worldly trouble and labour, were not like to have more Learning than the holy Scriptures taught them.

2. And this appeareth by the forecited Canons of Counsels, which forbad Pastors, even almost three hundred years after Christ, to read the Gentiles books. By which the former custome of the Church may easily be perceived. And also by abundance of reproaches which are cast upon some Hereticks in the Ancients writings, for being too much skilled in Logick and other of the Gentiles Learning.

3. And it appeareth by the parity of writers of the second and third Centuries.

4. And also by the paucity of famous Divines that are mentioned in the Histories of those times.

5. And above all by the plainness and simplicity of those that are described and of their writings. I speak not in any contempt of them for this (perhaps we value common learning now too highly) But only to tell you the true History of those times. No doubt but many poor men among us, (divers Weavers and some Plowmen, of the Church which I was removed from, for instance) are able to pray, and teach as well as most of those who are by Eusebius extolled as the famous Bishops of the second and third age; and to write as Methodical, pious, weighty tractates, as any that were then written by men that neither conversed with the Apostles, nor had been bred up in Philosophy: That I say not as Clemens Romanus himself, or Ignatius, or Irenæus, yea or Cyprians, Epistles are. Yea, or as many of the ages following; even as holy Macarius, Ephrem, Cyrus, Synisius, (a Philosopher) Isidore, Pelusiota, and many more have written since. If this be not believed, how many Lay-men could I name who have written more accurately and judiciously, and as far as the writings shew, as piously as any of these? And that not only Learned Lay-men, but men that had neither many Languages nor Philosophy. And if the books then written were very few, and of those very few that were written by any but Bishops or Philosophers,

Z   losophers,

losophers, and those few so plaine as we see they are, (the best of them far below the writings of abundance of late Latin and English and French writers, that were but Presbyters), you may easily judge of what parts the rest of the Presbyters of those times were, that never wrote.

And from hence you may gather the reasons, 1. Why so few Volumes are left us written in the two first ages. 2. And why the Churches had then so many Presbyters. (Whatever Doctor *Hammond* say to the contrary without any proof.) It was easy to find such Christians as afore-decribed, who might competently guide the rest by Doctrine, worship, discipline and example: Though to find Learned men was hard. 3. And you may see why so many Hereticks boasted so much of their higher knowledge, and Platonical &c. speculations, as accounting the Orthodox to be ignorant men. 4. And you may see why so few were Champions for the truth. 5. And why there were so many parties and divisions, when the Elders were many and less judicious. 6. And you may see how the opinion of Ecclesiastick meer Ruling Elders came up; and how to expound *Pauls*, 1 *Tim.* 5. 17. *Especially them that labour in the Word and Doctrine.* For it was but here and there a Learned or special gifted Christian, that was able solemnly and ornately to Preach, decide hard cases and controversies, confute Hereticks, and guide the Churches in difficult cases. And the rest did sit about the Bishop as his assistants, and Preach and officiate at his direction, and oversee the people from man to man; being of the same order and office with the Bishop, but not of the same parts, and therefore not equal in the exercise.

7. And therefore lastly hence you may see, the reasons of the first fixed particular Church *Episcopacy*: Those few that were Philosophers or eminently qualified (being scarce enow to make one for every Church) did by their gifts overtop the rest in the due esteem of all the people: Who were bound to esteem him wisest that was wisest, and to yield more to his judgment than to others that knew less: And this inequality of gifts usually lasted as long as life; and therefore so did the inequality of esteem and reverence. And both the people and the inferiour gifted Pastors, obeyed the Law of God in nature, and readily gave honour to whom honour was due. And when one was dead finding another fit to excel the rest, they accordingly preferred him before the rest, even as an excellent Physician would be by the patients, and by all the younger and more ignorant Physicians, that are not carryed away with pride. And this did easily (as all things else) turne into formality under pretence of order, and come to seem a kind of *Office*. But when difference required it, I know not but that all this was well done, except that they foresaw not the degenerate tyranny that would afterward hence arise.

This present experience openeth to us to the day. What did set up *Luther*, and *Melancthon*, and *Illyricus*, but their eminent parts? What else

elſe gave _Zuinglius_ and _Oecolampadius_ the Preſidencie at _Zurich_? What elſe did ſet up _Calvin_, and _Beza_ at _Geneva_? And _Knox_ and _Henderſon_ in _Scotland_? And all our Parſthes that have Chappels and Curates ſhew it here in _England_: Where one man for his worth is thought meeteſt to have the Benefice and chief cure; but others may be choſen by him and placed under him, and maintained by him (by the Biſhops allowance) as his curates.

And indeed it was ſo long before Academies made a ſufficient ſtore of men of ſufficiencie for every Presbyters place, that for four or five hundred years, there were few bred up to competent Learning, except either under Heathens, or elſe in a Biſhops houſe, or here and there as an Auditor of ſome one rare Teacher. _Clemens Alexandrinus_, as a Diſciple of _Pantænus_ and _Origene_ of _clemens_, and ſome few others, came to Learning, as auditors in that _Alexandrian_ School: But few other places beſides _Alexandria_ had any ſuch School of a long time, in ſo much as _Nazianzen_, _Baſil_, _Greg. Niſſen_, _Chryſoſtome_, &c. were taught at _Athens_, by _Lybanius_ and ſuch other Heathens; And _Ambroſe_, _Auguſtine_, and many others, were in a manner αὐτοδίδακτοι, ſelf taught, ſo that it was not poſſible then to have many Learned men ordinarily for one Church (or congregation) And yet many Presbyters certainly they had. Which is the true cauſe that one Learned man was made an Overſeer and Guide to the reſt, who were his Curates or Aſſiſtants, gifted like our wiſer ſort of the Lai-y, but of the ſame Office and order with him; And this Biſhop was the uſual Preacher, and the other did learne of him to Preach, and grew up under him as Scholars; and he that came to greateſt abilities under him, was choſen for a Biſhop to another Church that wanted, but not without his own Biſhops conſent, which made the debate in Councels ſo frequent, whether a Presbyter might remove to another Church, or be choſen for a Biſhop of another Church? And an _African_ Council giveth it as a Reaſon why that Biſhop that had able Presbyters, ſhould not refuſe to let one go to be a Biſhop elſewhere, becauſe where there were many fit to be Presbyters, there were but few men fit to be made Biſhops, which implieth that they took it not then for a meer place of order, where one man of equal parts was for Unity to rule the reſt, but for a neceſſary difference of exerciſing the ſame Office, becauſe of the different abilities of the Officers: Which was not only to keep an order by diſparity of places, but to educate the Presbyters to greater abilities, and to manage Gods work in each aſſembly more skilfully and guide the Church more prudently, and defend the truth more powerfully, than common unlearned Presbyters could do.

Now let it be for the preſent granted that for ſuch reaſons _Epiſcopacy_ in each Church was juſtly ſetled, and call it an order or a degree as you pleaſe; It will be a difficult queſtion, what ſhall be judged of thoſe that have the ſame place and Title, without the ſame Qualifications and precedencie of parts? Becauſe the Reaſon of his power faileth. If one be choſen Biſhop to keep out Hereſie, and he prove a Heretick, and the Presbyters Orthodox, what is his power to that end? If one be choſen Biſhop to keep out Schiſm, and he prove a Schiſmatick or Sect-Maſter, and the reſt concordant, what is his power? If one be made Biſhop to teach the people better than the Presbytres, and to teach the Presbyters themſelves, and to defend truth and Godlineſs, and he prove more ignorant than the Presbyters, and Preach not to the thouſandth or hundredth part of his Dioceſe once in all his life, nor to any at all paſt once in many weeks or months or years, and if he do but ſilence the Miniſters that are abler and farr more pious than himſelf, what

Z 2   power

power hath he as a Bifhop to thofe ends? Sure I am that *difpofitio materiæ is neceffary* as *fine quâ non, ad receptionem formæ*. If one be made a School-maſter, that cannot teach the Scholars haiffo much as they know already, but hath need to learne of them, and yet will neither learne of them, nor fuffer them to learne without him, I know not well how farr he is their Schoolmaſter indeed. If one be made a Phyſician, that knoweth not half fo much as I do, I fhould be loth for Order fake to venture my life upon his truſt. Nor yet to venture my own life and others in a Ship that had an ig-norant Pilote, when the Mariners had more skill, but muſt not ufe it. Or-ders and Office that are appointed for the work's fake, effentially fuppofe ability for that work. And without the neceffary qualifications, they are but the Carkaffes or images of the office (but of this before).

Therefore it is that the Chriſtian flocks could never yet be cured, by all the art or tyranny that could be ufed, of the efteem of *real Wifdome* and *Godlinefs*, and preferring it before an *empty title*, or a *pompous fhew*, and from fetting lefs by *Ignorance* and *Impiety* venerably *named* and *arrayed*, then by felt evidencing worth; nor from valuing a Shepherd that daily feedeth them, from a Wolfe in Sheeps cloathing, that hath Fangs and bloody jawes, and fleeceth and devoureth the flock (with the Shepherds.)

And hence we may fay that *God himfelf* ufeth *to give Bifhops* to the Church; whether men will or not; while he giveth them fuch as (*Jerome*) Luther, *Melanckhorn, Bucer, Calvin, Zanchius, &c,* Who had *Epifcopal ability,* and *really did that* which Bifhops were firſt appointed for, while the Bifhops would have hindered them and fought their blood They *taught* the peo-ple, they *bred up young Miniſters,* they *kept out Herefies and Schifmes,* they *guided the churches* by the light of Sacred truth, and by the power of Reafon and Love: And who than was the Bifhop? who is the real Architect he that buildeth the houfe, or he that hath the title, and doth nothing unlefs it be hindering the builders?

To this already faid I add but two more intimations, which I defire the fober impartial Reader to confider. 1. Writing is but a mode of Preaching: And of the two it is worfe to have inept Sermons in Publick Affemblies (and fo Gods worke and worfhip difhonoured), than to have inept bookes in private. And no doubt, the Paſtors overfight extends to publick and pri-vate. Now while the meer worth of bookes without any Authority, com-mendeth them to the world, though fometimes with fome few, giddy Pam-phlets are accepted, yet that is but for a fit; and ordinarily the Book-fellers fufficiently reſtrain all that are not of worth, becaufe they cannot fell them. But if a Bifhop muſt impofe on all the people what bookes they muſt read, in many Kingdoms it will be for the Pope and Maffe, in others for Exorcifm and Confubſtantion, &c.

2. Is not order for the the thing ordered? *Epifcopacy* is for the Churches benefit by the Bifhops eminent gifts and parts. But if the Bifhop be of low-er parts, than the Paſtors (and an Envious Malignant hinderer of their work), Quere, Whether the order (being humane) ceafe not, *ubi ceffat fub-jecti difpofitio & relatio ad finem;* when the end and the pefons capacity ceafe.

I I. But how the world by the countenance of Emperours was invited to come int the Church? How worldly wealth, power and honour did indue them? How Bifhopricks were made baites for the proud and tyrannical and Covetous? How fuch then fought them and fo the worldly Spirit had the rule, and altered *Epifcopacy,* I fhewed in the Hiſtory before.

C H A P.

THE
Second Part.

Having in the former Part laid down thofe Grounds on which the Applicatory Part is to be built, and fubverted the foundations of that Diocefane frame which we judge unlawful, I fhall now proceed to give you the Application, in the particular Reafons of our judgment, from the Evils which we fuppofe this frame to be guilty of.

CHAP. I.

The clearing of the ftate of the Queftion.

THE occafion of our difpute, or rather Apology, is known in *England.* 1. Every man that is ordained Deacon or Presbyter (or licenfed a Schoolmafter) muft fubfcribe to the Books of Articles, Liturgy and Ordination, as *Ex animo that there is nothing in them contrary to the Word of God.* And by the late Act of Uniformity [*that he doth affent and confent to all things conteined in, and preferibed by the faid books* as fince altered (we think for the worfe.)

2. In the year 1640 the Convocation formed, printed and imposed a new Oath in these words (after others) [*Nor will I ever give my consent to alter the Government of this Church, by Arch-Bishops, Bishops, Deans, Arch-Deacons, &c. as it stands now established, and as by right it ought to stand.*]

3. After this the Parliament in the Wars imposed a Vow and Covenant on the Ministers and People contrary to this called the *Et cetera Oath* ; which Vow contained a clause to endeavour the extirpation of this Prelacy. In the *Westminster* Assembly before it passed, many Learned Divines declared that they would not take it as against Prelacy unexplained, lest it should seem to be against all Episcopacy, which was not their judgment, they being for the primitive Episcopacy. To satisfie these men (that else had protested against it, and the Assembly been divided, the *Scots* and some others being against all) the additional Titles of Deans, Chapters, &c. were put in as a description of the peculiar English frame of Prelacy which they all agreed against. Since His Majesty's Restoration, there are many Acts made against the belief of an obligation by this Vow. One is made for a change in Corporations, requiring a Declaration by all in any place of Trust, [*that there is no obligation on me or any other person from the said Oath, Vow or Covenant*] even absolutely no obligation at all without exception of the clauses that are for the Protestant Religion, for Repentance of our sins, against Popery, Heresie, Schism, Prophaneness, &c. The Act of Uniformity imposeth it on all Ministers, &c. to declare or subscribe that there is no *obligation* from that Vow on me or any other person to endeavour at any time any alteration of Government in the Church.] The Vestry Act imposeth the like on all Vestry men ; and so of others.

4. All Ministers swear to obey the Bishops *in licitis & honestis*, which is called the Oath of Canonical Obedience.

5. And last of all an Act past at *Oxford* by which we are to be banished five miles from all Cities and Corporations, and all places where we have preached, and imprisoned six months in the Common Jail, if we come nearer any of them, except on the Road, till we have taken an Oath [*that we will not at any time endeavour an alteration of the Government of the Church,*] (which plainly importeth as much objectively as the *Et cetera* Oath of 1640 ; Though *not endeavouring* be somewhat less than *not consenting*.) And so black a Character is put upon the Non-conformists, with a [*some of them*) in the beginning of the said Act, that all Reason, Religion and Humanity obligeth us for the satisfaction of our Rulers, for the vindication of our selves, and for the just information of posterity, plainly and truly to lay open our Case, even those reasons for which we forbear that Conformity ; and by so doing, incurr all this, besides the greater loss of our Ministerial Liberty, to labour for the saving of the peoples souls, and the edifying of the Church of God.

What is said in the beginning may sufficiently inform the Reader, 1. That it is not every man's Cause that is called a Non-conformist, no nor a Presbyterian, or Independant that I here maintain. 2. That I am not writing a Justification of the Covenant, 1. As to the Act of Imposing. 2. Or of taking it. 3. Nor as to the obligation of it to any thing unlawful. Leaving such matters

as

as alien to my work. 3. And that I am not so rash as to assert that it obligeth any man, *to endeavour* (in his place and calling) *any change of our Church Government*, no not of a Lay-Chancellor's use of the Keys, whatever I think, Because it is made a matter of so grievous penalty by an Act. All that I have to do is, to enquire whether the Diocesane Prelacy as now stated, be so lawful that we may take all these Oaths and Subscriptions to it, and so necessary that the King and Parliament have no power to change it, or make an alteration if they please, and we endeavour it by obeying them if they should command us.

And I go upon such Principles as Doctor *Burges*, Master *Gataker*, and many others in the Assembly, that were ready to protest that they were not against the Primitive Episcopacy, no nor a moderate one that did not in all things reach it.

I will rather be guilty of Repetition than of leaving the rash or heedless under a pretext for their mistake or calumny.

My own judgment is as followeth. 1. *That every particular Church, (consisting of as full a number as can associate for true personal Communion in Worship and holy living)* should be guided by as many Pastors or Elders (of the same Office) as the number of souls, and the work requireth.

2. That it is lawful, (if not usually laudable and fit) if these Presbyters consent that one among them who is wiser and fitter than the rest, be statedly their Guide, Director, or Moderator; in the matters of Doctrine, Worship and Discipline in that Church, for order and concord, and for the peoples sakes and their own : And especially that in Ordinations they do nothing without him.

3. That these particular Churches with their Bishop and Presbytery are Independant, so far that no other Bishop or Church hath a Divine Right to Govern them, saving what is anon to be said of General Pastors or Visiters, and the power of each Minister in the Universal Church, as he is called.

4. That as to the Communion of several Churches among themselves, these particular Churches are not Independent, but must hold Concord and Correspondency by Letters, Messengers or Synods as there shall be cause.

5. That in these Synods it is lawful and orderly oftentimes to make some one the Moderator or Guide of their debates. And that either *pro tempore*, or *quamdiu sit maxime idoneus*, or *durante vita*, as true Prudence shall discern it to be most conducible to the end.

6. That where the Churches Good and the calling of the Infidel World requireth it, there should be itinerant Ministers, like the old Evangelists, *Silas*, *Apollo*, *Timothy*, *Titus*, &c. to preach the Gospel, and gather Churches, and help their Pastors. And if such be not necessary in any place, yet the fixed Pastors should when there is cause be itinerant, and help to convert the Infidels and Hereticks, and do both the general and particular work.

7. That the judgment of Antiquity moving me much, but more the Argument from the necessity, [that the same form of Government be continued in

A 2   its

its ordinary parts, which Chrift at firft fetled in the Apoftles, and is not proved repealed] do move me to incline to think that the Apoftles muft have fuch Succeffors, as general Planters and Overfeers of many Churches. And who fhould (before all particular Bifhops) have a chief hand in the ordaining of particular Bifhops and Paftors, and removing them as the Churches good requireth (As the Seniors have in the *Bohemian Waldenfes* Government.) And though I am yet in doubt my felf, whether fuch general Minifters, or Arch-bifhops be *jure divino*, of Chrifts inftitution, I do not deny it, or contend againft it: And though I would not affert or fwear to their right, I would obey them.

8. That all this Church-power is to be exercifed only by *Gods word*, managed by convincing Reafon, Love and good Example, and that no Bifhops or Arch-bifhops have any power of Corporal Coaction ; Nor fhould give Church Communion to any but Voluntary Confenters ; nor fhould mix and corrupt the exercife of the Keys, with unfeafonable interpofitions of the Sword even in the Magiftrates own hand.

9. But yet that the King and Magiftrates are the Rulers by the Sword over all Paftors and their Flocks, to fee that all men do their duties, and to regulate them by Laws about holy things, fubferviently to the Kingdom and Laws of Chrift, and in confiftence with the prefervation of the Office of the Miniftry and real liberties of the Flocks.

10. And therefore, though we think Churchmen ufually very unfit for any Magiftratical Power, yet we fhall obey as his Minifters any whomfoever the King fhall commit any part of his power about Church matters to ; and promife them due obedience as fuch.

And fo you fee what *is not* the Queftion now to be debated.

But the Queftion is [*Whether the prefent Church Government in* England *(as diftinct from the Kings and Magiftrates part) be fo good or lawful, that we fhould fwear or fubfcribe our approbation of it, our obedience to it, or that we will never (in our place and calling) endeavour an alteration of it (no though the King command us) and that every man in the three Kingdoms that vowed to endeavour fuch alteration, is fo clearly and utterly difobliged, as that all ftrangers that never knew him may fubfcribe or declare that he is difobliged, or not obliged to it by that Vow.*

CHAP.

CHAP. II.

*The first Argument against the English Diocesans;
That their form (*quantum in se*) destroyeth the particular Church Form of God's Institution, and setteth
up a Humane Form in its stead.*

ARGUMENT I.

WE cannot subscribe or swear to that form of Church Government as
good or lawful, which in its nature excludeth or destroyeth *the very specifical nature of the particular Churches which were instituted by the Holy
Ghost, and setled in the primitive times, and is it self a humane form set up in
their stead.*

But such we take the present *Diocesane form to be :* Ergo,

The Major will be denied by very few that we have now to do with. And
those few that will deny it, must do it on this supposition, 1. That the Holy
Ghost did institute that particular Church Form which is destroyed but *pro
tempore.* And Secondly, That he allowed men since to set up one or more
of their own in its stead. But the disproof of this supposition will fall in more
fitly, when I have shewed what Church Form was first setled.

The Minor I thus prove.

The Species of a particular Church which the Holy Ghost did institute, was [one
Society of Christians united under one or more Bishops, for personal Communion in
publick worship and holy living.]

The Diocesane English frame is (destructive of or) *inconsistent with this species of
a particular Church.*

Ergo, *The Diocesane English frame is inconsistent with* (or destructive of) *the
Species of the Holy Ghosts institution.*

In the Major, 1. By [Bishops] I mean, Sacred Ministers authorized by
Divine appointment, to be the stated Guides of the Church, by Doctrine,
Worship and Discipline, under Christ the Teacher, Priest and Ruler of the
Church. Whether he have a superior Arch-Bishop I determine not ; Nor now
whether he may ordain Pastors for other Churches.

What I mean by [*Personal Communion*] and whether it be consistent with
divers Assemblies, I have fully shewed before. I mean, that the said Churches
were no more numerous than our English Parishes, nor had more Assemblies ;
Or no more than could have the same personal Communion, and that there
were never any Churches *infimæ vel primæ speciei*, which consisted of many
such stated Assemblies.

I shall

I shall therefore now prove, 1. That the Churches of the Holy Ghosts institution were no more numerous, or were such single Congregations. And that they had each such Bishops and Pastors will be proved partly herewith, and partly afterward.

2. And that such Churches do *tota specie* differ from the Diocesane Churches, and from our present Parish Churches as they define them, and are inconsistent with them. And the first I shall prove, 1. From the Holy Scriptures. 2. From the Confessions of the Diocesanes. 3. From the testimony of Antiquity. All proving fully that the ancient Episcopal Churches were but such single Societies or Congregations as I have described, and such as our Diocesses of many hundred Churches are different from, and inconsistent with.

CHAP. III.

That the primitive Episcopal Churches of the Holy Ghosts Institution, were but such Congregations as afore described.

THese following particulars set together, I think will by the Impartial be taken for full proof.

1. In all the New Testament, where ever there were more stated societies than one, for publick worship as afore described, they are called [*Churches*] in the Plural Number, and never once [*a Church*] in the Singular Number; except when the *Universal Church* is mentioned which containeth them all. This is visible in *Act.*9.31.[and 14.41.and 16.5. *Rom.*16.4, and 16. 1 *Cor.*7.17. and 11. 16. and 14. 33,34. (unless that mean the several meetings of the same Assembly at several times) and 16. 1, 19. 2 *Cor.* 8. 1, 18, 19, 23, 24. and 11. 8,28. *Gal.* 1. 22. 1 *Theff.* 2. 14. 2 *Theff.* 1. 4. *Rev.* 1. 4, 11, 20. and 2. 7, 11, 17, 29. and 3.6, 13, 22, 23. and 22. 16.

If any say, how prove you that all these were but single Congregations, I answer, 1. It is granted me by all that these plural terms [*Churches*] included many single Congregations. 2. I shall prove anon that the most of the particular Churches named in Scripture were but such Congregations. 3. And no man can give me any proof that a Society consisting of divers such Congregations is any where called [*a Church*] singularly : And therefore we are not to believe that the plural term meaneth many such singulars, as are no where singularly named.

2. Particular Churches are described so in Scripture as fully proveth my aforesaid limitation and description. As 1 *Cor.* 11. 16, 18, 20, 22. *When ye*
come

come together in the Church I hear that there be divisions among you. A Church consisted of such as came together.

When ye come together into one place, this is not to eat the Lords Supper. And it is the *Assemblies* that are called Churches, when he saith [*We have no such custom, nor the Churches of God.*]

So 1 *Cor.* 14. 4. *He that prophesieth edifieth the Church*] that is, the Assembly that heareth him, and not many hundred such Assemblies that are out of hearing.

Verf. 5. *Except he interpret that the Church may receive edifying.*

Verf. 12. *Seek that ye may excel to the edifying of the Church.*

Object. *May not the whole Church be edified* per partes ? *Anf.* Yes, but it must be *per plures vel diversis vicibus.* Not at once by the same man, if the far greatest part of the Church be absent.

Obj. *But is not the whole man edified (naturally or morally) by the edification of a part ? Answ.* Yes, if it be a noble part : Because the whole man being naturally One, by the unity of the soul or form, there is a natural Communion and Communication from part to part : But one Corporation in a Kingdom, may be edified or enriched without the wealth or edification of the rest. And this Text plainly speaketh of Immediate Edification of *that Church that heareth,* and this at once, and by one speaker.

So Verf. 19. *In the Church I had rather speak one word with my understanding, that I may teach others.* Here the *Church* is plainly taken for the *Assembly.*

Verf. 23. *If therefore the whole Church be come together in one place, and speak with tongues,*] what can be more expresly spoken to shew that it is not only a part of the Church, but the *whole* which cometh together into one place.

So Verf. 24. *If there be no Interpreter let him keep silence in the Church.*]

So Verf. 34. *For God is not the Author of Confusion, but of Peace, as in all the Churches of the Saints.*

So Verf. 14. *Let your women keep silence in the Church, for it is a shame for women to speak in the Church.*

So Act. 11. 26. *A whole year they assembled themselves with the Church, and taught much people.*

Act. 14. 27. *When they were come, and had gathered the Church together, they rehearsed all that God had done by them.*

Act. 15. 3. *And they were brought on their way by the Church,*] which must signifie such a number as might be called the Church, when part was but for the whole, at least.

Act. 2. 1. *They were all with one accord in one place ;* which it's like was all the Church with the Apostles.

Verf. 44. 46. *And all that believed were together, And they continuing daily with one accord in the Temple,* &c.

Act. 4. 31, 32. *And the place was shaken where they were assembled together. And the multitude of them that believed were of one heart, and of one soul.*

Act. 5. 12. *And they were all with one accord in* Solomon's *Porch, and of the rest durst no man joyn himself to them.* .

If.

If any here fay that fo many thoufands could not be of one Affembly, I have anfwered it before. 1. I have preached (as was fuppofed) to ten thoufand at once. 2. Some of our Parifhes that have but one Church, are thirty thoufand, fome forty thoufand, fome fifty thoufand. 3. There were ftrangers at *Jerufalem* from all parts. 4. The next Verfe faith [*There came alfo a multitude out of the Cities round about unto* Jerufalem.] 5. The multitude were not yet perfectly embodied, and were quickly fcattered.

Col. 4. 16. *When this Epiftle is read among you, caufe that it be read. alfo in the Church of the Laodiceans,* &c. It is not [*to the Church*] for then you might have faid that fo it may be if the Church confifted of many Affemblies: But it is [*in the Church*] which intimateth that the Church was but one Affembly. And fo that of *Coloffe* anfwerably.

All thefe Texts and others fuch plainly tell us whether a Church there was one Affembly or many hundred.

3. This is made yet much more evident, by the Scriptures defcription of a Bifhops work; even fuch as the Apoftles then appointed over every Church. 1. They were to be the ordinary publick prefent teachers of all the Flock which they did overfee. 1 Theff. 5. 12, 13. *Know them which labour among you and are over you in the Lord, and efteem them highly in love for their work fake.* Thofe then that were over every Church, were prefent with the Church, and *laboured among them* (which they could not do in one of our Dioceffes, faving as a man may be faid to labour among a Kingdom, or the World, becaufe they labour in it.)

Heb. 13. 8, 17, 24. *Remember them which have the rule over you, which have fpoken to you the word of God. Obey them that have the Rule over you, and fubmit your felves, for they watch for your fouls as they that muft give account.* So that a Church was no bigger than the Bifhops could *fpeak the word of God to, and could watch for their fouls.* But I never faw the face of the Bifhop of the Diocefs where I live, and know but very few men in his Diocefs that ever did fee him.

2. And this care was to extend to the particular perfons of the Flocks. *Act.* 20. 20, 28, 31. *I taught you publickly, and from houfe to houfe. Take heed to your felves, and to all the Flock over which the Holy Ghoft hath made you Bifhops, to feed (or rule) the Church of God,* &c. *Remember that by the fpace of three years I ceafed not to warn every one night and day with tears.*

1 Pet. 1. 2, 3. *The Elders which are among you I exhort who am alfo an Elder, feed the Flock of God which is among you, taking the overfight thereof, not by conftraint,* &c. that is, faith Doctor *Hammond* [*The Bifhops of your feveral Churches I exhort, take care of your feveral Churches, and govern them, not as Secular Rulers by force, but as Paftors do their Sheep by calling and going before them, that fo they may follow of their own accord.*] See alfo Doctor *Hammond's Annot.* on *Heb.* 13. 7, 17. 1 *Theff.* 5. 12, 13. And faith Doctor *Jeremy Taylor,* of *Repent. Pref.* [*I am fure we cannot give account of fouls of which we have no notice.*] (O terrible word to the undertakers of fo many hundred Churches, and fo many thoufand or ten thoufand fouls which they never knew!)

This

This made *Ignatius* (as after cited) say, that *The Bishop must look after or take account of each person as much as Servants and Maids.*

Object. *But there may be more in a Parish than a Minister can know.* *Answ.* If a Parish may be too large for a Bishops work, how little reason have they to make a Church, and take the Pastoral Care of many hundred Parishes? 2. We must judge by the ordinary common case. In a Parish a Minister may know every one, except it be some few strangers or retired persons, or except it be a Parish or Church of too great a swelling bigness: But in a Diocess of many hundred Churches, it is not one of a hundred that the Bishop will ever know. 3. I know by experience what may be done, whatever slothful persons say; I had a Parish of about three or four thousand souls; (A Market Town with twenty Villages) and except three or four Families that refused to come to me, (whom yet I knew by other means) I knew not only the persons but the measures of all or almost all their understandings, in the Town, and my assistants in the Villages knew the rest, by personal conference, each family coming to us by turns. 4. And where a Church is too large for one, there may be and must be assistant Ministers, and that may be done by many, which cannot be done by one alone.

Object. *So may a Bishop and his Presbyters in a Diocess.* *Answ.* In a Diocess of many Churches, the Presbyters only know the people, and do the Ministerial Office for them, except in some one or few Churches where the Bishop dwells and sometimes preacheth: But in the same Church, all the Ministers preach to the same persons ordinarily, (*per vices*) and they all know them, and all watch over them, though they assist each other in particular offices for them. There is much difference between a School-master and his assistants in the same School, and one School-master only with several Ushers in many hundred Schools. As there is between a Master, Mistriss, and Steward ruling the same Family, and one Master with Stewards ruling many hundred Families; (of which more anon.)

3. Another part of the Bishops work in those times was to Baptize: For it was part of the Apostles work. *Matth.* 28. 19, 20. And how great a work that was, to try the peoples due preparations, and to see that they did understandingly and seriously what they did, I desire no other proof than the great care taken in all the ancient Churches of this business, which brought up the Custom of baptizing but twice a year.

Object. *The Apostles baptized three thousand at once.* *Answ.* The Jews were supposed to be bred up in the knowledge of other parts of Religion, and wanted only the knowledge of the true Messiah, and his Salvation, which might be taught them in a shorter time than the Gentiles could be taught the whole substance of Religion, that knew but little: Therefore as soon as the Jews were convinced of the true Messiah and the righteousness of Faith, and consented to the Covenant, they might be baptized. 2. The extraordinary effusions of the Spirit in that time, did make a shorter preparation sufficient. At least Baptizing must be an addition to the Bishops work.

4. As the Apostles laid hands on Believers to convey the Holy Ghost, so the Prelatists think that the Bishops then *Confirmed Believers* with Imposition of hands, saith Doctor *Hammond* on *Heb.* 13. *1.* To teach, exhort, confirm and impose hands, all which were the Bishops office in that place.] And O what a work it is to know the persons of many hundred Parishes to be capable of Confirmation, and so to confirm them (of which more afterward.)

5. I need not prove that the Bishops then were the Masters of the Assemblies, and called them, appointing time and place, as the Rulers of the Synagogues did : which sheweth that they were present with the Church Assemblies.

6. The Bishops administred the Lords Supper (as all confess) and therefore must have some Pastoral notice of the fitness of all the Church to receive it : which intimateth sufficiently the extent of the Church.

7. They went before the Assemblies usually in performance of the publick worship : They prayed with them, and praised God : And Doctor *Hammond* thinks that in all this in Scripture times, they had not so much as a Presbyter to assist them.

8. They admonished the unruly and disorderly, and received Accusations, and openly reproved and excommunicated the Impenitent. And O, how great a work is it to deal with one Soul aright as must be done, before it cometh to Excommunication ! Much more with all in a Parish. Much more in many hundred Parishes.

9. It is confessed that it was the Bishops work to absolve the penitent publickly. And then he must judge of their Repentance : and then he must try it : And for how many thousand can a Bishop do this, with the rest ?

10. The Bishop did dismiss the Congregation with a Benediction (as is maintained by those that we dispute with) and therefore must be present in it.

11. They were to visit and pray with the sick, *and all the sick to send for them to that end,* Jam. 4. 14. *If any be sick among you let him call for the Elders of the Church, and let them pray over him*] saith Doctor *Hammond* [*Because there is no evidence whereby these (inferior Presbyters) may appear to have been brought into the Church so early, And because the visiting of the sick is anciently mentioned as one branch of the office of Bishops ; therefore it may very reasonably be resolved, that the Bishops of the Church, one in each particular Church, but many in the universal, are here meant.*] Though I am far from believing him that the sick person is bid to send but for one, when the term is plural, or that he must send for many out of other Churches, I will take his concession that this was the Bishops work.

12. Lastly, They were to take care of the poor, and of the Contributions and Church stock, saith Doctor *Hammond* on *1 Cor* 12. 28. *The supreme trust and charge was reserved to the Apostles and Bishops of the Church. So in the 41st. Canon of the Apostles, the Bishop must have the care of the moneys, so that by his power all be dispensed to the poor by the Presbyters and Deacons ; and we command that he have in his power the Church Goods.* So *Justin Martyr, Apol.* 2. *That which*

which is gathered is depofited by the Præfect or Bifhop, and he helpeth or relieveth the Orphans and Widows, and becometh the Curator and Guardian of all abfolutely that be in want. So *Ignatius* to *Polycarp, After the Lord thou fhalt be the Curator of the Widows.* And *Polycarp himfelf fpeaking of the Elders or Bifhops, They vifit and take care of all that are fick, not neglecting the Widows, the Orphans and the Poor.*] So far Doctor *Hammond.*

So that by this time it is eafie to fee how great the ancient Churches were ; yea, and how great they were to be continued ; when all this is the Bifhops Office and Work. We are willing that they have Diocefses as big as they can do this work in, even with a *Confefsus* of afsifting Presbyters. There is no one of all thefe twelve alone that a Bifhop can do for a Diocefs of many score or hundred Churches. How much lefs all thefe fet together ? Nay, what one confiderable Parifh would not find a Bifhop with divers afsiftants work enough in all thefe kinds, if it be faithfully done ?

As for the doing of it *per fe aut per alium,* I have fo far confuted it before, as that I may be bold to tell them now, that they may alfo receive the reward *in fe aut in alio :* And if he that will not work fhould not eat, *quære* whether they fhould eat *per alium.*

I add, *If all this* as Doctor *Hammond* maintaineth was made by the Spirit in the Apoftles the Bifhops work, if they may make new Church-Officers to commit part of their work to, there may be twelve forts of Officers made by them for thefe twelve parts of their work. And then we fhall better underftand them.

Whatever is the work of a Bifhop as a Presbyter, every Presbyter may and muft do, according to his ability and opportunity : But whatever belongeth to a Bifhop as a Bifhop, cannot be done by another, either Lay-man or Presbyter. Therefore let us have but Bifhops enough to do it, or elfe confefs that it is no necefsary work.

So great a truft as the Gofpel and mens fouls which Chrift hath committed to Bifhops, may not be caft upon others without his confent that did commit it to them. But they can fhew no confent of Chrift to make new Officers to do their work by. *Timothy* was to commit the fame to others which he had received, 2 *Tim.2.2. The things thou haft heard of me among many witnefses, the fame commit thou to faithful men, who fhall be able to teach others alfo.* And who knoweth not that if a Tutor commit his work ftatedly to another, he maketh that other a Tutor ? And fo if a Phyfician commit his work ftatedly to another, or a Pilot, or the Mafter of a Family, he maketh the other a Phyfician, a Pilot, a Mafter ? And fo if a Bifhop or Presbyter commit his work ftatedly to another, he maketh that other a Bifhop or Presbyter. And then that Bifhop or Presbyter fo made is himfelf *obliged* as well as *empowred,* and the work that he doth is his own work, and not his that delivered him his Commifsion. So that this doing thefe twelve parts of a Bifhops work *per alium* is a meer mockery, unlefs they fpeak unfitly, and mean the *making* of all thofe to be Bifhops as they are, or elfe by perfidious ufurpation cafting their truft and work on others. For if they could prove that God himfelf had inftituted the *Species* of *Sub-presbyters*, it would be to do *their own work*, and not another mans.

My next proof of the limitation of Churches in Scripture times is, that Deacons and Bishops were distinct Officers appointed to the same Churches. The Church which the Deacon was related to, was the very same, and of the same extent, with the Church which the Bishop was related to; as is plain in all Texts where they are described; *Act. 6. 1 Tim. 3. Tit. 7. &c.* But it is most clear that no Deacon then had the charge of many hundred Churches, or more than one such as I have described: Therefore neither had the Bishop of that Church.

They that have now extended the Office of the Deacons further, and have alienated them from their first works, of attending at the Sacred Tables, and taking care of the Poor, cannot deny but that this was at least a great part of their work in the Scripture times and some Ages after (at least when *Jerome ad Evage.* described the Offices of the Presbyters and Deacons.) And was any man then made a Deacon to a Diocess? or to many hundred Churches? or to more than one? Did he attend the Tables of many Churches each Lords day at the same time? If you say that there were many Deacons, and some were in one Church and some in another, it is true: that is, They were in several Assemblies, which were every one a true Church, and they were oft many in one Assembly: But there was no one that was related to *Many* stated Church Assemblies; nor to a Church of a lesser size or magnitude than the Bishop was.

5. And that there was no Church then without a Bishop (one or more) is evident from *Act. 14. 23. They ordained them Elders in every Church;* compared with other Texts that call them Bishops: And Doctor *Hammond* sheweth that these Elders were Bishops. And indeed it was not a Church (in a proper political sense) that had no Bishops formally or eminently. No more than there can be a Kingdom without a King, a School without a School-master, or a family without a Master.

Object. *They are called Churches Act. 14. 23. before they had ordained Elders.*

Answ. 1. It is not certain from the Text, for the name might be given from their state *in fieri* or which they were now entring into. 2. If it were so, it is certain that the appellation was equivocal, as it is usual to distinguish the Kingdom from the King, the School from the School-master, the Family from the Master, but not in the strict political sense of the words, for that comprehendeth both. 3. The truth is, they were true political Churches before. For they had temporary unfixed Bishops, even the Apostles and Evangelists, that converted them, and officiated among them. Otherwise they could have held no Sacred Assemblies for holy Communion and the Lords Supper, as having none to administer it. The fixing of peculiar Bishops did not make them first Churches, but made them setled Churches in such an order as God would establish.

6. Lastly, The setling of Churches with Bishops in *every City, Tit. 1. 5.* doth shew of what magnitude the Churches were in the Scripture times. For, 1. It is known that small Towns in *Judea* were called Cities. 2. And that

Creta

Crccte which was called *Hecatompolis*, as having an hundred Cities, muſt needs then have ſmall ones, and near together. 3. And it is a confeſſed thing that the number of Converts was not then ſo great, as to make City Churches ſo numerous near as our Pariſhes are.

And if the conſideration of all this together, will not convince any, that the Churches that had Biſhops in Scripture times, conſiſted not of many ſtated Aſſemblies as afore deſcribed, but of one only, and were not bigger than our Pariſhes, let ſuch enjoy their error ſtill.

CHAP. IV.

The ſame proved by the Conceſſion of the moſt Learned Defenders of Dioceſane Prelacy.

Though the Scripture Evidence be moſt ſatisfactory in it ſelf, yet in controverſie it much eaſeth the mind that doubteth, to find the Cauſe fully and expreſly granted, by thoſe that moſt learnedly defend thoſe conſequents which it overthrows : And if I do not bring plain Conceſſions here, I will not deprecate the Readers indignation.

1. Among all Chriſtians, the Papiſts are the higheſt Prelatiſts ; And among all Papiſts the Jeſuits ; and among all the Jeſuits *Petavius*, who hath written againſt *Salmaſius, &c.* on this Subject. *Petavius, Diſſert. Eccleſiaſt. de Epiſcop. dignit. & juriſd. p. 22.* concludeth his firſt Chapter in which he had cited the chiefeſt of the Fathers ; [*Hactenus igitur ex antiquorum authoritate conficitur primis temporibus, Presbyterorum & Epiſcoporum non tantum appellationes, ſed etiam ordines, in eaſdem concurriſſe perſonas, iidem ut eſſent utrique.*] i. e. *Hitherto it is proved by the Authority of the Ancients, that in the firſt times, not only the Names, but the Orders, of Presbyters and Biſhops did concur into the ſame perſons, ſo that both were the ſame men.*] And if ſo,I ſhall ſhew the conſequents anon.

And *pag.* 23. He thus beginneth his third Chapter, as opening the only neceſſary way to avoid the Scripture Arguments againſt Epiſcopacy, [*Si quis omnia illa ſcripturæ loca diligenter expendat, id neceſſario conſequens ex illis eſſe ſtatuet, eos ipſos, qui ibi Presbyteri vocantur, plus aliquid quam ſimplices fuiſſe presbyteros, cujuſmodi hodieque ſunt : nec dubitabit, quin Epiſcopi fuerint iidem, non vocabulo tantum, ſed re etiam & poteſtate.*] i. e. [*If any one will diligently weigh all thoſe places of Scripture, he will conclude that this is the neceſſary conſequent of them, that thoſe that are there called Presbyters were ſomewhat more than ſimple Presbyters, and ſuch as now they are : and he will not doubt but the ſame men were Biſhops, not only in name, but in deed and in power.*]

1. Petavius.

Pag.

Pag. 24. [*Exiſtimo Presbyteros vel omnes, vel corum plerofque ſic ordinaios eſſe ut Epiſcopi pariter ac presbyteri gradum obtinerent.*] *I think, that either all or moſt of the Presbyters were ſo ordained, as that they obtained both the degree of Biſhop and of Presbyter.*] Which he proceedeth to ſhew that he thinks was done that there might be a ſtore of Biſhops prepared for all Countries. Pag. 25. he thus far differs from Doctor *Hammond*, but not from the truth, as to hold, that [*Plures in eadem Ecclesia velut Epheſina Epiſcopi fuere.*] [*There were many Biſhops in one Church, as in that of* Epheſus.] Which he taketh for a particular Church, and not a Province; and ſaith, that the ſimple manners of the Church would then bear this, till Ambition had depraved men, and Charity and Humility and the imitation of Chriſt waxed cold : then came that which *Hierome* ſpeaketh of, that *For a remedy of Schiſm one was choſen out of the company of Presbyters, and ſet above the reſt.*

So Pag. 26. *In eadem capit paſſim ambo conferebantur.* And p. 27. *Hoc ſi ita eſt, quid aliud reſtat niſi ut penes eoſdem (Nam plures una in Ecclesia fuiſſe tales, iiſdem ex locis argumentum ducitur) tam nomen illud duplex, quam conveniens nomini poteſtas & authoritas utraque fuiſſe dicatur.*] that is [*If this be ſo, what elſe remaineth, but that both the double name, and the agreeable double power and authority, be ſaid to have been in the ſame perſons (for that there were many of them in one Church, may be proved from the ſame places.)*

And Pag. 95, 96, 97, 98, 99. he ſheweth out of *Juſtin Martyr*, firſt, [*That all things in the ſacred Aſſemblies and Sacraments were done by the Biſhop alone ; and that he was the Curator and Moderator both of the Sacraments to be adminiſtred, and of teaching the people, and of the Churches money. The Biſhop conſecrated the Sacraments, and by the Deacons adminiſtred them to the people. He prayeth and preacheth. He had the care of the Church-moneys, and kept them with it ; he relieved the Orphans, Widows, Sick, Priſoners, Travellers,* &c. And from *Tertullian*, that *the Chriſtians received not the Sacrament from the hands of any but the Biſhops.* (Were there not then as many Biſhops as Church-Aſſemblies?) And that they chiefly did baptize.

And p. 112. he citeth the *Can. 7.& 8.Concil. Gangrenſis*, which anathematizeth thoſe that without the Biſhop's conſent *durſt give or receive the Church Oblations,* &c. And p. 141. out of *Proſper de vita contempl. c. 20.* that a Biſhop muſt excel in knowledge, *that he may inſtruct thoſe that live under him.* And p. 144, 145, 147. he citeth *Can. 3. Concil. Arelat. 3. an. 813.* [*That every Biſhop in his own Pariſh do perfectly and ſtudiouſly teach the Presbyters and all the people, and not neglect to inſtruct them.*] And *Concil. Turonenſ. 3. Can. 4. Let every Biſhop diligently ſtudy by ſacred preaching to inform the flock committed to him, what they muſt do, and what they muſt avoid.* And *Concil. Rhemenſ. 2. Can. 14. That Biſhops preach the Word of God to all.* And *Concil. Cabilonenſ. 3. Can. 1.* [*That Biſhops be diligent in reading, and ſearch the myſteries of Gods Word, that they may ſhine by the brightneſs of Doctrine in the Church, and ceaſe not to ſatiate the ſouls ſubject to them, by nutriment of Gods Words.*] And p. 147. That in the *formula* by which the Kings of *France* committed Epiſcopacy to any, it is ſaid, *You ſhall ſtudy by daily Sermons to edifie, or poliſh, the people committed to you, according to Canonical Inſtitution.*

And

And *ibid. Can.* 19. *Concil. Constant. in Trullo,* [*The Church Presidents must every day, but especially the Lords day, teach all the Clergy and people, the things that belong to piety, gathering from the Scriptures the sentences and judgments of verity.*]

And *p.* 149. he citeth *Concil. Lateran. sub Innoc.* 3. *c.* 10. allowing Bishops to take helpers in preaching when business or sickness hindred them. And *p.* 150, 152, 153. he mentioneth it as somewhat rare, that at *Alexandria* Presbyters preached, and at *Antioch Chrysostom,* and at *Hippo Augustine,* while *Flavianus* and *Valerius* were Bishops.

I do not cite all this now as to prove the sense of Antiquity, but the sense of *Petavius,* who plainly intimateth that the Churches were no larger of a long time, than that a Bishop might preach to all the Clergy and People every Lords day; and that in Scripture times all or near all the Presbyters were Bishops (which is it that we contend for;) and consequently you may judge what the Churches were.

And though it still look much farther than Scripture times, I will shew you what *Petavius* thought of the Magnitude of City-Churches, even near four hundred years after Christ, in *Epiphanius's* days, in his *Animadvers.* on *Epiphan. ad Hær.* 69. *p.* 276. [*Singularem tunc temporis Alexandriæ morem hunc fuisse, vel saltem paucis in Ecclesiis usurpatum, &c. i.e. That this was a singular custom of* Alexandria, *or at least used in few Churches, you may hence conjecture, because he so expresly mentioneth this custom as peculiar to the Alexandrian Church : to wit, that in the same City there should be many Titles, to each of which should be assigned a proper Presbyter, who should there perform the Church Offices. But yet the same was formerly elsewhere instituted; that is, at* Rome *: where the Presbyters did every one rule his own people, being distributed by Titles (that is, setled Sub-Assemblies. To them the Bishops on the Lords days sent Leaven, or hallowed Bread in token of Communion.*] See what a shift they were at first put to, lest the several Assemblies should seem several Churches. For it is not to be imagined that this was done to signifie that common Christian Communion which they had with all other Christian Churches, but that nearest Communion which belongeth to those that are embodied under one Pastor, or the same Pastor in Common, that is one particular Church Even as if these divers Altars or Tables were at a distance in the same Church, and the Bishop would signifie the Union of the several Companies in the same Society, by sending some of the Bread which he had blessed to them all.

But *Petavius* proceedeth [*Non dubito majoribus duntaxat in urbibus, &c. I doubt not but that it was in the Greater Cities only that there were more* (than one) *Titles within the bounds (or Liberties) when within the same Walls, they would not be contained and meet together; and so had Presbyters put on the several Churches. But in the smaller and less frequented Cities, there was one only Church, into which they all did come together. Of which sort were the Cities of* Cyprus. *And therefore* Epiphanius *noteth the custom of* Alexandria, *as a thing strange to his Countrymen and unusual. Hence was the original of Parishes; which word was transferred from the Country Churches to the City Churches.* And adding the πάχοι with

their

their Bishops or Curators setled in *Rome* by *Servius Tullius* he saith, *Quibus Christianorum in agris Paræciæ quam simillimæ fuerunt ; Nam & illie ἐπίσκοποι, &c.* To which the Parishes of the *Christians* in the Countries were most like : For there also were *Bishops*, or rather (*Chorepiscopi*) rural Bishops placed of old : which some *Latine* interpretations of the Canons call the Vicars of the Bishops, but others far more rightly than they, the Country, or Village (*Bishops*) (of which more after.)

So that you see in *Petavius* opinion, even when *Epiphanius* wrote, the ordinary Cities of the World had but one Assembly in each City and Suburbs ; And only some extraordinary Cities (of which only *Alexandria* could be named by *Epiphanius*, and *Rome* also by *Petavius*, and no more by any other Author) had divers setled Titles under their several Presbyters : And even those Titles in those two Cities were but Chappels, like our Parish Chappels, received consecrated Bread from the Bishops Church, lest they should think that they were a distinct body of themselves. Yea, and that the Villages that had Assemblies had their proper Bishops. And so I dismiss *Petavius* with thanks, for his free Concession.

2. *Bishop Downame*   2. My next Witness is Bishop *Downame*, the strongest that hath written against Parish Bishops for Diocesanes ; who, *lib.* 1. *cap.* 1. (before recited) saith, [*Indeed at the very first Conversion of Cities, the whole number of the people converted, being somewhere not much greater than the number of Presbyters placed among them, were able to make but a small Congregation.*] And *cap.* 6. *pag.* 104. [*At the first, and namely the time of the Apostle* Paul, *the most of the Churches, so soon after their Conversion, did not each of them, exceed the proportion of a populous Congregation.*] Though this reach not so low as *Petavius* Concession, it is as much as I need to the present business.

3. *Master Mede.*   3. My third Witness shall be that learned moderate man, Mr. *Joseph Mede*, who in his discourse of Churches, *pag.* 48, 49, 50. saith, [*Nay more than this, it should seem that in those first times before Diocesses were divided into those lesser and subordinate Churches which we now call Parishes, and Presbyters assigned to them, they had not only one Altar to a Church or Dominicum, but one Altar to a Church, taking Church for the Company or Corporation of the faithful united under one Bishop or Pastor : and that was in the City or place where the Bishop had his See and Residence. Like as the Jews had but one Altar and Temple for the whole Nation, united under one High Priest. And yet, as the Jews had their Synagogues, so perhaps might they have more Oratories than one though their Altar were but one, there namely where the Bishop was. Die solis, saith Justin Martyr, omnium qui vel in oppidis vel ruri degunt in eundem locum Conventus fit. Namely as he there tells us to celebrate, and participate the holy Eucharist. Why was this ? but because they had not many places to celebrate it in. And unless this were so, whence came it else that a Schismatical Bishop was said, Constituere or collocare aliud altare ? And that a Bishop and an Altar are made correlatives ? See St. Cyprian, Epist. 40, 72, 73. de unit. Eccles. &c.* So that Mr. *Mede* granteth that every Church that had a Bishop, had no more

more people than communicated at one Altar. To which purpose he goeth on further to *Ignatius* Testimony, of which anon.

4. Bishop *Bilson's* Testimony, *Perp. Gov. cap. 13. pag. 256.* See after- 4. Bilson. ward.

5. *Grotius* is large in his endeavours to prove, that not only every City had 5. Grotius. a Bishop, but also every stated Assembly, of which there were divers in one and the same City, and that the Government was not suited to the Temple way, but to the Synagogues; and as every Synagogue had its chief Ruler, of which there were many in a City, so had every Church in a City its Bishop; and that only the Church of Alexandria *had the custom of having but one Bishop in the whole City.* Thus he *de Imper. Sum. Pot. p. 355, 356, 357.* And in his *Annot. in 1 Tim. 5. 17.* [*Sed notandum est tena urbe, sicut plures Synagogas, ita & plures fuisse Ecclesias, id est conventus Christianorum : & cuique Ecclesiæ fuisse suum præsidem, qui populum alloqueretur & Presbyteros ordinaret : Alexandriæ tantum eum fuisse morem, ut unus esset in tota urbe præses qui ad docendum Presbyteros per urbem distribueret, docet nos Sozomenus, l. 1. c. 14. & Epiphanius, &c.*]

Thus *Grotius* thought that of old every stated Assembly had a Bishop that had power of Ordination. I confess I interpret not *Zozomen* nor *Epiphanius* as *Grotius* doth, nor believe I that he can bring us frequent proof of two Churches with Bishops in one City (much less many;) unless in Doctor *Hammond's* instance before and after mentioned. But the rest I accept.

6. I may take it for a full Concession from Bishop *Jeremy Tailor*, which is 6. Bishop before cited, though in few words; *Præf. Treat. of Repent.* [*I am sure we can-* *Jeremy* *not give account of souls of which we have no notice.*] And I am sure a full Pa- *Tailor.* rish is as many as a more able and diligent man than ever I was, can take such notice of as to do the Pastors Office to them.

7. But the last and greatest Champion for Diocesanes is Doctor *Hammond,* his 7. Doctor Concessions are mentioned before; but now are purposely to be cited : But re- Hammond. member still that we are yet speaking but of the matter of Fact.

In his *Annot.* in *Act. 11. 30.* he saith, [*Although this Title of* πρεσβύτεροι *Elders, have been also extended to a second Order in the Church, and now is only in use for them under the name of Presbyters, yet in the Scripture times it belonged principally, if not alone to Bishops, there being no evidence that any of the second order were then instituted ; though soon after before the writing of* Ignatius *Epistles there were such instituted in all Churches.*

(Though so suddain a change be unlikely, I pass it by.) In his *Dissert p.208, 209, 11. cap. 10. sect. 19, 20, 21. & 11. sect. 2. &c.* he saith, [*Prius non us-quequaque verum esse quod pro concesso sumitur (in una civitate non fuisse plures É-piscopos.) Quamvis enim in una Ecclesia aut cætu plures simul Episcopi nunquam fuerint, nihil tamen obstare, quin in eadem civitate duo aliquando disterminati cætus fuerint, a duobus Apostolis ad fidem adductis, &c.* as I have before more large-ly cited him.

C   Yea,

Yea, *Differt. Epift. Sect.* 30, 31. he will have the queftion ftated only of a Bifhop [*in fingulari Ecclefia*] *&* [*in fingulari cœtu.*] *The controverfie is not, Quibus demum nominibus cogniti fuerint Ecclefiarum rectores ; fed an ad unum in fingulari Ecclefia, an ad plures poteftas, ifta devenerit ? Nos ad unum fingularem præfectum, quem ex famofiore Ecclefiæ ufu, Epifcopum vulgo dicimus, poteftatem iftam in fingulari cœtu ex Chrifti & Apoftolorum inftitutione, nunquam non pertinuiffe affirmamus.* So that it is a Bifhop of one Affembly or Church which Doctor *Hammond* will have the queftion ftated about. 2. And fuch a Church or Affembly as great Cities a while had divers of, and fo divers Bifhops. 3. And this was after the Scripture times ; for they had divers Bifhops with a divers Clergy. 4. But that in Scripture times, the Order of Sub-Presbyters cannot be proved inftituted. 5. And in his Annotations he expoundeth all the Texts of the New Teftament of Bifhops that mention Presbyters. 6. But in his Anfwer to the *London* Minifters, not daring yet to hold that they were of Humane and not of Divine Inftitution, he holds that they were inftituted in the end of St. *John*'s days after all the Scripture was written (which was about two or three years before his death) and fo were of Divine Inftitution, though all the reft of the Apoftles were dead.

Before I apply this I will fubjoyn his words of more numerous Witneffes to our opinion with himfelf, for he faith.

8. All the Divines in the fame Caufe.

8. Doctor *Hammond* of the reft, *Vindication againft* London *Minfters,* pag. 104. [*And though I might truly fay that for thofe more minute confiderations or conjectures, wherein this Doctor differs from fome others, he hath the fuffrages of many of the learnedft men of this Church at this day, and as far as he knoweth of all that embrace the fame Caufe with him.*]

I purpofely pafs by fuch Bifhops as *Cranmer, Jewel, &c.* and fuch conformable Divines as Doctor *Whitaker, Fulke, &c.* as being not high enough to be valued by thofe that I have now to do with. As *Jewel, Art.* 4. p. 171. fheweth that every Church muft have one Bifhop and but one, and out of *Cyprian* that the *Fraternitas univerfa* was to chufe him ; *Et Epifcopus delegatur plebe præfente — de univerfæ fraternitatis fuffragio, Epifcopatus ei (Sabino) deferretur* : And mentioneth the Refcript of *Honorius* the Emperor to *Boniface,* that [*If two Bifhops through divifion and contention happen to be chofen, we will that neither of them be allowed as Bifhop ; but that he only remain in the Apoftolick Seat, whom out of the number of the Clergy, Godly difcretion, and the confent of the whole Brotherhood, fhall chufe by a new Election.*] How big yet was the Church even then ?

Now all this being afferted, 1. It is evident that they hold that in Scripture times, no Church confifted of more than one ordinary ftated worfhipping Affembly. 2. And that every fuch Affembly had a Bifhop. For if there were no Presbyters, there could be no Affembly but where a Bifhop was prefent : for the Lords days were then ufed for publick Worfhip ; and the people could not do that without a Minifter, for they had Communion in the Lords Supper

every

every Lords day: And therefore they muſt have a Biſhop, or have no ſuch Worſhip. And Doctor *Hammond* departeth from *Petavius* in holding that no Church had more Biſhops than one : So that *de facto* he granteth all that I deſire, 1. That the Churches were but ſo many Aſſemblies having each a Biſhop. 2. And that no Sub-Presbyters were inſtituted in Scripture times. And by what right the change was made we ſhall enquire anon.

CHAP. V.

The ſame proved by the full Teſtimony of Antiquity.

THat the particular Churches, *infimæ ſpeciei vel ordinis*, (of which combined Aſſociated Churches were conſtituted) were no larger than is before deſcribed, and had but *Unum Altare*, I ſhall prove Hiſtorically from Antiquity.

I. And Order requireth that I begin with *Clemens Romanus*.

But let the Reader ſtill remember that while I cite him and others oft cited heretofore by many, I do it not to the ſame end, as they who thence prove that Biſhops and Presbyters were then the ſame ; but to prove the Churches to be but ſuch ſingle Congregations as are fore-deſcribed, *Ep. ad Cor. pag.* 54, 55. [Κατὰ χώρας ἒν ἐ πόλεις κηρύσσοντες, καθίςονται ἀπαρχὰς αὐτῶν, δοκιμάσαντες τῷ πνεύματι εἰς ἐπισκόπους ἐ, διακόνους τ῀ μελλόντων πιςεύειν.] *i.e. Per regiones igitur & urbes verbum prædicantes, primitias eorum ſpiritu probantes, Epiſcopos & Diaconos eorum qui credituri erant conſtituerunt.*] Here are theſe concurrent evidences to our purpoſe. 1. In that he ſpeaketh only of Biſhops and Deacons, and neither here nor elſewhere one ſyllable of any other Presbyters but Biſhops, it is apparent that in thoſe times there were no Subject-Presbyters diſtinct from Biſhops in being : Nor could Doctor *Hammond* any other way anſwer *Blondel* here, but by confeſſing and maintaining this, and ſo expounding *Clemens* as ſpeaking of Biſhops only before other Presbyters were in the Church. And if ſo, then there could be none but Churches of ſingle Aſſemblies then, or ſuch as one man could officiate in : becauſe there was then no more to do it.

2. In that *Cities and Countries* are made the Seats of theſe Biſhops : for though ſome would make them to be mentioned only as the places where the Apoſtles preached, the obvious plain ſenſe of the words is connexive of preaching and conſtituting Biſhops : by preaching they made believers in Cities and Countries, and over thoſe believers they placed Biſhops and Deacons ; which implieth it to be in the ſame places. And whereas ſome would ſtrain the word [χώρας] to ſignifie *Provinces*, and not *Country Villages*, it muſt then, as diſtinct from Cities, have meant [*many Cities*] and ſo have ſetled *Biſhops and Arch-*

Biſhops,

Bishops, intimating Subject-Presbyters under them : But here is no such word or intimation : Yea, when the *Countries* are made first the Place of the Apostles *preaching* (as they confess) let any impartial man judge whether this be like to be the sense [*They preached in Provinces*, that is; in the *Cities of Provinces*, and in Cities.] And if there were Country Churches and Bishops setled by the Apostle's, its easie to see that each particular Church-Assembly had a Bishop, when even the City Churches themselves were no bigger than *Petavius* and others mention.

3. *Ad hominem*, Though I believe that the [τῶν μελλόντων πιστεύειν] *eorum qui credituri erant*, be intended only to signifie the subsequence of believing to their preaching, yet waving that, to them that suppose it to intend the subsequence of *believing to making Bishops*, it must needs imply that the Churches then consisted but of few, and were yet to be filled up : But whether one Bishop to have many Churches is a question which must be otherwise and *aliunde* decided.

4. The magnitude of the Churches is plainly intimated, when he saith. *p. 57.* [τὰς ἐν κατασταθέντας, &c. · *Constitutos itaque ab illis vel deinceps ab aliis viris celebribus cum consensu universæ Ecclesiæ qui inculpate ovili Christi inservierunt, &c.*] If the Bishops were chosen by the *Consent of all the Church*, it was no greater a Church than would and did meet to signifie their consent ; and not such as our Diocesses now are.

5. Also the same is intimated by pag. 69. [*If it be for me that Contention, Sedition and Schisms arise, I will depart, I will be gone whither you will, and will do what shall by the people be appointed ; only let the Sheep-fold of Christ live in peace with the Presbyters appointed over it.* By which words it is evident, that it was such a particular *Ovile* or Church, where the *Will* of the *people* might be declared as a matter that bore much sway. But who can think that this is spoken of many Congregations, where the peoples Will could not easily be signified.

And it is farther manifest in that it was but for *the sake of one or two* that the Church of *Corinth* moved this sedition against the Presbyters (called also Bishops,) pag. 62. Now how many Congregations that Church consisted of, where the interest of one or two was either so far concerned or so powerful, it is easie to conjecture ; set all these together, and judge impartially.

I add (though out of season) that it was none of the Apostles meaning that those whom they made Bishops of such single Churches, without a subject Order of Presbyters, should make such an Order of subject Presbyters, and make themselves the Bishops of a Diocesane Church without any Bishops under them. For pag. 57. he saith, [*And our Apostles by our Lord Jesus Christ knew, that contention would arise about the name of Episcopacy; and for this cause being endued with perfect fore-knowledge, they appointed them aforesaid, and left the Courses (or Orders) of After-Ministers and Offices described, that other approved men might succeed in the place of the deceased, and might execute their Offices.*] So that it was the same places and the same Offices which those ordained by the Apostles had, in which others must succeed them, which therefore were *described* by the Apostles, and not into others.

To,

To confirm my Exposition of *Clemens*, note, that *Grotius* himself *Epist.* 182. *ad Bignon.* giveth this as a reason to prove this Epistle of *Clemens* to be genuine. *Quod nusquam meminit exortæ illius Episcoporum authoritatis, quæ Ecclesiæ consuetudine post Marci mortem Alexandriæ, atque eo exemplo alibi introduci cœpit: sed plane, ut Paulus Apostolus ostendit, Ecclesias communi Presbyterorum, qui iidem omnes & Episcopi, consilio fuisse gubernatas.*] that is, *Because he no where maketh mention of that excelling authority of Bishops which began to be introduced at Alexandria by the custom of the Church, after the death of Mark, and in other places by that example: But he plainly sheweth, as the Apostle Paul doth, that the Churches were governed by the Common Council of Presbyters, who were also Bishops.*]

Note also, as aforesaid, that Doctor *Hammond* in *Dissert.* granteth as to matter of fact, that *Clemens* speaketh but of the Bishops of single Congregations, whom he also calleth Presbyters, there being no other in the Church of *Corinth.*

II. My next Witness is *Pius* Bishop of *Rome*, in *Epist. Justo Episcopo*; in *Biblioth. Patr. Tom. 3. pag. 15.* mentioning only Bishops and Deacons: of which Doctor *Hammond* making the same Concession, still granteth that hitherto Bishops had but single Churches. (Of this more anon.)

III. My next and greatest Witness is *Ignatius*, in whom (to my admiration) the Diocesans so much confide, as that *quasi pro aris & focis* they contend for the authority of his Epistles. I am as loth to lose him as they are: therefore I will not meddle in *Blondel's* controversie (against whom they say Doctor *Pierson* is now writing.) In his Epistle to the *Philadelphians* he saith, [΄Εν Θυσιαστηριον πᾶςη τη ἐκκλησια, η̌, εἰς ἐπισκοπῷ ἅμα τῷ πρεσβυτεριω, η̌, τοῖς διχκόνοις τοῖς συνλδλοῖς μȣ.] [*There is to every Church one Altar, and one Bishop, with the Presbytery and the Deacons my fellow servants.*] I am not able to devise apter words to express my sense in. He saith not this of some one Church, but of all; nor yet as of an accident proper to those times of the Churches minority; but as of the Notes of every Churches Individuation or Hæcceity as they speak. The Unity of the Church is characterised by *One Altar*, and *One Bishop* with the Presbytery and Deacons. If [πᾶςη τη εκκλησια.] were out, it would not alter the sense, being plainly implied. Bishop *Downame's* Exposition of Θυσιαστηριον as if it signified *Christ*, is so forced and contrary to the evidence of the Text, that his own party quite forsake him in it, and he needeth no confutation. For who ever before dreamed that the *Unity* and *Individuation* of each particular Church, consisted in having *one Christ*, who is the common Head of all Churches? *One Christ to every Church and one Bishop*, would signifie that every Church must have one several Christ, as well as one several Bishop. Nor is Θυσιαστηριον so used by the Ancients, except when the Context sheweth that they speak by allusion of Christ. Master *Mead's* plain and certain Exposition and Collection I gave you before; the same with ours.

As

As for them that say that many Congregations might *per vices* come to one Altar to communicate, I answer, 1. Let them make Churches as big as can thus communicate and spare not ; though there be neceffary Chappels or Oratories befides. 2. But remember that every Church ufed to worfhip God publickly and to communicate, at leaft every Lords day ; and that there was but *One Altar* to each Church, and therefore but one Communicating Congregation. Doctor *Stillingfleet* in his Schifmatical Sermon is for my Expofition.

Object. *It is meant of one Species of Altars, and not one Individual.*

Anfw. Then it is meant alfo of one Species of Bifhops in each Church, and not of one Individual.

Object. *The practice of the Churches after fheweth that they took it not for a fin, or Schifm, to have feveral Altars in a Church.*

Anfw. I talk of nothing but *matter of fact* ; it was the note of *One Church* when thofe Epiftles were written : whether the Author was miftaken *de jure*, or whether after Ages grew wifer, or rather had fewer Bifhops and more Altars for the fake of Carnal Intereft, I judge not.

The fame Author *Epift. ad Smyrn.* faith [*Ubi utique apparet Epifcopus, ibi & multitudo fit : quemadmodum utique ubi eft Chriftus Jefus, illic Catholica Ecclefia :*] as *Ufher's Lat. Tranf.* or [πᾶσα ϛϱατιὰ] *omnis exercitus cæleftis.* And the Context fheweth that this *multitudo* or *plebs* is the Church which the Bifhop overfeeth. Therefore *ubi Epifcopus ibi Ecclefia fuit,* and fo every Church had a prefent Bifhop.

So in *Epift. ad Magnef.* he bids them [*All unitedly* (or as one) *run together to one Temple of God, as to one Altar, to one Jefus Chrift.*] So that every Church had one *Temple* and one *Altar* to which (as a note of their Union in Chrift) the whole Church muft unanimoufly come.

So in *Epift. ad Trull.* he faith [*Et Epifcopus typum Dei Patris omnium gerit ; Presbyteri vero funt confeffus quidam, & conjunctus Apoftolorum cætus ; fine his Ecclefia Electa non eft : Nulla fine his Sanctorum Congregatio ; nulla Sanctorum Collectio. Et poftea, Quid vero aliud Sacerdotium eft (vel Presbyterium) quam facer cætus, Conciliarii & affeffores Epifcopi? Quid Diaconi, &c.*] So that it is hard more plainly to exprefs a thing in words, than this Author expreffeth, that not only *de facto* every ftated worfhipping communicating Congregation had their Bifhop, Presbyters and Deacons, but that *de jure* it ought to be fo : And that there was no lawful Church Affembly for Worfhip, without the Bifhop and his Presbyters ordinarily ; and one Altar and one Bifhop were the Notes of one Church.

And *Epift. ad Polycarp.* [*Sæpe Congregationes fiant : ex nomine omnes quære : fervos & ancillas ne defpicias (ut Tranf. Lat. Ufh.)* i. e. *Keep often Congregations : Enquire* (or *look after) all* (or *every one) by name : defpife not the Servants and the Maids.*] And how many Congregations at once that Church then had, or how great it was, when the Bifhop himfelf was to look after every one by name, even the Men-fervants and the Maids, I leave to their judgments who are willing to underftand the truth.

Since the writing of this (about thirteen years) I have seen *Isaac Vossius* his *Florentine Ignatius, Edit.* 2. and also had some speech with Bishop *Gunning*, confidently denying that by ἐν θυσιαςήριον is meant one material Altar or place of Communicating : I will therefore review the Texts of *Ignatius* according to *Isaac Vossius*, and answer this Bishops confident assertion.

I. *Epist. ad Smyrn. p.* 4. Πάντες τῷ ἐπισκόπῳ ἀκολϑϑεῖτε, *&c. Omnes E-piscopum sequimini ut Jesus Christus Patrem ; & Presbyterium ut Apostolos ; Diaconos autem revereamini ut Dei mandatum. Nullus sine Episcopo aliquid operetur corum quæ conveniunt in Ecclesiam : Illa firma Gratiarum actio* (εὐχαριςίx) *reputetur, quæ sub ipso est, vel quam utique ipse concesserit : ubi utique apparet Episcopus, illic multitudo sit : quemadmodum utique ubi est Jesus Christus illic Catholica Ecclesia : Non licitum est sine Episcopo neque baptizare, neque agapen facere.*

Here it is evident, 1. That by τὸ πλῆθϴ, *the Multitude*,] is meant the assembling multitude, and not distant people many miles off.

2. That by φανῆ *apparet*, is meant the personal visible appearing presence of the Bishop. And so that every Church-Assembly had a present Bishop ordinarily.

3. That by εὐχαρισία, is meant the Churches joyful laudatory Communion, of which the Lords Supper was a chief part. And so that the *Eucharist* was usually celebrated with and by the Bishop, and never but by his particular allowance to the Presbyters ; not only a general allowance to do it commonly as Parish Priests do without him, but to do it in his Assembly either in case of his absence, or need, or as assisting him.

4. That by τ̄ συμφόϨων εἰς τὴν ἐκκλησίxν is meant *the matters and persons of* the particular Assembly : And so that every such Assembly had a present Supervisor or Bishop.

5. That by ἀκολϑϑεῖτε, is meant a local going whither he goeth, and an imitation of him as present ; and so that they had his visible presence.

6. That the prohibition of baptizing and holding their Love-feasting Meetings without him, signified not only [*without his general licence at a distance*] but as no Servants must do great matters in the house without the Master, so it implieth here his ordinary presence and particular approbation of the single persons fitness for Baptism, and his conduct of their Love-feasts, and his allowance in case of necessary absence.

7. That the same Assemblies had a Bishop, Presbyters and Deacons. For the same multitude is to follow the same Bishop, Presbyters and Deacons : And how could one Parish follow all the Presbyters of all other Parish Churches of a Diocess whom they never knew? And it is certain that it was the same Church that the *Presbytery* and *Deacons* here mentioned had : But Deacons were appropriated only to single Churches, and the people of one Parish-Assembly, were not to follow or obey the Deacons of all other distant Parish Churches.

8. And after he saith, [*Salute I eo dignum Episcopum, & Deo decens Presbyterium , & conservos meos Diaconos & singillatim & communiter omnes.*] Which plainly signifieth that it was the same City Church in *Smyrna* that

that had a Bishop, Presbytery and Deacons: For the scattered Presbyters of many distant Parishes cannot be meant by the Presbytery which is supposed present with the Bishop and Deacons.

II. The next in the *Florentine* Copy is the Epistle to *Polycarpe*, where he saith to the Bishop, [" *Let not the Widows be neglected: Next after the Lord,* " *be thou the Curator of them: Let nothing be done without thy Sentence: and do* " *thou nothing without God: and what thou dost let it be well stable: Let Congre-* " *gations be often made: seek all by name: despise not Servants and Maids: speak* " *to my Sisters to love the Lord, and be subject in flesh and spirit to their Husbands,* " *and to the men to love their Wives. And the Men that marry, and the Women that* " *are married, must make their union with the sentence of the Bishop,* &c.]

Here it is evident, 1. That it was a Church of which *Widows* were a part that is here meant : But *Widows* then were special parts of particular Parish-Churches, and not common to a Diocess of many such.

2. It was such a Church where the Bishop himself was to take care of all the Widows, and see that they were not neglected : And that could not be done to a Diocess of many score or hundred Parishes.

3. It was a Church where the Bishop as present could see to all that was done.

4. It was a Church that was oft to assemble or be congregate : which a Dio-cess never doth : For it is *frequent Congregations of the same persons* that is here commanded or desired.

5. It was a Church so assembled that the Bishop could by name take an ac-count who was absent by his own eye : Yea, even of the Servant-men and Maids.

6. And such as the Bishop could himself marry all that were married in it, or at least be their particular Counsellor therein : And exhort all Husbands and Wives to their duties.

7. He after saith, [" *I am of one soul with them that are subject to the Bishop,* " *Presbyters and Deacons.*] Signifying that these three were the present Officers of one and the same particular Church.

III. The next is the Epistle to the *Ephesians* ; where, 1. *Pag.* 17. he willeth them *to love their Bishop, and all of them to imitate him:* which supposeth that they knew him (and so doth not one in an hundred in most of our Diocesses, nor ever see his face.)

2. *Pag.* 19. He tells them that [" *They agree in the Sentence of the Bishop,* " *and so doth the worthy Presbyters agree with him, as the strings of a Harp ; and* " *therefore in their consent and confounding love Jesus Christ is sung : and they are* " *all made a Chore, that being consonant in consent, receiving in unity divine melody,* " *they might with one voice sing by Jesus Christ to the Father that he may hear them,* " *and know by whom they do good.*] Where it is most plainly signified that it was a Church which sung to God by Christ in one Chore, in unity of concent-ing voice, under one Bishop and his Presbytery and Deacons present and con-ducting them. 3. After

3. After *pag. 20.* he praiseth them for being [*confonant in Unity* with the Bishop, " *For if any be not within the Altar, he is deprived of the Bread of God :* " *For if the prayer of one or two have fo great force, how much more that which is of* " *the Bifhop and all the Church ? He therefore that cometh not to the fame, is proud* " *and condemneth himfelf. And by how much you fee the Bifhop filent, reverence him* " *the more : for we muft receive every one that the Lord of the houfe fendeth, as him* " *that fent him : you muft therefore look upon the Bifhop manifeft (or vifibly prefent)* " *as to the Lord.* Onefimus *praifeth your Divine Order.*]

Here it is plain that it was a Church where many, yea all the Church joyned prefentially in prayer with the Bifhop, which a thoufand Parifhes (nor two) do not.

4. It was a Church where the Bifhop was feen by all when he was filent ; and fo reverenced for his filent prefence.

5. It was a Church, which they that wilfully abfented themfelves from were felf-condemned : But a man can be but in one Parifh at once.

6. It was a Church where they might all fee Τὸν ἐπίσκοπον ἄδηλον, the Bifhop *manifeft,* that is, *Perfpicuum, vifible.*

7. It was a Church where all that had the Sacred Bread were [*within the Altar,*] that is, the one *Sacrarium,* or place of communicating in the Eucharift.

8. And this was their εὐταξία, the Order of their Affembly.

After *pag. 25.* he faith [" *Haften therefore to affemble frequently, for the Eu-* " *charift (or thankfgiving) of God, and for Glory : For when you oft meet for the* " *fame thing, the powers of Satan are deftroyed, and his perdition loofed in the concord* " *of your faith.*]

9. Here it is plain that it was a Church that ufed to meet together for the Eucharift ; manifefting therein the concord of the faith of all the Church.

And after *pag. 29.* he faith, [" *Becaufe they who according to Man, do all by* " *name meet commonly in Grace in one faith, and in Jefus Chrift, in your obeying the* " *Bifhop, and Presbytery, with an undivided mind, breaking one bread,* &c.]

10. Here it is fignified that the Bifhop and Presbytery were all prefent as Guides in one Affembly, which was that Church which they fupervifed.

11. And that it was fuch a Church that brake one Bread, profeffing one faith, in prefence, with undivided minds. So plainly doth this Epiftle decide our controverfie.

IV. The next Epiftle is *Ad Magnefios.* In which he faith, " *Canto Ecclefias* " *in quibus Unionem oro Carnis & Spiritus. Union of Flefh fignifieth local Com-* " *munion.*

2. *Pag. 31.* he faith, [" *I am dignified to fee you by* Dama *your Bifhop wor-* " *thy of God, and the worthy Presbyters* Baffus *and* Apollonius, *and my fellow* " *Servant* Sotion *the Deacon, whom I enjoy becaufe he is fubject to the Bifhop and* " *Presbytery,* &c.]

By which words it is plain that this Church which had a *Bifhop, Presbytery* and *Deacon,* was a Parochial Church that had prefential Communion with them, and not as our Dioceffes.　　　D　　　3. *Pag.*

3. *Pag.* 33. Having mentioned the Bishop he saith, [" *Because in the afore-* " *said persons I behold all the multitude, in faith and love I warn you, study to do* " *all in the concord of God, the Bishop presiding in the place of God, and the Presby-* " *ters in the stead of the Confession of the Apostles, and the Deacons,* &c.

Which sheweth that it was a Church where Bishop, Presbyters and Deacons sate together in presence.

4. And after it's said, [" *Let there be nothing among you which may divide (or* " *separate) you ; but be united to the Bishop and Presidents,* &c. Which sheweth the same present Presidency as aforesaid.

5. *Pag.* 33. He repeateth [*without the Bishop and Presbyters do nothing*] which no reason can interpret of any Presbyters but the present.

So 6. *Pag.* 34. [" *Let nothing else seem reasonable proper to your selves ; but* " *one Prayer for the same thing, one deprecation, one understanding, one hope in love-* " *and undefiled joy.*]

Which importeth their present Communion in Prayer and Profession.

7. He addeth, [" *All of you run (or meet) together into one Temple of God,* " *as to one Altar.*] This needeth only an impartial Reader, and it's plain.

8. And *pag.* 37. [" *With your worthily honoured Bishop, and the worthily* " *Complexe Spiritual Crown of your Presbytery, and the Deacons,* &c.] Where no Presbyters are mentioned but the Bishops Presbytery which sate about him in the Church, called the *Complexe Corona.*

9. He addeth *ut unio fit carnalis & spiritualis,* that is, of present *bodies* and of *minds.*

V. The next is the Epistle to the *Philadelphians :* where praising them for their union with their Bishop as the strings of a Harp, he saith, [" *Study there-* " *fore to use one Eucharist* (or Thanksgiving) that is, to joyn all together in the " Eucharistical Communion :) *For there is one Flesh of our Lord Jesus Christ,* " *and one Cup* (that is, which is there Sacramentally represented and given) *in-* " *to Union of his Blood, one Altar, and one Bishop, with the Presbytery and the* " *Deacons my fellow Servants ; that what you do, you may do according to God.*]

Here one Church is notified in its Unity by these marks.

1. *That they all joyn in one Assembly for the Eucharist.* Which signifieth one Body and Blood of Christ. 2. And that there be one Altar for this Communion. 3. And one Bishop. 4. And one Presbytery with his Deacons with him.

But here Bishop *Gunning* saith, *It is not meant of one material Altar.*

Answ. 1. It must be noted that (as Master *Mede* and others have observed) Θυσιαςήριον is used in Church Writers for the Chancel, *Sacrarium,* or place where the Altar stood, as well as for the Altar it self: Into which place the Communicants only were admitted ; to which form our Chancels are made.

2. And to be *intra Altare* is usually meant of being one *admitted to that Eu-charistical Communion.* 3. And though as we give the Sacrament in private houses to the sick, and have Chappels for the weak and distant, so might some great Churches then, and yet have but one Chancel, Altar or place for the

Com-

Communion of the whole Church; 4. The exprefs words, and the Context and fenfe fully fhew that it is perfonal prefent Communion that is here fpoken of, and therefore in one place. 5. The common ufe of the word in other Writers, fheweth it, (as being *intra vel extra Altare*, and fetting up *Altare contra Altare*, that is feparated Affemblies for fuch Communion. (6. The moft learned and famous Expofitors fo expound it; fuch as Mafter *Mede* before cited, and Arch-Bifhop *Ufher* and others. 7. The Contradictors can feign no other probable fenfe. For,

1. If by the Altar they fay is meant [*One Chrift,*] 2. or one *Species of Altars*, thefe are before confuted, and are palpably falfe. He that is in another part of the World may come to an Altar of the fame fpecies, which is nothing to the unity of a particular Church here fpoken of. 3. If they fay, *It is called one Altar* becaufe under *one Bifhop*, this maketh not *many to be one*, no more than many Temples. And if tropically it were fo meant, it would be but a vain repetition, *One Bifhop* being mentioned befides. And it is an Altar which the Bifhop with his Presbytery is fuppofed to be prefent at, which cannot be *All in a Diocefs called One.* Partiality can give no other probable fenfe.

Object. 1. *One Church it is known had many Altars.*

Anfw. Not then; no nor long after except at *Rome* and *Alexandria*: and then they were but as parts of Chappels, and not of Churches.

Object. 2. *It is faid alfo, There is one Body of Chrift and one Cup, which cannot be meant literally.*

Anfw. It is well called *One* agreeably to our prefent fence: For, 1. It is one and the fame Bread, though not one piece, which is there prefent, confecrated and divided to them all; and one Cup or prefent quantity of Wine which is there diftributed among them. 2. And it is *One body and blood* or facrificed Chrift, which is in every Church reprefented and offered by *One Bifhop at one Altar.* This doth but confirm our Expofition. But what can be fo plain as to convince the prejudiced and unwilling?

2. *Pag.* 45. he willeth [" *the Church to fend a Deacon to Antioch as other neighbour Churches fent Bifhops, and fome Presbyters and Deacons.*] And can any man think that a Diocefs met to chufe a Deacon to go on a vifit, or that it was a Diocefane Bifhop that was fent by a Diocefs, yea that all thefe neighbour Churches that fent them were fo many Diocefſes?

VI. The next is the Epiftle *ad Trallefios.* Where he faith of the Bifhop that came to him, [*That he faw all the multitude in him;*] that is, the Affembly. And as before he bids them, [*Do nothing without the Bifhop, and be fubject to the Presbytery; and that as to the Counfel of God, and Conjunction of Apoftles*] adding, [*For without thefe the Church is not called:*] what can be plainer to fhew that it was a Church that had a prefent *Bifhop and Council of Presbyters conjunct, without whom the Church was not lawfully called together?* So that every Church had fuch.

2. And *pag.* 50. he faith again, [*Not inflated, but being infeparable from God, Jefus Chrift, and the Bifhop and the Orders of the Apoftles* (that is, the Confefs of

Presbyters)

D 2

Presbyters) *He that is within the Altar is clean; and he that is without the Altar is not clean; that is, he that doth any thing* (in the Church) *without the Bishop, Presbytery and Deacon, is not clean in Conscience :* which plainly sheweth that every *Church-Assembly* had a guiding Bishop, Presbytery and ministring Deacon.

3. *Pag.* 52. he faith, [*I salute you from* Smyrna *with the Churches of God, which are present with me :*] He had not then the presence of many Dioceffes; nor were Bishops alone ufed then to be called Churches : Therefore they were Church-Affemblies which he vifited, and were with him, and about him.

4. Again he repeateth, [*Be subject to the Bishop and Presbytery, and love one another with an inseparable heart.*] Which hath the fenfe aforefaid.

VII. In the Epiftle to the *Romans,* the words of the Church prefiding *in locho chori Romanorum* is much fpoken of already by many.

The Epiftles afcribed to him have much of the like kind ; as *Epift. ad Tarfenfes, pag.* 80. *Ad Antiochenos, pag.* 86, 87, 88. The *Epift. ad Heroum Diaconum* calleth the Presbyters of *Antioch* Bishops who baptize, facrifice and impofe hands.

So *Epift. ad Philippenfes, pag.* 112.

If after all this evidence from *Ignatius* any will wrangle, let him wrangle : what words can be plain enough for fuch ? And what a blind or blinding practice is it, which too many Writers for Prelacy have ufed ? to pretend *Ignatius* to be for them, who is fo much and plain againft them ? And to tofs about the name of a Bishop and Presbytery, as if all that was faid for a Parochial Bishop and Presbytery (that is, in a Church affociated for perfonal prefential Communion) were fpoken for fuch a Diocefane Prelacy as putteth down and deftroyeth all fuch Churches, Bishops and Presbyteries.

And what falfhood is it to perfwade the World that we are againft Epifcopacy becaufe we would have every Church to have a Bishop, and would not have all the Churches in *England* except Diocefane, to be unchurched and turned into Chappels or Oratories ? When yet we refufe not to fubmit to more general Overfeers of many Churches, to fee that the Paftors do their duty, and counfel and exhort them to it, whether appointed hereto by the Magiftrate, or the confent and choice of many Churches.

IV. *Juftin Martyr's* Teftimony is trite, but moft plain, and not to be evaded. Ἐπεῖτα προσφέρεται, &c. *Poftea fratrum præpofito panis & poculum offertur — Poftquam præpofitus gratias egit totufque populus faufta omnia acclamavit ; qui inter nos Diaconi vocantur dant unicuique partem panis & calicis diluti, fuper quos facta eft gratiarum actio, atque etiam deferre finunt abfentibus — Die folis urbanorum ac rufticanorum cœtus fiunt, ubi Apoftolorum prophetarumque literæ quoad fieri poteft præleguntur : Ceffante Lectore Præpofitus verba facit adhortatoria — Pofthæc confurgunt omnes & preces offerimus : quibus finitis profertur panis, vinum & aqua : Tum præpofitus quantum poteft preces offert, & gratiarum actiones : Plebs vero Amen accinit. Inde confecrata diftribuuntur fingulis, & abfentibus mittuntur per Diaconos :*

tonos : Ditiores si libeat pro sua quisque voluntate conferunt : Collecta deponuntur apud præpositum : Is subvenit pupillis, viduis, & propter morbum aliamve necessitatem egentibus, vinctis quoque & peregrinis, & in summa curator sit omnium inopum. Thus *Justin Apolog.* 2. Where he describeth the Church State and Worship which we desire, as plainly as we can speak our selves. Note here, 1. That whether the Country-men and Citizens had several Churches or met in one City Church, it sheweth that they were but single Congregations. For every Church had a present Bishop : (For Doctor *Hammond* maintaineth that by the *Præpositus* here is meant the Bishop, and so do others of them.) 2. This Bishop performed the Offices of the day, every Lord's day, praying, preaching and administring the Lord's Supper, &c. 3. All the Alms of the Church was committed to the Bishop at present, (and therefore he had not many hundred or any other Churches under him where Presbyters did all receive the Alms.) 4. He was the common Curator of all the Poor, Orphans, Sick, &c. which could not be for more than one of our Parishes : (And let the Bishops take as big a Church as they will do all this for, and spare not.) 5. And the Deacons bringing the consecrated Bread and Wine to the absent in token of Communion with the same Church and Bishop, sheweth that there were not under him many other absent Congregations, that had no other Bishop of their own : Nor did the Deacon carry it to such Congregations through the Diocess. In a word, here is a full description of a Congregational Church and Bishop.

Saith Master *Mede* before cited, of these words, [*As the Jews had their Synagogues, so perhaps might they have more Oratories than one ; though their Altar were but one, there namely where the Bishop was. Die solis omne* &c. (here he cites these words,) *Namely as he there tells us, to celebrate and participate of the Holy Eucharist. Why was this ? but because they had not many places to celebrate in.*]

V. *Tertullian* is as plain and full : *Apol. c. 39. Corpus sumus de conscientia religionis, & disciplinæ unitate, & spei fœdere : Coimus in Cœtum, & Congregationem, ut ad Deum quasi manu facta precationibus ambiamus orantes — Cogimur ad divinarum literarum commemorationem.— Certe fidem sanctis vocibus pascimus : spem erigimus, fiduciam figimus, disciplinam præceptorum nihilominus inculcationibus densamus. Ibidem etiam exhortationes, castigationes, & censura divina. Nam & judicatur magno cum pondere, ut apud certos de Dei conspectu ; summumque futuri judicii præjudicium est, siquis ita deliquerit, ut a Communicatione orationis & Conventus & omnis Sancti Commercii relegatur : Præsident probati quique Seniores, &c.*

And *de Corona Milit. cap. 3. Eucharistiæ Sacramentum, & in tempore victus, & omnibus mandatum a domino, etiam antelucanis cœtibus ; nec de aliorum manu quam præsidentium sumimus.*

And further, [*Aquam adituri itidem, sed & aliquando prius in Ecclesia sub antistitis manu contestamur, nos renunciare Diabolo & pompæ & angelis ejus.*]

In all these words (and many more such in *Tertullian*) it is evident, 1. That then a Church was a Congregation met for holy Worship, and not many hundred

dred Congregations making one Church *prime ordinis.* 2. That this Church had ordinarily a Bishop present (not present in one Congregation and many hundred without.) 3. That the Bishop baptized, and took the Confessions of the Baptized, and performed the ordinary Worship, and administred the Lords Supper. (Doctor *Hammond* himself maintaineth that it is the Bishop that *Tertullian* speaketh of.) 4. That Discipline was exercised in those Church Assemblies, and therefore the Bishop was present.

5. They took the Sacrament from none but the Bishops hand (save that the Deacon distributed it as from him) which proveth that the Bishop was present, when ever the Sacrament was administred. 6. They had these Assemblies every Lords day. All which set together plainly sheweth that then every Church had a present Bishop, (ordinarily) and was no more than one Congregation, met for such Communion as is described.

Cyprian in the Separation of Feliciss. and five Presbyters Epist. 44. (ed. Goul) pag 93. saith, [Deus unus & Christus unus & una Ecclesia —— Aliud Altare constitui, aut Sacerdotium novum fieri prater unum Altare & unum Sacerdotium non potest.

VI. And even in *Cyprian's* time the alteration was not great: *Epist.* 68. (*Edit. Goulart.*) *p.*201. he saith, [*Propter quod plebs obsequens præceptis dominicis & Deum metuens, &c.*] i. e. [*For which cause the people that are obedient to* " the *Lords Commands and fear God, ought to separate themselves from a sinful Pre-* " *late (or Bishop) and not to be present, at the Sacrifices of a Sacrilegious Priest ;* " seeing they have the greatest power either of chusing worthy Priests, or of re- " fusing the unworthy : which very thing we see coming down by Divine Au- " thority, that the Priest, the people being present, be chosen (or appointed) be- " fore the eyes of all, and by the publick judgment and testimony be approved " worthy and fit. And so going on to prove the Divine Right hereof he ad- deth, " which was before done so diligently and cautelously, the people being " all called together, lest any unworthy person should creep into the Ministry " of the Altar, or the place of Priesthood. For that the Unworthy are some- " times ordained, not according to the Will of God, but according to the pre- " sumption of Man ; and that these things are displeasing to God which come " not of legitimate and just Ordination, God himself doth manifest by the " Prophet *Osee*, saying, *They made themselves a King, but not by me :* And there- " fore it is diligently to be observed, and held of Divine Tradition and Apo- " stolical Observation, which with us also and almost all the Provinces is held, " that for the right celebrating of Ordinations, all the next Bishops of the same " Province do come together, to that people over whom the Bishop (or Prelate) " is set, and that the Bishop be appointed them, (or assigned) the people being " present who fullyest know the life of every one, and have throughly seen the " act of every ones Conversation : which also we saw done with you in the Or- " dination of *Sabinus* our Colleague, that the Office of a Bishop was given " (or delivered) him, and hands imposed on him, in the place of *Basilides*, " by the suffrage of the whole Fraternity, and by the judgment of the Bishops " that had met together and had sent you Letters concerning him.

And before *Sect.* 4. *Deus instruit, &c.* " God instructeth and sheweth that " the Ordinations of Priests (that is, Bishops) ought not to be done but under the " Conscience (that is, present sight and consent) of the assisting people, that the

Laity

" *Laity being present,* either the crimes of the bad may be detected, or the me-
" rits of the good predicated, *and that Ordination be just* and legitimate, which
" was examined by the suffrage and judgment of all.—

The Case is so plain in *Cyprian* that *Pamelius* himself is forced thus to confess
[*Non negamus veterem Electionis Episcoporum ritum, quo plebe præsente, immo &
suffragiis plebis eligi solent.   Nam in* Africa *illum observatum constat ex electione*
Eradii *successoris D.* Augustini *de quo extat Epistola ejus* 120.   In Græcia *ætate*
Chrysostomi *ex lib.* 3. *de Sacerdot.   In* Hispaniis *ex hoc* Cypriani *loco, &* Isi-
dor. *lib. de Officiis.   In* Galliis *ex Epist.* Celestini, *p.* 2.   Romæ, *ex iis quæ su-
pra diximus Epist. ad* Antoniam.   *Ubique etiam alibi ex Epist.* Leonis 87.   Et
perdurasse eam consuetudinem ad* Gregor.1. *usque ex ejus Epistolis ; Immo ad tempora
usque* Caroli & Ludovici *Imper.at. ex* 1. *lib. Capitulorum eorundem satis constat ; Verum Plebi sola suffragia concessa, non electio quæ per subscriptionem fieri solet.— Hoc
enim potissimum tunc agebatur, ut invito plebi non daretur Episcopus.—*

. From hence now the quantity of their Churches may easily be gathered.
1. The people must be present.   2. And this must be *All the people, the whole
Laity* of the Church.   3. They give their testimony of the life of the ordained.
4. They are supposed all to know his conversation.   5. This is the common
custom of the Churches, in *Africa* and all other Countries.

Now I leave it to the consideration of sober minds how many Churches, or
Congregations could do all this ? Whether it was many hundred Churches
that never saw the person, nor one another, that were to meet in one Church
or place, to do all this ? Or rather the Inhabitants of a Vicinity, using to assemble for Communion, when even our *Greater Parishes* now are more than
can thus meet and do all this ?

2. Note also that when *Cyprian* imposeth it on the same people that chuse
their Bishop, also *to separate from one that is wicked,* and not communicate with
him in the Sacrament, it is most evident to him that is willing to understand,
that this Bishop was to be the Teacher of all the people of that Church, and
was to administer the Sacrament to them in the Congregation, and they had
ordinary communion with him : For how else should they be called on *to separate from him,* in the Sacrifice (as it's called.)   Doth he command a thousand or a hundred distant Churches to separate from the Sacrifices of that Bishop, who never had local Communion with him (unless perhaps once in
their lives as with a stranger.)   The Impartial can hardly read these words,
and not understand them.

Two Objections are here made.   1. Obj. *All the People is put for all present,
which is a part.*

Answ. By such interpretations let God or Man say what they will, it will
signifie but what the Reader please.   The Context and many concurrent expressions shew that(though business or sickness might hinder some Individuals)
it was the main body of the Congregation which is called *Plebs Universa,* or
else it will be nonsense.

2. Object. *But if the same were the custom till the days of* Charles *and* Lodo-
vick, *then it could not be all the people, for then it's known that the Dioceses were
larger : Therefore it must be but all that belonged to the Cathedral.   Answ.*

Anſw. 1. Even till their days Chriſtianity had not been received by the whole Cities or Pariſhes, in the greateſt part of the Empire; but (according to the liberty then given when none were forced to be Chriſtians) the Chriſtians were but few in many great Countries. It was long ere they were the greater number of the Inhabitants in *France* and *Flanders*; longer in *England*; and longer in *Germany,* and *Hungary,* and *Poland*; and longer in *Sweden* and *Denmark,* &c. 2. That it was no Cathedral Society diſtinct from other Congregations under the ſame Biſhop in *Cyprian*'s time, is moſt evident: There being no ſuch diſtinction intimated, but contrarily all the Biſhops Church or Flock is ſpoken to: And how ſhould one part of the Church come to have a right to chuſe and refuſe the Biſhop more than all the reſt? And in all ordinary Dioceſes it was ſo long after: But it is true that at *Rome, Alexandria* and the greater Churches, where the cuſtom was continued, and yet the multitude of the people was ſo great that they could not half meet in one place; thoſe that were forwardeſt crowded together, and oft committed Riots and Murders (as at the Election of *Damaſus,* and others,) till by this, the cuſtom was changed to avoid ſuch tumults; and thoſe that would not be in the Crow'd ſtayed at home: And the neareſt Neighbours commonly were they that met.

Object. But do not we ſee that a whole County can meet to chuſe Parliament Men?

Anſw. 1. No: It is only the *Freeholders* who are comparatively but a ſmall part of the County. 2. It is in a Field, or Streets, and not in a Church. 3. It is commonly to judge of their Suffrages by comparing by the eye, the magnitude of the diſtinct Companies when they ſeparate, or elſe by taking their Votes Man by Man in a long time, and not to do all in their hearing, and by their Counſel, as in this Caſe. 4. I have been at great Aſſemblies for ſuch Elections of Parliament, in the Fields; and I never ſaw more together than have heard me preach in one Aſſembly, nor half ſo many as ſome *London* Pariſhes do contain: much leſs as a Dioceſs.

There is a great deal more in *Cyprian* to prove the thing in queſtion, *Epiſt.* 3, 6, 10, 11, 13, 14, 26, 27, 28, 31, 33, 40. which would be tedious to the Reader ſhould I recite it. *A primordio Epiſcopatus mei ſtatuerim nihil ſine conſilio veſtro & ſine conſenſu plebis meæ privata ſententia gerere—— Prohibeantur offerre, acturi apud nos, & apud confeſſores ipſos, & apud plebem univerſam cauſam ſuam.*] *Hæc ſingulorum tractanda ſit & limanda plenius ratio, non tantum cum Collegis meis, ſed & cum plebe ipſa univerſa:—— Vix plebi perſuadeo, immo extorqueo, ut tales patiantur admitti—— Secundum veſtra divina ſuffragia, Conjurati & ſcelerati de Eccleſia ſponte ſe pellerent.—*] By theſe and many ſuch paſſages it is evident that even the famous Church of *Carthage,* under that famous Biſhop was no greater than that all Church Affairs might be treated of in the hearing of all the Laity, and managed by their conſent, and the Quality of each Presbyter and Communicant, and their faults fell under the Cognizance of the whole Church; not as Governors, but as intereſſed for their own welfare, as the words declare.

VII. And

VII. And here I think I may seasonably cite the Constitutions called. Apostolical ; which if not written by *Clement*, were certainly for the most part of them very ancient, as being before *Athanasius* who mentioneth them. And the Learned and Sober *Albaspinæus*, *Observ. Lib.* 1. p. 38. saith, [*De constitutionibus istis nemini dubium esse debet, quin probus juxta & antiquus liber sit ; certoque affirmare possum trecentis primis eo ecclesiam Græcam, tanquam rituali & Pontificali usam esse ; Quique eas attente legerit, eadem de illis quæ de canonibus judicabit, additas, viz. decursu temporum primis novas, quemadmodum & novæ leges & constitutiones in regimine Ecclesiæ, novis occasionibus enatis, factæ sunt.*] that though they were not written by *Clement* or the Apostles, yet they were that Summary of Apostolical or Christian Discipline, which the *Greek* Churches much used for the first three hundred years ; and that Additions were made by degrees. But I cite them for nothing but the History, wherein they are of great account to acquaint us with the state of the Church in those times.

Lib. 2. *cap.* 18. It is said, that [*Omnium Episcopus curam habeat, & eorum qui non peccarunt, ut non peccent, & eorum qui in peccatis sunt, ut peccasse pæniteat : ait enim Dominus, Videte ne contemnatis unum ex pusillis istis. Item pænitentibus condonare oportet peccata.— Quocirca curam omnium suscipe tanquam rationem de pluribus redditurus : Ac sanos quidem conserva, lapsos vero mone, & qui in jejunio premens, leva in remissione, & eum qui luxit recipe, cuncta Ecclesia pro eo deprecante, &c.*] And much more works he adds : Whereby it appeareth that the Bishoprick was no greater than that he could take a personal care of every member, over the meanest, sound and unsound : And that it was one Assembly where all did intercede for the restoring of the Penitent.

So *cap.* 20. opening the Bishop's duty to the Laity, he repeateth, *Omnes monens, omnes increpans, &c.* And *ibid. Medice ergo Ecclesiæ Domini adhibe medicinam cuique ægrotantium convenientem : Omnibus modis cura, sana, factos sanos redde Ecclesiæ ; pasce gregem, non per vim, neque imperiose, cum ludibrio & despectu quasi dominatum teneas, sed tanquam bonus pastor in sinum ac complexum agnos congrega & oves gravidas hortare.*

And it concerneth them to know well what they do, for *cap.* 2. *Scitote quod qui eum, qui injuriam non fecit, ejicit, aut qui se convertit non recipit, fratrem suum occidit, & sanguinem ejus fudit, sicut Cain sanguinem fratris sui fudit ; cujus sanguis, qui ad Deum clamat, requiretur. - Similiter eveniet ei qui ab Episcopo suo sine justa causa fuerit excommunicatus : Qui tanquam pestiferum ejicit eum qui est extra culpam, is quidem sævior est interfectore.— Violentior est ipso homicida qui corpus perimit, is qui innocentem ex ecclesia ejicit.*

Et cap. 25. *Oportet ut qui in Ecclesia assidui sunt eos Ecclesia alat* (viz. *Pontificem, Sacerdotes, Levitas.*) where the Assembly is the Church which maintaineth the Bishop and Presbyters.

And *cap.* 26. It is the Bishop that to all the Church is, *Minister Verbi, scientiæ custos, Mediator Dei & vestrum in iis quæ ad eum colendum pertinent* (that is, officiateth in Church Worship :) *hic est magister pietatis ac religionis ; hic est secundum Deum pater vester, qui vos per aquam & Spiritum sanctum regeneravit, &c.*

E   *Epis-*

Episcopus igitur vobis præsideat, ut dignitate Dei cohonestatus, qua clerum sub potestate sua tenet, & toti populo præest, Diaconus vero assistat huic, &c. So that a Bishops Church was no greater than that he could be the constant Teacher, Guide, Baptizer, &c. of them all.

And *cap.* 27. All the Oblations were to be brought to the Bishop himself, by themselves that offered, or by the Deacons. *Immo primitias quoque & decimas & quæ sponte offeruntur; is enim probe novit afflictos & cuique tribuit, ut congruit; ne quis eadem die aut eadem hebdomade bis aut sæpius accipiat, alius vero nihil penitus.* So that the reason why all the Offerings, Tythes and Gifts in his whole Diocefs were brought to the Bishop himself was, because he was well acquainted with all the Poor of his Diocefs, and was every day to relieve them, and fee that one did not receive twice the same day, or the same Week, and another have none. How many hundred Churches think you had a Church then in the Belly of it? and how large was such a Diocefs?

And *cap.* 28. In their Love-Feasts the Bishop was to have always his special part of the Feast, even fent him if he were absent. Sure if his Diocefs had six hundred or a thousand Parishes and as many Feasts, and some of them as far off as I am from the Cathedral Church (about fourscore Miles) it will cost more the Carriage of the Bishop's Supper than it is worth, and it will be cold, and it is well if it ftink not by the way. And the Presbyters that were all to have a double portion also of the Feast, are called *tanquam Consiliarii Episcopi & Ecclesiæ Corona, funt enim Consilium & Senatus Ecclesiæ.* So that it was but one City Congregation yet that had Bishops and Presbyters and Deacons, &c.

And in *cap.* 30. and many Chapters there is mentioned often the Bishops doing all without any help fave the Deacons, which would make one think that *de facto* Doctor *Hammond* was in the right, and that some of the Constitutions were written when in most Churches there was no Presbyters with the Bishop but Deacons only.

Cap. 32. If the Deacon knew any to be poor, he must tell the Bishop, and do nothing without him. How large was this Diocefs? *cap.* 34. This Bishop must be loved as a Father, feared as a King, honoured as a God, offering him our Fruits and the works of our hands for his Blessing; giving him as God's Priest our First-fruits, Tythes, First-fruits of Corn, Wine, Oyl, Apples, Wool, and all that God shall give us.] Was all this carried him from many hundred Parishes, many score Miles?

And *cap.* 36. The Bishop's Church was no farther off than that all the Members were to come to it in the morning before they went to any work, and at Evening when they had done. How big was this Diocefs?

Cap. 44. The Deacon is to be the Bishop's Eye, and Ear, and Mouth, and to help him, that he may not be overwhelmed with his work: If he had a thousand fubject Presbyters, one Deacon's help only would not have been named.

Cap. 56. The Bishop is to fee that this Deacon fpeak Peace to every one that entreth into the Church to worship. Which implyeth that he was prefent in the Church.

Cap. 57. The defcription of a Church Order is, that the Bishop's Seat be in
the

the midſt, and that the Presbyters ſit on each ſide of him, and ſo for the reſt. And the Order of Officiating was, [that (the Deacons ſeeing all orderly keep their Seats) the Reader firſt read the old Scriptures, and the Deacon or Presbyters the Goſpels; then that the Presbyters exhort the people, not all at once, but one by one, and laſt of all the Biſhop, &c.] Theſe were then the Churches; where every Altar had a Biſhop.

So cap. 50. *Cum doces Epiſcope, jube & mone populum frequentare quotidie Eccleſiam mane & veſpere, ut omnino abeſſe nolit, immo aſſidue conveniat, neque Ullus ſubducendo ſe Ecclefiam mutilam faciat, & a corpore Chriſti unum membrum decerpat: Neque enim de ſolis Sacerdotibus dictum eſt, ſed potius quiſque Laicus, &c.* So that a Biſhop's Dioceſs or Church was ſo great, as that no one Lay Member ſhould be abſent Morning or Evening.

Lib. 4. *cap.* The Biſhop had the particular care of all the Pupils, Widows, Labourers, Weak, Naked, Sick, Virgins, &c. And *cap.* 5. He is to know well who they be that offer all the Oblations; and is to reject the Oblations of all the Wicked: For *cap.* 7. Let the Poor have never ſo much need, it's better periſh by Famine, than receive any thing from the Enemies of God, which may be contumelious to his Friends.]

Lib 8. *cap.* 4. The Ordering of a Biſhop muſt be (*de quo nulla eſt querela; & qui ſit a cuncto populo ex optimis quibuſque electus, quo nominato & placente populus in unum congregatus, una cum Presbyteris & Epiſcopis præſentibus, die Dominico, conſentiat. Qui vero inter reliquos princeps Epiſcopus, percontetur Epiſcopos & populum, an ipſe ſit quem præeſſe petunt? &c.* So that all the people of the Church came together to chuſe and conſent to the Biſhop: no greater at that time was a Dioceſane Church.

Cap. 12. *His peractis dextram & levam ejus ut diſcipuli Magiſtro aſſiſtant.*—— This is part of the Common Rubrick (of the beſt and eldeſt Liturgy that I know of recorded by Church Hiſtory) for the celebrating the Sacrament. So that it ſuppoſeth a Biſhop to be then preſent in all Churches that had an Altar and Sacrament. The reſt of the Liturgy, *lib.* 8. ſuppoſeth ſtill the ſame preſence of the Biſhop. *Cap.* 35. *Congregabis Epiſcope Eccleſiam ad veſperam, &c.* It would be too long to recite all the Biſhops part in the ordinary Offices of the Aſſembly. It is hence plain that in thoſe Ages (unleſs it were very few; perhaps only *Rome* and *Alexandria*) no Biſhops had more ſtated Aſſemblies or Churches that had Altars, or communicated, than one.

VIII. The Canons called the Apoſtles run juſt in the ſame ſtrain with the Conſtitutions: And though by ſome of them it is apparent that (at leaſt) all of them are not ſo old as many think, (As that which intimateth that Rulers ſet up Clergy-men, &c.) yet they were elder than our Compound Dioceſane Churches. For *Can.* 5. It is ſaid. [*Omnium aliorum primitiæ Epiſcopo & Presbyteris domum mittuntur; non ſuper altare: Manifeſtum eſt autem quod Epiſcopus & Presbyteri inter Diaconos & reliquos Clericos eas dividant.*] By which and many ſuch paſſages it is evident that there was then but one Altar and one Biſhop with his Presbytery and Deacons in a Church, as in

Ignatius's

Ignatius's time : and that they all lived on the same Altar, together with the rest of the Gifts of the Church, *Vid. & Can.* 58.

The *Can.* 32. saith, [*Siquis Presbyter contemnens Episcopum suum, seorsim collegerit & altare aliud erexerit, nihil habens quo reprehendat Episcopum in causa pietatis, aut justitiæ, deponatur, quasi principatus amator existens.--- Hæc autem post unam & secundam & tertiam Episcopi obsecrationem fieri conveniat.*] The same is in the *Can.* 5. *Concil. Antioch.* And to set up *aliud Altare, & Altare contra Altare* is the Phrase used then by many Writers, and Councils, to signifie a dividing and separating from the Church, and setting up an Antichurch ; All which sheweth that then a Bishops Church had but one Altar.

IX. *Dionysius* (whoever or whenever he wrote) doth so describe the Bishops work as sheweth that he had but one Church and Presbytery to assist him. *Cap.* 4. *de Ecclef: Hier.* he tells us that [*The Præfecti did baptize those that were converted,*] and the Presbyters and Deacons did but assist him : And it is a very long manner of baptizing which he there describeth, and all the Church were called together to it, and joyned in it. And this was in times when the Infidels were to be brought in, and converted, and baptized at Age, where Examinations, Professions and Circumstances made it so long a work, as this alone would have proved his Church to be no greater than aforesaid : much more with the rest of the work which he describeth.

X. But Councils give the surest testimonies to such matter of fact : *Concil. Agath. Can.* 4. *Siquis etiam extra Parochias, & ubi legitimus est ordinariusque conventus, Oratorium habere voluerit, reliquis festivitatibus ut ibi missam audiat, propter fatigationem familiæ, justa ordinatione permittimus. Pascha vero, Natali Domini, Epiphania, Ascensione Domini, Pentecoste, & natali Sancti Johannis Baptistæ, & siqui maxime dies, in festivitatibus habentur, non nisi in civitatibus, aut Parochiis audiant.* This being decreed so late, when Christians were increased in the Countries, alloweth them, to avoid wearinefs in travelling with their Families too far, to have Chappels or Oratories in the remote parts of the Country (but so that they come all to the City or Parish Church on all the greatest Festivals.) Which sheweth that then the Church was but one Assembly which all could joyn in to hear the word.

And that each of these City and Parish Churches had a Bishop of their own, is apparent in what followeth, [*Can.* 30. *Benedictionem super plebem in Ecclesia fundere aut pœnitentem in Ecclesia benedicere, Presbytero penitus non licebit ;* that is, [*It shall not at all be lawful for a Presbyter to pronounce the Blessing on the people in the Church, or to bless a Penitent in the Church.*] Now these being (or one at least) performed in every Church Assembly, when a Presbyter is forbidden to do them, it is implied that a Bishop was present to do it himself : and so that every communicating Assembly had a Bishop.

And it's said, *Can.* 31. *Missas die Dominico secularibus totas audire speciali ordine præcipimus ; ita ut ante benedictionem sacerdotis egredi populus non præsumat, quod si fecerit, ab Episcopo publice confundatur.* So that there must be a daily pronunciation

ciation of the Blessing each Lords day, and that not by the Presbyters but the Bishop, who must rebuke them that go out before it ; which sheweth that each Church had a Bishop.

And after, [*Qui solemnitatum, id est Paschæ & natalis domini vel Pentecostes festivitatibus, cum Episcopis interesse neglexerint, quum in civitatibus communionis vel benedictionis accipiendæ causa positos se nosse debeant, triennia communione priventur Ecclesiæ.*] By which it appeareth that in a City there were no more Christians or Church-members, than could congregate with the Bishop on the Festivals for Communion ; when all the neglecters were to be deprived of the Communion for three years.

XI. The Council at *Eliberis Betic. An.305.* had nineteen Bishops, twenty six Presbyters, and the Deacons, *& omnis Plebs* stood by : which intimateth that these twenty six Presbyters and the Deacons were the main body of the Clergy under the nineteen Bishops ; which was not two Presbyters to a Bishop ; why else should the Deacons and all the Laity be there, if not all the Presbyters ? And supposing that *Plebs omnis* here signifie not strictly *all the Laity*, yet it intimateth that the Churches were no greater than that so great a part of their Laity was there, as that Phrase might be well used of ; which cannot be of our Compound Diocess.

XII. *Concil. Gangrens. cap. 7. No one was to receive the Oblations of Fruits, and the First-fruits, due to the Church, out of the Church.* And *cap. 8. None was to receive them but the Bishop, or he whom the Bishop appointed.* This sheweth the quantity of the Diocess, and that every Church had one Altar and one Bishop.

XIII. In a *Roman* Council *sub Silvest.* it's said, [*Ab omni Ecclesia eligatur consecrandus Episcopus, nullo de membris Ecclesiæ intercedente, & omni Ecclesia conveniente : & nulli Episcopo liceat sine cuncta Ecclesia a novissimo gradu usque ad primum ordinare Neophytum Silvester Papa dixit, A nobis incipientes moderamine lenitatis judicare, commonemus ut nulli Episcopo liceat quemlibet gradum Clerici ordinare aut consecrare, nisi cum omni adunata Ecclesia, si placet : & dixerunt Episcopi, placet.* What can be more fully said, [*Let the Bishop to be ordained be chosen by all the Church, no one of the Members of the Church being wanting, and all the Church meeting together. Let it be lawful for no Bishop without the whole Church to ordain.*———*Not to ordain or consecrate any degree of Clergy-Man, but with the whole Church together in one.* And how great then were the Churches, when even at *Rome* and all about it, *The whole Church united, and every member could meet together at every Ordination and Consecration ?* I scarce know how a testimony can be plainer.

XIV. The *Concil. Sardic.* which first began to befriend the Grandeur of the *Roman* Bishop, was it that first forbad Bishops to be ordained in *small Villages :* yet note that even there it was not absolutely forbidden to all Villages ; but only

only to such Villages and small Cities where *one Presbyter* was enough : But they allowed a Bishop to the Cities. [*Quæ Episcopos habuerunt, & siqua tam populosa est Civitas vel Locus* (mark *Locus* as distinct from *Civitas*) *qui mereatur habere Episcopum.*] So that if there were but people enough for more than one Presbyter, they allowed them a Bishop.

And *Can.* 14. It is decreed that, [*As no Lay-man must be above three Weeks from Church, so no Bishop from his own Church at another place.*] Whereas if a Bishop have many Churches, or many hundred, or a thousand, he could be but at one in a Year, or two, or three, or more, if he did nothing but travel from parish to Parish. Only in the next Canon, those that have Farms or Lands in the Country are dispensed with for three Weeks to be absent from their own Churches, so they go to another.

XV. In the Epistle of the 1. *Concil. Nic. ad Eccles. Ægypt.* (*in Crab. pag.* 262. *T.* 1.) Presbyters were to be made, [*Solummodo si videantur digni, & populus eos elegerit, condecernente simul & designante maxime* Alexandriæ *Civitatis Episcopo.*] Still the people that had the choice were no more than could meet to chuse.

And even in the *Arabick* Canons ascribed to this Council by some of late it's said, *Can.* 72. *Sic Episcopi & Sacerdotes si Civitates suas & Altaria propter alia majora relinquerent, male facerent* ; which shews that each City even then had but one Altar or Meeting for Sacramental Communion : though when these were written, there were other Churches in Villages that had Altars.

And in *Pisan. Can.* 57. *Archi-presbyter in absentia Episcopi honoretur tanquam Episcopus, quia est loco ejus, & sit caput Sacerdotum qui sub potestate ejus sunt in Ecclesia.* The Bishop then was but such a Head of Priests in the same Church, as an Arch-Presbyter might be in his absence.

And *Cap.* 9. The Vote of the whole Diocess without the Arch-bishop shall not serve to chuse a Bishop, though all gathered together.

XVI. The *Concil. Vasense* granted leave for Presbyters to preach and Deacons to read Homilies in Country Parishes, which sheweth both that Bishops were the ordinary Preachers to their whole Flocks before, and that these Parishes were yet but new, and perhaps but Chappels that yet had not Altars and the Lord's Supper.

XVII. *Binnius* in *Concil. Ephes.* 1. *To.* 2. *cap.* 20. saith, [Dalmatius *told the Emperor that there were six thousand Bishops under the Metropolitan sent to the Council that were against* Nestorius ;] And there was a great number on the other side with *Johan. Antiochen.* who cast out *Cyril* and *Memnon.* How great think you were these Bishops Dioceses ?

XVIII. *Concil. Carth.* 3. *cap.* 39. & 40. (*in Crab*) some would have had many (twelve) Bishops at each Bishop's Ordination ; but *Aurelius* desired it might be but three, because [*Crebro & pene per diem Dominicum ordinationes habemus,*] they

had

had Ordinations almoſt every Lord's day, and *Tripoli* had but five Biſhops. How big were theſe Dioceſes where the Biſhops could meet almoſt every Lord's day for Ordinations ; and five under *Tripoly* was an exceeding ſmall number.

•And *cap.* 40. If a Biſhop were accuſed at his Ordination, the Cauſe was to be tried, *In eadem plebe cui ordinandus eſt* ; And ſurely it was not to be in many hundred Congregations at once or *per vices.*

XIX. *Concil. Antioch.* (before this) *Can.* 5. *(pag.* 321 *.in Crab) Siquis Presbyter aut Diaconus Epiſcopum proprium contemnens, ſe ab Eccleſia ſegregaverit & ſeorſum colligens Altare conſtituit (vel in ſecunda edit. & privatim apud ſe collectis populis Altare erigere anſus fuerit, &c.)* This theweth, 1. That the Presbyters then joyned with the Biſhop in the ſame Church. 2. And that then each Church had but one Altar, and to erect another Altar elſewhere, was to ſet up another Church.

Can. 8. *Presbyteri qui ſunt in agris Canonicas Epiſtolas dare non poſſunt----Chorepiſcopi autem--- dare poſſunt.----* This theweth that then the Country Villages had *Chorepiſcopos* with Presbyters.

Can. 10. *Qui in vicis vel poſſeſſionibus Chorepiſcopi nominantur quamvis manus impoſitionem Epiſcoporum perceperint, & ut Epiſcopi conſecrati ſint, tamen Sanctae Synodo placuit, ut modum proprium recognoſcant, in gubernent ſibi ſubjectas Eccleſias earumque moderamine curaque contenti ſint.* This theweth that then the Churches in Villages had their Biſhops, though under the City Biſhops.

Can. 16. A Biſhop that put himſelf *into a vacant Church* without the conſent of a perfect Council, where muſt be the Metropolitane, muſt be caſt out, *etſi cunctus populus quem diripuit cum habere delegerit :* which theweth that the *whole people* were no more than could meet to chuſe him.

Can. 17, 18, 21. imply the ſame ; *Epiſcopus ab alia Parochia non migret ad aliam, nec ſponte ſita inſiliens, nec vi coactus a populo, nec ab Epiſcopis neceſſitate compulſus : Maneat autem in Eccleſia quam primitus adeo ſortitus eſt.* A Church and a Pariſh are here the ſame ; and no greater than that the people could be the compellers, which implieth their concurrence, which could not be in a Dioceſs of many hundred Churches ; but in one only.

Can. 23. *The Goods of the Church are faithfully to be kept :* which alſo are to be *diſpenſed by the Judgment and Power of the Biſhop, to whom is committed the people, and the ſouls that are congregated in the Church: and it's manifeſt what things belong to the Church, with the knowledge of the Presbyters and Deacons that are about him, who cannot but know what are the Church Goods,* &c. Here 1. The Church contained only *the ſouls that were congregated in it,* and not many Congregations. 2. All the Church Goods were known to the Presbyters and Deacons, ſo that the Biſhop did diſpoſe of them while he lived, but could alienate none at his death : which theweth that it was but one Church or Congregation, where the Biſhop and Presbyters joyned in the Miniſtry.

Cap.

Cap. 25. hath the fame Evidence : The Bifhop difpenfeth all the Goods and Lands of the Church, to all that need, but muft not appropriate them to his Kindred, *&c.* but ufe them by the confent of his Presbyters and Deacons.

XX. *Concil. Carthag.* 4. *cap.* 14. The Bifhop's dwelling was to be near the Church. (But if he had many Churches, they would have told which.) *Can.* 17. The Bifhop was to exercife the care of Government of Widows, Orphans, and Strangers by his Arch-Presbyter and Arch-Deacon (which fheweth that they had not many Churches; where each appropriate Presbyter and Deacons did it.)

Can. 22. The Peoples confent and teftimony was neceffary to every Clerk ordained : (which fheweth how large the Churches or People were.)

Can. 35. The Bifhop is ordered to fit above the Presbyters in the Church, and in their Confefs; but at home to know himfelf to be their Colleague : which fheweth that they were all belonging to one Church, and not to many far from each other.

XXI. *Concil. Laodic.* Presbyters muft not go into the Church (or *Sacrarium* as the other *Ed.*) before the Bifhop, nor fit in the Seats, but *muft go in with the Bifhop, or fit in lower Seats* (till he comes.) Which fheweth that they were all in one Church. And if there had been many Churches diftant where there were no Bifhops but Presbyters only, it's like that Cafe would have been excepted, as well as is the Cafe of the Bifhop's [*Sicknefs and Peregrination.*] See *Binnius* three Verfions, *To.* 1. *pag.* 292. and *Crab's* two *Vol.* 1. *pag.* 310.

Can. 28. Forbidding the *Agapæ*, or Church Feafts to be made in the Church, implieth that other Houfes could contain the Church Members. And *Can.* 58. Forbidding *Oblationes fieri vel celebrari in domibus ab Epifcopis vel Presbyteris,* doth fhew that till they built Chappels there was but one Congregation in a City, which was where the Bifhop was.

XXII. *Decretum Innocent.* 1. *P. Rom.* (*in Crab, Vol.* 1. *pag.* 453.) *Dicit, De confignandis infantibus manifeftum eft non ab alio, quam ab Epifcopis fieri licere : Nam Presbyteri licet fint Sacerdotes, Pontificatus tamen apicem non habent, &c.* And for how many one Bifhop can do this with all his other work alfo, you may judge.

XXIII. (To look back,) *Concil. Carthag.* 2. *Can* 3. decreeth, [*Chrifmatis confectio, & puellarum confecratio a Presbyteris non fiant : Vel reconciliare quenquam in publica miffa, Presbytero non licere.*] (*Crab. pag.* 424.) But this being an ordinary publick work, this fuppofeth the Bifhop ftill prefent in every Church to do it, and to have a Church no more numerous than he could do it for : whereas if Difcipline were but moderately exercifed according to the ancient Canons, there could not be fewer than many hundreds in a day for the Bifhop either to excommunicate or abfolve in this Diocefs where I live, *Leg. Albafpin. Not. pag.* 268. And the fourth *Can.* fortifieth this by this exception, *Si quifquam*

quam in periculo fuerit constitutus & se reconciliari divinis altaribus petierit, si Episcopus absens fuerit, debet utique Presbyter consulere Episcopum, & sic periclitantem cum præcepto reconciliare. Where note that *reconciliari altaribus* is the Phrase for being reconciled to the Churches : And that no Presbyter might do it but in case of the persons danger, the Bishops absence, and with the Bishops Command : Which still sheweth that the Bishop was usually present. And as *Albaspineus* noteth, a Presbyter might not do it for a dying Man, till he had consulted the Bishop, and told him all the case, and had his Command : Which supposeth him *near* (for the man may be dead before our Ministers can ride to the Bishop and have his Commission) and supposeth the Church to be but small.

XXIV. To make short, and leave no place for doubting, I will joyn several Canons which decree that [No Man shall be a Clerk to two Churches, nor an Abbot to two Monasteries, nor a Bishop to two Cities or Churches.]
So *Concil. Oecumen. Nic.* 2. *Can.* 15. *(in Bin. pag.* 394.) *Clericus ab hoc deinceps tempore, in duabus Ecclesiis non collocetur. Ab ipsa enim domini voce audivimus, non posse quenquam duobus dominis servire.*
And *Concil. Chalcedon. Can.* 10. *juxta* Dionys. *Non licet Clericum conscribi in duabus simul Ecclesiis.* And though then the *Can.* 17. sheweth that there were *Singularum Ecclesiarum Rusticæ Parochiæ vel possessiones,* yet these were but like our Chappels, and not called *Churches,* but only the Bishop's Church. And if the Secular Power made any place a City, it was thereupon to follow the Secular Order. So of Abbots, *Concil. Venet. Can.* 8. *(in Crab, pag.* 948.) no one was to have two Monasteries ; *Vid. Concil. Agath. Can.* 38.
And *Photius & Balsamon Nomocan. Tit.* 1. *cap.* 20. *pag.* 21. *Ne in una Provincia duo Metropolitani, aut in una Civitate duo Episcopi, aut in duabus Civitatibus unus Clericus----* *Neque in duabus Civitatibus quis potest esse Episcopus.*] Excepting only (even then) *Episcopum* Tomensem : *Ille enim reliquarum Ecclesiarum Scythiæ curam gerit,* (Because the Christians were few, and from under the *Roman* Power.) [*Et* Leontopolis Isauriæ *sub Episcopo* Isauropolis *est.*] He addeth, [*Porro* 35 *Const. tit.* 3. *l.* 1. *Cod. c.* 3. *&c.* ait, [*Eum qui quamcunque veterem aut recens conditam civitatem, proprii Episcopatus jure, aliove privilegio privat, tametsi Principis permissu id faciat, infamia notat, multaque bonis constitutio ; ac simul inceptum irritum facit.*] So that no City new or old might be deprived of its Privilege of having a Bishop. Now seeing Corporations and Market Towns are in the old sense *Cities,* and seeing Parish Churches such as ours are true Churches (as Communities) how many Cities, and how many hundred Churches have many Bishops now? He addeth, *C.m.*15. *Conc.*7. and saith [*Si non permittitur cuiquam in duabus Ecclesiis Clericum fieri, multo magis præsul duo Monasteria non moderabitur ; Quemadmodum neque unum caput duo corpora.* Therefore by parity of reason much less should one Church-man or Bishop be the head of many hundred or a thousand Bodies, without any subordinate Head or Bishop under him. Why may not an Abbot as well rule a thousand Monasteries, *per alios non Abbates.* as a Bishop a thousand Churches *per alios non Episcopos?*

F

Above

More *Testimonies* of *Councils* added to the former Chap. 5.

UPon the Review, finding some confiderable Evidences from Councils before omitted, fome fhall be here added.

1. The *Roman* Clergy called a Council at *Rome, Bin. pag.* 158. &c. faith, that in the *Interregnum* they had the charge of the Univerfal Church : and *Cyprian* wrote to them as the Governors of the Church of *Rome,* when they had been a year or two without a Bifhop. And their Actions were not null.

Cypr. l. 1.
Ep. 66. 2. A *Carthage* Council with *Cyprian* condemn even a dead man called *Victor,* becaufe by his Will he left one *Fauftinus* a Presbyter the Guardian of his Sons, and fo called him off his Sacred Work to mind Secular things. Did this favour of Bifhop's Secular Power, Magiftracy or Domination ?

3. How came the *Carthage* Councils to have fo many hundreds in fo narrow a room or fpace of Land, but that every πόλις Corporation or big Town had a Bifhop ? *Anno* 308. at a *Carthage* Council the very Donatifts had two hundred and feventy Bifhops. And at *Arles* two hundred Bifhops heard the Donatifts Caufe.

4. The *Laodicean* Council decreed, *Can.* 46. that the Baptized fhould learn the Creed, and on *Friday* repeat it to the Bifhops or Presbyters :] which implieth that a Bifhop was prefent with every Church.

And *Cap.* 57. It is ordained that thenceforth [*Bifhops fhould not be ordained in fmall Villages and Hamlets, but Vifiters fhould be appointed them : But fuch (Bifhops) as had heretofore been there ordained fhould do nothing without the Confeience of the City Bifhop.*] Which implieth, 1. That every big Town had a Bifhop. 2. And Villages before.

5. *Epiphanius, Hær.* 68. *pag.* 717. &c. faith, That *Peter* feparated from *Meletius* in the fame room, and as *Meletius* went to the Mines, *he made new Bifhops, and gathered new Churches* ; fo that in feveral Cities there *were two* (Bifhops and Churches :) Which implieth that they were Congregations for Perfonal Communion.

6. The *Nicene* Council, *cap.* 8. alloweth Rural Bifhops then in ufe, (whom *Petavius* proveth to have been true Bifhops.)

7. *Greg. Nazianz. pag.* 528. &c. fheweth how Churches were enlarged and changed when the ftrife began between *Mea & Tua, Antiqua & Nova, Nobilior & Ignobilior, Multitudine Opulentior aut Tenuior.*

8. After *Lucifer Calaritanus* ordained *Paulinus, Antioch* had long two Bifhops, half being his Flock, and half cleaving to *Meletius.*

9. *Nazianzen* had in the great City of *Conftantinople* but one of the fmall Churches, (the *Arians* having the greater) till *Theodofius* gave him the greater : And thofe Hearers he was Bifhop over.   10. A

10. A Council at *Capua* ordered that both the Bishops Flocks in *Antioch* (under *Evagrius* and *Flavian*) should live together in Love and Peace.

11. Many Cities tolerated *Novatian* Bishops and Churches among them, and oft many other Dissenters. Which sheweth that but part of the City were one Church.

12. The Council at *Carthage* (called the last by *Binius*) decreed that [*Reconciliation of Penitents* (*as well as Chrisme and consecrating Virgins*) *is to be done only by the Bishops, except in great necessity*: (For how many Parishes can a Bishop do all this and all the rest of his Office?) And *when Christians were multiplied they that desired a Bishop where was none before, might have one.* But else *aliud Altare is again forbidden to be set up.*

13. Another *Carthage* Council decreeth, *Can.* 15. That *the Bishop have but vile or cheap Houshold-stuff and a poor Table and Diet, and seek Authority or Dignity by his Faith and desert of Life.* *Can.* 19. *That he contend not for transitory things though provoked.* *Can.* 23. *That he bear no Cause but in the presence of his Presbyters: else it shall be void that is sentenced without them, unless confirmed by their presence.* (Note, this being a constant work required a constant presence: and it is not a selected Chapter of Presbyters that is named : And must those of many hundred Parishes dwell in the City, or travel thither for daily Causes of Offenders? &c.) *Can.* 28, & 30. Bishops unjust Sentence void : and Judgment against the absent.

14. A Council at *Agathum*, *Can.* 3. saith, [*If Bishops wrongfully excommunicate one, any other Bishop shall receive him :*] Which implieth that the wronged person lived within reach of a Neighbour Bishop's Parish : For it doth not bind him to remove his Dwelling : And leave to go daily twenty or forty Miles to Church is a small kindness.

And I have already cited, *Can.* 63. *If any Citizens on the great Solemnities, Easter, the Lord's Nativity or Whitsuntide, shall neglect to meet where the Bishops are (seeing they are set in the Cities for Benediction and Communion) let them for three Years be deprived of the Communion of the Church.*] So that even when Churches were enlarged, yet you see how great a part of them met in one place.

15. Divers Canons give the Bishop a third or fourth part of all the Church Profits; And if those Churches had been as big as our Dioceses, it would have been too much of all Conscience.

16. A Synod at *Carpentoratte* decreed, that the Bishop of the City shall not take all the Country Parish Maintenance to himself : Which implieth as the former, that his Country Parish was small.

17. A Council at *Orleance, Anno* 540. decree, *Can.* 3. about ordaining a Bishop, that [*Qui præponendus est omnibus, ab omnibus eligatur.*] The Dioceses yet were not so large, but that *All met to chuse.*

18. So *Concil. Byzazon.* saith, it must be [*By the Election of all.*]

19. Another at *Orleance, Anno* 545. saith, [*No Citizen must celebrate Easter out of the City, because they must keep the principal Festivities in the presence of the Bishop, where the holy Assembly must be kept.* But if any have a necessity to go

F 2 abroad,

abroad, let him ask leave of the Bishop.] Here is but one City Assembly, and Individuals must be known to the Bishop, and ask his leave to go abroad.

And *Can.* 5. saith, [*A Bishop must be ordained in his own Church which he is to oversee.*] Which implieth that he had but one Church and Country Chappels.

20. Another *Orleance* Council hath the like, deposing all Bishops that come not in by common consent : And requiring them both in their Cities and Territories to relieve the Poor from the Church-House.] Let us have such Dioceses as the Bishop can do this for, and we consent.

21. A Synod at *Paris*, *Can.* 8. says, [*Let no Man be ordained a Bishop against the Will of the Citizens, nor any but whom the Election of the People and Clerks shall seek with plenary Will : None shall be put in by the Command of the Prince.*] &c.

22. King *Clodoveus* called a Synod at *Cabilone*, which *Can.* 10. decreeth, [That all Ordination of Bishops be null that was otherwise made than by the Election of the Comprovincials, the Clerks, and the Citizens.]

23. The *Const. Trul. Can.* 38. sheweth how the unhappy changes were made, decreeing, [*That whatever alteration the Imperial Power shall make on any City, the Ecclesiastical Order shall follow it.*] And so if the King will make every Market Town a City, it shall have a Bishop : And if he will make but one or two cities in a Kingdom, there shall be but one or two Bishops : And if he will make one City Regent to others, that Bishop shall be so. Thus *Rome, Constantinople, &c.* came by their Superiority. But *Hierome* telleth us the contrary ; that the Bishop of *Tanais*, or any small City (like our least Corporations) was of equal Church-Dignity with *Rome* (or the greatest.)

24. The same Council, *Can.* 78. repeateth that, [*All the Illuminate* (that is, Baptized) *must learn the Creed, and every* Friday *say it to the Bishop and Presbyters.*] I hope they did not go every *Friday* such a Journey as *Lincoln, York,* or *Norwich* Diocess, (no nor the least in *England*) would have put them to ; nor that the Bishop heard as many thousands every *Friday,* as some of ours by that Canon should have heard.

25. *Anno 693.* at a *Toletane* Council, King *Egica* writeth a Sermon for them, and therein tells them, that [*Every Parish that hath twelve Families must have their proper Governor* (not a Curate that is no Governor.) *But if it be less, it must be part of another's Charge.*]

26. *Anno 756.* Pipin called a Council in *France,* whose *Can.* 1. is, that [*Every City must have a Bishop.*] And (as is beforesaid) every Corporate Town was a City.

27. In the Epitome of the old Canons sent by Pope *Adrian* to *Carolus Magnus,* published by *Canisius,* the eighth *Antioch* Canon is, [*Country Presbyters may not give Canonical Epistles, but the* Chorepiscopi.] By which it appeareth that the *Chorepiscopi* were Bishops, as *Petavius* proveth (in *Epiphan. Arrius.*)

And *Can.* 14, 15. That [*No Bishop be above three Weeks in another City, nor above two Weeks from his own Church.*] Which intimateth that he had one single Church.

And

And *Can.* 19. That when a place wants a Bishop, he that held them must not proudly hold them to himself, and hinder them from one ; else he must lose that which he hath.

28. The same Canons say (*Can.* 94.) If a Bishop, six Months after Admonition of other Bishops, neglect to make Catholicks of the people belonging to his Seat, any other shall obtain them that shall deliver them from their Heresie.] So that, 1. The Churches were not so big but that there might be divers in one Town. 2. And converting the People is a better Title, than Parish Bounds.

29. It is there also decreed, [That no Bishop ordain or judge in another's Parish : else it shall be void :] And they forbid [Foreign Judgments, because it is unmeet that he should be judged by Strangers, who ought to have Judges of the same Province chosen by himself.] But our Diocesanes are Strangers to almost all the People, and are not chosen by them. See the rest.

Also another is, that every Election of Bishops made by Magistrates be void : yea, all that use the Secular Magistrate to get a Church must be deposed, and separated, and all that joyn with him : Also if any exact Money ; or for affection of his own, drive any from the Ministry, or segregate any of his Clergy, or shut the Temple.

30. A Council at *Chalone* under *Carol. Magn.* the *Can.* 15. condemneth Arch-Deacons that exercise Domination over Parish-Presbyters, and take Fees of them : as matter of Tyranny, and not of Order and Rectitude. And *Can.* 13. saith, [It is reported of some Brethren (Bishops) that they force them whom they are about to ordain to swear that they are worthy, and will not do contrary to the Canons, and will be obedient to the Bishop that ordaineth them, and to the Church in which they are ordained : Which Oath, because it is very dangerous we all agree shall be forbidden.] By which it appeareth that, 1. The Dioceses were not yet so large as to need such subordinate Governors as ours have : Nor 2. Were Oaths of Canonical Obedience to the Bishop and Church yet thought lawful, but forbidden as dangerous.

31. A Council at *Aquisgrane*, under *Ludov. Pius*, wrote an excellent Treatise gathered out of the Fathers, to teach Bishops the true nature of their Office, which hath much to my present use, but too long to be recited.

32. Upon *Ebbos* Flight that deposed *Lud. Pius*, the Arch-Bishoprick of *Rhemes* was void ten Years, and ruled by two Presbyters, *Fulk* and *Hotho* : who were not then uncapable of governing the Flock : but it is not like that they governed Neighbour Bishops.

33. *Canisius* tells us of a *Concilium Regiaticinum*, and *Can.* 6. is, [That the Arch-Presbyter examine every Master of a Family personally, and take account of their Families and Lives, and receive their Confessions : And *Can.* 7. That a Presbyter in the absence of the Bishop may reconcile a Penitent by his Command, &c.] Which shew that yet Dioceses were not at the largest.

34. A Council at *Papia*, *Anno* 855. order yet, [That the Clergy and People chuse the Bishops : and yet that the Laity on pretence of their electing power trample not on the Arch-Presbyter, and that Great Men's Chappels empty not Churches.

35. Yea,

35. Yea, Pope *Nicholas*, *Tit.* 8. *c.* 1. decreeth that no Bishops be ordained but by the Election or Consent of the Clergy and People.] When they became uncapable of the ancient Order, yet they kept up the words of the old Canons.

36. This is intimated in the old Canons repeated at a *Roman* Council, *Anno* 868. [*That if Bishops excommunicate any wrongfully, or for light Causes, and not restore them, the Neighbour Bishops shall take such to their Communion till the next Synod:*] Which was the Bishop of the next Parish or Corporation, and not one that dwelt in another County out of reach.

And *Can.* 72. *Because the Bishops hindred by other business, cannot go to all the Sick, the Presbyters (or any Christians) may anoint them.* How big was the Diocess when this Canon was first made? Who would give his *business,* rather than *Distance, and Numbers, and Impossibility,* as the reason why the Bishop of *London, Lincoln, Norwich, &c.* visit not all the Sick in their Diocesses?

37. *Anno* 869, till 879. was held a Council called General at *Constantinople.* The *Can.* 8. is, [*Whereas it is reported that not only the Heretical and Usurpers, but some Orthodox Patriarchs also, for their own security have made men subscribe,* (that is, to be true to them) *the Synod judgeth that it shall be so no more ; save only, that Men when they are made Bishops be required as usual to declare the soundness of their Faith : He that violateth this Sanction, let him be deprived of his Honour.*]

But these later instances only shew the Relicts of Primitive Purity and Simplicity, more evidently proved in the three first Centuries.

38. And he that will read the ancient Records of the Customs of Burying, will thence perceive the extent of Churches : Doctor *Tillesly* (after cited) affirmeth *(pag.* 179. against *Selden)* that *The Right of Burial place did first belong to the Cathedral Churches :*] And Parish Churches began so lately (as now understood, having no Bishops, and distinct from Cathedrals) that they could not be there buried, before they were built and in Being ; which saith *Selden,* began in *England* seven hundred years after Christ ; here one and there one; as a Patron erected it : *Selden* of Tythes, *pag.* 267. Yea, in seven hundred he findeth but one of Earl *Puch* in *Beda* ; and in *Anno* 800. divers appropriate to *Crowland* ; and so after. And it was the Character of a Parish Church to have *Baptisterium & Sepulturam, (pag.* 262.) So that before a Bishop's Church however called, had but one place that had *Baptisterium & Sepulturam :* Yea, long after that Parishes, had very few Members in most places, so long was it e'er the People were brought to Christianity : And they were then, as our Bishops make them now, not proper Churches, but Chappels of Ease. *Selden,* (*ibid. pag.* 267.) tells you that *Ralph Nevil* Bishop of *Chichester* and Chancellor of *England* requested of the King that the Church of Saint *Peter* in *Chichester* might be pulled down, and laid to another Parish, because it *was poor, having but two Parishioners.* Sure it was never built for two Persons : But it's like many were Heathens : Or if not so then, in the Years 700 and 800 they were so, (Though Master *Thomas Jones* hath well proved that the *Brittish*

Churches

Churches were far extended before *Gregory* sent *Auſtine*, and that our Biſhops and Religion are derived from them :) Even at *Tours* in *France* in the days of Saint *Martin*, notwithſtanding all his Miracles, the Chriſtians were not ſo many as the Heathens, at leaſt till one publick Miracle towards his later time convinced ſome.

CHAP. VI.

The ſame further confirmed by the Ancients.

I. **E**Uſebius *Demonſtrat. Evangel. pag.* 138. ſaith, [When he conſidered the Power of Chriſt's Word, how it perſwaded innumerable Congregations of Men, and by thoſe Ignoble and Ruſtick Diſciples of Jeſus, μυρ εκτρςοι εκκλησιαι numeroſiſſimæ Eccleſiæ were conſtituted, not in certain unknown and obſcure places, but erected in the moſt famous Cities, (*Rome*, *Alexandria* and *Antioch*) through all *Egypt* and *Lycia*, through *Europe* and *Aſia*, εν τε κωμαις τε και χωραις, και παντοιοις εθνεσι.——in Villages and Countries or Regions and all ſorts of Nations.] By this it appeareth that Villages had Churches then.

II. Though of later date, conſider the Hiſtory of *Patrick's* Plantation of Churches in *Ireland :* who is ſaid himſelf in his own time to have three hundred ſixty five Churches, and as many Biſhops, and three thouſand Presbyters ; as *Ninius* reporteth. Not only *Thorndike* taketh notice of this, but a better Author, *Uſher de Eccleſ. Brit. Primord. pa.* 950. And *Selden* in his Comment on *Eutychius Origines Alex. pag.* 86. from *Antoninus* and *Vincentius*, thus mentioneth it, [*Certe tantum in orbe terrarum tunc temporis Epiſcoporum ſegetem mirari forſan deſinet, quiſquis credidevit, quod de B. Patricio Hibernenſi Antoninus & Vincentius tradunt ; Eum ſcilicet ſolum Eccleſias fundaſſe* 365. *totidemque Epiſcopos ordinaſſe, præter Presbyterorum* 3000. *Qua de re conſulas plura apud præſtantiſſimum virum* Jacobum Uſſerium, *&c.*] So that here was to every Church a Biſhop and near ten Presbyters. (No Man will doubt but the Biſhops themſelves were taken out of the better ſort of the Laity, and the Presbyters of the ſecond ſort ; and all below many private Chriſtians now among us.) And were there three hundred ſixty five Cities think you in *Ireland ?* Yea, or Corporations either ? It's eaſie to conjecture what Churches theſe were.

III. All Hiſtory, Fathers, and Councils conſent, that every City was to have a Biſhop and Presbytery to govern and teach the Chriſtians of that City and the Country people near it ; which is but a Pariſh or Presbyterian Church. For the word πόλις ſignifieth in the old common uſe, any big Town, yea
little

little Towns that were diftinct from Country Farms and fcattering Villages : fo that all our Corporations and Market Towns are *Oppida* and fuch Cities as πόλις fignified.   Therefore even by this Rule we fhould have a Bifhop to every fuch Town.

1. *Crete* was called *Hecatompolis*, as having an hundred Cities, as *Homer* faith it had.   And what kind of Cities were thofe? Which were to have an hundred Churches and Bifhops (in a fmall Ifland?)

2. *Theocritus Idyl.* 13. *de laudibus Ptolem. verf.* 82. faith, that he had under his Government thirty three thoufand three hundred and thirty πόλεις, Cities: And if fo, they muft be as fmall as our Boroughs, if not fome Villages : certainly he had not above twice the number of Cities eminently fo called that *Stephanus Byzantinus* could find in the whole World, in his Book, περὶ πόλεων.

Tit. 1. 5. Ordain Elders in every City. 3. He that will perufe and compare the Texts in the New Teftament that ufe the word πόλις (above fixfcore times) and fee *Grotius* on *Luk.* 7. 11. &c. fhall foon fee that the word is there ufed for fuch Towns as I am mentioning, if not lefs.

IV. *Sozomen,* *lib.* 5. *cap.* 3. tells us, that *Majuma* which was *Navale Gazæ*, being as part of its Suburbs, or the adjoyning part but twenty *Stadia* diftant, was, becaufe it had many Chriftians, honoured by *Conftantine* with the name of a City, and had a Bifhop of their own.   And *Julian* in malice took from them the honour of being a City, but they kept their Bifhop for all that.   It had the fame Magiftrate with *Gaza*, and the fame Military Governors, and the fame Republick ; but was diverfified only by their Church-State. For, faith he, each had their own Bifhop, and their own Clergy, and the Altars belonging to each Bifhoprick were diftinct : And therefore afterward the Bifhop of *Gaza* laboured to fubject the Clergy of *Majuma* to himfelf, faying, that it was unmeet that one City fhould have two Bifhops : But a Council called for that purpofe, did confirm the Church-Right of *Majuma*.

V. *Gregory Neocæfarienfis* called *Thaumaturgus*, was by force made Bifhop of that City, where all the Chriftians were but feventeen at his Ordination : fuch was the Bifhop's Church.   And when he had preached and done Miracles there till his Perfecution, there is no mention of any Presbyter he had with him ; but of his Deacon *Mufonius* that fled with him. (Though when he died he left but feventeen unconverted.)*

A Village, faith Eufeb.l.5.c. 16. Vid. Baron. an. 233.n.10. And when he had converted fome at *Comana*, a fmall Town near him, he did not fet a Presbyter over it, and make it part of his own Diocefs, but appointed *Alexander* (the Collier) to be their Bifhop ; and that over a Church who were no more than met and debated the Cafe of his Election and Reception.   See *Greg. Nyffen. in Orat. in Greg. Thaumat.* & *Bafil de Spirit. Sancto,* *cap.* 19. & *Breviar. Roman. die* 15 *Novemb.* & *Menolog. Græc.*

VI. *Concil.*

VI. *Concil. Nic. Oecum.* 1. *Can.* 13. decreeth that every one that before death defireth the Sacrament, was to have it from the Bishop : One Ed. in *Crab* faith, *Generaliter omni cuilibet in exitu posito, & poscenti sibi Communionis gratiam tribui, Episcopus probabiliter ex oblatione dare debebit.* The other Ed. faith, [*Et cura & probatio sit Episcopi.*] We are content that the Dioces be as great as the Bishop will perform this for, to examine all such dying men, and give them the Sacrament, or send it them after his diftinct Examination.

VII. *Gregor. Nazianz. Episi.* 22. *pag.* 786. *To.* 1. perswading the Church of *Caesarea* to chuse *Basil* for their Bishop, sendeth his Letters to the Presbyters, the Monks, the Magiftrates, and the whole Laity.] And though I doubt not but by that time there were Country Congregations, by this the magnitude of the City Church may be gathered, where the whole Laity could be consulted, and could chuse.

And *Basil* made this *Gregory* his chief friend Bishop of *Safimis*, a small poor dirty Town : And yet *Gregory* himself it seems had in some near Village a *Chorepiscopus* with Presbyters and Deacons ; as in *Glycerius* his Cafe appeareth, *Epist. Greg.* 205. *pag.* 900, 901.

And *Nazianzum* where he plaid the Bishop under his Father (two Bishops at once, one in Title, the other in Practice without Title) was but a small Town.

VIII. *Basil* an Arch-Bishop was fo much againft enlarging Dioceses, and taking in many Churches to one Bishop, that he taketh the advantage of the difference between him and *Anthymius* to make many Bishops more in his Diocefs over small places : yea, it seemeth some places were fo small as that they never before had any Paftors at all : as appeareth by *Gregory Nazianzene*, *Epist.* 28.

IX. *Theodoret* tells us, *lib.* 4. *cap.* 20. *Hist. Eccles.* that even in the great *Alexandria* the Presbyters and Deacons were all but nineteen when *Lucius* came to banish them to *Heliopolis*, a City of *Phaenicia* ; which City had not one Chriftian in it. By which it appeareth, that even then under Chriftian Emperors, Chriftianity was not received by the multitude, when some Cities had not a Chriftian.

X. *Theodor. ib. l.* 4. *c.* 16. faith, that when *Eulogius* and *Protogenes*, the Presbyters of *Edessa*, were banished to *Antionone* in *Thebais*, they found the moft of the people Heathens, and but few of the Church ; yet had that little number a Bishop of their own.

XI. *Id. l.* 4. *c.* 20. In *Peter* Bishop of *Alexandria's* Epiftle (wherein he sheweth such actions then done by the Soldiers in scorn of the Godly, proclaiming Turpitude not to be named under the name of scornful Preaching, as

G

have

have been done by others lately among us) it's said of *Lucius*, [*Qui partes Lupi nequitia & improbe facti agere impense studebat, quique Episcopatum, non consensu Episcoporum Orthodoxorum in unum convenientium, non suffragiis vere Clericorum, non postulatione Populi, ut sacri Ecclesiæ Canones præscribunt.*] So that great Patriarch himself was chosen *Postulatione Populi*, as shewing the custom of all the Churches ; which beginning when the people were but one Congregation, continued as it could in some degree when they came like a Presbyterian Church (for even then it was no otherwise) to have many Congregations.

XII. *Id. c. 22.* saith that [*Valens* found the Orthodox even in the great Patriarchal City of *Antioch*, in possession but of one Church, which good *Joviniañ* the Emperor had given them ; of which he dispossessed them. And when they met afterwards to worship God at a Hill near the City, *Valens* sent to disturb them thence.] And *Cap. 23. Flavianus* and *Diodorus* Presbyters (*Meletius* the Bishop being banished) led them to a River side, where they congregated, till they were thence also driven by the Emperor. And *Flavianus* when he could not preach, collected Matter, Reasons and holy Sentences, (as Sermon-Notes) for others to preach (in the *Gymnasium Bellicum*) where they resolved to meet whatever came on it. Then *Aphraates* a Monk taught them, and when *Valens* told him that Monks must pray in private, and not preach in publick, *Aphraates* told the Emperor that he had set the House of God our Father on fire, and troubled the Church, and therefore he was called to its publick help (to shew how far they obeyed a silencing Emperor.) By all which it appeareth that even then the Orthodox Patriarchal Church of *Antioch* was but one Assembly which met in one only place at once.

XIII. *Id. l. 4. c. 29.* When *Terentius* the Emperor's victorious General, (being Orthodox) was bid by the Emperor to ask what he would of him as a Reward, he asked but *One Church* for the Orthodox, and was denied it, which intimateth their numbers.

XIV. *Dolicha* where *Eusebius* made *Maris* Bishop, was *parvum Oppidum*, a little Town (and infected with Arianism,) where an Arian Woman killed *Eusebius* with a Tile when he went to ordain *Maris* Bishop. *Theodor. lib. 5. cap. 4.*

XV. *Euseb. Eccles. Hist. l. 5. c. 16.* tells us that *Apollonius* saith of *Alexander* a Montanist Bishop, that the Congregation whereof he was Pastor, because he was a Thief, would not admit him.] By which it appeareth that his Church was but one Congregation.

And *l. 7. c. 29.* The Synod of *Antioch* say of *Dionysius Alexandr.* that he wrote not to the person of *Paulus Samosatenus* ; but to the *whole Congregation* (that is, his Church. And they say [He licensed the Bishops and Ministers of the adjoyning Villages and Cities to preach to the People.] Which sheweth what Dioceses and Churches then were.

XVI. *Socrates.*

XVI. *Socrates, l. 1. c. 8.* tells us that *Spiridion* was at the same time a Bishop and a Shepherd.] And whether his Parish was one Church or many hundred you may easily judge, when so holy a Man could spare time all the Week to keep his sheep.

XVII. When *Constans* the Emperor affrighted *Constantius* to restore *Athanasius, Constantius* craved of *Athanasius* that the Arrians in *Alexandria* might have one Church to themselves : *Athanasius* told him, It was in his power to command and execute ; but craved also a request of him, which was that in all Cities there might also be one Church granted for them that communicated not with the Arrians : But the Eastern Arrian Bishops hearing that, put off the decision of both the Requests.] By which a willing person may conjecture at the quantity of the Episcopal Churches in those times.

XVIII. Even in *Ambrose's* days the great Church of *Milan* was no greater than could meet in one Temple to chuse a Bishop : And *Ambrose* was chosen by them. *Socrat. l. 4. c. 25.*

And *Baronius,* in *Vita* Ambrosii *ex* Paulino, saith, (*pag. 9.*) [*Quod solitus erat circa Baptizandos solus implere, quinque postea Episcopi tempore quo decessit vix implerent.*] What then was all the rest of his work? and how many Churches could he thus oversee ?

And the Arrians, for whom the Emperor made all that stir with *Ambrose,* were so few in *Milan,* that when the Emperor would have had one Church for them, and could not get it by fair means or force, *Ambrose* thus jesteth at the Empress and the Arrian *Gothes ; Quibus ut olim plaustrum sedes erat, ita nunc plaustrum Ecclesia est ; Quocunque foemina illa processerit, secum suos omnes extus vehit.*] Her Coach is their Church ; and which way soever she goeth, she carrieth all her Congregations with her.

Ambros. de Offic. To. 4. c. 1. sheweth that teaching his Church is the Bishop's Office : And *de initiandis,* c. 2. p. 163. *To.* 4. he saith to the baptized person, [*Vidisti illic (in Sacrario) Levitam, vidisti Sacerdotem, vidisti summum Sacerdotem.*] In which he intimateth that the Bishop (as the Chief Priest) was present in the Church with his Presbyters at Baptizings. Which sheweth that they had not a multitude of Churches without Bishops. And *de Sacram. l. 1. c. 1.* how the Bishop himself must touch with Oyl the Nostrils of all that were baptized, with other Ceremonies after mentioned, sheweth that he was usually present at every Baptism.

And *de Sacram. l. 3. c. 1.* he giveth the reason why he did wash the Feet of all that were baptized, and the Church of *Rome* did not, *Vide ne forte propter multitudinem declinarit.*] [Perhaps they decline it because of the multitude.] But all the Diocess of *Milan* (as a Bishoprick, not as an Arch-Bishoprick) had no such multitudes, but that besides all his other work, *Ambrose* could have time to wash the feet of every one that was baptized.

And

And *cap. 3. Ecclesiæ contuitu & consideratione te ipse commenda* — The Church was present then. And to shew by his work what his Church was, he celebrated the Sacrament daily : *Accipe quotidie quod quotidie tibi prosit : sic vive ut quotidie merearis accipere : Qui non meretur quotidie accipere, non meretur post annum accipere.*

And how he discharged all this you may perceive, *de Dignit. Sacerdot. cap. 3. Episcopus non aliud nisi Episcopalia opera designat, ut ex bono opere, magis quam professione noscatur, plus meriti esse Episcopum quam quod nomine, vocitetur. Quia sicut nihil esse diximus Episcopo excellentius, sic nihil est miserabilius si de sancta vita Episcopus periclitetur, si Sacerdos in crimine teneatur.* (He thought not as too many now do, that the Name and Seat of Bishop or Priest can do more to hallow Persecutions, Worldliness and other Crimes, than the Crimes can do to unhallow the Bishop or Priest.)

And *lib. 5. To. 4. pag. 180.* having mentioned [*The Husband of one Wife,*] he addeth, [*Si vero ad altiorem sensum conscendimus, inhibet, duas usurpare Ecclesias.*] A Bishop must no more have two Churches than a Husband have two Wives. But some Bishops imitate *Solomon*'s Lust rather than his Wisdom, and will have above a thousand Churches, as Wives or Concubines.

Adding, *Qui stipendiis tantum contentus Ecclesiæ suæ, penitus non ambiat quæ novit esse superflua.* Covetousness hath enlarged Dioceses.

And *cap. 5. Cum dominatur populis, & anima servit Dæmoni.* When he Lords it over the people, his own Soul is a Slave to the Devil.

And *cap. 6. pag. 18. Nam quid aliud interpretatur Episcopus nisi superinspector ? Maxime cum solio editiore in Ecclesia resideat ut ita cunctos respiciat, ut & cunctorum oculi in ipsum respiciant.*] So that it is from the oversight of one Congregation where he sits among and above the Presbyters, that he is called a Bishop, and not from Churches which he *overseeth* indeed, but *seeth* not, and might well be said to be an *Overseer* in our vulgar sense, as it signifies one that overlooketh or observeth not, were he, as many now.

And of so small a place as *Forum Cornelii,* instead of committing it to a subject Presbyter, he saith, (*Epist. 63. p. 111. ad Constant. Arausicorum Episcopum*) *Commendo tibi fili Ecclesiam, quæ est ad forum* Cornelii, *quo eam de proximo invisas frequentius, donec ei ordinetur Episcopus.*

And *pag. 117. Ad Eccles. Vercellens. post obitum* Eusebii *Epist.* he writeth to them thus to chuse another, *Quanto magis ubi plena est in nomine domini Congregatio ; ubi Universorum Postulatio congruit, dubitare vos nequaquam oportet, ibi dominum Jesum & voluntatis authorem, & petitionis arbitrum fore, & ordinationis præsulem, vel largitorem gratiæ.*] So that this famous Church was no greater than that all the people could meet and agree in the Choice or Postulation of a Bishop.

So *To. 4. de Pænitent. l. 5. c. 15. Tota Ecclesia suscipit onus peccatoris cui compatiendum & fletu, & oratione & dolore est.* By which it seems that *all the Church* (that is, so great a part as might be called all) was used to be present each meeting when Penitents lamented their sin.

And

And in *To. 3. p. 183.* in 1 *Cor.* 11. he faith, that the Angels before whom the Women in the Church muft be veiled, are the Bifhops as God's Vicars?] which intimateth that ordinarily every Church-Affembly was to have a Bifhop prefent.

And *ibid. Hoc notat qui fic in Ecclefiam conveniebant, ut munera fua offerentes advenientibus Presbyteris, quia adhuc rectores Ecclefiis non omnibus locis fuerant conftituti, &c.* And *p. 161.* in *Rom. 1. 2. Propterea Ecclefiæ fcribit, quia adhuc fingulis Ecclefiis Rectores non erant inftituti.* By which you may conjecture what he thought of the magnitude of Churches then.

Tom. 3. p. 89. He fo far acknowledgeth the People to have elected him, that he calleth them on that account *his Parents*, who in other refpects were his Children, (in *Luk.* 18.) *Vos mihi eftis Parentes, qui Sacerdotium tuliftis: Vos inquam Filii, vel Parentes: Filii finguli, Univerfi Parentes.* (Like *Hooker's Singulis Major, Univerfis Minor.*) Where you fee, that the whole Church (and not a thoufandth part) did chufe him Bifhop.

And *To. 3. p. 180.* in 1 *Cor.* 14. *Verum eft, quia in Ecclefia* (that is in every Church) *Unus eft Epifcopus* (not in hundreds of Churches.) For he faith, *ibid.* in 1 *Cor.* 12. *Et quia ab uno Deo Patre funt omnia, fingulos Epifcopos fingulis Ecclefiis præeffe decrevit.*] He decreed that there fhould be to every Church a feveral Bifhop.

When I cite all this of the ftate of that famous Church of *Milan*, where the Emperor himfelf did oft refide, and which prefumed to differ in Cuftoms from *Rome*, I leave you to gather how it was before Chriftian Emperors, and in all the ordinary Churches.

XIX. *Auguftine* was chofen by the people, and brought to the Bifhop to be ordained. *Vit. cap.* 4. And *cap.* 5. *Valerius* the Bifhop gave him power to preach before him contrary to the ufe of the *African* Churches, but according to the cuftom of the Eaftern Churches.] Which fheweth that *Auguftine* while Presbyter (and fo other Presbyters ordinarily) was in the fame Congregation with the Bifhop, and not in another. And upon this other Churches took up the fame cuftom.

And *cap.* 21. it's faid, [*In Ordinandis Sacerdotibus & Clericis Confenfum majorem Chriftianorum, & confuetudinem Ecclefiæ fequendam effe arbitrabatur :* — And *cap.* 25. *Cum ipfo femper Clerici una etiam domo & menfa, fumptibufque communibus alebantur, & veftiebantur.* Yea, he ordered juft how many Cups in a day his Clergy-men with him fhould drink ; and if any fware an Oath he loft one of his Cups. (Through God's Mercy fober Godly Minifters now need no fuch Law.) By this it evidently appeareth that the Church which he and his Presbyters ruled, was not many hundred, but one Congregation, or City-Church : There being no mention of any Country Presbyters that he had elfewhere, as far as I remember.

And when *Auguftine* was dying, the People with one confent, accepted of his choice of *Eradius* to be his Succeffor ; *Epift.* 110. *pag.* 195. To recite all that is in *Auftin's* Works intimating thefe Church-limits, would be tedious.

XX. *Epi-*

XX. *Epiphanius's* Teftimony I have before mentioned, as produced by *Peta-vius*, that there were few Cities, if any befides *Alexandria* in thofe Countries that had more than one Congregation ; and particularly none of his own. And Doctor *Hammond* trufteth to him and *Irenæus* to prove that the Apoftles fetled fingle Bifhops in fingle Congregations in many places without any Sub-Presbyters.

XXI. *Socrates, l. 5. c. 21.* faith, [The Church of *Antioch* in *Syria* is fituate contrary to other Churches : for the Altar ftands not to the Eaft, but to the Weft.] Which Speech implieth that (befides Chappels if any) there was but one Church that was notable in *Antioch* ; while he calleth it [The Church at *Antioch*,] without diftinction from any other there.

XXII. *Socrates, l. 7. c. 3.* tells us a notable ftory of *Theodofius* Bifhop of *Synada*, who went to *Conftantinople* for Power to perfecute *Agapetus* the *Mace-donian* Bifhop in that City. But while he was abfent *Agapetus* turned Orthodox, and his Church and the Orthodox Church joyned together. and made *Agapetus* Bifhop, and excluded *Theodofius :* who made his Complaint of it to *Atticus* the Patriarch of *Conftantinople* (a wife and peaceable Man) who defired *Theodofius* to live quietly in private, becaufe it was for the Churches good.] (May fuch caufes oft have fuch decifions, and Lordly troublefome Prelates fuch fuccefs.) By which ftory you may guefs how many Congregations both Parties made in *Synada*.

XXIII. *Socrates, l. 7. c. 26.* tells us that *Sifinnius* was chofen Bifhop of *Conftantinople* by the Laity againft the Clergy. And *cap.* 28. *Sifinnius* fent *Pro-clus* to be Bifhop of *Cyzicum* ; but the People chofe *Dalmatius* and refufed him.] And this cuftom of the *People's Choice*, muft needs rife at firft from hence, that the whole Church being but one Congregation was prefent : For what Right can any one Church in a Diocefs have to chufe a Bifhop for all the reft, any more than the many hundred that are far off, and uncapable to chufe ?

XXIV. *Sozomen's* Teftimony (even fo late) is very obfervable ; *lib. 7. cap.* 15. who mentioning the differences of the Eaft and Weft about *Eafter*, and inferring that the Churches fhould not break Communion for fuch Cuftoms, faith, [*Frivolum enim & merito quidem judicarunt, confuetudinis gratia a fe mutuo fegregari eos qui in præcipuis Religionis capitibus confentirent : Neque enim eafdem traditiones per omnia fimiles in omnibus Ecclefiis quamvis inter fe confentientes, reperire poffes.*] And he inftanceth in this, [*Etenim per Scythiam cum fint Civitates multæ, unum duntaxat hæ omnes Epifcopum habent* (I told you the reafon of this Rarity before) *Apud alias vero nationes reperias ubi & Pagis Epifcopi ordinantur : Sicut apud* Arabes *&* Cyprios *ego comperi.*] He fpeaketh of his own knowledge : No wonder then if *Epiphanius* be to be interpreted as *Petavius* doth, when in *Cyprus* not only the Cities had but one Church, but alfo the
Villages

Villages had Bishops. To these he addeth the Novatians and the *Phrygian* Montanists. And let none think their instances inconsiderable. For the Montanists were for high Prelacy, even for Patriarchs, as in *Tertullian* appeareth. And the Novatians were for Bishops, and had many very Godly Bishops, and were tolerated by the Emperors even in *Constantinople*, as good People and Orthodox in the Faith : And *Novatus* was martyred in *Valerian's* Persecution, as *Socrates*, *l.* 4. *c.* 23. saith.

XXV. Even *Clemens Roman.* or whoever he was that wrote in his name, *Epist.* 3. sheweth that Teaching the People is the Bishop's Office, and concludeth (in *Crab*, *p.* 45.) *Audire (Episcopum) attentius oportet & ab ipso suscipere doctrinam fidei ; Monita autem vitæ a Presbyteris inquire, a Diaconis vero ordinem Discipline :* By which Partition of Offices it is evident, that the Bishop only and not the Presbyters then used to preach to the Church, and that the Presbyters (though *ejusdem ordinis*, and not Lay-Elders) used to instruct the People personally, and give them *Monita vitæ :* and that they were all in one Church together, and not in several distant Churches.

XXVI. *Paul* himself telleth us that *Cenchrea* had a Church, and the Scripture saith, They ordained Elders in every Church : And though *Downame* without any proof obtrude upon us, that it was under the Bishop of *Corinth*, and had a Presbyter of his to teach them ; yet of what Authority soever (in other respects) the Constitutions called *Clements* or the Apostles be, they are of more than his in this ; where *lib.* 7. *cap.* 46. in that old Liturgy, *Lucius* is said to be Bishop of *Cenchrea*, ordained by the Apostles.

XXVII. *Gennadius de viris illustr. l.* 1. *c.* 10. saith, that *Asclepius* was *Vici non grandis Episcopus*, Bishop of a Village not great.

XXVIII. Saith *Cartwright*, Four or five of the Towns which were Seats of the Bishops of the *Concil. Carthag.* which *Cyprian* mentioneth, are so inconsiderable that they are not found in the Geographical Tables.

XXIX. And saith *Altare Damascen. p.* 294. *Oppidum trium Tabernarum Velitris vicinum* was a Bishop's Seat for all the nearness and smallness of the Towns : And *Gregor. lib.* 2. *Epist.* 35. laid the Relicts of the wasted Church to the Bishoprick of *Veliterno*.

Castrum Lumanum had a Bishop till *Gregory* joyned it to *Benevatus* Bishop of *Micenas :* (and so had many *Castra* ordinarily.)

Remigius did appoint a Bishop within his own Diocess when he found that the number of persons needed it : *Viz. apud Laudunum clavatum Castrum suæ Diœceseos.* Of *Spiridion* the Bishop of *Trimithantis* I spake before.

XXX. *Theoph. Alexand. Epist. Pasch.* 3. *in Bibl. Pat. To.* 3. concludeth thus, [*Pro defunctis Episcopis in locis singulorum constitui. In urbe* Nichio *pro* Theopen pto ɽempto Theodofius ; *In* Terenuthide Aifinthius ; *In oppido* Geras *pro* Eudæmone Pirozus ; *In* Achæis *pro* Apolline Mufæus ; *In* Athrivide *pro* Ifidoro Athanafius ; *In* Cleopatride Offellus ; *In* Oppido Lato, *pro* Timotheo Apelles. And the nearnefs and fmallnefs of fome of thefe fheweth the Diocefes fmall.

The fame *Theoph. Alex.* faith, *Epift. Canon. Can. 6.* [*De iis qui ordinandi fient hæc erit forma, ut quicquid eft Sacerdotalis ordinis confentiat & eligat, & tunc Epifcopus examinet, vel ei etiam affentiente Sacerdotali ordine in media Ecclefia ordinet præfente populo, & Epifcopo alloquente, an etiam poffet ei populus ferre teftimonium : Ordinatio autem non fiat clanculum : Ecclefia enim pacem habente decet præfentibus fanctis ordinationes fieri in Ecclefia.*] Undoubtedly, as *Balfamon,* noteth by [Saints] is meant *fideles,* the People. Here then you fee that the Churches then were fuch where all the Clergy were prefent with the Bifhop, who ordained Minifters to a fingle Church where all the people could be prefent to be confulted.

XXXI. In the Life of *Fulgentius* it is faid, that *Plebs ipfius loci tibi fuerat Monafterium conftitutum differre fuam prorfus Electionem, donec inveniret B. Fulgentium, cogitabat* (where, the Bifhops refolved to ordain, though the King forbad it them.) And though the King perfecuted them for it, it is added, [*Repleta jam fuerat Provincia* Bizacená *novis Sacerdotibus, & pene vix paucarum plebium Cathedræ remanferant deftitutæ.*] And the Phrafe [*plebium Cathedræ*] doth fignifie a Bifhop's Seat in one Congregation of People. One *Plebs* was one Congregation ; and had its proper *Cathedram.*

XXXII. *Sozomen* (after *Socrates*) mentioning the diverfity of Church Cuftoms (as aforefaid) *l. 7. c. 19.* faith, that at *Alexandria* the Arch-Deacon only readeth the Holy Scriptures, in other places only the Deacons, and in many Churches only the Priefts, and on folemn days the Bifhops.] By which words it appeareth that then every Church was fuppofed to have a Bifhop, Priefts and Deacons prefent in their publick Worfhip. For the Bifhop on his folemn days could not be reading in many Churches (much lefs many hundred) at once.

XXXIII. *Hiftor. Tripartit. l. 1. c. 19.* (out of *Sozomen, l. 1. c. 14. Edit. Lat. Bafil. p.* 1587.) telleth us, how *Arius* feeketh (as from the *Bithynian* Synod) to *Paulinus* of *Tyre, Eufeb. Cæfar. & Patroph. Scythopol. ut una cum fuis juberetur cum populo qui cum eo erat, folennia Sacramenta Ecclefiæ celebrare,— Effe dicens confuetudinem in* Alexandria (*ficut etiam nunc*) *ut uno exiftente fuper omnes Epifcopo, Presbyteri feorfim Ecclefias obtinerent, & populus in eis Collectas folenniter celebraret.—*] [*Tunc illi una cum aliis Epifcopis, &c.*] By this (with what is faid before out of *Epiphanius*) it is undeniable that this (gathering of Affemblies by the Presbyters in the fame City, and adminiftring the Sacrament to them befides the Church where the Bifhop was) was taken to be *Alexandria*'s fingularity, even as low as *Sozomen*'s time. And yet note that here is even at *Alexandria* no mention of many Churches in the Countries at a diftance, much lefs less hundreds, thus gathered, but only of some few in that great City. And if even in a great City, and in *Epiphan.* and in *Sozomen's* days a 'Presbyter's Church was an *Alexandrian* Rarity, what need we more Historical Evidence of the Case of the Churches in those times?

XXXIV. *Ferrandus Diaconus, in Epist. de* 5. *Quæst.* saith to *Fulgentius,* [*Sanctos Presbyteros, Diaconos, beatamque Congregationem* (which was his Church) *saluto.*] And that you may again see what Congregation or Church that was, *In vita Fulgentii, cap.*17. *pag.* 8. it is said, that the *Plebs sought and chose him* (and that in despight of *Fælix* the ambitious Deacon, who sought the place, and sought the life of *Fulgentius.*) *Populus super suam Cathedram eum collocavit : Celebrata sunt eodem die Divina solenniter Sacramenta, & de manibus Fulgentii Communicans omnis populus lætus discessit.*] And if in the noble City of *Rusfe,* so late as the days of *Fulgentius,* the Bishop's Church-members were no more than could chuse him, set him on his seat, and all communicate that day at his hands, it is easie by this to judge of most other Churches.

XXXV. *Concil. Parisienf.* 1. (*in Caranz. pag.* 244. *Can.* 5.) saith, [*Nullus civibus invitis ordinetur Episcopus, nisi quem Populi & Clericorum Electio plenissima quæsierit voluntate ; Non principis imperio, neque per quamlibet conditionem Metropolis voluntate Episcoporum Comprovincialium ingeratur. Quod si per ordinationem Regiam honoris sui culmen pervadere aliquis nimia temeritate præsumpserit, a Comprovincialibus loci ipsius Episcopis recipi nullatenus mereatur, quem indebitè assumptum agnoscunt. Siquis de Comprovincialibus recipere eum contra indicta præsumpserit, sit a fratribus omnibus segregatus, & ab ipsorum omnium Charitate remotus.*] Here again you see how late all the Church was to chuse every Bishop ; *plenissima voluntate ;* and consequently how great the Church was. And were this Canon obeyed, all the people must separate from all the Bishops of *England,* as here all are commanded to do from all those Bishops that do but receive one that is put in by the King, and not by the free choice of all the Clergy and People of his Church. Note that *Crab (Vol.* 2. *pag.* 144.) hath it, [*contra Metropolis voluntatem :*] But both that, and *Caranza's* Reading, who omitteth [*contra*] seem contrary to the scope ; and it's most likely that it should be read [*Metropolis voluntate, contra Episcoporum comprov.*] *scilicet voluntatem.* It is the tighth Canon in Crab.

XXXVI. *Leo* 1. *P. Rom. Epist.* 89. *pag.* (*mihi*) 160. damning Saint *Hillary* Magisterially, yet saith, [*Expectarentur certe vota Civium, testimonia populorum, quæreretur honoratorum arbitrium, Electio Clericorum, quæ in Sacerdotum solent ordinationibus, ab his qui norunt patrum regulas, custodiri, ut Apostolicæ authoritatis norma in omnibus servaretur, quæ præcipitur ut Sacerdos Ecclesiæ præfuturus, non solum attestatione fidelium, &c. Et postea, Teneatur subscriptio Clericorum, honoratorum testimonium, ordinis consensus & Plebis : Qui præfuturus est omnibus, ab omnibus eligatur.*] And how great must that Diocess be, where all the Laity must chuse and vote? &c. It's true that *Epist.* 87. c. 2. p. 158. he would

H not

not have little Congregations to have a Bishop, to whom one Presbyter is
enough ; and no wonder at that time, that this great Bishop of *Rome*, (the
first that notably contended for their undue Supremacy in the Empire) was of
that mind ; who also *Epist.88.* saith of the *Chorepiscopi,* (*Qui juxta Can.* Neocæsar.
sive secundum aliorum decreta patrum iidem sunt qui & Presbyteri.) The falsehood
of which being too plain, *Petavius in Epiphan. ad Heref.* 74. *p.* 278. judgeth
that these words being in a Parenthesis are *irreptitious.*) And *ibid. Epist.* 88.
he saith that by the *Can.* all these things following are forbidden the *Chorepisc.*
and Presbyter, [*Presbyterorum, Diaconorum, aut Virginum consecratio, sicut constitutio Altaris, ac benedictio vel unctio : Siquidem nec erigere eis Altaria, nec Ecclesias vel Altaria consecrare licet, nec per impositiones manuum fidelibus baptizandis
vel conversis ex hæresi Paracletum Spiritum Sanctum tradere, nec Chrisma conficere,
nec Chrismate Baptizatorum frontes signare, nec publice quidem in Missa quemquam
pænitentem reconciliare, nec formatas cuilibet Epistolas mittere.*] By which it appeareth how big that Man's Diocess must be, who besides all his other work,
must be present to sign every baptized person, and reconcile every Penitent in
every Congregation. And it's worth the noting what kind of works they be
that the Bishop's Office is maintained for.

XXXVII. From the great Church of *Rome* (at its first Tide time) let us
look to the great Church of *Constantinople* ; even in the days of a better Bishop,
Chrysostom : Besides that they had long but one Temple, (of which anon)
Chrysostom saith in 1 *Thes.* 5. 12. *Orat.* 10. πρῶτον μὲν, &c. *Et primum debet
imperare & præesse volentibus & lubentibus, qui ei gratiam habent quod imperet,*
(*p.* 1472. & *p.* 1473.) *Sacerdos in hoc suum contulit negotium : Nulla est ei alia
vita quam ut versetur in Ecclesia— Qui Christum diligit, cujusmodicunque sit Sacerdos cum diliget, quod per eum sit veneranda affectus Sacramenta* ; (And Doctor
Hammond saith, this Text speaketh only of Bishops, 1 *Thes.* 5. 12.) *Et ibid.*
[*Pro te precatur, & dono quod per Baptismum datur tibi inservit, visitat, hortatur
& monet, & media nocte si vocaveris venit.*] And how many Parishes can a Bishop thus serve ? And how many score miles will they send and he go to visit
the Sick at midnight ?

And *Chrysost.* in 1 *Cor.* 14. *p.* 653. saith, *Conveniebant olim, omnes psallebant
communiter. Hoc nunc quoque facimus,* (They had no separating Choristers)
*sed tunc in omnibus erat una anima & cor unum : Nunc autem nec una quidem ani-
ma illam concordiam videris & consensum ; sed ubique magnum est Bellum. Pacem
nunc quoque precatur pro omnibus, is qui præest Ecclesiæ, ut qui in domum ingreditur
paternam, sed hujus pacis nomen quidem est frequens, res autem nusquam. Tunc
etiam domus erant Ecclesiæ* (though called Conventicles:) *Nunc autem Ecclesia
est domus, vel potius quavis domo deterior.* When Churches grew to be Dioceses
they grew worse than when they were in houses : But he that here is said *præesse Ecclesiæ* is he also that pronounceth Peace to them.

XXXVIII. *Gregory Nyssen.* speaking of the gathering of true Churches by
preaching, saith (in *Ecclesiast.* Hom. 1. *p.* (*mihi*) 93.) [*He is the true Preacher,
who*

who gathereth the dispersed into one Assembly, and bringeth those together into one Congregation (or Convention) who by various Errors are variously seduced.

XXXIX. He that readeth impartially *Beda's* Ecclesiastical History shall find that in *England* between six and seven hundred years after Christ they were but single Churches that had Bishops : For indeed the famousest and holiest of them in the Kingdom of *Northumberland*, were but *Scots* Presbyters, and such as were sent by them without any Episcopal Ordination; *(Aidan, Finan, &c.)* And though they did Apostolically preach in many places to convert the Heathen Inhabitants, yet their Churches of Christians were small : yet presently the *Roman* Grandeur and Ceremoniousness here prevailed, and so by degrees did their Church-form. Yet saith *Cambden, Brit. ed. Frank. p.* 100. When the Bishops at *Rome* had assigned several particular Churches to several Presbyters, and had divided Parishes to them, *Honorius* Arch-Bishop of *Canterbury* about the Year 636. first begun to distribute *England* into Parishes, as is read in the *Canterbury* History.] But it's plain in *Beda*, if he did then begin it, he went but a little way with that division.

The same *Cambden* also tells us, that the Bishoprick of *York* devoured seven Bishopricks, and the Bishoprick of *Lincoln* more, &c. Some Seats were but removed, but many Bishopricks were dissolved and turned into one, which yet were erected when Christians were fewer, saith *Isaackson Chronolog.* There was one at *Wilton*, the See at *Ramesbury*, one at *Crediton*, one at St. *Patrick's* at *Bodmin* in *Cornwall*, and after at St. *Germains*, one at *Selfey* Island, one at *Dunwich*, one at *Helmham*, and after at *Thetford*, one at *Sidnacester* or *Lindis*, one at *Osney*, one at *Hexham*, &c. And at this day *Landaff*, St. *Asaph's*, *Bangor*, St. *David's* are no Cities, where we have Bishops Seats, as notices of the old way.

XL. *Isidorus Pelensiota, lib.*1. *Epist.*149. to Bishop *Tribonianus* distinctly nameth the Bishop's Charge, and the calamity, if he be bad, that will befall himself first, and then the whole Church : Himself for undertaking and not performing, and the whole Church, ὅτι τοιούτῳ ἱερωσύνην ἀναξίας ἐπέδωκαν, *Quod hujusmodi viro Sacerdotium indigne mandavit.* The whole Church then was no bigger than to chuse the Bishop and be under his present inspection, as he intimateth.

And *Epist.* 315. to Bishop *Leontius*; [If thou tookest on thee the care of the Church, against thy Will, and art constrained by the Suffrages, and the Contentions and Hands of the People, God will be thy helper.——— But if by Money——— &c.

Lib. 3. *Ep.* 216. *p.* 342. He reckoneth up such and so much work as necessary for a Bishop as no man living can do for above one ordinary Parish. And frequently he describeth the City and Congregation at *Pelusium* as the place where the wicked Bishop and his wicked Priests together destroyed the interest of true Religion.

H 2 XLI. I

XLI. I conclude this with the words of *Eusebius* with the Collection of *Papirius Maffonus*, a Writer of the Popes Lives. [*Fabianus ab iis electus est ad Episcopatum urbis : Ac forte evenit ut in locum ubi convenerant Columba, e sublimi volans capiti ejus insideret, Id pro fælici signo accipientes magno consensu & alacritate animorum ipsum elegerunt : Hæc* Eusebius, *Hist. l. 6. Ex quo loco collegimus Electionem Episcopi Romani, non ad paucos, sed ad omnes olim pertinuisse. Pap. Maffon. in vita Fabiani, fol. 18 col. 2.*] And if all the whole People of the great Church of *Rome*, were then no more than could meet in one Room to chuse their Bishop, what were the rest of the Churches in the World ? and how many Congregations did they contain?

CHAP. VII.

More Proofs of the aforesaid Limits of Churches.

THe thing that we are proving is that every Bishop should have but one Church (supposing him to be no Arch-Bishop) and that this Church should be such and so great only as that there may be personal Communion in publick Worship and holy Conversation between the Members : and not so great as that the Members have only a Heart-Communion, and by Delegates or Synods of Officers.

As to our Historical Evidence of the matter of fact, it runs thus : 1. That in the first state of the Churches, it cannot be proved that any one Church in all the World consisted of more stated Communicating Assemblies than one, or of more Christians than our Parishes. But though through Persecution they might be forced (as an Independant Church now may do) to meet by parcels in several Houses sometimes in a danger, yet their ordinary Meetings when they were free was all together in one place : And *Unum Altare* was the note of their Individuation, with *Unus Episcopus*, when Bishops grew in fashion in the eminent sense.

2. That the first that broke this Order and had divers Assemblies and Altars under one Bishop were *Alexandria* and *Rome*, and no other Church can be proved to have done so, for about three hundred Years after Christ or near ; nor most Churches till four-hundred, yea five hundred Years after.

3. That when they departed from this Church temperament, they proceeded by these degrees. 1. They set up some Oratories, or Chappels (as are in our Parishes) which had only Prayers and Teachings without an Altar, Oblations or Sacraments in the City, Suburbs or Country Villages near, the People coming for Sacramental Communion to the Bishop's Church. 2. Afterward these

thefe Chappels were turned into Communicating Churches : But fo as that at firft the Bifhop's Presbyters (who lived fometimes in the fame Houfe with him, and always near him in the fame City, and were his Colleagues) did preach and officiate to them indifferently, that is, he whom the Bifhop fent ; and after that a particular Presbyter was affigned to teach a particular Congregation; yet fo, as that more of the Bifhop's Presbyters commonly had no fuch Congregations, but the moft of them ftill attended the Bifhop in his Church, and fate with him on each hand in a high raifed Seat, and whilft he did ufually preach and adminifter the Sacrament, they did but attend him and do nothing, or but fome by affifting Acts : as Lay-Elders do in the Presbyterian Churches ; principally employed in perfonal overfight, and in joyning in Government with the Bifhop. And thofe fame Presbyters who had Congregations, joyned with the reft in their Weekly Work, and made up the *Confeffus* or College of Presbyters. 3. And next that (and in fome places at the fame time) Communicating Congregations were gathered in the Country Villages, fo far off the City, as that it was found meet to leave a Presbyter Refident among them ; but under the Government of the City Bifhop and Presbytery, of whom he was one when he came among them. And all this while the Churches were but like our greater Parifhes which have divers Chappels, where there is liberty of Communicating. 4. After this when the Countries were more converted, there were more Country Parifh-Congregations fet up ; till they attained the form of a Presbyterian Church, differing only in the Bifhop ; that is, a certain number of the Neighbour Country Parifhes in one Confiftory (but with a Bifhop) did govern all thefe Parifhes as one Church ; that is, It was *many Worfhipping Churches* (as fix, eight, or ten, or twelve,) joyning to make up one governed Church. But at the fame time many Paftors and People being convinced of the Church-form which they had before been under, and of their own neceffity and privileges, did require the fame Order among themfelves as was in City Churches, and fo had their proper Bifhops, who were called *Chorepifcopi*, or Country Bifhops. But thefe Country-Bifhops living among the poorer and fmaller number of Chriftians, had not fo many Presbyters to attend them as the City-Bifhops had:So that fome Country Congregations had Bifhops and fome had none. And the Churches being chiefly governed by the Synods, who met for obliging Concord, to avoid Divifions; thefe Synods being made up of the City-Bifhops at firft, they there carried it by Vote to make all the Country-Bifhops under them, and refponfible to them : Which they the rather and the eafilier confented to, becaufe many obfcure and unworthy Fellows did infinuate into the efteem of the Country-Chriftians, who had no Bifhops near them to advife them better ; and fo became the Corrupters of Doctrine, and the Mafters of Sects and Herefies.

By this time one part of the Country Churches had Bifhops of their own, and the other had none, but only Presbyters under the City-Bifhops and Presbytery. But yet it was but few Neighbour-Parifhes, like our Market-Towns and the Villages between them that were thus under the City-Bifhop. For every fuch Town was then called a City in the larger fenfe as it fignifieth *Oppidum.*

Oppidum, and most such Towns had City-privileges too, which was no more than to be Corporations, and not to have a Nominal Eminency, as now some small places have above greater (as *Bath* rather than *Plimouth*, *Ipswich*, *Shrewsbury*, &c.)

Next to this, the Emperors being Christians, and desiring without force to draw all the People from Heathenism to Christianity, they thought it the best way to advance the Christians in worldly respects, which ever win on common minds. And so they endued the Churches and Bishops with such Honours and Powers heretofore described as were like to the Honour and Power of the Civil Governors in their kind. And the Bishops being thus lifted up, did first enlarge their own Dioceses as far as they could, and advance their Power; and the World came unchanged into the Church, both in Cities and Villages, (where the Christians were before so few, that many think the Heathens were called *Pagani* in distinction from the Citizens, who were Christian.) And then the Bishops put down the *Chorepiscopi*, as presuming too much to imitate their Power: And next to that, lest every Corporation or Market-Town having a Bishop, their Dioceses should not be great enough, and *ne vilesceret nomen Episcopi*, lest a Bishop's Name should not be honoured enough, but become cheap by reason of the number, and of the smallness of his Church, they first ordered that no such small Cities or other places as had People enough for but one Presbyter, should have a Bishop; and afterward by degrees put down many smaller Bishops Churches, and joyned them to their own: And so proceeded, by the advantage of Civil Alterations on Cities Names and Privileges, to bring themselves to the state that they are in, wherein one Bishop *infimi ordinis* (that is no Arch-Bishop) hath many hundred or above a thousand Churches and multitudes of Cities, called now but Corporations, Burroughs or Market-Towns.

I have repeated so much of the History, lest the Reader forget what it is that I am proving; and that he may note, that if I prove now that in later Ages they kept but the *Vestigia*, or Reliques of the former to prove how it was before their times, and if I prove but a Church of Presbyterian Magnitude to have so long continued, it sufficeth against that which we now call a Diocess: And that we do not play with Names, nor by a Diocesane Church, mean the same thing with a Parochial or Presbyterian; but we mean such as our Dioceses now are, where a Bishop alone with a Lay-Chancellor's Court, or with some small help of an Arch-Deacon, Surrogate, or Dean and Chapter, without all the Parish-Ministers besides, doth rule a multitude of distant Congregations, who have no proper Bishop under him. And now I proceed.

I. The *Chorepiscopi* which were at first placed in Country Churches where were many Christians, do shew what extent the Churches were then of: That these were really Bishops at first (whatever the aforesaid Parenthesis in *Leo* or *Damasus* say) most Writers for Episcopacy, Papists and Protestants do now grant; and therefore I may spare the labour of proving it: And whereas it is

said

said that they were but the Bishop's Deputies : I answer, even as Bishops are the Arch-Bishops Deputies ; that is, they were under them, but were really Bishops themselves : For if a Bishop may depute one that is no Bishop to be his Deputy, either a Presbyter also may depute one that is no Presbyter to administer the Sacraments, or not. If yea, then Lay-men shall come in and all be levelled, (For a Deacon also may depute his Office.) If not, then either a Bishop cannot do it, or else the Presbyter's Office is much holier than the Bishop's.

And that these *Chorepiscopi* Country-Bishops were not such Rarities as to invalidate my Proof, but very common, besides what is before said, is evident by the Subscriptions of many Councils, where great store of *Chorepiscopi* are found. And besides the names in our common Collections of the Councils, how it was in the *Egyptian* and Neighbour Churches at least (if not how it was at *Nice*) you may see in the *Arabick* Subscriptions published by *Selden* in his Comment on *Eutych. Orig. Alex.* pag. 93, 94, 95, &c. Num. 29, 31, 55, 64, 68, 119, 122, 128, 131, 179, 193, 215, 237, 241, 278. There are seventeen named. And the Canons made to curb and suppress them, shew that they were ordinary before ; as, *Concil. Laodic. Can.* 57. But they should rather have increased them, that Bishops might have multiplied as Churches or Christians increased, which was decreed here in *England* in the *cap.* 9. of the Council at *Hertford, per Theodor. Cantuar. referente Beda, lib.* 4. *Hist. Eccles. cap.* 5.

vid. Pittavium, in *Epip. hæres.* 69. p. 276, 277, 278, &c. *The chief champion of Prelacy strongly proveth that the Chorepiscopi were true Bishops.*

II. The very name *Ecclesia* which was first used before *Parochia* or *Diœcesis,* and still continued to this day, doth shew what the form of a Church then was, especially if you withal consider, that the name was communicated to the Temples or sacred Meeting-Places, which are also ordinarily called *Ecclesiæ;* which no Man doubteth was in a secondary sense, as derived from the People, who were the *Ecclesia* in the primary sense. And so even in our Tongue, the word Church is used for both to this day, as it is in many other Languages. Now it is certain that a part, especially a small part, (a hundredth or a thousandth part) of the Church is not the Church (unless equivocally.) Why then should the Temple be so called from the Church, when no Church at all, but a Particle only of a Church doth meet there? (For that the word, *Church,* in our Question is not taken for any Community or Company of Christians, but for a governed Society consisting of the governing and governed part, I have before shewed.) But, 1. A Church in its first and proper Notion being *Cœtus Evocatus,* An Assembly, or Convention or Congregation; (as distinguished from the Universal Church, which is so called because it is called out of the World to Christ the Head, and with him shall make one glorious Society,) how are those twenty or an hundred Miles off, any more a part of the Assembly where I live, than those at the *Antipodes* may be ? If you fly to one Governor, I answer; 1. So the Pope claimeth a Government at the *Antipodes.* 2. A Governor of many Assemblies may make them one Society, as to Government, but not one Assembly.

2. And

2. And certainly when Temples were first named *Churches*, it was not because those met there that were no *Churches*, but only Members of Churches: Nor is this Parish Church called a Church because some meet here that belong to the Church at *Boston*, *Lincoln* or *Grantham*; But to this day we cannot disuse our selves from saying, the Church of *Barnet*, the Church of St. *Albans*, of *Hatfield*, &c. yea, in the same City, we denominate the several Temples still several Churches.

Hesychius explaineth *Ecclesia*, by no other words than these three, σύνοδος, συναγωγὴ & πανήγυρις, which all signifie the Meetings of the People, and not Men that never see each other, only because one Man ruleth them.

Mr. *Mede* in his *Exercitat.* of Temples proveth largely that the places of Meeting are ordinarily by the Ancients called Churches, even in several Centuries. *Euseb. lib.* 8. *cap.* 1. saith, in every City they built spacious and ample Churches. And *Theophil. Antiochen. Autol.* saith, [*Sic Deus dedit mundo, qui peccatorum tempestatibus & naufragiis jactatur, Synagogas, quas Ecclesias sanctas nominamus, in quibus veritatis doctrina fervet, ad quas confugiunt veritatis studiosi, quotquot salvari, Deique judicium & iram evitare volunt.*]

So *Tertullian, de Idololat.* cap. 7. pag. 171. *Tota die ad hanc partem zelus fidei ingenuum Christianum ab Idolis in Ecclesiam venire, de adversaria Officina in domum Dei venire, &c.* The very *Name* there of a *Church*, and the naming of a single Temple thence doth signifie our supposition.

III. To this I may add the *Name* and * *Primitive Sense* of παροικία. For it signifieth a *Vicinity*, and *Parochus Vicinus*, a Cohabitant or Neighbour, as well as *inquilinus*, and is used in all the ancient Church-Writers as noting both a Sojourner (as Christians are in the World) and a Neighbour; so constantly in this later sense, not excluding the former. Else Men of several parts of the World might have been said to be πάροικοι, because *inquilini*, had it not also and specially signified Vicinity. To avoid tediousness of Citations, I refer the unsatisfied Reader but to *Gers. Bucer* against *Downam*, and the *Basil Lexicon* of *Henr. Pet.* in the word παροικία. And though the custom of calling a Church by the name παροικία continued when the Church was altered in magnitude to a large Diocess, yet that is so far from proving that this was the first and old signification, as that the word rather plainly leadeth us up to the *thing* and *sense* which first it signified. And therefore to this day, Etymology teacheth us more wit than in English to call a Diocess a *Parish*, but only a Vicinity of Christians: And when the *a Vicinity* is the English of the Word, why should Strangers that we shall never see or have to do with, any more than those in the uttermost part of the Land, be called our Parishioners or Neighbours?

IV. Another clear Evidence of the truth in question is the Paucity of Churches (or consecrated Meeting-Places) for many hundred Years after Christ: both before they were called Temples and after. Not that occasional Meeting-places were few (Houses, Fields, &c.) but appropriated consecrated

places

places called *Churches*, where there were *Altars*, or ordinary Church-Communion in the Lord's Supper. (Or rather it is doubtful whether the name of *Altars* with the form were introduced till two hundred Years after Chrift, which maketh fome the more queftion the Antiquity of *Ignatius* and *Clem. Conft.* and *Can. Apoft.*) I yield to *Baronius* (*ad An.57.*) that the Chriftians had Churches, that is, places confecrated for Church-Aſſemblies, under thoſe peaceable Emperors that went before *Dioclefian* : For *Eufebius* (befides others) expreſly telleth us fo : *Spaciofas & amplas conftruxerunt Ecclefias* : But I defire the Reader to mark his words. " *Lib.* 8. *cap.* 1. [A man might then have feen the Bi-
" ſhops of all *Churches* in great reverence and .favour among all forts of Men,
" and with all Magiſtrates : Who can worthily defcribe thofe innumerable heaps
" and flocking multitudes through all *Cities* and *famous Aſſemblies* frequenting
" the places dedicated to Prayer ? Becauſe of which Circumſtances, they not
" contented with the old and ancient Buildings, which could not receive them,
" have through all Cities builded them from the Foundation wide and
" ample Churches.] Here note, 1. That here is no mention of any more Churches than one in each City : *Cities* and *Aſſemblies* are numbered together. 2. That thefe Buildings are called *Churches*. 3. That thefe Churches were built greater than the old ones anew from the Foundation, becauſe the old ones were too narrow to contain the People : But not fuperadded to the old ones. 4. That the Biſhops are called *The Biſhops of all Churches* in relation to the fame kind of Churches as are here defcribed. So that then a Biſhop's Church met in one enlarged place.

Yet all thefe were no Temples ; but fuch as the filenced Miniſters have of late built in fome parts of *London* ; for the Chriſtians were in continual danger of the demoliſhing of them : which fell out in *Dioclefian's* time. But till this Calm which *Eufebius* here defcribeth, for about two hundred and fifty Years after Chriſt, the Chriſtians oft met in Vaults and fecret places, where they might be hid, and not in open Churches, unlefs now and then in a Calm between.

Platina in vit. Xifti, tells us, that even at *Rome* it felf about the Year 120. there were few found that durſt profefs the Name of Chriſt. And fee what he faith, *In Vita Clement.* 1. *& Anaclet. & Mantuan. lib.* 1. *faftor. de Clem. Anacl. Evarift. Alex. Xift. Calift. Urban. &c.* In whoſe times, Killing, Baniſhing and Perfecuting cauſed Scatterings, hidings, and as *Pliny* tells us many Apoſtaſies. See what *Gerf. Bucer* faith, *pag.* 221, 222, 223. of all the Ages now in queſtion about this matter : As *Tertullian* faith, *Apol. c.* 3. *adeo in hominibus innocuis, nomen innocuum erat odio :* Did the Rabble but fee or hear the Chriſtians, they were raged againſt them, and cried to the Judges, *Tollite impios.*

Saith *Polydor. Virgil. de invent. rer.* l. 5. c. 6. *Romæ non reperio quod fciam aliud antiquius templum ædificatum aut dicatum, vel ad ufum Sacrorum fuiſſe converfum, quam Thermas Novati in vico patricio, quas Pius Pontifex Praxidis eximiæ fanctitatis fœminæ rogatu, divæ Pudentianæ ejus Sorori confecravit ; qui fuit annus circiter* 150. But the name *Templum* here is not ufed by *Polydore* as by the Ancients,

I

cients, for a large and comely Fabrick. For, faith *Tertullian*, after that, *Apol. c. 37. Chriſtians leave Temples to the Heathens.* And faith Pope *Nicholas*, in *Epiſt de depoſitione Zachariæ & Rodoaldi Epiſc.* (recited in his Life by *Papir. Maſſonus, Fol. 132. Col. 2.*) [*Deinde propter frigidiorem locum in Ecclesia Salvatoris, quæ ab Authore vocatur Conſtantiniana, & quæ prima in toto terrarum orbe conſtructa eſt.*] You ſee that by this Pope's own Teſtimony, there was no Church in the whole World built before this one at *Rome* by *Conſtantine.* The meaning is, no large ſumptuous place called a Temple, but only commodious meaner Rooms or Buildings.

And the ſame *Pap. Maſſon. in Vita Bonifacii, fol. 55.* noteth that *Hierom* even in his time (ſo late) *Baſilicas Chriſtianorum tres tantum commemoraſſe.*

When upon the great increaſe of Chriſtians, but one odd Idol Temple even in *Alexandria,* was begged of the Emperor for the Chriſtians, *Ruffin. lib. 2. cap. 22.* and divers others tell us what tumult and ſtir it cauſed. And when *Euſeb. de Vita Conſtant. lib. 3. c. 49, 50.* tells us of his building of Churches except *Conſtantinople,* it is but one in a City, even the great Cities, *Nicomedia* in *Bythinia,* and *Antioch.* And *Socrat. lib. 1. cap. 12.* faith that even in *Conſtantinople* (which he made ſo great and beautiful that it was no whit inferior to *Rome,* and by a Law engraven on a Pillar, commanded that it be called *Second Rome,*) he built from the Foundation (but) two Churches, *Pacis & Apoſtolorum.*

I could find in my heart, were it not tedious, here to tranſlate all *Iſidor. Peluſiota's Epiſt. 246. lib. 2.* in which he openeth the difference between *Templum* and *Ecclesia,* and inveigheth againſt that Biſhop as no Biſhop, who cried up the Temple as the Church, while he perſecuted and vexed the Godly who are the Church indeed ; and againſt them that are for ſumptuous Temples and unholy ſcandalous Churches ; and tells us he had rather have been in the times when Temples were leſs adorned, and the Churches more adorned with Heavenly Graces, than in thoſe unhappy times when Temples were too much adorned, and Churches naked and empty of Spiritual Graces.

So that when there was but one Temple in a City, (except two or three) and when that was called the *Church,* becauſe it contained the *Church,* it's evident what the *Churches* then were.

V. The ancient *Agapæ* ſhew how great the Churches then were, when as all the Church did feaſt together : and theſe continued in *Tertullian's* time, in ſome places at leaſt : And ſeveral Church-Canons mention them after that. And *Chryſoſt.* faith (*Homil. de Oportet hæreſ. eſſe p.* (*mihi*) 20, 21. that in the Primitive times, there was a cuſtom that after Sermon and Sacrament, they all feaſted together in the Church, which he highly praiſeth. (But it was not many hundred Churches that feaſted in one Room.) And after he faith, [The Church is like *Noah's* Ark, but Men come in Wolves, and go out Lambs, &c.] ſhewing that by the *Church* he meant the *Aſſembly.* And after, [All have the ſame Honour, and the ſame Acceſs, till all have communicated and partaked of the ſame Spiritual Meat. The Prieſts ſtanding expect them all, even the

pooreſt

poorest Man of all.] (By this he sheweth what Church he meant, and how great the Church was.) *Et Serm.* 21. *pag.* 313. *Rodundat injuria in locum illum* ; *Ecclesiam enim totam contemnis* : *Propterea enim Ecclesia dicitur, quia communiter omnes accipit.* This doth not only shew what Church he meaneth, but fully confirmeth what I said before : that [*The whole Church was in that place :* *and that the place is therefore called the Church, because it commonly receiveth all.*] But note that this was not preach'd at *Constantinople*, but yet at the great Patriarchal Church of *Antioch*. *I know the learned Albaspinaus laboureth to prove that the Agapæ were not at the sacrament, and in that place : But he thinketh that they were meetings of the whole fraternity, and its like no house was much greater than the Church-house, so that this makes no difference.*

And I may add as to the former Evidences, *To.* 5. *Serm.* 52. *pag.* 705. when he had shewed that in the *Church* there must be no division, he expoundeth it by [ὁ μέν τοι τῆς συνόδου ταύτης ἑαυτὸν ἀπορρήξας.] [*Qui seipsum ab hoc conventu sejunxerit.*] So that the Assembly was the Church, and not a thousandth part of the Church only.

See more of the Churches feasting together in *Baronius ad an.* 57. *pag.* (ed. *Plant.*) 543. to spare me more labour about this.

VI. Another Evidence of the Limits of the ancient Churches is (that which I oft mentioned in the particular Testimonies) that every where all the People either *chose*, or expresly *consented* to their Bishops, and they were ordained over them in their sight. And this no more could do than could meet in one place ; and one part of a Church hath no more right to it than all the rest. The Consequence is evident : And for them that say, that it was only the Parishioners of the Cathedral Church that voted ; I answer, Now Cathedrals have no Parishes, and heretofore the Cathedral Parish was *the whole Church*. The Testimonies fully prove that it was *All the Church* or *People* that were *the Bishop's Flock :* And for some hundreds of Years there were no Parishes in his Diocess but one, and therefore no such distinction. *Pamelius*'s heap of Testimonies, and many more, for the matter of fact I have already cited : And however some talk now to justifie the contrary course of our times, it is so clear and full in Antiquity that the People chose their Bishops, at first principally, and after secondarily after the Clergy, having a Negative Voice with them, and their Consent and Testimony ever necessary, even for eight hundred Years at least, that it would be a needless thing to cite any more Testimonies of it to any versed in the Ancients. Papists and Protestants are agreed *de facto* that so it was. See *Cyprian, lib.* 4. *Epist.* 2. of *Cornelius* ; *lib.* 1. *Epist.* 2. of *Sabinus* ; and *lib.* 1. *Epist.* 4. *Euseb. Hist. lib.* 6. *cap.* 29. tells us that *Fabian* by the People was chosen to succeed *Anterus*. And *Cyprian* saith it was *Traditione Apostolica, vid. & Socrat. lib.* 4. *cap.* 14. *& lib.* 2. *cap.* 6. *& lib.* 7. *cap.* 35. *& Sozomen. lib.* 6. *cap.* 24. *& lib.* 8. *cap.* 2. of *Chrysostom* ; *& lib.* 6. *cap.* 13. *vid. & Augustin. Epist.* 110. *& Theodoret, Hist. lib.* 1. *cap.* 9. *in Epist. Concil. Nicæni ad Alexandr.* The Bloodshed at the Choice of *Damasus* was one of the first occasions of laying by that custom at *Rome*. And yet though they met not so tumultuously, they must consent. *Leo*'s Testimony I gave you before with many more. *Theodor. lib.* 5. *cap.* 9. of *Nectarius* sheweth that Bishops were then chosen, *Plebe præsente & universa fraternitate*, as *Cyprian* speaketh of *Sabinus*.

I 2   So

So the *Concil. Parisien.* even *an.* 559. But for more plentiful proof of this see, *M. A. Spalatenf. de Rep. Ecclef. lib.* 1. *cap.* 22. *n.* 10. & *lib* 6. *cap.* 7. & *lib.* 3. *cap.* 3 *n.* 12. &c. & *Blondel de Jure plebis,* more copiously, and *de Epif.* & *Presbyt.* & *Bilfon perpet. Govern. cap.* 15. & *lib.* of Christian Subjection oft.

And it is to be noted that when the People's Confusion had made them seem uncapable any longer to chufe : 1. This was long of the Prelates themselves, who by that time had so far enlarged their Churches, that the People were neither capable of doing their ancient Work and Duty, nor yet of being ruled by the Clérgy aright. 2. And when the People were reftrained from the Choice by Meetings and Vote, the Magiftrates in their ftead did undertake the Power. 3. And when it fell out of the People's hands into Great Mens, the Proud and Covetous who could beft feek and make Friends did get the Bifhopricks, whereupon the Churches were prefently changed, corrupted and undone. 4. And the fenfe of this moved the few good Bifhops that were left to make Canons againft this Power and Choice of Princes and great Men, decreeing that all Bifhops obtruded by them on the Churches fhould be as none, but be avoided, and all avoided that did not avoid them. And the *Roman* and Patriarchal party cunningly joyned with thefe honeft Reformers to get the Choice out of the Magiftrate's hands that they might get it into their own ; and fo Chrift's Church was abufed among ambitious Ufurpers. The Decrees againft Magiftrates Choice of Bifhops you may fee, *Can. Apoft.* 31. & *Decret.* 17. *q.* 7. *c. fiquis Epifc. Sept. Synod. c.* 3. *Decret.* 16. *q.* 7. *Oct. Synod. c.* 12. & *Act.* 1. & *c.* 22. *Decret.* 16. *q.* 7. *Nicol.* 1. *Epift.* 10. & *Epift.* 64. with more which you may find cited by *Spalatenf. lib.* 6. *cap.* 7. *pag.* 675, 676, 677.

And it is to be noted that (though ftill the Clergy had a Negative or firft Choice, yet) when they procured *Charles* the Great (who was to rife by the Papal help) to refign and renounce the Magiftrates Election, he reftored the Church to its Ancient Liberties, as far as enlarged Diocefes and ambitious Clergy-men would permit it. His words are thefe, [*Sacrorum Canonum non ignari ut in Dei nomine Sancta Ecclefia fuo liberius potiretur honore, affenfum ordini Ecclefiaftico præbuimus, ut fcilicet Epifcopi per Electionem CLERI & POPULI fecundum ftatuta Canonum de PROPRIA DIOECESI, remota perfonarum & munerum acceptione, ob vitæ meritum & fapientiæ donum, eligantur, ut exemplo & verbis fibi fubjectis ufquequaque prodeffe valeant.*] *Vid. Baron. To.* 11. *n.* 26. *Decret. Dift.* 63. *c Sacrorum.* Where note that, 1. he includeth the People of the *whole Diocefs.* 2. And doth this as according to the *facred Canons.* So that for Men to dream that only the Parifhioners of a Cathedral Church (which had no proper Parifh) or the Citizens only, were to chufe, is to feign that which is contrary to notorious Evidence of *Law* and *Fact,* as well as of the reafon of the thing. For where all are the *Bifhops Flock,* and chufe as *his Flock,* there *all the Flock* muft chufe, and a parcel can claim no privilege above all the reft.

VII. The.

VII. The next Evidence is this: In the first Age, it is very fairly proved by Doctor *Hammond*, that there were by the Apostles more Bishops and Churches than one in many Cities themselves: And if *one City* had more than one Church and Bishop, then much more many distant places, in Towns and Countries. That one City had more than one he sheweth by the distinction of *Jews* and *Gentiles* Churches: As *Peter* was appointed chiefly for the Jews, and *Paul* chiefly for the Gentiles, so he sheweth it very probable, that at *Rome*, *Antioch*, and other places they had several Churches. And thus he reconcileth the great differences about *Linus*, *Clemens* and *Cletus* or *Anacletus*. And especially on this reason, that they had not the same Language. And indeed when in great Cities there are Christians of divers Languages, it is necessary that they be of divers Congregations, unless you will have them *Hear*, as the Papists will have them *Pray*, they know not what. And though some might say, that though they be of divers Assemblies, yet they might have onely *One Bishop* to *Rule* them: I answer, 1. Dr. *Hammond* is more ingenuous, and acknowledges that the diversities of congregations and languages inferred a diversity of Churches and Bishops with their distinct Clergy. 2. And all Antiquity made Preaching or Teaching his flock as essential to the Bishops office as Governing them (of which next:) But he could not teach several Churches whose language he understood not.

VIII. Antiquity made the three parts of the Bishops office *Teaching*, *Worshipping*, and *Governing*, to be of the same extent as to the subject society under him. It was one and the same Church which he was ordinarily to *Teach*, to guide in *worship* (prayers, praise, sacrament) and to Rule by discipline (supposing still that we speak of a meer Bishop and not an Archbishop) I should weary the Reader to cite numerous testimonies for so notorious a thing. But it is known that the said Bishop neither is nor can be the *Ordinary Teacher*, and *Guide* in worship to a Diocese of a multitude of Churches, but to one or few at most. And he that peruseth ancient writers, shall find that the Bishop was not only to be a rare or extraordinary Teacher of his whole flock, but the *Ordinary* one: not only to send others, but to do it himself; till the enlargement of Dioceses changed the custome.

IX. Another evidence is this: In the first two Centuries, Deacons and Bishops were ever officers in the same Church: But Deacons were never then officers in more Churches (or stated assemblies that had Sacramental Communion) than one: therefore Bishops were not officers in more. No proof can be given of any Deacons that had the care (in their places) of many Churches, Parishes, or Societies of Christians. And when Dioceses were enlarged, it is notable that the Presbyter that was the *oculus Episcopi* in the Diocese is called the *Archdeacon*: Because originally he was but indeed a Deacon, the chief Deacon who was with the Bishop in one and the same Church; It being then *inauditum* for a Deacon to belong to many.

X. Another

. X. Another evidence is, The Great number of Bishops who out of a narrow space of ground, did usually assemble in the ancient Synods. I told you before out of *Crab* of *Sylvesters* number at *Rome*. *Binius* also hath the like words [*Sylvester collegit in gremio sedis suæ* 284 *Episcopos*] and that 139 of them were *ex urbe Roma vel non longe ab illa*. A hundred thirty nine Bishops in *Rome* and not far from it, had not such Dioceses as now.

Cyprian saith, *lib.* 1. *Ep.* 3. that *Privatus* was condemned *in Synodo Lambesitana* by 90 Bishops which was before Christianity was countenanced by Emperours, and were under persecution, yea, long before *Cyprian* wrote that Epistle.

For the examining of every ordinary cause of an accused Presbyter, *sex Episcopi ex vicinis locis*, six Bishops from the neighbour places, (not from 40 or fourscore miles distance) were to hear and determine, and three Bishops for the cause of every Deacon, *Concil. Afric. Can.* 20. so that no doubt but their Bishops were as near as our Market Towns at least, even when so few of the people were Christians as that all that space afforded but one great Congregation.

The sixth provincial Council at *Carthage* had 217 Bishops (whereas the General Council at *Trent* had long but 40.)

A Council of Donatists (Hereticks not so numerous sure as the Catholicks) at *Carthage*, mentioned by *Augustine, Epist.* 68. (about an. 308) had 270 Bishops. And when there were so great a number of Heretick Bishops, how many were there of the Catholicks and Donatists and all other sects set together? This one heresie had enow to become persecutours of the Catholicks, (beating them with clubs, putting out the peoples eyes by casting vineger mixt with lime into them, dragging them in the dirt) And yet they were the smaller number , and complained of persecution; and some Circumcellions killed themselves to make the Catholicks odious as persecutors (*Occisos auferunt luci, vivis auferunt lucem— Quod nobis faciunt sibi non imputant : & quod sibi faciunt nobis imputant inquiunt, Clerici Hippon. ib. ad Januarium.*) Certainly here were Churches no bigger then, than our smaller Parishes.

And *Augustine cont. Gaudentium* saith, there were innumerable Bishops in *Africa* that were Orthodox. (And it was but a corner of *Africa* that were Christians, and in the *Roman* Empire here meant.)

Victor Uticensis in persecut. Vandal. sheweth that in that part of *Africa* 660 Bishops fled; besides the great number murdered, imprisoned, and many tolerated. The like may be said of *Patricks* Irish Bishops before mentioned, and many others, who plainly were Parochial Bishops.

XI. Another evidence is, The way of Strangers communicating then by way of Communicatory Letters , or Certificates from the Church whence they came, which were to be shewed to the Bishop of the Church where they desired to communicate : But was it many hundred Churches that they must thus satisfie? or must they travail to the Bishop with their Certificate, before they must communicate in any one Church within 20. 30. 40.

or

or 50. miles of him ? Doubtless an impartial Reader will think, that it was but a Bishop of the same City-Church which he desired Communion with, to whom the Certificate was to be shewn. See what *Albaspinæus* saith of these Letters, *ex Concil. Laodic. c.* 41. *Concil. Antioch. c.* 1. *Concil. Agath. can.* 52. *Concil. Eliber. c.* 58. in his observat. p. 254, 255.

XII. Another evidence is the ancient phrase describing a Schism by *Altare aliud erigere*, to set up *another Altar*, or to set up Altar against Altar. And to separate from that Altar was to separate from that Church : which implyeth, that there was but one Altar in a Church ; and multiplying Altars was multiplying Churches.

XIII. Another evidence was the late division of Parishes : The idle story of *Evaristus* dividing Parishes at *Rome*, *Gerf. Bucer* hath fully confuted. It is most certain that except at *Alexandria* and *Rome*, it was long before they were divided. Sir *Rog. Twisden Histor. Vindicat. c.* 3. *p.* 9, 10. saith that it was under *Theodore A. B. C.* that Parochial Churches began (mark *Begin*) to be erected here in *England*, and the Bishop of *Rome* greatly reverenced in this nation *&c.* out of a *MS.* in Trinity Hall *Cambridge*. And it was 668 as *Beda* tells us before *Theodore* was Ordained Bishop. The evidence in history of the Lateness of Parish divisions is past doubt.

And whereas the usual answer is, that there may be Dioceses without Parishes ; I answer, It is not the *Name* [Diocese] that is the thing in question, but the Church-state. While there was but one Altar, there was but one place of ordinary Church Communion in the Lords Supper. And when there were more places with Altars erected, they could not be, nor were long without their proper affixed Presbyters (as *Arius* his Case sheweth and as is confessed) And when that was done, they were Parishes in our sense : And till that was done, some one Presbyter was sent from the Bishop as he pleased ; and then all the Parishes in the Diocese must needs be under one Presbytery as well as one Bishop. There were no setled Congregations for ordinary Church Communion, besides the Bishops Church-meeting, till Parishes were divided : if not by *space of ground*, yet by the *distinction* of Temples and People, which is the thing intended. There could be no such thing as a Diocesane Church in the sense that we oppose it in, that is, One Church with a Bishop *infimi ordinis* (having none under him) made up of a multitude of Communicating Churches with their Subpresbyters, yea such as are no part of the Bishops Confessus or Presbytery for the Government of that Church.]

XIV. The next evidence is, the ancient custom of *All his Presbyters sitting in one seat with the Bishop in a semi-circle in loco eminentiore on each hand of him and the Deacons standing under or below them :* which is so ordained by Councils (as *Carth.* 4. *Can.* 35. *&c.*) And the thing is commonly reported in the ancients. And this being put usually as of his Presbyters in common, who were his assistants and colleagues , and with whom he Governed the Churches, without

So Sr. Hen. Spelman Concil. p. 152. saith, in Th odor time about An 672. Parish divisions here began. Seld. of Tythes proveth that the division of Parishes in England began but about 700 years after Christ. And Dr. Tillesly doth not deny the time, but thinketh that though Patrons (as Selden saith) might probably begin this, yet Bishops also had a hand in it.

without mentioning any excepted Presbyters belonging to diftant Parifhes. It is apparent that the Bifhop then had ordinarily but one affembly. The fame I may fay of the many Canons, that fhew what the Presbyters are to do in the Church, which imply his prefence: But I have mentioned many of them before.

XV. Another evidence is, the cuftom of the Presbyters dwelling in the fame houfe with the Bifhop (fingle) as in a Colledge ; which not only in *Hippo*, but in very many other places was then ufed : and they dwelt near the Church, where that was not ufed (As when they had wives, or the Bifhop had his *Epifcopam* as the *Concil. Turon.* 2. calleth her, and alloweth it.)

Tolet himfelf, *de Sacerdotio lib.* 5. *cap.* 4. *n.* 15. *pag.* 722. confeffeth this faying, [*In Ecclefia Primitiva ufque ad tempora Auguftini & Hieron. Epifcopum & Clerum folitos vivere in communi : unde bona quæ vel ex decimis, vel ex fidelium devotione offerebantur, erant indivifa, & fubdebantur diftributioni Epifcopi, quæ partim ipfi, partim Clero, partim fabricæ, partim pauperibus obveniebant. Poftea vero quando quifque per fe vixit, talia bona divifa funt in quatuor partes, prima Epifcopo fervata, fecunda Clero, tertia fabricæ, quarta pauperibus.*] And fure that Church then was no bigger than that Colledge did officiate to.

XVI. And that which thefe words of *Tolet* recite, is the next evidence, *viz.* The way of *maintenance* in thofe times. 1. They lived on Oblations moftly : And thefe oblations are ever mentioned as offered but upon *One Altar*. 2. Thefe Oblations were all brought to the Bifhops hands, and diftributed by him or his appointment. 3. The Firft-fruits, and Tythe that came next were alfo in his hands. 4. And fo were all the Gifts, and all the *Prædia* or Church glebe. 5. All thefe are mentioned as given to One Church only, and not many. 6. The diftribution was as aforefaid, fome fourfold, fome-time three-fold ; of which *Spalatenfis* reciteth the decrees fo fully, that I will not tire the reader with reciting them. 7. And it was the *Fabrica of One Church* only that the Bifhop was to give the fourth part to maintain (And were many hundred fabricks more forgotten ?) 8. And it was a *prefent Clergie*, and not men fetled a long way off, that he was to make diftribution to. 9. And when he was to have the firft fourth part himfelf, who can think that this is meant that men muft carry the fourth part of the Hay, and Corn, and Wood, and Pigs, &c. from all the Parifhes through fuch Diocefes as ours, and the fourth part of all the Glebe rents ; This would make the Bifhoprick indeed feem to worldly minded men to be worth the venturing of their fouls for ; And they muft have fo many fcore or hundred barns full, as might tempt them to fay, *Soul take thine cafe, eat drink and be merry, &c.* But the evidence fpeak-eth plainly.

Of this fee an excel-lent Tract of Church Benefices; by Pad. Paul Sarpi, tranflated by Dr. Den-ton confir-ming many things be-forefaid.

XVII. Another evidence is this : That when firft new Communicating Af-femblies were erected even in the fame Cities with the Bifhops, the faid Bifhops did devife this new trick of their own heads, to fend to that Affembly fome Bread hallowed

hallowed by themselves ; And this was first to comfort (as they said) the Presbyters and new Congregation, left they should think themselves cut off from their Bishops Church and Communion. 2. To hold their interest in the people by this handle of their own making. Of these *Eulogiæ* the *Can. Concil. Laodic.* 14. speaks, as *Petavius* and others think : *Pet. xv. in Epiph. ad heres. 69. pag. 276. saith, [Romæ, ubi per titulos distributi presbyteri suos quique populos regebant : Ad eos Episcopi Dominicis diebus fermentum sive benedictum panem in Communionis symbolum mittere consueverant.*] And the passage which he citeth out of *Innocent ad Decentium cap.* 5. is very full, [*De fermento vero quod die Dominico per Titulos mittimus, superflue nos consulere voluisti : cum omnes Ecclesiæ nostræ intra civitatem sint constitutæ : Quarum Presbyteri quia die isto propter plebem sibi commissam nobiscum convenire non possunt, ideo fermentum a nobis confectum per acolythos accipiunt, ut se a nostra communione, maxima illa die non judicent separatos.*] That *Melchiades* ordained this, *Damasus* his pontifical book saith ; which was about *An.* 313. But *Baronius ad An.* 313. largely openeth all the business, and sheweth that this *fermentum* was hallowed leavened bread, which was not the Eucharist, but a devised sacrament (as *Innocent* calleth it) of Union and Communion : confirming this which I have said : And *ex Can.* 14. *Concil. Laod. &c.* he sheweth that it was used also in the East : And to this notable passage of *Innocent* [*Omnes ecclesiæ nostræ infra civitatem sunt constitutæ*] all the Popes Churches were within the city, he saith, (*p.* 97.) [*De titulis tantum intelligit, ad quas fermentum mitti solebat, non quidem quod non essent in suburbiis aliæ complures ecclesiæ atque sanctorum memoriæ, sed nulla prorsus Titularis, in quam populus colligi consueverit. Cujus rei causa aut se non mittere fermentum ad Presbyteros per diversa cœmeteria constitutos, quod illi plebem sibi subditam quam colligerent, non haberent.*]

Here you see, 1. That there were more Temples than Congregations, or Parishes, being erected as Monuments in honour of the Martyrs. 2. That there were no Congregations or Parishes, but within the City. 3. That this device of holy bread came upon the division of Parishes ; and therefore as one was new then, so the other could not be old.

XVIII. Another evidence is the state of Cathedral Churches, which as many Episcopal Antiquaries say, were first the sole Churches of the Bishops Charge or Diocese ; and that Parish Churches were since built one after another, as Chappels be in Parishes, by those that could not come so far : And that the present Government of the Cathedral by the Dean and Chapters, under the Bishop, is the evident relict of the old Episcopal Government, and truly telleth us what it was : To pass by many others, I will now recite but the words of *Holingshead* our Historian, a Clergy-man, *Chron. Vol.* 1. *p.* 135. *Col.* 1. [" Those Churches are called Cathedral, because the Bishops dwell

first belong to the Cathedral Church] *and herein the custome of our Kingdom and others was not determined. And if the Diocese was such as that all were to be buried at the Cathedral, it was not so big as one of our Parishes in* London, *which are fain to take other ground for burial ; and their Church was not the tenth part of the living as auditors.*

K

And it : a considerable part which T. Tillotsley against Selden saith (p. 179 [T right of place di place di neat

"near them. At first there was but ONE CHURCH in every JURIS-
"DICTION, whereinto no man entered to pray, but with some ob'ation
"towards the maintenance of the Pastor — And for this occasion they were
"built very huge and great : for otherwise they were not capable of such mul-
"titudes as came daily to them, to hear the word and receive the sacraments:
"But as the number of Christians increased, so first Monasteries, then finally
"Parish Churches were builded, in every jurisdiction ; from which I take our
"Deanry Churches to have their original, now called Mother Churches, and
"their Incumbents Archpriests ; And the rest being added since the Conquest,
"either by the Lords of every Town, or zealous men loth to travail far,
"and willing to have some ease, building them near hand unto these Dean-
"ry Churches, all the Clergie in old time of the same Deanry were appoin-
"ted to repair at sundry seasons, there to receive wholsome ordinances, and
"to consult of the necessary affairs of the whole jurisdiction, if necessity so
"required : And some image thereof is yet to be seen in the North parts. But
"as the number of Churches increased, so the repair of the faithful to the Ca-
"thedral, did diminish, whereby they are now become, especially in their
"nether parts, rather Markets and shops for merchandize, than solemn places
"of prayer, whereunto they were first erected.] I need to say no more
of this.

XIX. The next evidence is, That when Churches first became Diocesane
(in the sense opposed) they were fitted to the form of the Civil Government ; And Dioceses and Metropolitanes, and Patriarchs, came in at the same
door : The very name διοικησις was long unknown in a sacred sense, and
was after borrowed from the Civil divisions, when the Church was formed
according to them.   And as *Altare Damasc. p. 290.* saith, *Vox διοικησις
ut refertur ad piscopum,ignota fuit Eusebio & superioribus seculis :* And the word
Parish was also before used in our narrower sense, for a vicinity of Christians.
And as *Grynæus* saith in *Euseb. p. 1. not. 3. Euseb. promiscue usurpat hæc duo vo-
cabula παροικι κ, εκκλησια.

And that a Diocesane as such (thus formed to the *Roman* Civil form) and a
Metropolitane and Patriarch, yea, and the Pope as the Prime Patriarch in the
Empire, are all of Humane institution, and all of the same original and right,
there are few Protestants that do deny. 1. The reason of the thing plainly sheweth it. 2. Their beginning at once sheweth it. 3. And that they were never
any of them setled out of the *Roman* Empire, where that form obtained, except
that they setled here and there one on the verge of the Empire to have some
care of the neighbour countreys, till after that the *Roman* name and power invited small countreys adjoyning to them to imitation.   And Bishop *Bilson* of
Chr. Subject. often tells us that Metropolitans and Patriarchs are of Humane institution.

Godwin a Bishop, in the Lives of the *English* Bishops, *de Convers. Brit.c.3. p.30.*
saith, *Quis tam imperitus est ut non intelligat, post mortem Tiberii fluxisse multos
annos, ne dicam seculum unum aut alterum priusquam Cardinalis, Patriarchæ,*

aut.

aut Metropolitani nomen in Christianorum ecclesiis auditum est] He might have added, *aut Diocesani*, for they were built by the same hand on the same foundation. I do not mean that an Apostolical General Ministry was so new, but a Diocesane of many Churches, as *Episcopus infimi gradus*. Multitudes of Papists and Protestants attest the novelties of these foresaid ranks. Two testimonies of the Papists are so notable, as that I will not pass them by.

Cardinal *Cusanus* (that Learned Prelate, and proud enough) *li. de Concord. l. 2. c. 13.* saith, [*Omnes gradus Majoritatis & Minoritatis in ecclesia juris positivi esse.*] And therefore concluded that the Papacy is removeable from *Rome*.

Nay the very Canon Law it self, saith, *Decret. Par. 1. dis. 22. c. 1. c. omnes,* [*Omnes sive Patriarchii cujuslibet apices, sive Metropoleon primatus, aut Episcopatuum Cathedras, vel ecclesiarum cujuscunque ordinis dignitates, instituit Romana ecclesia.*] what need we more witness? It is from *P. Nicolaus* his decretal. And though a man might suspect that he meant only of the personal Institution of the particular Patriarchs, Metropolitans, &c. yet the context sheweth the contrary, and that it is the species, office or place that he speaketh of; Because the opposite assertion is, that the *Roman* Churches dignity was founded by God himself: And the next *Cap. 2.* is that, *not the Apostles, but the Lord himself gave the Roman Church its primacy.*

XX. The next evidence is, That we rarely read of any Bishops preaching in any Church but One, unless he was driven out of it by persecution, or unless it were in another Bishops Church. If I should except only the great Patriarchal Churches out of all the world, and that only as late as 400 or 500 years after Christ, when Emperours had helpt to increase the Churches, no impartial man would take that for any debilitation of my proof. And yet I shall not easily yield to that exception. In *Antioch* and *Jerusalem* I think it will hardly be affirmed, that the Bishop used to preach to any Congregation but One: In Great *Constantinople* (equalled to *Rome*) when find you *Chrysostome* any where but in one Church, except when violence hindred him, and then the same Congregation followed him? Indeed the *Novatians* had a Church there, and perhaps there was some bye Congregation or two of Christians, who all communicated in the Bishops Church, and therefore were but as Chappels. But go into all the rest of the world, and the case will be plainer, (except *Rome* and *Alexandria.*) Even *Basil* an Archbishop is not found a Teacher ordinarily any where but to his Church at *Cesarea* ; nor *Gregory* but at *Nazianzum* (when he went from *Constantinople* and from *Sasimis* ;) and so of the rest, no not *Ambrose* in the great city of *Milan*: And let it move none that *Milan* and some other Cities had more Temples than one, for as *Baronius* before cited tells us, there were then many Temples built as Monuments in honour of the Martyrs, that were not *Tituli*, nor had any Parish or Congregation belonging to them. When find you *Augustine* teaching in any Church but one (in *Hippo*) as part of his charge? Of *Epiphanius* I need not speak, seeing it is confest that in *Cyprus* no City had two Churches in his days, and that it was their

Leg. plura apud *Gers. Bucer* pag. 231, 232, 233, 234, 235,

their cuftome to place Bifhops in villages, (as *Socrates, Sózomen,* and *Nicephorus* agree.) So that the matter of fact is certain : except four or five Churches (if fo many) in all the world 400 years after Chrift, and except but two or three hundred years after Chrift, you will find no Bifhop in any Church but one, as part of his own Charge.

But the confequence inferred hence will be denied, becaufe the other Parifhes might be taught by Subpresbyters without him. *Anfw.* But I would ask, 1. Whether all the reft of the Parifhes were not the Bifhops Charge ? yea part of his Church, yea equally with the other part ? As to what *Onuphrius* and others fay of the ftations, and the Bifhops going from Church to Church, 1. It was fcarce any where but in *Rome* : 2. It was of later times : ·3. It was only in the City : 4. It was· commonly the fame auditors that followed him to feveral Churches.

And it's true that other Bifhops went to the memorials of the Martyrs oft, and had as monuments more Churches than affemblies. And it's true that of later times, certain Canons bind the Bifhops to vifit all their Parifhes : And the eldeft oblige him to vifit all the people : which fheweth that yet his Docefe was not great.

If he be the Bifhop of the Church, and the office of a Bifhop be to guide the Church, in *Worfhip,* and by *Difcipline,* then he is bound to do this to all the Church : indeed if you make but a meer Presbyter of him, then as many may divide the work between them, fo each might know his proper part, (as things ftood when Parifhes or Chappels were divided) But if a Bifhop, as fuch, be the uniting head as the King of a Kingdom, he muft be equally. related to the whole.

But if it were not *equally,* who can believe that there was fo great a difference in the parts of the fame Church, as that one parcel of them only fhould have right to their Bifhops prefence, teaching, worfhipping, and perfonal guidance, and ten, twenty, an hundred, a thoufand other parcels have no right at all ? What ! a Bifhop of a whole Church, not at all obliged to Teach, or Guide in perfonal worfhipping, any part of that Church but one ? Some great change was made in Churches before men could arrive at fuch a conceit ? Even now among us, a Bifhop taketh himfelf (by the conftraining Law of man, which is his Rule) to vifit his Diocefe once in three years : (I do not mean one Church of fourty or an hundred in his Diocefe, much lefs to preach himfelf ufually in thofe few Towns he comes to ; but to call his Curate Priefts together, and to fet one of them to preach his Vifitation Sermon.) But where find you this done by three Bifhops in the world for 300 years after Chrift, unlefs that Archbifhops vifited the Bifhops Churches under them ? Now they fay there have been Bifhops in *England* who have once in three years confirmed fome children abroad throughout their Diocefe (I do not mean one of two hundred.) but where find you that then the Bifhop went out of his City to do this ?

2. My next queftion therefore is, Whether the Bifhops of thofe times were not at leaft as confcionable and careful and laborious in their offices, as any now are,

are, if not much more? What! not a *Gregory*, a *Basil*, a *Chrysostome*, an *Augustine*, a *Fulgentius*, a *Hillary*, &c. What! not they that preached almost daily? They that write so strictly of the labours of the Ministery? They that lived so austerely, and favoured not the flesh; that speak so tenderly of the worth of souls? And would all these, think you, undertake to be Bishops of a whole Church, and yet so leave the whole work upon others, as never to come among them and teach them, and examine them, nor give them the Sacrament in all the Parishes of the Diocese save one? This is not credible.

If you say that in *Alexandria* it was certainly so, that distinct congregations were committed to the Presbyters, I answer, 1. Yet so as that they might any part of them (as living in the same city) come and hear the Bishop when they would: 2. They might communicate with him *per vices* if they would: 3. They were all bound to do so at the great festivals of the year: 4. They were all personally governed by the discipline of the Bishop and Presbyters conjunct in Council: But of this next.

XXI. Another evidence is that the whole *Plebs* or people of the Bishops charge (till Churches were setled under Presbyters far off in the countreys) were bound by the Canons to come to the Cathedral Church, and communicate with the Bishop at Easter, Whitsuntide, and some other such festivals, even after they were distinguished into several Auditories and Communicating Assemblies under Presbyters; which I have before proved from the particular Canons: which certainly proveth that the Dioceses were no more than could assemble in one place.

XXII. Another evidence is that Presbyters did but rarely preach in the two or three first ages (except in *Alexandria*, or in some few Churches which had got some extraordinary men; *Chrysostome's* preaching at *Antioch*, *Augustin's* at *Hippo*, while they were but Presbyters, are noted as unusual things. And it is said of *Augustine* (as forecited) that it being not usual in other Churches, for the Presbyters to preach in the Bishops presence, the example of that Church (by the humility of the honest Bishop who preferred his abler Presbyter before himself) did lead many other Churches into the same practice. *Spalatensis* and many others have given large proofs, that the Bishops and not the Presbyters were the ordinary preachers in their Church. * *Filesacus* saith, *De Episcop. authorit. cap.* 15. *Sect.* 1. *pag.* 344. | *Episcopus consuevisse ex ambone verba facere, refert Concil. Lateran. sub Martino, & Concil. Trull. c.* 33. *Permissum deinde Presbyteris, quanquam non passim, nec in quibuslibet ecclesiis: Diaconis olim id concessum* ...

I may add also as another evidence, that in the beginning few were able ...

* time, Confirmation was closely joyned to Baptism, and therefore ordinarily none were Baptized but by a confirmer, or in his presence: And the Bishops say, that only Bishops did confirm: And if so, then let it be considered, to how large a Diocese a Bishop could be present at every Baptism: Yea if Confirmation had been at a greater distance, seeing all that were baptized were confirmed, it is easy to know for how many one Bishop cannot do this. Did our Bishops use it they would know. I do not think that in this city one person of ten or 100 is confirmed though the Bishop dwell among them. Perhaps in some Dioceses not one of 1000 for we rarely hear of any at all.

sam,

fum, fed raro —— *& p. 351. ait,* [*Balfamon juris Graco-Romani li 2. cap. 9.
in Alexii Commeni Bullis ; Populum docere folis eft datum Epifcopis: & magna
ecclfix Doctores Patriarche jure docent.*] Thefe were like our Canons as he fhews
at large ; and this was in later ages when a Bifhop might teach *per alium.* — And
*p. 351, 352. Concil. Trull. c. 64. docet ex Greg. Nazianz. folis Epifcopis conve-
nire concionari & fanctas fcripturas interpretari ; Presbyteris vero non nifi Epifcoporum conceffione.* Of the Bifhops teaching fee the numerous citations in *Filefacus cap. 1.*

And if any be ftumbled at the name *Presbyteri Parochiani* ufual in the Councils and Fathers, as if they were Countrey Presbyters, who preached then in
other Churches? I have before cited a Canon which gave leave to Presbyters to
preach in the countrey villages, intimating it was rare heretofore. 2. *Filefacus* faith, *ibid. p. 562, 563.* [*Sed ut quod res eft libere eloquar, & illo avo & an-
teriore, cum Parochia vox vulgo etiam pro Diacefi ufurpatur* (that is for all the
Bifhops Charge) *credo Presbyteros Parochianos dictos fuiffe, non aliter ac fiquis
Diacefanos pronunciaret, hoc eft, In hac Parochia feu Diacefi ordinatos & titulatos.*]

But furely whilft Presbyters rarely preached, there were either Churches that
had no preaching (which cannot be proved) or elfe few Affemblies that had
not Bifhops.

Obj. But then you make Lay Elders of the Presbyters.

Anf. They were the abler fort of Chriftians ordained to the fame Minifterial
or Sacerdotal Office as all true Minifters are : But few of them being Learned
men, and able to make long Sermons, were imployed only as the Bifhops
affiftants, as elders are among the Presbyterians : who if they would but ordain
thofe Elders, and let them have power over the word and Sacraments, though
only to exercife it under the Bifhops or chief Paftors guidance, when there was
caufe, they would come nearest to the ancient ufe.

XXIII. And it feemeth to me an evidence that the Churches then were
(ufually) but as narrow as I affert, that the *Presbyters* were to abide with the
Bifhop, and attend him in his City Church. For if you fuppofe them able to
Teach or guide a flock themfelves, (as fome were fuch, as *Auguftine, Macarius,
Ephrem Syrus, Tertullian, &c.*) it is fcarce credible to me that the Bifhop
In the fub- would fuffer fuch worthy perfons to fit among his Auditors, when there were
fer ptions many countrey congregations that needed their help. For that the Church was
of Councils fo fupplied with Preachers as that befides all thefe Presbyters in the Bifhops
you fhall Church, there were enow for all the reft of the countrey Parifhes as now, is
find fome- contrary to all the intimations of Church-Hiftory. And therefore when we
time a read of fo many Presbyters with the Bifhop, before we read of many or fcarce
Bifhop and any elfewhere, furely there were no people that needed them.
one Deacon,
fometime a
a Bifhop
and a Pref- XXIV. And yet (though great Cities had many with the Bifhop) I may
byter, as at add that the *paucity of Presbyters under the generality of Bifhops, fheweth that
Arles, id.* their Dioceses then were but like Parifh Churches with their Chappels : Or
Spelman. elfe *Aurelius* and the other Bifhops in the *Carthage* Council needed not have
p. 42. been

been in doubt whether thofe Bifhops that had but one or two Presbyters, fhould have one taken from them to make a Bifhop of, which was yet affirmatively decreed, *becaufe there may be more found fit to make Presbyters of, where it's hard to find any fit to be Bifhops.*

I will fpeak it in the words of the learned Bifhop *Bilfons Perpet. Govern. c.* 13. *p.* 256. ["In greater Churches they had great numbers of Presbyters : In "fmaller they had often two, fomewhere one, and fometimes none. And "yet for all this defect of Presbyters, the Bifhops then did not refrain to im- "pofe hands without them. The number of Presbyters in many places were "two in a Church, as *Ambrofe* writeth on **1** *Tim.* 3. fometimes but one. In "the third Council *Carthag.* when it was agreed that the Primate of that City "might take the Presbyters of every Diocefe and Ordain them Bifhops for fuch "places as defired them, though the Bifhop under whom the Presbyter before "lived were unwilling to fpare him, *Pofthumianus* a Bifhop demanded, [what "if a Bifhop have but one only Presbyter, muft that one be taken from him ?] "*Aurelius* the Bifhop of *Carthage* anfwered, One Bifhop may Ordain many "Presbyters, but a Presbyter fit for a Bifhoprick is not eafily found : where- "fore if a man have but one only Presbyter, and *fit for* the room of a Bifhop, he "ought to yield that one to be Ordained. *Pofthumianus* replied, Then if ano- "ther Bifhop have a number of Clerks, that others ftore fhould relieve him. "*Aurelius* anfwered, Surely as you helped another Church, fo he that hath "many Clerks * fhall be driven to fpare you *one* of them, to be ordained by   * *not many* "you] A Diocefe fuch as is intimated here, we do not ftrive againft.   *Churches.*

XXIV. Another evidence is that when ever we read of perfecution turning the Chriftians out of their Churches, you ever find them gathered into one Con- gregation, when they could have leifure and place to meet in, and ufually a Bifhop with them ; unlefs he were banifhed, imprifoned, or martyred, and then fome Presbyter fupplied the place : or unlefs they were fcattered into many little parcels And you find no talk of the perfecution of multitudes of Countrey Presbyters afar off, but of the Bifhop with his City Presbyters and Church. To which add that it was *One Church* ftill, which rejected, obtru- ded Bifhops, and refufed to obey the Emperour who impofed them. All this is manifeft in *Gregory Neocæfar.* his flight with *Mufonius*, and the ftate of his Church : In the Cafe of *Bafil* ; and of *Lucius* the obtruded Bifhop at *Alexan- dria*, and in the Cafe of *Antioch* before defcribed, and of *Rome* it felf. It's tedious to cite numerous teftimonies in a well known cafe. If *Alexandria* was in fuch a cafe, or near it, I hope you will doubt of no other Churches. And that with this you may fee what *Conventicles* the Chriftians kept when the Emperours forbad them. and how refolutely the Bifhops preached when the Emperours filenced them, I will recite the words of *Baronius* himfelf, and in him of *Dionyfius Alexandr. apud Eufeb. lib.* 7. *c.* 10. & *c.* 17. and *Cyprian ep.* 5. &c. in *Baron. ad an.* 57. *p.* 542. that thofe who cry out againft Preaching and Con- venticles, when they are but ftrong enough to drive others out of the Temples, may better underftand themfelves.

Signando .

[*Siquandv, &c.* If at any time so vehement a persecution did arise, that the
" Chriftians by the Emperours edicts, were utterly excluded from the Churches
" and affemblies, notwithstanding, little regarding such things, they forbore
" not to come *together in One*, in holy affemblies, whitherfoever there was op-
" portunity. This *Dionyf. Alexand.* Bifhop witneffeth writing to *Germanus*
" when he mentioneth the Edicts of *Valerian* forbidding the Affemblies. [But
" we by Gods affiftance, have not abftained from our accuftomed Affemblies
" celebrated among our felves. Yea, I my felf did drive on certain brethren to
" keep the affemblies diligently, as if I had converft among them.] And he
" writeth the fame alfo to *Hierax* when he was banifhed [When we were per-
" fecuted by all and put to death we celebrated the Feaft with joyful minds;
" and any place appointed us for feveral forts of fufferings, (as the woods, the
" defert folitudes, the toffed fhips, the common Innes, the horrid prifon) did
" feem fit to us in which we might keep our folemn Affemblies with the great-
" eft joy.] That they held their Affemblies and offered facrifice ufually (when
" it was permitted them) in the prifons, *Cyprian* witneffeth : But the Acts of
" the holy Martyrs do fullier fignifie it ; efpecially thofe moft faithful ones called
" *Pro-Confular* , which were taken by the publick Notaries. Certainly the
" Gravel-pits afforded them advantage for the celebrating of their publick Af-
" femblies, in the time of perfecution, efpecially at *Rome*, where in the dig-
" ged gravel there remain many fubterraneous ample receffes : Though when
" the perfecution was vehement, they were thence alfo excluded ; as the letters
" *P. Cornelii ad Lupic. Epifc. Vien.* teftifie, faying , [Chriftians may not *miffas*
" *agere*, keep their meetings for Church worfhip publickly, no not in the vaults,
" (or pits) So much of the Churches and publick affemblies of the Chriftians
" *&c.* faith *Baronius.*

Which *Polyd. Virgil* fecondeth *c. 6.* yea the Bifhops durft fcarce be feen in
the ftreets fo hot were the perfecutions, as *Eufeb. lib. 6. cap. 31.* Therefore, as
I before noted, they had yet no capacious Temples, as *Illyricus* well gathereth,
Catalog. Tefti. verit. p. 112. But they began to have days of peace and liberty
under *Alexand. Severus, Gordian. Philip, Galienus, Flavius, Claudius, Aureli-
anus, Probus*, and then they did enlarge their too fmall rooms, to that defcribed by *Eufeb. lib. 8. c. 1.*

XXVI. Another evidence is, that Monafteries were built before Chappels
and Countrey Parifh Churches, and far more numerous, fo that we frequently read of Monafteries under a Bifhop with their Abbot, or Presbyter, when
we read little or nothing of Parifh Churches in the Countries. under him.
And if thefe had been as common, why are they not as much mentioned in
the ancient records of the Church ? The Egyptian Monks, and thofe in *Judea*,
and thofe in *Britain*, in *Beda*, and the life of *Hierome, Fulgentius*, and abundance fuch witnefs this.

XXVII. Another

Sti Leo 1.
Epist. 88.
p. 159. So
Lib. pœni-
tential.
Thtodori
Cantu. in
Spelman.
p. 155.

Concil. A-
relat. 1.
c. 21.

Conc. Laod.
c. 57.

XXVII. Another evidence is the Canons, that none but a Bishop must publickly reconcile a penitent, nor pronounce the blessing in the Church, &c. Of which before in particular Canons.

XXVIII. Another evidence is that Presbyters or Bishops were not to remove from the Places they were Ordained in: But those places of old were single Churches; (usually in Cities with the suburbs that could come to the same Church, as Dr. *Field* saith.) *Concil. Arelat.* 1. cited by *Spelman, pag.* 40. (because we had 3 Brittish Bishops there) [*In quibuscunque locis ordinati fuerint Ministri, in ipsis locis perseverent*] And *ipse locus* was not a circuit of 40 or 50 or 100 miles long, but the Bishops Parish or Vicinity. Of the Bishops not removing (without a Synod) many Councils speak.

XXIX. Another evidence is that the Canons which take down the *Chorepiscopi* and turn them to *periodeutæ Visitors*, or Itinerants, and which forbid the making of Bishops in small Cities, or villages, 1. Were of late date, 2. And were in aspiring times, and had a reason answerable, *ne vilescat nomen Episcopi*; 3. And therefore intimate that it was otherwise before (as I have before shewed.)

XXX. A Separatist or Schismatick was then known by his withdrawing from his proper Church; and so was an Apostate or deserter: And he that stayed away certain days was to be excommunicate; And they that fall into sins and never present themselves to the Church, to shew their penitence, even when they fall sick and desire Communion, shall not have it till they shew fruits worthy of repentance, saith *Concil. Arelat.* 1. *Can.* 22. But 1. in our way, when the Church that I am of is an hundred miles long and hath above a thousand Parishes, who can tell when a man is at the Church, and when he is not, unless you make half a years work to examine the matter in a thousand Assemblies? 2. And a man may wander, and never be in the same Assembly once in three years, and yet be still in his own Church because the Doese is the Church: 3. Unless the Bishops presence as well as remote relation be necessary; And then no man cometh to Church, but he that cometh where the Bishop is, for *ubi Episcopus ibi Ecclesia*: And the Parish Church is with them no Church, unless equivocally as a Community. For as Learned Dr. *Field* saith, (and they must all say) [*None are to be ordained, but to serve in some Church: and none have Churches but Bishops; all other being but assistants to them in their Churches.*] *Lib.* 5. *c.* 27. *p.* 139. Therefore they call the Parish Priests the Bishops Curates; and Dr. *Field* maketh the Bishops Church or Diocese and a *particular* Church all one. If then one Parish priest of a thousand be an Arrian, Antinomian, Socinian, Papist, Seeker, &c. he that separateth not from that one Priest and Parish meeting, separateth not from his Bishops Church, nor any particular Church: For his Church is a country, which while he is in, he is no Separatist, if he join with any part of it.

L

XXXI.

XXXI. But my greatest evidence which I trust to above all the rest is, The greatness of the Bishops work, which no mortal man can truly and faithfully discharge and do for a Diocese in the opposed sense, nor for more than one of our greater Parishes. I have recited some of the particulars before, and I shall again have occasion to do it more at large: I now only name these parts.

1. To be the ordinary Baptizer, or still present with all that are Baptized, (to anoint their nostrils, &c. as aforesaid.). 2. To be the Confirmer of all the baptized in all the Diocese. 3. To be the ordinary preacher to his flock, and to expound the Scriptures to them. 4. To be the only publick reconciler or absolver of all penitents. 5. To be the publick Priest, to be the Guide of the people in publick worship, and to administer the Lords Supper. 6. To take particular account and care of all the peoples souls, and admonish, teach, and exhort them as there is special need. 7. To be the Excommunicator of the impenitent (or ever one and the chief.) 8. To Ordain all Ministers and Subministers. 9. To oversee and rule the Clergy. 10. To receive all Oblations, Tithes, Gifts, and Glebes, and be the distributer of them. 11. To visit the sick in all his flock. 12. To take a particular care of all the poor, the sick, the strangers, the imprisoned, &c. as their Curator. 13. To keep almost daily, but constantly weekly Assemblies for all the publick offices. 14. To keep Synods among his Colleagues, Bishops, and Presbyters. 15. To try and hear Causes with the Bishops, and Synods, and with his Presbyters at home, about all scandals, &c. that come before him, (of which one Town may find him work enough, the convincing and gentle reproof and exhortation will take up so much time.) 16. The looking after and convincing or confuting Hereticks. 17. The reconciling disagreeing neighbours. 18. The confecting of oyl and holy bread, &c. to furnish all his Presbyters with. 19. The Benediction of Marriages, and Solemnizing of Funerals; with a multitude of other Ceremonies. 20. And besides all this, the right government of his own house (And if he had Children, the education of them) 21. The oversight of all the Schools and educating young men for the Ministery (there being then no Universities to do it.) (That the Schools were under his care, you may see proved in *Filesacus*) 22. The Consecrating of devoted Virgins (to say nothing of Altars and other utensils) 23. The oversight of the Monasteries. 24. The writing of Canonical Epistles (as they called them) to Great men, to other Churches, &c. 25. The granting of Communicatory Letters. I have named all that come suddenly to my memory, but it's like not all. And how many Parishes, how many hundred thousand souls can one man do all this for, think you?

I will not tire you with citing out of *Isidore*, *Gregory*, *Ambrose*, *Chrysost*. &c. the strict Charges terribly laid on Bishops, but only now recite the Preachers words whose Oration *Eusebius* giveth us, at the dedication of a new Church, *Histor. Eccl. l.* 10. *c.* 4. It is *Paulinus* Bishop of *Tyre*. In which he tells them that it is the work of Bishops [*Intime animarum vestrarum theoriæ videre & introspicere, ubi experientia & temporis prelixitate unumquemque vestrum exacte inquisivit, studioque & cura cunctos vos honestate & doctrina quæ secundum pietatem*

est,

est, instruit.] It was then thought a Bishops duty to be intimately acquainted with the minds of his flock, and exactly enquire after every one of them, even menservants and maidservants by name, faith *Ignatius*, as cited before.

All this was then the Bishops work: Almost all this (except the Ceremonies) Dr. *Hammond* proveth industriously belonged to the Bishop. Let him faithfully do it all, and let his Diocese then be as big as he please.

I might have added *Concil. Arelat.* 1. c. 16. that people are to be absolved in the same place where they were Excommunicated, which intimateth it must be only in the Bishops Church. And in *Synod. Hybernic. Patricii* (in *Spelman* p. 52.) All that was more than necessary to a poor man that had a Collection was to be laid on the Bishops Altar,] which implyeth that each Church had one Bishop and one Altar. And *c.* 21. [*& non in Ecclesiam ut ibi examinetur causa*] And *c.* 25, 26, 27. no Clergy-man but the Bishop to dispose *c. 4, 5.* of Church offerings; *& Clericus Episcopi in Plebe novus ingressor, baptizare & offerre non licet, &c.* with much more which intimateth what Churches were of old.

But so much shall suffice for proof of the *Minor* of the first Argument, that our Diocesane Form, 1. taketh down the Church Form of Gods Institution, and the primitive Churches possession : 2. And setteth up a humane form in its stead, yea one only Church instead of a thousand or many hundred.

And therefore I add

CHAP. VIII.

That the Diocesans cause the errour of the Separatists, who avoid our Churches as false in their Constitution; and would utterly disable us to confute them.

WHen the *Brownists* say that our Churches are no true Churches, they do not mean that they are not Societies of mens devising; but that they are not Societies of Gods Instituting. And this they prove upon the principles of the Diocesans thus : If your Churches be of Gods Institution (*de specie*) it is either the Parish Churches, or the Diocesane Churches that are so : But neither the Parish-Churches, nor the Diocesane : *Ergo.*

1. That the Parish Churches are not such, they prove because by the Diocesans own confession, they are no Churches at all, except equivocally so called : It is one of their own principles, (and we grant it) that *Episcopus & Plebs* Constitute a Church, as a *King* and *Subjects* constitute a Kingdom, and as a

Schoolmaster

Schoolmaster and Scholars make a School: and as a Master and houshold make a Family. And that *ubi est Episcopus* (as *Cyprian* saith) *ibi est Ecclesia*; which is nothing but *Plebs pastori adunata*. And that a people without a Bishop (truly so called) are but a Church equivocally, as Scholars without a Master are a School, or as a company of Christians in a ship or house accidentally met, and praying together are a Church, &c. And as Dr. *Field* before cited, saith, *None but a Bishop hath a Church : all others are but his assistants*, or as commonly called his Curates. Therefore when a Prelatist pleadeth that our Parish Churches are true Churches (either of Gods or mans institution) they do forsake the principles of their party (as now maintained) or they contradict themselves, or they play with equivocations and ambiguities.

II. And that a Diocesane Church, which is one composed of the carcases of multitude of mortified Churches, is not *jure divino*, having said so much to prove my self, I will not stay to tell you how easily the Separatists may prove it. So that for my part as much as I have written and done against them, I profess I am not able to confute them on the Diocesane grounds, but would be one of them if I had no better.

Quest. *How then must they be confuted?*

Ans. Thus or not at all by me. A Presbyters office is not to be judged of by the Bishops will or description, but by God's the institutor. As if the King describe the Lord Mayors office in his Charter; If the Recorder or whoever giveth him his oath, and installeth him, shall misdescribe the office, and limit it, and say falsly you have no power to do this or that; This will not at all diminish his power, as long as it is the Charter that they profess to go by. He shall have the power which the King giveth, and not which the investing Minister describeth. If a Parson presented to a Benefice, shall be told by the Bishop at his institution, the Tithes or Glebe are but half yours, this shall not diminish his Title to the whole. So when God hath described the Ministers office, it shall be what *God* saith it is, and not what the Ordainer saith it is. And God maketh the Pastors of each particular body of fixed Communicants, united as aforesaid, to be really a Bishop (or at least the chief of these Pastors, or the sole Pastor:) And therefore the Church to be truly and univocally a Church of Divine institution : Though it were never so much granted that Archbishops were over them, as the Apostles were over those *Acts* 14. 23.

And then when the Parish Churches are once proved true Churches, whether the Diocesane be so or not, is nothing to our controversie with the Separatists. But for my part I cannot confute the lawfulness of a Diocese as consisting of *many* particular Churches with their Bishops, as I can a Diocese which hath put them all down.

CHAP.

CHAP. IX.

The second Argument : from the Deposition of the primitive species of Bishops, and the erecting of a humane inconsistent species in their stead : A specifick difference proved.

ARGuMENT II.

A Humane inconsistent species of Bishops erected instead of the Divinely-instituted species thereby deposed, is unlawful. But such is the Diocesan species now opposed —— *Ergo.*

I have hitherto charged it with the changing of the *Church Form :* Now of the form or species of Bishops. And here I need not add much to the former, because they are coincident, and in proving the one I have already proved the other.

A Bishop of one Church united for Individuals Communion, and a Bishop of one Church united only for Communion in *specie actionum,* are not the same. But because I hear many say that *Magis & Minus non variant speciem,* And that a Greater and a Lesser Diocese *make* neither the Church, nor Bishop to be of a different *species,* I am here to prove the contrary.

And first let it be remembred in what predicament the things in question are, a Church and a Bishop : That is, They are *relations.* Then let it be remembred what goeth to the essence and definition of a Relation, that is, The Relate, the Correlate, the Subject, the *Fundamentum* (or as some speak the *Ratio fundandi* also) and the *Terminus.* Now where these are not the same, or any of these, then the Relation is not the same : because where an essential ingredient is wanting, the essence is wanting.

Again it must be remembred that many Natural Relations are so founded in an act past, that the Relation resulteth from it without depending on any thing future. As God is Creator *quia jam creavit , Pater est qui genuit.* But there are other Relations which are founded in meer *Undertaking, Mandate authority,* and *obligation* to *future actions :* As he is a Tutor, a Schoolmaster, a Judge, a Chancellor, a Pilot, a Bishop, a Husband, *&c.* who by *mandate* and *undertaking* is *authorized* and *obliged* to such and such works, implyed in the names. And in these cases, there is nothing more specifieth the offices than the *work* of the office, which is, its *nearest End.* And these nearest ends are ever essential to such Relations ; whether you will call them the *Termini* or *End,* or by what other name, we contend not.

And

And therefore *Aquinas* and all, 1.2. *q.* 18. *art.* 2. and others commonly agree, that the *Object* and the *End* do specifie humane acts.

But *remote ends* may be the same in Acts, (and so in Offices) of the same species ; It proving but a Generical agreement (which yet may be in *specie subalterna.*) All humane Acts should have the same ultimate end, that is, The pleasing of God in the resplendency of his Glory, and the felicity of man. Yet this maketh them not all of the same *infimæ specici.* All Government intendeth the *common good* ; and yet there are different species of Government. All Church Government is for the good of the Church, and for the killing of sin, and the promoting of faith and holiness : And yet there are different species of Church Governours.

Aqu. 1. 2.
q. 18. art.
3. 5. & 10.
& q. 72.
art. 9. &
Cajet. &
Medin.ib.
But besides the *Object* and *End*, (which all agree to) there are by Schoolmen and Casuists, said to be *circumstances*, which may also *specifie* Moral acts. The seven named by *Cicero* in *Rhetor.* are, *Quis, Quid, Ubi, Quibus auxiliis, Cur, Quomodo, Quando* : And *Aquinas* and others tell us that these circumstances communicate special Goodness or evil to actions. *Vid. P. Soto in relect.* §. *in fine de bonit. & mal. act. Greg. de Valent. tom.* 2. *qu.* 13. *puncto* 4. *Jos. Angles in Florib.* 2. *sent. d.* 37. *q.* 3. *a.* 5. *p.* 2.

Greg. Sayrus in Clav. Regia Lib. 2. *Cap.* 3. *pag.* 54. giveth us these two notes to know when circumstances specifie actions.

1. *Quando Circumstantia novam conformitatem, aut deformitatem actui tribuit ; ita ut peculiariter conveniat vel repugnet rectæ rationi, novam speciem constituit : Rat. Quia in hoc casu circumstantia transit in rationem objecti ——— 2. Quotiescunque circumstantia non respicit specialem ordinem rationis in bono vel malo nisi præsupposita alia circumstantia a qua actus moralis habet speciem boni vel mali quam solam intra eandem speciem auget, vel diminuit, reddendo actum illum meliorem aut pejorem, toties circumstantia illa aggravans vel diminuens, non autem speciem mutans, censenda est : ut quantitas v: g. magna vel parva in furto.*

Note also that though *Relatio in forma relationis, non recipit magis & minus* ; e. g. *Titius non est magis Pater quam Sempronius* ; Yet *quoad subjectum, & aliquando quoad fundamentum & correlatum*, it may *recipere magis & minus*, so that *magis vel minus* shall change the *species.* This is in such cases, wherein the alteration of Quantity altereth the *Capacity* of the subject *quoad finem essentialem.* For as in Physicks, besides the Matter, the *Dispositio materiæ* (which *Aristotle* calls *Privation*) is necessary *ad formam recipiendam* (which is comonly called A third Principle ; but I would call it, the *Conditio necessaria* of the *Material Principle* ;) so in Relations there must be the *Dispositio necessaria subjecti*, or else there can no relation result. E. g. to the being of a *house*, some quantity is necessary to the *End*, that is, habitation ; And therefore it is no *house*, except equivocally which is no bigger than an egg-shell : So to the being of a Ship, of a Church, &c. that which is no bigger than a nutshell is no Ship or Church, though you call it so or Consecrate it, &c. And on the other side, It is not a spoon, a dish, a ladle, a pen, which is as big as a Church, a Ship, a House. Yea a Ship and a Boat do differ in *specie*, though both have the same End, (safe passage over the waters by portage) by the circumstantial differences of the End and Subject.

So

So also in Societies; the whole world, or a Kingdom is too big to be a Family: And a Family is too little to be a Kingdom. *Pagus,Vicus, Civitas, Regnum* differ principally in their *Ends*, and next in their Quantity of the subject matter, because every quantity is not capable of the same Essential End.

These things being premised, for the use of such ignorant Lads only as know them not, who may possibly study the controversie, I proceed to my proofs.

I. And I will begin (though it be weakest in it self) with an Argument *ad hominem*; For with the men that I now deal with, I shall take that to be the most effectual argument, which is fetcht from their interest, and fitted to their wills. I remember that once when an Army was resolved for Liberty of Conscience, for all that professed the fundamentals of *faith in God by Jesus Christ*, and the Parliament appointed some of us to draw up a Catalogue of fundamentals, (which I thought was best done by giving them the Sacramental Covenant, the Creed, Lords Prayer, and Decalogue) a good man, (with others of his mind) would needs have many more fundamentals, than I was for, and among others, (*That to allow our selves or others in known sin, is inconsistent with salvation* (or is damnable) I told him that I would not dispute against it, but undertake to make him cast it by without dispute: And when they would not believe me, but went on, I did all that I promised presently with telling them, You know that the Parliament take Independency to be a sin, and they will say, If we allow or tolerate them, they here pronounce the sentence of damnation on us under their own hands] *Dictum factum*; we had no more of that fundamental.

I have greater confidence of prevailing with Diocesans by such an argument: In taking the Covenant, in the *Westminster* Assembly, it would not pass till the parenthesis describing the English *species* of Prelacy was inserted; because many declared that they were not against all Episcopacy, but only the present English *species*. Accordingly those that took the Covenant in that sense, take not themselves bound to endeavour the extirpation of all Episcopacy but only of that *species*: And they that would have conformed on the terms of the Kings Declaration about Ecclesiastical Affairs, went on this supposition that the *species* of Prelacy was altered by it. Now I put these questions to the Diocesans. *Quest.* 1. If a Usurper by power should take down all the Diocesans (and their lands, Lordships, and Courts) and turn them into Parish Bishops, and say, I alter not the *species* but the degree, would they believe him? *Quest.* 2. If one that thinketh himself obliged by the Vow or Covenant against this *species* only, should think that he answereth his obligation, if he procure no other alteration than is made in the Kings forenamed Declaration, would they tell him, You alter not the *species* unless you totally extirpate Episcopacy: (supposing that he had power to do it.) *Quest.* 3. Seeing most that we speak with who conform, and who take or plead for the *Oxford* Oath [*Never to endeavour any alteration of Church Government*] do tell us that the meaning is only that we will not endeavour to alter the present *species*, which is *Episcopacy*, and not the appurtenances, as Chancellors, &c. I ask, If it should please the King to take down

down all Diocesanes, and to set up only a Bishop in every Parish or Independent Church,& say, I change not the *species*; or if I believed that this were a Change of the English *species* of Church Government I would not do it : what answer would they give to this ? *Quest.* 4. If a Conformist or one that hath taken that Oath, shall say, I did subscribe and swear only not to endeavour an alteration of the *species*, but not of the degree: Therefore I will do all that I can to take down Diocesans, and to set up Congregational or Parochial Bishops in their stead, will you tell this man that indeed by so doing he endeavoureth not to change the *species* ? *Quest.* 5. Seeing many of the greatest opposers of Prelacy, do consent to a Congregational or Parochial Bishop, will you grant that these are not at all your adversaries as to the *species* of Church Government, but only as to the degree or extent of Diocefes? These cases are practical : Therefore take heed how you resolve them, lest you do that which you are unwilling of. *Quest. 6.* And I may ask, Why is it that many deny that it was a Parliament of Episcopal men, that raised the Army against the King, only because in the Proposition sent to *Nottingham* they would have had Episcopacy reduced to what is there intimated, and would have had their power shortned ? Come, come, deny not the plain truth, If *magis & minus non variant speciem*, Parliament men, yea, and the Learnedest part of that Synod who took down Bishops, were Episcopal men, yea, Prelatists as you are, for they were but for a Gradual alteration at the beginning of their war, till they were carried further by necessity and interest. *Quest.* 7. And I ask you also, why, and with what front do you call us all Presbyterians, who offered Bishop *Ushers* Model to the King and you in 1660. as the terms of Concord ? Is it against your Consciences meerly to make us odious with you know whom ? what can it be better, if you grant that we are not only for Episcopacy *in genere*, but even for the same *species* with your selves? Yea, those that are against Bishop *Ushers* Model, and are only for Congregational or Parish Bishops, are it seemeth even for your *species*: And are they not then Episcopal as well as you ? So much *ad hominem* ; now *ad rem*.

II. *Where the specifying Ends differ, there the Species of Relations differ. But in the Churches and the Bishops in question the specifying Ends differ : Ergo &c.*
I will first manifest the truth of the Minor (for the Major is unquestionable) of *Churches*, and next of Bishops.
1. The ends of a particular Church as described by us are these : 1. Communion sensible and external ; 2. And that local or presential ; 3. And that personal by all the body of the Church ; 4. And that in the same Individual acts of Gods publick worship. 5. In watching over, or helping each other towards Heaven, by provoking each other to love and to good works, and if a brother offend to tell him of his fault ; to comfort each other, and to live together in holiness, love and peace. 6. To be related to the same Pastors, as those that are their Ordinary Teachers, Governours and Guides in publick worship, as labouring amongst them and being ensamples to the flock. 7. To hold a distant Communion with the neighbour associated concordant Churches, and

and particularly with those nearest them of the first order of Composition; of which association this particular Church is a part, for Communion of Churches as they are themselves a Society for Communion of Individual Christians in a single Church.

2. Now the ends of our Diocesane Churches are not one of all these. For 1. Their Communion is internal in Faith and Love; such as we have with the Abassines. 2. It is distant only, and not presential at all: For as Diocesane we never see each other, it's like in our whole lives. 3. It is not *personal* (as external and sensible) but only by the intervention of Delegates, Messengers, Officers or Synods, or such. 4. It is only *in eadem specie* of publick worship and sacred actions that we have Communion, but not in the same Individual actions of worship: And so we may have Communion with the *Antipodes*, while we believe the same Scriptures and Creed, and use the same Sacraments, &c. in *specie*. 5. We have no converse with one another at all as Diocesane: (though as Parochial we may) we never meet together, pray together, hear together, exhort or watch over or help each other: If a Brother trespass we tell him not of his fault, &c. for we never know one of five hundred in the Diocese, no more than men of another Countrey. 6. We hear not the same Teachers; we have not the same Guides to resolve our doubts, and to instruct us as we need; We have not the same Priests to joyn with in Gods publick worship: But he that Teacheth and officiateth in one Church, hath no power in another: Only we have the same Bishop to call (not the people before him to teach and warn and comfort them, but) the Parson and Churchwardens; or rather the same Lay-Chancellor and his Court, and the same Canons (for silencing our Ministers, Excommunicating many conscionable Nonconformists, &c.) which not only all the Diocese hath, but all the Land. Not one of many hundreds of the Diocese ever seeth the Bishop in all his life. 7. A Diocese is it self a compound of particular Churches associated (Though mortified *quantum in Diocesanis*;) And therefore cannot be a constitutive part of such a first order of Association, as a particular Church may be or is. These are the differences in *the Ends*.

Now lay all these together, and try, whether the differences in so many parts of the *Ends* of the Society, make not a Specifick difference in Societies. Whether [a company of Christians associated with the same present Pastors, for presential personal Communion in Gods publick worship, Sacraments, Teaching, and Guidance, and for mutual assistance in holy converse and living, &c. and cohabiting in a *vicinity* capable of this converse and Communion] be a Society of the same species with [A company of Congregations associated (or rather never associated) to hold a distant Communion in the same *species* of Belief, Prayer, Sacraments, &c. under several appropriate Pastors, not living (*ut Parochiani*) in any such vicinity as may *render* them capable of any of the foresaid present assistances or Communion: (unless in travail men accidentally come together as we may do with men of other lands.)] It is notorious that these *Essentiating Ends* of the two sorts of Societies are distinct; and therefore the Societies are essentially distinct.

M   Even

Even as a City, Burrough, or Corporation, are part of a Kingdom, and are specifically distinct societies from the Kingdom. (For the Parts may have a proper subordinate specification, which all set together may constitute one more comprehensive *species*: As a Clock, and the several wheels and parts of that Clock may differ in *specie*, though not as coordinate *species*) A Kingdom may possibly be no bigger than a City : But yet the form of a Kingdom and of a City do differ in the *Ends* of the Societies. So a Family in *specie* differeth from a City, which is compact of many Families : so a Troop differeth in *specie* from a Regiment, and a Regiment from an Army, a Colledge from an University, a bed-chamber which is part of an house from an house, though yet it's possible that a house may be but one room, and an University but one Colledge, and an Army but one Regiment, &c.

Now let us enquire whether *de jure divino* there ought to be such a Society as I have described, associating for personal present Communion and assistance as aforesaid. And this I have fully proved before Chap. 3. *Act. 14. 23. They ordained them Elders in every Church. 1 Thes. 5. 12, 13. Know them that labour among and are over you in the Lord, and highly esteem them in love for their works sake : and be at peace among your selves. Heb. 13. 7. 17. Remember them which have the rule over you, who have spoken to you the word of God. Act. 20. 28. Take heed to your selves and to all the flock, &c. v. 31. I ceased not to warn every one night and day with tears. 20. publickly and house by house. 1 Pet. 5. 1, 2, 3. The Elders that are among you, &c. feed the flock (not a particle of the flock)Mat. 18. 15. If thy brother trespass against thee, tell him his fault between thee and him ; If he hear thee not, take two — If he hear not them, tell the Church* —* If with Sel-den, de Synedr.* and the *Erastians* by the Church were meant the *Sanhedrim*, it would tend to the confirmation of what we plead for ; considering how thin both Council (and Synagogues), were, and in how small places. But against that sence, see Galaspies *Aarons* Rod, &c.

Heb. 10. 22. &c. Forsake not the assembling of your selves together, But exhort one another —— *1 Cor. 11. When ye come together in the Church, 1 Cor. 14, &c.* See the Text as forecited Chap. 3.

It is then manifest that Churches associated for such present Communion of Christians, is of Gods appointment, which *Thorndike* in a set Treatise proveth to be the ground of Discipline.

2. Next I will shew that the Bishops of such a particular Church and of a compound Diocese are offices specifically different (*a finibus.*)

1. The Bishop of a particular Church is related to another Correlate, specifically distinct from the said Diocesane : Therefore his office is specifically distinct. The Antecedent is before proved, and the Consequence no sober man will question.

2. And their works are specifically distinct.

1. The work of the one is, 1. To be the ordinary publick Teacher of the Church ; 2. To Congregate the Church ; 3. To be their Guide in present worship ; 4. To give them the Lords Supper ; 5. To watch over and guide them personally in their conversation ; and so of the rest forenamed.

2. The

2. The work of the other is, 1. To send Curates to be the ordinary Teacher, and Guides, and Priests to the people ; even to each Parish one. 2. To have a Lay Chancellors Court to trouble them in a secular mode, and to judge men to excommunication and absolution. 3. To visit some Towns in his Diocese, and there to call together the Clergy and Churchwardens, once in three years, (or a year if he please.) 4. To have an Archdeacon to keep some kind of Courts under him in certain places, by himself or his official. 5. To grant Licences to Marry: 6. And to preach : 7. And to eat flesh in Lent. 8. To suspend or silence Preachers. 9. To lay his hands on Children or others, for the Ceremony of Confirmation; perhaps on the thousandth or five hundredth part of his Diocese, (though *de jure* he should do it to every one) 10. To preach as oft as he please in his Cathedral, or where he will.

But as for the aforesaid work of a Bishop of a particular Church, he is not to do it, nor any one part of it, that I know of. For whereas the *true office* of such a Bishop is (as Dr. *Hammond* in his *Annotat.* well describeth it) by a Ministerial participation to subserve Christ to his whole flock in the threefold work of a teacher, a Priest, and a Ruler, he doth no one part of all. 1. Instead of Teaching *his flock*, he (if he be one of the extraordinary best) doth only publickly preach once or twice a week to the thousandth or five hundredth or hundredth part of his flock: (But so do very few of them, but some it may be once in a month or a year) And as to the personal care of their Souls, he hath not one Parish that he taketh the care of, to teach them personally. 2. He seldom doth officiate in publick Prayer, Praise, and Sacrament to any part of his flock : And when he doth, it is but to a particle of the foresaid proportion : But when others do it, he saith, He doth it by them. 3. He doth not at all govern his flock with that which is the true Pastoral Government ; which is in person among them to guide them, and resolve their doubts, and admit those to Communion that are fit, and refuse the unfit ; To admonish all the scandalous and unruly, as personally known to him, to watch over them and confirm the weak, and refel seducers when they come among them. But instead of this, he never seeth them, (as to the main body of his flock) nor knoweth them, but summoneth their Teachers and Church-wardens, (and such as others that dwell among them, or his Apparitors will accuse to him) to come before his Lay-Chancellours Court, as aforesaid, and in his Visitation to meet him : so that here is none of the same work no nor Government it self, but another kind of Government.

And here note, 1. That the foresaid three parts of the office (Teaching, Worshipping, and Ruling) are all *Essential* to the office ; so that if he wanted but *any One* of them, he were not an Officer of the same *species* with those that have them all, much more if he have but One, yea, not One of all.

2. That the *flock* or *Church* is not to be denominated from a small or inconsiderable part of it, but from the main Body. Therefore he that is the Teacher but of one Congregation of a thousand, or many hundreds, or scores, is not to be therefore called, the Teacher of that Church or Flock, which consisteth of

so

fo many Congregations: And fo alfo for Worſhip and Perſonal conduct, He is not a Prieſt to that flock,&c. Much leſs when he undertaketh not one Pariſh.

Obj. *So you may ſay of one of the old City Churches, ſuch as* Alexandria *where the Biſhop preached but to one Congregation; or of our Pariſhes that have Chappels, where the Curate teacheth in the Chappels; or wherever there are many Presbyters to a Congregation: All do not preach, at leaſt to all the people.*

Anſ. 1. I doubt not but *Alexandria* and all ſuch places, ſhould have had many Churches and Biſhops, as the Chriſtians grew too many to be in and under one.

2. But yet when they had ſeveral Churches and Presbyters, the people were not at all tyed to their own Pariſhes, but might come to hear and joyn with the Biſhop as oft as they pleaſed: which though they could not do all at once, they might do by *turns*, ſome one day and ſome another: And fo they did. So that ſtill they had perſonal Communion with him, though not every day. 3. And they lived in Vicinity, where they were capable of Converſe, and perſonal notice, and private help from one another. 4. And the Presbyters all joyned in perſonal overſight or Government of the whole flock, and were each one capable of perſonal admonition and exhortation to any member. 5. And thoſe that attended the Biſhop and did not frequently officiate in the chief actions, yet were preſent with the Church, and aſſiſted him in officiating, and were ready to do the reſt when-ever he appointed them or there was need: fo that though *quoad exercitium* they did not the chief parts of the work every day, or uſually, yet, 1. it was all the three parts of the *Paſtoral office* which they did, and undertook to do, in ſeaſon: 2. And that to the ſame Church in perſon by themſelves. So that though Churches that ſwell to a diſordered bulk, are not in that perfect order as more capable Societies may be; yet whileſt their Communion is perſonal, preſent, as aforeſaid, the Church *ſpecies* is not altered as in our Dioceſes it is.

III. *A divers fundamentum vel ratio fundandi, proveth a diverſity of Relations: But a true Pariſh Biſhop and our Dioceſanes have fundamenta that are in ſpecie divers; And fo have a particular Church and a Dioceſane Church: Ergo,* a Pariſh Church and Biſhop, and a Dioceſane Church and Biſhop are *ſpecie divers.*

The Major is undeniable. The Minor I prove by ſhewing the diverſity.

1. The *Fundamentum* of the Relation of a Particular Church, is either 1. Of the Relation of the Church to God: 2. Or their relation as fellow members one to another: 3. Or of their joynt relation to their Paſtors or Biſhops: 4. Or of their Biſhops or Paſtors relation to them. For certainly a Church is not only compounded of various Materials, but its *form* is a compounded of theſe *Four Relations* ſet together, and every one is Eſſential to it (And he that cannot diſtinguiſh cannot underſtand.) Now every one of all theſe compounding Relations, is founded in a *mutual conſent.*

1. The Relation of the Members, Paſtors, and the whole Church to God is founded in *Gods conſent and theirs: Gods* is ſignified 1. By his Scripture Inſtitution and Command: 2. By his qualifying and diſpoſing the perſons: 3. By his providential giving them opportunity: 4 And *ad ordinem*

where

where it can be had, by the Ordainers (as to the Paſtors relation) who are Gods miniſters to inveſt them in the office; 5. And by his moving the hearts of the People to conſent (which belongeth to the giving of opportunity.)

The Relation of all theſe to God, is ſecondarily founded in their own conſent (that it may be a *Contract:*) The Paſtors expreſs *theirs,* in their *Ordination* in general, and in their *Induction* or fixing in that particular Church, to the Ordainers, and to the people. The members expreſs *their conſent,* either plainly in a Contract, or *impliedly* by actual convention and ſubmiſſion, and performing of their duties.

2. The Relation of the members to each other, is founded in their ſaid Explicite or Implicite conſent among themſelves, joyned to their foreſaid conſent to God.

3. The Relation of the Members to their Paſtors, is founded Remotely in the ſaid ſignification of Gods will, by his *Word* and *Providence,* and by the Ordainers, (for they are but Miniſters, and operate but by ſignifying Gods will.) And *nextly,* by the mutual conſent of the People and the Paſtors.

4. The Relation of the Paſtors to the flock is accordingly founded, 1. Remotely in the ſaid ſignification of Gods will by his *Word, Gifts, Diſpoſition, Opportunity,* and by the *Miniſtery* of the *Ordainers:* 2. And nextly by the conſent of Paſtors and People. Thus is a particular Church-relation founded, and all theſe parts are neceſſary thereunto.

But as for our Dioceſane Churches, which have no particular Churches under them, nor Biſhops, but only Congregations with ſeveral Curates, being not *politically* and properly Churches, (For I meddle not with ſuch A. Biſhops Dioceſes as conſiſt of many true Churches with their proper Biſhops) let us ſee from what foundation they reſult.

. 1. As to their Relation to God, he never expreſſed his *Conſent,* nor *owneth* them (that ever I could hear proved) And therefore the Fundamental Contract is wanting. Thoſe that go Dr. *Stillingfleet's* and Biſhop *Reynold's* way, and ſay, No Form of Government is of Gods appointment, do grant that the Dioceſane form is not: But that the Congregational form is, I have fully proved. Therefore they have not the ſame Foundation.

2. And as to the Relation of the Members of a Dioceſe to one another, there is no mutual conſent truly nor ſeemingly ſignified by them: what ever ſome few may do, who are not the Dioceſe, it is certain that the Dioceſe as ſuch do neither *Explicitely* nor *Impliedly* by word or deed expreſs any ſuch Church conſent, but rather the clean contrary. For 1. Their *Dwelling* in the Dioceſe is no more a profeſſion of conſent, than the Chriſtians dwelling in *Conſtantinople* ſheweth them to be Mahometans: For their Anceſtors there lived, and they have no other dwelling.

2. Their chooſing a Parliament who conſent is no proof of their conſent. 1. Becauſe it is not paſt a ſixth or tenth or twentieth part of the Members that chooſe Parliament men. 2. Becauſe they never intend to chooſe them for any ſuch uſe as to be the chooſers of their Religion, or Church, and to diſpoſe of their Souls: But only to regulate Church matters according to Gods word, which
when

when they go againſt, they go beyond, and againſt the peoples conſent.   As in chooſing Parliament men, we do not truſt them to chooſe husbands and wives and Maſters and ſervants for all the people : Nor can we commit that truſt (for the choice of our Religion or Church) to others ſtatedly, which Gods Word and Nature have bound us to uſe our ſelves.   Or if ſuch miſchooſe for us, they diſoblige us from accepting their choice. I am ſure the Papiſts think not that they chooſe Parliament men to chooſe a Church for them : Nor would the Prelatiſts think ſo, if the Parliament ſhould prove Presbyterian, Independent, Anabaptiſts, or Papiſts.

3. The Dioceſe doth not *ſignifie Conſent* to a Church relation, by the Church-wardens or accuſed perſons coming to the Chancellors ~or Biſhops Courts.   For 1. It is but a ſmall number comparatively that do ſo.   2. They are compelled , and are well known to come full ſorely againſt their wills : They are undone if they refuſe : And ſubmiſſion and patience, are not ſub-jection nor conſent.   3. They moſt commonly profeſs to come to theſe Courts in obedience to the King, and as they are empowered by him, and ſtrengthened by his ſword : And not at all as Church-Paſtors, empowered by Chriſt : For who taketh the Chancellor to be ſuch ?

4. The appearance of the Clergy at the Biſhops Viſitation , and their Conformity, is no proof of the peoples conſent. For the Miniſters are diſtinct perſons, and have a diſtinct intereſt, and are no way empowered to ſignifie the peoples conſent.

5. Yea, they ſhew their diſſent, 1. By being ſo backward to be made Church-wardens : 2. So backward to take their Oaths : 3. So backward to preſent : 4. So backward to appear at their Courts. 5. Doing it on a civil account as obeying the Kings Officers. 6. So few of them ever coming to a Biſhop to be inſtructed, reſolved, yea or for the ceremony of Confirma-tion.

So that the people can never be proved to conſent to a Dioceſane Church State.

And if they had, that is not the ſame as a conſent to a Congregational or Pariſh Church State.

3. The ſame I need not ſay over again as to the Dioceſane Biſhop, Chan-cellor and Archdeacon : They conſent to the Pariſh Miniſters where they are tolerable, by word or daily attendance in Gods worſhip : But I know *England* ſo well as that I know that as they never chooſe their Biſhops, or Chancellors, (but the King chooſeth them, and a Dean and a few Prebends *pro forma* con-ſent) ſo they are never called to expreſs their conſent, nor do any conſidera-ble part of the Dioceſe uſually conſent indeed ; ſome never mind ſuch matters : others ſay, the King may put in whom he will ; it is no act of theirs : others had rather have a good one than a bad one, but had rather yet have none at all, eſpecially of late ſince ſo many hundred Miniſters are ſilenced. And ſome would have Biſhops to ſilence the Miniſters, and ſome are for them on a better ac-count.   But it's no conſiderable part of the Dioceſe that ſignifieth Conſent. And as for the formal demand to the ſtanders by at the Conſecration, whether

any

any of them have any thing against the Bishop, it's a ceremony fitter for a stage, than to come here into an Argument.

4. And as for the Bishops and Chancellors relation to the People, when it wants the word of God, and his consent, and the peoples consent, and hath but the Kings collation, the Deans and Chapters formal consent, and the Prelates and Conformist Ministers consent, I may well conclude that here is not the same *Fundamentum* as is of the Parochial and Pastors Church relation.

IV. And where there is not the same Relate and Correlate, there is not the same Relation. But a Parochial Church and Pastor, and a Diocesane Church and Pastor, are not the same Relate and Correlate. *Ergo.*

If they be, let them become Parochial Bishops and be still the same. But what I have said of the difference of *Ends* and *Foundations* proveth this; a Combination of Christians into one Church *primi ordinis* for personal Communion, is not the same with a Combination of Congregations for Communion mental or by delegates only. And so of the Bishops of these several Churches.

V. If a Congregational Church or Pastor be of the same *species* with our Diocesane Churches and Prelates, then a Church that extendeth through all the Kingdom, yea to many Kingdoms, yea to the East and West Indies or Antipodes may be of the same *species* also (and so its Pastor.) And so the Pope and his Church may be of the same, (as to the magnitude) But the consequent is false : *Ergo,* so is the antecedent.

The consequence in the Major is evident, because there is *eadem ratio* ; For their reason of denominating a Church *One* is because it hath *One* Bishop ; and by their Principles there may be one Bishop to a Province, to a Kingdom, to an Empire, to the World.

When all the subordinate Bishopricks were taken down to make up this Diocesane Church of *Lincoln* which I live in, the Church was *One,* which before was many. And if all the Bishops were taken down except the two Archbishops, the two remaining Churches I confess would be of the same *species* with a Diocese. Yea, if there were but One Church and Bishop in the Land. And why might not all *Europe* on these terms make one particular Church ? If you say, Because they are not under one King, I answer, 1. That's no reason : A King is a Civil extrinsick Accidental head of a Church as a Church ; and not a Constitutive Head : But a Bishop is an Intrinsecal, Ecclesiastical Constitutive head, without whom it is no Church (unless equivocally.) 2. Ten Kings may agree to give way to One Bishop in all their Kingdoms (as they have done to the Papacy.) 3. The Roman Empire was bigger than *Europe* : Why then might not that have been one only Church of the same *Species* with a Diocese ?

If they say that it is because one man is not capable of doing the work of a Bishop for so many Countreys. I Answer, *Per se,* he cannot do it for the hundredth part of a Diocese : *Per alios* he may do it for all *Europe* : It is but appointing some who shall appoint others, who shall appoint others, (and so to the

the end of the chapter) to do it. There is but one *Abuna in Abaffia* to Ordain, (though numerous Bishops, who have not the Generative faculty ; which *Epiphanius* makes to be the difference between a Bishop and a Presbyter, that the one begets Fathers and the other but Sons : Their Countrey was converted by an Eunuch.) It would be a notable dispute whether all the rest be true Bishops or not (I think Yea ; the Prelatists must think Nay.) And yet *Brierwood* saith that *Abaffia* (after all its great diminutions) is as big as *Italy, France, Spain,* and *Germany.* And doth not the Pope govern *per alios* yet far more, and pretend to govern the whole Christian World? while he sendeth one to *Goa,* another to *Mexico,* (and *Oviedo* to *Abaffia,* would they but have received him.)

Obj. But he hath other Bishops under him, therefore he is not *ejusdem speciei* as a Diocese. *Answ.* But the *Abuna* hath no Ordainers under him. And the Bishop hath Chancellors, Deans, Arch-deacons, Surrogates, Officials, and sometimes in the days of old had *Suffragans* too, under him. (*Quest.* Was a Diocese then, *One Church,* or two ?) And what if a Patriarch or Pope put down all Bishops under him, and exercise his power only by other sorts of officers ? (They that can demise, grant, let, what parts they please of their own office, may devise enow.)

And seeing it would not alter the *species,* what if it should please the King and Parliament to put down all the Bishops of *England* save *One*? I hope the Bishops would not take that to be against the Canon of 1640. nor against the *Oxford* Oath [of never endeavouring to *Consent* or *Alter* the *Church Government*] (if it could have been past to be taken by the Parliament) Because the *species* is not altered : And they tell us Nonconformists to draw us to Swear, that they mean but the *species.* I make no doubt but at the rates of our present Ordinations, One Bishop or *Abuna* with Chaplains enow, may Ordain Priests enow, (and too many of all conscience) for all the Kings Dominions ; and may silence preachers enow, and may set up Chancellors, Surrogates, and Arch-deacons enow to do the present work. And it's pity that the land should be troubled with so many when one would serve. I confess I would either have *more* or *fewer* had I my wish.

And as for my Minor proposition, let him that thinketh it wanteth proof, when he hath considered what is beforesaid, and how personal present Communion in all Gods Church-worship, differeth from the Communion of associated Congregations by messengers, &c. think so still, if he be able so egregiously to err.

But I must not so leave our Prelatists. I know that it is the common trick of Sophisters, when they cannot make good an ill cause, to carry it into the dark, or start a new controversie, and then they are safe. A Papist will wheel about into the wilderness or thickets of Church history, and ask you what names you can give of your Religion in all Ages, that one proposition of your Syllogism may contain much of a Horse load or a Cart load of Books, and then I trow he hath done his work, if women be the judges. And others use to carry the question *a rebus ad verba :* And so it is in the case in hand. But it is not the name of a *SPECIES* that shall serve your turn. We know how hard
it

it is in Physicks, to determine what it is that specifieth; and much more in Morals, Politicks and other Relatives. But Let the Logical notion of a *species* lie at your mercy : It shall suffice us, that you may not make so great a change of the Church-orders and Government of Gods institution, as to turn a thousand or hundred Churches into one ; and to deprive all Parishes or Churches Consociate (or present Communion, of the priviledge of having a Bishop of their own to Teach, Worship, and Govern them presentially and *per se.* As if all the Arch-bishops in the Roman Empire had put down all the Bishops, and called themselves the Bishops of the Churches. Of which more anon.

CHAP. X.

Whether any form of Church Government be instituted by God as necessary ? or all left to humane prudence ?

Obj. **B**Ut *Doctor* Stillingfleet *hath invincibly proved that God hath made no one form of Church Government necessary, but left the choice to humane prudence.*

Answ. I. If so, Why should we all swear to this *one form*, that we will never endeavour *to alter it*? or (as the *& cætera* Oath) never *consent* to the *alteration* of it, when we know not but the King may alter it, or command us to endeavour it ? Must there be such *swearing* to the perpetuating an alterable unnecessary thing?

II. The word [*Form*] signifieth either the essentials of Church policy, or the Integrals, or accidents which Christ himself hath setled : Or else it signifieth only some mutable accidents or modes; which God hath left to humane prudence. Of the first we deny mans power to change them. Of the later we grant it.

1. It is undeniably of Divine institution that there be ordinary publick Assemblies for Gods solemn worship, and the peoples edification. 2. And that Ministers of that office which Christ hath instituted, be the officiating Guides in these Assemblies. 3. And that Cohabiting Christians be the ordinary stated bodies of these assemblies, and not live loosely to go every day as they please from Church to Church, but ordinarily when they can, be setled members of some one Church (To which cohabitation or vicinity, is one *dispositio materiæ*) 4. And that each of these Churches have their proper fixed Pastors, and should not take up with unfixed various passing Ministers, unless in cases of necessary unsetledness.

Act. 2. 1. 42, 44, 46 Heb. 10. 22, &c. & 13. 7, 17, 24. Act. 14. 23. & Act 23. 1 Thes. 5 12, 13. 1 Cor. 5. 14. 16, 20.

N

unſetledneſs. 5. And that theſe ſetled Paſtors ſhould live among the People, and watch over them perſonally, and know them, and be known of them in doctrine and enſample, as to the main body of the flock. 6. That theſe Relations and Communion be by mutual conſent of the Paſtors and the body of the flock. 7. That theſe mutual Relations of Gods appointment and their own conſent do conſtitute them a ſpiritual ſociety of Divine inſtitution. 8. That this Communion muſt be (as our Creed calleth it) a Communion of Saints: that is, of men profeſſing Chriſtianity and Holineſs, and ſeeming ſuch : And muſt extend to a free Communication to each other, for the ſupply of corporal neceſſities ; And to a mutual aſſiſtance of each other in holy living. 9. That therefore there muſt be ſome to diſcern and judge whether the perſons that would enter this Society and Communion, be Profeſſed ſeeming Chriſtians and Saints or not ? And whether they revolt by Hereſie or wicked lives from their profeſſion ? And whether they be impenitent in theſe revoltings ? And therefore having opportunity by preſence or nearneſs to know them and the witneſſes, muſt judge of the credibility of reports or accuſations ? And muſt admoniſh the offenders, and ſeek by all poſſible conviction and exhortation, with patience to draw them to Repentance : And if no perſwaſion will prevail, to refuſe to admit them to the Communion of the Church, and to deliver them the Sacrament of Communion, and to tell them openly of their ſin and danger, and pronounce them lyable to Gods wrath till they do repent, and to charge the Church to avoid Communion with them. 10. It is the particular Paſtors of thoſe Churches, to whoſe office all this belongeth. 11. If that Church have more Paſtors than one, they muſt do all this work in concord, and not divide nor thwart each other. So that as many Phyſicians undertake one Patient, as each one ſingly of the ſame office, and yet muſt do all by agreement, unleſs ſome one ſee that the reſt would kill the patient ; ſo it is in this caſe. 12. All theſe particular Churches muſt in their vicinities and capacities, live in Concord, and hold ſuch a correſpondency, and Communion of Churches for mutual ſtrength and edification, as tendeth to the common good of all : The means of which are Meſſengers, Letters, and Synods as there is occaſion. All theſe twelve particulars I doubt not but ſo judicious and worthy a man as Dr. *Stillingfleet* will eaſily concede. And indeed the ſumme of them is granted in his book. And then whether you will call this a Form of Government or not, how little care I for the meer name ? 13. I may add this much more, that All theſe Congregations are under the extrinſick Government of the Magiſtrate, as Phyſicians are : And he only can rule them by the ſword and force.

But then we will agree with Dr. *Stillingfleet* or any man, that God hath left all theſe things following without a particular determination to be determined according to his General Laws. 1. Whether this Parochial or Congregational Church ſhall always meet in one and the ſame place ; or in caſe of perſecution or want of room, or by reaſon of the Age, Weakneſs, and diſtance of ſome Members, may have ſeveral houſes or Chappels of eaſe, where ſome parcels may ſometimes meet, who yet (at leaſt *per vices*) may have perſonal preſent
Communion.

Marginal notes (left column): 1 Pet. 5. 1, 2, 3. 1 Tim. 3. & Tit. 1. 5, &c. 1 Cor. 16. 1, 2. 1 Cor. 11. Mat. 28. 19, 20. Mat. 18. 15 Tit. 3. 10.

Communion with the rest. 2. Whether a Church shall be great or small, that is, of what number it shall consist, supposing that it be not so *great* or *so small* as to be inconsistent with the end. 3. How many Pastors each Church shall have. 4. Whether among many One shall be a Chief, and upon supposition of his preeminence in Parts, Grace, Age, and Experience, shall voluntarily be so far submitted to by the rest, as may give him a Negative voice. 5. Whether such officers of many Churches, shall consociate so as to joyn in Classes or Synods stated for number, time and place. And whether their meetings shall be constant, or occasional *pro re nata*. 6. Whether One in these meetings shall be a stated Moderator, or only *pro tempore*, and shall have a Negative voice or not, in the circumstantials of their Synodical work. 7. Whether certain Agreements called Canons, shall be made voluntarily to bind up the several Members of the Synods to one and the same way in undetermined circumstances of their callings; or as an agreement and secondary obligation to their certain duties. 8. Whether these Associations or Synods shall by their Delegates constitute other provincial or larger associations for the same Ends: Who those Delegates shall be. Whether one in those larger Synods also shall have such a Negative as aforesaid. All these and such like we grant to be undetermined: And if they will call only such Humane modes and circumstances by the name of Forms of Government, we quarrel not *de nomine*, but *de re* do grant that such kind of Forms or Formalities are not particularly determined of in Gods word.

9. And besides all these, whether successors of the Apostles in the ordinary part of their work, as A. Bishops or General Ministers having the care of many inferiour Bishops and Churches, be not *Lawful*, yea, of *Divine right*, or whether they be unlawful is a question which all Nonconformists are not agreed on among themselves, so great is the difficulty of it. But for my own part, being unsatisfied in it, I never presumed to meddle in any Ordinations, lest it should belong to Apostolical A. Bishops only; and I resolved to submit herein to the order of the Church wherever I should live.

III. But if you hold that Dr. *Stillingfleet*, Bishop *Reynolds*, and all those Conformists who say that no Church Form is *jure divino necessaria*, do extend this (as expresly they do) to the Diocesane Form, Let it be observed, 1. That we plead for no more than we have proved, (and they will confess I think) to be *jure divino*. 2. And that we plead against *swearing* and *subscribing* to nothing but what they themselves say is not of Gods institution. 3. That the proper Prelatists affirm it to be of Divine Institution, or else they will renounce it. 4. That the preface of the book of Ordination to which we must subscribe or declare Assent and Consent, doth make this Episcopacy to be a distinct Order from Presbyters, as a thing certain by Gods word. This therefore I wonder how they can subscribe to, who say no Form is *jure divino*: I am sure they *perswade* us not to subscribe it, while they disprove it.

And I would have leave to debate the Case of the Church of *England* a little with these Humanists, and to ask them, If no Church Form be of Gods making, 1. Why may not the King and Parliament put it down as aforesaid?

2. But

2. But specially who made the Form of the Church of *England* which we must swear to ——— If another Church, then that other was not of the same Form; otherwise that Form was made before, which is a contradiction. If it was of another Form, I ask, what it was? and who made the Form of that other Church which made this Church Form? and so to the Original? If Bishops or Synods made it, still they were parts of a Church, or of no Church If of no Church, what Bishops were those, and by what power did they make new Church Forms that were of none themselves? If an Emperor or King first made them, either he was himself a member of a Church, or of no Church. If of a Church, what form had that Church? And why should not that first form stand? And who made that form? and so *ad originem*. If he was of *no Church,* how came he by power to make Church forms, that was of none himself? *Nemo dat quod non habet.* It's no honour to Prelacy to be so made. And were they Christians or no Christians that made the Diocesane Form? If Christians, were they *orderly* Christians, or rebellious? If orderly, how happened it that they were of no Church themselves, when the Apostles setled so much of Church Form and Order, as I have before named? If rebellious, they were a dishonourable original of Diocesanes.

And if the *Church Form* be not of *Divine institution,* then the *Church* it self is not. For *forma dat nomen & esse.* And so the cause is given up to the *Brownists* by these Learned moderate men, so far as that there is no *Church* in *England* of *Divine institution.* Were it not that when in general they have said that *no Church Form* of Government is so Divine, they again so far unsay it, as to confess the Parish Churches or Congregations with their Pastors to be of Divine institution and of continued necessity.

All that is to be said by and for them is this, That the Apostles were the makers of the English or Diocesane Form, but not of that only, but of the Presbyterian (and Independent) also; and so made no one necessary but left all indifferent: Or that they made one of these Forms as mutable, allowing men to change it.

Answ. But 1. I have proved what they made; Let them prove that they made any other, of a different sort, not subordinate or supraordinate, if they can. 2. And let them prove the mutability of that which they made, and their power to change it, which they assert. Till one of these is proved, we are or should be in possession of that which was certainly first made.

I am bold to conclude this argument with the speech of a *bold* but a wise and holy man, *Joh. Chrysostome de Sacerdotio lib.* 3. *pag.* (*mihi*) 48. *cap.* 15. [*And when some* (Bishops) *have obtained that prefecture of a Province not belonging to them*, *and others of one* FAR GREATER THAN THEIR OWN *proper* STRENGTH CAN BEAR, THEY CERTAINLY BRING TO PASS, THAT THE CHURCH OF GOD SEEMETH NOTHING TO DIFFER FROM AN EURIPUS (*or a confused turbulent changeling thing*). —— *& pag.* 49. AND DO NOT THESE THINGS DESERVE GODS THUNDERBOLT A THOUSAND TIMES? ARE THEY NOT WORTHY TO BE PUNISHED WITH
THE

THE FIRE OF HELL? NOT THAT *hell* WHICH THE HOLY
SCRIPTURES THREATEN TO US; BUT EVEN OF ONE
THAT IS FAR MORE GRIEVOUS.] Forgive the words, my Lords;
They are not mine but *Chrysostome's*: or if you will not forgive the citing of
them, I will bear it as he did the like. Only I will abate you in my prognostication, or sentence, that *far sorer hell fire* than the Scripture threatneth, supposing this will be sharp enough, even for the most dispersing, silencing persecuting Prelate; and imputing those words to honest *Chrysostome's* vehement
Oratory. And I'le tell you what went next before these words, [*And they do
not only take in the unworthy* (into the Priesthood) *but they cast out the worthy:
For as if they had agreed both ways to spoil the Church of God, and the first cause
were not enough to kindle the wrath of God, they add the second, or worse, to the
former. For I judge it equally pestilent to drive out the Profitable, and to take in the
unprofitable : which certainly they do, that the flock of Christ may from no part
either find consolation, or be able to take breath*] O what would this man have
said had he lived now in *England* !

C H A P. XI.

*Argument 3. From the destruction of the order of Pres-
byters of Divine Institution, and the Invention of a
new order of Sub-half-Presbyters in their stead.*

ARGUMENT III.

THE *office of Presbyters instituted by the Holy Ghost containeth an Obligation and
Authority to Guide by Doctrine, Worship, and Discipline the flocks committed
to their care : But the office of a Diocesane, being one only Bishop over many score
or hundred Congregations, is destructive of that office of Presbyters, which containeth
an obligation and authority to Guide by Doctrine, Worship, and Discipline, (or
the exercise of the Church keys) the flocks committed to their care. Therefore the
office of such a Diocesane is destructive of the office of Presbyters instituted by the Holy
Ghost.*

The Major is thus proved by the Enumeration of the Acts which contain
the general office, and by the proof of the General power extending to those
Acts: *viz.*

1. They

1. They that had the Authority and Obligation to exercise the Church keys in the Scripture sence, had the authority and obligation to Guide their flocks by Doctrine, Worship, and Discipline. But the Presbyters of the Holy Ghosts institution had the authority and obligation to exercise the Church keys, in the Scripture sence: *Ergo* they had authority and obligation to Guide their flocks by Doctrine, Worship, and Discipline.

2. Again: The office which contained an *Authority* and *Obligation* to Teach, Exhort, Rebuke, publickly and privately, to judge of persons baptizable and to baptize them, to Pray, Praise God, and administer the Lords Supper to the Church, and to judge of them that are to receive it, to watch over them privately, and publickly to Excommunicate the obstinately impenitent, and absolve the penitent, doth contain authority and obligation to Guide that flock by Doctrine, Worship, and Discipline. But such is the Office of Presbyters as instituted by the Holy Ghost. — *Ergo* — &c.

Here note 1. That I am not now medling with the Questions, Whether such Presbyters hold this power in subordination to any superiour Bishops ; nor whether there lie any appeal from them to a higher power in the Church ? 2. Nor am I now questioning, Whether in Scripture sence Bishops and Presbyters are all one in Name or thing.

3. But that which I maintain is, 1. That there is no proof in Scripture that God ever instituted any order of Presbyters which had not the forementioned power of the keys. 2. And that God did institute such an Order of Presbyters as *had* that power, *de nomine & de re.* And 3. That the Diocesane Office destroyeth such, and setteth up others in their stead. What God instituted I will prove 1. Out of the Scripture records, 2. Out of the History of the Church which long retained them, in some degree.

CHAP.

CHAP. XII.

That God instituted such Presbyters as had the foresaid power of the Keys, in Doctrine, Worship, and Discipline; and no other, proved by the Sacred Scriptures.

THat God instituted such Presbyters and no other, I shall prove by the enumeration and perusal of all the Texts of Scripture which mention them, (*viz.* as instituted in the New Testament, and now in force.)

Act. 14. 23. *When they had Ordained them Elders in every Church* — Compared with *Tit.* 1. 5. *That thou shouldest Ordain Elders in every City, as I had appointed thee* — 7. *For a Bishop must be blameless as the steward of God.* And his *power* is described *v.* 11, 13. *Ch.* 2. 1, 7, 15. and 3. 10. intimate it. Compare this with 1 *Tim.* 3. 1, 2, 5, 6.

1 *Tim.* 5. 17. *Let the Elders that rule well be counted worthy of double honour; especially they who labour in the Word and Doctrine:* compared with 1 *Cor.* 9. 14. *Gal.* 6. 6. which shew that preaching the Gospel was their work, as well as Ruling the Churches under them, as 1 *Cor.* 12. 28. *Eph.* 4. 11, 12. *Rom.* 12. 7, 8. intimate.

Acts 20. 17, 28. *He sent to Ephesus and called the Elders of the Church* — *Take heed to your selves and to all the flocks over the which the Holy Ghost hath made you overseers,* (or Bishops) *to feed* (or rule) *the Church of God which he hath purchased with his own bloud. v.* 31. *Therefore watch &c. v.* 35. *So labouring, ye ought to support the weak.*

Acts 11. 30. *They sent it to the Elders by the hands of Barnabas and Saul. Acts* 15. 2. 6. 22, 23. *To the Apostles and Elders* — *And the Apostles and Elders came together to consider* — *Then pleased it the Apostles and Elders with the whole Church* — *The Apostles, Elders, and Brethren send greeting* — See *v.* 25, 28.

Acts 16. 4. *The decrees which were ordained of the Apostles, and Elders which were at Jerusalem.*

Acts 21. 18. *The day following Paul went in with us unto James, and all the Elders were present* —

1 *Tim.* 4. 14. *Neglect not the gift which is in thee, which was given thee by prophecy, with the laying on of the hands of the Presbytery* —

1 *Pet.* 5. 1. *The Elders which are among you I exhort, who also am an Elder, — Feed the flock of God which is among you, taking the oversight* (or Episcopacy) *thereof, not by constraint but willingly* — *Neither as being Lords over Gods heritage, but being ensamples to the flock. And when the chief Shepherd shall appear* —

2 *Joh.*

2 *Joh.* 1. *The Elder to the Elect Lady ------*

Whether those Texts, 1 *Tim.* 5. 1. *Rebuke not an Elder. v.19: Receive not an accusation against an Elder*] speak of an Elder by Office or by Age, is uncertain ; if it be by *Office,* the other Texts describe them.

Jam. 5. 14. *Is any man sick? Let him call for the Elders of the Church.* All these Texts shew that every Church had Elders by the institution of the Holy Ghost : That they were the Teachers, Worshippers, Rulers, and were among the people, present with their flock, personally doing their Offices, &c. And the Scripture mentioneth no other that I can find.

And of this I have Dr. *Hammonds* full confession, *Annotat. in Act.*11. *& dissert.* before cited : with all those whom he mentioneth of his party and mind. And as for them of the contrary opinion, they tell us that in Scripture times the Names Presbyter & Bishop were common : And that the word [Bishops] sometimes signified all the Presbyters (the Bishops as Presbyters and the Subpresbyters) as in *Phil.* 1. 1,2. And that the word [Presbyters] sometimes signifieth the Bishops only, and sometime both conjunctly : But they are none of them able to give us any one instance with proof, of a Text which speaketh of Subject Presbyters? (I mean subject in Order or degree to Bishops of the single Churches, and not subject to the Apostles and General officers.) And while we prove that God appointed such entire Presbyters as are here described, and they cannot prove against (Dr. *Hammond* or us) that any one text speaketh of a lower order or rank, I think we need no other Scripture evidence.

CHAP. XIII.

The same confirmed by the Ancients.

AS for Humane testimony, the heap is so great brought in by *Dav. Blondel,* that I have the less mind to say any more of it ; But shall only (besides all that is said before on the by) recite a few of those testimones which most convinced my own understanding in the reading of them in the Authors themselves, leaving others to take what they see best out of *Blondels* store.

I. I know that somewhat may be said against what I shall first cite, but I think not of sufficient force. I begin with it, though not first in time, because first in Authority. The 1. *Concil. Nicen.* in their Epistle to the Church of *Alexand.* and all the Churches of *Egypt, Libya,* and *Pentapolis,* thus decree concerning those that were Ordained by *Meletius,* (as *Socrat. lib.* 1. c. 6. translated by *Grynæus*) *Hi autem qui Dei gratia & vestris precibus adjuti ad nullum lium schisma deflexisse comperti sunt, sed intra Catholicæ & Apostolicæ Ecclesiæ fines ab erroris labe vacuos se continuerint, authoritatem habeant tum Ministros ordinandi, tum eos qui clero digni fuerint nominandi, tum denique omnia ex lege & instituto Ecclesiastico libere exequendi*] Now ordaining Ministers and nominating men for the Clergy, are acts which, if any, shew Presbyters to be Rulers in the Church.

Obj. 1. *Perhaps it is Bishops ordained by* Meletius *that are here spoken of: or Bishops with the Presbyters respectively.*

Answ. There is no more in the Text but this, [*They decreed further touching such as were entred into holy Orders by his laying on of hands, that they, after confirmation with more mystical laying on of hands should be admitted into the fellowship of the Church, with this condition that they should enjoy their dignity and degree of Ministry, yet that they be inferiour to all the Pastors throughout every province and Church ---- Moreover that they have no authority to elect the Ministers approved by their censures, no not so much as to nominate them which are to execute the Ecclesiastical functions, nor to intermeddle with any thing touching them that are within Alexanders jurisdiction, without the consent of the Bishop of the Catholick Church.*] And then they add as afore, that those that fell *not into Schism* (as they did) *shall have authority to Consecrate Ministers, and nominate such as shall be thought worthy of the Clergy.* Now that it is Presbyters and not Bishops that are here spoken of appeareth. 1. In that it is without any note of eminency said to be [*such as were entred into Holy Orders.*] 2. In that it is such as so entred by the Laying on of *Meletius's* hands: Whereas a Bishop must be ordained by the hands of *three Bishops.* And the Schism of one of the three, would not have frustrated the Ordination, if the other two stood firm in the Catholick Union. 3. Because it is the priviledge of Presbyters that is denyed them: Though they be not degraded, they are to be below all other Pastors in every Church: which cannot be, that they shall be Bishops below all Presbyters. 4. Because the consent of the Bishop of the Catholick Church (where they shall come) is necessary to their officiating. But if it could have been proved that Bishops had been here included, yet while Presbyters also are included, it will not invalidate the testimony. But indeed here is no such proof. I confess that *Nicephorus* (a less credible Author) seemeth to apply it to Bishops Ordained by *Meletius*: But no such thing can be gathered out of *Sozomen,* either *Tripart. lib.* 1. *c.* 18. where he describeth *Meletius* and his party, or *Tripart lib.* 2. *c.* 12. where he reciteth the same Epistle that *Socrates* doth. But I would pretend to no more certainty than is evident.

Yet I doubt not that they were not to Consecrate Ministers alone without the Bishop.

II. *Pius Episcop. Roman. in Biblioth. Pat. Tom.* 3. *p.* 15. *Epist. Justo Episcopo inquit,* [*Presbyteri & Diaconi non ut Majorem, sed ut Ministrum Christi te observent ------ salutat te senatus pauper Christi apud Romam constitutus: saluta omne Collegium fratrum qui tecum sunt in Domino ------* And *epist. prima eidem Justo,* he reckoneth *Timothy* and *Mark* with the *Presbyters* educated by the *Apostles.* Now if they were of the *Senate,* the *Colledge,* and the same name *Presbyters* as Bishops had, we have no reason to think that they had not the power of the keys.

O   III. *Tertullian*

III. *Tertullian de pœnit.* to caſt himſelf *down* at the *feet* of the *Presbyters*; which implyeth that they had the power of the keys for Abſolution : And thoſe whom he calleth [*Seniores*] *Apolog.* managed the Diſcipline, and that not in a Chancellors Court, but in the ſame Congregations where and when they Aſſembled for publick worſhip. If any will ſay that Biſhops are here included, I will not deny it; But if they will ſay that when he nameth the *Seniors* and Presbyters without diſtinction, that he *excludeth* all ſave the Biſhop alone, I ſhall not believe that *Tertullian* ſpeaketh ſo un-intelligibly. Unleſs they will follow Dr. *Hammond* and believe (as I do not) that there was yet but *One* Presbyter, who was the Biſhop in a Church, or in moſt Churches : which *de facto* would be for us.

IV. The Teſtimonies of *Clem. Roman. Ignat. Juſtin Martyr,* may be gathered out of the words forecited. *Hierom's* Teſtimony in this caſe is ſo plain and full, and trite in every writing (*Epiſt ad Evagr. & paſſim,* making them the *Apoſtles Succeſſors,* and the *ſame* with the Biſhops, except only in ordination) that I will not trouble you with reciting it.

Epiſt. 28.
p.64.Edit.
Goulartii.

V. *Cyprian* neither would nor could govern his Church without the concurrence of the Presbyters : (before cited) *De Gaia deſideraſtis ut de Philumeno & Fortunato hypodiaconis & Favorino acolutho, reſcribam: cui rei non potui me ſolum judicem dare ; cum multi adhuc de Clero abſentes ſint; nec locum ſuum vel ſero repetendum putaverint, & hæc ſingulorum tractanda ſit & limanda plenius ratio; non tantum cum collegis meis, ſed & cum plebe ipſa univerſa. Epiſt.36. (edit. Goulart.*) He ſheweth that it is the Clergies duty, to take care of the widows, the ſick, the poor, the ſtrangers: (he the Biſhop was then abſent.) So alſo *Ep.37.* And *Epiſt.*10. he reprehendeth the Presbyters for reconciling and abſolving the Lapſed overhaſtily and with neglect and contempt of the Biſhop; but not as if the work were not their office work to do : Nay he giveth us this full plain teſtimony, that even in this publick Abſolution *in foro exteriore,* the true cuſtom of the Church was for the Biſhop and his Presbyters together to impoſe hands on the penitent and ſo abſolve them, receive them, and give them the Sacrament. *Pag.* 30. ſaith he, *Nam cum in minoribus peccatis*

The next
Epiſ. 7. is
worthy to
be read of
all that
ſuffer for
the truth
to keep
them from
pride, un-
rulineſs,
and ſcan-
dal. and ſo
is the 8.

agant peccatores pœnitentiam juſto tempore, & ſecundum diſciplinæ ordinem, ad exomologeſin veniant, & per impoſitionem manus Epiſcopi & Cleri. jus Communionis accipiant ; Nunc credo tempore, perſecutione adhuc perſeverante, nondum reſtituta Eccleſiæ ipſius pace, ad Communicationem admittuntur, & offertur nomen eorum, & nondum pœnitentia acta, nondum exomologeſi facta, nondum manu eis ab Epiſcopo & Clero impoſita, Euchariſtia illis datur.]

Epiſt. 5. *p.* 15. He writeth to the Clergy in his abſence to do the work of Diſcipline, even their own part and his, and (as no man doubteth but they did the whole work in the publick aſſembly when he was abſent ſo long time, ſo (that you may ſee what kind of Chappel meetings they had) it being the cuſtome for encouragement of ſufferers, to go to the Confeſſors

and.

and visit them and there celebrate the Sacrament,) he perſwadeth them that the people may not go crowding by great companies at once, leſt it ſtir up envy, and they be denied entrance (it's like they were in Priſon) and loſe all while they are inſatiable to get more : But that one Presbyter and one Deacon go one day, and another another day by turns, becauſe the Change of perſons, and viciſſitude of meeters would break the envy : and all ſhould be done in meekneſs and humility.

But the words I inſiſt on are, [*Peto vos pro fide & religione veſtra, fungamini illic &* Veſtris *partibus &* meis, *ut nihil vel ad diſciplinam vel ad diligentiam deſit.*] And if the whole work of Diſcipline be ſuch as is partly their own part, and partly what they may do in the Biſhops abſence in his ſtead, it is within the power of their function : For a Lay-man or a Deacon cannot do all the Presbyters work in his abſence.

And *Epiſt. 6. p. 17.* Having exhorted the ſufferers or confeſſors not to grow proud by it, and lamented that ſome after ſufferings grew inſolent and were a ſhame to the Church, he addeth (*Nec a Diaconis aut Presbyteris regi poſſe,*] Shewing that even the Government of the Confeſſors belonged to them both in their places: And of himſelf he ſaith to his Presbyters, *Solus reſcribere nihil* potui, *quando a primordio Epiſcopatus mei ſtatuerim nihil ſine conſilio veſtro, & ſive Conſenſu Plebis mea , privata ſententia gerere — ſed cum venero ---- in Commune tractabimus ——* As to them that ſay, This was only *Cyprians* arbitrary condeſcenſion, I anſwer, 1. He ſaith *Non potui,* And 2. he elſewhere ſpeaketh of it as due, 3. It agreeth with the Canons and cuſtomes of thoſe times: 4. *Cyprian* pleadeth ſo much for the Biſhops prerogative, that we have little reaſon to think him both ſo ſubmiſſive and imprudent, as to bring up ill cuſtomes, and teach the Miniſters and people to expect that as their part which belonged not to them, and ſo to corrupt the Church.

And in the *Ep. 11. p. 32.* again he ſaith [*Ante exomologeſin graviſſimi & extremi delicti factam, ante manum ab Epiſcopo & Clero in pænitentem impoſitam, offerre lapſis pacem & Euchariſtiam dare, id eſt ſanctum Domini corpus profanare audeant ------*

The ſame he hath again *Ep. 12. p. 37.* (with an *examinabuntur ſingula praſentibus & judicantibus vobis* (that is, the people, to ſhew how great the Church was.)

Afterward *Ep. 14.* he directeth the Presbyters to abſolve thoſe by Impoſition of hands themſelves without him that are infirm and in danger, but that the reſt muſt be publickly reconciled in the Church *praſente & ſtantium plebe.* To recite all of this nature in *Cyprian,* would be too long.

VI. I will add next a General Teſtimony *viz.* the conſtant cuſtome of all Churches, even *Rome* it ſelf, where the Presbyters have Governed without a Biſhop in the intervals, when after one Biſhops death another was not choſen. As before the choice of *Fabian's* ſucceſſor you may ſee by the Epiſtles of the *Roman* Clergy to *Cyprian. Marcien* was expelled by the *Roman* Presbytes

ſide

sede vacante, Epiphan. Hæref. 42. And if they had the power over one another, more over the flock.

See Inftan-ces in Blondel. §. 3. p. 183, 184.

And I need bring no particular proofs of this: For when Biſhops have been baniſhed, impriſoned, dead, and the ſeat vacant a year, yea, divers years to-gether (as it hath been at *Rome*) was the Church no Church all that time? Had it no Government? Was there no power of the Keys? Was the Church laid common to all? This inftance is ſo full as nothing can be ſaid againſt it, but that it was in *Caſe of Neceſſity.* But that only proveth that it is the Presbyters office work, though out of a caſe of neceſſity they muſt do it with the Biſhop, and not without him. But a Lay-man may not do a Presbyters proper work on ſuch a pretence. However the Church by this practice hath declared it's judgment in the caſe.

VII. *Concil. Carthag.* 4. *Can.* 23. is [*Ut Epiſcopus nullius cauſam audiat abſque præſentia Clericorum ſuorum ; Alioquin irrita erit ſententia Epiſcopi, niſi Clericorum præſentia confirmetur.* If it be ſaid that here is no mention of their *Conſent,* but of their *Preſence* only, I anſwer, It is a preſence neceſſary to the Confirmation of the Biſhops ſentence : and the preſence of Diſſenters would rather *infirm* the ſentence (more than their abſence) than confirm it. And the conjunct Canons ſhew that it is *Conſent* that is meant. For,

Can. 32. it's ſaid [*Irrita erit donatio Epiſcoporum, vel venditio, vel commutatio rei Eccleſiaſticæ, abſque conniventia & ſubſcriptione Clericorum :* where ſuch a *Connivence* is meant as is joyned with *ſubſcription.* And if *ſubſcription* of the Presbyters was neceſſary in theſe caſes, no leſs than *Conſent* is meant in the other.

Which is yet more apparent by thoſe following Canons, which forbid the Biſhop to *Ordain* without his Clergy, or to accuſe any of them but by proof in a Synod, or to ſuffer a Presbyter to ſtand while he ſitteth. And the Canons that place the Biſhop *in conſeſſu Presbyterorum ;* and ſet him in the midſt of them in the ſame ſeat in the Church, and call him their Colleague : The Canons which make the Presbyters Governours of the Rural Churches, and make the Deacons ſervants to them, of which the number is too great to be now recited ------

Note it is not conſilio but concilio.

Even here *Can.* 22. it's ſaid [*Epiſcopus ſine Concilio Clericorum ſuorum Clericos non ordinet : Ita ut Civium aſſenſum & conniventiam & teſtimonium quærat.*] And if not *ſine concilio* *, then not *contra conſilium.* And if the conſent of the Laity be neceſſary, ſure the Clergies is ſo too.

Can. 29. *Epiſcopus ſi Clerico vel Laico crimen impoſuerit, deducatur ad probationem in Synodum. Can.* 30. *Caveant Judices Eccleſiæ ne abſente eo cujus cauſa ventilatur ſententiam proferant ; quia irrita erit, imo & cauſam in Synodo pro facto dabunt.* And if a Biſhop muſt not ſo much as *accuſe* but in a Synod on proof, much leſs might he be judge alone.

Can. 33. appointeth that Biſhops or Presbyters ſhall be invited to preach, and conſecrate the Oblation, when they come into ſtrange Churches] So far there was no difference.

Can.

Can. 34. Ut Episcopus in quolibet loco sedens, stare Presbyterum non patiatur.

35. Ut Episcopus in Ecclesia & in consessu Presbyterorum sublimior sedeat. Intra domum vero Collegam Presbyterorum se esse cognoscat.

Can. 36. Presbyteri qui per Diœcesses Ecclesias regunt, &c.

Can. 37. Diaconus ita se Presbyteri, ut Episcopi ministrum esse cognoscat. vid. & Can. 38, 39, 40.

Yea even in Ordination it is said, *Can. 2. Presbyter quum Ordinatur, Episcopo cum benedicente, & manum super ejus tenente, etiam omnes Presbyteri qui præsentes sient manus suas juxta manum Episcopi, super Caput illius teneant. Et Can. 3. Diaconus quum ordinatur solus Episcopus, qui eum benedicit, manus super caput illius ponat: quia non ad Sacerdotium sed ad ministerium consecratur]* So that Priesthood was to be conferred by the hands of Priests, and the Bishop's alone was not enough; But Deacons might be Ordained by a Bishop without Presbyters.]

What need I tire the Reader with other Councils testimonies? when this, though called Provincial having 214 Bishops, and among them *Aurelius, Augustine, &c.* is no less valuable than any General Council in the volumes of the Councils.

VIII. In the Arabick Canons of the *Concil. Nic.* I. (which I cite not for their justification, but as testifying the matter of fact in the times of which they were written whensoever it was) it's said, *Can. 47.* After one Bishop is forbid to absolve him that another hath Excommunicated [*Eadem Lex erit de Sacerdote, id est, Ut nullus Sacerdos solvat aut liget quem alius Sacerdos solverit aut ligaverit, quamdiu ille qui solvit aut ligavit vixerit: Post mortem vero successor ejus solvet cum mortuus ligavit: sed debet Episcopus præesse huic negotio----- Neque convenit ut Episcopus aut Archiepiscopus solvat aut liget eum, qui digne a Sacerdote solutus aut ligatus sint, quamdiu ille qui solvit aut ligavit vixerit.*] Here you see the Priest may bind and loose, and that *in foro Ecclesiastico* : yea so fast that no Bishop or Archbishop may loose or bind contrarily during his life. Then Presbyters had the keys.

And *Can. 57.* (according to other Canons cited before) they say.[The Arch-Presbyter in the Bishops absence shall be honoured as the Bishop, because he is in his place ; and let him be the Head of the Priests, who are under his power in the Church, with all that the Archdeacon is over.] And if one Presbyter may Rule the rest as a Bishop, the Government of the flock is not above their Order or place. If it be said that he doth it as the Bishops Deputy, it is answered oft enough before. Spiritual Power (or Pastoral) is deputable to none but such as are of the same Order: which is not properly a deputation.

IX. Presbyters had power to Baptize and to celebrate the Lords Supper, Therefore they had power to judge who were Baptizable, and who were capable of the Lords Supper : For 1. Else they would not do it as Christs Ministers, but as the executioners of anothers judgment. And if so, they may give both Sacraments to Turks and Infidels if they be bid. And then indeed the Priest is not the Baptizer or Consecrater Morally, but the Bishop doth

it

it by the Prieſt : All which are falſe. And a Presbyter may preach and Baptize in any Infidel Kingdom, where no Biſhop hath any Dioceſe, and this as an ordinary caſe (in *Turky, Tartary, China, Japan, &c.*) And what Biſhop ſhall there tell him *whom* to Baptize where there is no Biſhop ? And the power of Baptizing is the firſt and greateſt Key of the Church, even the Key of admiſſion.

And they that do among us deny a Presbyter the power of judging whom to Baptize and give the Lords Supper to, do not give it to the Biſhop (who knoweth not of the perſons) But the Directive part they commit to a Convocation of Biſhops and Presbyters ; and the Judicial partly to the Prieſt, and partly to a Lay-Chancellor.

X. *Epiphanius Hæreſ.* 75. ſaith, [The Apoſtles did not ſet all in full order at once : And at firſt there was need of Presbyters and Deacons ; by whom both Eccleſiaſtical affairs may be adminiſtred : Therefore where no man was found worthy of Epiſcopacy, in that place no Biſhop was ſet] By which it appeareth that he thought that for ſome time ſome Churches were Governed without Biſhops : And if ſo, it there belonged to the Presbyters office to govern.

Whereto we may add the opinion of many Epiſcopal men, who think that during the Apoſtles times, they were the only Biſhops in moſt Churches themſelves. And if ſo, Then in their long and frequent abſence the Presbyters muſt be the governours.

XI. That many Councils have had Presbyters, yea many of them is paſt doubt : Look but in the Councils ſubſcriptions and you will ſee it. A Synod of ſome Biſhops and more Presbyters and Deacons gathered at *Rome*, decreed the Excommunication of *Novatianus* and his adherents, *Euſeb. lib. 6. c.43.*

Noetus was convented, judged, expelled by the Seſſion of Presbyters, *Epiphan. Hæreſ.* 47. c. 1.

See a great number of inſtances of Councils held by Biſhops with their Presbyters in *Blondel, de Epiſc. ſect. 3. p.* 202. Yea one was held at *Rome præſidentibus cum Joanne* 12 *Presbyteris, An.* 964. *vid. Blond. p.* 203, 206, 207.

Yea they had places and votes in General Councils: Not only *ut aliorum procuratores,* as *Victor* and *Vincentius* in *Nic.* 1. but as the Paſtors of their Churches, and in their proper right. I need not urge *Selden*'s Arabick Catalogue in *Eutych. Alex.* where there were two perſons for divers particular places : or *Zonaras* who ſaith, There were Prieſts, Deacons and Monks ; nor *Athanaſius* a Deacon's preſence: Even of late the Council of *Baſil* is a ſufficient proof.

XII. The foreſaid Canons of *Carthage* which are ſo full, are inſerted into the body of the Canon Law, and in the Canons of *Egbert* Archbiſhop of *York,* as Biſhop *Uſher* and others have obſerved.

XIII. *Hierom*'s

XXIII. *Hierom*'s [*Communi Presbyterorum Concilio Ecclesiæ gubernabantur,*] seconded by *Chryfostome* and other Fathers, is a trite, but evident testimony.

XIV. That Presbyters had the Power of Excommunications see fully proved by *Calderwood, Altar. Damasc. p.* 273.

XV. *Basil*'s, *Anaphora Bibl. Pat. Tom.* 6. *p.* 22. maketh every Church to have Archpresbyters, Presbyters, and Deacons, making the Bishop to be but the Archpresbyter.

C H A P. XIV.

The Confessions of the greatest and Learnedest Prelatists.

I. **T**He Church of *England* doth publickly notifie her judgment, that Church Government, Discipline, and the power of the Keys is not a thing aliene from or above the Order of the Presbyters, but belongeth to their office. **1.** In that they allow Presbyters to be members of Convocations (and that as chosen by the Presbyters.) And whereas it is said, that the Lower house of Convocation are but Advisers to the Upper, I answer, All together have but an advising power to the King and Parliament; But in that sort of power, the lower house hath its part, as experience sheweth.

2. There are many exempt Jurisdictions in *England*, (as the Kings Chappel, The Deanry of *Windsor*, and *Wolverhampton*, *Bridgenorth*, (where six Parishes are governed by a Court held by a Presbyter) and many more, which shew that it is consistent with the Presbyters office.

3. The Archdeacons who are no Bishops exercise some Government; And so do their Officials under them. The Objection from Deputation is answered.

4. The Surrogates of the Bishops, whether Vicar General, Principal Official, or Commissaries, are allowed a certain part of government.

5. They that give Lay-Chancellors the power of Judicial Excommunication and Absolution, cannot think a Presbyter uncapable of it.

6. A Presbyter *pro forma* oft passeth the sentence of Excommunication and Absolution in the Chancellors Court when he hath judged it.

7. A Presbyter in the Church must publish that Excommunication and Absolution.

8. By allowing Presbyters to baptize, and to deliver the Lords Supper, and

to keep fome back for that time, and to admit them again if they openly profefs *to repent and amend their naughty lives*, and to abfolve the fick, they intimate
that the Power of the Keys belongeth to them, though they contradict themfelves otherwife by denying it them.

9. And in Ordination the Presbyter is required to exercife difcipline: And
the words of *Act.* 20. 28. were formerly ufed to them [*Take heed to your
felves and to all the flock, over which the Holy Ghoft hath made you Overfeers* (or
Bifhops) *to feed* (or Rule) *the Church of God* : Whence Bifhop *Ufher* gathereth that the Churches fence was that the Presbyters had a joynt power with
the Bifhop in Church Government. And though lately *Anno* 1662. this be
altered, and thofe words left out, yet it is not any fuch new change that can difprove this to have been the meaning of them that made the book of Ordination,
and that ufed it.

II. Archbifhop *Cranmer* with the reft of the Commiffioners appointed by
King *Edward* the Sixth for the Reformation of Ecclefiaftical Laws, decreed
the adminiftring Difcipline in every Parifh by the Minifter and certain Elders;
Labouring and intending by all means to bring in the ancient difcipline. *Vid.
Reform. Leg. Ecclef. tit. de Divinis Officiis cap.* 10. And our Liturgy wifheth
this *Godly Difcipline* reftored, and fubftituteth the Curfes till it can be done.
And the fame *Cranmer* was the firft of 46 who in the time of King *Henry* the
Eighth affirmed (in a book called *The Bifhops Book*, to be feen in *Fox's*
Martyrology,)that the difference of Bifhops was a device of the ancient Fathers,
and not mentioned in Scripture. And of the opinion of *Cranmer* with others in
this point, his own papers publifhed by Dr. *Stillingfleet Irenic.* p. 390,391,&c.
are fo full a proof, that no more is needful.

III. Dr. *Richard Cofins* in his Tables fheweth how Church Difcipline
is partly exercifed by Presbyters, and by the Kings Commiffion may be much
more. And it is not aliene to their office.

IV. *Hooker Ecclef. Pol. lib.* 5. pleadeth againft the Divine fettlement of
one form of Government : And *lib.* 7. *Sect.* 7. *p.* 17, 18. he fheweth at large
that the Bifhops with their Presbyters as a Confefs governed the Churches:
And that in this refpect, [*It is moft certain truth, that the Churches Cathedral
and the Bifhops of them are as glaffes wherein the face and very countenance of Apoftolical antiquity remaineth yet to be feen,notwithftanding the alterations which tract of
time and courfe of the world hath brought*. And much he hath elfe-
where, which granteth that the Presbyters are Church governours, though not
in equality with the Bifhops.

V. Dr. *Field*, *lib.* 5. *c.* 27. fhewing how the Apoftles firft limiting and
fixing of Paftors to particular Churches, was a giving them Jurifdiction,
faith, [*this affigning to men having the power of order, the perfons to whom they were
to minifter holy things, and of whom they were to take the care, and the fubjecting
of*

of such persons to them, gave them the power of *Jurisdiction which they had not before.*]

And [*As another of my Rank cannot have that Jurisdiction within my Church as I have, but if he will have any thing to do there, he must be inferiour in degree to me ; so we read in the Revelation, of the Angel of the Church of Ephesus, &c.*] So that with him a Bishop is but one of the Presbyters, of the same Rank, having the first charge of the Church, (as every Incumbent in respect to his Curates) and so above his Curates in Degree.]

And [*As the Presbyters may do nothing without the Bishop, so he may do nothing in matters of greatest moment without their presence and advice. Conc. Carthag. 4. c. 23. ----- It is therefore most false that* Bellarmine *saith, that Presbyters have no power of Jurisdiction ——— For it is most clear and evident, that in all Provincial Synods Presbyters did sit, give voices, and subscribe as well as Bishops : ----- And the Bishops that were present (in General Councils) bringing the resolution and consent of the provincial Synods of those Churches from whence they came, in which Synods Presbyters had their voices, they had a kind of consent to the decrees of General Councils also : and nothing was passed in them without their concurrence.*

And Chap. 49. [*The Papists think that this is the peculiar right of Bishops : But they are clearly refuted by the universal practice of the whole Church, from the beginning : For in all Provincial and National Synods, Presbyters did ever give voice and subscribe in the very same sort that Bishops did ; whether they were assembled to make Canons of Discipline, to hear Causes, or to define doubtful points of doctrine : And that they did not anciently sit and give decisive voices in General Councils, the reason was, not because they have no interest in such deliberations and resolutions, but because seeing all cannot meet in Councils that have interest in such business, but some must be deputed for and authorized by the rest, it was thought fit that the Bishops -----*] So here are Bishops *authorized* by Presbyters as their Deputies in the greatest affairs in General Councils.

And c. 30. he sheweth instances of Concil. Antisiodor. c. 7. Tarrac. c. 13. Concil. Tolet. 1. & ex Gregor. l. 4. ep. 88. Synod. Eliber. &c.

He proceedeth to prove this by instances, *Concil. Later. sub Innoc. 3. &c.*

VI. Even Archbishop *Whitgift* maintaineth (as Doctor *Stillingfleet* hath collected, *Iren. pag.* 394.) that [*No kind of Government is expressed in the word, or can necessarily be concluded thence : ------No form of Church Government is by the Scriptures commanded to the Church of God (or prescribed.)*] And Doctor *Stillingfleet* there citeth * many testimonies, to prove this the judgment of the Church of *England* : And if so, it must be only men and not God, who make any difference between a Presbyter and a Bishop in the point of Jurisdiction.~

* King James, Dr. Low, Ep. Bridges, Cosins, Sutliffe, Crakenthorp, Hales, Chillingworth, &c with Chemnitius and many Lutherans and Calvinists.

VII. Bishop *Bilson Perpet. Govern. p.* 16. c. 391. saith, [*The Synod of Antioch which deposed* Paulus Samosat. as *Eusebius* sheweth *lib.* 7. c. 38. & in Concil. Eliber. about the time of the first Nicene Council sate Bishops and Presbyters, even 36. In the second Concil. Arelat. About the same time subscribed twelve Presbyters besides Deacons. So in Concil. Rom. sub Hilario & Gregor. where*

P

where 34 Presbyters subscribed after 22 Bishops. And in the first sub Symmach. where after 72 Bishops subscribed 67 Presbyters: So in the third, fifth, and sixth, under the same Symmachus, Felix had a council of 43 Bishops and 74 Presbyters. The Concil. Antisiod. c 7. saith, Let all the Presbyters being called come to the Synod in the City. *]

* By this judge how big the Diocese was.

Concil. Tolet.4. c.3. saith, Let the Bishops assembled go to the Church together and sit according to the time of their Ordination: After all the Bishops are entred and set, let the Presbyters be called, and the Bishops sitting in a compass let the Presbyters sit behind them, and the Deacons stand before them. Even in the General Council at Lateran sub Innoc.3. were 482 Bishops, and 800 Abbots and Priors conventual, saith Platina.] Thus Bilson and more.

VIII. To the same purpose writeth the *Greatest* Defender of Prelacy Bishop *Downam*, *Def. lib.* 1. *c.* 2. *sect.* 11. *pag.* 43, 44. and the places before cited out of him, professing that the Bishop hath but a *chief* and not *sole* *jurisdiction.*

IX. Bishop *Ushers* judgment is fully opened in his Model which we offered to the King and Bishops in vain, and which he owned to me with his own mouth.

X. Because the citing of mens words is tedious, I add, that All those whom I cited *Christ. Concord. p.* 57, &c. to shew that they judge the Presbyters Ordination may be lawful, and valid, do much more thereby infer that they are not void of a Governing power over their own flocks. *viz.* 1. Dr. *Field lib.* 3. *c.* 32. 2. Bishop *Downam Def. lib.* 3. *c.* 4. *p.* 108. 3. Bishop *Jewel Def. of Apol.* Part 2. *p.* 131. 4. *Saravia De divers. Min. Grad. cap. p.* 10, 11. 5. Bishop *Alley Poor mans Libr. Prelect.* 3. & 6. *p.* 95, 96. 6. Bishop *Pilkington.* 7. Bishop *Bridges.* 8. Bishop *Bilson, Of Subject. p.* 540, 541, 542, 233, 234, &c. 9. *Alex. Novel.* 10. *Grotius de imper.* 11. Mr. *Chisenhall.* 12. Lord *Digby* (then a Protestant.) 13. Bishop *Davenant Determ. Q.* 42. *p.* 191, 192. 14. Bishop *Prideaux, cont. de Disciplin. Eccles. p.* 249. 15. Bishop *Andrews.* 16. *Chillingworth.* To which I add 17. Bishop *Bramhall* in his Answer to *Mileterius's* Epistle to the King. 18. Dr. *Steward's* Answer to *Fountains* Letter. 19. Dr. *Fern.* 20. *Mason* at large. 21. Bishop *Morton Apolog.*

XI. *Spalatensis* is large to prove the power of the Keys to belong in common to Presbyters as such. I cited the words before, *Lib.* 5. *c.* 9. *n.* 2. & *c.* 2. *n.* 48, &c.

XII. Even *Gropperus* the Papist pleadeth in the Council of *Trent* for the restoring of Synods of Presbyters instead of Officials, (the thing so much detested in *England*, as that all we undergo must rather be endured) yet saith *Gropperus* [Restore the Synodals which are not subject to so great corruption, removing those

those Officers by whom the world is so much scandalized, because it is not possible that Germany should endure them.] The Spaniards and Dutch-men willingly heard this, but not the rest. *Hist. p. 334. lib. 4.*

XIII. The opinion of *Paulus* himself, the author of that History, is so fully and excellently laid down, of the Original of the Bishops grandeur, and of the manner of introducing the Ecclesiastical Courts by the occasion of Pacifications, Arbitrations, and *Constantines* Edict, as that I intreat the Reader to turn to and peruse *p. 330, 331, 332, 333.*

XIV. *Filesacus* (a Learned Papist) copiously proveth from Councils that Presbyters were called the *Rectors* of the Churches, *pag. 560.* And more than so, that they were called *Hierarchici* and *Prelates,* and *had* place in Councils, especially Provincial, *p. 576, 577, 578. Pag. 574.* he citeth *Concil. Aquisgr.* saying, *Presbyteri qui præsunt Ecclesiis, de omnibus hominibus qui ad eorum Ecclesiam pertinent, per omnia curam gerant. Pag. 576.* he proveth they were called Prelates abundantly. *Pag. 577. Episcoporum instar suam habebant plebem regendam.*

XV. Mr. *H. Thorndike* is so large in defending the Presbyters Governing power, and that as grounded on the power of Congregating, in his *Form of Primit. Gov. and Right of Church, &c.* that it would be tedious to recite his words. *Pag. 98.* he saith, [*The power of the Keys belengeth to the Presbyters and is convertible with the power of celebrating the Eucharist, and that's the Reason why it belongeth to them* (*Nothing could be spoken plainer to our use.*)

And *p. 128. The power of the Keys, that is, The whole power of the Church, whereof that power is the root and source, is common to Bishops and Presbyters.*]

And *Right of Ch. p. 126, 129, 130, 131.* he faith much more to confirm this by testimonies and instances of antiquity.

XVI. The great *Jo. Gerson* is cited to your hand by the same *Filesacus* as shewing that Curates were Hierarchical, *Quia eadem opera Hierarchica eis incumbunt quæ & Episcopis :* And more out of *Gerson, de Concil. Evangel. & de stat. Ecclesiastic. tit. de statu Curatorum consid. 1. & 4, &c.*

XVII. I will end all in the fullest testimony for these times, His Majesties Declaration concerning Ecclesiastical Affairs, before the passing of which it was examined by his Majesty and the Lord Chancellor, before Dukes, Lords, Bishops, Doctors of their party, and many of us also that are now silenced, and after all two great Bishops with Bishop *Reynolds* and Mr. *Calamy* appointed by the King to joyn with two Lords to see that it were worded according to the Kings expressed sense. And it faith *p. 11; &c.* [*Because the Dioceses, especially some of them are thought to be of too large extent, we will appoint such a number of Suffragan Bishops in every Diocese as shall be sufficient for the due performance of their work *.* 3. No Bishop shall Ordain or exercise any part of jurisdiction which appertaineth*

* But no one in all the land was appointed to this day.

P 2

appertaineth to the censures of the Church without the advice and assistance of the Presbyters: And no Chancellors, Commissaries or Officials as such, shall exercise any act of Spiritual Jurisdiction, in these cases, viz. Excommunication, Absolution, &c. ——— [As to Excommunication our will and pleasure is, that no Chancellor, Commissary, or Official Decree any Sentence of Excommunication or Absolution —— Nor shall the Archdeacon exercise any Jurisdiction without the advice and assistance of six Ministers of his Archdeaconry, whereof three to be nominated by the Bishop, and three by the election of the major part of the Presbyters within the Archdeaconry. 4. To the end the Dean and Chapters may the better be fitted to afford counsel and assistance to the Bishops both in Ordination and other offices mentioned before, &c. —— Moreover an equal number to those of the Chapter of the most learned, pious, and discreet Presbyters of the same Diocese annually chosen by the major Vote of all the Presbyters of that Diocese present at the Election, shall be always advising and assisting together with those of the Chapter in all Ordinations and every part of Jurisdiction which appertains to the censure of the Church, and at all other solemn and important actions in the exercise of the Ecclesiastical Jurisdiction wherein any of the Ministery are concerned. —— And our Will is that the great work of Ordination be constantly and solemnly performed by the Bishop and his aforesaid Presbytery ——— 5. We will take care that confirmation be rightly and solemnly performed by the information and with the consent of the Minister of the place: Who shall admit none to the Lords Supper till they have made a credible profession of their faith, and promised obedience, &c.—— Besides the Suffragans and their Presbytery, every Rural Dean ——— together with three or four Ministers of that Deanry chosen by the major part of all the Ministers within the same, shall meet once in every month, to receive such complaints as shall be presented to them by the Ministers and Church-wardens of the respective parishes, and also to compose all such differences between party and party, as shall be referred to them by way of Arbitration, and to convince offenders, and reform all such things as they find amiss, by their Pastoral Reproofs and Admonitions, if they may be so reformed. And such matters as they cannot by this Pastoral and perswasive way compose and reform, are by them to be prepared for and presented to the Bishop; At which meeting any other Ministers of the Deanry may if they please be present and assist. Moreover the Rural Dean and his Assistants are in their respective divisions to see that the children and younger sort be carefully instructed by the respective Ministers, &c.] See the rest.

This was the judgment of his Majesty, &c. 1660. And on these terms we were ready to have Conformed and United with the Prelatists so far as to go in the peaceable performance of our Offices. But that very Parliament who gave his Majesty thanks for this his Declaration, did lay it by, so that it was never done, but other Laws established which we feel.

Obj. You do but obtrude on us your own opinions: For when you had drawn up most of those words, his Majesty was fain to seem for the present to grant them you, for the quieting of you.

Answ.

Answ. 1. If we did offer such things, let the world judge what we fought by them. 2. There is most of that about Rural Deanries put in (I suppose by the Bishops consent who were to word it) after it went from us, and after the King had done with it, on *October* 22. 1660. 3. Whoever motioned or desired it, by this it appeareth that his Majesty and those that counselled him, did not then think the work of Jurisdiction, Excommunication, Absolution, no nor Ordination, to be aliene to or above the office of the Presbyter. And if that be no part of his Pastoral work, they would not have appointed it him.

Yet finally let the Reader note, that though my proofs have reached as high as the power of Canon-making, Jurisdiction, Court-excommunications and Ordination ; Yet it is no more than the power of Pastoral *Guidance* of our particular Parish Churches, and not to be forced to administer all holy things (Sacraments, Absolutions, &c.) contrary to our consciences, at other mens will who know not our people, and not to those that we know to be utterly Ignorant, Infidels, Scandalous, and Impenitent, that I am here pleading for.

I conclude therefore boldly after all this proof, that the *Presbyters office which was instituted by God, and used by the ancient Churches, contained an obligation and Authority not only to Teach and Worship, but also the rest of the Power of the Keys, to Rule the Churches committed to their care, (not by the sword or force, but) by a pastoral perswasive power, judging who is to be taken in and put out, and what persons are fit objects for the respective exercises of their own Ministerial acts :* (which was the thing I was engaged to make good.)

CHAP. XV.

Whether this Government belonging to the office of Presbyters, be in foro Ecclesiæ & exteriore, *or only in* foro Conscientiæ & interiore.

THe last shift that some Prelatists have, is to distinguish between the *forum internum Conscientiæ, pænitentiale,* and the *forum externum Ecclesiasticum,* and to tell us that indeed *Presbyters have the Power of the Keys in private* or in the first sense, but not in *Publick* or in the second.

Answ. 1. Note that the question is not whether they have the sole power, or the chief power, or with what limitations it is fit for them to exercise it, nor what appeals there should be from them ; But whether the power of the Keys be part of their office.

2. That

2. That the question is not of the power of Governing the Church by the sword, which belongeth to the King, and is Extrinsick to the Pastoral office, and to the being of the Church (As protecting the Church, punishing Church-offenders corporally, &c.) For this is proper to the Magistrate, and belongeth neither to Bishops nor Presbyters as such. We claim no part with the Prelates in any such secular Government as their *Courts* use, except when they come to Excommunication and Absolution : At least no coercive power at all.

3. All the question is of the power of the Keys of Admission, Conduct and Exclusion ; of judging who shall have Sacraments, and Church-Communion with our assemblies ? that is, Who shall be pronounced fit or unfit for it, by our selves ?

And that this belongeth to Presbyters *in foro publico Ecclesiæ*, I prove,

1. Because they are *Publick officers*, or *Pastors over that Church*, and therefore their power of the Keys is a publick Church power, else they had none of the Keys as Pastors of that Church at all : For the Keys are to *Let in* and *put out* ; They are the Church Keys : and he that hath power only to speak secretly to a single person, doth not thereby take in to the Church or put any out, nor Guide them publickly. A man that is a Minister (at least) may convince, satisfie, comfort any mans conscience in secret, of what Church soever he be, even as he is a member of the Universal Church. But he that is a publick Officer and Governour of the Church may publickly Govern the Church. But a Presbyter is a publick officer and Governour : Ergo.

2. The rest of his office may be publickly performed, *Coram Ecclesia*, and not in secret only : He may Preach to the Church, Pray with the Church, Praise God with them, Give them the Sacrament : Therefore by parity of Reason he may publickly exercise discipline, unless any by-accident *pro tempore* forbid it.

3. Else he must be made a meer *Instrument* of another, and not a rational free Agent and Minister of Christ : Yea perhaps more like to an Asse who may carry Bread and Wine to the Church, or like a Parrot that may say what he is bid, than a man who hath a discerning judgment what he is to do. I must publickly baptize, and publickly preach and pray, and publickly give the Lords Body and Blood : And if I must be no Judge my self to whom I must do this, then, 1. Either I may and must do it to any one (without offending God) to whom the Bishop bids me do it : And if so, I may Excommunicate the faithful and curse Gods children, and absolve the most notoriously wicked, if the Bishop bid me. And how come they to have more power than King *Balak* had over *Balaam* ? or than a Christian Emperour had over *Chrysostom* ? He that saith to the wicked, Thou art righteous, *Nations shall curse him, people shall abhor him*, *Prov.* 24. 24. Wo to them that call evil good and good evil ! But what if the Bishop bid them ? If I may not preach lies or heresies if the Bishop bid me, then I may not lyingly curse the faithful nor bless the wicked if he bid me. If I may not forbear preaching the Gospel meerly for the will of man, when God calleth me to it, much less may I speak slanders, yea

and

and lie in the name of God, when men bid me. The *French* Priest did wiselier than so, that being bid from the Pope to Curse and Excommunicate the Emperour, said, *I know not who it is that is in the right, and who is in the wrong, but I do Excommunicate him that is in the wrong whoever he be.*

2. Or else, it will follow that I am bound to sin and damn my soul thereby, whenever the Bishop will command me : which is a contradiction.

3. Or else it will follow that I am a beast, that am not to judge or know what I do, and therefore my acts are neither sin nor duty.

4. If he have not the Keys to use publickly *in foro Ecclesiæ* he hath no power of Excommunication and Restitution at all : For to Excommunicater is publickly to notifie to the Church, that this person is none of them, nor to be communicated with, and to charge them to avoid his company.

5. The Bishops themselves put the Presbyters to proclaim or read the Excommunication : and if this be any Ministerial or Pastoral act, certainly it is *in foro Ecclesiæ.*

6. Most of the Acts before named as their concessions, as to be in the Convocation, *&c.* are acts *in foro publico.*

7. The full proofs before brought from Antiquity, of Presbyters sitting in Councils, Judging, Excommunicating, *&c.* are of *publick*, not private exercise of the Keys.

8. They are the same Keys or Office power which Christ hath committed to the Pastors, even the Guidance of his Church, to feed his lambs : And *ubi Lex non distinguit non est distinguendum.* Where doth Christ or Scripture say, You shall use the Keys of Church-power privately, but not in the Church, or publickly ?

9. All this striving against *Power* in the Ministers of Christ, is but striving against their *duty, work,* and the *ends* and *benefits* of it : He that hath no *Power* for publick discipline, hath no *obligation* to use it ; and so he is to neglect it : And this is it that the Devil would have, to keep a thousand or many hundred Pastors in a Diocese from doing the publick work of Discipline : And as if he could confine Preaching to Diocesans only (And I verily believe they are better of the two at Preaching, than at Discipline) he knoweth that it is but few souls of many thousands that would be taught : Even so when he can confine Church discipline to the Diocesanes, he knoweth how little of it will be done. And who will use his wit, learning and zeal, to plead his cause, and his parts and office thus to serve his designs and gratifie him, who considereth what it is to be a Bishop, a Christian, or a man ?

CHAP. XVI.

That the English Diocesane Government doth change this office of a Presbyter of Gods institution into another (quantum in se) of humane invention.

I Come now to prove the Minor proposition of my Argument ; That the Diocesane Government deposeth the Office of Presbyters which God hath instituted (as much as in them lieth) By which limitation I mean, that if we would judge of the Power and Obligation of Presbyters, as the Prelatical constitution *de facto* doth describe it, and not as God describeth it contrarily, we must take it for another thing.

For the proof of this it must 1. be considered what is Essential to the office, and 2. How somewhat Essential is taken from them.

I. And 1. we grant (as before) that no Action whatsoever, as performed at the present, or for some excepted season, is Essential to the Pastoral office : A man ceaseth not to be a Preacher or Pastor, as soon as the Sermon is done and he is out of the Church. When a man is asleep or in a journey, he endeth not his office : Nor yet when he is interrupted by business, sickness, or persecution. Yea, if he were so sick, as to be sure never to exercise his office more, he keepeth the Title with respect to what he hath already done.

2. Yet *Exercise* as *Intended* and as the Relative end or *Terminus* of the Obligation and *Authority*, is Essential to the Office : For when it is a Relation which we question, and that consisteth in *Obligation* and *Authority*, there is no doubt but it is *ad aliquid*, and is *specified* by the *Action* or *Exercise* to which men are *Obliged* and *Authorized*. (As a Judge, a Souldier, a Physician, are) And it being a *Calling* which we speak of, and that *durante vita & capacitate*, it must be such *Action* as is intended to be *Ordinary*, and *Constant*. He that *Consenteth* not to do the work of a Minister, and that for more than a trial or a present occasion, and is not *Obliged* and *Authorized* to that work, at least statedly as his intended ordinary course of life, is no Minister of Christ : which *Paul* well expresseth by that phrase *Rom.* 1. 1. *Separated to the Gospel of God.*

3. As God in creating man made him in his own Image, so did *Christ* in making Church Pastors : Therefore he saith, *As my Father sent me, so send I you : And he that receiveth you receiveth me*, and he that *despiseth you despiseth me,*

me, and — *him that sent me, Luke* 10. 16. And they are *Embassadours to beseech men in his name and stead to be reconciled to God,* 2 *Cor.*5.19,20. And Christ himself is called the Angel of the Covenant, and the Apostle and high Priest of our Profession, and the Great Prophet, and the Bishop of our Souls, and the good Shepherd, and the great Shepherd or Pastor of the flock, and the Minister of the Circumcision: And he was a Preacher of the same word of life as we are: And he administred the same Sacrament of Communion as we do.

Now as the Office of Christ had these three Essential parts, *viz.* to be the *Teacher,* the *High Priest,* and the *Ruler* of the *Church;* so hath (not only the Apostles, but) every true Pastor in his place (as is proved) this threefold subserviency to Christ. 1. They will confess themselves, that He is no true Pastor who hath not *Authority* and *Obligation* (which set together are called a *Commission*) to be a *Teacher* of the Church. For though some men may be so weak as that they can Teach but by Reading, Catechizing, Conference, or very short defective immethodical Sermons: And though where a Church hath *Many,* the Ablest may be the usual publick Preachers, and the rest be but his assistants : Yet I never found any proof of Elders that were not Teachers by office as well as Rulers, and had not Commission to Teach the flock according to their abilities, and might not Preach as the need of the Church required it, however the *weaker* may give place to the *abler* in the exercise of his office. Because his office is an *Obligation* and *Authority* to exercise his Gifts as they are, for the Churches greatest edification.

2. And it will be confessed that he is no Minister or Pastor who is not Commissioned by Christ to be the Churches Guide in publick Worship, in Prayer, praise, and Sacrament of Communion: However where there are many, all cannot officiate at once.

3. Therefore all the doubt remaineth whether the power of the Keys for Church Government, such as belongeth to Pastors, be not as *Essential* as the rest ; I say the *Commission,* the *Authority,* and the *Obligation,* (though violence may much hinder the exercise) And this I have proved before and must not stay to repeat it. Only 1. God doth not distinguish, when he giveth them the Keys and office. Therefore we must not distinguish. 2. The very signification of the words [*Keys, Pastor, Presbyter, Overseer, Steward, &c.*] do not only import this Guiding, Ruling power, but *notably* signifie it, as most think *more notably* than the *Worshipping* part of their office. 3. Dr. *Hammond* and all of his mind confess that in Scripture these words are applyed to no one person or office, that had not the Governing as well as the Teaching and Worshipping power. 4. The truth is, the Teaching, and Ruling, and Worshipping power, are inseparably twisted together. Ruling is done (not by the sword here, but) in a Teaching way by the Word: As a Physician may 1. read a Lecture of health to his Patients, 2. and give every one particular directions for his own cure ; and this last is called Governing them : So when the same Pastor who Teacheth all generally by Sermons, doth make his applications to mens persons and cases particularly,

Q

it

it is Governing the Church: as when a man is impenitent, he doth Excommunicate him only by teaching him and the Church, that such persons as are so impenitent are under the wrath of God, and uncapable of Church Communion, and therefore requiring the Church as from Christ, to avoid that person, and declaring him to be under the wrath of God till he repent, and requiring him to forbear Communion with the Church. And so in other acts of Government. And as in Worshipping, the Pastor *delivereth* the Sacrament of Communion, so it must belong to him to *Give it* or *Deny it*. 5. And indeed the ancient Churches had usually more Pastors than Assemblies, by which means every Presbyter could not daily preach and officiate. But yet they were so constant Assistants in the Government, as hath occasioned so many to think that it was mere Ruling Elders who joyned with the Bishops in those times. And *Paul* himself saying 1 *Tim.* 5·17. *The Elders that rule well are worthy of double honour, especially they that labour in the word and doctrine*, doth plainly imply that there were *fewer* who were thus *Labourers in the word* and *doctrine* than that *Ruled well*. For indeed the following practices of the Churches expoundeth this Text, when the Churches having few Learned or able Speakers, he that could speak or preach best, did preach ordinarily, and was made Chief or Bishop, and the rest helped him in Government, and other offices, and taught the people more privately, and preached seldomer when the Bishop bid them and there was need: (Being yet of the same office.)

Obj. *Why then may they not now be forbidden publick Government in foro Ecclesiæ exteriore?*

Answ. 1. Our question is not chiefly what part of the exercise of their proper office may be *restrained* on just occasion; But what it is which truly belongeth to their office. 2. It is one thing to forbid it them *pro tempore*, and another statedly (for this changeth the Office.) 3. It is one thing to forbid a man *Preaching, Praying*, or *Exercise of Discipline* in a Church where there are many, and all cannot speak at once, and his restraint is for the better doing of the work, and the avoiding of confusion: And another thing to forbid a single Pastor of a Parish Church, with all his Curates, to do it, when there is no other there, nor near the place, that knoweth the people, to do it; but it must be undone. 4. And indeed the case of Discipline in this differeth from Preaching and officiating in Worship: Two men cannot do the later at once in the same Congregation, without confusion and hinderance of Edification: But ten men or twenty may consult and consent to the acts of Discipline. So that by Reason, Scripture, and Antiquity it is clear, that if any one part were more essential to the Presbyters office than the rest, it would be the *Authority* and *Obligation* to Rule *the flock* by the word of God, and exercise the Church Keys of Discipline.

II. Now that this power is here taken from them (notwithstanding all the forecited Concessions or Confessions that it is due to them) I prove.

I. I might

I. I might premise, that *Ubi non est idem fundamentum, non est eadem relatio: At, &c.* There is not the same *foundation, therefore not the same Relation.* For 1. Here is not the same *Election*, no nor *Consent*. I opened this before. Though all Antiquity gave the Church the *Election* of her own Pastors, yet we make not that necessary to the *being* of the office, or relation to them : So there be but *Consent*. But we take *Consent* of the Church to be necessary to any mans Pastoral Relation to that Church (though not to the Ministry in general as unfixed.) For, seeing it is not possible to *Exercise* the office without the *peoples Consent*, it cannot be *assumed* as over them without their Consent : Because that which cannot be *Exercised* should not be undertaken to be exercised. But with us, commonly, the *Patron chooseth, and the Bishop approveth, instituteth*, and giveth him induction, and so he is fully setled in title and possession in their way, without any of the peoples knowledge or consent.

Obj. You choose Parliament men who make these laws, and your Ancestours consented to Patrons power : Therefore you consent.

Answ. This seemeth a jest, but that the business and execution make it a *serious* matter to us. 1. It cannot be proved that all the Churches or people gave the Patrons that power. 2. We never intended to consent that Parliaments should do what they list, and dispose of our Souls, or of that which is necessary to the saving of our Souls. 3. Else you may as well say that we consent to be Baptized and to receive the Sacraments, because the Parliament whom we chose consenteth to it : And so we may baptize Infidels because their great grandfathers consented that all their posterity should be Christians: And you need no discipline to keep men from the Sacrament, if *Noah* consented that all his posterity should fear God and serve him and so be saved. Many men are jested *out* of their faith and salvation, but none are thus jested *into* it. Sin is a mockery, but so is not piety. 4. Our forefathers had no power to represent us by such consenting. If they could oblige us to Duty by their Authority, they cannot be our substitutes for the performance of duty, any more than for the possession of the reward. 5. What God himself hath laid upon the *Person* or existent *Church*, they cannot commit to another if they would themselves, because the obligation was personal, and they have not Gods consent for the transmutation. We cannot serve God by proxy, nor be happy by proxy.

Obj. But how unfit are the common people to choose their Pastors : They are ignorant, and partial, and tumultuous. Do the children beget their own father, or the sheep choose their own shepherd ?

Answ. 1. No : but wives choose their own husbands, and Patients choose their own Physicians, and Clients their own Advocates, and servants their own masters, &c. Similitudes run not on four feet. If all the Church of Christ besides the Prelates and their Curates, be as brutish as sheep and as silly as infants (in comparison of them) then they have talkt reason in their similitude. Else ——— 2. Is it not notorious in *England* that no Congregations have had more Learned and holy Paftors, than where the People have had their choice? I defire *London* but to confider it (nay they know it by great experience) what men hath *Aldermanbury* had, Mr. *Calamy*, Dr. *Stoughton*, Dr. *Taylor*, and fo before? What men hath *Blackfryers* had, Mr. *Gibbons*, Dr. *Gouge*, and many formerly? So alfo *Antholins*, *Lincolns*-Inn, *Greys*-Inn, the *Temple*, &c. But the truth is, that is an excellent perfon to us, who is an odious or contemptible perfon to the high Prelatifts. If he will preach as *Heylin* writeth, and make the people believe that Prefbyterians are Rebels, and Difciplinarians are feditious brainfick fellows, and ftrict living is hypocrifie, and praying without book and much preaching is Fanaticifm, and that none are worthy to preach the Gofpel who will not fwear to be true to this Prelatical intereft: that drunkennefs in a Conformable man is a tolerable infirmity, and their ignoranteft nonfence is fitter to fave fouls or Edifie the Church, than the labours of a Learned Holy Nonconformift; that *Calvin* was a Rogue, and *Cartwright*, *Amefius* and all fuch as they, difcontented factious Schifmaticks, unworthy to preach or to be endured; This is a fon of the Church, and an excellent perfon with the men in queftion. But it is the man that Learnedly and Judicioufly openeth the word of life, that clofely and skilfully and ferioufly applyeth it, that is an example of Holinefs, Sobriety, Love, Meeknefs, Humility, and Patience to the flock, who fpareth no labour or coft or fuffering for the faving of mens fouls, who is for the wifdom which is firft pure and then peaceable, &c. This is the Paftor that is excellent in our eyes. And of fuch I have oft wondred that the common people fhould ufually choofe far better than the Prelates do. But the truth is, Wifdom and Goodnefs have their witneffes even in the confciences of natural men, which *Faction*, *Pride*, and *Flefhly intereft* doth bribe or filence, and cannot endure.

3. But what's all this to us? We plead not now for the neceffity of the peoples Elections, but only for their *confent*: If the Patrons as now, or the Clergy as formerly be the Nominators, or Electors, yet fhould the peoples *confent* be acknowledged neceffary in the fecond place.

4. For who is fitter to *choofe*, or *refufe*, or *confent* at leaft, than he whofe everlafting intereft lieth at the ftake? It is their own foul that muft be faved or damned? And in good fadnefs do thefe Diocefans love the fouls of all the people better than they love their own? Do you make them believe this, by not feeing one of a thoufand or many hundred of your flock once in all the time of your lives? Doth the filencing of fo many Minifters fhew it? Chrift will have all men at age in Covenanting, Baptifm, and the Lords Supper, to be Chufers or Refufers for themfelves, becaufe (as *Clem. Alexandr. Strom.*1. faith,) they have free will, and it is themfelves that muft have the gain or lofs, that muft be in heaven or hell for ever. What if a Prelate, a Parliament, a Patron, or a forefather, chufe Mafspriefts or Hereticks for us, muft we accept the choice? Is this our *bewaring of falfe prophets, and of the leaven of the Pharifees, and our trying all things, and letting no man deceive us, &c.*

5. But how unfit is this objection for a Prelates mouth or pen? Are
you

you the Church Governours? Is all this contention that you may have the Keys alone, without the parish Ministers? And is this the fruit of all your Government, that the common Church members are so mad, so bad, so untractable, that they are not fit to be free Consenters to them that are to Teach and Guide them to salvation? Who then is this Church Ruine and Abomination long of but your selves, who *have* and only *will have* the Keys? Have you not fine Churches and members, that are not fit to choose no nor consent to their own Guides? Why do you not take care that the Churches by discipline may be better constituted? As none should be Pastors who are not fit for the duty of Pastors, so none should be members who are not fit for the duty of members. It's excellent Government inded to keep such in the Church as are unfit to be there, and then fetch an argument from their unfitness for their neglect of their duty, and your depriving them of their power? As if you should choose none but ideots (or most such) to be Jury men, and then argue thence, that they are unfit for so great a trust, and so the people must lose their liberties.

6. There are among the ignoranter sort of the people, usually divers sober and good men, and the rest use much to hearken to them.

Obj. But *what if the people will not consent to any but a Heretick or intolerable person?*

Answ. 1. The former answers serve to this: You do fairly to keep such people in the Church? But as the Foreigner wondered in *Henry* the Eighth's days, to see at once some hanged for being Papists, and some burnt for being Protestants, and cried out *Dii boni quomodo gentes hic vivunt*! So it is such another case to see at once the same Prelates forcing the *unwilling into the Church* and to the *Sacrament*, as if this would or could save them (if their Church be salvation) in despight of them, even on pain of undoing, and perpetual imprisonment; And yet Excommunicating and casting out those that are *willing* to stay in; As if *Consent* were a mark of an aliene and a reprobate, and unwillingness the mark of worthiness.

2. Such as you here describe are not fit to be members of a Church. If they will not Consent to Church priviledges and duties, they should be without the doors. And you may force them to *bear Teaching* whether they are *willing* or not; But you cannot make them Godly nor bring them to *heaven*, nor give them right to Church Communion and Sacraments whether they will or not. So much of Election and Consent.

2. Moreover the *Ordination* differeth from that of Gods institution. For Presbyters are now Ordained commonly neither by Archbishops, Bishops or Presbyters of Christs institution (in their way.)

1. The Bishops themselves profess that they Ordain not as Presbyters. For they say such have no power of Ordination. 2. They are not Bishops of Christs institution as is before proved; but of another *species*, which half themselves confess to be but humane. 3. They are not Archbishops, because they have no Bishops under them. And so having not their power of Ordination as Officers of Gods making, they have no power from him to Ordain.

Obj.

Obj. By thefe two laft differences you feem to give up the Caufe to the Separatifts: *Anfw.* The Prelatifts do fo; but fo do not we: 1. Becaufe whether the Prelates will or not, the people *ex pofi facto do Confent* to every worthy Paftor. 2. Becaufe we judge of Parifh Minifters as God defcribeth them, and therefore as true Bifhops: and confequently take the Prelates for a kind of Archbifhops whatever they call themfelves. 3. And there is no honeft Minifter but hath the Confent of fome neighbour *Minifters* and of the *People:* And though impofition of hands be a laudable Ceremony, yet it is not that, but *mutual Confent of themfelves* and the *Paftors* and *People* in which their external call confifteth, as is before faid.

II. The different Correlates and *Termini* make different Relations. The Churches which the ancient Presbyters were related to, were true entire Churches, (however their work might be parcelled among the members.) But according to the Prelates platform, each Presbyter hath his charge over no Church of Chrift at all, but only over a hundredth, fix hundredth or thoufandth part of a Church; having no more to do with all the reft than if they were of another Diocefe.

III. But I come to the point intended: That they take from the Presbyter his effential *Obligation* and *Authority* appeareth,

1. In general, they commonly affirm, that the Governing power belongeth not to them; and that they are but the Bifhops Curates: By which they mean not only that the Bifhops rule them: but they fay that the Bifhop doth *Teach* all his Diocefe *per alios,* even by thefe his Curates. And accordingly they have lately blotted out of their Litany [*Bifhops, Paftors, and Minifters of the Church*] and have fubftituted [*Bifhops, Priefts, and Deacons*] left the Priefts fhould be fuppofed Paftors. But they altered not the Collect for all *Bifhops and Curates.* And they have put out of the Office for Ordination of Priefts, *Act.* 20. 28. Now what a Presbyter doth in the *perfon* of the Bifhop and as his inftrument, that he doth not in the diftinct perfon of a Presbyter: He that payeth money or delivereth poffeffion in his Mafters name, doth it not in his own. So that if really they mean as they fay, that *quoad perfonam legalem quamvis non naturalem,* it be the Bifhop that doth *Teach* and *Officiate per alios,* then no Presbyter is indeed endued with any power of Teaching, Officiating, or Ruling in the perfon of a Presbyter, but only to be the Servant and Inftrument of the Diocefane.

2. No Presbyter hath power to judge whom he fhall *Baptize,* or whom to refufe; but is to Baptize all without any exception that have Godfathers and Godmothers, who will but fay the words in the book. The *Canon* 78. is [*No Minifter fhall refufe or delay to Chriften any Child according to the book of Common prayer, that is brought to the Church to him upon Sundays or Holidays to be Chriftened* ———— *Elfe fufpended three months from his Miniftry.* (Yea, that is it that pays for all.) So *Can.* 79. he is bound to do in houfes in cafe of danger.

Yet

Yet-Can. 29. *No Parent shall be urged to be* P R E S E N T *nor be admitted to answer as Godfather for his own child.* Now the Liturgy requireth not any Godfather to Adopt the Child, and take it for his *own :* Nor doth it allow us to refuse the Children of Turks, Jews, or Heathens ; And if these *Godfathers* be known Atheists, Turks, Jews or Heathens, or the filthiest Adulterers or wicked persons, if they did ever in their lives receive the Sacrament, and will say as the Book bids them, the Priest cannot refuse the Child. But if the godliest Parent can get none to be such Godfathers or Godmothers, his Child must not be Baptized. I told the Bishops my self that I had a notorious Infidel boasted that he would bring his Child to be baptized, and say the words of the book, and see who durst refuse it ; And I was answered that if the Child had Godfathers, there was no scruple but I should Baptize him : But when I ask, what if these Infidels (profesedly such) be the *Godfathers,* and say before-hand ; I will say those words and refuse me it you dare] they have nothing to say, that common reason should regard. Now he that is but sent to Baptize those (even all whomsoever) that others bid him baptize, and hath no more discerning or judging power of the persons capacity, than a Lay-man hath, is in this no Presbyter, but a Prelates messenger or servant.

3. They have no power to instruct, admonish, or reprove in secret or publick or in their own houses, any one Ignorant Heretical Infidel, Atheistical or scandalous wicked man, that will but refuse to speak with them or to hear them. And yet he must give this person the Sacrament, at least till he prove that by him which his refusal to speak to him maketh impossible to be publickly proved. If I have great reason by some private occasional speech or report to believe, that many of the Parish know no more of Christ than Pagans do ; or that they among their own companions (who will not accuse them) profess Atheism, Infidelity, or Heresie ; or if after scandalous fames I would admonish them to repent ; If they refuse to speak with me, or suffer me not to come and speak to them, I have no remedy ; but must still continue them in the Communion of the Church.

Obj. You would not have such men feed your self.

Answ. But I would not be free. I then my self, to give him the Sacrament of Communion as his Pastor, who refuseth to speak with me or to hear me as his Pastor ; but would have power to refuse that Pastoral administration to him that refuseth the rest.

4. They have no power to judge of the fitness of any one for the Sacrament of the Lords Supper, in point of knowledge, faith, or Covenanting with God, nor whether he understand what the Sacrament is, any more than an Infidel or idiot ; so be it the Bishop do but confirm him (in his childhood) or he will say that he is ready to be confirmed. Indeed all are required to send their children to be Catechised ; But 1. few Ministers use it : 2. few persons in a parish come. 3. If they refuse, we cannot prevent their farther communicating. 4. It is but to say over the words of that Catechism which they are

called

called to ; which experience tells us children will do like Parrots, without understanding what they say : And we must not ask them any other questions.

It is true also that they who are confirmed by the Bishop should bring a Certificate from the Minister that they can say the Creed, Lords prayer, Commandments, &c. But they may choose, and not one of many doth it. I went my self at thirteen years of age or fourteen, to the worthy Bishop *Morton* with the rest of the School-boyes without any Certificate, and without any examination he hastily said as he passed on three or four lines of a prayer over us, when I knew not what he said : And after this, no Minister can refuse any one at age the Sacrament. The Rubrick saith, They should openly own their Baptism, *&c.* But few do it, and none can be refused for not doing it. And so the transition from the number of Infant members into the number of the adult, is made without the Ministers *Consent* (Though the Kings Declaration once yielded to the contrary) And Communicants croud upon him in utter ignorance, because they were Baptized in Infancy : Nay few in a Parish (not one of many hundred of my acquaintance) is ever confirmed by the Bishop at all, so much as ceremoniously, or regard it.

5. They have no power to choose what Chapter they will read to the Church in publick (though a word before the Homilies *lib.* 2. seemed once to allow it them) But every day in the year even week-days and Holidays they are tyed up to the Chapters imposed on them, though *Bell and the Dragon, Judith, Susanna, Tobit,* and other Apocryphal writings be appointed for Lessons, even about 106 Chapters of the Apocrypha in two months : And though any scandal or other occasion in his Church would direct him, to choose some other subject for the peoples good.

6. He hath no power to choose what words to use in his publick prayers to God : no not to use any that are not written for him to read out of the book. And though custom hath so used Ministers to pray without book in the pulpit, yet this is but connived at because it cannot easily be remedied : One of them wrote a book against it, as answering that part of our *Savoy* Reply 1660 : Dr. *Heylin* hath largely laboured to prove that it is contrary to the Canon, which indeed doth seem express against it : And that's not all ; However their Consciences digest it, all the Conformists in *England* do subscribe as *ex animo* a covenant or promise [*that they will use the form in the said book prescribed in publick prayer and administration of the Sacraments, and no other.*] Canon. 36. Mark, *No other :* And the Bishops that endure this are forced to say, that these *Pulpit prayers are not the Churches prayers but our own :* But yet they are [*Publick prayers*] and therefore I doubt a breach of the Canon-Covenant.

7. A Presbyter as such hath no power to preach the Gospel. The words of his Ordination do but give him power to preach when he shall be *lawfully called :* yea his Presentation, Institution, Induction and possession of a Pastoral Charge, do not all make up this *Lawful call* , nor may he preach one
Sermon

Sermon after all this, till he have a particular Licensing Instrument from the Bishop. So that he preacheth not meerly as a *Presbyter* nor as a possessed Incumbent, but as *Licensed* by the Bishop.

8. When he visiteth the sick, he hath no *Power* left him to judge, Whether the person be penitent and fit to be Absolved or not ? But if the wickedest liver will but say or swear that he repenteth of Swearing, of Adultery, of Perjury, though such expressions or circumstances be such as plainly tell a present Minister, that he hath nothing like to a serious repentance, yet must this Minister be forced even in Absolute words to Absolve him from all his sins: When a Popish Confessor would require more. I do not in all this lay the fault that this Minister hath not power *to keep away any of these persons, from Baptism , Confirmation, the Lords Table, Absolution , &c.* but only that he hath *no Power* to forbear his *own action* and application, and leave them to others that are satisfied to do it : Nor not so much as to delay till he give a reason of his doubt to his Lord Bishop.

In the new Rubrick is added [If he humbly and heartily desire it] But if he will but say so, the Priest must not judge.

9. When he buryeth the dead, he hath no power to judge so far as to the performing or restraining of his own act, whether the deceased person must needs be declared and pronounced blessed. Three sorts of persons he must deny Christian burial to. 1. Those that die unbaptized, (though they be the Children of the holiest Parents) 2. Those that kill themselves (though they be the faithfullest persons of godly and blameless lives, who do it in melancholy , deliration, a phrenzy, feaver, or distraction.) 3. All that are Excommunicate, (though by a Lay Chancellor,) for not paying their fees, or though it be because they durst not take the Sacrament from the hands of an ignorant, ungodly, drunken Priest, to whose ministery neither they nor other of the Parish did ever consent ; or that it be the Learnedest Godly Divine that is excommunicate for dissenting from the Prelatists.

But all others without any exception that are brought to Church, they must bury with a publick Declaration that they are saints, *viz.* [*That God in mercy hath taken to himself the soul of this our dear brother*] (And without Holiness no man shall see God.) (So great difference in Holiness there is between the Holy Church of *Rome* and ours, that they Canonize one Saint in an age by the Pope, and we as many as are buryed by the Priest.) Though it was the most notorious Thief or Murderer, or the most notorious Atheist, or Infidel, or Heretick, who either writeth, or preacheth or disputeth that there is no God or no life to come, or useth in his ordinary talk to mock at Christ as a deceiver, and to scorn the Scriptures as nonsence and contradiction, or though it be a Jew who professeth enmity to Christ ? Much more if it be a common blasphemer, perjured person, adulterer, drunkard, a scorner at a godly life, &c. who never professed repentance, but despised the Minister and his counsel to the last breath, yet if he be brought to the Church for buryal, the Priest must pronounce him *saved* in the aforesaid words, so be it he be not Excommunicate (of which sort of late there are too great numbers risen up, in so much that the sober Prelatists themselves cry out of the growth and peril

R

of

of Atheism, Infidelity, and most horrid filthiness, and profaneness.) The words of the Canon are *(Can 68.)* [*No Minister shall refuse or delay to bury any corps that is brought to the Church or Churchyard (convenient warning being given thereof before) in such manner and form as is prescribed in the book of Common Prayer. And if he shall refuse— except the party deceased were denounced Excommunicated* Excommunicatione majori *for some grievous and notorious crime, (and no man able to testifie of his repentance) he shall be suspended by the Bishop of the Diocese from his Ministry by the space of three months*] But the New Rubrick in the Liturgy saith, [*The office ensuing is not to be used for any that die unbaptized, or Excommunicate, or have laid violent hands on themselves.*] The Office saith, [*Forasmuch as it hath pleased Almighty God of his great mercy to take unto himself the Soul of our dear brother here departed, &c.*] And [*We give thee hearty thanks that it hath pleased thee to deliver this our brother out of the miseries of this sinful world.*]

And yet as self-contradicters and condemners, if any man do but say of one that hath been openly against the Prelates or Conformity, that he was a godly honest man, (much more one that was against the King, and especially a downright Traitor who so lived and died impenitently) they take it for a heinous crime, (as in the latter case they well may do) And yet (except those whose quarters they set up upon the gates, or deny Christian burial to by the Magistrate,) the poor Priest must pronounce them all at the Grave to be the Bishops dear brethren and saved as aforesaid.

10. They have no Power to give the Sacrament of Communion with Christ and his Church, to any the most Learned holy Christian, who dare not receive the Sacrament kneeling, (for fear of bread-worship in appearance, &c.) which (though I think is unwarrantably scrupled, yet) hath so much of Universality and Antiquity as maketh it ill beseeming those same men who cry up the *Church Councils, Customes,* and *Antiquity,* to cast out of Communion those that conform to all these, for so doing. For who knoweth not by *Can.* 20. of *Concil. Nic.* 1. and the consent of Antiquity, that they took it for a custome ? and tradition and Canon for the Universal Church, that none should at all adore God kneeling on any Lords day in the year, nor on any week-day between Easter and Whitsunday.

11. They have no power to forbear denying the Sacrament of Communion to any how faithful and holy soever, who is against the Diocesanes Confirmation, and is unwilling that those whom he taketh to be no true Bishops should use that which he taketh (as used by them) to be no true Ordinance of God, but a taking of his name in vain ; or if on any other account he be *unwilling* of it : For the new Rubrick is, [*There shall none be admitted to the holy Communion, until such time as he be Confirmed, or be ready and desirous to be Confirmed.*] So that it is not actual confirmation which they think necessary. But [*a Desire of Confirmation*] by the imposition of the Diocesanes hands, is made a thing necessary to Christian Church Communion.

12. As it is before said that he hath no power to judge who shall be Confirmed,

firmed, and admitted into the Rank of Communicating members, so he hath no power at all effectually to keep away the grossest offenders, or to forbear his own actual putting the Sacrament into their hands. For though the Canon seem to favour his power, and the Rubrick say somewhat the same way, yet it is to be noted, 1. That whereas the Rubrick alloweth him to *advertise* the *scandalous not to come* to the Sacrament, yet it is only the contentious that have injured others and are not reconciled, whom he is plainly enabled to refuse. 2. Among those that he may advertise not to come, the grosly ignorant (who know not what Christ or the Sacrament is) the Atheist, Infidel and Heretick are not numbred at all; but [*an open and notorious evil liver, or that hath done wrong to his neighbours*] 3. And if he be never so wicked, yet unless also [*The Congregation be thereby offended*] the Curate cannot hinder him, or so much as advertise him not to come. And so if only a few Godly persons be offended, they are not the Congregation; or if the Minor part be offended, they are not the Congregation: And how shall the Minister know whether the Major part be offended : For he hath no power to ask them, much less to put it to the Vote : And the Major part will never come to him nor be accusers ? And if the Major part (which is no wonder) be themselves so Ignorant, Heretical, or ungodly as not to be offended, but rather to take the Sinners part, then the Curate must give them all the Sacrament, and hath no remedy. 4. And he that must not live in Taverns, Alehouses, Play-houses, or other places of wickedness (specially if he live as *Chrysostome* did, who never did so much as eat with any one in his own house) may have most of his Communicants to be abominable and flagitious, before it will be Notorious to him : for (as is said) He hath no power to call any to witness any thing, that are unwilling. And few will be willing to enrage their neighbours, when they foreknow that it will do more hurt than good. 5. And if he do refuse any one, he is bound to become an Informer, and to *give an account of the same to the Ordinary within fourteen days at the farthest.*] Whenas, 1. Perhaps he may dwell many score miles off; 2. And have his studies and all other business on his hands: 3. And must then bring his proofs, when he is not enabled to examine any witness nor take proof of that which to all others is notorious. 4. It is a great doubt whether the Sinner have not his remedy at Law against him to his undoing, if he lay not by all his other business to prosecute the proof to the utmost. And if he do lay by the rest of his work that while, the Bishop may undoe him or suspend him. 5. By this means he shall more exasperate the Sinners (by prosecuting them to such a Court as the Prelates) and harden them against all profiting by his Ministry, than if by his Pastoral office he had himself first lovingly convinced them, and suspended them only till they repent. 6. When he hath all done, if the sinner pay his fees and say, *He repenteth*, the Chancellor is to *Absolve* him : And so the Curate doth only to his own vexation and the Sinners hurt, deny him the Sacrament but once. And if the wrath

R 2   or or scorns of the Sinner shew that he was far from true Repentance, the Curate cannot deny him the Sacrament the next day, nor ever after, till he not only again commit the same sin (Adultery, Perjury, Drunkenness, &c.) but till it be again notorious, and he will be again at the same trouble in the prosecution. 7. And there are few great Parishes in *England* where there are no Swearers, Drunkards, Railers, Fighters, Fornicators, Adulterers, and such like enow, to hold a Curate work through the whole year to prosecute them, though he lay by almost all his other work : so that by this way, if he keep such from the Sacrament, he must keep all away by ceasing his Ministerial work. 8. The Curate cannot refuse him till he hath *called* and *advertised him* ; whereas the person may refuse to come to him, at least by pretending business and other excuses. All these things make this which seemeth his most confiderable power, to be in effect but next to none.

13. The Curate hath no power when any person is obstinate and impenitent in the most notorious scandal or heresie, or endeavoureth to pervert others, to admonish him before all, that others may beware, nor to call him openly to Repentance.

14. Nor hath he any power to judge who shall be Excommunicated as impenitent, be the crime never so heinous or notorious : no not so much as to concur in this power with any Bishop, Chancellor or Presbyters ; any more than any Lay-man hath. He can but Accuse them, and so may an Apparitor or Church-warden : or Read the Bishops or Chancellors Excommunication, as he doth the Kings Proclamations, or as the Clerk doth other writings.

15. He hath no power to *absolve publickly* any person Excommunicated, no more than a Lay man ; but as aforesaid to read the Absolution.

16. He hath no power to forbear his own act of Reading an Excommunication against the faithfullest and most religious persons in his Parish, whom it shall please the Bishop or Chancellor to Excommunicate, (that is, usually, a Nonconformist, or a Churchwarden who dare not swear to their large books of Articles, to persecute the Nonconformists, &c. or one that appeareth not at their Courts, or a poor man that doth not pay their fees, &c.) The poor Curate must read the Curse against them.

17. He hath no power himself to forbear the open Reading of an Absolution of the most impenitent wicked man, whom it shall please the Chancellor to absolve. And how easily that is procured for any man, that is but Rich and Conformable, is well known.

18. The Curate hath no power so much as to Baptize the holiest believer or the Child of such, as do but fear least it be a Sin to use the Transient Image of the Cross, as a humane symbol of Christianity, and an engaging dedicating sign, that he [will not be ashamed to profess the faith of Christ crucified, and manfully to fight under his banner against the Devil, the world and the flesh, and to continue Christs faithful servant and souldier to his lifes end.] If the person to be baptized were a Turk, or
a Jew,

a Jew, who both hate Idolatry, and should be so scandalized at this *Transient Image* and *humane Symbol*, as that they would rather never be Christians or be Baptized, than receive it ; yet must the poor Priest let them go without Christianity, rather than Baptize them without this Image of a Cross, unless he will be suspended from preaching Christs Gospel to the ignorant that they may be saved. But if he will *bear that*, he may do what he will ; that so poor souls may be the losers.

19. If the commonest whore or wicked woman come to be Churched, as they call it, after child-bearing, the Priest must use all the Office of thanksgiving, without first expecting her repentance, as if she were the chastest person : And must give her the Sacrament.

20. To conclude, no Priest as such (till Licensed) hath power [*to take upon them to expound in his own Cure, or elsewhere* (and therefore not to his family, or any one of his ignorant neighbours) *any Scripture, or matter, or Doctrine ; But shall only study to Read plainly and aptly, without glossing or adding the Homilies, &c.*] Are these Authorized Priests, that may not so much as tell a Child the meaning of his Catechism, or any Article of the Faith ? No though an ignorant person ask him ? The Priests lips should preserve knowledge , and the Law should be enquired of at his mouth, for he is the messenger of the Lord of hosts. But an English Priest may not expound any *Matter, Scripture, or Doctrine* but barely Read, till the Bishop License him.

Obj. If they be not able, it will do more harm than good.

Answ. Will the righteous God be always mocked ? and suffer men to make merchandice of Souls, and to vilifie them and set them at cheaper rates than they would do a goose, a pig, or a dog ? Is this a fit answer for those that are their Ordainers ? under whose examination and hands all men enter into the Ministery ? Will they say that they can get no better ? What, not when they have made so many Canonical Engines to keep out better ? What, not when such as *Cartwright, Hildersham, Amesius, Parker, Dod, Ball, &c.* are cast out as unworthy ? When so many hundred were silenced in Queen *Elizabeth* and King *James*'s days ; and Eighteen Hundred of us now ? When the Bishops have got so many Laws to hinder us from Preaching in publick and private, and to banish us five miles from all Cities, Corporations, and places where we have preached ? When none but their *sworn Curates, Subscribers, Declarers, &c.* may preach, yet can they get no better ? Will they keep up a Ministry whom they will themselves so ignominiously stigmatize, as to tell the world, that none of them all, as Presbyters, may be endured to expound any *Scripture, Doctrine, or Matter*, but barely to Read ? Yea as if they would disswade them *from all Learning* of Humanity or Divinity as needless or hurtful things, they say [*he shall only study to Read plainly and aptly.*] So that he that studieth for any more than to *Read*, doth break the Canons of the Prelatical Church.

Also

Alſo a Prieſt as ſuch hath no power to judge what Garments he ſhall wear, nor of what colour at home or abroad.

He hath no power to judge in what houſe he may inſtruct or pray with any of his flock : nor when ſo much as with his Church in publick, or with any ſick or afflicted neighbour in private, to *Faſt* and *Pray* : But they are all ſtraitly forbidden to preach or adminiſter the Sacraments, (except to the ſick) in private houſes : To preach or officiate in any room ſave a Conſecrated Chappel, even in a Noblemans houſe ; To keep publick or private faſts ; To give the Sacrament to any that are not of their own Pariſh, at leaſt if they go from their own Prieſt, becauſe he never ſtudied more than to Read : They have not power to admit any other, how Learned and Holy ſoever, to preach in their Churches, as Presbyters, without Licence. All theſe ſhew their Prieſtly power.

Obj. But a Surrogate may Excommunicate.

Anſw. 1. That is but ludicrous *pro forma*. 2. Or elſe it is but their ſelf-condemnations while they allow one Presbyter of a thouſand, to do that which all the reſt are forbidden. The ſame I ſay of Arch-deacons, and peculiar Ordinaries.

Object. They make Canons in Convocations, and chooſe Convocation Prieſts.

Anſw. 1. It is but *two Prieſts* of many hundred that are in a Convocation : And what's that to all the reſt. 2. Chooſing is not a Governing act. Where the people chooſe Kings and Parliament men, it proveth not that they have any Government themſelves. The Laity ever formerly choſe their Biſhops, and yet were no Biſhops nor Church Rulers. 3. It is in the Biſhops power to fruſtrate their choice. For when they have choſen four, he may put by two of them. In this great Convocation which hath new moulded our Liturgy, which hath formed the Engines that have done what is done, the great and famous City of *London* had not one choſen Clerk in the Convocation. (No wonder then if they Conform not, as not being bound by their own Conſent) For when they choſe Mr. *Calamy* and my ſelf, the Biſhop refuſed us both (which I am ſo far from mentioning in diſcontent, that I take it to have been a greater Mercy than I can well expreſs) 4. I take not Canon-making to be any conſiderable part of the Paſtoral Office. If two of many hundred, have power to pleaſe the Plural Number of Prelates, Deans, and other Dignitaries (whom they cannot over-vote) by ſerving them againſt the Church and their Brethren, doth that prove that Presbyters as ſuch have the Governing power of their flocks?

I am not ſtriving for a power of Ruling one another, much leſs of Excommunicating Kings and Magiſtrates, nor a power of making Laws, or

Ruling

Ruling Neighbour Churches : But only a power of Guiding their own flocks, and judging of their *own* actions. Yea, and that not as Ungoverned or without Appeals : But as Ruled by Magiftrates, confociated for Concord with other Paftors, and Ruling Voluntecrs. And if Archbifhops alfo Rule them by Gods Laws, we fhall fubmit.

C H A P.   XVII.

That the great change of Government hitherto defcri-
bed (the making of new fpecies of Churches, a
new Epifcopacy, and a new fort of half-fub-presbyters,
with the Depofition of the old, was finfully done, and
not according to the intent of the Apoftles.

THere are two pretences (and no more that I know of) made to juftifie all this foredefcribed change. The firft is by Dr. *Hammond* when he was hard put to it at laft, in anfwer to the *London* Minifters, which is, *That Subpresbyters were Ordained in Saint* John's *time, and therefore by him. The fecond is ordinary, that though* de facto *the Apoftles fetled but fingle Paftors (without Sub-presbyters at leaft) over fingle Churches or Affemblies, yet this was not done with an Obligatory purpofe, for the fo fixing of it ; But only* de facto, pro tempore, *as a State of immaturity, with a purpofe and intent, that it fhould grow up to the change of this maturity.*

I. To the firft Pretence I anfwer.   1. What probability is there that one Apoftle when all the reft were dead, fhould make fo great a change in their Church Orders? Either it was part of the Apoftolical Commiffion and work to fettle Church Offices and orders for Government, or not.   (as to the *fpecies*, if Chrift had not before done it ; or to fettle it by revealing what Chrift did command them ; either from *Chrift's mouth*, or the *Spirits* infpiration, to fettle the Catholick Church, as *Mofes* did the Jewifh.) If it were none of *their Commiffioned Office work*, then it was none of *John's* : And then it is done fo as may be yet undone.   But if it were *John's* work it was *Theirs* ; And if theirs, why did they not perform it ? Even while they
had

had that promise, *Matth.* 15. 20, 21. *Where two or three are gathered together in my Name, &c.* And, *If two of you agree of a thing, &c.* If you say that *there was no need till they were all dead,* I answer, It is a Fiction. The greatest numerous Church at *Jerusalem,* had more need of more than One to officiate among them, (and so had *Ephesus,* *Antioch,* *Corinth,* &c.) than most Churches else had in St. *John*'s days. And were all the Apostles so negligent and forgetful?

2. What proof is there that St. *John* did make this change? It is either by *Scripture* that it is proved, or by *History.* 1. Not by Scripture: For 1. No Scripture mentioneth S. *John*'s doing it. 2. Dr. *Hammond* and his followers confess that it was not done (as can be proved) in Scripture times. And Chronologers suppose that there was but a year or two, between his death, and the end of Scripture times, that is, the writing of his Apocalypse. And is it probable that he began so great a Change the last year of his life?

2. And History maketh no mention of it at all. (For I am ashamed to answer their nonconcluding reason, from St. *John*'s bringing a young prodigal to a *Presbyter* to be educated, or his Ordaining Presbyters, when it is no more than is said of the other Apostles.) Let them give us, if they can, any Satisfactory proof, that S. *John* alone, a year or two ere he died, made this new *species* of Presbyters and Churches, that we may believe it to be of God. But blind presumptions we dare not trust.

3. None of the Ancient Churches, Councils or Doctors (that ever I could find) did ever hold that Subpresbyters were instituted by St. *John* alone, and these changes made by him: How then shall we think that men of yesterday can tell us without them, and better than they, and contrary to them, the history of those times?

4. By as good a course as this, what humane corruption may not be defended, and Scripture supposed insufficient to notifie Gods Church-institutions to us? When there is nothing said in Scripture for them, the Papists or others may say that S. *John* made this or that Change when all the rest were dead: But why must we believe them?

5. And the Church hath rejected this plea already long ago. When *Papias* pleaded that he had the Millenary Doctrine from St. *John* himself, and when the Eastern Churches pretended his Authority for their time of *Easters* observation ; here was incomparably a fairer shew of St. *John*'s Authority than is produced by Dr. *H.* in the present case: And yet both were over-ruled by the Consent of the Churches.

II. And that it cannot be proved to be the Apostles *intentions* that their establishment herein should be but temporary, and left to the will of man to change, I have largely proved in my *Disput.* 1. of Church Government long ago. I now only say,

1. *That*

1. That which the Apostles did in execution of a Commission of Christ, for which he promised and gave them his infallible Spirit, was the work of Christ himself and the Spirit, and not to be changed but by an Authority equal to that which did it. But such was the setling of the *species* of Churches and Elders. *Ergo—&c.* The Commission is before recited from Scripture, and so is the promise and gift of the Spirit to perform it.

2. Where there is full proof of a Divine Institution by the Apostles, and no proof of a purpose that men should afterward change it, or that this institution should be but for a time, and then cease; there that Institution is to be supposed to stand in force, and the repeal, cessation, or allowed mutation to be feigned. But there is full proof of a Divine institution by the Apostles that Preesbyters with the power of Government were placed over single Churches (and no other faith Dr. *H.*) And there is no proof brought us at all, of either Repeal, Cessation, or Allowance for mutation——*Ergo &c.*
——They confess *de facto* all that we desire, *viz.* 1. That there was then none but *single Churches* or Congregations under one Bishop. 2. That there were no Subpresbyters. Let them now prove the Allowance of a Change.

3. That supposition is not to be granted which leaveth nothing sure in the Christian Churches and Religion: But such is the supposition of a change of the Apostles Orders in these points. *Ergo.*

If the after times may change these Orders, who can prove that they may not change all things else of supernatural institution? As the Lords day, Baptism, the Lords Supper, the Bible, the Ministry yet remaining, *&c.* And if so, nothing is sure.

Object. Christ himself instituted these, and therefore they may not be changed.

Answ. 1. It was not Christ himself that wrote the Scripture, but his servants by his Spirit. 2. Christ himself did that *mediately* which his Apostles did by his *Mandate* and *Spirit.* Matth. 28, 20. The *Spirit* was given them to bring all things to their remembrance which he had spoken to them. And to cause them to Teach the Churches all things which Christ had commanded them. And as Christ made the Sin against the Holy Ghost to be greater than that which was but directly against his humanity, and as he promised his Disciples that by that Spirit they should do greater works than his, so that which his *Spirit* in them did establish, was of no less authority, than if Christ had personally established it.

4. By this rule the Prelates themselves may be yet taken down by as good authority as the Apostles other settlement was changed: For if it was done by Humane Authority, there is yet as great Humane power to make that further change: Wherever they place it, in Kings, Bishops, or Councils, they may yet put down Bishops, by as good authority as they put down what the Apostles set up; and may set up more new orders still, by as good autho-

S

rity

rity as they set up these half-presbyters : And so the Church shall change as the Moon.

5. That which is accounted a reproach to all Governours is not without proof to be imputed to God, and his inspired Apostles. But to make oft and sudden changes of Government, is accounted a reproach to all Governours : *Ergo*—

For it is supposed that they wanted either foresight and wisdom to know what was to be done, or Power to maintain it. To make Laws and set up Churches, Officers, and Orders, this year, and to take them down, and set up new ones a few years after, seemeth levity and mutability in man : And therefore must not without cause and proof be ascribed to God. And the rather because that *Moses* Laws had stood so long, and the taking down of them was a scandal very hardly born : And if the Apostles that did it, should set up by the Spirit others in their stead, to continue but till they died, this would be more strange and increase the offence.

6. There was no sufficient change of the *Reason* of the thing, Therefore there was no sufficient reason to change the thing it self (if Prelates had had Authority to do it.) If you say, That in Scripture times there were not worthy men enow, to make Subpresbyters and Bishops both of : I answer, It is notoriously false, by what Scripture speaketh, 1. Of the large pourings out of the Spirit in those times : 2. Of the many Prophets, Teachers, Interpreters, and other inspired speakers which were then in one Congregation, *Act.* 13. 1, 2. And 1 *Cor.* 14. Insomuch that at *Corinth Paul* was put to limit them in the number of speakers, and the exercise of their gifts. 2. And it's known by history and the great paucity of Writers in the next age, that when those miraculous gifts abated, there was a greater paucity of fit Teachers, proportionably to the number of Churches, than before. 3. And who can prove that if there had been more men, the Apostles would have made a new Order of Presbyters, and not only more of the same Order?

2. Obj. *But the Churches grew greater after than before ?*

Answ. 1. Where was there three Churches in the whole world for 300 years so numerous as the Church at *Jerusalem* is said to have been in Scripture ? 2. If the Churches were more numerous, why might they not have been distributed into more particular Churches ? 3. Or how prove you that Presbyters should not rather have been increased in the number of the same Order, than a new Order invented ? 4. This contradicts the former objection : For if that Churches were so small and few before, it's like there might have been the more gifted persons spared to have made two Orders in a Church. 5. And what if in *Constantine*'s days the Churches grew yet greater, than they did in the second, or third age compared to the Apostles ? will it follow that still more new *Orders* may be devised, as Subpriests were ?

7. There

7. There are *worser* reasons of the change too visible : And therefore it is not to be imputed to a secret unproved mental intention of the Apostles. In Christs own time, even the Apostles themselves strove, who should be the greatest. False Apostles afterward troubled *Paul* by striving for a superiority of reputation. *Diotrephes* loved to have the preeminence. Sect-masters rose up in the Apostles days : *Acts* 20. 30. *Of your own selves shall men arise, speaking perverse things, to draw away disciples after them.* Some caused Divisions and Offences contrary to the Doctrine which they had learned, *Rom.* 16. 17. In *Clem. Rom.* time the Church of *Corinth* was contending about Episcopacy and superiority, even Lay-men aspiring to the chair. *Peter* seemeth to forefee what Pastors would do, when he forewarneth them not to Lord it over Gods heritage, 1 *Pet.* 5. 1, 2, 3. *Victor* quickly practised the contrary when he Excommunicated the *Asian* Bishops. See *Grotius* his complaint of the early and ancient pride, contention, and tyranny of the Bishops, *De Imper. sum. Pot. p.* 360, 361. *Novatian* with *Novatus* quickly shewed this spirit (if they be not wronged) at *Rome* and *Carthage* ; and so did *Felicissimus* and his partners against *Cyprian.* What stirrs were there for many ages between the *Cecilians* and the *Donatists* ? What horrid work was there at the *Concil. Ephes.* 1. And *Concil Chalcedon. & Concil. Eph.* 2. between the contending Bishops on each side ? The reading of the Acts would make a Christians face to blush. What strife between *Anthymius* and *Basil* for a larger Diocese ? What work against *Nazianzen* to cast him out of *Constantinople* ? What sad exclamations maketh he against Synods, and against these Names and Titles of preeminence and higher seats, wishing the Church had never known them ? And yet he was angry with his friend *Basil* for placing him in so small a Bishoprick as *Sosimis.* What abundance of Epistles doth *Isidore Pelusiota* write to *Eusebius* the Bishop and *Sosimus* and the other wicked Priests, detecting and reproving their malignity, drunkenness, and horrid wickedness ? And how sharply doth he lament that a faithful Ministry is degenerate into carnal formal Tyranny , and that the Bishops adorned the Temples under the name of the *Church,* while they maligned and persecuted the Godly who are the Church indeed ? How lamentable a description doth *Sulpit. Severus* give of the whole Synods of Bishops that followed *Ithacius* and *Idacius* ? And in particular of *Ithacius* himself, as a fellow that made no conscience of what he said : And what did *Martin* think of them who avoided all their Communions to the death, and would never come to any of their Synods ? Especially because by stirring up the Magistrate against the Priscillianists, they had taught the vulgar fury to abuse and reproach any man that did but read, and pray, and fast, and live strictly, as if he were to be suspected of Priscillianism (which *Hooker* himself complaineth of, *Pref.*) And *Ambrose* also did avoid them. What bloody work did *Cyril* and his party make at *Alexandria* ? What a man was *Theophilus* after him ? What work made he against *Chrysostom* ? What a Character doth *Socrates* give of him ? What insolence and furious zeal did *Epiphanius* shew in the same

cause,

caufe, in thrufting himfelf into the Church of *Chryfoftom* to ftir up his hearers to forfake him ? *Hierom* had a finger in the fame caufe: His quarrels with *Johan Hierofol.* with *Ruffinus*, his abufive bitternefs againft *Vigilantius*, &c. are well known. The multitudes of Canons for preferving the grandeur of Patriarchs, and Metropolitanes, and Prelates, on one fide, and for keeping fmall Cities without Bifhops, *ne vilefcat nomen Epifcopi*, and for reftraining Pride, felf-exaltation, enlargement of Diocefe, encroachment on each other, on the other fide, do all fhew the difeafes that needed fuch a Cure, or that had fuch a vent. In a word the Bifhops never ceafed contending, partly for their feveral opinions and errours ; and partly for preeminence and rule, till they had brought it to that pafs as we fee it at this day, between *Rome* and *Conftantinople*, and the moft of the Chriftian world. From all which it is moft apparent that *Pride* and *Contention* were cured but in part in the Paftors of the Churches: And that the remaining part was fo ftrong and operative, as maketh it too credible that there were ill caufes enow for enlarging of Diocefes and getting many Churches into one mans power, and fetting up a new Order of half-fubpresbyters ; And that the event of fuch a change is no proof that it was the *Intent* of *the Apoftles*, that this change fhould be made when they were dead ; no more than you can prove that all this turbulent *pride* and *ftrife* was intended by them.

If any fay, that it is not probable that fo foon after the Apoftles all the *Churches* would confpire in fuch an error : I anfwer, If all thefe things before mentioned were not done, or if matter of known fact may be denied as improbable, then that objection hath fome fence. To which I add,

8. I have proved that this change was not made at once, but by flow degrees: No nor made fo foon as is pretended, nor fo univerfally, but in long time, except at *Alexandria* and *Rome* ; It was long before the Churches knew it.

9. And I think none will deny but other things were taken up as the Traditions of the Apoftles, and all the Churches cuftomes, which yet are now rejected as no fuch thing. To fay no more of *Eafter* and the *Millennium*, there were five ceremonies which were accounted the Churches univerfal cuftomes, and traditions, and none was to omit, *viz.* not kneeling in adoration on the Lords days, Adoring towards the Eaft, the White Garment, the Milk and Honey and the Chrifm to the Baptized : But were thefe fuch ? *Socrates, Sozomen*, and *Nicephorus* tell us great Reafons to believe that (whatever fome fay) the time of Eafter, the Faft of Lent, and many other obfervances, and among others the largenefs or fmallnefs of Diocefes, were no Laws of God or the Apoftles, but ufages voluntarily and diverfly taken up, in feveral places, in which no Chriftians fhould condemn each other, but allow a liberty of diffent and difference, without breach of Charity or peace.

10. Moreover it is a clear proof that the Apoftles intended no fuch change, in that they left no Rule, Inftructions or Directions for it, nor for the calling of the new fort of Presbyters, nor for their performance of their places. They

left

left full directions for the *Ordination* and *Regulation* of Bishops, called Pesbyters, and for Deacons, not leaving out so much as Deaconesses ; And would they have wholly omitted all instructions for the new order of Presbyters, and Prelates, *&c.* if they had intended them ?

11. To put all out of controversie, God hath told us that his setled orders are for continuance. *Eph. 4. 11, 12, 13.* Such Offices as Christ hath given to the Church, are for the perfecting of the Saints, for the work of the Ministry, for the edifying of the Body of Christ, till we all come to the unity of the Faith, and the knowledge of the Son of God, to a perfect man, *&c.* If God do give some to lay the foundation, and some to build thereon, yet he leaveth not men to make new Officers besides all these, to do his appointed work. *Timothy* had charge to propagate the same Doctrine, and the same Church orders, even to the coming of Christ, *1 Tim. 6. 13, 14. 2 Tim. 2. 2.* and *1 Tim. 3. Tit. 1.5. Heb. 10. 23, 24, 25.* But of this I desire the Reader to see full proofs in my 2. sheet for the Ministry.

12. Lastly, the holy Scripture is a perfect standing Rule for all things necessary to Salvation, and Divine Faith and duty, and to Church worship and Communion. If not, what is ? And where shall we find it ? And what stop shall we make of our additions, if there be no Law or Rule to govern the universal Church ? And who are they that have power to Rule the Church universal ? See my *Key for Catholicks, against the claim of Pope and General Councils.* But if it be, then the adding and altering is presumption, except in circumstantials which God hath left to mans determination : And then why must we swear never to alter unnecessary circumstances, were they such ?

CHAP.

CHAP. XVIII.

The fourth Argument, From the Impoſſibility of their performance of the Epiſcopal Office, in a Dioceſane Church ; And the certain excluſion and deſtruction of true particular Church Government, while one man only will undertake a work too great for many hundreds.

ALl that I have ſaid hitherto is far ſhort of this one Argument, from the notorious unqueſtionable miſchiefs which the oppóſed frame of Prelacy doth infer ; not probably, but certainly ; not only where Biſhops are bad, but with the beſt ; not in ſome Churches, but in all.

ARGuMENT IV.

That Form of Prelacy is not lawful and to be ſworn to, which maketh the Epiſcopal Office impoſſible to be performed, and certainly deſtroyeth and nulliſieth true particular Church Government wherever it obtaineth. But ſuch is the oppoſed frame.

None will deny the Major but the *Eraſtians*, who think that the Magiſtrate only is the Church Governour (which as to forcing Government is true) And they that ſo think, muſt needs be againſt Biſhops otherwiſe than as they are *Preachers* or *Magiſtrates*. Therefore I may let them paſs.

The Minor I am to prove by parts.

It muſt be remembred, that I have ſhewed how great the Dioceſes are, and that no work proper to the Office of a Biſhop can be done by a Lay-man, or any but a Biſhop. And have prevented the pretence of doing it *per alios*. And now I muſt ſhew more fully than in the former breviate, what the work of a Biſhop is; And then you ſhall ſee whether it be not impoſſible. And left you think I preciſely feign more work than God hath put upon them, I will take it out of Scripturè and Dr. *Hammonds* Annotations.

I. The *Teaching* of the Flock. II. The Prieſtly worſhipping of God with them. III. The Government of them by Diſcipline, are the three parts of the Biſhops Oiſice, as hath been proved.

L The

I. The *Teaching* of the Flock is, 1. *Publick Teaching* them in their Sacred Assemblies, by expounding and applying the word of God. 1 *Pet.* 5. 2, 3. *Feed the flock of God which is among you, taking the oversight thereof, &c.* saith Dr. *Hammond,* [The Bishops of your several Churches, I exhort —— take care of your several Churches and govern them, &c.]

Heb. 13. *Remember them which have the rule over you, who have spoken to you the word of God.* Dr. *H.* [Set before your eyes the Bishops and Governours that have been in your Church and preached the Gospel to you ——] *Acts* 20. 7. *Upon the first day of the week when the Disciples came together to break bread, Paul preached to them ——] *Matth.* 24. 45, 46. *Who then is a faithful and wise servant whom his Lord hath made ruler over his houshold to give them meat in due season.*]

1 *Thes.* 5. 12. *We beseech you brethren to know them that labour among you and are over you in the Lord and admonish you, and to esteem them very highly in love for their works sake.*] D. *H.* [Pay (your Bishops) as great a respect as is possible for the pains they have taken among you.]

1 *Tim.* 5. 17. *The Elders that rule well are worthy of double honour, especially they that labour in the word and doctrine.*] D. *H.* [Let the Bishops that have discharged that function well, receive for their Reward twice as much as others have, especially those that preach the Gospel to whom it was news, and also continue to instruct congregations of Christians in setled Churches.]

1 *Tim.* 3. 2. *A Bishop must be —— apt to teach.*] D. *H.* [One that is able and ready to communicate to others the knowledge that himself hath.]

2 *Tim.* 4. 1, 2. *I charge thee before God and the Lord Jesus Christ who shall judge the quick and the dead at his appearing, and his kingdom, preach the word, be instant in season, out of season, reprove, rebuke, exhort with all long-suffering and doctrine.*] See Dr. *H. Annot.*

And can one Bishop be the publick Teacher of a thousand, a hundred, or many Churches: Can he feed them, and give them their meat in due season? where one of a thousand never heard his voice nor saw his face? Is the *flock* with them or among them? Can you say to his Diocese, *I beseech you know the Bishop that laboureth among you and admonisheth you, and esteem him highly in love for his works sake?* Will they not say you mock them, and that they cannot *know* him whom they never saw; nor love him for his work and admonition among them, that never was among them, that never workt with them, that never admonisht them; but only that one of many hundred saw him, and heard a Visitation Sermon in one City or market Town once in three years, or a year at most. Must many hundred Congregations that never heard him, give him double honour that preacheth sometime to one Congregation a hundred or twenty miles from them, and this as their Instructing Elder? Judge of the possibility of this.

2. The Bishops are also bound to private helps, instruction, counsel, and to watch over all the flock, and every particular member of them; as a Father must

muft look to every Child, and a fhepherd to every fheep, and a Phyfician to every Patient.

Acts 20. 20, 28, 31. *I taught you publickly and from houfe to houfe — — Take heed therefore to your felves and to all the flock over which the holy Ghoft hath made you Overfeers, to feed the Church of God, which he hath purchafed with his own bloud ------- Therefore watch, and remember that by the space of three years, I ceafed not to warn every one night and day with tears*] D. H. [*Inftructing both in the* Synagogues, and in private Schools, and in your feveral houfes whither I alfo came ----- Wherefore ye that are Bifhops or Governours of the feveral Churches, ------ look to your felves and the Churches committed to your truft, to rule and order all the faithful Chriftians under you.]

Col. 1. 28. *Whom we preach, warning every man, and teaching every man in all wifdom, that we may prefent every man perfect in Chrift Jefus.*] *Heb.* 13.17. *Obey them that have the rule over you and fubmit your felves, for they watch for your fouls as thofe that muft give account.*] D. H. [Obey thofe that are fet to Rule over your feveral Churches, the Bifhops, whofe whole care is fpent among you, as being to give an account of your proficiency in the Gofpel.]

I before cited *Ignatius* telling the Bifhop that he muft enquire after every one by name, even fervants and maids. And Dr. *Jer. Taylor* who faith, *No man can be accountable for them that he knoweth not (or cannot know.)*

Now is it poffible for a Bifhop to do this : To inftruct, overfee, counfel, one of many hundreds of the flock? who know him no more than one in another kingdom? Is this paftoral teaching of particular Souls, to have an Apparitor call one of a thoufand when he Conformeth not, or offendeth, to a Chancellors Court; How little know they what the work of a Paftor is that think fo?

3. Bifhops muft teach the flock by their own *vifible example*; By holy fpeaking and holy living before their flocks. *Heb.* 13. 7. [*Remember them which have the rule over you, who have fpoken to you the word of God, whofe faith follow, confidering the end of their converfations.*] D. H. [Set before your eyes the Bifhops ------ obferve their manner of living.] If it were the Pope at *Rome*, we might caft a conjecture by the report of that great liar *fame*, Becaufe it is a place that we hear often from in the Curranto's and Gazets : But no Gazet telleth us of the life of our Bifhop. And how fhall thofe *obferve their manner of living*, who know not whether they be alive or dead, till a Minifter is to be filenced, or a new Bifhop doth fucceed the old? You may as well bid us obferve how they live in the *Weft-Indies*.

1 *Pet.* 1. 5. 3. *Neither as being Lords over Gods Heritage (or having dominion over your charges) but being enfamples to the Flock.*] D. H. [Walking Chriftianly and exemplarily before them.] What ! before them that never faw or heard them? Before men of another Countrey, that may fwear and not repent with *Peter*, *We know not the man?* What ! be *examples* to them that are out of the notice of their words and lives? But if really you think that fame is fufficient, 1. It muft be of perfons and things not too far off. 2. It muft be

in

in a Golden age or another world, where good men are not hated and calumniated, and where bad men if Great are not extolled, and where false reports be not easily believed and reported ; where a vile person is contemned, and those that fear the Lord are honoured ; Where the faithfullest Pastors are not the object of Great mens jealousie, of bad mens malice, of dissenters and contentious mens backbitings and reproch, and are not made the drunkards song, nor the scorn and off-scouring of all things, and where he that reproveth or departeth from evil, doth not make himself a prey ; or at least where malignity, worldliness, and lying are not the predominant humours of the Age. When you have secured us of a true fame, we will make the example of a stranger of another land or Diocese,(as soon as one of this Diocese as strange to us) the exemplar of our lives.

4. Another part of the Bishops work is to preach to those without that are uncalled, as he hath opportunity: To labour in the *word* and Doctrine, 1 *Tim.* 5. 17. saith Dr. *H. To preach the Gospel to whom it was news :* which made Dr. *Donnam* and other Prelatists say That the City and Territories are their Diocese even when few of them are converted, that they may first convert them and then govern them ; and Dr. *H.* to Note out of *Clem. Rom.* that they are made Bishops over the Infidels that should after believe. And doubtless they must do their best to call the unbelieving and impenitent to Christ.

And how much of this will a Bishop have time to do, that hath the work of a Diocese of Christians on his hands?

5. It is the work of a Bishop to Baptize, or at least to judge of those that are to be Baptized, *Matth.* 28. 19. *Go and disciple me all nations baptizing them.* And Dr. *H.* thinketh that no Presbyter, but Bishops baptized in Scripture time, because there were then no other existent. And it is too evident in Antiquity (by what I before cited) that no child or aged person was usually baptized without a Bishop(when Bishops came up,) at least they used to anoint their nostrils, &c. with holy oyl. And doubtless they that Baptized or admitted to baptism, did examine them of their faith, and resolutions, before they took them into the Covenant and Vow of God. And how many hundreds in a year can the Bishop do this for, besides all his other work ?

6. It is by the English Canons and Rubrick the Bishops duty to confirm all that were baptized : many think it is meant in *Heb.* 6. 1, 2. Our Bishops take it for a proper part of their work. And they that must confirm them according to our Liturgy, must know their understanding, and receive their profession of their faith, and standing to their Baptismal Covenant, which requireth some time and labour with each one, for him that will not make a mockery of it. Look into the Bills of *London,* which tell you how many are born every week ; and thence conjecture how many hundreds in a year the Bishop hath in that Diocese to Confirm, and consequently in other Dioceses proportionably? Or if that will not inform you, try over *England* where you come, how many are (though but cursorily as a hasty ceremony) confirmed at all? Whether it be one of many hundreds? And set this to the rest of the Bishops work.

7. It is the Bishops work to defend the truth against gainsayers, to confute

T   and

and stop the mouths of Hereticks and contradicters, and confirm the troubled and wavering minded in the faith: not by fire and sword, nor by a quick prohibition of others to preach; but by sober conferences, and weight of evidence, and by Epistles as *Paul* did, when they are not at hand, yea even to other Churches: and as one that is *gentle to all men, apt to teach, patient, in meekness instructing them that oppose themselves, if God peradventure will give them repentance to the acknowledging of the truth,* 2 *Tim.* 2.24, 25. And shall the Bishop do this for many hundred Churches? While he is defending the poor flock against Papists, Quakers, Arrians, Socinians, Infidels (alas how numerous are the deceivers!) at *Newark*, or *Gainsborough*, or *Boston*, what shall they all do between that and *Barnet*, or the remotest part of *Buckinghamshire*?

II. The second part of the Bishops office is to be the peoples *Priestly guides* in Gods worship: principally in the publick Assemblies, and oft in private, *viz.*

1. To confess the peoples sins and their own: To be their own and the Churches mouth in prayer, thanksgiving and the praises of the Lord. And in how many hundred Congregations at once will they do this?

2. To consecrate and distribute the Sacrament of Communion; and consequently to discern who are fit for it. And in how many Churches at once will he do this?

3. To bless the Congregation at the end of every meeting. All these I have before proved that the ancient Bishops did; and Dr. *Hammond* saith, No other in Scripture times; And what Ubiquitary shall do this.

4. And in private it is the Bishop that *must visit* the sick, that must be sent for by them all, and must pray with them. As Dr. *H.* at large proveth, *Annot.* in *Jam.* 5. I have told you before how well and for how many he is able to do this, in one of our Dioceses. If that serve not turn, I pray you if you are foreigners, ask English men what number it is of sick men in a Diocese that are visited and prayed with by the Bishop? Compare them with the Bills of Mortality in *London*, and judge proportionably of the rest, whether he visit one of many thousands of such as die, to say nothing of all the sick that do recover.

5. And it is the Bishops work to receive all the offerings, first-fruits, tythes, and other maintenance of the Church, as the Canons before cited say. And see Dr. *H.* on *Act.* 2. c. and *Act.* 4. 33, 34, 35, &c.

6. It was the Bishops work to take care of all the Poor, Orphans, Widows, Strangers, as the Canons cited shew; And Dr. *H.* on 1 *Cor.* 12. 28. c. saith [*The supreme trust and charge was reserved to the Apostles and Bishops of the Church.*] So in *Can.* 41. *Apost.* A Bishop must have the care of the moneys, so that by his power all be dispensed to the poor, &c. where he citeth *Just. Mart.* and *Polycarp.* for a particular care. I have before told you that if the poor of every parish be not relieved till the Bishop take notice of them, few of the poor in *England* would be any more for Bishops, than for famine, nakedness, and death.

III. But the principal thing which I reckon impossible, and is, and must be destroyed by Diocesanes, is the *Government of all the particular Churches,* (or Parishes) in the Diocese.

Where

Where note, 1. That I speak not of the Magistrates Government, 2. Nor of that General Inspection by which an Archbishop or General Pastor overseeth the inferiour Bishops with their flocks, as a general Officer doth the Regiments and Troops in his Army, which have Colonels and Captains of their own. But I speak of the particular Church Government of the Bishops of single Churches, like that of Captains over their own troops, or rather Schoolmasters in their several Schools.

And I the rather mention this because Bishops making it more proper to themselves, than *Teaching* or *Worship*, must hold, (were they confident with themselves) that they can less delegate it to others.

The exercise of the Keys are 1. For entrance by Baptism. 2. By confirmation (rightly understood, as in a peculiar Treatise I have opened it) 3. By Reproof, Consolation, Excommunication, and Absolution of particular persons, which I am now to speak of.

Where distinctly note I. What the work is Materially, II. In what manner it must be done, III. On how great a number of persons.

I. 1. To receive accusations and informations of all the great and perilous heresies, crimes, and scandals in the Diocese.

2. To judge of the credibility of the witnesses (hardly done by a stranger) and of the validity of their proofs. For Councils themselves have petitioned the Emperours, that ungodly persons might not be witnesses, who make so small a matter of other sins, as that they may be supposed to make but little of false witnessing. Else an Atheist or Infidel or man of no conscience (as he never need to miss of Church preferment, for want of conforming to mens wills, so) he may be master of the fame, liberty, and lives of all honest men, at his pleasure, and govern them that govern Church and State. Therefore Bishops themselves must difference between witnesses : And to say, I know an honest man that knoweth an honest man that saith they are honest men, is a poor satisfaction in comparison of personal knowledge. Much less to trust the whole trial to another.

3. He must hear the accused person speak for himself. For there is no judging till both are heard.

4. He must rebuke false accusers, and justifie the innocent, and vindicate their good name.

5. He must by convincing arguments and melting affections, labour to bring the sinner to Repentance.

6. He must desire the Church to be witnesses of his faithful admonitions, and to avoid the like crimes and impenitence themselves, and to pray God to give Repentance to the offender.

7. He must publickly declare the impenitent excommunicate, and bind him over to answer it at the bar of God, and set Gods terrors before his Conscience.

8. He must try and judge of the Truth of the Repentance of those that say they do repent (where all the ancient rigorous Penances came in.) And not trust every incredible saying, I Repent.

T 2   9. He

9: He muſt receive thoſe publickly into the Church that truly repent , or credibly profeſs to do ſo ; and muſt comfort him with the declaration of the pardon of his ſin.

10. He muſt perſwade the Church to receive him into their affections and Chriſtian Communion, and to eſteem and uſe him as a Brother again.

11. And as to the *Manner*, all this muſt be done, 1. with great Prudence and diſcretion ; elſe the Church may ſoon be ſet on fire, (as by a confeſſion of a Deacons adulteries at *Conſtantinople, &c.*) 2. It muſt be done with *deliberation* and *througheſt* acquaintance and information of the truth : elſe raſh and haſty judgments, and believing knaves will diſgrace the Biſhop, and injure the juſt, and gratifie the wicked, & breed uncurable breaches between ſo unjuſt a Biſhop and the flock. 3. It muſt be done with the greateſt *ſeriouſneſs, reverence,* and *gravity* ; As knowing that the honour of God and Religion and the Church lieth on it, and the comfort or recovery of the ſouls of men, and the preſervation of the reſt.

It is not a Chancellors check, nor ſaying, *do you repent,* and will *you pay your fees,* that diſpatcheth ſuch a work as this. It requireth much skill, and time and patience. Poor ſinners muſt not be taken in a paſſion ; nor is it imperious frowns that melt men into true Repentance : The opening of the nature of the ſin, and the aggravation, not reproachfully but convincingly ; the awakening of a ſecure hardened ſinner, with the terrors of the Lord ; the drawing him home by the opening of the motives of Love and mercy ; do all require greater *skill,* and *holineſs,* and *love* to *Souls,* than moſt Biſhops have that ever I was acquainted with ; much more than a Lay-Chancellor hath, who is the man that doth the work, that never pretended to be a Divine.

I muſt profeſs for my own part, that when I did this with others for one Pariſh, it called for more *skill,* and holy *affections,* and conſequently more convinced me of my weakneſs, by far, than publick preaching to the people. The heart of an honeſt judge will be turned within him, before he paſs the ſentence of death on an offender. And before we paſs the ſentence of Excommunication, our bowels muſt yearn over poor ſouls, and all means be tried to recover them.

And here it is not the cleareſt witneſs of the crime that will ſerve turn : For men are not to be excommunicated for any ordinary crime, unleſs it have *impenitency* and *obſtinacy* added to it. And therefore the work of the Biſhop is (not like a ſecular Court to judge only of the *fact* and *fault,* but) to judge of mens repentance or *Impenitence.* And that is a thing that cannot be done by a few Lordly awful words.

You will ſay, *Becauſe of all this we judge that ordinary Prieſts are not to be truſted with ſo great a work, but a few wiſe and Reverend Prelates.*

Anſ. 1. I never yet knew the beſt Biſhop that was to be compared for ability in this work to many a Pariſh Miniſter that I have known : Nor did I ever know One Biſhop tolerably fit for it, who had not for a conſiderable time been a laborious Pariſh Miniſter. Thoſe that come from the Univerſities to be Noblemens and Biſhops Chaplains, and ſo get the Tythes of two or three rich Benefices, and then are made Prebends, Deans, and Maſters of Colledges ; and then are made Biſhops, may read, and talk of all this work ; but know no more what

what it is indeed than I know how to build an house.

2. An experienced Minister that liveth upon the place and knoweth all the persons and witnesses, hath incomparable advantage above a strange Prelate.

3. One that is their familiar and ordinary Teacher, whom they neither contemn, nor fear with a carnal awe, for fear of punishment, may discern whether Repentance be credibly serious; which he that aweth them by greatness and terror shall never know: For almost all the veriest beasts will there profess Repentance, though they come home with redoubled malice against the persons that would have reformed them: Only a man that believeth he is in the right will incur the Bishops wrath for not confessing that he is in the wrong.

4. But yet our Caution is far greater than the Bishops; For because this requireth so much *skill* and *faithfulness*, we would have no one Man trusted with it (except in a case of necessity, when a Church can have no more) For in the multitude of Counsellers is safety: We would have every Church have a *Consessus* of *Presbyters* (and if one be a Bishop we contend not against it) And we would have it done in the presence of the Seniors of the flock, who know the persons, that so if one should want skill or truthiness, he might be helpt by others, or hindred from doing wrong. And if all this will not do, we would have the next Synod of neighbour Pastors to have a final audience of the case.

And now let any thing except utterly blinding *Pride* and *Partiality* be judge; WHETHER A *CONSESSUS* OF MINISTERS IN THE PRESENCE OF THE SENIORS OF THE FLOCK, WHO ALL KNOW THE PERSONS, be not liker to JUDGE RIGHTLY IN ONE PARISH, where also a neighbour Synod may review the case, than ONE STRANGE PRELATE or CHANCELLOR FOR A DIOCESE OF MANY CHURCHES, WHERE HE KNOWETH NOT THE PERSONS:

Especially when this Chancellor and all the Proctors and Officers of the Courts do live (in wealth) upon the *Trade*, and therefore must manage it as a trade: When in the way that we desire, no Presbyter, nor Synod, should have one farthing for all his pains; but his comfort in obeying God, and endeavouring the Churches good and mens salvation.

Alas Lord, How long shall Christs enemies be the Pastors of his flocks? and the seed of the serpent be the great instruments that must break the serpents head, and the lovers of sin be they that must be the suppressers of it, and those employed to teach men knowledge, who themselves will not know, and to preach up holiness who cannot endure it? To willing minds these things are plain.

Church Discipline hath its effect on the Consciences of men, and these things take as they come with spiritual *life, light* and *love*. We see in our Preaching, how much all work is lost, which is done proudly, unskilfully and marred in the manner. And true Pastoral discipline must work just as Preaching must do, it being but a more particular application of the same word, to persons and causes. *Athanasius Patriarcha Constantinop.* in his fifth Epistle for the residence of Bishops (*Bibl. Patr. T. 3. p.* 159.) saith of constant preaching [*Hæc nocte dieque debent singuli Pastores gregibus suis inculcare, quæ tam necessaria sunt, quam est respirare animanti: Necessarium inquam omnia judicia & testimonia Dei denunciare; ita ut ab* hæc *hoc est prosperitas & opulentia*, And in his three last Epistles he counselleth the Emperor to force those Bishops to *Preaching* and *Vigilancy*, that will not do it without force.

And indeed, unjust Excommunications most hurt the Excommunicators. Read *Nicon's* Epistle *ad Euch. de injusta Excommunicatione*, proving that an unjust Excommunication bindeth not another, but falleth on the Excommunicators head.

But the sad truth is, that it's usual with the Prelates to confess the vanity of their own Spiritual power, and to call it a leaden sword, which would but be despised, if it were not backt with the Magistrates sword, which is the very thing they trust to.

But of this anon.

III. And lastly, let it be considered objectively what work it is that every Bishop hath to do : and then you shall see whether it be possible.

1. As to the number of Sins *in specie*. 2. As to the number of Sinners.

1. Such sins as are in other Countries, and as are condemned in Scripture are among us also. 1. As to Intellectual evils, we have ignorant persons who neither know what Christ or Christianity is, or what a Sacrament is, or what are the Essentials of Faith. We have Atheists that think there is no God, or say so at least ; we have more Infidels, that deride Christ and Christianity : we have impious persons who make a mock of Godliness : we have Quakers and Familists, and Seekers, who either deny the Scripture to be Gods word, or true, or say Scripture, Church and Ministry are lost, or turn Scripture into an Allegory, or that prefer the light within every man, Heathens and all, as sufficient without it ; and Enthusiasts and true Fanaticks who trust to inward Revelations and impulses instead of Gods word. We have Papists, we have Antinomians, Libertines, and more Sects which the Bishops themselves can name you, and overcharge.

2. And for more voluntary sins, we have almost all the breaches of all the commandments : We have open enemies of preaching, praying, sacraments, family duties, catechizing, the Lords days holy observation : Common scorners of those that fear to sin, and diligently seek God. We have (if the Bishops could know them) malignant persecutors, that would force Gods servants to most odious sins, that hinder Christs Ministers from doing the work to which they are devoted, and from preaching to sinners the Gospel of Christ, and calling them to Repent and live. We have idolaters, false worshippers, blasphemers, perjured persons, common prophane swearers, and cursers, and liars ; and we have children despisers and dishonourers of their parents, and servants of their masters ; and subjects of Princes and Rulers, (and whether of Bishops and Pastors, let the Bishops judge :) Profane families ; husband and wife living in open enmity or wrath : we have murderers, fighters, railers, such as maliciously seek the ruine of others, great and small oppressors, thieves, defrauders, adulterers and fornicators, filthy speakers, gluttons, drunkards, such as waste their lives in gaming, plays, and idleness, false-witnesses, Simoniacal, bribe-takers, subverters of justice,

to

to say nothing of the notorious effects of gross *uncharitableness, covetousness,* and *pride.* These and more than these are here.

2. And for the number of sinners ; 1. Conjecture by the number of persons : 2. And then by the commonness of the sins.

1. I have before oft told you that some Dioceses have many hundred Parishes, some above a thousand ; and in the lesser sort of these Parishes, commonly there are in some 50, in most 100 or 200 families ; and in the greater and Market Towns, there are in some of the lesser about 1000 souls, in the middle sort about 2000 or 3000 or 4000 ; and in the bigger about 5000 or 6000, and some few 10000 : And in the greatest Parishes of all in *London,* some 20000, some 40000, some 50000, and it is said in some many thousands more.

2. And for the sins, 1. The Bishops themselves say, that Atheism, Infidelity, and derision of Scripture and Religion aboundeth among such as I will not name : 2. They say themselves that Rebels, and Quakers, and Seekers, and Enthusiasts, *&c.* are so many as that they know not what to do with them. 3. They say themselves that Papists so increase, as that they give out their hopes to swallow up all. 4. One sort which they call Schismaticks, as being against their interest, they really exercise their power against : and find that this one sort are more than they know what to do with. 5. The number that malignantly labour to make all *seriousness* and *diligence* in *seeking God,* to become a scorned hated thing, and make it to seem meer self-conceitedness and hypocrisie, and to keep people from obeying God, is so great, as we cannot reckon them. 6. The number of the grosly ignorant is lamentably great. 7. Common swearers and cursers are usually met with in our ordinary converse. 8. How common drunkenness is, let lamenting Parents, grieved wives, and beggered families tell you. 9. Whether fornication and adultery (rarely heard of till of late, comparatively) be now grown common, if not in fashion, I leave the Prelates themselves to judge. 10. To pass by all the rest, *Whether serious credible Repentance* (though not expressed by the ancient severe penances) be now a common thing, for these or many other sins, I am content that any English man be judge, that ever laboured to bring men to Repentance, and knoweth what Repentance is.

And now by this conjecture 1. How many thousands (I say not the Bishop who puts it off, but) the Lay-chancellor hath to stand at his bar at once, if discipline were tolerably exercised. 2. How many years, the accusers and offenders were like to wait before a cause could be heard. 3. Or how spiritually, powerfully, meltingly this Lay-man (that never preached) is like to draw all these thousands to Repentance. 4. What the Sinner and the Church shall do till the year come that they can be heard. 5. Whether it be possible for any such thing as true Pastoral conviction, exhortation, discipline, to be ever exercised on them at all, while that new sins, even heinous ones are still committed ; and the Bishop or Chancellor or Surrogate, that had a thousand, or ten thousand sinners at once to speak to, when he could deal but with six or seven in a day (if he did nothing else,) shall before he can examine their cases have thousands more (of their and others) to examine.

So that nothing of this nature can be more notorious, than that our controversie with

with the Bishops is but such as these: Whether the Lord Mayor alone shall not only oversee all the Families in the City, but be the *Only Governour* of them, so that Husbands, Parents, and Masters, shall only teach and exhort their families, but the Lord Mayor alone shall rule them, as to their daily *works*, their *speeches* and their lives.

Or, whether the City and the whole Diocese shall have but one Schoolmaster, who shall be the sole governour of all the Schools in all those hundred parishes, 20, or 40, or 100 miles distant, and the Schools shall have under him only Curate Ushers, who shall only teach the boyes as far as they are willing to learn, and for all their untractableness, disobedience, absence, and faults, shall present their names to a Chancellors Court, set up by the sole ruling Schoolmaster.

Or whether all the Colledges in the University shall have no Governour but the Vicechancellor, and the rest be but Tutors to the Voluntiers.

Or whether all the Patients in a Diocese shall have but one Physician, to govern the Patient by prescripts, and under him only Apothecaries to carry about his medicines and directions? Indeed if it were the Physicians work to play the Soldier, and cut all their throats, it might be done in a short time. But healing requireth more ado. And if it were the Bishops or Chancellors work to do no more, than to read an accusation, and say, Do you Repent, and (as some do, because they must be thrice admonished,) to say at once, *I admonish you, I admonish you, I admonish you, I excommunicate you*; or to do as the Pope doth, *Interdict* whole *Kingdoms at once*, (as *Herod* killed all the children in hope that he should meet with Christ among them,) then a few hands might do the work. But whether it be possible to exercise the discipline of Christ, in their Diocesan way on one of a thousand, let the impartial judge: As also whether that Church be fitlier said to be governed or ungoverned where one of a thousand is governed indeed, whenas it is the body of the people, and not one of a thousand, that is called the Church.

C H A P.

CHAP. XIX.

The same Impoffibilty proved by Experience.

THey fay Experience is the teacher of fools : But O how well were it for the Churches of Chrift, if their Reverend Bifhops (who think themfelves only meet to govern them) had but learnt by it, thefe 1300 years, at leaft. The Experience which I offer you is,

1. That of the ancient Churches : what work the enlargement of their Dioceffes, and growing great by the greatnefs of their charge made quickly by the deftruction of true difcipline, abundance of forecited teftimonies fhew. To which what fad complaints might I add out of *Socr t s Chryfoftome. Ifidore Pelufiata.* and many others: which made *Gregory Nazianz. Orat. 1.* Say fo much of the difficulty of a Bifhops work, and to depofe himfelf when contentious men were ready to depofe him, and to wifh fo earneftly that there had never been greatnefs and Priority and difference of Seats as Upper and Lower among the Paftors of the Churches being tired with their contentious pride and envy, even of the Orthodox themfelves : who inftead of doing the work, contended for power and preeminence.

I cited fome of *Chryfoftomes* fayings before, *de facerdot.l 3 c 16.17.* where he fheweth the greatnefs of a Bifhops work, and p. 57. So p. 58. *Nifi quotidie Epifcopus omnium domos circumierit, in hac parte vel eas fuperans, quibus nullum aliud ftudium eft quam in foro verfandi deambulandique, hinc omnino offenfiones infinitæ emergent : Neque enim ij foli qui ægrotant, fed & qui fani funt, invifi fe volunt : Ad quod non religionis ac pietatis, fed honoris dignitatifque potius nomine plurimi fibi vendicant. Ac fi quem forte contigerit ex ditioribus potentioribufque Chriftianis ecclefiæ ufu hoc æque communi ita urgenti, ab Epifcopo frequentius invifi, hic protinus Epifcopus palpatoris atque adulatoris notam fibi inurit.* Chryfoftome fpeaketh like a man that knew by experience what a Paftors work is : And if our Bifhops muft go to every houfe, how many years pilgrimage would it be to go but once through all their Dioceffes ?

Bernard, faith *Epift. 82. Cum præfideant urbibus valde populofis, & cætus, ut ita dicam, patrias, propriæ Diocæfes ambitu circumcludant, occafione inventâ ex quacunque veteri privilegio, fatagunt ut vicinas fibi fubdant civitates, quatenus duæ, quibus vix duo Præfules fufficiebant, fub uno redigantur antiftite.* And the doleful lapfe of difcipline hereupon all Hiftory witneffeth.

Which made *Erafmus* fay, *Ecclef. lib. 1. Quantum negotii credimus effe, cum præter vicos & pagos, viginti frequentes & amplæ civitates* (fuch as our big Market Towns) *uni parent antiftiti-- Et multorum præfulum ditio tam late patet, ut fi quam maxime forent expediti omnibus mundanis negotiis, non poffent tanta in in omnibus oppidis Concionari ; quum hodie una civitas quamplures requirit Eccle-siastes :* How much less will one perform all the rest of the Bishops work?

Saith *Musculus Loc. Commun. de Minist. p. mibi* 438. [Quare viderint E-piscopi, *&c.* [*Let Bishops look to it, who when they cannot* (or do not) *rightly Minister to one Church, extend their power, not to some few Churches, but to whole Provinces.* Let them read *Chrysostome* on *Tit* 1. *Per civitates,* in every City, *&c.* These things made *Luther* say *adverf. falfo nominatum ordinem E-piscop. To.2.p.*310. Perinde habet, &c. *It is with these wicked ungodly Bi-shops all one as if the Devil himself, should mitred and ringed sit in the chair and himself rule the people.*

And Bishop *Hooker* in 8 precep. saith, Et certe si jam vigeret antiquus ille erga populum amor, *If they had the ancient Love to the people, they would them-selves confess that there is more work in one City, than the best men can easily do.* They know well enough that the Primitive Church had no such Bishops till the time of *Silvester the first.* (I cite this *ex Altar. Damascen* having not the Book at hand.

Filefacus tells us, *ex Concil. Triburicufi c.* 26. *Relata est coram sancta Synodo quaeremonia plebium, eo quod sint quidam Episcopi nolentes ad praedicandum, vel ad confirmandum suas per annum parecias circuire, de Orig. parec. p.* 537. What would they have done if they had been in our times.

See *Isidore Peluf. Ep.*246. *l.2.p* 236. teaching Bishop *Eusebius* (and *Theo-dosius*) what a Church is, who had to far lost the true Episcopacy, as to take *walls for men,* and to abuse and scorn the true Church or godly people: while the Walls were adorned, as if Christ had come from Heaven more for [*Walls* than *Souls*] *&c.* of which before.

In a word, nothing is more evident than that true Discipline was shut out at the times and in the degrees as Dioceffes were enlarged ; and that in *Africk* and other places where the Churches or Dioceffes were more small and numerous, discipline was best preferved.

II. The second sort of experience is, that almost all the Reformed Churches, who have found the Pastoral work and Discipline particularly to be so great, as that less than all the Parish Ministers concurring could not perform it. 1. Those Churches which with *Calvin* set up Presbytery, ex-clude no Pastor from the Governing part ; but took in Elders of the people to help them, because experience had told them that all the Ministers were too few : what then would one Bishop and Chancellour or Vicar have been able to do ?

2. The Lutherans who set up superintendants, commonly so set them over the Pastors as not to take away the true Pastoral power of governing their particular flocks, as finding by experience, that the old way of Pre-lacy would not do it : And usually they join Magistrates with them, as they also in the Palatinate did. And it is such a moderate superiority which is exercifed in *Hungary, Transilvania,* and in *Poland* till the Papists rooted them out thence.

3. The Helvetian Divines exercife a certain meafure of power in keep-ing the unfit from the Sacrament; but not what they judge to be the

Churches

Churches duty, because the Magiſtrate never would conſent: That the Paſtors are for it, as needful to the right ordering of the Churches you may ſee in *Polani: Syntag.* at large, and in moſt of their Divines of *Baſil, Bern, Zurich,* &c. I will now only cite the honeſt hearty words of *Muſculus* above 100 years ago, becauſe he was a man moſt clear and candid, and that did mancipate his judgment neither to *Luther, Calvin,* nor any party as ſuch; but took liberty to differ from them all as in the points of Redemption, perſeverance, &c.) At *Bern* in his *Loci Commun. ed.* 1567 *p* 421. He proveth *Biſhops,* and *Presbyters* and *Doctors,* and *Paſtors* to be all one. And *p.* 422. that in the Apoſtolick Primitive Church they governed the Church in common, being ſubject to no head or preſident. But after the Apoſtles dates as *Hierome* ſaith to avoid ſchiſm, but as he thinketh more out of a deſire of Majority; one got the name and preſidency of a Biſhop: But, ſaith he [*whether this counſel did profit the Church or not, by which ſuch Biſhops were introduced, as Hierome ſaith by cuſtome rather than by truth, of divine diſpoſition, to be above the Presbyters. it hath been better manifeſted to after ages, than when this cuſtome was firſt brought in: which we muſt thank for all the inſolency, wealth and tyranny, of the Principal and Equiptral Biſhops, yea for the corruption of all the Churches, which if Hierome had ſeen, undoubtedly he would have known that it was the deviſe, not of the Spirit of God, to take away ſchiſms as was pretended, but of Satan himſelf to lay waſte and deſtroy the ancient Miniſters for feeding the Lords flock: whereby it might come to paſs that the Church might have not true Paſtors, Doctors, Presbyters and Biſhops but under the masks of thoſe names, idle-bellies, and magnifick Princes, who will not only not themſelves feed the people of God with ſound Apoſtolick Doctrine, but alſo take care by moſt wicked violence, that it be done by no one elſe. By this deviſe of Satan it is brought to paſs. that inſtead of Biſhops. the Churches have potent Lords and Princes, for the moſt choſen out of the order of Nobles and great men. who being upheld by their own and their kindreds power, may domineer over the flock of God as they liſt.*

And *p.* 423. *The office appointed to the Biſhops that came after the Apoſtles times was to preach to the people, to adminiſter the ſacred things, to preſcribe repentance to take the care of the clergy and the people both in City and Country, to ordain, to wit, to take care that the goods of the Church be rightly kept and diſpoſed, and to take the patronage of Church matters with Princes. And if the Biſhops had but ſtood here, it had been better with the Church: Or if the Prelates and Paſtors of our times would return to theſe Canonical Rules, there might be hope that the Eccleſiaſtical State and order might poſſibly be repaired; and the controverſies of theſe times might be ended by the word of God——* Hence it is plain that the office of true Presbyters and biſhops in the Church of Chriſt is, to feed the Lords flock with ſound Doctrine, and to be truly Paſtors and Teachers. But now the falſe Biſhops pretend a Paſtoral Cure, when going to the Aſſembly-Offices they are, as they ſay it, Epiſcopally cloathed. They put on a white ſtole, longer than ordinary; with a girdle (not ſuch as John Baptiſt wore, &c. —— *The mask of Paſtors thus decked, doth not feed the flock of God,*

but performeth the Church service in such a gesture, Ceremony and dialect, that all
the matters of the Church may be nothing else than certaine vaine and pompous
shewes ——— so that if one of the Apostles were there, he would never so much as
dreame that this were the Episcopal feeding of the Lords flock. Thus the
'Bishop doing once or twice a year doth Sufficiently performe his Office, what e-
'ver he do the rest of the time. The ordination of Ministers and other things
'accounted Ecclesiastical, he committeth partly to his suffragane, and partly to
'his Vicar, or Chancellor. The office of Teaching he committeth to some Doctor
'or Monk, so sworne, as that he shall not dare to speake a word (or hisse) be-
'sides what is prescribed him in the formes of Lawes.

Thus far I confess he speakes of the Popish Bishops: But who would
believe he meant not ours that had seen them? And how little do they
differ? Well you shall next hear him speak of Protestant Bishops.

'Pag. 425 [Let us now come to other Ministers, Pastors and Bishops, di-
'vers from these, who do nothing in the Church of Christ but Preach and teach :
'They have certaine daies of the weeke on which they Preach: And that is well :
'They Preach only out of the holy Scriptures: And that will too. But this is
These are not 'not well, that very many of them speak formally and coldly, and not from
our Bishops. 'the heart ; so that what Seneca somewhere saith, agreeth to them ; Animum
'non faciunt, quia animum non habent. They make not men hearty (or
'serious) because they are not so themselves : And that of the Roman Orator,
'thou wouldst never talk thus, if thou speakest from the heart : Nor do they
'accommodate the word of God to the Hearers, by pertinent and profitable di-
'stribution, but they think they have well performed their office, if they have
'any how spoken out the hour. In the mean time, they observe not the peoples
'mindes and lives, much lesse do they reforme them : Nor do they take care
'how the people grow in the knowledge of God, the faith of Christ and in true
'Godlinesse: They apply not themselves to the study of the Scriptures, nor per-
'swade the people to read them in their houses ; they neither take care of the poor
'and strangers nor visit the sick, as little caring how and with what faith they de-
'part: And thus they discharge their Ministry neither faithfully, prudently nor
'profitably. It is indeed of great moment that they bring not strange Doct-
'rine into the Church ; but teach the Scripture Doctrine; and that they use
'not superstitious rites, but are not content with simple administration of the Sacra-
'ments, according to the custome of the Primitive Church. But in this they
'are to be blamed, that they do things right and profitable, not from the hearts,
'but sleightly, as on the by, and what is accordingly to be else done by a faith-
'ful Minister they wholly neglect. While they thus Minister, they do not indeed
'bring Errour and superstitions into the Churches, as in the foregoing ages was
'done. But in the mean time, inclining to the other extreme, they take the
'course which by degrees will bring the people into that indifferency in Religions
'which is the most pestilent, and to drink in Epicurism the waster and extinguisher
'of all religion. Wherefore I beseech them in the Lord, that they fully performe
'and discharge their Ministry, and not thus by the halves] Thus far he describeth our ordinary better sort of the Clergie, but not our Bishops.

'And

'And Pa. 431. [*They that labour more to keep up the authority of Bishops, than*
'*to save the people, when they cannot convince the Ministers, called by the Magistrate,*
'*of error, do raise a question about their calling, (being themselves neither lawfully*
'*chosen nor called) saying, what Suffragane ordained you minister? what Bishop cal-*
'*led you to the office? As the Priests by Christ. They questioned not his work,*
'*which they could find no fault with, but his power — so these, where*
'*they cannot by Gods word defend their own errours and abuses, nor disprove our*
'*true doctrine, they fly to the Episcopal power and authority, as if they did pos-*
'*sess any such unblamable and lawful power, when they neither discharge the of-*
'*fice, nor have the power of true Bishops; wherefore let no true sincere Minister*
'*of Christ regard the barking of these men, but as content with the testimony of his*
'*Conscience, and his calling to teach by the Lawful Magistrate, go on in the Lords*
'*work with alacrity of spirit.*]

Here he addeth the manner of their calling, at *Bern*, by the election of
the Pastors and confirmation of the Magistrates, and reception of the
people, that you may know what he meaneth by the Magistrates
Call.

'And p. 436. having told us, that *Christianity falleth where the election*
'*and Pastoral care of the Ministry falleth*, he addeth. [*But now they that endea-*
'*vour to put out the light of truth, boast much of the power of Bishops, Arch-*
'*Bishops, Metropolitanes, Patriarcks, and the Roman Pope; where if you urge*
'*them to it, they are not able to prove by any truth of divine institution, that so*
'*much as this first ministerial power (of Ministring in the Church) is in those*
'*Bishops, Arch-bishops, Metropolitanes, Patriarcks or Pope, that is, in these Church*
'*Lords (Satrapes). Let them prove that these are true Ministers of Christ.*
'*I strive not about Episcopacy (simply) in it self, whether it be to be numbred*
'*with Christs true Ministers: But the controversie is whether such Bishops as our age*
'*too patiently tolerateth are to be numbred with Christs true Ministers; It is great-*
'*ly to be feared, lest in the day of judgment they will hear that dreadful word*
'*from God, Depart from me ye workers of iniquity, I know you not*]

I have added more of *Musculus* then directly concerneth the point now
in hand, because I would take him all together. And because the Helvetians are not accounted Presbyterians, I add *Bullinger, Decad.* 5. *Serm.* 3. *p.*
(mihi) 377. 378. and *Serm.* 4. *p.* 38^. Where he sheweth that *Diocesan*
Bishops have not the sole power of ordination, that Presbyters and Bishops were the same and had the same work, and the horrid abuses, that
came into the Church by the degenerating of Episcopacy: And *Decad.* 5.
Serm, 10. *p.* 491. '*that in latter Ages, Prelates and Bishops, snatching by ty-*
'*ranny that power of excommunication, to themselves which before was used by*
'*the Pastors in Synods in common, and sacrilegiously using it against the first insti-*
'*tution, had turned a wholsome medicine into deadly poyson, and made it abs-*
'*minable to good and bad. But I may not recite all.*

Wigandus was no Presbyterian, being superintendent of *Magdeburgh*
first, and after of *Wismaria*, and after of *Jene*, and after Bishop *Pomeranien-*
sis; nor yet *Math. Iudex.* yet go they the same way as may be seen, *Sy-*

A a 3   *tagm.*

tagm. p. 1049. *de excom. p.* 1114. *de Ecclef. p.* 1135. *de Minift.* Should I cite all that is faid by thofe that never were called Presbyterians, about the degeneration of Epifcopacy, the largenefs of their charge, the ruine of difcipline by their tyranny, ambition and grafping wealth and titles, when they neither will nor can perform the work, I mean by *Luther, Melancton, Illyricus, Chytræus Tzegedine, Bucer, Zuinglius, Oecolampadius, Gryneus Aretius, Gualther, Pet. Martyr, Aræus, Chenmitius, Pelargus,* &c. I fhould but over-weary the Readers patience. I only add that if the Churches of *France, Belgia, Geneva* and the reft of the Presbyterians, and the Churches of *Tranfilvania, Hungary* and formerly, *Poland* (that were Orthodox) and *Bohemia, Brandenburgh Saxony,* the Palatinate, &c. that fet up another fort of Epifcopacy, had found, that the old or Englifh fpecies would have done the Minifterial works it is not credible that they would all have rejected it.

III. The third part of that experience which I alledge is the Bifhops own.

1. This is fignified by their confeffions before named,

Ar. Bifhop *Ufhers* reafons for the ancient ufe of Epifcopacy with their Presbyters who fhall be acknowledged true Church Governours over their flocks, is fetcht from the need of fo many to the work. And Mr. *Stanley Gower* late of *Dorchefter* was wont to profefs (being long intimate with him) that he protefted to him that he took a Bifhop to be but *primus Presbyterorum,* of the fame order, and every Presbyter a Governour of the flock: And when he afked him, why then he would be a Primate as he was, he told him that he took it not for any part of his office as inftituted by Chrift but for a Collateral Dignity which the King was pleafed to beftow on him, for the more advantageous difcharge of his Spiritual Office.

What Bifhop *Jewels* opinion was to the like purpofe is plain enough in his works,

Bifhop *Reignolds* (that now is) profeffed to me his opinion to be the fame, when he took the Bifhoprick, and when he faw Dr. *Stillingfleets* book, that no form of Church Government is prefcribed in Scripture, profeffed that it was always his opinion; And joyned with us in our propofals for Bifhop *Ufhers* Model.

Dr *Stillingfleet* in his *Irenicon* hath faid fo much againft the *Jus Divinum* of our Prelacy as can never be anfwered.

I have talked with many of the Bifhops and Epifcopal Conformifts my felf of thefe matters, and I do not remember that ever I fpake to one accounted a Learned man, that did not confefs when driven to it, that the *Greatnefs of the Diocefes,* and the Chancellors Government by the Church Keyes, were caufes of fo great a lapfe of difcipline, as is to be groaned under: And can fhew us no probability, if poffibility of reftoring it, while it fo ftands. And yet they would have us fubfcribe and fwear *never to endeavour any alteration of the Church Government :* not excepting in our place

and

and calling, by petition, or otherwise, no though the King commanded us.

Bishop *Hall* in his *Mod.Offer* doth confess the faultiness, and desires reformation: and in his excellent *Peace-maker*, would take up even with a presidencie *durante vita*, as sufficient to reconcile us.

Dr. *Hammond* himself oft complaineth of the lapse of discipline, and the clergies and peoples vices thereupon.

The Liturgy wisheth the godly Discipline restored, but doth it not, as if in our case it could not be done.

Abundance of their Writers lament the scandals of clergy and people which have abounded, of which I shall say somewhat more anon.

2. And this is yet plainlier confessed by the *Actual omission* of discipline: We need not to dispute whether that can or be ever like to be done, by our Prelacy, which is *no where done, and never was done, no not by any one man of them*, not excepting the very best; so that if they had not come neer the Erastian opinion in their hearts, and thought this use of the Keyes to consist but in bare Teaching, or the rest to be of no great need, it had not been possible that they should have quieted their Consciences. Or at least, if they did not do it, by saying, I cannot help it; It is not long of me: As Bishop *Goodman* layeth it on the King in the case of Chancellours, and most lay it on the Church-Wardens and Ministers for presenting no more: But all must confess that little is done besides the troubling of Nonconformists. It is not one of a thousand in a Diocesse, I am confident, that ever is brought under the exercise of Church discipline that ought to be; Nor one of many thousand that should be so according to the ancient Canons of the Churches. If I should give no other instance, than the ordinarie neglect of all Gods publick worship (Preaching, Prayer and Sacraments) in publick, Churches or any other Religious Assemblies, I do not think but ten thousand persons in this Diocesse, and twenty thousand, if not fourty, in *London* Diocesse are guilty, that were never questioned by the Church.

I may therefore argue thus: That which never was done by any one Bishop in *England*, being the confessed work of their office is naturally or Morally Impossible to be done (or if it have a possibility it is as bad as none, when it never was once reduced into act) but the true exercise of Church discipline on all or the hundredth or many hundredth person that it is due to, was *never done by one Bishop in England, that can by any credible History be proved* (since the deformation or reformation) Ergo.

The strength of the Major is plain. 1. From the Bishops own mouths who use to praise themselves as the Wisest, Learnedst and best of the Clergie, and therefore fitter to be trusted with the Government of the Church than all or any of the Presbyters (though but under them) And they would take it heynously if we question their wisdome, conscience or honesty, and if they are all or most so good, sure it is long of the

state

ſtate and conſtitution of their places, and not long of their perſons, that their very proper work is made but a ſhaddow and a dream.

2. But though this be but *ad homines*, yet really we have had very worthy and excellent perſons to be Biſhops; what a man was *Jewell*? Arch-biſhop *Grindal* had Godlineſs enough. and reſolution too to make him odius, and favoured Lectures and Preaching, *&c.* Enough to bring him down, if *Cambden*, *Godwin* or *Fuller*, are to be believed: but never could do this work of diſcipline, upon one of hundreds or thouſands under him. We had an excellent Arch-Biſhop-Abbot afterwards, good enough to be reproached by *Heylin*, and to ſuffer what I need not mention, but never able to do this work. What Learned, Judicious worthy men, were his Brother *Robert Abbot*, and after him *Davenant*, Biſhops of *Salisbury*? And how good a man was peaceable Biſhop *Hall*, ſo *Uſher* in *Ireland*, *Moron* and many more? But no ſuch thing was done by any of them? what ſhould I ſay now of Biſhop *Reignolds*, and Biſhop *Wilkins*, Men Learned and extraordinary honeſt in theſe times: But let any man enquire whether any ſuch thing as the diſcipline in queſtion is exerciſed on the thouſandth Criminal in their Dioceſe ? Indeed we have heard in Biſhop *Reignolds* Dioceſe of a great number cenſured for Nonconformity: And it is his praiſe that it was not his doing; but his Chancellours (though heretofore Judge Advocate in *Fairefaxes* or *Cromwells* Army.) And to ſay now that it is long of Church-Wardens, Chancellours, *&c.* Is but to ſay that the Church is corrupted, the Epiſcopal diſcipline almoſt quite caſt out, and all the remedy is to ſay, It is long of ſomebody : Like the Phyſician whoſe Praiſe was, that his patients dyed according to the rules of art; or the nurſe whoſe praiſe was, that though moſt of the Children periſhed, it was long of themſelves or ſomebody elſe.

IV. But the fulleſt experience, which ſo far ſatisfieth me that all the books in the world cannot change me in this, *is my own, and the reſt of my Brethren in* the Miniſtry. I have lived now (through Gods wonderful mercy) threeſcore years wanting leſſe than four * In all this time, whilſt the Biſhops ruled, I never heard one man or woman called openly to repentance for any ſin ; nor one ever publikely confeſs or lament any ſin ? Nor one that was excommunicate in any Country where I came , except the Nonconformiſts : Nor did I hear of any but one man to my remembrance , who did formal penance for Fornication, I doubt not but there have been more: But the number may be conjectured by this. I lived under a great number of drunken and ignorant Curates that never preached, and Schoolmaſters, my ſelf, and many more were round about us, that were never troubled with diſcipline, or caſt out. I never lived where drunkards and ſwearers were not common ; but never one of them underwent the Churches diſcipline : But thoſe that met to faſt and pray, and went to hear a Sermon two miles off, when they had none at home. But yet this is the laſt of my conviction. When

Now ne w-
fixty five
I have late-
ly heard
two excom-
municated
for teaching
School and
being mar-
ried with-
out Licenſe,
and a third
no cauſe
named.

When I undertook a Paſtoral charge my ſelf, I kept with me two Miniſters to aſſiſt me (at one Pariſh Church and a ſmall Chappel): I had three Godly Juſtices of Peace in the Pariſh, who to countenance our diſcipline kept their monthly meeting at the ſame time and place. I had four ancient Godly men that performed the office of Deacons: I had above twenty of the Seniors of the Laity, who without pretence of any office, met with us to be witneſſes that we did the Church and ſinners no wrong, and to awe the offenders by their preſence: Theſe met once a month together, we had almoſt all the worthy Miniſters of the Country agreeing and aſſociated to do the like in their ſeveral Pariſhes as far as they were able; that unity might the more convince offenders: We had in the ſame Town the next day after our monthly Town-meeting, an Aſſembly of a dozen or twenty ſuch Miniſters, to edifie each other, and that thoſe might be tryed by them and before them, whether we could perſwade them to repentance, who could not be prevailed with by our ſelves: And, which was our caſe incomparably beyond all this, the times nor our judgment allowing us to uſe diſcipline upon none but ſuch as conſented to our office and relation to them, we told them that we had all agreed only to exerciſe ſo much of diſcipline as Epiſcopal, Presbyterians and Independants had no controverſie about (ſome of the Epiſcopal joyning with us) and that we would exerciſe it in all our flocks, but we could be Paſtors to none againſt their wills; whereupon of about 5000 perſons, 1800 or more of which were at age to be Communicants, all refuſed to do any more than hear me preach, (for fear of diſcipline) except about 600 or a few more. Theſe 600 were the moſt underſtanding Religious part of the Pariſh, all the groſly ignorant, and the Common Swearers, and all the Drunkards and ſcandalous perſons were among the refuſers, except about five or ſix young men that had got ſuch a Love to tipling that they could not leave it. Theſe hid their tin a while: But could not long: Yet the trouble and work that theſe five or ſix men made us, ſometimes by Drunkenneſs, ſometimes by fighting, ſometimes by ſlandering their Neighbours, or ſuch like was more than it is caſy for an unexperienced perſon to believe. So hard was it to bring them to a Confeſſion of their ſins or to ask thoſe Forgiveneſs whom they groſly wronged, that when we endeavoured with all our skill to convince them, and uſed both gentle exhortation, and alſo opened to them the terrors of the Lord, when we prayed before them that God would give them repentance, when their own Parents and relations joyned with us, all would not make them confeſs their ſin, but we were forced to caſt them out of our Communion (for the moſt part of them). And among all the reſt there were ſome that ſometimes would need admonitions, and reconciliations with one another, which found us ſome work. But if we had but been troubled with all the other (1000 or 1200 as was ſuppoſed) of the Pariſh, and ſo with all the Swearers, railers, Common Drunkards, ſome Infidels, &c. What work ſhould we have had ? So much as I dare confidently ſay that (without

out being half so strict and troublesome as the Ancient Canons were) all we could not possibly have done more in the work of discipline, than Govern that one Parish. Nor could we have done so much, but with such omissions as nothing but disability would have quieted our Consciences under.

And that you may know that I give you not my single experience, the rest of the honest Ministers of the County. 1. Sometimes durst not associate with us, because the scandalous persons of their Parishes were so many and so masterly and fierce, as that they were not able (they thought) to exercise any discipline among them. 2. Some that did joyn with us were fain to do as the Independants, and gather out some of the best to be their flock as to Communion in the Sacrament, and let the rest live quietly as bare hearers, because the offenders were so many that they durst not exercise discipline on them. 3. Some did even give the Sacrament to all promiscuously how scandalous soever, to avoid the difficulties of exercising discipline. 4. And all over the land they were faine to take the same course with these sorts aforesaid, yea and more, too many quite forbear the Sacrament, because they could not keep away the scandalous. 5. And too many took up the way of Separation, and gathered Churches out of these Churches, according to their several opinions, because the Parishes were so bad, that they thought them uncapable of discipline. Though yet the truth is. 1. Many such made them worse than they were. 2. And took the course that was easiest to them, by avoiding the most difficult part of their work; 3. And they were led to it by over valuing *Expressive parts* in some of the people, and unvaluing the *good desires* of some that wanted such *Expressions*.

And if we that found discipline too hard a work for us to exercise in our several Parishes, should have dreamed that one of us, was sufficient to have exercised it on a thousand or many hundred such Parishes (by our selves and Chancellors) O what Monsters of ignorance, should we have been.

CHAP. XX.

Objections against Parish Discipline answered.

Obj. 1. **Y**Ou make this discipline seem more needful than it is. *A Church may be a true Church without it. The Helvetians use very little of it at all.*

Ans. 1. The *Helvetian* Divines write for it, though with lenity and they are for denying the Sacrament to the Impenitently wicked, which is not nothing; and they are for Pastoral admonition of the persons that are scandalous. And the rest the Magistrates hinder them from, and

partly

partly undertake themselves. And verily I take it to be much more in-ingenuous to let the Magistrate do what he can, and to pretend to no more discipline, than to talk for it, and never use it.

2. A Man may be a true man though he have the Palsie, Dropsie, Gout or Stone, or be dismembred. And are these therefore indifferent things?

3. Whether discipline be needful judge after these Reasons. 1. Other-wise *Bishops* are not *needful* to exercise it, nor any other Pastors, but bare Preachers. Why should Lordships, wealth and honours, be allowed Bi-shops for that which is not needful? 2. If it be *needful* to be exercised on Ministers, why not on the People also? And if not on Ministers, why have there so great numbers been silenced, suspended, and troubled? Sure somebody thinketh, that our silencing is needful. 3. If it be not need-ful, why did the universal Church use it, and that so strictly from the be-ginning? And why do they that say this, pretend a reverence to the Anci-ent Churches, to the Councils, the Canons, and the Bishops of those times, who went ten times further in their Severities than we do. 4. It is need-ful by Precept and Divine Canon as may be seen, *Lev.* 19. 17. *Matth.* 18. 15, 16, 17, 18. 1 *Cor.* 5. *Tit.* 1. 13. *and* 2. 15. *and* 3. 10. 1 *Tim.* 3. 5. 15. *and* 5. 19, 20, 21. 22, 24. 2 *Tim.* 3. 5. *and* 4. 2. 2 *Thes.* 3. 6, 14. 5. It is needful to the honour of God, our Creator, Redeemer, and Sanctifier, that he may be declared Holy in the Holyness of his Church, and not by our allowed wickedness be represented as an unholy friend to sin. 6. It is needful to the Churches honour, that it be not as a very stie and sink of wickedness as the Infidel World. 7. It is needful to the Churches beauty, safety, and felicity, that God may delight in it, and not forsake it, as he hath done most of the East, nor make them miserable by his judg-ments. 8. It is needful to the Honour of Holiness it self, which will be vilified if we difference not the precious from the vile. 9. It is needful to the Conviction and Conversion of *Mahometans*, and other Infidels and Heathens, who now are kept in their Infidelity, by seeing that Christians as are bad or worse than themselves; and would be more drawn to Christ, if the holy Lives of Christians, and holy State of Churches did invite them. 10. It is needful to the comfortable Communion of Saints, as it is professed by us in our Creed. 11. It is needful to prevent the infection of the Church, and the increase of sin; seeing a little leaven leaveneth the whole lump, and he that toucheth pitch will be defiled by it. 12. It is needful to encourage and strengthen the Faithful, when they see by this *præjudicium futuri judicii*, as *Tertullian* calleth it, the difference that God himself will make. 13. It is an Essential part of the Pastoral Office to have the *Power* of Discipline: And what is the *Power* for but the *Work?* yea *Power* and Obligation are essential to his Office. 14. It is needful to the Holy Administration of Sacraments, and other parts of Divine Worship, that Holy things be not given to Dogs. 15. It is needful to convince the ordinary careless sinners among us, that seeing a difference put between

the

the good and bad, they may not think that preaching is but idle talk and falfhood, and that they are as fafe as others. 16. It is needful to keep the better people from offending God by their familiarity and communion with the notoriously wicked. 17. It is needful to break the Serpents head, that in Chrifts Church the Devils-works may be renounced and caft out, and fin be publickly made a fhame, as the Devil out of the Church endeavoureth to do by *Truth* and *Holinefs*. 18 It is needful to the eafe and peace of Magiftrates, that they may not be overwhelmed with the cares, troubles, dangers, that come by multitudes of Wicked Men; but the Paftors labours with the voluntary may prevent much of the Magiftrates trouble with the involuntary. 19. It is needful to the fafety of Commonwealths and Kingdomes, that they be not poyfoned by wickednefs, and fo expofed to the judgment of God. 20. And laftly, it is needful to the fcandalous Sinners themfelves, that they may not be fuffered to die and perifh in their fin, but have all poffible means ufed to bring them to repentance, that they may be faved. Confider whether all thefe Reafons prove not Difcipline to be needful.

Object. II. *But till Conftantines time there was no Chriftian Magiftrate, which made it then needful: But fince the cafe is not the fame.*

Anfw. 1. Down then with Bifhops now, if their work be needlefs. But why then were they fet fo much higher, and had fo much more power fince the dayes of *Conftantine* then before? 2. Are you wifer than all the Councils (*Nice, Ephef. Chalced. Conftance*, &c.) which have ever fince made Canons for Difcipline? 3. Again, try whether none of the foregoing reafons, be ftill in force. 4. Read *Galafpies Aarons* Rod, which fully proveth the continued need of difcipline.

Object. III. *But difcipline is not to be ufed on all that deferve it, but only one now and then, one to be a terror to the reft: You are for too much ftrictnefs, rigidnefs and feverity.*

Anf. 1. I am not for half the rigidnefs and feverity of the Ancient Bifhops and Churches, who made the penitents waite at the Church doors, and caft down themfelves with cryes and tears to beg abfolution and readmiffion, and in many cafes to waite thus many years together, and in fome, till their death bed. I am for accepting the firft credible profeffion of Repentance: Iam for gentle exhorting them and praying for them long before we caft them out. I am not for troubling any for fmall faults: Nor for bringing any mans fecret fins to light, or making them more publick than he maketh them himfelf; I am not for impofing fuch penances as the Papifts do. And is a ftrictnefs fhort of theirs intolerable to you, that pretend to be more holy than they? Yea more, I am not for the ufe of difcipline at all, where it is notorious to true reafon that its like to do more harme than good. And is all this too much ftrictnefs? But I amnot for keeping it out, and then making fuch pretences, nor for caufing the inconveniences, and then pleading them againft the duty.

2. The

2. The Scripture and Canons do not bid you reprove or suspend or reject one blasphemer, or drunkard of many ; but all that are such : And do you say that God and Councils dissembled, and bid us do that which they would not have us do ?

3. To censure one of a hundred or a thousand, yea, or twenty offenders, will be no terror or warning to the rest ; who will look to scape that which falleth on so few.

4. When one of so many only is censured, the Church will be still under most of the forementioned danger and defilement ; and this much will not reach the End.

5. Partiality is an odious Character of injustice and should not be found in civil judges ; much less in the Churches of Christ. And it will but harden and enrage those persons whom you deal with, when you enable them to say, *you censure me, and let many others alone, in the same sin. Is this your Church justice, or rather malice to me?*

Obj. IV. *You confess your self that it is so hard to use discipline in one Parish, that most Ministers did neglect it when the Bishops were out : And why blame you the Bishops then for neglecting it ?*

Ans. 1. We were to deal with the Parishes in that defiled and unruly state as the Bishops left them : And all great works must have time to be done in. And at last the reformation prospered apace, till they pull'd it down. 2. We were to make use of such Ministers as the Bishops left us, and of young men who were newly come from the Universities. And men cannot get wisdom interest, experience and resolution in a day. 3. The remaining respects which the people had to the Prelates and their way was a hindrance to us that desired to meddle herein with none but consenters. 4. A great number of Sectaries, raised by the distastes of the Prelates wayes, did also hinder us. 5. Yet it was than *possible and feasible* to Ministers that were wise and willing to do so much as might very much attain the ends of discipline, though not so much as they desired. 6. But is this an Objection fit for the Prelatists to make ? or doth it not encrease their condemnation ? what would you say to a Physician, a Pilot, a Schoolmaster, that should say, *It is not an hundred Physicians, that can do what should be done for all the Patients in this City; nor an hundred Pilots that can well govern all the Navy; nor an hundred Schoolmasters that can well Govern all the Schools in the Diocess : Therefore I will get them all turned out, and I will be the only Physician* (with my Apothecaries) *the only Pilot* (with my Seamen) *the only Schoolmaster* (with my Moniters and Ushers) *my self; for the work can be but left undone?* Such rule the Churches must have while God for our sins will suffer it.

The doing it *per alios* is oft enough answered before.

Obj. V. Many Parish Ministers are young, and raw and unfit to govern. *Ans.* 1. They are unfit who make this Objection, who bring and keep such in, and call so many hundred out that are better (lo ever ignorant malice slander them) 2. This also may be said against their preaching, much

Bb 3

more

more: For, 3. They may Rule with others, when they cannot preach by others. 4. There may be appeals to the next Synod (or Prelate if you will have it so).

Obj. VI. *You would have a Priest to be a Pope in his Parish.* Anf. I can call this Objection no better than grofs Impudency: For, 1. Its a Contradiction: A Pope is a Head of the Univerfal Church: And fo it is faying, *that we make every Minifter a Head of the Univerfal Church to his Parifh.* 2. We defire more Presbyters than One in a Church. 3. We defire Appeals to the next Synod: and is that to be a Pope? 4. Is not one Minifter as able to Rule a Parifh, without the help of affiftants and Synods, as one Prelate to Rule many hundred Parifhes, who likely is a worfe man than the Minifter? Impudent pride will perhaps fay no.

CHAP. XXI.

The Magiftrates Sword is neither the ftrength of Church difcipline, nor will ferve inftead of it, nor fhould be too much ufed to fecond and enforce it.

THefe three affertions I will prove diftinctly. 1. *The Magiftrates Sword is not the chief ftrength of true Church difcipline.*

I add this, becaufe this is the Prelatifts laft Objection, that *its true that the Keys are but* brutum fulmen *and a leaden fword without the Magiftrate: For almoft all men will difpife it: Who will come to our Courts if they may choofe? Who will regard our Excommunications? Do not the people now defpife them? what then would they do if they had their wills? when we have excommunicated the Schifmaticks, They will Excommunicate us again.*

The greateft Prelatifts who write to me and fpeak with me, ufe thefe very words themfelves. To which I anfwer.

1. If we prove that Chrift hath inftituted difcipline, and that for fuch noble ends as aforementioned, it is little lefs than blafphemy thus to reproach it: As if Chrift had no more Power, Wifdome or Goodnefs, than to ordain fo vain and unprofitable a means, to fuch high and neceffary ends.

2. The objection doth but exprefs a carnal mind, which regardeth only carnal things, and thinketh as bafely of all others, as if nothing moved them but the intereft of the flefh; And as if Gods favour or difpleafure, and the authority of his word and Minifters were of no force or regard even with the Church of Chrift.

3. The objection inviteth Kings to put down all Bifhops, except

Preachers

Preachers and Magistrates; For why should they put the people to so great charge and trouble, especially when they love the *Prelates so little* as to keep them up to wield a Leaden Sword, and to brandish a *brutam fulmen*, and to make a noise to no more purpose; yea to rob the Magistrate of the honour of his proper work, and to make the deluded people believe that those things are done by a *brutum fulmen* which really are done by the Civil power.

4. This objection bitterly reproacheth all the ancient Churches and Bishops, and all General and provincical Councils, and all the Cannons and ancient discipline of the Churches; As if they had troubled the world to no pupose and all their discipline had been vain.

5. The objection is notoriously confuted, in that the Discipline was more powerful and had better effect, before *Constantius* time than afterwards, and was much more strictly exercised against sin. And that which so long did more without the Sword, than afterward by it, doth not receive its efficacy from the Sword.

6. A *natura rei* there is as much of Divine Authority, as much of the power of his Precepts *Prohibitions, Promises,* and threatnings, as much of Heavenly inducement, as much of the terrors of Hell, as much of internal goodness of holyness, and evil of sins, as much of Soul interest in what the Minister propoundeth for mens conviction, as there is, when it is backt with the Magistrates Sword. And if all these have no force, Christianity must be a dream, and able to do no good in the world; which better beseemeth *Julian, Celsus* or *Porphyry, Symmachus,* or *Eunapius,* to say, than a Bishop.

7. By this objection the Prelatists openly confess that their Churches consist of men so carnal as are not moved by Divine authority without the Sword: And consequently what Pastors they have been to the Churches, and how they have governed them; and what they allow us to expect from their discipline for the time to come.

8. By this Objection they condemn themselves and justifie the Nonconformists: For why should we *Swear* that we will never endeavour any alteration of so *brutish* an Office, as if the King and Parliament could not take down such an useless thing? And why should so many hundred Ministers be forbidden to Preach Christ, for not assenting, consenting and Swearing to such a vaine and brutish power?

9. By this they give up their cause to the Presbyterians, and Independents; Confessing that their discipline is uneffectual; when as we that plead for another frame, desire not the Magistrates Sword to interpose, and desire to use discipline on none but Voluntiers. And either the discipline which we desire hath *some* efficacy, or none. If none, what need they fear it, or hinder it, or silence so many hundred Ministers, and write and strive, and all to keep men from using such a *brutum fulmen* which can do no harme. But if they confess that our discipline
hath

hath efficacy, and theirs hath none, what do they but directly call us to seek the alteration which we are required to abjure?

10. Lastly by this objection they shew themselves too ignorant of the nature of *Church*, and *discipline*, and *Sacrament* and *Ministery*: Or else they would better know how far Volunteers are proper objects of Church discipline, and have the right to the privileges and Communion of the Church.

II. *The Magistrates Sword will not serve instead of Church discipline.*

1. Else Christ would not have instituted another office for it.

2. Else it might serve also instead of Ministry, Preaching and Sacraments.

3. The nature of it tendeth not directly to convince men of Errours to lead them into truth, to move them by heavenly motions, and to bring them to true repentance and godlyness. But this will be fuller proved under the next; and is confessed by all save the *Erastians*.

III. *The Magistrates Sword should not be used too forwardly or too much to second or enforce Church discipline; much less to be its life and strength, and inseparably twisted with it.* I mean,

1. No unbeliever should be forced to say he is a Believer, and to professe the Christian faith.

2. None upon such profession should be forced to be Baptized.

3. None that hath no right to Church Communion in the Sacrament should be forced to receive it.

4. None that Apostatizeth from Christ should be forced falsly to professe that he is still a Christian.

5. None that are at age should be forced to stay in the Church by local presence or relation as a member of it, who is not willing, and the practice of the Papists who force no Heathens to be Christians, but afterward force Christians by fire and Sword, and burn them that were Hereticks, Schismaticks, or Apostates is self contradicting and self condemning; God having left man as much unto his own choice for *continuing* as for *Entring* into the Church: And as for *Obedience* to Rulers, Infidels may owe it to Christian Kings, as well as Christians: And none but Magistrates can use the Sword to punish either.

6. No Magistrate should punish a Mans body, meerly because he is Excommunicate, and so punished already. Nor should he be made a meer executioner to the Bishop without hearing, trying and judging the Cause himself, in order to his own execution.

7. No Magistrate should force an Impenitent sinner to lie and say he doth repent, that thereby he may be admitted to the Church Communion and Sacrament, but it is the force of Gods word that must try his Repentance.

But yet I acknowledge. 1. That Magistrates and Parents and Masters may

may force their Subjects to use those means which tend to make them Christians, as to hear Preaching, Conference or disputations, or to read convincing books: But with these two Cautions. 1. That it be but when it is like or hopeful to do more good than harme. 2. That it be by wise and moderate means of constreint, and not hang or burn them to convert them.

2. Accordingly Magistrates, Parents, and Masters, may use the like force with their Subjects who are Christians, to cause them to use the foresaid meanes (of hearing and Reading and conference) for the cureing of their dangerous errours or sinful lives.

3. And I doubt not but Magistrates may punish men Corporally for their crime according to the nature of them, and even for the same that the Church hath excommunicated them. If one be excommunicated for Treason, Murder, Theft, Swearing, Prophaning the Lords day, and holy things &c. it followeth not that the Magistrate may not also meddle with him.

4. And we doubt not but Magistrates may Restraine false Teachers, from seducing others, and drawing them from God to sin.

5. And the Magistrate may and ought to encourage Ministers in the use of the Church Keyes, and to preserve them from the violence of wicked men.

7. And they may make a difference in their favours and rewards, between Christians obedient to God and their Pastors, and Infidels, excommunicate, impenitent ones, and Apostates, by denying honors and preferments and rewards to the worse, which he giveth to the better sort of men.

But yet as to the Cases before denied, especially the forcing men by fire, sword, and imprisonment to say, they believe and repent, and to take the Sacrament and other Church priviledges, and making this the strength of Church discipline, I have all this against it.

1. No force should be used to the hindering and destruction of Christs ordinance of discipline and his Church Laws. But such it would be in the case in hand. For Christs fundamental Covenant is, that the true willing penitent and believer shall be a member of his Church, or those only that credibly profess to be so (at age) He that will may freely drink of the water of life. *Nemo invitus fit Christianus* : so that to say, that any man hath right to the mystical Church priviledges, but *Consenters*, or any man hath right to the visible Church priviledges, but *credible Professors of consent*; is to contradict the very condition of the Covenant of life, which is the sum of all the Gospel. Its true, you may compel some men to duty, but you cannot compel them to be *happy*.

But to force them by perpetual Imprisonment, confiscation and the sword, to say that *they are Christians*, or *repent, consent* or *are willing*, and so to give them absolution and Church-communion, is to make Christs ordinance of none effect. For true *discipline* is to *make* them *penitent* and *willing*

C c

ling

ling, and then to *use them* as fuch : But, 1, It is not *credible* that that perfon is *truly* penitent and willing to be a Chriftian, or have Church-communion, who will not be perfwaded to confent by all that can be faid by the Paftors from the word of God, but yet on the rack or to prevent *undoing* will fay, I confent. This is contrary to the nature of true Repentance. 2. Or if it did not make this forced confent utterly incredible, yet it utterly croffeth the ends of Church difcipline, which is to difcern the *voluntary penitent*; which force fo obfcureth that no man can tell whether the perfon be credibly penitent or not. If I left a Legacy to fo many that are Lovers of the Church, and its Communion, and my Executors fhould get the Magiftrate to hang, or Imprifon or undo certain men that are accufed as Enemies of the Church, unlefs they will fay, *we Love the Church*, I think my Will would be ill performed, if thofe men had my Legacy, that were forced to fay fo.

2. No man fhould be forced to his own fin and diftruction. But he that is forced to take the Sacrament when he is unwilling and had rather be without it, in likelihood is forced to his fin and deftruction : For even the Liturgy telleth the unworthy that they eat and drink damnation to themfelves, and that the Devil may enter into them as he did into *Judas* : And who is unworthy if the unwilling are not ?

3. Force is not fitted to caufe *love* and *willingnefs* ; therefore men fhould not be forced to take a Gift, which Love and willingnefs is the condition of ; men ufe not to fay, Love me or I will hang thee or imprifon thee: This feemeth to make a new way of Preaching which Chrift never made.

4. Chrifts terms are felf-denial, Crofs-bearing and forfaking all and following him for the hopes of heaven : But this feemeth a new and contrary Gofpel, as if Chrift had faid ; He that will be my difciple rather than be imprifoned or die, fhall be faved or received.] Chrift faith : *He that forfaketh not all that he hath cannot be my difciple*, Luk.14.33. This way, faith [*He that will come to the Church-communion rather than forfake all fhall be my difciple*]. Chrift faith [*He that loveth any thing; even his life more than me, cannot be my difciple.*] This way faith, [He that loveth life, credit, wealth, liberty fo well as that he will rather receive the Sacrament than lofe it, fhall be my difciple] Chrift faith, *except ye repent ye fhall all perifh.*] This forceth a Minifter to abfolve a wicked man, as if he fhould not perifh, if he will but rather fay [*I repent*] than lofe his liberty and eftate. God faith [*He that loveth the World, the love of the Father is not in him*]. This way faith [Do but Love the world fo well as to fay and do any thing to keep it, and then Paftor and people fhall number thee with the Lovers of the Father.] God faith ; *The carnal mind is enmity to God and is not fubject to his Law nor can be.*] This way faith [If thy carnal mind make thee fay or do any thing to fave thy liberty or money, thou art an obedient Son of the Church and of God.] And is not this to fet up a new Gofpel, Gal.1.7.8,

5. And

5. And this way compelleth men to lie and play the Hypocrites, when we may discerne it is so. Mr. *Capel* of *Temp:* would perswade us that a lie thus *differeth* from most other sins, that it is so *evil in it self, as that it cannot in the very act be lawful.* When a man against all per-swasion, saith or sheweth you, that *he doth not believe in Christ, or doth not repent, to say* to that man, [*Say thou believest, or Repentest, or thou shalt be confiscate and lie in jaile*] is plainly to say [*Lie or suffer*] I deny not but that in some cases a man may be examined when it is foreknown that he will lie. But its one thing to force him to examination and an-swer, and another to force him *to that particular answer.*

6. It is a compelling men to pretend to that which we cannot compel them to, that is, *to have a Right to so great a benefit as Absolution and Church Communion.* Force giveth no man *Right to the Benefit,* and their force should not compel him falsly to pretend a *Right.*

7. It confoundeth the Church and the world : Whilest every man is made a member of the Church that had but rather tell a lie and take bread and wine, than be undone, what wicked man on earth will not do the same (unless he be so Consciencious that mistake and Conscience hindereth him) Is there any Infidel, Heathen, Atheist, Murderer, Traytor, or Sensualist, in the world that will not do it ? What should hinder him that believeth there is no God, to do thus rather than be undone ? Is it so hard a word to say in a Chancellours Court [*I repent*] and deride and curse them when he is gone out ; or is a *bit of Bread* and a *Sup of Wine* so hard for a Glutton or Drunkard to get down, as that any of them would rather lie in jaile. 1. So that by this course the Church and the Infidel world are made *equal,* and no man can prove that any *Mahometan* Congregation is not as good, as to the persons, as such a Christian Congregation : For what *Mahometan* would not say and do this rather then be undone ? unless he be a Consciencious one, who is not so bad as those Christians that have no Conscience. 2. And by this meanes no conjecture can be made of the real members of the Church. Thousands may be driven in at the doors, but we have no means to perceive whither any of them indeed be Christians.

8. And hereby the Church and the Christian Religion are greatly dishonoured, while this odious *stigma* is made the marke of a visible member, [One that had rather say he is a Christian and repenteth, than lie in a jaile]! Is this a laudable description ?

9. And hereby *Mahometans, Jews* and *Heathens* are hardened in their Infidelity and reproach of Christ, while Christians are such as these.

10. It putteth every consciencious Minister into a snare, and trou-bleth his Conscience, or turneth him out, when he must put the Sacrament into the very hand of every man that had rather take it than be imprisoned ; and must read the Absolution of every one that had rather say, [*I repent*] than be undone.

Cc 2

11. It

11. It hindereth the comfort of the faithful in Church Communion to know that this is the meafure and Character of thefe with whom they muft hold that Communion, which is called the Communion of Saints.

12. It deftroyeth Church unity and Love. For every vifible member of the Church being a feeming Saint, fhould be loved with the fpecial Love which belongeth to Saints, by us who are not Searchers of the heart. But who that is not out of his wits can by any obedience to the Church, be brought to Love all thofe as *feeming Saints*, who will choofe a Sacrament before a jaile? He that cannot believe them fuch, cannot Love them as fuch.

13. It will ftrengthen them that Separate from us as no Church, and make it not fo eafy to prove that we have any Church, as elfe it would be; when they fhould argue [*Where there is no credible Profeffion of Faith and repentance there is no true Church: But &c. Ergo.* The Major is undenyable. * The Minor indeed is not true, becaufe many do *Voluntarily* profefs, and fhew their *Voluntarinefs* other waies. But no thanks to them that teach the accufers thus to argue [*When the Laws of Profeffion are Profefs or lie in jayle, there is no credible (* Voluntary *) Profeffion : But &c.* The Major *they* prove, *Non effe & non apparere* here are equipollent: But *under fuch a law no voluntarinefs and Credibility is apparent :* Ergo — And I know but this anfwer to the Minor, it is apparent otherwife, though not by that forced profeffion, becaufe multitudes daily fhew that they approve of what they do.

As they that tooke the Covenant unwillingly now maintaine that therefore it binds them not.

14. Force tendeth rather to *hinder mens Repentance and Love to the Church:* For *Fear* breadeth *Hatred;* or at leaft *Hurt* doth. Kindnefs breedeth Love. God winneth our Love by mercy: And we are fo to win the Love of others. Give a man but a box on the ear or flander or wrong him, and try whether it will make him Love you; to fay, *Love Chrift and the Chriftian or I will undo thee and lay thee in jaile,* is the way to make him hate them.

15. And the *Office* of the Paftors is fuch *as that truth* and *Goodnefs* are the wares which they expofe to finners choice, and *Light* and *Love* are the effects which *Spirits Word and Miniftry* are appointed to produce: And by *Light* and *Love* they muft be wrought. Therefore no Minifter doth his work, or doth any good to fome, if by *Light* and *Love* and holy *Life,* he help not the people to the fame. And therefore the adjunction of *Jayles* and *confifcations,* is fo contrary to his Office and defigne as obfcureth or deftroyeth it. (Though *Enemies* may be reftrained, and *peace kept* by force.)

16. True difcipline cannot be exercifed this way, not only as its loft in the confufion of powers (as a little wine in Wormwood juice) but becaufe the *Number* and *quality* of the Church members will make it impoffible. Enemies and rebellious carnal minds are not fubject nor can be to the Lawes of Chrift; you may affright them to a Sacrament,

ment, but *one of them* will make a Minister such work, who will but call them to credible repentance for their crimes, and will renew those crimes so oft till he be excommunicated, and will so hate those that excommunicate, as will tell you what can be done, when *all* such are forced unwillingly into the Church. Of this I have spoke at large in my Book of *Confirmation.*

17. It tendeth greatly to harden the sinners in the Church in their impenitence, to their damnation : when they shall see, that let one swear and curse and be drunk every day in the week, if he will but say, I repent, rather than lie in Jayl, he shall be absolved by the Chancellour in the Bishops name, and have a sealed pardon delivered him in the Sacrament, by the Minister who knoweth his wicked life. How easie a way to Heaven (which leadeth to Hell) do such good-natured (cruel) Churches make men?

Obj. *The Minister is to refuse the scandalous.*

Ans. Not when he is absolved by the Chancellour.

Obj. *But if he sin again, he may refuse him again.*

Ans. How far that is true, I shewed before. But *not when he is absolved again.* And he may be absolved *toties quoties*, if he had, but rather say, *I repent*] than lie in Jayle.

18. Let but the ancient Canons be perused, and how contrary to them will this course appear? The ancient Churches would admit none to absolution and communion after divers greater crimes, till they had waited (as is aforesaid) in begging and tears, and that for so long a term and with such penitential expressions, as satisfied the Church of the truth of their repentance. It would be tedious to recite the Canons. How great a part of *Cyprians* Epistles to the Churches of *Carthage* and *Rome*, are on this subject? reprehending the Confessors and Presbyters for taking lapsed persons into Church Communion before they had fulfilled their penitential course? And what a reproach do they cast upon all these Bishops, Churches and discipline, who say, *That sinners must be taken into communion, if they will prefer it before a Jayle* Though they love a *Whorehouse*, an *Ale-house*, a *Play-house*, a *Gaming house*, yea, a *Swine-Stie* better than the *Church*, yet if they do not love a *Jayle with beggery* better, they shall be received.

19. Even when Christian Emperours had advanced Prelates, and given them (though not the sword yet) the aid of it in the Magistrates hand to second them, they never used it to force any to the Communion of the Church, but only to defend them, and to repress their adversaries. Yea when Prelates themselves began to use the sword, or to desire the Magistrates to serve them by it, it was not at all to force men to say : *They Repent and so to be absolved and communicate* ; But only to keep hereticks from their own assemblings, and from publishing their own doctrines or maintaining them, or from being Pastors of the Churches. And yet now men will force them to be *Absolved* and *communicate.*

And how great mischiefs did even so much use of the sword in matters of Religion as was the *punishment* of Hereticks then being (though they

were.

were not forced into the Church.) *Socrates* brandeth *Cyril* of *Alexandria*, for the first Prelate that used the sword ; and what work did he make with it ? He invaded a kind of secular Magistracy. He set himself against the Governour *Orestes*, and under his shadow those bloody murthers were committed on the Jewes; who also killed many of the Christians. The Monks of Mount *Nystra* rose to the number of 500, and assaulted the civil Governour and wounded him ; and *Amonius* who did it was put to death by *Orestes*: and *Cyril* made a Martyr of him; till being ashamed of it, he suffered his memorial to be abolished.   And when *Hypatia* a most excellent woman of the Heathens, was famous for her publick teaching of Phylosophy, *Peter*, one of *Cyrils* Readers became the head of a party of that Church, who watched the woman, and dragg'd her out of a Coach into a Church, stript her of her cloaths, and tore her flesh with sharp shells, till they killed her, and then tore her members in peices, and carried them to a place called *Cynaron* and burned them, for which we read of no punishment executed, *Socrat. lib.* 7. c. 13. 14, 15. And it was this *S. Cyril* who deprived the Novatians of their Churches, and took away all the Secret treasure of them, and spoiled the Bishop *Theopompus* of all his fortunes, *Socrat. l.* 7. c. 7.

*Theophi. lus his Si. sters son and successor.

What his Nephew and Successor *Theophilus* was and did, you have heard before and shall hear more anon.

What the ancient Christians thought of using the sword against Hereticks (though they compelled them not to the Church and Sacrament) any man that readeth their Writings may see, viz. *Tertullian, Arnobius, Lactantius* and abundance more.   And the case of S. *Martin* towards *Ithacius* and *Idacius*, I have oft enough repeated : Only I cannot but note the imprudency of *Bellarmine*, who *de Scriptor. Eccles. de Idacio* (falsly making *Idacius* to be the same with *Ithacius*, when he was but one of his associates) doth tell us that *Idacius* fell under the *reprehension* and *punishment* of the Bishops (*in eo reprehensus & punitus ab Episcopis fuit, quod Priscillianum apud seculares accusaverit & occidi curaverit*] whereas *Sulpitius Severus*, telleth us, that all the Bishops of the Synod joyned with them, and one S. *Martyn* and one French Bishop more disowned and refused them, and *Martin* would have no Communion with them to the death (save that once at the Emperours perswasion he Communicated with them to save a prisoners life, which was given him on that condition, and yet was chastised by an Angel even for that.) And *Ambrose* at *Milan* also disowned them (as you may read in his life); and when the deed was done, the Christians spake ill of *Ithacius* and *Idacius* for taking that new and bloody way, which before the Churches commonly disowned, but they pretended that they did not cause this execution.

And the same *Sulpitius* tells you, that when this new way of seeking to the Emperour, was first set on foot by *Ithacius* and his Synodists, the Priscillianists quickly got the handle of the sword, and by a Courtier got even *Gratian* to be on their side against the Bishops.

And

And yet that was not all the mischief, but when *Maximus* had killed *Gratian*, it was this pleasing of these bloody Orthodox Prelates which he trusted to as his means to possess the Empire, and so punished the Priscillianists to please them, and serve himself of them (of which more anon.)

But you may see here that *Bellarmine* himself seemeth to disown Bishops seeking to Magistrates to punish Hereticks; As if he had forgotten their bloody Inquisition and Massacres. And *Baronius iavit. Ambros.* would perswade us that *Ambrose* (who was of *Martins* mind) did not disown the punishment of hereticks by the sword, but he would not have Churchmen seek it. As if it were not evident enough that it was the *thing it self* that he and *Martin* were against, and that *Martin* was reproached by the Prelates as a factor of Hereticks, for travelling to *Maximus* Court and importuning him to *save* them. And as if the Inquisitors did not *seek* to the Magistrate, and more, even Judge, and execute the sword themselves.

Its true that *Augustine* was at last for the use of the sword against the Donatists. But its as true. 1. That he wrote much before against it. 2. That it was so much against the Churches former judgement and practice that he was fain to write his Apology and reasons. 3. And that the Donatists, Circumcellians used frequent and cruel violence against the Christians that were Orthodox (or Cecilians) and catch'd their Presbyter in the streets of *Carthage*, dragg'd him in the dirt, and abused him cruelly two Church daies before they let him go, with many such outrages: Yea, the Catholicks could not go safely in the streets for them; And among other devises, they mixt Lime and Vinegar together, and cast it in mens eyes as they passed in the streets, to put out their eyes: And they were so mad that they wounded and killed themselves to bring *odium* on the Catholicks: And they were so numerous, that they called themselves the whole Catholick Church. 4. And *Austin* did never desire the Magistrate to force them to the Sacrament, but to defend the Church, and repress their insolencies. 5. And yet the whole Clergy joyned first in a representation of all this to the Donatists Bishop *Januarius* as being an old experienced peaceable man, and to desire him to remedy it, before they would fly for aid to the Magistrate (all this you may see in their Epist. to him *inter Augustini Epistolas.*

And what work did the Arrians make with the Orthodox, when they had got the Emperours sword to serve them. Nay indeed it was the Arrians who did first set this work on foot (after the Jewes and Heathens.) They so depopulated the Churches by it in the daies of *Constantius* and *Valens*, that they seemed all to be turned Arrians, and the Orthodox party seemed to be almost conquered if not extinct. And their *Sergius* the Monk that instructed *Mahomet*, set him by this way of the sword on that extirpation of Christianity, which hath so dolefully prevailed in the Eastern Empire: And so great was the swords success against the faith of

the

the Trinity, that *Philoftorgius* of Old, and out of him *Sandius* of late, would make us believe that almoſt all the ancient Biſhops indeed were Arrians.

But the faddeſt inſtance of the miſchief of too much ſerving Church-men by the ſword, is the caſe of the Papal faction : when *Cyril* had begun the trade at *Alexandria*, faith *Socrates*, [*Epiſcopus Romanus non aliter atque Alexandrinus quaſi extra ſacerdotis fines egreſſus , ad ſecularem principatum erat jam ante delapſus*] (it ſeems *Rome* had the primacy in a Sanguinary Prelacy;) *And*, faith he, Then Pope *Celeſtine* firſt took their Churches from the Novations, and compelled their Biſhop *Ruricola* to keep their meetings privately in houſes : And though the Biſhops commended them as Orthodox, yet they ſpoiled them of their fortunes, *Socrat. l. 7. c. 11.* ſo impatient are armed Prelates of any that are not of their mind and way, how horeſt otherwiſe ſoever they acknowledge them.

But, alas, ſince then what ſtreams of blood have been ſhed to back the Romane diſcipline ? How many hundred thouſand of the *Waldenſes* and *Albigenſes* did they murther ? How many thouſands in *Belgia, France, Germany, Poland, Ireland,* &c. And when at firſt they precariouſly got the Magiſtrates to ſerve them voluntarily with the ſword, at laſt they would *conſtrain* them to it, as their duty ; and ſuch a duty as they muſt perform on pain of loſing their dominions : For the Pope having firſt excommunicated them, next may give away their dominions to others, as is fully expreſſed, *Concil. Lateran. ſub. Innoc. 3. Can. 3. & Concil. Rom. ſub. Gregor. 7.* And do I yet need to ſay more, what miſchief hath come by overmuch backing Church diſcipline by the ſword ? If I do, let this be the cloſe, that God knoweth how many Great men and Commanders are now in Hell, for the perſecutions and murders, which Church men have thus drawn them to.

2. Laſtly, moſt certain this courſe (of forcing all men into the Church and to the Sacrament by priſon and ſword) will keep up perpetual diviſions in the Churches. The more religious ſort of people will ſtill in all ages be flying away from ſuch Churches as from a Peſt-houſe, or infected place, or ruinous houſe that's ready to fall. The unexperienced Prelates think that it is but ſome few preachers that teach the people ſuch ſtrict opinions, and if thoſe were cut off all would be well : But their ignorance is the Churches plague and their own. 1. There is ſomewhat in Scripture that perſwadeth them that God hateth all the workers of iniquity ; and that holineſs and unholineſs are as Light and Darkneſs, and that he that nameth the name of Chriſt muſt depart from iniquity, and that the impenitent and ſcandalous muſt be avoided and aſhamed, and hereticks after a firſt and ſecond admonition, and that he that bids them *Good ſpeed* is partaker of their evil deeds, and that a little leaven leaveneth the whole lump, and therefore the wicked muſt be caſt out, and muſt be to us (if obſtinate after admonition) as Heathens and Publicans ; Theſe are not the words of phanaticks but of Chriſt. 2. There is ſomething in the

said

newborn foul which is contrary to wickednefs, and which inclineth men to an enmity with the Serpents feed as fuch, though a love to them as men that are yet capable of grace and which difpofeth men to obey all the forefaid words of Chrift. 3. And there is in the people more than in the Paftors, fome remnants of ignorance, which makes them more liable to ftretch thefe words of Chrift too far, and by miftake to run further from wicked men than God would have them. But when they fee the Wildernefs called the Garden of God, and the wicked not only tolerated in the Church, but forced into it by the Sword, and fo the Church to contain the world, and to be as vicious as Infidels ; (what ever men fhould do,) I dare confidently prophecy what they *will* do ; All the Prelates in the world, no nor all the godly that' preach, will never prevent it, but every age will bring forth new divifions, and the ftricter fort will be ftill flying from fuch Churches as thefe, to worfhip God in purer focieties ; And if you are angry with the Scriptures, and with the Papifts, keep them from their knowledge, you muft do fo alfo by the Creed, Lords Prayer and ten Commandments, or elfe the very Article of [*the Communion of Saints*] and the praying [*Thy Name be hallowed, thy Kingdome come, thy Will be done in earth as it is heaven*] with the precepts of *Holinefs* and *Righteoufnefs*, will have the fame kind of operation.

Obj. *But in the Church of* Rome, *there is unity and concord, and no Sects, and therefore that fheweth us what the fword may do.*

Anf. 1. But the Church of *Rome* is it felf but a fraction, divided from the reft of the Church. Do they not differ fufficiently from the *Greeks, Armenians, Abaffines,* &c. Did they not drive from them *Germany, Belgia* and the reft of the Proteftants ? Yea, even by their cruelty, fo far was cruelty from preventing it ? The Anabaptifts, and many other Sects may be at one among themfelves, and yet not at one with any others.

2. Are you willing of a concord in your Churches upon the fame terms as the Church of *Rome* hath it ? What, with the fame ignorance and ungodlinefs ; Locking up the Scriptures, in Latin Prayers and Maffes, and a Catholick Tyrant or Ufurper, and all this procured by the blood of fo many hundred thoufands, and kept up by the fame Love-killing means ? would you indeed have fuch a concord ? *Et cum folitudinem facitis, pacem vocabitis,* as *Tertullian* fpeaketh.

3. But indeed the Church of *Rome* hath one other means for concord which you want ; and that is various houfes and orders of Monafticks. Ignorance and prophanefs will ferve for the concord of the worft ; but there will be ftill fome who believe and forethink of a life to *come,* and therefore will be religious ; and for thefe when they cannot have communion with the wicked, this politickly holy Church hath provided this expedient : every one that will be Religioufer than the reft, hath a hive or fociety to flie to at their choice, and may betake themfelves to that which is moft ftrict or moft fuited to their own conceits. And if you would make Independant Churches to be like fuch Monafteries, where the Religioufer fort may

Dd

have

have Communion with one another, you may do much to prevent a further breach.

Object. II. *But the sword will prevail with the most: In the changes of Religion in* England *and elsewhere, the People have alwayes changed with the be King.*

Answ. 1. Men may seemingly leave an ill way with the King: Because they are wicked that walk in it, and therefore can say any thing. But men will not so easily leave a *good way* when a King shall leave it; Because they that are in a good way are often *Good men,* and true to God, and hold *Truth* and *Goodness* faster than bad Men hold Error and Evil. 2. Indeed this is the way to have a Church onely of perfidious wicked Men, who will turn to any thing with their tongues (because they will not turn to God with their hearts): And to have no true Christian left among you: for such fear not them that can kill the body onely, in comparison of him that can damn the Soul, *Luke* 12. 4. 3. Do not *France,* and all the Churches, and *Our selves at this day fully shew you the falseness of this Objection.*

CHAP. XXII.

An Answer to the Objections. 1. *No Bishops no King.* 2. *And of the Rebellions and Seditions of those, that have been against Bishops.*

I Come not for your own sake to meddle with such matters as these, but you put a necessity on us, by making us odious by such pretences.

1. To the first I answer, 1. Were not all the very Heathen Emperors heretofore, and are not all the Heathen Kings still, Kings, and as great as others, without Bishops? And may not Christian Kings much more? 2. If the Presbyterians had said, *no Presbyters, no King,* you would have taken it for treasonable; as if they had threatned that the King shall not be King, unless they may have their way, and shall not the King be King unless you may be Bishops? 3. What is in the nature of the thing to warrant this assertion? Presbyterians own every text and Article for Monarchy as the Prelatists do, even as ever any Christian Council or Confession asserted, as far as we can learn. They plead no other divine right for their offices, than our Prelates do. And (save what some of them have held by the Magistrates own gift) they pretend to no power over any mans body or purse. Many of them and the Independants, meddle no further than their own Congregations. What is in all this against Kings? That an Aristocratical Church Government may not live quietly under Monarchy, or a Monarchial Church Government under Aristocracy, is an asserted fiction, without all proof. Otherwise by the same reason you would perswade *Venice, Holland* and all such Governments, that Prelacy may not be endured under them.　　　　　　　　　　　　　　　　　　　　　4. But

4. But what if it were all as true as it is false? What is it to those Nonconformists that craved Bishop *Ushers* Episcopacy? The question is but whether a humble Bishop in a Parish or Market Town, without any Lordship or great revenews, or interest in the sword, may not live as safely and obediently under Kings, as our Lord Bishops? Yea in very deed most of the Independant Churches themselves have a kind of Episcopacy, whether they own the name or not: For usually one single Pastor hath as much as a Negative voice in the mannagement of all disciplinary affairs.

II. But the answer to the second will fuller answer this. 1. Do you not know that where Prelacy is at the highest, there Kings and Emperours have been at the lowest? Do you not know how the Papal Prelacy at the present usurpeth one part of their Government: and is ready to take away the other when they can, when ever Kings displease them? Can any thing be said to hide this by him that readeth, but the two forenamed Councils (*Later. & Rom. sub Gregor.* 7.) Did Prelacy preserve those Emperors of the *East* that suffered by it? Doth it now preserve the Emperour of *Moscovy*, where the Patriarks interest is pretended in the rebellion? Did it preserve *Frederick*, and the two *Henries* of *Germany*? or *Henry* 3. and 4th. of *France*? Did it preserve the Kings of *England*, *Will.* 2. *Hen.* 2. and 3. *John*, &c. from their wars and troubles? Did it preserve the Kingdome of *Navar* to the right Lord? What should, I say, more of this after the copious instances of *H. Fowlis*? and after that volume of *W. Prin.* of the *English* Prelates Treasons? Read it and judge.

2. What people more peaceable and obedient to their superiors, for instance than the Helvetian Ministers have been? who yet have no such thing as Bishops.

3. Dr. *Pet. Moulin* Junior, one of your selves in his answer to *Philanax Angl.* hath said enough to confute most of the Calumnies against the Reformed Churches in this point.

4. Who knoweth not, that even in the ancient Churches, and that when Episcopacy was thriving apace, yea and by and among the Bishops themselves, yea some that were good men and are now Sainted, yet tumults, seditions, rebellions, and contentions troubled the Churches, and the Emperours and Magistrates, as frequently as of later times, which I mention not to abate the honour of those better Christians, but 1. To shew you, that all this was done under Prelacy, and therefore it was not want of Prelacy, or averseness to it that is to be taken for the cause. 2. That these distempers were found in the best times, and among the purest Churches, and therefore are not to be now thought strange, or taken for a mark of a bad religion.

I will not repeate what I said but even now of the horrid tumults and blood shed at *Alexandria*, their cruel Murdering of *Hypatia*, and the insurrection and sedition even of the Holy Monks, and Saint *Cyrils* Sainting of the executed actor of violence on the Governour.

Dd 2 What

What work his Predecessor Saint *Theophilus* made against Saint *Chry-sostome*, how *Epiphanius* acted his part ; how Saint *Hierome* was of their party ; how even the Orthodox Bishops in several Synods opposed and deposed those two excellent Bishops of *Constantinople Gregory Theol.* and *Chrysostome*, hath been said before.

Even at the Election of *Chrysostome, Theophilus* went about by all means to discredit him, and to preferr to the place one *Isidore* a Priest of his own Church. And that you may know how Loyalty prevailed against the owning of Tyrants when they got the better you shall further hear why *Theophilus* set so much by this *Isidore*, because he undertook for him a perillous piece of service (saith *Socrates li. 6. c. 2.*) viz, ‘ [When the Emporour *Theodosius* waged War with *Maximus* the Ty‘rant, *Theophilus* sent *Presents* directed to the Emperour with two Let‘ters (one to *Theodosius* and one to *Maximus*) charging *Isidorus* to pre‘sent him that got the better with the gift and one of the Letters. *Isi-*‘*dore* being careful of his business, went diligently about this feat, got ‘ him to *Rome*, and hearkeneth after the Victory : But his fetch was ‘ not long ere it was found out ; for his Reader, that accompanyed him ‘ stole away his Letters. Whereupon *Isidore* being afraid to be taken ‘ with the manner, took his heeles in all hast to *Alexandria* : This was ‘ it that made *Theophilus* labour so earnestly for *Isidore* : But all that ‘ were of the Emperours Court preferred *John* to the Bishopprick : And ‘ afterwards when as many charged *Theophilus* with heynous crimes, ‘ and presented to the Bishops (then present) libells and Articles against ‘ him , some for this thing and some for that ; *Eutropius* one of the ‘ Emporours Chamber having gotten the Articles and Inditements, ‘ shewed them to *Theophilus*, bad him choose whether he would Create ‘ *John* Bishop , or stand at the Barr and answer to the Crimes that ‘ were laid to his charge. *Theophilus* was so afraid with this that present‘ly he consented to the installing of *John*].

What would have been said of one of us now, if we had not only complyed with a victorious Tyrant, but also so jugled with presents and double Letters before hand. I did my self disowne *Oliver Cromwel* openly to his death ; and yet because after twelve years possession of the Usurpers, I did but Dedicate two Bookes to his Son *Richard*, whom I never saw nor heard from, only to encourage him to befriend truth and unity against Papists and Sectaries, who then threatened all, (and this when the Royalists themselves gave out that he was Really for the restoration of the King) this is made the odious Crime in me, as a thing deserving greatest Infamy.

Do I need to recite how great *Leo* himself and other *Roman* and *I-talian* Bishops owned the *Barbarian* Conquerours? No wonder than if they too early took *Theodoricus* for their King set over them by God, who was a better man than the rest, and had at last a better Title.

‘ Saith

'Saith *Socrates* further *li. 6. c. 7:* [When the Common-wealth of the
'*Roman*-Empire, was tossed with these troublesome stormes of Rebelli-
'on, such as were promoted to the reverend function of Priest-hood
'were at distraction among themselves, to the great slander of Christi-
'an Religion: Then was one set against the other; the original of which
'pestilent Schism came from *Egypt*, and the occasion was as followeth.
'There was a question broached a little before, whether God were
'a body, made after the likeness and forme of man? Or whether he
'were without body, and void of all Corporal shape. * Hereof
'there arose sundry contentions and quarrels: While some affirmed this
'and others that: Some of the rudest and unlearned sort of Religious men
'thought that God was Corporeal, and of the forme and figure of man:
'But the greater part condemned them with their Heretical opinion, af-
'firming that God had no bodily substance or shape. Of which opinion
'was *Theophilus* Bishop of *Alexandria*; so that in the hearing of the whole
'Congregation he inveighed bitterly against the Contrary ---- The wor-
'shippers of *Egypt* understanding this, left their Religious houses, came
'to *Alexandria*, flocked about *Theophilus*; condemned him for a wick-
'ed person, and sought to bereave him of his Life. *Theophilus* being
'made privy to their Conspiracy, was wonderful pensive, devised how
'he might scape their hands and save his life. As soon as he came
'into their presence he saluted them Courteously, and said thus to them:
'When I fasten mine eyes on you, methinks I see the lively face of
'God. With these words the rash heat of the unruly Monkes was de-
'layed, and they said, *If that be true that thou sayest, that the Counten-*
'*ance* of God is no otherwise than ours, accurse then the works of *Ori-*
'*gen*: For divers of his books do impugne our opinion: But if thou
'refuse to do this, assure thy self to receive at our hands the punish-
'ment due to the impious and open Enemies of God: Nay, saith
'*Theoph.* I will do that which seemeth good in your eyes] Thus you
see what the Monks were. But will you see what *Theophilus* was.

'It followeth [The Religious, houses in *Egypt* were overseen of four
'worthy men, Brethren, *Dioscorus, Ammonius, Eusebius,* and *Euthemius,*
'Their great fame and excellency made *Theophilus* force them out of
'their beloved solitude, and make *Dioscorus,* a Bishop, and two other
'to live with himself ---- At last, their Consciences were pricked,
'perceiving that the Bishop was set upon heaping and hoarding of mony.
'* and that all their labour tended to gathering, they would no longer
'dwel with him but got them into the desert ---- As soon as *Theophilus*
'understood that they abhorred his manner of living, he was wonder-
'fully incensed, and promised to work them a displeasure --- and being
'prone to anger and revenge, bestirred himself against them and endeavour-
'ed by all means to work them mischief. And he began to despight
'*Dioscorus,* the Bishop, for it grieved him to the gutts that the Worship-
'pers made so much of *Dioscorus* and reverenced him so highly (To be-
                                                                        'shorter

What should such Religious men be now called, that had no more knowledge, so great errour and so great fury and tumul-tuating re-bellion.

Saith Dr. Hammer in his Margin, This is. so p hath more fel-low in ke world]

D 3

shorter than *Socrates*) *Theophilus* not knowing else how to be revenged, set the Monks against him and his Brethren, and accuseth them of holding contrary to the Scripture, that God had no body, hands, or feet, and so taketh on him to be of their opinion, till he had set them altogether by the ears : And the ignoranter Monks being the greater number he took their side, and so they went first to it by zealous reproaches, one part calling the other *Originests*, and the other part calling them *Anthropomorphites*, and at last it came to a *deadly Battel. And*, saith Socrates, *Theophilus perceiving, that his fetches framed after his will went with great power towards the Mount* Nitria, *where there religious houses stood, and aided the Monks against* Dioscorus *and his Brethren : And the Religious men thus beset with great danger had much ado to save their lives.*] Socr. l. 6. c. 7.

Did ever Presbyterians commit such an unchristian and inhumane vilany as this, by such false dissimulation and malice ? And here we see how the quarrel began against *Origens* Works, not for the passages that are truely culpable, but for the sounder parts ; and how it came to pass that *Chrysostome* was not so forward to condemn them as his Condemners did require him to be.

Theodoret. lib. 4. Hist Eccl. c. 13. Tells us that when the Emperour *Valens* his order was brought to *Eusebius Samosatenus* for his removal and banishment, *Eusebius* tels the Officer, *That if the People should know it, they would drown him in the River* (Euphrates) and therefore contrived to slip away by night.] What would they say, if our Churches were such as this orthodox Episcopal Church was?

Theodor. lib. 3. c. 13. The Virgins openly sung in reproach of *Julian* the Emperour [*Rate illum consceleratum tyrannum contemnendum esse & omnium irrisione ludendum*] judging that wicked Tyrant to be contemned and made a mocking stock by all. And yet he was a lawful Emperour and none of the cruellest Persecutors.

Theodor. l. 3. c. 13. When the People of his Church had found out *Eusebius* their banished Bishop, they earnestly perswaded him to return, contrary to the Emperors Edict, and not to suffer his flock to be left to the Wolves (which were the Bishops set over them by the Emperour). And is not this more than the people are now condemned for, who only hear the Ministers privately ?

Cap. 14. When the Emperors Arrian Bishop was set over them, not one of all the People, rich or poor, servant or labourer, husbandman or Artificer, man or woman, young or old, would come as they used to the Church, nor come in sight of the Bishop, nor speak with him: But though he lived very modestly, he came to the Church (place) alone. They would not bathe with him nor bathe in the same water , but throw it first into the Channel ; when he left the City (this was *Eunomius*). Do our hearers deal as harshly as this ?

Afterward when *Lucius* was set over them, the Children in the streets did burn their ball, because his Asses feet had touched it.

Id.

Id. ib. c. 16. When the Bishop of *Edessa* was removed and another set over them, the people frequented private meetings in the Suburbs. And when the Emperour commanded his Prefect, *Modestus*, to take Souldiers and disturb them, and drive them away, the women ran with their Children hoping to die with them. And *Eulogius* the Presbyter asked, *Was the Emperour made Priest when he was made Emperour?*

And how the Presbiters and People of *Antioch* continued their meeting whether the Emperour would or not, though he disturbed them by Soldiers.

Theodor. c. 17. Basils answer to the Prefect, when he offered him the Emperours favour, was, that Children were to be so talk'd to, but Men bread up in divine studies, would suffer any death rather than suffer one syllable of divine Truth to be blemished. *Quod autem ad Imperatoris amicitiam,* &c. But as for the Emperors friendship I much value it (saith he) joyned with godliness, but if it want that, I say, it is pernicious. In one of us this answer would have been enough to make us seem as bad, as it made *Basil* esteemed good.

Id. 11. c. 19. When the forenamed *Lucius* was made Bishop of *Alexandria,* and *Peter* their Bishop put out, the People would come to the Church place, though he persecuted them as he had done the other, *& omnes pariter ceperunt Lucium convitiis lacerare,* they all began to tear *Lucius* with revilings, because he persecuted the Monks of *Egypt.*

Id. l. c. 38. Audas a Bishop in *Persia* demolished their Temple (or *Pyreum*) by violence: For which the Emperour of *Persia* killed him, and destroyed all the Christian Churches.

Id. l. 4. c. 21. When *Moses* was desired by Queen *Mavia* to be her Bishop among the *Saracens,* he would not let *Lucius* ordain him, because he had persecuted good men, But said to him (*Quis impius non tua causa conventus Ecclesiasticos petulanter infestatus est? Quis e laudatorum virorum numero non parte exulavit? Quam immanitatem barbaram, malefici abs te in dies singulos admissa nen superarunt?*) Do Nonconformists speak more harshly to our Bishops?

Theodoret himself frequently calleth *Julian* a Tyrant. *cap.* 22. The Heathens kept their Feasts openly; *Telis autem Apostolicæ doctrinæ propugnatoribus, tyrannus iste se hostem præbuit.* And, when he was dead, they openly rejoyced at his death.

Id. cap. 30. l. 4. With what bold language doth *Izaak* tell *Valens* of his fighting against God, and casting out his Ministers, and Gods fighting against him, and what he would be sure to meet with at the end, if he kicked against the pricks.

Lib. 5. c. 17. The Christian people of *Thessalonica* rose, and killed some of *Theodosius* his Officers, which provoked him by his Souldiers to kill seven thousand of them, for which *Ambrose* brought him to do open pennane.

To mention all the blood shed at *Rome* (as at *Damascus* election and else) elfe) and *Constantinople*, and *Alexandria* would be tedious, even that which was shed on the account of Bishops.

Lucius Calaritanus was a pious Bishop; but so hot for separation from those that had been *Arrians*, that he is numbered for it with the Hereticks, though an orthodox Bishop.

The *Novatians* were Episcopal, and so were the *Donatifts*, and yet how have they been judged of for their Schifin I need not tell: *Apollinarius* father and son, *Paulus Samofatenus*, *Nestorius*, *Diofcorus*, *Eufebius*, *Nicomed*, *Theodorus Mopfuest*, and how many more Bishops have been Arch-hereticks and the caufe of tumults and diffensions. The very reading over the acts of the General Councils, efpecialy *Eph.* 1. and 2. *& Calced.* is tremendous. It was to be a Bishop, that *Maximus* made fo peftilent a ftir at *Conftantinople* and *Alexandria* againft *Gregory Theolog.* Yea they tell us themfelves, that it was becaufe he could not be a Bishop that *Aerius* fpake againft Bishops, fo peftilent a thing hath the defire of fuch Eifhopricks been.

Theodotus the Bifhop would not fo much as joyn in Prayer with *Bafil* morning or evening, becaufe he had but communicated with Bifhop *Euftathius* upon his fair profeffions, *Bafil. Epift.* 43. *Admir: ad Terentium Comit.*

The contention between fuch excellent perfons as *Eufebius Cæfar* while Bifhop, and *Bafil* : while Presbyter, was very fad and fcandalous.

The contention between *Bafil* and *Euthemius* about the extent of their Diocefs was no lefs.

The People of *Cæfarea* would have torn in peices, *Eufebius* the Prefident, the Emperors own Unkle, for *Bafils* fake, if he had not hindred them.

The Church of *Neo-Cæfarea* wrangled with *Bafil* for his *Pfalmodie*, and even avoided him as if he had been an Heretick, fee *Bafils Epift. ad mer.* 4. to *Julian*, what language he there ufeth to the Emperour : Not that I judge him, but wifh you to judge equally of the actions of thofe times and ours. See *Bafil Ep.* 82. *Theodor. l. 5. c.* 19.

The *Antiochians* for a Tax under *Theodofius* the great, did tumultuate and kill the Magiftrates, and deftroyed the Statue of *Placilla* the good Emprefs.

In the Weft good *Ambrofe* at *Milan* (was not filenced as we are, but) by an Orthodox Emperour defired and commanded to deliver the *Arrians* poffeffion but of one Church : and he refufed to do it, and to forfake that Church (or Temple) or deliver the Veffels till they fhould be taken by force. *Vit. Ambrof. per Baron. p.* 6. whereas we all left our Churches at a word. Nay though he would not refift the Emperour, he would rather die than deliver up the Church.

When he was celebrating Gods Worfhip he was fain to break off, to refcue an *Arrian* Prieft out of the hands of the Orthodox people, who had laid hold on him: For which multitudes were laid in prifon and Irons, and accufed of Sedition, and great Calamity followed to the

Church,

Church , and this from *Valentinian* an Orthodox Emperour.

Ambrose. saith when he refused to deliver up the Temple, *Ea quæ sunt Divinæ Imperatoriæ potestati non esse subjecta* (If *Baronius* say true); but mine I shall yield to him]. But we hold that even Temples (as well as Bishops) though dedicated to God, are under the Civil power of the Empour.

When *Ambrose* was desired but to quiet the people, he answered *It is in my power not to stir them up; but it is God that must quiet them*] So great was his interest in the people that the Emperour said he was a *Tyrant*, and that the people would deliver himself bound to him, if *Ambrose* did but bid them. Yet had *Ambrose* been the man that had gone on his Embassie to *Maximus*, and kept him from coming into *Italy* in pursute of *Valentinian* which made *Ambrose* say .[*Non hoc Maximum dicere quod Tyrannus ego sum Valentiniani: qui se meæ legationis objectum queritur ad Italiam non potuisse pervenire.*]

And because the late revolutions in *England* are made by some Prelates the pretence for the silencing of the 1800 Ministers, of whom one of ten never medled with Warrs, being fallen again on this case of *Maximus*, let it be noted how like he was to *Cromwel*, saving that it was not the Sectaries, but the Bishops that he studyed to please and rise by. When *Gratian* the Emperour befriended the *Priscillianists*, *Maximus* to please the Bishops persecuted them to the death. When *Valentinian* by *Justina* the Empresse meanes did persecute or trouble *Ambrose* for refusing to deliver a Church to the *Arrians*, and also other Orthodox Bishops as well as *Ambrose*, *Maximus* gave to *Ambrose* and the Bishops the Honour of keeping him out of *Italy*, and letting *Valentinian* scape: Yea, wrote his Letters to *Valentinian* for the Orthodox Bishops, telling him how grievous a thing it is to persecute the Ministers of God, and when under his father they went for faithful Ministers. *Quæ tanta mutatio, ut qui antea sacerdotes, nunc sacrilegi judicantur! Iisdem certe præceptis, Iisdem Sacramentis dilatis; Eadem fide credunt, qua antea crediderunt. An pietas Venerabilis mihi serenitas tua conceptam semel in animis religionem quam Deus ipse constituit posse evelli?* And proceedeth to shew what disorders and contentions must needs follow when there be a shew of persecuting Christians and Ministers] Upon this message of *Maximus*, *Valentinian* being afraid of him, the persecution ceased; and *Ambrose* must be sent again on the Embassage to *Maximus* to stop him: But when as the Bishops of *France* and *Germany* owned him, and *Ambrose* would not communicate with those Bishops (no more than *Martin*) saith he, *cum viderem me abstinere ab Episcopis qui communicabant ei, vel qui aliquos devios licet a fide* (that is the *Priscillianists*) *ad necem petebant, jussit me sine mora regredi.* See here that *Ambrose* as well as *Martin* separated from the Communion of the multitude of Bishops for owning *Maximus*, and for seeking to the Magistrate to draw his sword against the *Priscillianists*, whom *Sulp. Severus* calleth *Gnosticks* : When as many among us , have by words and

writting

writing provoked Rulers to draw the sword against us that differ, in no one point of doctrine from the Articles of the English Church.

And the said *Maximus* and the Bishops did so close, that only one *Hyginus* a Bishop is mentioned, and *Theognostus* besides *Ambrose* and *Martin* that rejected *Maximus*, and refused Communion with the Synod and Bishops, and was banished also for so doing. By which you may see, 1. That Bishops can comply with usurpers that will be for them as much as Presbyters, 2. And that all is not unwarrantable separation or schism, which Bishops call so, when these three shall separate from so many.

And saith *Baron. in vita Ambrof. Maximus ut Tyranni nomen vitaret, perinde atque fidei Catholicæ tuendæ caufa bellum illud fufcepiffet, in hereticos pugnam convertit, & Catholicos facerdotes quibus valuit honoribus & officiis eft profecutus, p. 24. Maximus* raiseth that war for the Orthodox Bishops to save them from the persecution of their lawful Prince, and sets himself to do them all the honor he could, and to pull down the hereticks.

And these were the Halcionian daies which *Ambrose* himself declareth and magnifieth, even when *Maximus* had suppreft the Arrians [*En tempus acceptabile! quo non hiemalibus perfidiæ caligantis pruinas annus riget, nec altis nivis, &c. ibid.* Reader was not that time more strange than ours? that *Ambrose* muft be so loyal as to save his Prince and Country from a ufurper: and yet so pious as to be perfecuted by his Prince, and he and his brethren saved by that same ufurper, and openly give praife to God for the great felicity of the Church which it received by that same ufurper whom he so refifted? Is it not pity that things should be so ftrangely carried?

And that yet you may see more into this bufinefs, *Paulinus in vit. Ambrof. p.40.* tells us, that *Maximus* took juft a name to himfelf as *Cromwel* the Protector did. [*Maximus Procuratorem fe reipublicæ nomine, præfuiffe confiteretur.*] He would rule as the Procurator of the Common-wealth.

Well! But this is not all the ufurpers that rofe up in thofe daies. *Eugenius* soon becometh more terrible than he (who once was but a Schoolmafter.) And how doth this loyal S. *Ambrose* carry it? when he had got of *Theodofius* a pardon for all that took part with *Maximus*, even his Army except two or three, yea and benefits too, yet did not this holy loyal man think it finful to write thus to the Tyrant *Eugenius*, [*Epiftol.l.2.p.103. Clementiffimo Imperatori Eugenio, Ambrofius Epifcopus*; Bishop *Ambrose* to the moft Clement Emperour *Eugenius*. And thus concludeth, [*In his vero in quibus vos rogari decet, etiam exhibere fedulitatem poteftati debitam, ficut & fcriptum eft, cui honorem, honorem, cui tributum, tributum: Nam cum privato detulerim corde intimo, quomodo non deferrem Imperatori?*] i. e. But in these 'matters where it becometh us to petition you, we muft also give the dili-'gence due to power: as it is written, honor to whom honor, tribute to 'whom tribute: For when I honored you, when you were a private man 'from the inwards of my heart, how should I not honor you an Empe-'rour?]

Reader do not only judge of my two Epiftles to *Rich. Cromwell* by these

these passages, but even of theirs that submitted to *Oliver* himself: and yet Judge of the inferences that are raised by our accusers.

Should I but recite the words of submission of *Bishops* to usurpers, yea of *Gregory* the Great and such of the highest note, it would be over tedious to the Reader, who I doubt will think that I have been too long in this unpleasant History already.

2. But this I must need add *ad homines*, 1. That it hath been the Bishops themselves that have been the grand cause of our Church divisions and separations: what advantage they have given the separatists I shewed before. I am sure in the Congregation where I once was teacher, and the Countrey about, nothing that ever came to pass hath so inclined the people to avoid the Prelates, as their own doing, especially the silencing and reproaching their ancient teachers whom they knew longer and better than the Prelates did.

2. That it was a Parliament of Episcopals and Erastians, and not of Presbyterians, who first took up Armes in *England* against the King.

3. That the General, and chief Officers of the Parliaments first Army were scarce any of them at all Presbyterians, but Episcopal by profession, saving some few Independants.

4. That the Lord Lieutenants of the several Counties, were almost all Episcopal, save three Independents.

5. The Major Generals of the several By-armies in the Counties were almost all Episcopal.

6. The Assembly of Divines at *Westminster* were all save eight or nine Conformable.

7. Most of the Episcopal men of my acquaintance took the Covenant, that could keep their places by it, or at their composition.

8. I knew few of them that took not the engagement it self, *against King and house of Lords*, meerly for liberty to travail about their business, when we that ran a greater hazard by refusing, never took it; but many were cast out of their Churches, and their government in the University Colledges for refusing it. These and many more such unpleasant things, I have fully proved elsewhere, being constrained by the false accusations of implacable men, to mention that which I had far rather silence.

9. And what hand the Londoners, the Presbyterian Ministers, and Gentlemen, and people had in bringing in the King was once known and acknowledged.

And General *Monks* Colonels and Captains were so many of them Presbyterians, when they cast out the Anabaptists, from among them in *Scotland* and marcht into *England* and restored the King, that as I knew divers of them to be such, so far as I could learn from others, the chief strength of them were such or so inclined.

10. And though many of the Parliament were suppos'd Presbyterians long after, who were Episcopal at the raising of the Army, yet could not

the

the late King *Charles* I. be rejected and judged and put to death, till most of the Parliament were violently secluded and imprisoned by the Army. And as soon as they were but called together again, it was they (in Parliament and Council of State) that opened the door for the Kings restitution.

But while the matters of the Church of Christ, and the decision of religious controversies, and the liberty of Christs Ministers to preach his Gospel, must be laid upon state revolutions, and where Bishops that can neither accuse Christs Ministers of heresie, ignorance, negligence, covetousness, pride, nor scandalous immoralities, shall run to the old methods; and perswade Kings that these men are not for their profit, that they are pestilent fellows and movers of sedition among the people, that they prophecy not good of Kings but evil, and that they would set up another King, one *Jesus*, and therefore are not *Cæsars* friends, these malicious projects may silence Ministers, and prosper, while our sins are to be punished, and the peoples, contempt of the Gospel and their ingratitude are to be chastised. But the wicked servant that saith, my Lord delayeth his coming, and beateth his fellow servants, and eateth and drinketh with the drunken, will see that his Lord will come in a day, that he looked not for him, and will cut him a sunder, and give him his portion, with hypocrites (for their dead Image of Religion will not save them) there shall be weeping and gnashing of teeth, *Matth.* 24.48,49,50,51.

CHAP. XXIII.

Four double charges I have now proved against the foredescribed Diocesane form of Government, the least of which alone is enough to prove it utterly unlawful.

1. THat it overthroweth the ancient Species of Churches, and setteth up another sort of Churches, in their place; and sets up *one Church* of that kind instead of many hundreds.

2. That it overthroweth the ancient office of a Presbyter; by taking away one part of his work (*viz.* Government) which as much belongeth to him as the rest : And maketh a new office of subject Presbyters, which God never made.

3. That it overthroweth the ancient sort of fixed Episcopacy, (as distinct from Itinerants and Arch-bishops); taking down a thousand or very many Bishops, even the Bishops of particular Churches, and instead of them all setting up but one over all those Churches; as if all Bishops were put down, and the Archbishops only take all their charges and work upon them.

4. That it maketh the Discipline or Government instituted by Christ, in the very matter of it to become impossible and impracticable, and so exclud-

excludeth it, under pretence that they are the only persons impowred for it ; and they set up a kind of secular Courts and Government in its stead; and so are practically Erastians.

I shall conclude all with these *Consectaries* which follow what is already proved.

Conf. 1. Such *Diocesane* principles greatly strengthen the Brownists cause, who deny us to have any Church or Ministry of divine institution : as is before shewed. And as for them that say [No form of Church Government is of divine institution]. *Ans.* 1. It is well, that they are forced to except both the universal and the particular Churches, and expound this only of Associations of Churches. 2. It is well that yet they confess that the *office* of Pastors is of Divine institution ; who are made Church Governours by Christ. 3. But it is scant well that yet they subscribe to the book of *Ordination*, which asserteth the Divine right of three distinct orders, if they do not believe it. 4. And these also too much gratifie the Brownist, who affirmeth that we have no Churches of Divine institution, and thinketh that it is no fault to separate, but from a Church of humane invention.

Conf. 2. To say that no man High or Low is bound in his place and calling to endeavour a Reformation of such a Church-Government, and so to justifie the neglecters and opposers of all such Reformation is to draw upon a mans self the guilt of so much pollution, and of the ruin of such a multitude of souls, as should make that Conscience smart and tremble, which is not seared and past all feeling.

Conf. 3. To swear or subscribe, or say and declare, that though millions should swear to endeavour such a reformation, in their places and callings, by lawful means, there is no obligation lieth on any one of them from that Vow or Oath : So to endeavour it, is —— The Lord have Mercy on that Land, City or Soul that is guilty of it ——

Conf. 4. All carnal interest and all carnal reason is on the *Diocesanes* side, and all the lusts of the heart of man, and consequently all the Devil can do : Therefore while carnal Christians make a Religion of their lusts and interest, and pride, and covetousness, and idleness are more predominant, than the fear of God and the love of souls, no wonder if the *Diocesane* cause prevail with such.

Conf. 5. A truly sanctified heart knoweth the nature and worth of Grace, and the nature and weight of the Pastoral Office, and is devoted to God and the good of souls, and contemneth the ease and pleasures of the flesh and the riches and the honours of this World, and is the best argument in the World against such *Diocesane* Prelacy; and must at least be *weakned* before it can subscribe never to endeavour to amend it.

Conf. 6. No wonder if the most serious zealous practical sort of Christians are ordinarily against such *Diocesanes* Prelacy, when it hath the described effects and that those among themselves.

Conf. 7. No wonder if the principal work of such *Diocesanes* be to silence faithful preachers and persecute zealous Christians, where they had e-

Ee 3　　　　　　　　　　　　　　　　　　　　　　spoused

efpoufed a caufe fo contrary to the intereft of Godlinefs that all thefe are unreconcilable thereto: Speak not of any other Prelacy.

Conf. 8. Take but from fuch Prelacy the plumes which it hath ftolen from Magiftrates and Presbyters, and it will be a naked thing, and fimply a name.

Conf. 9. If Magiftrates were not the Prelates Executioners or feconded them not by writs *de excommunicato capiendo, &c.* fuch Prelacy would give up as dead, or aweary of it felf.

Conf. 10. The ill Mixtures of force and fecular power, corrupteth Church Difcipline, and depriveth it of its proper nature, ufe and force, maketh it another thing, or undifcernable.

Conf. 11. Though in cafes of neceffity civil Rulers may truft Church men with part of their power about religion, it is far better out of neceffity that they keep it wholly to themfelves. And let them thunder their excommunications without any power of the Sword.

Conf. 12. Such Bifhops and Arch-Bifhops as overthrow not the Churches officers, and difcipline of Chrift, muft be fubmitted to by all peaceable men, though we cannot prove them as fuch to be of Divine inftitution.

CHAP. XXIV.

Some teftimonies of Prelatifts of the late ftate of the Church of England, left we be fuppofed partial in our defcription of it.

I. FOr the true underftanding of the late ftate of the Church of *England*, the Reader may find fome light, in the Lord *Falklands* Parliament *Speeches*, and Sir *Edward Dearings*, and in *Heylins* own Hiftory of the Sabbath, with *Pocklingtons* Sunday no Sabbath, and the Bifhop of *Lincolnes* book of the Holy Table name and things, and Dr. *Heylens* anfwer to him; And the fame *Heylins* Hiftory of Arch-Bifhop *Laud*: and from Mr. *Thornedicks* four laft bookes.

II. To what common fcorne all ferious Godlinefs was brought by the rabble through the abufe of the name *Puritane*, ufed by the Prelatifts to make odious the Nonconformifts, is after fhewed out of Bifhop *Downame*, and Mr. *Robert Bolton*, who is large and frequent in it.

III. Bifhop *Halls* Confeffion of the corruptions in the Church Governours and Government in his Modeft offer and Peacemaker, and his difclaiming thofe that deny it, I have cited elfewhere.

IV. *Williams* Arch-Bifhop of Yorke, *Morton* Bifhop of *Durham* with many other Epifcopal Divines of greateft name and worth, did affem-

bl.

ble in *Westminster* and collected a Catalogue of things needing reformation in Discipline and worship, which are to be seen in print.

V. A Prelatical Divine in a Treat: called *Englands faithful Reprover and Monitor*, thus speaketh to his prelates and Pastor pag. 60, 61. &c.
' And *now with what depth of sorrow* ought we to recount your past errours,
' partly through neglect of duty, partly through abuse of power ——
' * were the faithful in your trust? did ye diligently instruct the ignor- *Ithaclaus*
' ant? severely punish the disobedient? Endeavour to reclaime those that
' walked disorderly and contrary to the Gospel —— That ye were vio-
' lently bent against Action and Schisme, against singularity and Non-
' conformity, all confess ; a few excepted who thought nothing too
' much, yea nothing enough in this kind, how opposite soever to Christi-
' an mildness, prudence and Conscience : But in the mean time, by reason
' of your Connivence or Supineness in the Episcopal office, Ignorance and
' Superstition every where misled the people, and caused them to wan-
' der in darkness, not knowing whither they went. Profaness like a
' rank pernicious weed overspread the field and Vineyard of the Lord
' --- And the prophane and vicious lives of those who stood up in defence
' of your Government * occasionally gave increase and added strength *Most of*
' to the opposite factious party, who alledged this as one main ground *the pro-*
' of their separation from the Church, that those who adhered to it, *phane.*
' were for the most part unworthy to have Communion with any orderly
' well governed Congregation of believers, because of their loose and
' scandalous manner of living, which because they could not redresse,
' they did pretend at least they were bound thus to shun and avoid as
' hateful to God and to good men. Wherefore ye did not carefully se-
' perate between the precious and the vile * but consulting with flesh and *1. Yes but*
' blood what ye were to do in this case, thought in humane Policy to *the, did, by*
' break the power of one party, by strengthening the hands of the o *persecuting*
' ther * or not binding and restraining them with the Cords of Ec- *the rest. 2.*
' clesiasticall discipline. Thus while you opposed Profaneness against *not because*
' Schism * or did let that loose at this, or secretly favoured and upheld *they were*
' it in hope to suppresse the later by the former, the one grew too strong *Diocesans,*
' by the violence of opposition for your selves, and both for the Church *and would*
' in order to peace and holiness. As for your labour in the work of the *too may*
' Ministry, how little it hath been for many years together, it is even a *of them*
' shame to mention, some of you wholly exempting your selves, from *hated the*
' this necessary burden of their calling, for ease and pleasure: Others *best.*
' supposing it a task and employment too low and inferiour for them ---- *baist.*
' The rest for the most part, slightly or seldome bearing it with their *O good*
' shoulders, and laying it aside presently, as that which concerned o- *Bishop.*
' ther men, and not themselves any longer then they listed ; And thus far
' had been pardonable with men, had care been taken to see this work
' duely performed by the Clergy ---- But alas there were not wanting
' of you, who did not only wink at the wilful neglect of their inferi-

' FOUR.

'our brethren in this point of Ministerial duty: But did countenance
'and favour such as were most peccant therein, judging them most a-
'verse from faction, who were least conscious * Of Preaching to the peo-
'ple, and fairest friends to the present Government, who were loose
'enough, God knoweth, in their office and conversation. Whence it
'came to pass that very many who were for you in the time of Tryal,
'were ignorant and dissolute men, * dishonourable to your party, and
'indeed to the Christian Religion, which they did continually profane
'by their words and workes: So unsuitable is humane policy with
'Evangelical simplicity, and unsuccesful when it is used to support the
'regiment thereof. And instead of sending forth meet Labourers into
'the Lords harvest, fit Pastors into his flock, you sent those that were
'idle Shephards, loving to slumber, given to sleep, altogether like your
'selves, carelesse of the Lords Heritage, either unwilling if able or if
'willing unable, or neither willing nor able, rightly to divide the word
'of truth, giving them their portion in due season. As for those to
'whom God had given both ability and will, to preach the word, ye per-
'mitted them not the free use and exercise of their gifts; but forbade
'them to teach the people as oft as they saw it convenient or necessary
'for their Edification. And though you did at first commend to them,
'the way of Catechizing the younger sort --- yet afterwards, I know not
'upon what grounds or for what reason, you so far limited and restrain-
'ed the Minister in this pious and profitable practice, that ye did in a
'manner take away the key of knowledge, or make it uselesse for them, so
'that they could not enter in thereby.

'And pag. 69. [of this I am assured, that nothing was reformed after-
'ward in your ordinations, it being as free and indifferent for all who
'came, as ever ---- p. 70. 71. 72. [The like excuse some frame for the
'grosse corruptions of your prerogative Courts, for commutations, un-
'just, partial and unreasonable Censures of Excommunication, for un-
'lawful (to say no more) suspension of the meaner sort from ordinances
'of Jesus Christ, for non-payment or rather disability of paying pecuniary
'mulcts and fees imposed on them, and without Equity exacted of them,
'by your prophane and greedy officers. They pretend the power of the
'Chancellour to be distinct and separate from that of the Bishop, in many.
'points of spiritual Jurisdiction, and so exempt from it and uncontroulable
'by it, however proving illegal and exorbitant in the proceedings there
'of;—— And surely it may seem strange to any considerate person, that
'ye who did so much strain your authority for the introducing of new
'Ceremonies into the Church of Christ (favouring of superstition, and be-
'getting jealousies in mens minds of Popish innovations intended by you,)
'without prudence or Conscience, and used it so rigorously for the enforc-
'ing of the old upon many ill affected to the observation of them, absolutely
'requiring conformity to the Church Liturgy in every point, of all
'men, (notwithstanding *rebus sic stantibus & profligata disciplina* * some
'formes

'former thereof were not appliable to divers persons) would not ex-
'tend it to the utmost measure for the rectifying those great abuses
'which had by insensible degrees crept in, and corrupted the true Primi-
'tive discipline———— But Court employments, State flattery, and sinful
'Complyances with great persons, were the main lets, which hindred
'you from the due discharge of your office, both in preaching the word,
'and exerciting the Rod of Christ, according to his mind and will, while
'ye thought in carnal reason, such means as these most effectual for the
'acquiring and retaining of your greatness, and despised those which the
'prudent simplicity of the Gospel did offer and commend unto you: Where-
'fore it is no wonder if vice did reign there where flattery did abound,
'and that in the chief Ministers and Messengers of truth, if injustice and
'oppression did bear sway,———— If men were secure in their sins, where
'peace was proclaimed———— where a prophane Company heard nothing
'for the most part decried in the Pulpit but *Faction*, from which perhaps,
'alone they were free. And what could be expected from the common
'people, but blind ignorance love of pleasures more than God———— when
'ye their chief Leaders caused them to err, not only through your
'negligence, but also by your example.———— And I would to God some
'of you had not proved false and deceitful to your brethren, whom ye
'perverted from the way of truth and peace, by your own departing
'from it———— continuing fast friends to the world—— ye were carnal
'your selves and walked as men, shewing them the way to heaven with
'hearts and eyes fixed upon earth. For who more immoderate in their
'care for the things of this life than you? Who more eager in the
'pursuit of riches and honor, more tenacious in withholding good from
'the owners thereof, than your selves? Who were more set upon the u-
'sual course of enriching above measure, and raising your families on
'high? If a dignity or office fell within the Compass of your Diocess,
'who was presently judged of you more worthy to possess and manage
'it, than a Son or a Nephew, or a Kinman, or an Allie, though they
'were many times altogether uncapable of the honor and trust to which
'ye preferred them in the house of God, either they wanted ability of
'parts requisite thereunto, or had not as yet attained to maturity of
'years, being not much past their nonage, as we have known some of
'them to be, or in all respects undeserving persons. And yet men of
'age, and experience, eminent for learning, and piety, must stand un-
'veiled before such as these, to receive directions, and commands from
'them, to whom they were able and fit to give the same: who through
'the just judgment of the Almighty, have since been as much and more
'scorned--- than they do now scorn others, every way their superiour,
'but in place.]

Here he citeth such like words also even from Bishop *Andrews, Conc: ad
Cler.* with his prediction of the fall of their order, for their vicious lives.
. So p. 6. [To this specious design, an open way seemed to be made by

F f   the

the great profanefs and vicious living of the oppofite party, who while they were zealous for conformity to the ordinances of men, and thought a main part of Chriftian duty, to depend upon the obfervation of them, did allow themfelves carnal liberty inviolating the precepts and commandements of God. And this they did, as from the inbred corruption, which is common to all men ; fo likewife from a private fpirit of oppofition againft the adverfaries of their caufe].

And p. 10 11. Speaking of advantages againft the Bifhops and their party, faith he [' This perchance was not the meaneft, that they might ' thus check and fhame the open prophanefs, grofs impiety, irreligi-' on and fin of their profeffed adverfaries : The which (to fpeak truth) ' was fo eminent oft times and notorious in many of them, as might ftar-' tle a meer natural Confcience to hear or behold it ; and caufe therein an ' abhorrence from their courfes, (fo oppofite as well to right reafon, as ' fanctifying grace) much more in a mind inlightened, though with the ' fmalleft ray of Evangelical truth. For what could be more ftrange or ' hateful to men, in whom was any fpark remaining of common grace or ' moral virtue, and who were not wholly poffeffed with Atheifm, and car-' ried on with fulleft bent to libertinifm, and ungodly practice, than to ' hear thofe that profeffed themfelves the followers of Chrift, fcoffing at ' the pureft acts of his worfhip, blafpheming or prophaning his holy name, ' by cauflefs Oaths, fearful imprecations, direful execrations, and fuch like ' fpeeches, not to be expreffed again without horror and amazement. And ' not only fo but glorying likewife in this their abominable wickednefs, ' and in other of like damnable nature; in lafciviousnefs, lufts, excefs of ' wine, and ftrong drinks, revellings ; wherein they thought it ftrange that ' others ran not with them to the fame excefs of riot, fpeaking evil of ' them.—— How much did this their apparent and overdaring impudence ' in fin, commend and grace the feeming Saint-like * converfation of their ' adverfaries, [of fome of them, we cannot without manifeft breach of ' charity judge of them otherwife, than that they were fimple harmlefs ' well meaning men, who being offended (and not without caufe) at the ' corruption of the times, and fcandalous lives of many in the facred of-' fice of the Miniftry.——] And indeed their ftrict conformity in other ' refpects to the precepts of the Gofpel, with their conftancy in fuffering ' for the defence of their caufe, did argue as much to moderate men and ' not poffeffed with prejudicate hatred of their opinion and perfons : For ' fuch as thefe could never be induced to entertain a good conceit of them, ' no not in the leaft meafure ; but judged their beft actions to be counter-' feit and falfe, and thought their greateft fuffering to proceed from pride ' and contumacy of fpirit—— Now as it comes to pafs between thofe ' that extreamly hate one another, that they endeavour as much as in ' them lieth, to be unlike each other in manner of life, fo it fared in this ' cafe.——

Leave it to God to judge of the fecrets of the heart.

And p. 27. 28. (The flack hand of ecclefiaftical difcipline, was another.

' ther caufe of the general ignorance and prophanefs of thefe times ;
' which reached no further for the moft part, to the inferior Clergy (how
' peccant foever otherwife) than in difconformity to Epifcopal orders ,
' Provincial or Synodical Conftitutions touching external government :
' Neither did it call people to a due account (if any) of their proficiency
' in the knowledge of Chrift Jefus, or cenfure them for non-proficiency
' therein, yea fcarcely for grofs and fcandalous crimes, if they were per-
' fons known to be well affected to the prefent Government———]

' And of the change fince in 1653 when Bifhops were down, he faith,
' p. 29 [I can fpeak it on my own knowledge, that a Town of good note in
' the Weftern parts of the land, not far diftant from the Sea, heretofore
' famed for all manner of riot, and diforder, by this courfe of late years
' hath been reduced to that order and difcipline, that it is a rare matter to
' fee a man there at any time diftempered with wine and ftrong drink, or
' to hear a rafh Oath proceed from any mans mouth, no not when there
' is moft frequent concourfe of people thither from all the neighbour-
' ing parts.

Such changes through Gods mercy were not rare, till Prelacy returned.
Reader, I cite, the words of this author fo tedioufly, becaufe many would
perfwade thofe that knew not thofe times that none of this was true on
either fide ; And becaufe the Author was a very high Prelatift, writing
openly againft their adverfaries, 1653.

VI. Dr. Gauden, after Bifhop of *Worcefter*, *Hiera fpift. pag.* 287. faith,
' [I neither approve or excufe the perfonal faults of any particular Bi-
' fhops, as to the exercife of their power and authority; which ought
' not in weighty matters to be mannaged without the prefence, Council,
' and fuffrages of the Presbyters, fuch as are fit for that affiftance. The
' want of this S. *Ambrofe*, S. *Hierome*, and all *fober* men * juftly reprove, † *He mak-*
' as unfafe for the Bifhops and Presbyters and the whole Church. For in *eth our Pre-*
' multitude of Counfellors is fafety and honor. I am fure much good they *lates no fo-*
' might all have done, as many of them did, whom thefe touchy times *ber men.*
' were not worthy of———]

' And p 262. 263. [They have taught me to efteem the ancient
' and Catholick Government of Godly Bifhops, as Moderators and Prefi-
' dents among the Presbyters in any Diocefs or Precincts, in its juft mea-
' fure and conftitution for power paternal duty exercifed, fuch as was in
' the perfecuting, pureft and primitive times. ———] Juft fuch we offered
' them in Bifhop *Ufhers Model*, ——— p. 263, [I confefs after the example
' of the beft times and judgment of the moft learned in all Churches, I
' alwayes wifhed fuch moderation on all fides, that a Primitive Epifco-
' pacy (which imported the authority of one grave and worthy perfon,
' chofen by the confent, and affifted by the prefence Counfel and fuffrages
' of many Presbyters) might have been reftored or preferved in this
' Church; And this not out of any factious defign, but for thofe weigh-
' ty reafons which prevail with me].

F f 2　　　　　　　　　　　　　　　　　Add

Add to this, what he faith in *Hookers* life of the late Bifhops, and remember that this man was one of the Keenest Writers againft the adverfaries of the Bifhops in his time; And that though he was made a Bifhop and great when the King was reftored, yet he was the only Bifhop of them all that in our conference at the *Savoy*, did defire and endeavour by fuch conceffions to have reconciled us altogether.

VII. I muft not tire the Reader with more fuch long citations, I next wifh him to fee Mr. *Alesburies Treatife of confeffion, p.* 21.24 28,104,105, 169. Where he defcribeth the ancient difcipline, and fheweth from our own Prelates that it is every particular member of the flock that the Paftor fhould perfonally know and counfel; And fee how far we are from this.

VIII. But none of thefe fpeak of the times that we are now fallen into: It can hardly be expected that any of their own party fhould yet dare to fpeak againft them: yet in private talk how common is it? But becaufe it will be too tedious to recite the words, I defire the Reafon to perufe a Book called *Icabod*, or the five groans of the Church, which in fharpnefs and high charges upon the Prelates fince their return, exceedeth all that are before cited. And that you may know that he is fufficiently Epifcopal, one of his accufations of them is for accepting fo many into the Church now that were lately againft conformity: I know the man who is faid to be the Author, and know him to be conformable to this time, and in poffeffion of a benefice in the Church.

IX. Let the Reader remember that the divifion between the Conformifts and Non-conformifts began at *Frankford* in Queen *Maries* days, and that Dr. *Ri. Coxe* was the man than began this ftir againft the Englifh Church there, by his forcible obtruding the Common-Prayer book on them, and that long led that party; And let him read in *Caffander* his 20th. Epiftle where he will find that the faid Dr. *Coxe* when he was made Bifhop of *Ely* in Queen *Elizabeths* time, wrote to *Caffander* for directions about fetting up Crucifixes or croffes in the Churches; and *Caffander* inftructeth him in what fhape the Crofs is to be made: And his *Prec. Ecclef.* gave us fome of our Collects.

X. Yea, when the Popifh Prelacy is defcribed, it is fo like to ours that when Dr. *Baftwick* and others wrote againft the Italian Bifhops, ours take it as fpoken of them. Hear Bifhop *Jewl*, Serm. on Mat. 9. 37 38 . [*But the labourers are few, I fay, not there are but few Cardinals, few Bifhops, few Priefts, that fhould be preachers, few Archbifhops, few Chancellors, few Deans, few Prebendaries, few Vicars. few Parifh Priefts, few Monks, few Fryers; For the number of thefe is almoft infinite—— And p 198. And what fhall I fpeak of Bifhops? Their cloven Mitre fignifieth perfect knowledge of the old and new Teftament; Their Crofiar ftaff fignifieth diligence in attending the flock of Chrift. Their purple boots and fandals fignifie that they fhould ever be booted and ready to go abroad through thick and thin to teach the Gofpel.—— But, alas in what kind of things do they bear themfelves as Bifhops? Thefe myftical titles and*
fhews

shews are not enough to fetch in the Lords harvest : They are garments more meet for Players than for good labourers —— whatsoever apparel they have on unless they will fall to work Christ will not know them for Labourers. —— Pag. 144. *The Christians in old time, when they lived under Tyrants, and were daily put to most shameful deaths, and were hated and despised of all the world, yet never lacked Ministers to instruct them. It is therefore most lamentable that Christians living under a Christian Prince, in the peace and liberty of the Gospel should lack Learned Ministers to teach them, and instruct them in the word of God : This is the greatest plague that God doth send on any people.*

To which, I add on the by, that if any say, we would labour if the Bishops would give us leave.] Though the charge against them thus intimated is grievous (and it were better for that man that offendeth one of Chrsts little ones, much more that hindereth multitudes from their duty in seeking mens salvation, that a Mill-stone were hanged about his neck, and he were cast into the depths of the Sea) yet that this will not excuse men from the preaching of the Gospel to the utmost of their power, see Bishop *Bilson* himself Asserting, *viz.* that silenced Ministers should not therefore give over preaching, in his *Christian subject*.

XI. Yea, read but *Cæsars* description of the Heathen Druides, and tell us, whether their Character agree not better with the Prelacy which hath prevailed in the Churches these seven hundred years at least, than Christs Character in the Scripture, save onely that it is Christianity which they profess. *Cæsar* Comment. lib. 6. p. 72. [*In omni Gallia, &c.* '*In all France there are two sorts of men in some number and honour (for* '*the common people are accounted almost but as servants, which of them-* '*selves dare do nothing, nor are used in any consultations, most of them be-* '*ing pressed with debts, or the greatness of tributes, or the injuries of the* '*more powerful, do give themselves in servitude to the nobles, who have all* '*that power over them as Lords over their servants : And of these two* '*sorts, one are Druides, the other Knights. The former are interested in* '*Divine affaires, they procure publick and private sacrifices; they interpret* '*Religions : To these flock abundance of young men for discipline; and* '*they are with them in great honour : For they determine of almost all* '*controversies private and publick; And if any crime be committed, if mur-* '*der be done, if there be any controversies of inheritance or bounds, these* '*men determine them, and do award rewards and punishments. If any* '*private person, or the people stand not to their award (or decree) they for-* '*bid them the sacrifices. This is with them the most grievous punishment.* '*Those that are thus interdicted are accounted in the number of the ungod-* '*ly and wicked : All men depart from them, and fly from their presence and* '*their speech, lest they get any hurt by the contagion: nor is any Right (or* '*Law) afforded them when they seek it, nor any honour done them. And*

F f 3

' over all these Druides there is one in chief, who hath the highest authority
' among them. When he is dead, if any one of the rest excel in worthi-
' ness, he succeedeth: But if there be many equal, he is chosen by the suffrage
' of the Druides: And sometimes they contend for the principality by Arms.
' At a certain time of the year in the borders of the Carnuti (Chartres)
' which is counted the middle of all France, they have a Confess (or Con-
' vocation) in a consecrated place; Hither come all that have controversies
' from all parts, and obey their judgments and decrees. It is thought that this
' Discipline was found in Brittain, and there translated into France. And
' now they that more diligently would know that business, for the most
' part go thither to learn it. The Druides use not to go to the Wars, nor
' do they pay tribute with the rest. They have freedome from warfare, and im-
' munity of all things: Being excited by so great rewards, many flock to this
' discipline of their own accord; and many are sent by their parents and
' kindred. They are reported to learn there abundance of Verses: Therefore
' some continue at learning twenty years; And they think it not lawful to
' commit them to writing; for in other publick matters and private accounts,
' for the most part they use the Greek Letters. It seemeth to me that they
' do this for two causes: because they would not have their discipline (or
' learning) made common (or brought to the Vulgar) nor those that learn it,
' neglect their memories by trusting to writings; which befalls the most, who by
' the help of writings, remit both their diligence in learning and their memory.
' This especially they perswade that souls die not, but after death pass from
' some to others: And by this they think that men are chiefly excited to virtue,
' neglecting the fear of death. Many things also they dispute and deliver to
' youth about the Stars, and their motion, of the magnitude of the world, and
' of the earth, of the nature of things, of the force and power of the immortal
' Gods.] So far Cæsar, which I repeated as offering it to consideration,
whether the foresaid Prelacy for Grandure be not liker to these Druides,
than to Chrilts Ministers who must be the servants of all? And yet whether they are not far more negligent in the exercise of discipline? And
whether this Discipline, which shameth sin, by thus distinguishing the
Godly and upright from the ungodly and wicked, be not of the very light
of nature, and found much in Brittain before Christianity, and therefore
should not be hated and banished by Christian Bishops, who pretend that
their office is instituted for that very use and end.

CHAP.

CHAP. XXV.

The Ordination lately exercised by the Presbyteries in England is valid : Ergo Reordination unnecessary.

That *valid ordination* is not to be *repeated*, is agreed on by *Protestants* and *Papists* : It is one of the ancient Canons called the Apostles, Can. 67. [*Siquis Episcopus aut Presbyter aut Diaconus secundam ab aliquo ordinationem acceperit, deponitor, iam ipse, quam qui ipsum ordinaverit.*

Arg. 1. *The way of Ordination which was valid in the Primitive Church is valid now.*

But the way of Ordination by meer Presbyters was valid in the Primitive Church : Ergo *it is valid now.*

The *Major* needs no proof, at least to the point in hand.

The Minor, I prove.

1. From *Hieromes* frequently cited words in his Epistle to *Evagrius,* where he tells us, that the *Presbyters of* Alexandria *from the daies of* Mark *till* Heraclas and Dionysius *made or ordained their own Bishops.* Having shewed that Bishops and Presbyters were of one office, he addeth. [*Quod autem postea unus electus est, qui cæteris præponeretur, in schismatis remedium factum est, ne unusquisque ad se trahens Christi ecclesiam, rumperet : Nam & Alexandria à Marco Evangelista usque ad Heraclam & Dionysium Episcopos, Presbyteri semper unum ex se electum. in excelsori gradu collocatum Episcopum nominabant : Quomodo si exercitus Imperatorem faciat : aut Diaconi eligent ex se quem industrium noverint, & Archidiaconum vocent.*] Where note, 1. That *Hierome* undertaking to shew how *Bishops* were made at *Alexandria,* mentioneth no other making of them but this *by the Presbyters:*

2. That [*Presbyters made Bishops*] is brought by *Hierome* as an Argument to prove the *Identity first*, and *nearness after* of their power.

3. That he ascribeth to the *Presbyters* the *Election,* the *placing* of him in a higher degree, and the *naming* of him a Bishop.

4. And that he distinguisheth the *Presbyters* making of a Bishop thus *anciently,* from that which *followed* Heraclas and Dionysius, which was by *episcopal ordination* or *consecration.* Which observations are sufficient to answer all their objections that will perswade men that *Hierome* speaketh but of *Election.*

2. This testimony is seconded by a more full one of *Eutychius* Patriark of *Alexandria,* who out of the Records and Tradition of that Church,

in

in his *Arabick Originalls* thereof faith as followeth [*according to* Seldens *Translation* in his Commentary pag. 29. 30.* [*Constituit item Marcus Evangelista duodecem Presbyteros cum Hanania, qui nempe manerent cum Patriarcha, adeo ut eum vacaret Patriarchatus eligerent unum è duodecim Presbyteris cujus capiti reliqui undecim manus imponerent, eumque benedicerent, & Patriarcham eum crearent: & dein virum aliquem nisi quem eligerent, cumque Presbyterum, secum constituerint loco ejus qui sic factus est Patriarcha, ut ità semper extarent duodecim. Neque desiit Alexandriae institutum hoc de Presbyteris, ut scilicet Patriarchas crearentur Presbyteris duodecim, usque ad tempora Alexandri Patriarchae Alexandrini, qui fuit ex numero illo* 318. *Is autem vetuit ne deinceps Patriarcham Presbyteri crearent, & decrevit ut mortuo Patriarchà convenirent Episcopi qui Patriarcham ordinarent. Decrevit item ut vacante Patriarchatu, Eligerent sive ex quacunque regione, sive ex duodecim illis Presbyteris, sive aliis, ut res ferebat, virum aliquem eximium, cumque Patriarcham crearent; atque ità evanuit institutum illud antiquius, quo creari solitus a Presbyteris Patriarcha, & successit in locum ejus decretum de Patriarchà ab Episcopis creando.*

Here you fee in the moft full expreffions that the *Presbyters Election, imposition* of hands and *Benediction* created their Bifhop or Patriark; and alfo *chofe* and *made* or *ordained another Presbyter* in his roome, and fo ordained both *Presbyters* and *Bifhops.*

3. The Tradition or Hiftory of *Scotland* telleth us that their Churches were long governed by *Presbyters* without *Bifhops*, and therefore had no *ordination* but *by Presbyters.*

Hector Boethius Hiftor. Scot. li. 7. *fol.* 128. 6 [*Ante Palladium populi suffragiis ex Monachis & Culdeis Pontifices assumerentur.*]

John Major *de geftis Scotorum li.* 2. *cap.* 2. Saith [*prioribus illis temporibus per sacerdotes & monachos sine Episcopis Scoti in fide eruditi funt.*

Jahan. Fordonus *makes this the curome of the Primitive Church: Scotichr. li.* 3. *cap.* 8. *Ante Palladii adventum habebant Scoti fidei Doctores ac Sacramentorum Miniftratores Presbyteros folummodo vel Monachos, ritum fequentes Ecclefiae primitivae.*

Which Bifhop Ufher reciting (*de primordiis Ecclef. Brit. p* 798. 799 800.) Saith *Quod postremum ab iis accepiffe videtur qui dixerunt* (*ut* Johan. Semeca *in gloffa decreti Dift.* 93. *cap. Legimus*) *quod in prima primitiva Ecclefia commune erat officium Episcoporum & sacerdotum, & nomina erant communia & officium commune fed in fecunda primitiva ceperunt diftingui & nomina & officia. So Baleus Script. Brit. Cent.* 14. *cap.* 6.

All which affure us that then only Presbyters could *ordaine* where there were no other, the fame we may fay of the *Gothick Churches* according to *Philoftorgius Eclog. li.* 2. *c.* 5. That were for feventy years after their converfion without a Bifhop. *Ulphilas* being the firft.

4. *Columbanus* was no Bifhop but a Presbyter and Monk, nor his Succeffours that yet *Ruled* even the *Bifhops*, as *Beda* notcth, *Hift. li* 3. *c.* 4. *&* 5. *Habere folet ipfa Infula Rectorem femper Abbatem Presbyterum, cujus*

cujus jure & omnis provincia, & ipsi etiam Episcopi, ordine inusitato deleant esse subjecti juxta exemplum primi Doctoris illius (Columbani) qui non Episcopus sed Presbyter extitit & Monachus.]

And these Presbyters did not only *ordaine* (as being the *only Church Governours*) but they sent *Preachers* into *England*, and *ordained Bishops* for *England* at King *Oswalds* request, as *Beda* at large relateth Ecclef. *Hist.l.3.c.* 3. 5. 17. 21. 24, 25. The Abbot and other Presbyters of the *Island Hy*, fent *Aydan* [*& ipfum effe dignum Epifcopatu ipfum ad erudiendos incredulos & indoctos mitti debere decernunt* — *Sicque illum ordinantes ad prædicandum miferunt &c.* Succeffit vero ei in Episcopatu *Finan, & ipfe illo ab Hy Scotorum infula ac monafterio deftinatus. c. 17. & cap. 25. Aydano Epifcopo de hac vita fublato. Finan pro illo gradum Epifcopatus a Scotis ordinatus & miffus acceperat &c.* So cap. 24. &c. You will find that the Englifh had a *Succeffion of Bishops* by the *Scotifh Presbyters ordination* : And there is no mention in *Beda* of any *diflike* or *fcruple* of the lawfulnefs of this courfe.

Segenius a Presbyter was *Abbot of Hy* (*cap. 5.*) when this was done And (*cap. 4.*) it appears that this was their *ordinary cuftome*, though in refpect to the Churches that were in the *Empire*, it be faid to be, *more inufitato*, that Presbyters did Govern Bishops : but none queftioned the validity of their ordinations. And the Council at *Heradford*, fubjecteth *Bishops in obedience to their Abbots.*

And the firft *reformers* or *Proteftants* here called *Lollords* and *Wicklififts* held and practifed ordination by *mere Presbyters*, as *Walfingham* reports *Hift. Angl. An.* 13. 89. and fo did *Luther* and the Proteftants of other Nations, as *Pomeranus* ordination in *Denmark* fhews, and *Chytræus Saxon Chron lib.* 14. 15. 16 17.

5. *Leo Mag. Epift.* 92. cited by *Gratian*, being confulted a *ruftico Narbonenfi, de Presbytero vel Diacono qui fe Epifcopos mentiti funt ; & de his quos ipfi clericis ordinárunt,* anfwered [*Nulla ratio fuit ut inter Epifcopos habeantur qui nec a clericis funt electi, nec a plebibus expetiti, &c.* — yet thus refolveth of their ordination [*Siqui autem Clerici ab ipfis Pfeudo- Epifcopis in eis Ecclefiis ordinati funt, quæ ad proprios Epifcopos pertinebant, & ordinatio eorum cum confenfu & judicio prefidentium facta eft, poteft rata haberi, ita ut in ipfis Ecclefiis perfeverant.*] So that the *mere confent* of the proper Bishops can make valid fuch *Presbyters ordination.*

6. *Feliciffimus* was ordained *Deacon* by *Novatus* one of *Cyprians Presbyters, Schifmatically,* yet was not his ordination made *Null by Cyprian,* but he was *depofed* for *Mal-adminiftration.* See *Blondel* p. 312. 113.

7. *Firmilian* (in 75 Epift. apud Cyprian) Saith [*Neceffario apud nos fit, ut per fingulos annos feniores & præpofiti unum conveniamus ad difponenda quæ curæ noftræ commiffa funt, ut fi quæ graviora funt, communi confilio dirigantur This fhews that communi confilio importeth a confenting Governing Power) &c. Omnis poteftas & gratia in Ecclefiis conftituta, ubi præfident majores natu qui & baptizandi, & manum imponendi, & ordinandi poffident Poteftatem*] If

G g

any

any fay, *It is only Bishops that* Formilian *speakes of*; I answer, 1. He had a little before used the word (*Seniores*) (the same in sense with *Majores natu* here) as distinct from (*Prapositi*) to signifie either *all Pastors in general*, or *Presbyters in special*. 2. When he speakes of (*Majores natu*) in general, they that will limit it to Bishops, must prove it so limited; and not barely affirme it. 3. The conjunct acts of the office disprove that: It was the same men that had the power of baptizing.

8. The great Council of Nice (the most reverend Authority next to the holy Scripture) decreed thus concerning the Presbyters ordained by *Melitius* at *Alexandria* and in *Egypt* [*Hi autem qui Dei gratiâ & nostris precibus adjuti, ad nullum Schisma deflexisse comperti sint, sed se intra Catholicæ & Apostolicæ Ecclesiæ fines ab erroris labe vacuos continuerint, authoritatem habeant tum ministros ordinandi, tum eos que clero digni fuerint nominandi, tum denique omnia ex lege & instituto Ecclesiastico libere exequendi.*] If any fay that the meaning is that these Presbyters shall ordain and Govern with the Bishops but not without them, I am of his mind, that this must needs be the meaning of these words; or else they could not be consonant with the Church Canons: But this sheweth that ordination belongeth to the Presbyters office, and consequently that it is no nullity (though an irregulrity as to the Canons) when it is done by them alone *Socrat. lib.* 5. 6. *cap.* 6.

9. It is the title of the twelfth Canon *Concil. Ancyrani* [*Quod non oportet Chorepiscopos ordinare nisi in agris & villulis*] Now either these *Chorepiscopi* were of the order of Bishops or not; If they were, then it further appeareth how small the Churches were in the beginning that had Bishops, even such as had but *Vnum Altare*, as *Ignatius* faith; when even in the Countrey Villages they had Bishops as well as in Cities; notwithstanding that the Christians were but thinly scattered among the Heathens. But if they were not Bishops, then it is apparent that Presbyters did then ordain without Bishops, and their ordination was valid. And the *Vafrities* of the Prelates is disingenious in this that when they are pleading for *Diocesan* Churches, as containing many fixed Congregations, then they eagerly plead that the *Chorepiscopi* were of the order of Presbyters: But when they plead against Presbyters ordination; they would prove them Bishops. Read *& Can.* 10. *Concilii Antiocheni.*

10. Even in the daies of ignorance and Roman Usurpation, *Bonifacius Mogunt. alias Wilfred, Epist.* 130 (*Auct. Bib. Pat. To* 2. *p.* 105.) tells Pope *Zachary* (as his answer intimateth) that *in Gente Boiariorum* there, was but one Bishop, and that was one *Vivilo*, which the Pope had ordained, and that all the Presbyters that were ordained among them, as far as could be found were not ordained by Bishops, though that ignorant usurping Pope requireth, as it seemeth, that they be reordained, (unless *Benedictionem ordinationis* should signifie only the *blessing* or confirmation of their former ordination, which is not like) For he faith [*Quia indicasti perrexisse te ad gentem Boiariorum, & invenisse eos extra ordinem ecclesiasti-*

cum.

cum viventes, dum Episcopos non habebant in Provinciâ nisi unum, nomine Victito, quem nos ante tempus ordinavimus, Presbyteros vero quos ibidem reperisti, si incogniti fuerint viri illi à quibus sunt ordinati, & dubium est eos Episcopos fuisse, an non, qui eos ordinaverunt, si bonæ actionis & catholici viri sunt ipsi Presbyteri & in ministerio Christi omnemque legem sanctam edocti, apti, ab Episcopo suo benedictionem Presbyteratus suscipiant & conficer mtur, & sic ministerio sacro fungantur.

11. Of old it was the Custom of the Church that Presbyters joyn with the Bishops in Ordination. *Concil. Carth. c. 3. All the Presbyters present must impose their hands on the head of the Presbyter to be ordained with the Bishop.* Which fully sheweth, that it is an act belonging to their Office, and therefore not null when done by them alone, in certain cases: and that it was but for order sake, that they were not to do it without a Bishop, who was then the Ruler of the Presbyters in that and other Actions.

And its worth noting, That *ib. Can. 4.* The Bishop alone without any Presbyters was to lay hands on a Deacon (though not on a Presbyter) *Because he was ordained non ad sacerdotium sed ad ministerium,* not to the Priesthood but to a Ministery or service, which plainly intimateth what Arch-Bishop *Usher* said to me, that *Ad Ordinem pertinet ordinare (quamvis ad Gradum Episcopalem ordinationes regere.*) The Priesthood containeth a power to ordain Priests; but the Episcopal Jurisdiction as such sufficeth to ordain a Deacon: Or that the Bishop ordaineth Presbyters, as he is a Presbyter(his Prelacy giving him the government of the action)but he ordaineth Deacons as a Ruler only.

See Stillingfleets tretr. p 373, &c.

Arg. II. Ordination by Bishops such as were in Scripture time is valid (and lawful). But the Ordinations in *England* now questioned, were performed by Bishops, such as were in Scripture times, *Ergo* the late ordinations in England (now questioned)are valid and lawful.

The Major speaking *de nomine & officio* is granted by all. The Minor I prove thus. 1. The Ordinations in *England* now questioned were (many or most) performed by the cheif particular Pastors of City Churches (together with their Colleagues or fellow Presbyters) that had Presbyters under them. But the Cheif particular Pastors of City Churches having Presbyters under them, were such Bishops as were in Scripture times : *Ergo,* the Ordinations in *England* now questioned were performed by Bishops such as were in Scripture times.

I must first here explain what I mean by [a particular Pastor] as in an Army or Navy a *General Officer,* that taketh up the *General care* of all is distinct from the *inferiour, particular Captains,* that take a *particular care* of every Souldier or person under their command ; so in the Church in Scripture times there were 1. *General Officers,* that took care of *many Churches* (viz. a *general care.*) And 2. perticular *Bishops* and *Presbyters* that were *fixed* in every *City* or *perticular Church,* that took a *perticular care* of every *Soul* in that *Church.* It is only *these last* that I speak of, that were

G g 2   Bishops

Bishops *infimi gradus*; not such as the *Apostles* and *Evangelists*; but such as are mentioned *Acts* 14. 23. and *Acts* 20. 28. *Tit.* 1. 5. *&c.*

Now for the *Major* it is notoriously known, 1. That ordinarily some of our Ordainers were *City Pastors*. 2. That they had Presbyters under them; *viz. one* or *more Curates*, that administred there with them, or in Oratories called Chappels in the Parish.

Πόλις is *Oppidum*, and our Boroughs and Towns Corporate are such Cities as are signified by that word: And there are few of these but have *more Presbyters* than *one*, of whom one is the *Cheif*, and the rest ruled by him. Besides, that one was oft-times President of the Assembly chosen by the rest. For. instance (if I had ever medled in Ordainings as I did not). 1. I was my self a Pastor of a Church in a City or Burough. 2. I had two or three Presbyters with me, that were ruled by me: so that I was statedly their Chief: I was statedly chosen by the neighbourhood associated Pastors to be their Moderatour (which was such a power as made Bishops at *Alexandria* before the *Nicene* Council.)

Now that such were *Bishops* (such as were in Scripture-times) I prove 1. By the Confession of the Opponents: Doctor *Hammond* and his followers maintain, that there were *no subject Presbyters instituted in Scripture times*; and consequently that a Bishop was but the *single Pastour* of a *single* ongregation, having not so much as *one Presbyter* under him, but *one* or *more Deacons* (which granteth us more than now I plead for:) and that afterwards when Believers were encreased, he assumed Presbyters in *partem curæ*: So that our Bishops which I plead for are of the stature of those *after Scripture times* in the Doctors sence. *De facto* this is granted.

2. The *Bishops in Scripture times* were ordained in *every City and in every Church*, Tit. 1, 5. and Acts 13. 23. So are ours. They had *the particular Episcopacy over-sight rule and teaching of all the Flock committed to them*, Acts 20. 28. (and if the Angel of the Church of *Ephesus* were one cheif, he was but one of these, and over these in the same Church and charge *J*. And so have our Parochial Pastours; *these very words*, Acts 20. 28. being read and applyed to them in their ordination. They had the *Keys of the Kingdom of Heaven* committed to them, and so have ours. If it be said, that these are but things common to the Bishop with the Presbyter: 1. What then is *proper to a Bishop?* To say [*Ordination*] is but to beg the question: And Ordination it self is not proper in the sense of *our own Church*, that requireth that Ordination be performed as well by the *laying on of the hands of the Presbyters*, as of the Bishop. 2. They use themselves to make the *governing* or *superiority* over *many Presbyters* to be proper to a *Bishop*.

3. *Those to whom the description of Bishops in Scripture belongeth are truly and properly Bishops. But the Description of Bishops in Scripture agreeth (at least) to the chief particular Pastors of City Churches, having Presbyters under them;* Ergo, *such are truly and properly Bishops.*

The Minor (which only needeth proof) is proved by an induction of of the several Texts containing such descriptions, as *Acts* 20. and 13.23. 1 *Tim.* 3. and 5.17. *Tit.* 1. 5. *&c.* 1 *Thsf.* 5. 12. *Hebr.* 13.7. 17, 24. 1 *Pet.* 5. 1, 2, 3. and the rest.

4. *If our Parochial Churches or at least our City Churches (those in each Town Corporate and Borough) be true Churches, then the cheif particular Pastors of them are true Bishops, but they are true Churches; Ergo.*

Still note, 1. That I speak of *Churches* as *governed Societies* in *sensu Politico*; and not as a Company of *private Christians,*

2. That I speak only of *particular Pastors*, or Bishops *infimi gradus*, and not of *Arch-Bishops*, and *General Pastors*. And therefore if they say *It is not the Presbyters, but the Diocesane, that is the cheif Pastor of your Parish Church* : I answer, there is none above the *Resident* or *incumbent* Presbyters, that take the particular charge and oversight : The Bishop takes but the *general charge*, as a *general Officer* in an Army. If they do indeed take the *particular Pastoral charge* of *every Soul* which belongs to the *Bishops infimi gradus*, then woe to that man that voluntary takes such a charge upon him, and hath such a charge to answer for before the Lord. If they say that the *Presbyters* have the particular charge for *teaching* and *Sacraments*, but the Bishops for *ruling*. I answer, 1. It is *Government* that we are speaking of, if they are Bishops *infimi gradus*, then there are no *Bishops or Governours under them*. And if so, then it is they that must perform and answer for *Government* of every particular Soul. And then woe to them. 2. *Governing and teaching are acts of the same Office by Chrissts institution*, as appears in 1 *Tim.* 5: 17. *Acts* 20. 28. *&c.* And indeed they are much the same thing : For Government in our Church sense is nothing but the explication of Gods Word, and the application of it to particular Cases : And this is *Teaching*. Let them that would divide, prove, that Chrisst hath allowed a *division*. If one man would be the *general Schoolmaster* of a *whole Diocess*, only to oversee the particular School-masters, and give them rules, we might bear with them : But if he will say to all the *particular Schoolmasters*, you are but to *teach*, and I only must *govern all your Scholars*, (when governing them is necessarily the act of him that is upon the *place*, conjunct with teaching, this man would need no words for the manifestation of the vanity of his ambition. The same I may say of the *Masters* of every Science, whose government is such as our Church Government is, not *Imperial* but *Doctoral*: yea of the *Army* or the *Navy* where the government is most *imperial*.

Now for the Argument. 1. The consequence of the Major is undeniable: because every such Society is essentially constituted of the *Ruling* and *Ruled* parts, as every Common-wealth of the *pars imperans* and the *pars subdita* : So every organized Church of the *Pastor* and the Flock.

2. And for the Minor, if they denyed both our *Parish Churches*, and our *City Churches* (that is those in Towns Corporate to be *true Churches*, they then confess the shame, and open the ulcer and leprosie of their way of governing, that to build up one *Diocesane Church*, (which is

not

not of Chrifts inftitution, but deftructive of his inftitution) they deftroy and pull down five hundred or a thoufand Parifh Churches, and many City Churches.

If they will alfo feign a fpecifique difference of Churches as they do of Paftors, and fay that Parifh Churches are *Ecclefiæ doctæ*, but Diocefan Churches are only *Ecclefiæ gubernatæ* of which the Parifh Churches are but parts: I anfwer, 1. The Scripture knoweth no fuch diftinction of ftated Churches : All *ftated* Churches for worfhip are to be governed Churches ; and the government is but guidance, and therefore to be by them that are their Guides. 2. I have before proved, that every worfhipping Church, that had *unum altare* was to have a Bifhop or Government by Presbyters at leaft.

Arg. III. That Ordination which is much better than the ordination of the Church of *Rome*, or of any Diocefane Bifhops of the fame fort with theirs is valid.

The Ordination now queftioned by fome in *England*, is much better then the Ordination of the Church of *Rome*, or of any Diocefane Bifhops of the fame fort with theirs, *Ergo* the Ordination now queftioned by fome in *England* is valid.

The Major will not be denied by thofe which we plead with ; becaufe they hold the Ordination of the Church of *Rome* to be valid, and their Priefts not to be re-ordained.

The Minor I prove.

If the Ordination, that hath no Reafon of its validity alledged, but that it is not done by Diocefane Bifhops, be much better than the Ordination of fuch as derive their power from a meer Ufurper of Headfhip over the univerfal Church, whofe fucceffion hath been oft interrupted, and of fuch as profefs themfelves Paftors of a falfe Church, (as having a Head and form of divine Inftitution), and that ordain into that falfe Church, and caufe the ordained to fwear to be obedient to the Pope, to fwear to falfe Doctrine as Articles of Faith, and ordain him to the Office of making a peice of Bread to be accounted no Bread, but the Body of Chrift, which being Bread ftill is to be worfhipped as God by himfelf and others (to pafs by the reft) than the Ordination now queftioned in *England* is much better than the Ordination of the Church of *Rome*.

But the Antecedent is true: *Ergo* fo is the confequent.

And for the other part of the Minor I further prove it : If the Office and government of the Romifh Bifhops and of any Diocefanes of the fame fort with them, be deftructive of that form of Epifcopacy and Church Government which was inftituted by Chrift, and ufed in the Primitive Church, then the Ordination now queftioned by fome in *England* is much better than that which is done by fuch Diocefanes.

But the Office and Government of the Romifh Bifhops and of any Diocefanes of the fame fort with them, is deftructive of that form of Epifcopacy topacy and Church Government, which was instituted by Christ and used in the Primitive Church. *Ergo* The Ordination now questioned by some in *England* is much better, than that which is done by such Diocesanes.

The Reason of the consequence is because the Ordination of Presbyters now in question is not destructive of the Episcopacy and Government instituted by Christ and used in the Primitive Church: Or if it were, thats the worst that can be said of it. And therefore if other Ordination may be valid notwithstanding that fault, so may it. *N. B.* 1. I here suppose the Reader to understand, what that Ordination is now, questioned in *England*: *viz.* Such as we affirm to be by Bishops, not only as Presbyters, as such are called Bishops, but as the cheif Presbyters of particular Churches, especially City Churches, having Curates under them, and also as the Presidents of Synods are called Bishops:

2. Note that all I say hereafter about Diocesanes, is to be understood only of those Bishops of a Diocess of many hundred or score Churches which are *infimi gradus*, having no Bishops under them, who are only Priests, who are denied to have any proper Church Government: And not at all of those Diocesane Bishops, who are Arch-Bishops having many Bishops under them, or under whom each Parish Pastor is *Episcopus Gregis* having the true Church Government of his particular Flock.

And thus because the Major is of great moment, I shall handle it the more largely.

The Viciousnes of the Romish Ordinations appeareth thus.

1. In that they commonly profess to receive and hold the Ordainers office and power from the Pope: The very office it selfe say the Italians being from him; And the application and communication of it to the individual subject being from him, say the Spaniards and French also. But the Pope as such hath no power to make Bishops at all: which I prove

1. Because the very office of a Pope as such is not of Christ, yea is against Christ and his prerogative and Law, and abhorred by him; *viz.* [An universal visible Vicar or Head of the Church on earth.].

2. Because on their own principles, the Pope can have no power, for want of uninterrupted succession of true Ordination, nothing being more plain in Church History scarce, than that such succession is long ago nulled by oft interruptions, as I have proved elsewhere, and as is by many Protestants proved.

3. Because the Work that they ordain their Priest to is Idolatry, even Bread worship; besides Man worship, and Image worship.

4. Because all their Priests are (in the *Trent* Oath) sworn to this Idolatry, and sworn to renounce all their Senses to that end, and to renounce the Scripture sufficiency; and to own the Papal Treasonable usurpation, which all are contrary to the Office of Christs Ministers.

Yet are those, that ordained at *Rome*, received by our Prelates, when they turn to us, without reordination, and their Orders are not taken.

taken by them to be null (which I difpute not now). Much lefs are the late Proteftant Englifh Ordinations null.

II. The Vicioufnefs of fuch other Prelates Ordinations, is proved by all that is faid againft their Calling it felf before. And further. 1. Thofe Prelates, that are chofen by Magiftrates and not by other Bifhops or the Presbyters of their Diocefs or People (what ftale hypocritical pretext foever there may be of the contrary) are by the Canons of the Univerfal Church no Prelates. But fuch are thofe in queftion : *Ergo*——

The Major (to omit many other Canons) I prove from *Concil. Nic.* 2. *Can.* 3. *in Bin To. 2. p. 293.* [*Omnem electionem, quæ fit a Magiftratibus, Epifcopi vel Presbyteri, vel Diaconi, irritam manere, ex Canone dicente, fi quis Epifcopus fecularibus Magiftratibus ufus, per eos Ecclefiam obtinuerit, deponatur & fegregetur, & omnes qui cum eo communicant : Oportet enim eum qui eft promovendus ad Epifcopatum ab Epifcopis eligi, quemadmodum a fanctis Patribus Niceæ decretum eft in Can. qui dicet* [*Epifcopum oportet maxime quidem ab omnibus, qui funt in provincia conftitui, &c.*]

Argument I V. Orders conferred by fuch as are in orders, and have the Power of Order equal with the higheft Bifhops, is valid. But the Orders lately conferred in *England* and *Scotland* by thofe called Presbyters, were conferred by fuch as were in Orders, and had the power of Order equal with the higheft Bifhop : *Ergo* The Orders lately conferred in *England* and *Scotland* by thofe called Presbyters, was valid.

As to the Major, I remember Arch-Bifh. *Ufher* told me himfelf that it was the argument by which he indeavoured to fatisfie K. *Charles* I. 1. That *Ordinis eft ordinare*, a man that is in orders as to the facred Priefthood, may *cæteris paribus* confer Orders ; it being like Generation or univocal caufation. 2. That *Hierom* tells us the Alexandrian Presbyters did more ; for they made their Bifhops : And at this day among the Papifts, men of inferiour Order muft with them ordain, or confecrate, or make their Pope. And Bifhops make Arch-Bifhops : How much more may men of the fame Order confer what they have, that is the Power of the Priefthood or Presbyterate. As Abbots (who are no Bifhops) have frequently done.

2. And for the Minor Bifhop *Carleton* hath thefe words in his Treatife of Jurisdiction *pag. 7. The Power of Order by all Writers, that I could fee, even of the Church of* Rome, *is underftood to be immediately from Chrift, given to all Bifhops and Priefts alike by their confecration ; wherein the Pope hath no priviledge above others* Thus teaches *Bonavent. in 4. fent. d. 17. q. 1. Auguft. Triumph. li. de poteft. Ecclef. qu. 1. a. 1. Joh. Gerfon li. de pot. Ecclef. Confid. 1.* Cardinal *Cufan. li. de conced. Cathol. 2. cap. 13.* Cardinal *Contarenus Tract. de Eccl. poteft. Pontif. Bellarm. lib. 4. de Rom. Pontif. cap. 22.*

In the Canons of *Elfrick ad Wolfin Epifc. in Spelman p. 576. l. 17.* Having fhewed that there are feven Orders (1. *Oftiarius.* 2. *Lector.* 3. *Exorcifta cista*, 4. *Acolythus*, 5. *Subdiaconus*, 6. *Diaconus*, 7. *Presbyter*) though the Bishop for Unity sake have the priviledge of Ordination and Inspection, yet he is there declared to be but of one and the same (7th.) Order with the Presbyter. *Hæc pluris interest inter Missalem Presbyterum & Episcopum, quam quod Episcopus constitutus sit ad ordinationes conferendas, & ad visitandum, seu inspiciendum, curanduumque ea quæ ad Deum pertinent, quod nimiæ crederetur multitudini, si omnis Presbyter hoc idem faceret. Ambo siquidem unum tenent eundemque Ordinem, quamvis dignior sit illa pars Episcopi.* This being the Doctrine of the Church of *England* even in the times of Popery, we have little reason (with the Preface to the book of Ordination) to say that it is manifest in Gods word that they are distinct *orders*. For as it is added *Can.* 18. *Non est alius ordo constitutus in Ecclesiasticis ministriis* (humane and all taken in) *præter memoratos septem istos* &c.

   Dion. Petavius Theolog. Dogmat. To. 4. par. 2. Tomi. 3. *Append.* c. 2. p. 677 [*Alterum est, quod nunquam iterare illam* (ordinationem) *licet ut cum ab hæresi ad Catholicam Ecclesiam revertuntur, qui vere ordinati, eis denuo manus imponitur.* And what ordination is valid among the Papists, see in *Johnsons* answer to my Questions.

FINIS.

POSTCRIPT

Promiscuous additions to the Chapter, 4. of part second out of Mr. Gilbert Burnet's *booke called,* The Vindication of the Church of *Scotland, &c.*

'PAg. 304. 305. Let me here send you to the Masters of
'Jewish Learning; particularly to the eminently learned
'Dr. Lightfoot, who will inform you that in every *Synagogue*
'there was one peculiarly charged with the worship, called *the*
'*Bishop of the Congregation,* the *Angel of the Church,* or the Mini-
'ster of the Synagogue. And besides him there were three who
'had the Civil judicature, who judged also about the receiving
'of proselites, the imposition of hands, &c. And there were o-
'ther three who gathered and distributed the almes. Now the
'Christian Religion taking place as the Gospel was planted in
'Cities where it was chiefly Preached, these formes and orders
'were reteined, both names and things.

'Pag. 306. --- These Presbyters were as the Bishops Children,
'educated and formed by him, being in all they did, directed by
'him and accountable to him, and were as Probationers for the
'Bishoprick, one of them being alwaies chosen to succeed in the
'seat, when vacant by the Bishops death. Now all these lived
'together as in a little Colledge, thus the Churches were planted
'and the Gospel disseminated through the world. But at first
'every Bishop had but one Parish, yet afterwards when the
'numbers of the Christians increased, that they could not con-
'veniently meet in one place, and when through the violence
'of persecution they durst not assemble in great multitudes, the
The story 'Bishops divided their charges in lesser Parishes * and gave as-
of Evani- 'signments to the Presbyters of particular flocks, which was
tius deviding into Ti- 'done first in *Rome,* in the begining of the 2d. Century — And
tulos (much 'things continued thus in a Parochial Government, till toward
less proper Parishes) 'the end of the 2d. Century, the Bishop being chiefly intrusted
is confuted 'with the cure of Souls, a share whereof was also committed to
by the most knowing 'the Presbyters, who were subject to him, and particularly to be
Historians. 'ordained by him, nor could any ordination be without the
'Bishop; who in ordaining was to carry along with him the
'concurrence of the Presbyters, as in every other act of Ecclesi-
'astical jurisdiction.   'Pag.

' Pag. 308. 309. Corruptions broke in upon Church Officers,
' especially after the 4th. Centurie, that the Empire became
' Christian: Which as it brought much riches and splendor on
' Church employments, so it let in great Swarmes of corrupt
' men on the Christian Assemblies: And then the Election to
' Church offices, which was formerly in the hands of the people,
' was taken from them, by reason of the tumults, and disorders
' that were in these Elections, which some time ended in blood,
' and occasioned much Faction and Schism: And *Ambitus* be-
' came now such an universal sin among Churchmen, that &c.

    'Pag. 310. I do not alledge a Bishop to be a distinct office
' from a Presbyter, but a different degree in the same office, &c.

    'Pag. 320. As for the sole power of ordination and Jurisdicti-
' on, none among us claime it, but willingly allow the Pres-
' byters a concurrence in both these.

    'Pag. 322. That whole frame of Metropolitans and Patri-
' arks was taken from the division of the *Roman* Empire, which
' made but one great National Church.

    ' Pag. 331. I acknowledged Bishop and Presbyter to be one
' and the same office, and so plead for no new office-bearer in the
' Church --- The first branch of their power is their authority to
' publish the Gospell, to manage the worship and dispence the
' Sacraments: And this is all that is of Divine right in the Mini-
' stry; in which Bishops and Presbyters are equal sharers, --- but
' besides this the Church claimeth a power of Jurisdiction, of
' making rules for discipline, and applying and executing the
' same; All which is indeed suitable to the common laws of so-
' cieties, and the general rules of Scripture, but hath no positive
' warrant from any Scripture precept: And all these Constituti-
' ons of Churches into Synods, and the Canons of discipline, tak-
' ing their rise from the divisions of the world into the several
' provinces, and beginning in the 2d. and beginning of the 3d.
' Century, do clearly shew they can be derived from no Divine
' original, and so were a to their particular forme but of humane
' constitution. Therefore as to the managment of this Jurisdicti-
' on, it is in the Churches power to cast it into what mould she
' will --- But we ought to be much more determined by the Laws
' of the land --- In things necessary to be done by Divine pre-
' cept, since no power on earth can Cancel the authority of a
' Divine Law, the Churches restraints are not to be considered.

                      Pag.

'Pag. 335. I acknowledge that without Scripture warrant
'no new offices may be instituted.

'Pag. 337. I am not to annul these ordinations, that pass by
' Presbyters, where no Bishop can be had: And this layes no
' claime to a new office, but only to a higher degree of inspection
' in the same office; whereby the exercise of some acts of jurisdicti-
' on, are restrained to such a Method: And this may be done ei-
' ther by the Churches free consent, or by the Kings authority.

'Pag. 348. In *Augustines* time it appears from the journal of
' a conference he had with the Donatists, that there were about
' 500 Bishopricks in a small tract of ground.

'Pag. 30. Observe the Bishops were to be ordained in the
' presence of the people, where every one might propose his
' exceptions, yet the popular Elections were not wholly taken
' away, and at least the peoples consent was asked.

'Pag. 41. *Vossius*, from all the manuscripts of *Damasus* his lives
' of the Popes, shewes that S. *Peter* ordained both *Linus* and *Cle-*
' *tus*, Bishops of *Rome*, and after some enquiry into the matter he
' concludes, that at first there were three Bishops in *Rome* at
' once, *Linus*, *Cletus*, and *Anencletus*: in the next succession he
' placeth *Cletus*, *Anencletus*, and *Clemens*.

'Pag. 48. Among the *Jewes* where ever there were an hun-
' dred and twenty of them together, they did erect a Synagogue

'Pag. 49. At a conference which *Augustine* and the Bishops of
' that Province had with the Donatists, there were of Bishops
' 286 present, and 120 absent, and 60 Sees vacant: And there
' were 279 of the Donatists Bishops.

'Pag. 51. The *Gothick* Churches are said to be planted 70
' years before *Ulphilas* their first Bishop came to them (Pag. 50,
' He sheweth the like of the *Scots*.) By the streine of *Ignatius*
' Epistles, especially that to *Smyrna*, it would appear that there
' was but one Church, at least but one place where there was one
' Altar and Communion in each of these Parishes (which was
' the Bishops whole charge.]

'Pag. 56. The enlarging of the Diocesses hath *wholly altered*
' *the figure of Primitive Episcopacy*)

That the Bishops were chosen by the people, and by the Clergy and people, and at last not obtruded without the peoples
consent, Father *Paul Saript. de Beneficiis* oft tells you, and I have
fully proved by many Canons in my abstract of Church-history
of Councils.

FINIS.

.

Lightning Source UK Ltd.
Milton Keynes UK
UKHW031300101022
410237UK00010B/1664

9 781246 926629